THE BEAUTY OF THE INFINITE

THE BEAUTY OF THE INFINITE

The Aesthetics of Christian Truth

David Bentley Hart

WILLIAM B. EERDMANS PUBLISHING COMPANY
GRAND RAPIDS, MICHIGAN / CAMBRIDGE, U.K.

Wm. B. Eerdmans Publishing Co.

255 Jefferson Ave. S.E., Grand Rapids, Michigan 49503 /
P.O. Box 163, Cambridge CB3 9PU U.K.

Printed in the United States of America

08 07 06 05 04 03   7 6 5 4 3 2 1

Library of Congress Cataloging-in-Publication Data

Hart, David Bentley.
The beauty of the infinite: the aesthetics of Christian truth / David Bentley Hart.
p.   cm.
Based on the author's thesis.
Includes bibliographical references and index.
ISBN 0-8028-1254-6 (cloth alk. paper)
1. Philosophical theology.
2. Aesthetics — Religious aspects — Christianity.
I. Title.

BT55.H37   2003
230 — dc22

2003060789

www.eerdmans.com

Hunc Librum Insolitum atque Inusitatum
Solicandidae et Patricio
Nuncupo

Contents

CONTENTS

Acknowledgments

This book had its first life more than seven years ago, in the very different form of an academic dissertation; and, while it has developed and diverged considerably from that more callow original, between its infant and adult selves there remains a continuity of identity and purpose. Hence I should first thank those advisors and committee members who oversaw and collaborated in its birth: Larry Bouchard, Eugene Rogers, Robert Wilken, and John Yiannias (who is also my son's godfather). All, by their encouragements and discouragements, approbations and critical cautions, aided me in refining my argument and disciplining my method (to such degree, that is, as I am capable of discipline).

I wish also to thank the friends whose comments upon the text, at various stages of its incubation, and whose conversations with me concerning many and myriad things were of inestimable help in shaping this book: John Betz, Joseph Harder, T. Stuart Hinchliffe, R. Trent Pomplun, Brian Sholl, and Alfred Turnipseed. To this company I should add John Milbank, who — even at those times when we have been arguing over one thing or another—has been indefatigable in his generosity to me and my work.

And I owe no small measure of gratitude to a number of scholars who, through conversation and debate during a particularly crucial year, unwittingly aided me in the preparation of this book's final draft: Martin Bieler, Brian Daley, Paul Griffiths, Reinhard Hütter, P. Travis Kroeker, R. R. Reno, Philip Rolnick, Janet Soskice, and Carver Yu. Robert Jenson was especially patient and good-humored in allowing me to argue with him over my differences with him regarding how one should understand the relation between the immanent and economic trinities *(vide infra)*. Other names should no doubt be added to this list, but mine is a memory often culpably feeble.

I should add a special thanks to Bill Eerdmans for generously undertaking the publication of this book. His press — having emerged over the years as the most impressively diverse, ambitious, and catholic in the English-speaking theological world — scarcely needed the addition of a long and eccentric book by a scholar of small note to adorn its catalogue; and, given that the economics of theological publishing more and more forces publishing houses to insist on ever more compact and marketable texts, his sympathy for my project and willingness to grant it print and covers evoke my sincerest gratitude.

Finally, all thanks and love to my wife Solwyn for her longanimity in living with a husband whose fits of scholarly abstraction all too frequently distract him from more needful things and produce very little in the way of material advantage. And all thanks and love to Patrick too, whose arrival in my life midway between the completion of this book's first and last versions granted me the extreme privilege of receiving the world anew through his eyes, thus confirming me in my certainty that the intuition that initially prompted this project was indeed an intuition of the truth.

Слава тебе, Боже

Introduction

I. THE QUESTION

The rather prosaic question that initially prompted this long, elliptical essay in theological aesthetics, stated most simply, was this: Is the beauty to whose persuasive power the Christian rhetoric of evangelism inevitably appeals, and upon which it depends, theologically defensible? Admittedly, at first, such a question might appear at best merely marginal, at worst somewhat precious; but, granted a second glance, it opens out upon the entire Christian tradition as a question that implicitly accompanies the tradition's every proclamation of itself. Christianity has from its beginning portrayed itself as a gospel of peace, a way of reconciliation (with God, with other creatures), and a new model of human community, offering the "peace which passes understanding" to a world enmeshed in sin and violence. The earliest confession of Christian faith — κύριος Ἰησοῦς — meant nothing less radical than that Christ's peace, having suffered upon the cross the decisive rejection of the powers of this world, had been raised up by God as the true form of human existence: an eschatologically perfect love, now made invulnerable to all the violences of time, and yet also made incomprehensibly present in the midst of history, because God's final judgment had already befallen the world in the paschal vindication of Jesus of Nazareth. It is only as the offer of this peace within time, as a real and available practice, that the Christian evangel (and, in particular, the claim that Christ crucified has been raised from the dead) has any meaning at all; only if the form of Christ can be lived out in the community of the church is the confession of the church true; only if Christ can be practiced is Jesus Lord. No matter how often the subsequent history of the church belied this confession, it is this presence within time of an eschatological and divine peace, really incarnate in the

1

person of Jesus and forever imparted to the body of Christ by the power of the Holy Spirit, that remains the very essence of the church's evangelical appeal to the world at large, and of the salvation it proclaims.

A certain current within contemporary philosophy, however, asserts that violence is — simply enough — inescapable: wherever Nietzsche's narrative of the will to power has been absorbed into the grammar of philosophical reflection, and given rise to a particular practice of critical suspicion, a profound prejudice has taken root to the effect that every discourse is reducible to a strategy of power, and every rhetorical transaction to an instance of an original violence. From this vantage a rhetoric of peace is, by definition, duplicity; subjected to a thorough critique, genealogy, or deconstruction, evangelical rhetoric can undoubtedly be shown to conceal within itself the most insatiable appetite for control; the gesture by which the church offers Christ to the world, and bears witness to God's love for creation, is in reality an aggression, the ingratiating embassy of an omnivorous empire. Of course, if power's pathos were indeed the hidden wellspring of every act of persuasion, Christianity, as it conceives of itself, would be an impossible presence within history: the church as the earnest of the "peaceable kingdom" could never communicate itself in a way that would not contradict its own evangel, and the "city of peace" that the church tries (or at any rate claims) to be could never actually take shape, except mendaciously, as a dissimulation of power's arcane operations behind an apparent renunciation of power (such, at least, is Nietzsche's accusation in *The Genealogy of Morals*). What this book interrogates, then, is the difference between two narratives: one that finds the grammar of violence inscribed upon the foundation stone of every institution and hidden within the syntax of every rhetoric, and another that claims that within history a way of reconciliation has been opened up that leads beyond, and ultimately overcomes, all violence.

Nor, it should be added, can the question of rhetorical violence simply be ignored by theology, because the challenge raised by the Nietzschean reading of Christianity is one that the gospel implicitly invites: Christian thought has claimed from the first that in a world in bondage to sin, where violence holds sway over hearts and history, the peace of God made present in Christ is unique; the way, the truth, and the life that alone can liberate the world from the tyranny of greed, cruelty, egoism, and aggression is none other than a particular Nazarene rabbi put to death under Pontius Pilate. Precisely because the church has always explicitly maintained that the world lies under the authority of thrones, dominions, principalities, and powers whose rule is violence, falsehood, and death, over which Christ and Christ alone has triumphed, the suspicion that passes from Nietzsche to various "postmodern" theorists is justified. And insofar as the church has at its disposal no means whereby to corroborate its wildly implausible claim, except the demonstrative practice of Christ's

2

peace, it can scarcely be said incontrovertibly to have proved its case; in this regard, Christianity's record has been — to put it mildly — mixed. As Origen observed, the marvel of Christ is that, in a world where power, riches, and violence seduce hearts and compel assent, he persuades and prevails not as a tyrant, an armed assailant, or a man of wealth, but simply as a teacher of God and his love (*Contra Celsum* 1.30). Christ is a persuasion, a form evoking desire, and the whole force of the gospel depends upon the assumption that this persuasion is also peace: that the desire awakened by the shape of Christ and his church is one truly reborn as *agape,* rather than merely the way in which a lesser force succumbs to a greater, as an episode in the endless epic of power. Christian rhetoric, then, is already a question to itself; for if theology cannot concede the intrinsic violence of rhetoric as such, neither can it avoid the task of framing an account of how its own rhetoric may be conceived as the peaceful offer of a peaceful evangel, and not as — of necessity — a practice of persuasion for persuasion's sake, violence, coercion at its most enchanting. Such an account must inevitably make an appeal to beauty.

Beauty, that is, rather than simply "truth"; or, rather, beauty as inseparable from truth, as a measure of what theology may call true. Christian thought always already stands in what might be considered a "postmodern" position: if one conveniently oversimple definition (or aspect) of the postmodern is the triumph of (in classical terms) rhetoric over dialectic, or at least the recognition that the dialectical is always essentially rhetorical, theology should welcome this as a word of comfort. The great project of "modernity" (the search for comprehensive metanarratives and epistemological foundations by way of a neutral and unaided rationality, available to all reflective intellects, and independent of cultural and linguistic conditions) has surely foundered; "reason" cannot inhabit language (and it certainly has no other home) without falling subject to an indefinite deferral of meaning, a dissemination of signification, a play of nonsense and absence, such that it subsists always in its own aporias, suppressions of sense, contradictions, and slippages; and "reason" cannot embody itself in history without at once becoming irrecoverably lost in the labyrinth of time's interminable contingencies (certainly philosophy has no means of defeating such doubts). But Christian theology has no stake in the myth of disinterested rationality: the church has no arguments for its faith more convincing than the form of Christ; enjoined by Christ to preach the gospel, Christians must proclaim, exhort, bear witness, persuade — before other forms of reason can be marshaled. Lessing was undoubtedly correct, in his *Über den Beweis des Geistes und der Kraft,* to place Christ on the far side of that wide ditch that separates contingent historical facts from universal "truths" of reason; and no less than enlightened skepticism, theology has need of Lessing's ditch. Christian thought must remain immovably fixed alongside Christ, in his irreducible

3

particularity, and precisely insofar as the temper of "postmodernism" runs against confidence in universal truths of reason, postmodern theory confirms theology in its original condition: that of a story, thoroughly dependent upon a sequence of historical events to which the only access is the report and practice of believers, a story whose truthfulness may be urged — even enacted — but never proved simply by the processes of scrupulous dialectic. What Christian thought offers the world is not a set of "rational" arguments that (suppressing certain of their premises) force assent from others by leaving them, like the interlocutors of Socrates, at a loss for words; rather, it stands before the world principally with the story it tells concerning God and creation, the form of Christ, the loveliness of the practice of Christian charity — and the rhetorical richness of its idiom. Making its appeal first to the eye and heart, as the only way it may "command" assent, the church cannot separate truth from rhetoric, or from beauty.

Of course, to justify evangelical rhetoric by way of beauty as such, in the abstract, in no way serves to answer the question posed above. Who is to say that the beautiful is self-evidently free of violence or subterfuge? How can one plausibly argue that "beauty" does not serve the very strategy of power to which it supposedly constitutes an alternative? An "aesthetic" response to a postmodern insistence on the inescapability of violence is adequate only if it gives a coherent account of beauty within the Christian tradition itself; only if beauty belongs already to the Christian narrative, fully and consistently developed, and in such a way as to allay the suspicions it arouses, can the beautiful conceivably mediate Christian truth without the least shadow of violence. Only if the theme of beauty, as essentially peace, adheres to every moment of the Christian story, at its every juncture, without lapsing into equivocation, is Christian beauty one with Christian truth, rather than deceit, false enticement, aggression. It is just such a continuous theological account of beauty that is this book's task, and the conviction that guides it is that the Christian tradition embraces an understanding of beauty unique to itself: one in which the thought of beauty and the thought of infinity uniquely coincide. I shall argue that it is possible to see vast portions of Western philosophy, from antiquity to the present, as moving within the confines of two ontologies — two narratives of being — which are really only two poles of a single ontological vision, whereas the church's story of being — arising from Scripture and its own understanding of what has been revealed in Christ — is simply alien to the world this vision descries. And nowhere does this difference appear more starkly delineated than in the understanding of the infinite that becomes possible (indeed necessary) within Christian thought; the Christian infinite belongs to an ontology of original and ultimate peace, and as a consequence allows a construal of beauty and of peace inconceivable in terms of the ontology that Christian thought encountered first in various schools of pagan metaphysics, and encounters again in the thought of Nietzsche and his heirs. Hence the title of this essay: a defense of the suasive loveliness of Christian rhetoric, as the coincidence without contradiction of beauty and peace, can be undertaken according to the opposition between two narratives of infinity: one that conceives of the infinite in terms of a primordial and inevitable violence, and one that regards the infinite as originally and everlastingly beautiful.

II. TERMS EMPLOYED

Before proceeding, though, I should define certain of the terms that will appear with some frequency (and some occasional inexactitude) below. To wit:

1. "Postmodern," to begin with, is a term that will serve rather loosely to indicate a variety of styles, perspectives, prejudices, and premises for which no single word is truly adequate. "Postmodernity," for the purposes of this text, marks out a certain territory in current intellectual culture, a general convergence of various ideologies and methods, each of whose proponents might justifiably object to so tidy and comprehensive an abstraction, because all other terms that could be used — "poststructuralism," "late modernity," "deconstruction," etc. — suffer from too confined a range of associations. In the exceedingly elementary, and perhaps misleading, sense given the word above — the ascendancy of rhetoric over dialectic — the postmodern indicates an auroral astonishment following upon a nocturnal oblivion: the West at long last awakes from the nightmare of philosophy, even the last ghosts of Enlightenment reason having been chased away, to discover and rejoice in the irreducibly aesthetic character and ultimate foundationlessness of "truth." In a world of ungovernable plurality, composed of an endless multiplicity of narratives, there can be no grand metanarrative that extracts itself from, and then comes to comprise, all the finite and culturally determined narratives that throng the horizons of meaning; no discourse can triumph over the particularities of all the stories that pass one another by in the general congress of cultures; there is no overarching dialectic by which a single and rationally ascertainable truth might be set above all merely contingent truths. For Christian thought, this is not by any means a disheartening prospect. For if indeed God became *a* man, then Truth condescended to become *a* truth, from whose historical contingency one cannot simply pass to categories of universal rationality; and this means that whatever Christians mean when they speak of truth, it cannot involve simply the dialectical wresting of abstract principles from intractable facts. One may concede

5

from the outset that dialectic (especially when conceived as a Socratic discipline of "rational" disputation, in the course of which the authority of reason is invoked to persuade and gain an advantage over another) is often a kind of violence, insofar as it seeks to conceal its own reliance on rhetoric. The art of dialectic, assuming the aspect of a "neutral" rationality, dissembles its purely suasive intervals by submerging them within the sequences of its style; it achieves the appearance of seamless logic by way of a rhetorical effect, a ploy that makes all its unspoken premises and semantic instabilities invisible to its audience. Rhetoric *as such,* however, is (one could argue) transparently persuasive and consequently cannot actually *deceive;* it aspires to only a more compelling and fruitful fullness of style; it measures itself against a certain unattainable perfection of form; it overcomes distance simply by filling it with ornament, inveiglement, and invitation. This is, of course, an absurdly unsubtle distinction; obviously "rhetoric" refers as often as not to a game of conquest; its glory is all too frequently the false or monstrous glory of power, destiny, or empire. Still, while dialectical models of truth can never free themselves from a certain violence, this poses no very trying problem for theology. Rhetoric, however, is a different matter: Christian thought has no stake in the "pure" rationality to which dialectic seems to appeal — the Christian *ratio,* its Logos, is a crucified Jew — and cannot choose but be "rhetorical" in form; but it must then be possible to conceive of a rhetoric that is peace, and a truth that is beauty.

Where the discourse of fashionable postmodernism should become distasteful to theological reflection, in fact, is not in its alleged "relativism" or "skepticism," but in its failure sufficiently to free itself from the myths of modernity. Jean-François Lyotard has described the postmodern condition succinctly as "incredulity towards metanarratives":[1] an attitude commendable in itself, no doubt, but also one that can easily be translated into a dogmatic metanarrative of its own. In the terms presumed by this salutary dubiety, all the magisterial projects of modernity — political, philosophical, scientific, economic, social — are recognizably *modern* insofar as they attempt to ground their discourse in some stable, transhistorical process, method, set of principles, or canon of rationality; the "totalizing" tendency of modernity is as much in evidence in Descartes as in Kant, as much in Rousseau as in Marx, etc. (supremely, of course, in Hegel). The "modern" indicates not a single comprehensive narrative, but a single metanarrative ambition: a desire to transcend the conditioned finitude and contingency of stories by discovering the meaning, limits, and motives of *all* stories, by way of a representation of the absolute, the universal, or the rational. The "postmodern" condition, however, is an aware-

---

1. Jean-François Lyotard, *The Post-Modern Condition: A Report on Knowledge,* trans. Geoff Bennington and Brian Massumi (Manchester: Manchester University Press, 1984), xxiv.

ness that all metanarrative structures stand upon a shifting surface of dead and living metaphors, while all "truths" are endlessly fluid. So Nietzsche: "What, then, is truth? A mobile army of metaphors, metonyms, and anthropomorphisms — in short, a sum of human relations, which have been enhanced, transposed, and embellished poetically and rhetorically, and which after long use seem firm, canonical, and obligatory to a people: truths are illusions about which one has forgotten that this is what they are; metaphors which are worn out and without sensuous power; coins which have lost their pictures and now matter only as metal, no longer as coins."[2] Not that this is an extraordinary observation; one might learn as much from thinkers as diverse as Herder, Vico, various American pragmatists, even Anatole France; from no one more memorably than Wittgenstein.[3] Indeed, nothing would be more misleading than a catastrophist model of the "postmodern," which depicts it as simply a spontaneous reaction to modernity; it is, rather, the culmination of the critical tradition of modernity, and has evolved quite naturally from the same (metanarrative) ambition that led Kant to rewrite the project of philosophy as epistemology and ethics, consequent upon the collapse of metaphysics. And predictably (given its pedigrees), this rigorous soupçon or critical incredulity becomes yet another attempt to extract thought from the quagmires of narrative; it becomes a meta-metanarrative, the story of no more stories, so told as to determine definitively how much may or may not be said intelligibly by others who have stories to tell; it completes not only the critical but the metanarrative projects of modernity (which prove to be indistinguishable). This is where the temper of the postmodern often proves wanting in courage and consistency. The truth of no truths becomes, inevitably, truth: a way of naming being, language, and culture that guards the boundaries of thought against claims it has not validated.

A still more radical postmodernism, though, would free itself from the illusion that thought can occupy a place of mere critical suspicion. Critique is never merely doubt, but always a vantage (and advantage); it is always already principled, already dependent upon firm metaphysical assumptions, already a transcendental surveillance that has determined in advance the limits of every story's credibility. Below I shall explicitly or implicitly endorse many postmodern tendencies — forms of "antifoundationalism" and "antiessentialism," impatience with the dialectics of subjectivity, a sense of the unmasterable deferrals of language — but shall also champion themes against which many of

---

2. Friedrich Nietzsche, "From: 'On Truth and Lie in an Extra-moral Sense,'" in *The Portable Nietzsche*, ed. and trans. Walter Kaufmann (New York: Viking Press, 1954), 46-47.

3. See especially the notes collected in Ludwig Wittgenstein, *On Certainty*, ed. G. E. M. Anscombe and G. H. Wright, trans. Denis Paul and G. E. M. Anscombe (Oxford: Basil Blackwell, 1969).

postmodernism's proponents have quite pronounced prejudices: analogy, participation, revelation, and much else. And while I gladly praise any postmodern desire to give utterance to a genuine discourse of difference and distance, I shall also argue that the forms of postmodern theory addressed in this book, under the constraints of a dogmatically inflexible metaphysics concealed deep within them, can conceive of ontic difference only under the form of an ontological tautology, which reduces difference to mere differentiation (the indifferent distribution of singularities) and which suppresses the only real difference (the analogical) whose affirmation can liberate thought from "totality." This latter, more imaginative and radical thinking of difference belongs to the Christian logos.

2. The next term is "metaphysics," to which I shall delegate an equally spacious array of connotations, not because it is particularly rich in meanings, but because it is a word to which neither any stable, nor any very useful, meaning can be assigned. And yet it is in some ways indispensable. Whether written in the idiom of Kant, Heidegger, or Derrida, the practice of critique (and the postmodern might be defined as "critique without reserve") takes the end of metaphysics (or "onto-theo-logy," or "presence") as its impulse and task. But what is metaphysics? A simple belief in the "supernatural"? An illicit extension of terms proper to empirical perception (like causality) to "realities" transcendent of the conditions of perception? A discourse concerning the "cause of being" that perennially fails to think the "being of cause"? An attempt to erect a hierarchy within totality, so as to grasp both the boundaries and the inward mechanisms of being? The misconstrual of being as presence? The "double founding," of beings in Being and Being in a first being? An attempt to explain the world of appearances according to a "truer" world of substances and principles? All of this, as it happens, and more. Especially insofar as postmodern thought has absorbed the Heideggerian critique of "onto-theology," it tends to arrange a vast variety of narratives under this one word. But to quote Paul Ricoeur's rebuke of Heidegger:

> This inclosure of the previous history of Western thought within the unity of "the" metaphysical seems to me to express a sort of vengefulness — which this thinking, nevertheless, calls us to renounce — along with a will to power that seems inseparable from it. The unity of "the" metaphysical is an after-the-fact construction of Heideggerian thought, intended to vindicate his own labour of thinking and to justify the renunciation of any kind of thinking that is not a genuine overcoming of metaphysics. But why should this philosophy claim for itself alone, to the exclusion of all its predecessors, that it breaks through and innovates? It seems to me time to deny

oneself the convenience, which has become a laziness in thinking, of lumping the whole of Western thought together under a single word, metaphysics.[4]

I shall have occasion to address Heidegger's diagnosis of "onto-theology" below, but shall remark here that talk of the death of metaphysics, while certainly not devoid of meaning, is of little consequence to the tradition of Christian philosophy, as it concerns an ontology with which, for the most part, theology has had no dealings; and that, in its Heideggerian form especially, such talk (as I shall attempt to show) depends in equal measure on a defective history of Western philosophy and on a set of purely *metaphysical* fideisms. Undoubtedly, though, in a general sense the situation of Western thought is now one in which a certain critique of a certain "metaphysics" has been quite successfully prosecuted, but one of very limited scope: within the narrative of Western philosophy, with its myth of independent reason and the power of mind to transcend the limits of language and determine the limits of possible knowledge by the agency of unaided reason, metaphysical speculation (as a purely deductive enterprise of rational reflection) proves finally to be a contradiction of the terms of that narrative. This is the "nihilistic vocation" of the metaphysical, which Heidegger, in Nietzsche's wake, identified with such acuity. It is also as much as one may conclude from the Kantian retrieval of epistemic certitude from Humean skepticism: indeed, if all legitimate language of meaning must obey the logic of dialectical communicability (and assuming dialectic is not itself an arbitrary marshaling of metaphors), and if "knowledge" is only that which may be presented to a transcendental subjectivity, through the apparatus of empirical perception or by appresentation, then there is much that is impossible to say intelligibly. But this is finally a tautology: if one adopts the position of a certain account of how being, knowledge, and language are related, that is one's position — ultimately because one finds the particular depiction of the world it affords especially compelling, even inevitable, for reasons that are finally aesthetic. Nor does the postmodern soupçon of metanarratives take thought further than this. It sets limits to discourses of truth, even in advance of their articulations, but these limits are decisions that have been reached by philosophical reflection for purposes as much of control as of clarity.

To put the matter differently, the unity of metaphysics is a convenient fiction, a way to exclude other voices, other ways of naming the difference of being from beings or the relation of the one to the many. When, for instance, Jacques Derrida defines philosophy (as it has always been) as a discourse of "mastery

---

4. Paul Ricoeur, *The Rule of Metaphor: Multi-disciplinary Studies of the Creation of Meaning in Language,* trans. Robert Czerny et al. (Toronto: University of Toronto Press, 1977), 311.

over the limit *(peras, limes, Grenze),*"[5] or when he states that "philosophy is, within writing, nothing but this movement of writing as effacement of the signifier and the desire of presence restored, of being, signified in its brilliance and glory,"[6] one may even provisionally agree with him; but one should note that such observations can come to serve very quickly another discourse of "mastery over the limit," a jealous preservation of the *peras* against stories that would violate it.

> All dualisms, all theories of the immortality of the soul or of the spirit, as well as all monisms, spiritualist or materialist, dialectical or vulgar, are the unique theme of a metaphysics whose entire history was compelled to strive toward the reduction of the trace. The subordination of the trace to the full presence summed up in the logos, the humbling of writing beneath a speech dreaming its plenitude, such are the gestures required by an onto-theology determining the archaeological and eschatological meaning of being as presence, as parousia, as life without difference: another name for death, historical metonymy where God's name holds death in check. That is why, if this movement begins its era in the form of Platonism, it ends in infinitist metaphysics. Only infinite being can reduce the difference in presence. In that sense, the name of God, at least as it is pronounced in classical rationalism, is the name of indifference itself.[7]

It is difficult to elude the sweep of so comprehensive and grandiloquent a rhetoric, and more difficult still to make any claim, beyond the trivially factual, sentimental, or tautologous, that does not fall under its indictment.

In the course of one of his early critiques of structuralism, Derrida remarks, quite aptly, that "if *Le Cid* is beautiful, it is so by virtue of that within it which surpasses schemes and understanding";[8] by which he means to abjure metaphysical divisions of force from structure, in favor of an economy that would neither simply oppose the two nor subordinate the unique instance of a text to the canon of a synchronic order.[9] It is ironic then that, when it comes to identifying the metaphysical, Derrida (especially early on) reads like a thoroughgoing structuralist: he arranges every kind of discourse within a synchronic pattern of simple binary oppositions; he sees within the depths of

---

5. Jacques Derrida, *Margins of Philosophy,* trans. Alan Bass (Chicago: University of Chicago Press, 1982), x.

6. Jacques Derrida, *Of Grammatology,* trans. Gayatri Chakravorty Spivak (Baltimore: Johns Hopkins University Press, 1974), 286.

7. Derrida, *Of Grammatology,* 71.

8. Jacques Derrida, "Force and Signification," in Derrida, *Writing and Difference,* trans. Alan Bass (Chicago: University of Chicago Press, 1978), 18.

9. Derrida, "Force and Signification," 19-20.

stories that differ from one another drastically at the surface the same tension between immanence and transcendence, the same marks of a striving after immediate presence, the longing for the sound of the true voice or for the silence of the Same; within the flowing diachrony of innumerable beliefs, philosophies, and myths, he establishes his science. But it is necessary here to voice a protest: in every theology or system, every tradition or discursive practice, a story is being told whose peculiar force should be allowed priority over the abstract categories by which the critic might seek to reduce all narrative to the same bare framework of elementary functions. No less insidious than a "metaphysics" that strives to overcome difference, surely, is a structuralism that seeks to overcome the differences in such stories. Writes Derrida elsewhere: "There is no such thing as a 'metaphysical concept.' There is no such thing as a 'metaphysical name.' The metaphysical is a certain determination or direction taken by a chain. One cannot oppose it to a concept, but to a process of textual labor and another enchaining."[10] Such an approach, however, all too quickly liberates one from the tiresome labor of attending to particular names and concepts; it is much easier to speak in the abstract concerning "determination or direction," to consider (and ultimately dismiss) *the* metaphysical as a whole, while reducing all the changeable details of creeds and traditions to the strictly structural dynamism of their inner oppositions. The notion that behind every speculative, confessional, or mythic story lurks a single governing pathos, that onto-theo-logy rears its head wherever origins are invoked or presence is heralded, and that all Western (and, by implication, non-Western) discourses of truth express the same yearning for presence, the true voice, the origin, the father (or some other copula of the definite article and an abstract noun) repeats the very gesture of "metaphysics": it enacts a retreat from the bewildering world of difference to the secure simplicity of foundations. So long as he persists in reading all more or less "ambitious" tales as embodiments of the same suppressed and uniform motion, Derrida need never consider the real differences that distinguish each tale from every other: the difference of fathers from fathers, origins from origins, voices from voices. But, as with *Le Cid*, whatever makes Christian theology (for instance) beautiful is the force that is not accounted for by structuralist taxonomies. Of course, every age of Christian thought has borrowed freely from the metaphysical idioms in currency, but every appropriation has inevitably entailed a subversion: Christianity, by virtue of its sheer intractable historical particularity, has always come (even if belatedly) to govern every speculative reflection upon it, and no "metaphysical" scheme, as a consequence, has ever come to determine its meaning. Of

10. Jacques Derrida, *Dissemination,* trans. Barbara Johnson (Chicago: University of Chicago Press, 1981), 6.

course, a metaphysics offered in a vacuum, as the effect of a baseless speculative enterprise, might well merit Derrida's variety of critique, simultaneously structuralist and deconstructive; but if within a narrative, such as that of the Christian tradition, where the force of the story itself should expand into ever greater ranges of explanatory "background," even beyond what merely immanent investigation can certify, it is a kind of intellectual sloth to resort to abstract characterizations of the metaphysical as such rather than to attend to the narrative as a whole, to see whether it can fill itself out without lapsing into contradiction or gibberish. Once one withdraws one's thinking from this nubilous atmosphere of synchronic oppositions and abstractions and turns one's attention to the peculiar inherent continuities of particular narratives, any stable image of the metaphysical must dissolve. At this point, only, critique would overcome itself. This would be a true "deconstruction" without secret architectural aspirations of its own.

If, that is, this is the vantage that is desired. When, for instance, Lyotard elects to take the unrepresentable sublime — the sublime of Kant's third Critique — as the starting point of his aesthetics, in rebellion against the "totalizing" power of representation, and announces a war against totality (against the longing for all and one that has supposedly been the cause of so much terror this century), to be prosecuted by activating "differends,"[11] he not only fails sufficiently to acknowledge a certain advantage he thus gains over all discourse (after all, more absolute than any metaphysical account of what should be said is an intransigent insistence on what can never be said), but leaves a crucial question unanswered: Is it really possible, situated on this side of the sublime (so to speak), to distinguish metanarratives from narratives, the metaphysical from the empirical, the supernatural from the natural? Would not all such critical distinctions reside, necessarily, beyond the impenetrable veil of the "unrepresentable"? Would not a true sense of a sublime that renders all representation provisional and unfounded, all attempts at overarching synthesis absurd, also of necessity make it impossible to identify where the line of the sublime is located? This should be asked because Lyotard, despite his concern to loose discourse in all its irreconcilable differences, still presumes a knowledge of that point in any story where it becomes metaphysical, totalizing, and illicit — where it ceases to be a self-effacing and accommodating story, but begins to exhibit a longing for all and one. Similarly, Gilles Deleuze may seem quite humble when he suggests that the philosopher must henceforth put aside the desire to grasp the whole of things from above and instead become a creature of the

11. Jean-François Lyotard, *The Postmodern Explained: Correspondence, 1982-1985*, trans. Don Berry, Bernadette Maher, Julian Pefanis, Virginia Spate, and Morgan Thomas (Minneapolis: University of Minnesota Press, 1992), 10-11, 16.

surface, a "tick or louse," never allowing his or her thought to stray from the planes of immanence;[12] but Deleuze has quite rigid notions of where immanence, in general, comes to an end. In truth, though, thought that confines itself to an entirely "horizontal" axis of intelligibility could never have at its disposal means by which to determine where the immanent leaves off and the transcendent begins. One might plausibly argue that theology, dependent as it has always been upon the history of Jesus of Nazareth, has always been a discourse of the surface, a narrative without vertical perspective, lacking philosophy's buoyancy; the movement of theological thought from the realm of the "natural" to the "supernatural," the immanent to the transcendent, traverses a single, seamless narrative surface, and only from outside this narrative does it seem that the boundaries of the immanent have been breached. Theology is not an art that abstracts from history toward eternity, from facts toward principles, but one that — under the pressure of the history it is called upon to interpret — finds the sphere of its narrative expanding into ever greater dimensions of the revealed, crossing the line between the creaturely and the divine (and so that between the ontic and the ontological) because that line is already crossed, not symbolically but in fact, in the concrete person and history of Jesus. In Christian terms it is possible to identify a realm of the immanent only because it appears as a distinct mode within the discourse of divine transcendence, as a sphere of being that declares God's glory while, manifestly, not being God. Theological talk of the transcendent and the immanent is meaningful because it occurs *within* a continuous account of what has appeared within history, and not at the outward circumference of "reality." Deleuze's division of transcendent from immanent, however, can never be anything but an arbitrary foreclosure of thought and language, expressing a metaphysical certitude regarding the shape of the immanent and of the real. But, to subvert a Kantian axiom, one could actually never immanently determine where the furthest possible limits of the immanent must be set, because one's apparatus of knowledge is constrained not just by an assortment of analytic and synthetic a prioris or the anomalies of reasoning that bound them, but by an inescapable narrativity, an openness before an unforeclosed "more," which it may yet prove possible to tell. One might argue that too absolute a division of metanarratives from narratives, transcendence from immanence, narrative closure from the adventure of the trace partakes too obviously of a myth of origins, the idea of a place where language knows itself outside of its tropes and can determine what is a discourse of the real and what a practice of impossible speculation. Hence I shall proceed as if the critique of metaphysics is often only another metaphysics. And I shall ar-

---

12. Gilles Deleuze, *The Logic of Sense*, trans. Mark Lester et al. (New York: Columbia University Press, 1990), 133.

gue that, within the history of metaphysics, there occurred a theological "interruption" — a new account of being and of the infinite — whose effects profane philosophy still has not digested. More of that anon. Suffice it to say that I shall resort below to the word "metaphysics" equivocally and hope that its context will in every case be adequate to indicate its intended sense. While I shall concede neither the intrinsic violence of *the* metaphysical as such, nor even the ultimate coherency of the concept, I shall occasionally use the word in a fairly narrow critical sense, as a term descriptive of philosophy's various attempts to compose all of reality in its reflections under the form of a circumscribed totality, a panorama arranged before the gaze of theory; and at other times I shall employ it as a term innocent of any malign connotations, indicating merely that realm of conjecture that exceeds what is evident in the empirical order of discrete causes, *causae in fieri,* in order to speak of the ontological possibility — the *causa in esse* — of a world that is impotent to account for its own being.

3. Further to avoid some of the ambiguities in the term "metaphysics," I shall borrow from Emmanuel Levinas his distinction between "totality" and "infinity"; however, as will presently become clear, I have no sympathy for Levinas's thought, and so my use of this terminological couplet will prove quite subversive of his. By "totality" I mean the attempt to grasp the being of beings as a whole, immanent to and sufficient for itself, and to grasp all things and values — epistemic, moral, aesthetic — within the confines of this immanentism; and by "infinity" I mean what one desires when one seeks to see the totality as the gift of a true transcendence, granting the totality its essences, its existence, its values, and its transcendental properties from beyond itself, by the grace of participation and under the "rule" of analogy. "Totality," then, names a pathology, a desire to comprehend all of being in a single thought, as a single "meaning"; it does not, however, name (as it often seems to do for Levinas) being itself, or the "fold" of Being-beings.[13] It emerges wherever a division between the transcendent and the immanent is peremptorily drawn, or whenever one can say with certainty what the metaphysical is; totality is the science of the border, as it is defined according to authoritative representations (even, occasionally, representations of an unpresentable sublime). The God of Christian thought, though, is infinite, and respects no boundaries, but is — both transcendently and immanently — God. "Infinity," as Levinas uses the word, indicates a kind of purely ethical sublime, recognizably Kantian in its joyless rigor, and so jealously preserved against the idolatrous proclivities of human minds as to take on the characteristics of a gnostic myth; Levinas is anxious not to reinterpret

13. See Emmanuel Levinas, "God and Philosophy," in *The Levinas Reader,* ed. Seán Hand (Oxford: Basil Blackwell, 1989).

being in the light of infinity, but to escape altogether from ontology and phenomenology (which are irredeemable discourses, proper to the realm of graven images), and to follow instead the call of the ethical into the darkness of an infinite obligation whose only visible aspect is the contextless, unlocalizable, inescapable face of the other (I shall discuss this below). The Christian infinite, though, is "ethical" only because it is first "aesthetic"; it opens up being and beings — to knowledge or love — only within the free orderings of its beauty, inviting a desire that is moral only because it is *not* disinterested. For Christian thought there lies between idolatry and the ethical abolition of *all* images the icon, which redeems and liberates the visible, and of which the exemplar is the incarnate Word: an infinite that shows itself in finite form without ceasing to be infinite — indeed, revealing its infinity most perfectly thereby.

III. BEAUTY

A term still more elusive of definition is the one obviously most central to this text: "beauty." As it happens, beauty has fallen into considerable disfavor in modern philosophical discourse, having all but disappeared as a term in philosophical aesthetics.[14] In part this is attributable to the eighteenth-century infatuation with Longinus's distinction between the beautiful and the sublime, one of whose unfortunate effects was to reduce the scope of the beautiful to that of the pretty, the merely decorative, or the inoffensively pleasant; in the climate of postmodern thought, whose humors are congenial to the sublime but generally corrosive of the beautiful, beauty's estate has diminished to one of mere negation, a spasm of illusory calm in the midst of being's sublimity, its "infinite speed." There is, moreover, an undeniable ethical offense in beauty: not only in its history as a preoccupation of privilege, the special concern of an economically and socially enfranchised elite, but in the very gratuity with which it offers itself. There is an unsettling prodigality about the beautiful, something wanton about the way it lavishes itself upon even the most atrocious of settings, its anodyne sweetness often seeming to make the most intolerable of circumstances bearable: a village ravaged by pestilence may lie in the shadow of a magnificent

14. See, for instance, Mikel Dufrenne, *Phénoménologie de l'expérience esthétique,* 2nd ed., 2 vols. (Paris: Presses Universitaires de France, 1967); in this, perhaps the most influential and systematic text on aesthetic theory since Benedetto Croce's *Estetica* (and far superior), beauty is the one traditional aesthetic criterion for which the author evinces no real patience. Though he is willing to acknowledge the existence of beauty, in some sense, he can find no place for it within the scheme of aesthetics; for him it must remain the largely unspoken theme that haunts, but cannot guide, his phenomenology.

mountain's ridge; the marmorean repose of a child lately dead of meningitis might present a strikingly piquant tableau; Cambodian killing fields were often lushly flowered; Nazi commandants occasionally fell asleep to the strains of Bach, performed by ensembles of Jewish inmates; and no doubt the death camps were routinely suffused by the delicate hues of a twilit sky. Beauty seems to promise a reconciliation beyond the contradictions of the moment, one that perhaps places time's tragedies within a broader perspective of harmony and meaning, a balance between light and darkness; beauty appears to absolve being of its violences. But in an age when, by and large, a philosophical decision has been reached — correctly — that the violence of experience must not be placed within a context of transcendent reconciliation, but must simply be met by an earnest and wary ethical vigilance on the part of reflective intellects, beauty — conceived as a gracious stillness artificially imposed upon the surface of the primordial ontological tumult — mocks the desire for justice; if beauty is really no more than a diversion from the spectacle of worldly suffering, philosophy would be excruciatingly remiss not to assume the aspect of a kind of Brechtian theater, impatient with being's charms and the mystifying ministry of the beautiful. And frankly, there is from a strictly theoretical standpoint an infuriating imprecision (though one might prefer to say richness) in the language of beauty; the modern disenchantment with the beautiful as a concept reflects in part a sense that while beauty is something whose event can be remarked upon, and in a way that seems to convey a meaning, the word "beauty" *indicates* nothing: neither exactly a quality, nor a property, nor a function, not even really a subjective reaction to an object or occurrence, it offers no phenomenological purchase upon aesthetic experience. And yet nothing else impresses itself upon our attention with at once so wonderful a power and so evocative an immediacy. Beauty is there, abroad in the order of things, given again and again in a way that defies description and denial with equal impertinence.

More to the point, beauty is a category indispensable to Christian thought; all that theology says of the triune life of God, the gratuity of creation, the incarnation of the Word, and the salvation of the world makes room for — indeed depends upon — a thought, and a narrative, of the beautiful. Hans Urs von Balthasar claims there is a "Christian principle" made manifest in Christ — inseparable from the divine "content" of his identity — which, uniquely, does not oppose form to the infinite; "This," he writes, "makes the Christian principle the superabundant and unsurpassable principle of every aesthetics; Christianity becomes *the* aesthetic religion *par excellence*."[15] One might add that to

---

15. Hans Urs von Balthasar, *The Glory of the Lord: A Theological Aesthetics*, vol. 1, *Seeing the Form*, trans. Erasmo Leiva-Merikakis (San Francisco: Ignatius, 1982), 216.

grasp the aesthetic character of Christian thought is also to understand the irreducible historicality of the content of Christian faith: the *kerygma* that Christ
enjoins his disciples to preach is not some timeless wisdom, an ethical or spiritual creed fortified by the edifying example of its propagator, a *Wesen des
Christentums,* but a particular story, a particular Jew, a particular form. It is impossible, however, to offer a definition of beauty, either in the abstract or in
Christian thought; what can be done here, though, is to describe a general
"thematics" of the beautiful, a broad summary of the themes that will govern
the meaning of "beauty" in what follows. As will be obvious, the arrangement
of these themes is somewhat arbitrary; they are inextricably involved in one another, and might have been placed in an entirely different order of emphasis.
And because there is something tentative and tenuous in this list, each theme
can be given here only as a generality, to be made more concrete below. A certain degree of (one hopes, fertile) imprecision is inevitable, as these definitions
are points of departure, still inchoate, cumulative rather than deductive, offered
ex convenientia, for the sake of initial clarity rather than final synthesis.

1. Beauty is objective. This is asserted with neither any dogma nor any "science"
of the beautiful in view; there is no objective *thing* that can be isolated, described, and quantified in the manifold of experience whose name is beauty.
Nonetheless, beauty possesses a phenomenal priority, an indefectible precedence
over whatever response it evokes; it appears on the vastest of scales and on the
most minute, at once familiar and strange, near and remote; attempts to make it
obedient to a particular semantics inevitably fail, and expand uncontrollably
into an ever more inexact prolixity. The beautiful is not a fiction of desire, nor is
its nature exhausted by a phenomenology of pleasure; it can be recognized in despite of desire, or as that toward which desire must be cultivated. There is an
overwhelming givenness in the beautiful, and it is discovered in astonishment, in
an awareness of something fortuitous, adventitious, essentially indescribable; it
is known only in the moment of response, from the position of one already addressed and able now only to reply. This priority and fortuity allow theology to
hear, in the advent of beauty, the declaration of God's goodness and glory, and to
see, in the attractiveness of the beautiful, that creation is invited to partake of
that goodness and glory. So say the Psalms: "O taste and see that the LORD is
good" (34:8). Beauty thus qualifies theology's understanding of divine glory: it
shows that glory to be not only holy, powerful, immense, and righteous, but also
good and desirable, a gift graciously shared; and shows also, perhaps, the appeal
— the pleasingness — of creation to God. In the beautiful God's glory is revealed as something communicable and intrinsically delightful, as including the
creature in its ends, and as completely worthy of love; what God's glory necessitates and commands, beauty shows also to be gracious and inviting; glory calls

not only for awe and penitence, but also for rejoicing; God's ordinance is also ordonnance, so to speak. There is also a moral element in receiving the glory of God's work under the aspect of beauty: the beautiful fosters attachment that is also detachment, possession in dispossession, because it can be received only at a distance, only in letting be, as gift; where glory bestows itself as beauty, it consecrates otherness as good, and of God's goodness. All this said, however, the objectivity of beauty still does not make of beauty a particular object. The Christian understanding of beauty is analogical, in two senses: in the simple analytic sense, that whatever "beauty" means is grasped only by analogy, by constant exposure to countless instances of its advent, and through constant and continuous revision (this because, in theological terms, God is the "primary analogate" to whom beauty is ascribed); and in the more radically ontological sense, that beauty is not some property discretely inherent in particular objects, but indwells the analogical relationship of all things, each to the other, as a measure of the dynamism of their involvement with one another. The Christian use of the word "beauty" refers most properly to a relationship of donation and transfiguration, a handing over and return of the riches of being.

2. Beauty is the true form of distance. Beauty inhabits, belongs to, and possesses distance, but more than that, it gives distance. If the realm of created difference has its being for God's pleasure (Rev. 4:11), then the distance of creation from God and every distance within creation belong originally to an interval of appraisal and approbation, the distance of delight. God's pleasure — the beauty creation possesses in his regard — underlies the distinct being of creation, and so beauty is the first and truest word concerning all that appears within being; beauty is the showing of what is; God looked upon what he had wrought and saw that it was good. Within the world, beauty does not merely adorn an alien space, or cross the distance as a wayfarer, but is the true form of that distance, constituting it, as the grammar of difference. This presence of distance within the beautiful, as primordially the *effect* of beauty, provides the essential logic of theological aesthetics: one that does not interpret all distance as an original absence, or as the distance of differentiation's heterogeneous and violent forces, but that sees in distance, and in all the series and intervals that dwell in it, the possibility of peaceful analogies and representations that neither falsify nor constrain the object of regard. If indeed "metaphysics" names that species of discourse that strives to deny difference and overcome distance, then a proper understanding of beauty's place in theology may show how Christian thought eludes metaphysical ambitions, without sacrificing (as a prevalent philosophical prejudice often presumes one must) the language of analogy, reconciliation, or truth. For the first thought — more primordial than the difference between the same and the other, the transcendent and the immanent, or even Being and

beings — is the thought of the distance that opens up all differences, the interval between their terms, the event of their emergence; and in asserting that distance is originally the gift of the beautiful — rather than the featureless sublimity of will, or force, or *différance,* or the ontological Nothing — theology interprets the nature and possibility of every interval within being. At the level of ordinary experience, the distance within the beautiful is found in the space between oneself and the object held in one's regard, as well as the distance between that object and an infinite horizon; by this latter I do not mean a kind of noetic "foregrasp," an orientation toward a formless "infinite absolute" that surpasses the aesthetic even as it opens it up, but only that the object of attention, love, or awe is never finally, definitively *placed,* but is always serially consequent upon and open to an infinity of perspectives. Thus the infinite toward which beauty leads reflection, and which lays open the space in which every instance of beauty shines forth, is still itself beauty. And because the surplus of "meaning" in the beautiful consists in and urges attention toward this infinite content of distance, it allows for ceaseless supplementation: it is always unmoored, capable of disrupting stable hierarchies of interpretation, of inspiring endless departures and returns, and of calling for repetition and variation; it releases a continual distribution of meaning across the distance. No instance of the beautiful (say, the form of Christ) can be contained within a dialectical structure of truth, or recognized apart from its aesthetic series; it is always *situated* in perspectives, vantages, points of departure, but is never fixed, contained, exhausted, or mastered. The appeal — the rhetoric — of the beautiful, its excess over any form's singularity or isolation, is thus always composing and recomposing the distance. Because this distance that allows for an endless setting out from and homecoming to the object of attention belongs to beauty, the questions a theological aesthetics must ponder are what the shape of that distance is, what is its original content, how it is most truly inhabited and disclosed; for Christian thought the answer must, in every case, be peace.

3. Beauty evokes desire. This should be emphasized for two reasons. First, beauty is not simply the invention of a fecund, unpremised, spontaneous exuberance of will, a desire that preexists and predisposes the object of its velleity or appetite (as certain contemporary schools of thought suggest), but precedes and elicits desire, supplicates and commands it (often in vain), and gives shape to the will that receives it. Second, it is genuinely desire, and not some ideally disinterested and dispirited state of contemplation, that beauty both calls for and answers to: though not a coarse, impoverished desire to consume and dispose, but a desire made full at a distance, dwelling alongside what is loved and possessed in the intimacy of dispossession. Whereas for Kant, for instance, "interested" desire figures as the negation of the aesthetic and the ethical alike, as incompatible with

contemplative dispassion in the former case and with categorical obligation in the latter, for Christian thought desire — which includes interest — must be integral to both. It is the pleasingness of the other's otherness, the goodness that God sees in creation, that wakes desire to what it must affirm and what it must not violate, and shows love the measure of charitable detachment that must temper its elations; it is only in desire that the beautiful is known and its invitation heard. Here Christian thought learns something, perhaps, of how the trinitarian love of God — and the love God requires of creatures — is eros and agape at once: a desire for the other that delights in the distance of otherness. But desire must also be cultivated; the beautiful does not always immediately commend itself to every taste; Christ's beauty, like that of Isaiah's suffering servant, is not expressed in vacuous comeliness or shadowless glamor, but calls for a love that is charitable, that is not dismayed by distance or mystery, and that can repent of its failure to see; this is to acquire what Augustine calls a taste for the beauty of God (*Soliloquia* 1.3-14). Once this taste is learned, divine beauty, as Gregory of Nyssa says, inflames desire, drawing one on into an endless *epektasis*, a stretching out toward an ever greater embrace of divine glory. And, as Augustine also remarks, it is what one loves — what one desires — that determines to what city one belongs (*Enarrationes in Psalmos* 2.64.2).

4. Beauty crosses boundaries. Among the transcendentals, beauty has always been the most restless upon its exalted perch; the idea of the beautiful — which somehow requires the sensual to fulfill its "ideal" nature — can never really be separated from the beauty that lies near at hand. (In the thought of Plotinus, for instance, there is no simple division between beauty as idea and beauty as aesthetic experience.)[16] Beauty traverses being oblivious of the boundaries that divide ideal from real, transcendent from immanent, supernatural from natural, pleasing from profound — even, perhaps, nature from grace; "Crossing these boundaries so forgetfully," remarks Balthasar, "belongs to the essence of the beautiful and of aesthetics almost as a necessity."[17] Beauty defies our distinctions, calls them into question, and manifests what shows itself despite them: God's glory. For Christian thought, beauty's indifference to the due order of far and near, great and small, absent and present, spiritual and material should indicate the continuity of divine and created glory, the way the glory of heaven and earth truly declares and belongs to the glory of the infinite God. As the particular diction of the grammar of glory that commends it to the delight of the creature, beauty shows nature to be an intonation of grace and creation

16. See *Enneads* 5.8.9 and E. Krakowski, *L'Esthétique de Plotin et son influence* (Paris, 1929), 159.
17. Balthasar, *Glory of the Lord*, 1:34.

to be full of divine splendor. There is, moreover, a marvelous naïveté in the response most immediately provoked by the beautiful: neither in the Bible nor in patristic theology is God's goodness, truth, or lordship distinguished from his glory, savor, or awesome holiness; that God is good may be seen and tasted; and this means that a theology of beauty should not scruple to express itself at times as an ontology, an epistemology, or an ethics. Concerning the last, theology should ponder how beauty can compel morally by its excess: it is in the delighted vision of what is other than oneself — difference, created by the God who differentiates, pleasing in the eyes of the God who takes pleasure — that one is moved to affirm that otherness, to cherish and respond to it; there is an initial aesthetic moment of wakefulness in the ethical, which Christian thought can grasp in light of what it says of God's Trinity and his action in creation. Theology, finally, should be not only untroubled by beauty's prodigality, its defiance of so many orderly demarcations, but heartened by it: the beautiful, uniquely, displays the dynamic involvement of the infinite and the finite, the unmasterable excess contained in the object of beauty, the infinite's hospitality to the finite; and Christian thought, uniquely, must think the beautiful and the infinite together. Beauty crosses every boundary, traverses every series, and so manifests the God who transcends every division — including, again, that between the transcendent and the immanent.

5. Beauty's authority, within theology, guards against any tendency toward gnosticism, for two reasons: on the one hand, worldly beauty shows creation to be the real theater of divine glory — good, gracious, lovely, and desirable, participating in God's splendor — and on the other, it shows the world to be unnecessary, an expression of divine glory that is free, framed for God's pleasure, and so neither a defining moment in the consciousness of God nor the consequence of some defect or fall within the divine. Opposed to the private illumination of the *pneumatikos* and the sad remoteness of the call that issues from the alien god is creation's open and overwhelming declaration of God's glory, the beauty that fills and upholds heavens and earth, the divine goodness that expresses itself in light, flesh, and form. While the "knowledge" that every gnosticism offers is dialectical without remainder (that is to say, its content is actually exhausted by the negation of the world, leaving room only for fantastic mythologies of the self), beauty's address is rhetorical without restraint, negating nothing, simply unfolding ever more variously and intricately throughout the entirety of creation's display, resisting all reduction. God's glory and creation's goodness are proclaimed with equal eloquence and equal truthfulness in each moment, each interval within being, in an endless sequence of *excessive* statements of that glory and goodness. Gnostic dualism might seem a somewhat anachronistic concern, but the gnostic impulse belongs not only to antiquity: it has haunted every age

of theology as a persistent secret temptation. Wherever theology seeks to soothe those who are offended by the particularity of Christ, or struggles to extract a universally valid wisdom from the parochialism of the Gospels, a gnosis begins to take shape at the expense of the Christian *kerygma*.

The theology of Rudolf Bultmann provides perhaps the most striking example from the last generation of theology of how pervasive the inclination still is, and how thoroughly it depends upon a deficient aesthetics of creation. Generally speaking, of course, Bultmann's thought arrives late in the course of the "liberal Protestant" project, which for two centuries sought to abstract from the restive historicality of the *kerygma* some more universally valid content — religious, ethical, social — thus to convey Christ across to the more respectable bank of Lessing's ditch; the aims of this project were probably, from the first, both impossible and undesirable. And Bultmann's particular attempt to disclose the deeper "meaning" or "essence" within Christian "myth," coming when it does in this tradition, ventures far into those miasmal climes of the "existential" where meaningless terms — like "meaning" — and terms of dubious pedigree — like "authenticity" — flourish with the invincibility of weeds. But the real *danger* that Bultmann's thought represents is a gnostic etiolation of the gospel, its transformation into a fable of the soul, whose true meaning is a wisdom and peace vouchsafed inwardly, in the intactile depths of the self. His theology demonstrates with extraordinary clarity that to demythologize is not to demystify; its ultimate effect is not to ground faith in history or the worldliness of creaturely being, but to de-historicize, to unworld the soul, to make faith the experience of a mystical eschaton in perpetual advent, in the inner core of the present, imparted to the self in its most inviolable subjectivity. The church as a society in time (and society, therefore, as potentially the church) is displaced from the center of faith by the story of the self as a homeless wanderer seeking escape from history. Nowhere does this find clearer expression than in *Jesus Christ and Mythology,* Bultmann's brief reflection on the nature of history, myth, and faith, throughout which he treats history as a closed causal continuum (demonstrating little awareness of just how vague and metaphorical such a conception is) upon which the incursion of the "supernatural" could be only an "interruption" or "perforation";[18] and starting from so bluntly uncritical a position, he inevitably defines univocally as "myth" whatever is not recognizably immanent within this narrowly imagined chain of effects. Such a scheme can allow no real distinctions; everything that does not fit — whether it is as fabulous as the story of Eden or as complex as the story of the incarnation[19] —

18. Rudolf Bultmann, *Jesus Christ and Mythology* (New York: Scribner, 1958), 15.

19. Bultmann, *Jesus Christ and Mythology,* 17. Here, incidentally, Bultmann reproduces the error of Harnack and others by suggesting that the story of the incarnation obeys the dra-

is shrugged off with equal impatience, leaving nothing concrete behind but this closed continuum of causality — and causality, manifestly, does not save. But neither, obviously, can Bultmann simply "naturalize" God's saving action, as nature and history alike are for him closed off against every transcendence. And so, for him, the Christian story of salvation no longer really interacts with the world, but is partitioned off into the hidden depths of the self. It turns out, in the event, that the peremptory discrimination of myth from history actually denudes the particularity of history of value; the study of history must now become a metaphysical discourse of essences, mining the past for "the truth about human life."[20]

It is, of course, good to acknowledge that the geocentric view of the universe is incorrect, or that the spheres of the heavens do not physically separate the realm of the Most High from the world below, but Bultmann goes farther; his theology brings the entire weight of faith to rest upon a transcendental interiority by annihilating all aesthetic continuity between God and creation, and so necessarily terminates in a gnosticism that extracts from the mire of created contingency a purely spiritual, formless, inward, and unutterable wisdom, disabused of all illusion. Seen from the heart of this inward illumination, the beauty of the world is as nothing. To quote Bultmann himself:

> The idea of the beautiful is of no significance in forming the life of Christian faith, which sees in the beautiful the temptation of a false transfiguration of the world which distracts the gaze from "beyond." . . . If the beautiful is an image in which, in a certain sense, the puzzling, confused motion of life is brought to a halt and is made surveyable for the eye set at a distance from it, thus disclosing the deeper meaning for him (i.e. for man), then it is true for the Christian faith that it is not art that discloses the depths of reality, and that this is not grasped in a distanced act of seeing, but rather that this is grasped in *suffering*. The reply to the question posed in the human lot can never be objectified in a work of art but is always to be found in the enduring of suffering itself. The beautiful . . . is therefore, as far as the Christian faith is concerned, always something that lies beyond this life.[21]

---

matic morphology of certain preexisting gnostic savior myths; this is, however, at best extremely speculative: not only is there no evidence of such myths in existence prior to Christianity, the only gnostic systems in which such myths do appear (and they are fewer than one might imagine) are those that have been demonstrably influenced by Christian thought.

20. Bultmann, *Jesus Christ and Mythology*, 51.

21. Taken from Rudolf Bultmann's *Glauben und Verstehen: Gesammelte Aufsätze*, 4 vols. (Tübingen: J. C. B. Mohr, 1975), 2:137, cited in Hans Urs von Balthasar, *The Glory of the Lord: A Theological Aesthetics*, vol. 4, *The Realm of Metaphysics in Antiquity*, trans. Brian McNeil, Andrew Louth, John Saward, Rowan Williams, and Oliver Davies (San Francisco: Ignatius, 1989), 27 n. 11; I have borrowed the translation found there.

It is difficult not to see here a kind of barbarism, not solely of sensibility, but in regard to theological subtlety as well. Ignoring for the moment the troubling assumptions that beauty merely stills the tumult of existence, and that divine truth is something that lies in a "beyond" from which material beauty can distract the soul, it is sufficiently problematic that Bultmann the theologian is so concerned to plumb the "depths of reality" rather than properly to grasp its surface, as the fabric in which the glory of God is given marvelous, various, and motile expression; and it is astonishing how obviously the mysticism of *personal* suffering here has eclipsed the reality of distance, the need to behold, the interval of revelation and of otherness. And, as for the truth of art (whose beauty should not simply be distinguished from that of creation), it must be asked whether a knowledge not "objectified" in human artistry — invention, narrative, representation, craft — could conceivably be a knowledge of anything at all. In truth, for Bultmann, everything of significance occurs in the dawning, within a worldless subjectivity, of an inner apocalypse, a divine vocation at once both sublime and conformable to the dimensions of the self. One might liken this acosmic and immediate threshold or cusp between divine address and existential interiority to the knowledge of rational and moral freedom granted by the experience of the sublime in Kant's third Critique, or even to the twin sublimities that evoked Kant's awe, the starry firmament above and the moral law within, were it not that for Bultmann the firmament has been rendered all but mute. Whenever theology abandons the biblical notion of glory, it immediately succumbs to that venerable gnostic melancholy for which the sphere of fixed stars, the *stellatum,* is not the shining raiment of God cast over the heavens, but merely the final barrier through which the exiled πνεῦμα or *Fünklein* must pass in order to return to the πλήρωμα or *Abgrund Gottes.* This is the gnosis — with its distressingly easy leap across Lessing's ditch and, in consequence, over the world — that a theological aesthetics serves chiefly to resist; theology should take its lead from the "inauthenticity" of beauty, its superficiality, its exclusive dwelling in the intensity of surfaces, the particularity of form, and the splendor of created things.

6. Beauty resists reduction to the "symbolic." There are, of course, symbolic practices proper to the arts, and several senses of the word "symbol" that are theologically licit, necessary, and delightful; but beauty (the purely aesthetic) lies in the immediacy of a certain splendor, radiance, mystery, or allure; it plays upon the continuous insisture of a plastic, or lyric, or organic, or metaphoric surface. A "symbol" that truly constitutes a unified and "inspired" capture of this beauty, and genuinely makes it manifest in its particularity and in its capacity to reflect more than its particularity, is a thing to be desired, even revered. But symbol as I mean it here, in the abstract, is not this, but is rather always an

afterthought, a speculative appropriation of the aesthetic moment in the service of a supposedly more vital and essential meaning; the symbol is that which arrests the force of the aesthetic, the continuity of the surface, in order to disclose "depths"; it suspends the aesthetic in favor of the gnoseological, in order to discover something more fundamental than whatever merely "accidental" form might manifest it. The symbolic order, inevitably, is a taxonomic hierarchy, a metaphysics of the sign, and a discourse concerning inner truths; in the midst of the dynamism that beauty is — its interdependency, variety, difference, and distance — the symbolic occurs as that which stabilizes the individual aesthetic moment as a fixed property, a meaning, a kind of exchangeable capital or currency that stands *in lieu* of substantial wealth. To speak of symbols too freely is to speak like both a gnostic and a philistine, to alienate the aesthetic moment from its context of supplementarity, metaphorical deferral, cadence, and reference;[22] it is to imitate that most imperious idealist gesture of consigning the merely particular to the realm of the inessential, while turning one's eyes upward to seek out that clear lightning flash that will render the *semeia* of the world simultaneously transparent and adiaphoral. But the beautiful is prior to all schemes of isolable meanings: it is excess but never formlessness, a spilling over, jubilant, proclaiming glory without "explaining" it. For just this reason it fixes reflection upon the irreducibly particular, the momentary, fragile, and fortuitous. In the beautiful, when it is liberated from the "symbolic," a purely serial infinity is implied — such as Hegel dreaded — and the circular infinity of synthesis and transcendental reconciliation — such as Hegel heralded — is resisted. Beauty arranges the world not according to a logical or semeiological syntaxis or hypotaxis, obedient to a rigid hierarchy of accidental and essential, form and meaning, but according to a boundless and "superficial" parataxis, whose meaning *is* its ceaseless sequences of supplement, addition, variation, departure, and return: elliptical divergences, unanticipated convergences, whose effect is musical, not dialectical. In the moment of the beautiful, one need attend only to the glory that it openly proclaims, and resist the temptation to seek out some gnosis secretly imparted.

22. A few remarks of Vladimir Nabokov, who never tired of stating his distaste for "symbolic" theory, are oddly apposite here: "The notion of symbol . . . has always been abhorrent to me. . . . The symbolism racket in schools . . . destroys plain intelligence as well as poetical sense. It bleaches the soul. It numbs all capacity to enjoy the fun and enchantment of art. . . . In the case of a certain type of writer it often happens that a whole paragraph or sinuous sentence exists as a discrete organism, with its own imagery, its own invocations, its own bloom, and then it is especially precious, and also vulnerable, so that if an outsider, immune to poetry . . . , injects spurious symbols into it . . . , its magic is replaced by maggots." Nabokov, *Strong Opinions* (New York: Random House, 1973), 304-5. Harsh rhetoric aside, I shall want to suggest that — in a sense — God is a "certain type of writer."

The language of symbol has, unfortunately, worked considerable mischief in modern theology, particularly in the (still marginally influential) thought of Paul Tillich; to quote his memorable, if somewhat occult, formula: "While the sign bears no necessary relation to that to which it points, the symbol participates in the reality of that for which it stands."[23] This might be quite a salubrious analect, but Tillich's own practice makes it all too obvious that he entirely failed to understand in what sense his words were true. Of course, the advantage of vague talk concerning "symbol" is that it allows theology to prescind from the difficult details of particular narratives to the more governable realm of abstractions, but its price is often a denatured faith, a kind of docetism, wrapped in the apparel of a theoretical category: it is no longer the concrete details of the gospel narratives but the simple categories of universal or "spiritual" meaning that may be prized from them, that constitute the kerygmatic essence of faith. Inevitably, any attempt at a sophisticated "symbolic" reappropriation of faith's "essence" cannot help but obscure a host of necessarily fine (and crucial) distinctions; it is far too mechanical to accommodate the variety and complexity of the many narrative currents that flow through the discourse of belief. Consider Tillich's defense of the project of demythologization:

> [T]he primitive mythological consciousness resists the attempt to interpret the myth of myth. It is afraid of every act of demythologization. It believes that the broken myth is deprived of its truth and its convincing power. Those who live in an unbroken intellectual world feel safe and certain. They resist, often fanatically, any attempt to introduce an element of uncertainty by "breaking the myth," namely, by making conscious its symbolic character. Such resistance is supported by authoritarian systems, religious or political, in order to give security to the people under their control and unchallenged power to those who exercise the control. The resistance against demythologization expresses itself in "literalism." The symbols and myths are understood in their immediate meaning. The material, taken from nature and history, is used in its proper sense. The character of the symbol to point beyond itself to something else is disregarded. Creation is taken as a magic act which happened once upon a time. The fall of Adam is localized on a special geographical point and attributed to a human individual. The virgin birth of the Messiah is understood in biological terms, resurrection and ascension as physical events, the second coming of Christ as a telluric, or cosmic, catastrophe. The presupposition of such literalism is that God is a being, acting in time and space, dwelling in a special place, affecting the

23. Paul Tillich, *Systematic Theology*, vol. 1 (Chicago: University of Chicago Press, 1967), 239.

course of events and being affected by them like any other being in the universe. Literalism deprives God of his ultimacy and, religiously speaking, of his majesty. It draws him down to the level of that which is not ultimate, the finite and conditional. In the last analysis it is not rational criticism of the myth which is decisive but the inner religious criticism. Faith, if it takes its symbols literally, becomes idolatrous! It calls something ultimate which is less than ultimate. Faith, conscious of the symbolic character of its symbols, gives God the honor which is due him.[24]

Setting aside an unfortunate (if characteristic) hint of bigotry in this passage (Tillich's solicitude for abstractions like "the ultimate" is surely no less "idolatrous" than the belief that God's gracious acts in history are really occasionally *acts*), and setting aside its atrocious oversimplifications, the problem with Tillich's approach is that it does not actually clarify but merely reduces. This starkly stated alternative between thoroughgoing demythologization and thoroughgoing literalism looks altogether too much like simple critical indolence; one must at least have some feel for the difference between a story as openly fabulous — placed *in illo tempore* — as the narrative of Eden and a story as concrete as that of Christ's resurrection, which makes a disorienting (and scandalous) claim to historical actuality, with repercussions that can be described in terms of times and places. Tillich's method lacks the interpretive acuity that permits this absolutely necessary distinction. The reduction of so many of the differing contours of Christian faith to this same flat and featureless texture of the symbolic (which of course serves to preserve, rather than disrupt, "an unbroken intellectual world") requires a subordination of every concrete form to a "system" that resists the aesthetic precisely because it rests upon the assumption that some truth deeper than form has been grasped; but the content of Christian faith abounds in particularities, concrete figures, moments like the crucifixion, which cannot simply be dissolved into universal truths of human experience, but stand apart in their historical and aesthetic singularity. To speak of the cross of Christ or even the empty tomb as symbol merely arrests the power of expression — the aesthetic eruption, the linguistic radiance — that each releases, in order to make each explicable in the context of a neutral rationality; it stills the unutterable excess, at once historical and aesthetic, that belongs to both. But the crucifixion and resurrection of Jesus tell us nothing in the abstract about human dereliction or human hope — they are not motifs of a tragic wisdom or goads to an existential resolve — but concern first what happened to Jesus of Nazareth, to whose particular truth and radiance all the general "truths" of human experience must defer. The "symbol," extracted from the

---

24. Paul Tillich, *The Dynamics of Faith* (New York: Harper, 1957), 51-52.

complexities of its many contexts, is pure transparency, the paralysis of beauty, yielding before the figureless glare of an abstraction. Whatever remains irreducible in the symbol is also quite impotent, frozen in a great sea of "meaningfulness," drifting endlessly toward ideality. An "aesthetic" theology, however, actually helps guard the integrity of Christianity's historical specificity. And while a theology of beauty can make room for talk of "symbol" in many ways — in terms of sacrament, icon, or real presence — it must at all costs resist that odd confluence of the sublime and the evanescent that constitutes the "symbolic." At the outset, then, this book will move away from and against the "symbolic," its minor-key *Aufhebung,* and its disclosure of depths within depths. Theology should always remain at the surface (aesthetic, rhetorical, metaphoric), where all things, finally, come to pass.

If then a theology of beauty stands with the concrete and the particular, in defiance of any species of thought that places its faith in abstractions or generalities, it militates of necessity against practices that simply sort narratives into discrete categories of story and metaphysics, myth and meaning, symbol and reality, and then rest content; the more difficult practice of approaching narratives already prepared to be defeated by the unique, uncategorizable, and irreducible in each, is also the more fruitful (and charitable). Beauty, when not made subject to a symbolic economy, calls attention to those details of surface, those nuances and recalcitrant peculiarities, that distinguish one story from another, one narrative *moment* from another, and so discourages idle chatter concerning the "nature" of religious language or religious truth. If indeed Christianity embraces "the aesthetic principle *par excellence,*" then abstraction is the thing most contrary and deadening to the truth it offers. This provides perhaps the best definition of metaphysics, in the opprobrious sense of the word: an inexorable volition toward the abstract. "Metaphysics," so conceived, has no real name for beauty, and can account for it, if at all, only in terms of a formless ideality that is, aesthetically speaking, the only true deformity: the privation of form. God's glory, though, is neither ethereal nor remote, but is beauty, quantity, abundance, *kabod:* it has weight, density, and presence. Moreover, it has been seen in the form of a slave, revealed in a particular shape whose place in time and space is determinative of every other truth, every other beauty. In the end, that within Christianity which draws persons to itself is a concrete and particular beauty, because a concrete and particular beauty *is* its deepest truth.

IV. FINAL REMARKS

It would be impossible to enumerate all the sources on which this book draws. Gregory of Nyssa has influenced my thinking most. Though his originality as the first systematic thinker of divine infinity is now widely accepted, many aspects of his understanding of the infinite have yet, I believe, to receive adequate treatment. Moreover, there is in his thought — though he has occasionally been misrepresented as a kind of unreconstructed Christian Platonist — a revision of Platonic thought that is the most daring of his age, and one whose pertinence remains undiminished by the centuries. Said simply, Gregory's theology lies at the heart of this essay. If Nietzsche figures in its first part as the prototype of a certain kind of "postmodernist," Gregory figures in the second part as his antithesis: his account of desire and *epektasis* is offered as an answer to Nietzsche's account of the will to power and finite becoming, and his understanding of the infinite as an answer to a certain postmodern understanding of the sublime. Augustine, who wrote more concerning beauty than perhaps any other of the Western Fathers, and Maximus the Confessor, who wrote most beautifully concerning the relation of creation to the Logos, also influence these reflections. All theological aesthetics is adumbrated by Irenaeus; Bonaventure best understood the artistry — the rhetoric — of creation; and Athanasius and Anselm, in unexpected ways, grasped the beauty displayed in the language of salvation. Ultimately the metaphysical rationality of theological aesthetics is expressed by no one more perfectly than by Dionysius the Areopagite.

In modern theology, of course, the field of theological aesthetics is overshadowed by the towering achievement of Hans Urs von Balthasar, whose immense theological trilogy — in its successive stages of an aesthetics, a dramatics, and a logic — genuinely inaugurates a new kind of theological discourse, and abounds almost inexhaustibly in matter for theological reflection; my particular concerns in this project somewhat differ from his, but it would be quite appropriate were this essay read as a kind of extended *marginalium* on some page of Balthasar's work. John Milbank provides the question from which part 1 of this essay sets out, and his particular approach to a Christian "ontology of peace" has informed my argument throughout. And I must mention those modern Eastern Orthodox theologians and philosophers whose influence on this essay's style of thought runs too deep properly to measure; in particular, I should cite Vladimir Solovyov, Sergei Bulgakov, Pavel Florensky, Vladimir Lossky, Dumitru Staniloae, Pavel Evdokimov, and Alexander Schmemann. Though this essay may little resemble most texts on Orthodox theology (not least in its free use of Western sources), I am a member of the Eastern Church, and it is from that tradition principally that my argument, whatever its strengths or deficiencies, intends to derive its logic; from Byzantine worship and prayer, the heritage of patristic thought, and the writings of the theologians just named (not to mention many others) I have learned — as elsewhere I could not have done — that theology begins only in *philokalia:* the "love of beauty."

These debts having been acknowledged, and thereby a theological warrant for my aesthetic reflections having been claimed, it would be reasonable to ask why I have elected to write this essay in some sense *contra gentiles:* Why is it necessary for the first part of this book to address at such length current Continental philosophy, in its most "godless" forms? In part I proceed from the conviction that the centrality of beauty to theology should not need to be recovered, and that it does suggests that the condition of philosophical modernity must be confronted — its hidden prejudices unveiled, its customary language subjected to critique, its more arbitrary decisions decried — if theology is to be roused from its reticence on a matter that modern thought treats as trivial. That is at least the polemical rationale for my method; but there is another, perhaps more charitable explanation. Modern Continental philosophy is very much the misbegotten child of theology, indeed a kind of secularized theology; even at present its governing themes everywhere declare its filiation — ontology is concerned with the being of beings, phenomenology with truth as manifestation and the unity of knowledge and being, hermeneutics with interpretation and the transmission of texts; the questions of transcendence and immanence, the moral law, the transcendentals, the meaning of being, substance and event, time and eternity, freedom and fate, and the logic of history remain the essential matter of Continental thought. There are theologians who believe theology has something to learn from and contribute to the analytic tradition of philosophy (here I reserve judgment), but even if this is so the encounter would be a purely apologetic enterprise; there is no natural kinship. But theology is always already involved in the Continental tradition — its longings and nostalgias, its rebellions and haunting memories, its interminable flight from the Christian rationality that gave it life — and so is responsible for and before it; modern philosophy was born of some failure and some anguish within the language of faith, and so even its most strident rejections of faith are determined by Christian tradition, and by the Christian West's internal struggle against itself. This is the burden of consanguinity: theology cannot disown its history — or its children.

This said, my arguments are ultimately not so much apologetic as dogmatic; I do not, though, like to separate these things too absolutely. I presume that a credible defense of Christian rhetoric can be undertaken only from within Christian doctrine: because the church makes its appeal to the world first by pursuing its own dogmatics, by narrating and renarrating itself with ever greater fullness, hoping all the while that the intrinsic delightfulness (and of course, truthfulness) of this practice will draw others into its circle of discourse. I want less to refute the position against which I have set my argument, as refutation in strictly logical terms is an interminable task, than to point toward another grammar, an alternative rhetoric, a fuller vision, whose own inner rationality can argue for itself. Most "postmodern" critique, after all, achieves its ironic or clastic assault on the vestiges of Western metaphysics through the construction of alternate idioms; the idiosyncratic excesses that make many of its texts at once so daunting and so beguiling express a desire to subvert and weaken all those stable certitudes of Western thought that pervade and determine the language of philosophy. And this constitutes an invitation to theology to answer in kind, and so to follow a path already proper to its own tradition of kerygmatic proclamation. This essay attempts, with whatever obvious defects, the elaboration of a particular rhetorical idiom, an alternative style of address, by no means ideal, nor certainly adequate, but one obedient to the evangelical essence of Christian dogma (when, for instance, creation is considered below as music or as language, no precise argument is being advanced, but only another rhetoric, another depiction of being). This is not to say that I want to undertake "narrative theology" of the sort one associates with a certain "Yale school."[25] I dislike the tendency that certain adherents of this style of theology have of employing "narrative" as such as an "antifoundationalist" shelter against critique and against the ontological and epistemological questions that theology must address (inasmuch as it is a discourse concerning the Logos); I believe the Christian story is the true story of being, and so speaks of that end toward which all human thought and every natural human act are originally oriented, and so can and must speak *out of its story* in a way that is not "narrative" only, in a simple sense, and in a way that can find resonances and correspondences in the language and "experience" of those who are not Christian. And, I confess, I believe there is indeed the possibility of a consummation of all reason in a vision and a wisdom that cannot be reached without language, but is as much *theoria* as discourse; as such it is indeed "aesthetic" in the highest sense, a knowledge that is too intimately acquainted with what it knows ever to be reducible to mere explanation, but is also "rational" in the highest sense, in that it can "see" where and understand how other narratives fail the great theme of being, are too impoverished to speak the truth of reality's goodness, and simply lack the fullness and coherence that shows itself in the true. At this point the differences between vying narratives of truth are no longer simply in-

25. See, in particular, Hans W. Frei, *The Eclipse of Biblical Narrative* (New Haven: Yale University Press, 1974); and Frei, *Theology and Narrative: Selected Essays*, ed. George Hunsinger and William C. Placher (Oxford: Oxford University Press, 1993). For a treatment of the Barthian background, see David Ford, *Barth and God's Story* (New York: Peter Lang, 1981). See also Karl Barth, *Church Dogmatics* II, *The Doctrine of God* 1, trans. T. H. L. Parker, W. B. Johnston, Harold Knight, and J. L. M. Haire (Edinburgh: T. & T. Clark, 1957), 250.

adjudicable, and "narrative" is an inadequate word (but also, at this point, one is far beyond any truth this book can prove). Perhaps then it would be best simply to say that I assume that theology, even in its most purely evangelical moments, is most properly a practice of inner witness and *anamnesis*, a submission of language to the form of Christ revealed in the text of Scripture and in the unfolding tradition, but also one that seeks to find therein the true home of every "natural light." That the exemplary form of theology, and of the church's appeal to the world, should be this turn inward of dogmatic discourse that is also an opening out to what is beyond obeys a kind of trinitarian logic: just as the eternal "discourse" of God, the circumincession of the Persons in the infinite articulation of the divine utterance (Logos), opens "outward" to creation only according to its own eternal motion, expressed economically, so this dogmatic *diastole* and *systole* around the story of Christ has a power to include what is other within itself, through the mediation of the Holy Spirit who makes all words open to the Word that embraces every created difference.

Hence, in what follows I intend by no means to avoid "speculative" theology, even if I do mean to subordinate speculation to the narrative of the faith and the *regula* of common confession. Theology is not first a speculative science, but it is a hermeneutical labor that, in its fullness, positively demands speculative reflection as a necessary accompaniment. I distrust too absolute a distinction between narrative and metaphysics in theology; "narrative," as I would be content to use the word, would somewhat elide the distinction between metaphysics and story, myth and *kerygma*, gospel and creed; it is a category wide enough to accommodate every foliation of the Christian story, from the legendary to the most intensely theoretical. Moreover, too often modern theologians erect a disastrous partition between "biblical" faith and theology's chronic "Hellenism," as if the Bible were never speculative or as if hellenized Judaism did not provide the New Testament with much of its idiom; Hellenism is part of the scriptural texture of revelation, and theology without its peculiar metaphysics is impossible. The "metaphysical" — the doctrinal, the theologoumenal — does not occur simply as a reflective excess, at a distance from the figure of Christ, but is the inevitable filling out of the force released by his particularity. Confronted by the rhetoric of his form, one can respond only with a reciprocal rhetoric, which necessarily includes within itself an immense range of critical reflection, and which can never be adequate to its object. One always must say more. The force of such a rhetoric does not simply terminate at the frontiers of the speculative (it does, however, determine them). The Gospels and their metaphysical efflorescences, then, belong together in a condition of unschematizable textuality, and it is only by the dynamisms inherent in the tradition as a whole that orders of narrative priority may be determined (never definitively, of course). There is in the figure of Jesus, in his historical and textual singularity, already an overflowing fullness that surpasses invention and accident alike, that is already there past all interpretive striving; the form of Christ is already more than adequate and always answers theological impetrations; its aesthetic power contains the full scope of its truth and can always overwhelm through its sheer beauty. And if Christ was raised from the dead, the light shed by his form upon language and thought now always extends further than language or thought will ever reach.

What follows has three parts. The first concerns the question of violence, especially as raised in certain kinds of "postmodern" thought, and the challenge to Christian rhetoric that it implies. Much of this part is devoted to Nietzsche's treatment of Christianity and the figure of Christ, as it is the Nietzschean strain in the postmodern that is principally relevant here, and as Nietzsche remains the most spirited and inventive exponent of the ontology that a Christian thinking of the beautiful opposes. The second part, the heart of the essay, is a reading of the "Christian story" in four moments: Trinity, creation, salvation, and eschaton. My intention here is to describe beauty theologically, to demonstrate both that beauty belongs *continuously* to the Christian story (as, indeed, a chief element of its continuity) and that it appears there as peace: to show, in other words, that for theology beauty is the measure and proportion of peace, and peace the truth of beauty. Here the argument is made for the coincidence — unique, again, to Christian thought — of beauty and the infinite: peace and delight being the "cadence" of their unity. The third and briefest part then simply reverses the original question of rhetorical violence, and asks whether a characteristically postmodern account of truth and truthlessness might not actually serve to perpetuate certain styles of civic and political violence, while Christian evangelic rhetoric can yet be conceived (and perhaps practiced) as a gesture of peace.

It is in the nature of this project — at once narrative and argumentative, addressed to a manifold concern — that it cannot proceed in a strict deductive sequence; it does not attempt so much to construct a systematic aesthetics as to show how two grammars depart upon separate paths, upon which both beauty and the infinite are found in radically different forms. Two stories — two cities — are at issue, and each seeks to position the other; this book occupies a position within one of those stories, and tries to give an account of the prospect it opens upon the other, and upon the distance separating them. In form, then, my argument is meant to arrive at a conclusion that inverts the perspective from which the initial query is made; it moves from thesis to antithesis by way of a central diegesis, with no synthesis offered nor any wished for (synthesis, after all, redeeming only what it first dissolves, is the special province of "totality," and is generally demeaning to all parties). The diegetic interval, therefore, describes a line of flight, an exodus from one city to another, and whether the intervening distance (which is, in fact, the world) is regarded as a vast desert or a region of delights — wasteland or garden, exile or paradise — depends upon whether it is viewed from one city or the other. The conviction that prompts this book is that, whereas the story of violence simply excludes the Christian story of peace, the Christian story can encompass, and indeed heal, the city that rejects it: because that city too belongs to the peace of creation, the beauty of the infinite, and only its narrative and its desires blind it to a glory that everywhere pours in upon it. But if the Christian story is to be offered to the world as the gift of peace, it must be told in its fullness, without conceding any ground to the other narrative. It is in the entirety of the church's story that beauty is to be found, or else it is only a device — provisional, deceptive, and so violent — for ushering souls into the confines of an association whose nature it dissembles. Beauty must figure in the whole of the dogmatic deposit, as it articulates itself to itself, and not just in evangelical appeals to the world beyond; the allure of this beauty must of course be visible to those outside the circle of the faith, as it unfolds into fuller expression, but the Christian vision of beauty can be more truly recognized, more deeply understood, more richly explored, only as one is appropriated by the language in which it unfolds itself. And as this beauty is the proportion of the infinite, and so is inexhaustible, this recognition, understanding, and exploration never come to rest, but are able always to discover new intonations, new styles of rejoicing, new measures of delight.

PART 1

Dionysus against the Crucified

The Violence of Metaphysics and the Metaphysics of Violence

εἰδέναι χρὴ τὸν πόλεμον ἐόντα ξυνὸν καὶ δίκην ἔριν καὶ γινόμενα
πάντα κατ᾽ ἔριν καὶ χρεών·

HERACLEITOS

I. THE CITY AND THE WASTES

Such is its plasticity (if not, frequently, vacuity) that the term "postmodern" submits to innumerable employments, and any attempt to isolate within it some precise unity of reference is certainly hopeless. Yet the word, for all its vagueness, does seem at least to comprise a recognizable intellectual and cultural ethos, and if indeed we are situated somehow "after" modernity, it cannot be entirely fruitless to ask what this means — to ask, that is, precisely what we have left behind and what we have not. The past accompanies the present always, even when it is repudiated, and what we reject determines what we affirm.

One somewhat notorious answer has been proposed by John Milbank, who attempts, in his book *Theology and Social Theory,* to identify the prevailing discourses of postmodernist thought as variants of an "ontology of violence," a "single nihilistic philosophy" whose provenance can be traced most directly to Nietzsche and Heidegger, and whose most developed form has been variously propounded by Gilles Deleuze (with or without Félix Guattari), Michel Foucault, Jean-François Lyotard, and Jacques Derrida (and others). While Milbank is presumably aware of the many ways these philosophers differ from one another, he nowhere allows this to hinder his account: he is more concerned that the Christian narrative (and its "ontology of peace") be distinguished from and then advanced against the entire history of modern secular thought than that particular justice be done any given representative of secular reason, and so he pays scant attention to what, for his purposes, are little more than inconsequential and episodic divarications in the course of a single, comprehensive story. Nevertheless, there is considerable rigor and persuasive force in many of the moves within his argument, and he certainly does seem to expose an unsettlingly pervasive unanimity among the various thinkers he treats, a general and often unreflective agreement to the effect that there is of necessity an inescapable violence in the realm of difference — whether the account of difference be ontological, "genealogical," cultural, "grammatological," or other. Writes Milbank,

> Postmodernism . . . articulates itself as, first, an absolute historicism, second as an ontology of difference, and third as ethical nihilism. . . . its historicist or genealogical aspect raises the spectre of a human world inevitably dominated by violence, without being able to make this ghost more solid in historicist terms alone. To supplement this deficiency, it must ground violence in a new transcendental philosophy, or fundamental ontology. This knowledge alone it presents as more than perspectival, more than equivocal, more than mythical. But the question arises: can such a claim be really sustained without lapsing back into the metaphysics supposedly forsworn?[1]

Milbank's answer is that it cannot, and that the metaphysics to which it must resort is nothing other than a version of an ancient pagan narrative of being as sheer brute event, a chaos of countervailing violences, against which must be deployed the various restraining and prudential violences of the state, reason, law, warfare, retribution, civic order, and the vigilantly sentineled polis; it is, to employ the typology favored by the early Nietzsche, the story of Dionysus, over whose primordial, chthonic, and indiscriminate violences must be imposed the factitious, sacred, and precisely discriminating violences of Apollo. The novel and distinctly *postmodern* aspect of this reversion to the pagan myth of being is that, falling as it does on the far side of Christianity's "deconstruction" of "antique virtue" and of Christendom's failure to dissociate itself from the powers whose claims it had otherwise undermined, it tells this tale no longer from within the city walls and the temenos of Apollo, and even often affects the obstreperous, jubilant tones of the bacchante, reveling in an inebriate nostalgia for the Libyan wastes and the wild dance of Dionysus. And despite the fact that, to

---

1. John Milbank, *Theology and Social Theory: Beyond Secular Reason* (Oxford: Basil Blackwell, 1990), 278-79.

a man, the French quartet to which Milbank adverts espouses some form of emancipatory, "left-wing," and pluralist politics, "[these] neo-Nietzscheans cannot," he says, "wriggle out of the implication that while nihilism may be 'the Truth,' it is at the same time the truth whose practical expression must be fascism."[2] Having passed through Christian critique, and having been confined within Christianity's narrative of a primordial peace whereupon violence intrudes as an unnecessary, arbitrary, and sinful invention of the will, this "paganism" can reassert itself most purely (and with least implicit contradiction) only as a demystified and denuded celebration of force, an embrace of Dionysian chaos as the inward truth of Apollonian order, and terror as the inward secret of love.

Perhaps this is right; if nothing else, good intentions rarely retard the effects of malign metaphysics, and the ethical strain in postmodern thought is usually its emptiest gesture. Milbank merely echoes (among other things) Dostoyevsky's prognostications of post-Christian "nihilism's" ineluctable antinomianism, and if his language regarding the inevitability of fascism may be hyperbolic, he still correctly grasps the inescapable amphiboly of any "postmodern ethics" or "politics": if being is not also the good, but only "eventual," then force or tenderness, retreat, conquest, or charity are all equally "true." And power enjoys a certain greater eminence. Without denying the ethical seriousness of Derrida, the generally benign political intent of Lyotard, or the militant radicalism that flickers shapelessly about in the pages of Deleuze and Foucault, one must also acknowledge that none of it is sufficiently concrete to counter other possible impulses: there is no definitive means whereby any of these philosophers can restrain the gravitation of his rhetoric toward more forceful uses, except through an unconnected set of elective political and ethical commitments, and rarely have some of them been adequately circumspect regarding how close certain of their texts often come to the romantic nihilism that nourishes fascist passions. More to the point, though, if Milbank's is a plausible definition of the "postmodern" (and, at the level of ontology, it is), then one may go further and say that postmodernity, broadly speaking, neither subverts nor reverses metaphysics, but simply confirms it: it preserves a classic polarity within the metaphysical tradition, though it embraces one pole rather than (as is traditional) the other. It merely marks the triumph of Heracleitos over Parmenides, of the narrative of being as dynamic flow and aimless differentiation over the narrative of being as immobile totality. If indeed metaphysics, in its every manifestation, is really the attempt to erect a hierarchy within totality that will still the turbulence of difference, dam up the alluvial force of becoming, and scaffold Dionysian energy in a framework of Apollonian re-

2. Milbank, 279.

serve,[3] the collapse of metaphysics must be (for thought) the setting free of chaos and its prodigal play of creation and destruction. But a mirror preserves the image it inverts.

Perhaps then it is Hegel — the most ambitious metaphysician of all — rather than his critics, who effected the transition from the Parmenidean to the Heracleitean orthodoxy of the day: precisely because the Hegelian system is the most unrestrained, regal attempt to bring the dynamism of becoming into the fold of magisterial metaphysics, precisely because it absorbs time and history into the epic of the Idea, violence — indeed, warfare — is imagined as inextricable from being; strife, conflict, conceived as one or another process of negation, dialectical determination, and the endless labor of thought, belongs no longer to Plato's realm of the simulacra — ideality's defatigation in time and matter — but to being's truest, most necessary story: the diremption of Idea into finitude and the recuperation of finitude into *Geist*. On the one hand, it is here, where the architecture of metaphysics achieves its most splendid and elaborate effects, that it proves itself uninhabitable, as Kierkegaard observed, and becomes all too transparently an abstract violence enacted against the concrete innocence of becoming, the canopy of the "Same" cast over the extravagant openness of difference (or a cloud floating above an abyss). But on the other hand, it is also here that the strife of difference, along with the perishing of all that becomes, achieves a transcendental privilege of its own, essential to truth's inward determination. Even though Hegel's system is at once the triumph and reductio ad absurdum of Western metaphysics, if — *après le déluge* — ontological discourse is still confined by a rigid structuralism of the metaphysical to one or another pole of the opposition between Heracleitean and Parmenidean tropes, then the perceived failure of the system can be grasped by philosophical reflection only as the release of that prior ontological violence that every metaphysical scheme attempts to govern. Though the Hegelian system is essentially philosophy's most audacious imperial campaign to recapture territories lost to Christianity's "historicizing" narrative of truth, Hegel cannot (as Christian theology must) counterpose a true history and a false, a story of peace and a story of violence (there can be, in the system, no analogical interval between God and world), but must make the former the premise and the residue of the latter, so that peace and violence are convertible with one another as, on the one hand, the abstract repose of the Idea and, on the other, the concrete

3. See John Caputo, *Radical Hermeneutics: Repetition, Deconstruction, and the Hermeneutic Project* (Bloomington and Indianapolis: Indiana University Press, 1987), a text dominated by a kind of mysticism of "the flux," whose energies metaphysics is seen as trying always to subdue, and a text that also never questions the terms of this opposition, their narrowness, or their metaphysical pedigrees. See also Jacques Derrida, *Of Grammatology*, trans. Gayatri Chakravorty Spivak (Baltimore: Johns Hopkins University Press, 1974), 71.

process of negative determination. When metaphysics tries thus to incorporate being's violence into itself as a dialectical necessity, according to the logic of a higher reconciliation, an *Aufhebung,* but then fails through overreaching, totality withdraws but this now apparently inevitable violence remains. In this sense then, postmodernity would be merely the dialectical completion of the metaphysical project, the homecoming not of *Geist* but of a protean and capricious god for whom creation and destruction are as one. With the disappearance of the Idea, the flux of unlikeness does not abate, but overflows its banks; an ephemeral Parmenides yields to an everlasting Heracleitos; the intricate architectural ingenuity of Apollonian violence exhausts itself before the unmasterable pandemonium of Dionysian violence; Socrates drinks hemlock, but Athens remains — forever at war.

This is nothing very new. It may well be that every discourse of totality in the Western tradition — but especially as represented by the two great epochs of idealism, the Platonic and the Hegelian — springs from the ancient tension between an Ephesian and an Eleatic topology of being, and is destined therefore to imagine being under the form of either a synthesis between the two or a final definitive discrimination. In either case the limits of thought have been set from the start by this simple but inflexible antinomy. A different account of being, or of the infinite, simply cannot appear to view within so narrow a passage as that lying between Heracleitos and Parmenides (nor can any species of thought defined by loyalty to or apostasy from metaphysics recognize in the Christian infinite something that stands apart from this tedious but interminable opposition). Having failed to make Ephesus a colony of Elea, Hegel inadvertently inaugurated an Ephesian war of liberation. And perhaps Nietzsche was merely the first witness to this transition, the first to proclaim a gospel of salvation from one violence by another; his fable of God's death signified, after all, not only the disappearance of the Christian God from the horizon of human meaning, but the failure of philosophy's grand attempt to reidealize the world's being (which Christian thought had reduced to something gratuitous) and truth (which theology had rendered concretely historical): it was the fable of how Apollo once ventured forth beyond his city walls, intending to return in triumph, laden with spoils, but instead vanished in the immeasurable wilds of the exterior. But then, Nietzsche's is a narrative in which the Christian God has never truly figured and in the course of which the Christian story has never really been addressed; and the postmetaphysical flight from Apollo the tyrant to Dionysus the roisterer can have little or no consequence for Christian theology, because it is a tale told, and a war waged, between competing paganisms. By turning from the Hegelian logic of negation to an ethos of pure affirmation, Nietzsche at once demystified and forever consecrated violence: for *pure* affirmation, as could scarcely be otherwise within a discourse of defiant immanentism, must embrace the negative *as* the positive, being's *essential* positivity, its creative and wanton élan, in which violence participates not as dialectical negation — *Geist's* endless Sabbatarian probation — but as the world's essential, if atelic, creative power. Of course, Nietzsche's thought never was quite so purely affirmative as is often imagined:[4] his Dionysus gradually became a figure more than a little dialectical; nevertheless, insofar as a species of negation appears in Nietzsche's thought, it is not violence but peace — or, at any rate, the appearance of peace — that occupies the place of the negative: "peace" is always the stilling of a prior violence, a calculated accommodation, the hero's temporary, hard-won armistice, or a moment of ignoble passivity, during which the Dionysiac rhythm slackens or syncopates; peace dissembles force and beauty is a sober interval within the totality of a debauched sublime. And this story is certainly taken up — if also strained against — by much postmodern thought: being is being only in the tautological repetition, or eternal recurrence, of a collusion of force and chance; being is Dionysus's dismemberment and reassembly. This, at least, is the pagan metanarrative that Milbank — to return to his argument — extracts from Nietzsche (who does not resist) and from his disciples (who are somewhat more restive): πάντα χωρεῖ, οὐδὲν μένει — and all peace, civility, harmony, or beauty is accomplished by limiting a preexisting discord.

Milbank also, as has been noted, draws Heidegger into his critique,[5] albeit perhaps slightly less persuasively. Heidegger's rhetoric, in contrast to Nietzsche's, could scarcely appear more irenic: in his thought, both early and late, being always wears the aspect of openness, manifestation, *aletheia,* that which gives, shows, or lets be. From the "fundamental ontology" of *Being and Time* to the later writings' meditations upon the *Ereignis* or *es gibt* that gives being and beings to one another, being never loses its quality of luminosity, expansiveness, *Gelassenheit,* and peace; even the play of hiddenness *(lethe)* and *aletheia* has a strange tenderness about it. But this is precisely where Milbank grows

---

4. The Nietzsche of much of postmodernism is — as will be discussed below — Deleuze's Nietzsche, and Deleuze began his philosophical career in opposition, primarily, to the fashionable Hegelianism of his time (that of Alexandre Kojève principally, but also that of Gramsci and Sartre), and so made of Nietzsche his hero of the antidialectical and purely positive. One must, however, agree with John Caputo (in Caputo, *Against Ethics: Contributions to a Poetics of Obligation with Constant Reference to Deconstruction* [Bloomington and Indianapolis: Indiana University Press, 1993], 49-50) that Nietzsche made great room for the negative in his thought, not as fitting a teleological scheme, but certainly as part of the creative agon of being; Caputo is also correct to say that Deleuze early on sought to soften the rhetoric of strife in Nietzsche (50), though much of Deleuze's thought has consisted in a radicalization of that rhetoric as well.

5. Milbank, 296-302. The parenthetical numbers in the following text refer to Milbank's *Theology and Social Theory.*

restless. What he particularly objects to in Heidegger's account of the ontological difference is the notion of the "fall" (*Zug*) of being into one or another metaphysical contraction, its assumption of the limitations proper to one or another epochal situation; this is the tale "of the repetition of Being itself, its endless happening as the 'difference' of the various historical epochs, the various cultural orderings" (299), and it tends inevitably toward a very particular construal of difference as such:

> As both Jacques Derrida and Gilles Deleuze later say (in a more emphatic fashion), "difference" has now become the sole "transcendental" in both a "Kantian" sense that one assumes *a priori* that a radical heterogeneity, incompatibility, non-hierarchy and arbitrariness pertain amongst all knowable things, and in a "scholastic" sense that every thing really is constituted by such a radical heterogeneity. But if this is the case, then the *Sache,* the constant temporal mediation of the ontological difference, must itself be characterized by a rupture, an arbitrary break with the unanimity of Being. A unanimity which of course only "is" through this series of "breaks." (300)

For Milbank the notion that ontical presence *is* always the concealment of Being means that Heidegger's characterization of the proper method of ontological interpretation as a "doing violence," a *Gewaltsamkeit,* describes merely an appropriate response to the "primordial violence" of being's own essential caducity. "In [Heidegger's] later works . . . it is more and more insisted that Being only is, in the event of its own self-occlusion and the arbitrary series of differential breaks which constitute the battles of history, the replacement of one cultural regime by another" (300). And to treat the eventuation of ontological difference as somehow a declension, alienation, or suppression of being, rather than adopting, say, a theological vantage that regards this difference as the mysterious fold of the ontic's ontological contingency, which reflects the grace, splendor, and liberty of the God who is the source of all being, is a practice dictated not by philosophical necessity but by mere metaphysical prejudice. A being whose every showing is a withdrawal is univocal being, being that conceals as it reveals, making its every manifestation simply the violence of arbitrary rupture and contraction;[6] no analogical path opens between beings and being,

---

6. Milbank reads Heidegger's ontological difference as a new form of Scotist univocity (302), following the argument of Gillian Rose in *Dialectic of Nihilism: Post-structuralism and Law* (Oxford: Basil Blackwell, 1984). In point of fact, the *ens univocum* of Duns Scotus does not actually constitute an ontology (as here and elsewhere Milbank imagines it does), nor could one legitimately speak of being in Heidegger's thought as an empty, formal category indifferently embracing all beings as discrete substances. Still, he is correct on one score: Heidegger's ontology *is* univocal, in that the event of being is always simply the event of beings, being is conse-

nor any possibility of seeing being as a peaceful gift that *suffers* violence, upon which the strife of history accidentally impinges; Heidegger's *es gibt* excludes God's "It is good." The offense appears all the more grievous indeed in the light of the early Heidegger's appropriation (or plagiarism) of Kierkegaard's treatment of anxiety and use of the Augustinian reading of original sin (as aboriginal guilt) for the project of an analytic of *Dasein:* for once guilt is severed from the notions of the *privatio boni* — the nothingness of sin — and of the human will's quite contingent historical failure to remain directed toward God, and is inserted instead into an interpretation of the very nature of ontic "thrownness," guilt becomes nothing moral, absolute, or reparable, but only the inescapable condition of *Dasein* as such — as a result of a nothingness not dwelling in the will, but inherent in finite existence itself (301). This, from a theological position, cannot help but seem insidious: if sin is no longer that which intrudes upon being, but is more originally a guilt coterminous with being, then "alienation" or "transgression" is the very name of difference; the violence of history is inderacinable from existence if being is in some sense "violent" in the very event of its being.

Admittedly, Milbank's is too hasty a summary of a complicated issue; yet as idiosyncratic and inspissated as such a reading of Heidegger may seem — the emphasis appears, at first, so oddly placed — it is by no means one that should simply be dismissed. At least the substance of Milbank's complaint is clear: rather than a mere letting go of the world in its worlding, or a humble untying of the knots of metaphysics, the Heideggerian project is, both late and early, just another transcendental vantage on being, and one whose own metaphysical presuppositions confine philosophy within the narrative of a more subtle but more inescapable ontological violence: a univocal account of being, which makes out the ruptures in or transitions among manifestations of difference to be inadjudicable and arbitrary expressions of a being hidden by what has being. Ultimately I would endorse much of Milbank's reading here, if in somewhat altered terms. To speak of the "presencing" of beings as a "rupture" in the "unanimity" of being might make it seem as if Heidegger thinks of being as some *thing* from which other things must positively break out into the open, rather than as the sheer letting be of what is: not exactly something hidden made manifest, but the manifestation of the manifest, the uncontainable and inexhaustible power of manifestation itself. It is not entirely implausible to speak rather of the *kenosis* of being in Heidegger's thought. Nonetheless, if being's utmost generosity — in withholding itself, in "nothing-ing," so that beings may

---

quently not hierarchically related to beings, and being discloses beings only in its own nihilation (quite the opposite, as it happens, of Scotus's understanding of being as the infinite coincidence of the transcendentals in God's *"esse verum"*).

come to presence in the "juncture" of being and, in due order, give way to other beings — is merely its nothingness among beings, its "refusal" to appear as the absolute, being is not only not the plenitude of light into which love and knowledge may ascend, to discover the unity of truth, beauty, and goodness, but is in a sense darkness itself, the *dialectical* negation that perpetually, indifferently grants beings their finitude; and this is, if not violence itself, the tragic fatedness of violence. Being obviously neither embraces nor rejects violence or peace, cruelty or love: all *is* in the same way, and being illumines all things with the same empty effulgence. But then every "mittence" of being is, as Heidegger says, an "errance," for being gives light only by hiding and leading astray; as much as truth is a letting-be-manifest, it is also (as Heidegger also admits) a struggle of obscurity and light, *Erde* and *Welt*, so that peace and strife are inseparably joined. *Logos* must force *physis* into a gathered containment. More significantly though, no less than the Stoic image of the cosmos as an enclosed and finite totality in which every form is continually displaced by another, the whole under the arch of ἀνάγκη or μοῖρα, the later Heidegger's understanding of the destinal epochality of being's temporality ever more absolutely identifies the event of being not only with the coming to presence and "whiling" of beings, but with their annihilation. Like Hegel, Heidegger thinks truth as also, intrinsically, destruction. Indeed, the more the earlier concern regarding the difference of being from beings is superseded by the later concern regarding the event, the more Heidegger conceives of being under the regime of necessity. Only from the perspective of the "thinker" able to glimpse not only the appearance, but the mystery, of the event is there peace: the limpidity of being's openness mirrored in the thoughtful speech and poetic serenity of the philosopher, and the darkness of being's hiddenness recognized — not without a certain restrained dolor — as fate. There is an ontological "peacefulness" to which "thinking-thanking" responds, but true thought transcends the vulgar question of ontic peace, even amid wars and genocides: *aletheia* has its tragic costs. Perhaps, then, as a witness to the collapse of metaphysics, Heidegger was (contrary to his own reading of the matter) a thinker who was always only "on the way" to a place that Nietzsche had already reached.

II. THE VEIL OF THE SUBLIME

Another, somewhat less picturesque definition of postmodernity would be: the attempt of Western thought, in a time of utter disenchantment with all the beguiling promises of faith and reason alike, to unite the antimetaphysical moments in the thought of Kant, Nietzsche, and Heidegger in a single philosophical grammar (or habit), going beyond them, while still (for the most part) resisting despair, cruelty, or *destructive* nihilism. And yet another definition, closely if not obviously allied to this, would be: narratives of the sublime. The event of modernity within philosophy (which arrived, at least visibly, in the age of nominalism) consisted in the dissolution of being: the disintegration of that radiant unity wherein the good, the true, and the beautiful coincided as infinite simplicity and fecundity, communicating themselves to a world whose only reality was its variable participation in their gratuity; and the divorce between this thought of being, as the supereminent fullness of all perfection, and the thought of God (who could then no longer be conceived as being and the wellspring of all being, revealing his glory in the depth of splendor in which created things are shaped and sustained). This vision was so thoroughly and quickly forgotten (long before Heidegger would diagnose it, ineptly, as just another mode of the "forgetfulness of being") that being itself could now be conceived only in absolutely opposite terms: as a veil or an absence, thought or unthought, but in either case impenetrable — the veil that veils even itself, the empty name that adds nothing to the essence of beings, sheer uniform existence. And God's transcendence, so long as nostalgia preserved philosophy's attachment to "that hypothesis," could be understood now only as God's absence, his exile beyond or hiddenness within the veil of being, occasionally breaking through perhaps, but only as an *alienum* or an explanatory cause. Being, no longer resplendent with truth, appearing in and elevating all things, could be figured then only as the sublime.

That is one way of putting the matter, nor is it fanciful. Sublimity is in critical fashion, here on the far side of modernity; and it is — with whatever degree of conceptual alteration — the sublime of Kant's *Critique of Judgment* that has come to define the nature of this fashion. Which might suggest that by "postmodernity" we mean simply modernity grown fully self-aware. Whatever the case, the discourses we tend to recognize as critically postmodern, however little else they may share, all come sooner or later to depend upon one or another account of the "unrepresentable," the indomitably singular and eventual, the impenetrable and immemorial; and in each case it is this "reality," which precedes and exceeds the fragile frozen present of representation, that is accorded an unquestioned critical weight: the unrepresentable, the sublime, is somehow "true," while representation (whether eidetic or conceptual) must dissemble this prior and alien truth to achieve its quite necessary, but ultimately illusory, stability. Like Heidegger's "Being," it yields beings to thought precisely in its own occlusion, its own thoroughly immanent transcendence of sensibility and concept. Thought follows after — with a forlorn and ghostly anachrony — the event that it is destined always to have missed, lost, or forgotten, before it is itself the thought of anything at all. Even when Kant's sublime is not directly invoked, its logic (at least, construed in a certain way) is always presumed. For good reason: it repeats at the level of the aesthetic the first Critique's prohibition upon all metaphysical adventures beyond the realm of the theoretical, but more emphatically and creatively, transforming prohibition into a positive revelation of the limits and possibilities of thought and freedom. And when the Kantian sublime is explicitly treated as a "postmodern" theme, it proves itself a remarkably apt instrument for disclosing a fundamental commonality among otherwise unrelated streams of reflection (as is perhaps nowhere better demonstrated than in a slim but provocative collection of essays from 1988 called *Du Sublime*).[7]

Of course, Kant's own discussion of the sublime in the third Critique, however suggestive, is scarcely ambitious; it is quite brief, and reflects (as much as anything else) the formal expectation of the philosophy of his time that any theoretical aesthetics must address both beauty and sublimity; yet it is a distinctive treatment and clearly advances the project at the heart of the text: the integration of pure and practical reason. In examining, under the aspect of the beautiful, the peculiar rationality of the "aesthetic *a priori*" (whose judgments are only "subjectively universal"), Kant argues that the beautiful (understood as a judgment wherein imagination and understanding achieve a special and autotelic harmony) reveals the capacity of the aesthetic to mediate between sensibility and reason, as well as the rational power of the free play of the imagination. On turning to the sublime, however, Kant finds the harmony of aesthetic judgment (at least momentarily) disrupted. The imagination's occupation with the sublime, while still yielding a genuine sort of pleasure ("negative pleasure"), is nevertheless no longer play but serious labor; the sublime occurs for imagination as an inhibition of one's vital powers, followed by their yet more forceful release (*Critique of Judgment* §23). Unlike the beautiful, its manifestation is an intuition of the indeterminate, whether one encounters it in the incomprehensible vastitude of the "mathematical sublime" or in the incomprehensible natural power of the "dynamical sublime"; though, in fact, the true sublime properly resides nowhere in the things of sensibility (which can only suggest it), but only in the mind, which discovers, even in the instant of its rapture, its own essential superiority over all of nature (§23). In purely empirical terms, the sublime is suggested to us in moments when, presented by an immensity, grandeur, or force that exceeds representation — because it requires of apprehension *(Auffassung)* an "infinite" activity that surpasses the power of comprehension *(Zusammenfassung)*, which is itself dependent upon the inward

---

7. *Du Sublime*, ed. Jean-François Courtine (Paris: Belin, 1988); in English: *Of the Sublime: Presence in Question*, translated and expanded by Jeffrey S. Librett (New York: State University of New York Press, 1993).

synthesis of the sense of time and hence finite (§26) — reason must return from the realm of the sensible. But in so doing, it discovers in itself a super-sensible power that is infinitely free of and infinitely greater than the realm of representation. Precisely when the inner sense of time, exposed to comprehension's defeat, suffers violence at the hands of imagination's contrapurposive power of apprehension, reason discovers through its negative pleasure a deeper purpose within that violence: the entire vocation of the mind (§27). To realize this requires only a certain sacrifice (*Aufopferung*) in the realm of the aesthetic, in return for which reason receives word of its own boundless depths of supersensible freedom and might (§29), its capacity for rational concepts (to-tality, freedom, etc.) exceeding representation's scope. Thus practical reason "appears" within the theoretical, under the form of representation's failure and reason's triumph. At the moment of thought's overthrow, thought is restored to itself, is thrown back upon itself, and finds itself to be infinite; beyond nature's "veil of Isis," reason discovers itself, at home with itself, before and above all things. It is that moment, as Paul Guyer writes, when "God's creation is hum-bled before our free reason, and even the sublimity of God himself can be ap-preciated only through the image of our own autonomy."[8]

The impression a sober reading of Kant's treatment of the sublime should, in fact, leave is one of extraordinary rationalist triumphalism, a Prome-thean sense of the self's ultimate transcendence over all of nature, even its most awful and monstrous effects. This aspect of the third Critique, however, rarely survives in postmodern appropriations of Kant's text, which often allow the momentary appearance of something "irrational" or "unthinkable" in the midst of the critical project to carry them off toward regions of the "post-metaphysical" that one certainly cannot find in Kant's own patient cartography of thought's proper world. Still, the latter-day purveyors of the Kantian sublime can justly claim for themselves a certain fidelity to a pattern that Kant's account does indeed establish: insofar as there is any mediation between the discrete re-gions of the theoretical and the practical, it must occur under the form of a dis-ruption, one which in no way endangers the absolute distinction between the sensible and the morally good or essentially true, and thus the event of media-tion is one in which freedom, the good, or the true is merely intimated, by the end of aesthetic grace. Hence beauty's only "truth" is the truth of a certain power of judgment, while everything of graver import dwells beyond the aes-thetic altogether. The beautiful adumbrates nothing beyond the self, and thought must traverse it, even transgress it, to escape either triviality or illusion: the beautiful leaves off where the sublime begins, and the sublime itself falls

8. Paul Guyer, *Kant and the Experience of Freedom* (Cambridge: Cambridge University Press, 1993), 259.

away when it has sufficiently suggested to reason the *formless* power of the infinite. This nisus (from beauty to sublimity to infinity) is linear and irreversible, and the sublime serves as both median and partition, both indicating a continuity and assuring an inviolable division between the beautiful and the infinite. It is just this attempt at once to reconcile and preserve a presumed incompatibility between form and infinity that recurs, almost obsessively, in postmodern thought — even if it eschews such terms. However it trembles, whatever shadowy figures pass behind it, the sublime is a veil.

It is Lyotard who has devoted the most explicit attention to the Kantian sublime: he finds in it a category of the unrepresentable more radical than the less threatening "noumenon" of the first Critique; the earlier epistemological limit merely forbade metaphysical speculation regarding substances, but the latter (for Lyotard) describes a limit that actively draws in upon thought, until even the stability of representation and immanent formal teleology gives way; "the aesthetic of the sublime . . . comes about through the distension of beautiful forms to the point of 'formlessness' . . . and . . . , from that very fact, brings about the overturning, the destruction, of the aesthetics of the beautiful."[9] As Lyotard concisely puts it,

> Kant writes that the sublime is a *Geistesgefühl*, a sentiment of the mind, whereas the beautiful is a sentiment that proceeds from a "fit" between nature and mind, i.e., when transcribed into the Kantian economy of faculties, between the imagination and the understanding. This marriage or, at least, this betrothal proper to the beautiful is broken by the sublime. The Idea, especially the Idea of pure practical reason, Law and freedom, is signaled in a quasi-perception right within the break-up of the imagination and therefore just as much via a lack or even a disappearance of nature understood in this way. The *Geistesgefühl*, the sentiment of the mind, signifies that the mind is lacking in nature, that nature is lacking for it. It feels only itself. In this way the sublime is none other than the sacrificial announcement of the ethical in the aesthetic field. Sacrificial in that it requires that the imaginative nature (inside and outside the mind) must be sacrificed in the interests of practical reason (which is not without some specific problems for the *ethical* evaluation of the sublime sentiment). This heralds the end of an aesthetics, that of the beautiful, in the name of the final destination of the mind, which is freedom.[10]

The sublime opens up the interval between the realms of representation and ethics, the distance between representations of the intuited and the

9. Jean-François Lyotard, *The Inhuman* (Stanford: Stanford University Press, 1988), 136.
10. Lyotard, *The Inhuman*, 137.

unrepresentable event of intuition (between, in Lyotard's parlance, figuration and the "figural"), the space between signification and sense. It indeed shows how sensibility adumbrates (through its own failure) unrepresentable yet paradoxically conceivable notions like infinity or freedom; but, in addition, this recognition of the ungraspable surplus of *ethical* freedom, achieved through the sacrifice of the imaginative nature, should disabuse the theoretical consciousness of the notion that it can frame some species of master discourse — some metanarrative or critical *hors-texte* — which would lay hold of reality by combining all disciplines and perspectives in some single comprehensive wisdom: it should inspire the manumission of the "differends." More than that, sublimity is a spur to passion: an erotic surplus and an invitation that, by promising to thinking the thought of unrepresentable freedom, wakens it to its moral power. This failure of the concord of the faculties, then, is obviously more than an intimation of chaos; it prompts an awareness of ethical transcendence and allows thought to experience obligation (if not exactly as *the* moral law within, at least as a humble sense that the heteronomic and heterogeneous goods of experience cannot be reconciled, and should not then be made subordinate to a "total" narrative). The thought of the sublime thus belongs to a war upon totality, which claims to have had done with the ancient desire to make difference obey the plot of the universal, and which preserves thought's critical distance from every representation. Nor is the sublime merely an occasional sensation (as for Kant): sought for, it is at the very foundation of sensibility, in the instant of intuition. Occurring in the intensity of the immemorial event, prior to every transcendental act of comprehension, it helps thought achieve an extranarrative vantage from which the strategies of totality become visible.

In thus interpreting Kant's sublime as a kind of mist into which the close-knit company of the faculties ventures at its peril, and in which it cannot help but find itself dispersed, Lyotard goes well beyond Kant himself; for Lyotard the sublime is a moving limit, which not only describes the bournes of "comprehension" but continues to disrupt thought and discourse at the source; the sublime becomes not only a sentiment distinguishable from the apprehension of the beautiful, but an abolition of beauty, the revelation that beauty becomes lost in its own contradiction and vanity. Faith in the stable proportions of nature's forms vanishes, and the "teleological machine" is destroyed. Every interval within being somehow always already belongs to a sublime that enjoins not only an understanding of the impossibility of an adequate representation of the ethical or the true, but also an acknowledgment of the irreconcilable struggle between differing representations, and of the consequent need for claims to truth to restrict themselves to their limited spheres. Perhaps this reading of Kant is somehow faithful to the logic of the Critiques. But while it may be true that there is no universal genre of discourse that can regulate the conflicts that arise between differences,[11] that the differend as difference of opinion, idiom, or "language game" should be preferred to a consensus or reconciliation brought about under the form of ingratiating representations that merely "beautify" and becalm the space between, it should be noted that these truths are secured for reflection by a renunciation of reason that Kant would never have countenanced; for Lyotard the Kantian divorce between theoretical and practical reason (which the third Critique is intended to resolve) becomes an active and irresoluble hostility.

> Morality . . . intrinsically demands to be universally communicated, and it is analogous in this respect to the feeling of the beautiful. . . . As for the sublime, it escapes both demands for universal communication. . . . The Idea of the finality without concept of a form of pure pleasure cannot be suggested by the violent contra-finality of the object. The sublime feeling is neither moral universality nor aesthetic universalization, but is, rather, the destruction of one by the other in the violence of their differend. This differend cannot demand, even subjectively, to be communicated to all thought.[12]

But, if the chromaticisms of Lyotard's fantasia on the theme Kant has stated seem somewhat liberal, they pale in comparison to the strident and obsessively repetitive atonality of a rather notorious essay by Jacob Rogozinski called "The Gift of the World."[13] Kant occasionally speaks of the experience of the sublime as imagination's act of violence *(Gewalt),* but this word's function in his argument is both rhetorical and transitory; for Rogozinski, by contrast, "violence" is apparently the profound and guiding concern of Kant's analytic. Moreover, it is now a twofold violence: the violence both of "chaos" and of reason. According to Rogozinski, beauty appears in Kant's text as that moment in which imagination exults in its power to organize "chaos," but the sublime marks that moment in which all beautiful forms are undone and return to their primal indistinction, as the work of the imagination is destroyed (135-36). For Kant, "sublimity scatters the imagination or sets it to flight; broken and powerless, it recedes into itself" (140). When imagination thus does violence to reason, it provokes reason to respond with a contrary violence (and this is, among other things, the authentic form of the ethical); in the rupture of the bond between apprehension and comprehension, one discovers an essential incompati-

---

11. See Jean-François Lyotard, *The Differend: Phrases in Dispute,* trans. George Van Den Abbeele (Minneapolis: University of Minnesota Press, 1988), xii.

12. Jean-François Lyotard, *Lessons on the Analytic of the Sublime,* trans. Elizabeth Rottenberg (Stanford: Stanford University Press, 1994), 238-39.

13. In *Of the Sublime.* Parenthetical page references in the following text are to this work.

bility between imagination and the inward sense of time (141-42) that reveals the very act of representational synthesis to be a violent struggle with a restive exterior: "In its effort to retain the passivity of the past within the horizon of the present, to mask temporal difference beneath the appearance of a homogeneous flux, the violent synthesis of imagination works towards a leveling of time. In reducing time to a continuous and uniform series of nows, this synthesis submits temporality to the reign of presence, to the *maintenance* of time. Presence as such is violence. . . . Without this *transcendental violence,* which opens the horizon of phenomena, no phenomenon at all could appear and link itself to others in the cohesion of a world" (144). Rogozinski admits that Kant nowhere says that phenomenal temporality is actually illusory or vulgar, and that for Kant "this temporality is the condition of all objective truth"; but, that said,

> it is nonetheless dissimulating, and the truth it supports is initiated by means of a transcendental untruth. The time of phenomena masks the phenomenalization of time, the violent de-temporalization of time as form of phenomena. The violence of presence dissimulates itself in that — and in what — it presents. Each phenomenon can appear only by occulting this original violence, in re-covering the ecstatic fracture of time, temporal tearing of the imagination. The totality of phenomena — Nature — is the veil of Isis, the texture of which is woven of the thread of temporality. What weaves the veil is the violence of the imagination, concealed in the apparition of phenomena, in the luminous appearance of the world. The imagination is the violence of the veil, which veils itself and dissimulates itself under an illusory transparence. With respect to this beautiful appearance, the sublime would be the test of truth. Stretched to the extreme, to the breaking point, the hidden violence of the imagination becomes quasi perceptible, at the moment when it comes apart. The violent truth of the world, latent in each phenomenon, discovers itself in laceration. The sublime reveals the veil. (147)

And it is the "blind opacity" of this veil that yields truth, the unveiling of *aletheia* (147-48). So, for Rogozinski, hidden violence is met by the violence of appearance: this is the economy that grants the world, the obscuration of being in beings, the aggression of thought against the indeterminate, the endless war that is the secret power of peaceful proportion. Transcendental idealism's scission between phenomenon and noumenon, it turns out, is nothing less than the event of this conflict. "The violent 'rivalry' of imagination and reason then is nothing but a maddened play of the imagination with itself and the source of transcendental illusion. Not — as the tradition teaches from Plato to Malebranche — because the imagination is a 'deceptive power,' the 'enemy of reason,' but because it is pure reason itself, as the faculty of delirium. In the sublime failure of the imagination, metaphysical illusion deconstructs itself. The violence of finitude acknowledges its powerlessness to comprehend the infinite" (149). Still, the sublime affords an intimation of the infinite, nature's "total infinity as phenomenon," the supersensible substratum of nature that permits, within the violence of its unrepresentable economy, the representations of an ordered world. Form is a "pure gift," a unification of multiplicity achieved by limitation, the work of the pure forms of space and time — which Rogozinski calls "infinite form," the infinite power of form without contour, a sort of primordial confusion that is the absolute possibility of appearance. "It opens itself onto the entirety of the Maybe, the ideal of pure reason, which idolatrous metaphysics personifies and names God. The *Critique* is called upon to deconstruct this hypostasis, to discover beneath the veil of the idol the sublime chaos of the world" (152). But while the formless unity of this chaos evokes the unifying violence of imagination, the sublime marks that instant of failure when one discovers that the real force of unity is greater than and prior to imagination. "[C]haos is the supreme order: the finite figures of the phenomena mask the infinity of pure forms and only a radical disfiguration of the world reveals the world's Law. The *limen* of the sublime is the threshold of this passage" (155). This passage to the law of the world, which gives the world, is a passage to the supersensible; and here alone, presumably, all lawfulness finds its possibility: freedom, ethics, obligation. But here the essay leaves off.

One could, of course, simply disregard Rogozinski's essay as an annoying specimen of philosophical banality, an experiment in rhetorical extremism, or an eisegetical burlesque (the choices here are plentiful), but in its favor, "The Gift of the World" splendidly displays, within its very absurdity, the logical lucidity of its assumptions. Freighted as it is with so much of the jetsam of post-Nietzschean and post-Heideggerian Continental philosophy, it complements Lyotard's slightly less bibulous readings of Kant as an excellent example of a thoroughly logical extension of Kantian premises into what we tend to identify as postmodern convictions. Again, it is not implausible to say that the entire pathology of the modern and postmodern can be diagnosed as a multifarious narrative of the sublime, according to the paradigm of Kant's critical project: what pure reason extracts from experience and represents to itself is neutral appearance, separated by an untraversable abyss from everything "meaningful"; and what reason sees in appearance can have, obviously, no more eminent significance: beauty does not speak of the good, nor the good of being. Questions of the good, of being, of value, of the possibility of appearance itself do not so much exceed the world as stand over against it; truth is not, finally, the seen, but the unseen that permits one to see. With the dissolution of an ontology of the transcendent, of that infinite eminence in which what appears participates, every discourse that would attempt to speak not only of the things of the world but also of the event of the world must inevitably resort to the mysticism of the sublime and its dogmatisms: not a mysticism that seeks to penetrate the veil, but a mystical faith in the reality of the veil, an immanent metaphysics. And the only moral effort permitted by such a faith takes the form of paradox and tragedy. However one phrases the matter, this much is certain: insofar as the "postmodern" is the completion of the deconstruction of metaphysics, it usually depends upon one immense and irreducible metaphysical assumption: that the unrepresentable *is;* more to the point, that the unrepresentable (call it *différance,* chaos, being, alterity, the infinite . . .) is somehow truer than the representable (which necessarily dissembles it), more original, and qualitatively *other:* that is, it does not differ from the representable by virtue of a greater fullness and unity of those transcendental moments that constitute the world of appearance, but by virtue of its absolute difference, its dialectical or negative indeterminacy, its no-thingness. Between thought's representations and the unrepresentable "that" of the "event" there is an incommensurability, and sublimity marks the fated tragic *partage* of their union, the sacrificial economy of their collusion, as the symbol of their simultaneous divorce and marriage. That is why one can approach a definition of "postmodernity" by classifying many of its exemplary discourses under various accounts of the unrepresentable. I would isolate, perhaps arbitrarily, at least four such "narratives of the sublime." Thus:

1. *The differential sublime,* which might also be called the sublimity of exteriority. Stated simply, if metaphysics is the regime of immutability, presence, and interiority, the discourse of the unrepresentable "corrects" this by insisting upon the "priority" of change, absence, and exteriority — in short, difference. The imperative to *think difference* is the heart of the postmodern sensibility. In its more extreme, apocalyptic, and assured moments (especially in its simplified American academic variant), the postmodern proclaims itself as a repudiation of all the metaphysical vices: hierarchy, taxonomy, the whole apparatus of theory, law, government, and social convention, all that serves to localize, confine, and essentialize the different; idealism, priestcraft, inquisition, humanism, and grand unified theories; colonialism, tribalism, nationalism, and empire; authority, exclusivity, dogma, closure, and "Truth." Any attempt to still the Heracleitean flux by assuming the impossible vantage of a transcendent understanding or moral intuition of the nature of finitude is by definition complicit with schemes of power: such is the violence of metaphysics, whether it proceed in terms of *eidos, ousia, parousia, esse, ens, ego, Geist,* or *Sein,* and whether it employ strategies of categorization, participation, representation, resemblance, or analogy. Hence a robust postmodernism must surely be a discourse of libera-

tion, setting free the energy of the many, becoming, and the "differend."[14] And difference must be the first thought, conceived (though never grasped) before the thought of identity, defiantly advanced against every form of substantialization or classification, every epistemological tactic for drawing the different in under the sheltering eaves of the "Same." Difference must be thought ever anew, sustaining its critical distance from the tendency of every text (however liberating) to rationalize the "content" of difference, and must be thought in every way: regarding being, history, culture, science, language, ethics, politics, and the self; not only the difference of beings from being, or of one thing from (and so as determined by) another, but difference in every event of being, the difference of singularity as such, and of that serial repetition of the singular that displaces every presence into its own absence and reverberates within and disrupts the singular itself. The realm of difference is a region of freedom, chance, peril, escape, play, desire, absence, and innumerable paths of departure; it is the open horizon of becoming in its innocence, the homeland and the exile of the sign where an infinite array of signifiers — forever opaque to one another — excite and provoke one another into endless gaming; it is the land of unlikeness, liberated at last from an ancient empire and rejoicing in itself.[15]

While the theme of difference is a postmodern commonplace, the figure who has most rigorously thought it in terms of exteriority, without any *immediately* apparent relapse into a metaphysical discourse concerning the "ground" of differentiation, is Derrida. True, as time wears on, it becomes increasingly difficult to imagine that either Derrida's celebrity or his garrulity is quite proportionate to his philosophical contribution, but equally difficult to deny the scrupulousness with which he has pursued a single inversion of a Hegelian insight for decades without wavering in his resolve. Whether he speaks of difference, "writing," dissemination, erasure, absence, the trace, the *chora*, or whatever other term has arrived for him in the clearing, it is small effort to recognize behind these words the motions of the indefatigable engine of the Hegelian logic: diremption, negation, finitude, the exterior — although imagined now not as the middle moment in the circular adventure of the Concept, but as the original and irreducible difference, the primordial dispossession that permits thought to move and beings to be, without any "departure" from or "return" to plenitude: purest exteriority. Derrida's most effective early survey of the matter is his treatment of the difference — or *différance* — of writing, the constant differing and

14. An ideal introduction to the general atmosphere of this kind of postmodernism is Lyotard, *The Differend.*

15. I borrow this patois from various sources, in part from Derrida's essay "Structure, Sign and Play in the Discourse of the Human Sciences," in Derrida, *Writing and Difference,* trans. Alan Bass (Chicago: University of Chicago Press, 1978), 278-93, which ends with a rather notorious sequence, pitched in a tone whose chiliastic resonances Derrida has since disowned.

deferral of presence that *is* writing: difference, that is, in the absence that always precedes and unsettles "presence," the immediacy of self or other, the true voice, the moment of undiluted consciousness, or any direct intuition of the real, authoritative, or authentic. In Derrida's account of *archi-écriture* — with its perpetual displacement of meaning, a referral and deferral along an axis of interminable supplementation, dissemination, and slippage, never reaching the terminus of an achieved *reference,* prior to any present meaning — and in his treatment of the "trace," difference outstrips metaphysics in whatever direction it chooses to run — back to the origin, ahead to the ideal synthesis or eschaton, upward toward a Being unshaken by becoming, inward to the pure fount of a spiritual *memoria* more original than the cultural and linguistic archive that regulates and perpetuates the violences of the totality — because "writing" is always already there, as indeed, in each case, the enabling condition.

It is tempting to borrow here one of Milbank's aperçus. While accepting Derrida's "discovery" of an arche-writing that is not a consequence or transgression of an original immediacy of presence, and provisionally approving his talk of the "supplement at the origin" (the deferral of referral, signification's interminable supplementarity, which "constitutes" the "original"), Milbank still deplores the uniformity with which Derrida treats the originary supplement under the figure of an originary dissemblance; why not imagine an original supplementarity that, as in Gadamer's account, is at once the open interminable repetition whereby the origin is (rather than is merely recollected), but is also a faithful supplement of an origin that is itself pure giving?[16] Of course, Milbank is invoking a trinitarian rationality, according to which there is no *arche* without its logos, no logos without the open light of infinite *spiritual* "interpretation," and no necessary moment of alienation or negation anywhere herein; and so his question might appear at first more confessional than critical. Moreover, one could argue that he may be confusing the issue by considering the more purely "ontic" question of writing's discrete differentiations instead of the more "ontological" Derridean question of the differing as such, the prior condition of every instance of the different (Derrida would not necessarily deny the possible "peacefulness" of the supplement, but only the accord between *différance* and "presence"). But, in truth, this query is genuinely probative: having liberated himself from a mysticism of the origin without supplement, why does Derrida never quite abandon the language of transgression? Why is the immemorial motion of the writing "hand" that leaves the "trace" only as it withdraws so often depicted as a kind of primordial betrayal, violence, or alienation? Obviously this is partly garden-variety "dialectic," but one may yet wonder why Derrida seems still attached to the consequences of

---

16. Milbank, 308-9.

the enervating nostalgia he has cast off? If the great Western tradition of meta-physics is a violence that denies difference, must a postmetaphysical affirma-tion of difference merely reverse what it rejects? Must, indeed, the distinction of *différance* from presence be imagined in terms of dialectical priority, rather than of their mysterious concurrence within being's generosity? Derrida is aware of the impossibility of escaping metaphorical language, and nowhere does he claim a special authority for the metaphors he employs; but, then again, they have a certain power to exclude other turns of phrase, and for him writing (the exteriority of existence) is still always a prior violence, which opens the possibility of the world precisely through disruption. Could not Derrida con-sider supplementarity outside these inherited oppositions? This is not a cavil: it might be argued that this question misses the irony with which Derrida uses this language of absence, displacement, and concealment, the way in which he places all his terms "under erasure"; but what, in fact, is the real effect of such irony: What sort of gesture, in the end, is this act of placing words *sous rature?* Is it not perhaps a kind of effacement that still too ostentatiously calls attention to the effaced? Perhaps the very act of inscribing certain words with a *kreuzweise Durchstreichung* serves not only to indicate the places in a text where thought strains against the boundaries of language and tries to think at the margins by ironizing certain inescapable ways of speaking, but also to bind those words down securely to the page. It is a practice that can in fact redouble and reinforce the thinking it criticizes by determining absolutely what language must be used, even if in the negative; nothing so fortifies a concept as a "critical" distance from that concept's "literal" and unproblematic usage, because it is a distance by way of which thought may make an elliptical return to that concept — now demystified and so, paradoxically, indestructible. How can the figure of the visi-bly effaced *not* have the character of a "sublation," preserving what it negates, abstracting its idiom into an ever more unassailable eternality, progressively more devoid of graspable content, and progressively more authoritative?

When, for instance, in the course of his critical reading of Lévi-Strauss, Derrida finds an arche-writing already inscribed in the social codes of the Nambikwara, just where the structuralist anthropologist discerns echoes of a preinscriptional innocence, he finds it there precisely *as* violence.[17] From a theological standpoint, of course, this is quite understandable: Christian thought expects to find in every cultural coding a fundamental violence; no primordial innocence is displaced by the archive; but, perhaps fantastically, it treats this pervasive violence, inscribed upon being's fabric, as a palimpsest, ob-scuring another text that is still written (all created being is "written") but in the style of a letter declaring love. And while theology expects to find original

17. Derrida, *Of Grammatology,* 111-12.

sin in every society and will, it sees that sin not in writing as such but in a certain, very persuasive style of writing; but even within this history of violent inscription and violent erasure, other styles can renew themselves (however fleetingly) from a more original text, whose endless deferrals are still not transgressions. From the theological vantage, violence and dissimulation must be regarded as secondary: not to a mythical, unexplicated origin, a naked being given as *immediate* presence, mediated in alienation from itself, but to a being that is itself mediation, an arche-median prior to every reduction (manifest, one might add, in both its immediacy and transcendence, in that joyous concord of phenomenon and event that is the beautiful). But theology proceeds according to its own rationality; for Derrida, to speak in such terms would be to cross a limit that is the limit of being itself:

> The divergence, the *difference* between Dionysus and Apollo, between ardor and structure, cannot be erased in history, for it is not *in* history. It too, in an unexpected sense, is an original structure: the opening of history, historicity itself. *Difference* does not simply belong either to history or structure. If we must say, along with Schelling, that "all is but Dionysus," we must know — and this is to write — that, like pure force, Dionysus is worked by difference. He sees and lets himself be seen. And tears out (his) eyes. For all eternity, he has a relationship to his exterior, to visible form, to structure, as he does to his death. This is how he appears (to himself).[18]

Nor can this division be reconciled in the repose of spirit or the peace of an eschaton. Between force and structure (diachrony and synchrony, history and meaning, becoming and being, temporalization and presence) thought has apparently glimpsed that sublime instance that has awakened it to the economy: the necessary incommensurability and struggle between the world's power to appear and the appearance of a world, between the invisible sacrifice and the duplicitous spectacle. (But can one *see* this?)

2. *The cosmological sublime*, which is the form the discourse of the unrepresentable can take when the Nietzschean impulse predominates. The figure who here most forcibly comes to mind is Gilles Deleuze: a remarkably inventive philosopher, of such energy and originality that Foucault once asseverated that "perhaps one day, this century will be known as Deleuzian."[19] His philosophical project defies easy summary, and the neologisms that crowd the pages of his

18. In Derrida's essay "Force and Signification," in *Writing and Difference*, 3-30, here 28-29.
19. Michel Foucault, "Theatrum Philosophicum," in Foucault, *Language, Counter-Memory, Practice: Selected Essays and Interviews,* ed. Donald F. Bouchard, trans. Donald F. Bouchard and Sherry Simon (Ithaca, N.Y.: Cornell University Press, 1977), 165.

texts, and of those written in collaboration with Félix Guattari, are at once bracing and bewildering in their variety; but one can make a few general observations concerning the trajectory of his thought. For one thing, with Deleuze the thought of difference acquires a consciously metaphysical dimension — in the limited sense of a grounding of the physical in principles inherent in itself; his thought is a rigorous immanentist speculation on the original fecundity of "Chaos." Indeed, one might almost describe his philosophical vision as a kind of mongrelized Aristotelian monism, or (better) as an odd materialist Neoplatonism. Chaos stands in the place of the One; it is the absolute "simple" in which all forces are gathered in their virtuality, the one (Spinozan) substance that ramifies endlessly in an infinite variety of modalities; and this Chaos "expresses" or "explicates" itself through "ideas" — which Deleuze also calls "problems" — which comprise various virtual differential elements and the various "singular points" where these original differences coincide: points that are themselves actualized in the singularizing event of particular "intensities" of realization. Put more simply, "below" the schematizing extension of representable space is the absolute indifference of a *spatium;* below the extended presentness of representable time *(chronos)* lies the infinite linearity of time without dimension *(aion),* a perpetual divergence of past and future, without present (here Deleuze plunders the Stoics). And while all ideas and problems and intensities are "perplicated" in Chaos, Chaos must also express itself, for its very unity is a disruptive incongruity, a primordial inquisition of itself, that must obey the imperative of its own restless enigma. The *spatium* and the *aion* are explicated in the space and time of representation because the unexpressed ground is always subject to the original Question (rather than original "truth"), the "aleatory point" that traverses the whole body of the world, effecting infinitely many chance convergences of otherwise unrelated series of expression (say, a body and a phrase, a thought and a place, the taste of a madeleine dipped in tea and the memory of Combray, etc.); the Question, that is, evokes an infinite diversity of accidental "answers" or syntheses. We can apprehend these convergences and divergences under the form of "signs" (purely neural impressions, eluding reflective recognition), but not when we retreat to the ordered immobility of representations. Indeed — stretching his great inversion of idealism to the breaking point — Deleuze makes the unity of this expressive totality not any species of analogy, but just this activity of the aleatory point, which in its very aimlessness accomplishes three syntheses: the connective (within a given series), the conjunctive (between two series), and the disjunctive (of series from series); thus the order of the world is an original fortuity, and its rationality an original creative disorder.[20]

20. I am drawing my account from the two volumes in which Deleuze principally formulates his own immanent metaphysics: *Difference and Repetition,* trans. Paul Patton (New York:

Another, more concise description of his project might be as a "saving of the simulacra," the simulacrum being Plato's φάντασμα, which — as opposed to the εἰκών — is a poor or only superficial semblance of the ideal;[21] it is the refractory and amorphous moment of difference that occasionally slips out from beneath the hems of resemblance, analogy, and hierarchy, the reverberation of nonsense within the stable structure of sense, the free convulsion of sensation welling up within the serenity of representation, and the stress of becoming upon the firm outlines of being; but it is also that abrasive shock of contradiction that, according to the Socrates of the *Republic* (7.253a-d), is the very provocation to thought in the first place.[22] This marginal Platonic term, this concept of a force of degradation within matter and time that acts as the negated exterior of resemblance, and that awakens thought to the difference of the apparent from the real, becomes for Deleuze the principle whereby to invert not only Platonic speculative idealism but Kantian transcendental idealism and its posterity: because the simulacrum resists similitude, analogy, or even any form of structuralism, it is finally *the* unrepresentable. Whereas Kant's "concord of the faculties" of perception and thought traces a line from a passive capacity of intuition or sensibility to a representation accomplished through imagination and a prior understanding, the simulacrum suggests a prerepresentative experience, a *sentiendum*, that is nevertheless the real experience that at once founds and defies representation,[23] and that representation filters and diminishes. It is Deleuze's contention that the critical force of Kantian transcendentalism is hobbled by an idealistic representationalism, albeit one reoriented along the lines of common sense *(sensus communis)* rather than a metaphysics of the idea, and that the Kantian project can be brought to completion only by disrupting this lingering trace of essentialist thought; to this end Deleuze calls for a real thinking of difference through a derangement of the faculties of cognition and a precise attention to the unharmonizable experiences peculiar to each of them; these in turn point to the "molecular" elements of sensation that (prior to representation) emerge from the groundless space or chaos of becoming's unexplicated energies, only thereafter to be enfolded in the "molar" aggre-

Columbia University Press, 1994) and *The Logic of Sense,* trans. Mark Lester (New York: Columbia University Press, 1990); see also *Proust and Signs,* trans. Richard Howard (New York: George Braziller, 1972), for a fuller treatment of "ideas" and "problems."

21. See, in particular, the *Sophist* 234a-b, 246c.

22. The adoption of the simulacrum as a theme in the Deleuzean project is most fully developed in *The Logic of Sense:* see esp. appendix I: "The Simulacrum and Ancient Philosophy" (253-79).

23. The full treatment of Kant's epistemology, and a radicalization thereof, is developed in Gilles Deleuze, *The Critical Philosophy of Kant,* trans. Hugh Tomlinson and Barbara Habberjam (Minneapolis: University of Minnesota Press, 1984).

gates susceptible of recognition. As opposed then to a Platonic opposition between idea and likeness (as well as an Aristotelian distinction between essence and accident) on the one hand, and to a Kantian subordination of intuition to representation on the other, Deleuze proposes a neo-Stoic model of ideas as incorporeals or *lekta,* dwelling on the surface of the actual, as virtual solutions stretched like integuments over the singular and divergent points of original problems; and these surface ideas, "insisting" as they do upon the surface of a pure Bergsonian past — the veil of the "remembrance" — are already specters, recollections, images that are quite dead — that never lived. Actuality, in the virtuality of its depths, is formless, violent, disjoined, unsynthesizable, and incapable of analogy. Thought, then — as representation or analogy — does not encounter difference as a peaceful gift, offered up to transposition, but as a violent provocation, to which it reacts with a dissimulating representation (thus enacting a contrary violence); even meaning is a secondary effect that plays upon the surface of such corporeal intensities as words; sense is an incorporeal that comes about as an effect of nonsense, the fortuitous convergence of differing series of the corporeal upon the aleatory point, as it effects its nomadic distribution of singularities upon the virtual surface of the prerepresentational plenitude (the featureless "Body without Organs," which is only occasionally perceptible as such, in schizophrenic states of catatonia). Analogy, as a totalizing deception — to the effect that difference is an irenic hierarchy of substances, under the imperial ensigns of the idea — falters before the Dionysian creativity of the simulacral, whose violences cannot be subdued but only hidden, under the appearance of virtualities hovering above the empty flow of aionic time (whose other name is the time of Thanatos).[24]

Of course, were Deleuze's ontology merely an ontology of difference, so conceived, it would be an ontology of sheer incoherence; having denied himself the formidable explanatory tools of substance and analogy, he must give some other account of the continuity of the effects of Chaos, the ontic constitution of the order to which Chaos clearly gives birth, and to this end he employs a new category. "Repetition" is the term he chooses, taken originally from Kierkegaard's eponymously titled philosophic satire, where it is distinguished from "recollection": in this text the latter term names the very logic of philosophy, the Platonic anamnesis that struggles backwards, upstream against the motion of time and change, toward an imagined eternity more real than all the shadowy transience of the world, a spiritual realm secure against the onslaughts of

---

24. An elegant précis of Deleuze's metaphysics of becoming is found in chap. 3 of Ronald Bogue, *Deleuze and Guattari* (London and New York: Routledge, 1989), 55-80; this part of the book briefly and deftly summarizes the "grand synthesis" of Deleuze's early thought represented by *Difference and Repetition* and *The Logic of Sense.*

mutability; while the former describes the properly Christian notion of an eternity that lies ahead, an eternity to be gained by way of time and perseverance within change (a repetition within difference, of which identity is an effect).[25] Deleuze's rendition of "repetition," though, has been assimilated to his reading of Nietzsche's doctrine of eternal recurrence, which according to him, far from implying a circular reoccurrence of all that has gone before, means nothing other than fate's perpetual casting of the dice, the always repeated event of time itself, the occurrence of difference itself as dispersal and change, sealed within an inescapable circularity. For Kierkegaard repetition breaks from the past, not preserving but repeating anew, always differently; but repetition also concerns identity, the founding of a self within the turbulence of change. For Deleuze this "identity" is merely a metaphysical residue, another way of advancing the fiction of a stable subjectivity or soul; identity does not arise from repetition, except as a kind of rarefied phenomenal reduction; the return is therefore, in each instance, the happening of difference. But, as it is repetition, it repeats the effects of intensities, so long as they can be repeated. The future eternity of Kierkegaard's account, however, is torn in two: it is divided between a virtual futurity that is one of the two tensions of the barren infinity of the *aion* that, between them, form the fissure of the present, the infinitely divisible but apparently abiding *chronos*, and an eternity of the will, or rather an eternity willed by affirmation: Nietzsche's affirmation, at the point of despair, of the whole of being for now and all eternity. The force of becoming, of repetition, therefore, is properly called will to power. And identity is always serialized according to different sequences of becoming that at once converge and diverge, and is always fragmented into a plurality of desires (various functions of the desiring machines that compose the "individual").[26] Repetition for Deleuze is not even really a motion forward, just a motion from one to another identical incursion of difference; repetition imparts what is repeated in the form of loss, in a motion that shatters and then restores only as further shattering. It thwarts recollection (in the sense of an attempt to repeat in reverse, to establish the self, the mind, or

25. *Kierkegaard's Writings*, vol. 6, *Fear and Trembling* and *Repetition*, ed. and trans. Howard Hong and Edna Hong (Princeton: Princeton University Press, 1983), 131-33. See Caputo, *Radical Hermeneutics*, 11-35.

26. See Deleuze, *Difference and Repetition*. For Deleuze's interpretation of eternal recurrence, see Deleuze, *Nietzsche and Philosophy*, trans. Hugh Tomlinson (New York: Columbia University Press, 1983), 19-31, 47-72. See also Deleuze, *The Logic of Sense*, 58-65, for his appropriation of the Stoic distinction between *aion* and *chronos*. The language of "desiring machines" appears principally in Deleuze's texts written in collaboration with Félix Guattari; see the two volumes of *Capitalism and Schizophrenia: Anti-Oedipus*, trans. Robert Hurley, Mark Seem, and Helen R. Lane (New York: Viking Press, 1983), and *A Thousand Plateaus*, trans. Brian Massumi (Minneapolis: University of Minnesota Press, 1987).

the idea in an original and timeless setting), and leaves no room for substantial identity, presence, or analogy. And this is why it is most properly called "eternal return": it is not the perdurance of a discrete identity, but the whole event (the game) of the world, in its totality and power, eternally recurring as the one event, the creative force of chance.

This event of the return may also, according to Deleuze, be called the "univocity of being." While he is aware of and cites with approval the doctrine of ontological univocity usually ascribed (largely inaccurately) to Duns Scotus, it is Spinoza who exerts the most immediate influence over his use of the term: for Deleuze, as for Spinoza, the assertion that being must be said of all things "in the same voice" is an indispensable aspect of a thoroughgoing immanentism and "expressionism." While the "Scotist" version of univocity was intended to make intelligible the analogical attribution of like qualities to God and creatures,[27] claims Deleuze, the Spinozan, properly understood, makes all analogy impossible. Deleuze often prefers the more precise term "singularity of being," because the doctrine is intended to exclude all transcendence from the discourse of philosophy. However it is phrased, what remains at issue is difference; only a "monadological" doctrine of univocity, he contends, only a doctrine of being as a necessarily expressive singularity,[28] can preserve the purity of difference: as chance conjunction and disjunction. But for univocity the tendency to analogize, to essentialize, to place "essences" within a scheme of eminence and transcendence, would be free to devise metaphysical strategies for capturing the energy of chaos within a paralyzing totality. Of course, Deleuze has no need to retain Spinoza's "God" (a word that in the *Ethics* has already been conformed to a kind of naturalized version of the Qabbalism of the Florentine Academy). Deleuze's expressionism is, naturally, differential; his understanding of necessity is inescapable chance, the "necessity" of the dice throw and its uncontrollable result; hence, in place of Spinoza's complicative and explicative *Deus sive natura*, Deleuze extols Chaos, whose celebrant is the Antichrist or the Baphomet: "the 'prince of all modifications,' and himself modification of all modifications."[29] Analogy is excluded not only from the interval between immanence and an illusory transcendence, but from the nomadic distribution of diverging series within being; the doctrine of ontological univocity is simultaneously one of absolute ontic

27. See the *Commentaria Oxoniensia* 1.3.1-2; 1.8.3.

28. Deleuze's understanding and appropriation of Spinozan "expressionism" are laid out at great length in Deleuze, *Expressionism in Philosophy: Spinoza,* trans. Martin Joughin (New York: Zone Books, 1990).

29. Deleuze, *The Logic of Sense,* 296. Deleuze borrows this figure not directly from the odd legends regarding the "idol of the Templars," but from Pierre Klossowski's macabre Templar fantasy, *Le Baphomet* (Paris: Mercure de France, 1965); see *The Logic of Sense,* 280-301.

equivocity. "Univocity signifies that being itself is univocal, while that of which it is said is equivocal: precisely the opposite of analogy. . . . Opening is an essential feature of univocity. The nomadic distributions of crowned anarchies in the univocal stand opposed to the sedentary distributions of analogy. Only there does the cry resound: 'Everything is equal' and this 'Everything returns!'"[30] Theologically speaking, of course, Deleuze's understanding of analogy is excruciatingly unsophisticated; he obviously does not grasp, for instance, the tortured issue of the *analogia entis* (which, properly understood, cannot function as part of any simple scheme of resemblance, because it subjects every identity to the irreducible difference of the divine infinity); and his characterization of analogy — the equivocity of being, the univocity of attributes — entirely misrepresents the tradition, according to which neither being nor attributes are equivocal *or* univocal: both are *analogical.* But in terms of the simple binary proportion of attribution, which for him exhausts the matter of analogy, his logic is flawless: if the analogical is merely a discourse of attributive resemblance, it leaves behind a divine reserve, an unexpressed transcendence, and each actual analogy simply identifies abstract properties that may be ascribed to God and creatures alike; but for Spinoza (and himself) attributes are not mere properties, but the actual expressions of being, without reserve, and only by regarding being's attributes univocally can one affirm that all of them are full, direct, equal modes of expression.[31]

For Deleuze, such is the world, in its ceaseless transience and eternal eventuality: the will to power is the force of ontic becoming, while the eternal return describes the only possible ontology. If, though, this is the game of the world, and thought must now inhabit this interminable immanence of chaos, sealed within the necessary event, it might quite plausibly fall prey to sadness and simply withdraw into itself, impotent and disengaged; in the face of so terrifying and inescapable a power of becoming and perishing, only the highest power of the will can preserve itself intact: affirmation. This henceforth, holds Deleuze, must be the supreme philosophical ethos. Even as Zarathustra, when confronted by the terrifying thought of the eternal return and the abyss of meaninglessness it threatens to open up ("Ach, der Mensch kehrt ewig wieder!

30. Deleuze, *Difference and Repetition*, 304.

31. Deleuze, *Expressionism in Philosophy*, 45-57. Deleuze thinks analogy belongs to a "semeiological" (i.e., structuralist) rationality that makes language something distinct from being's expression, rather than the participatory mode of expression he treats it as being; see Michael Hardt, *Gilles Deleuze: An Apprenticeship in Philosophy* (Minneapolis: University of Minnesota Press, 1993), 67. At first glance this might seem to place Deleuze at a considerable remove from Derrida, but the effective difference is slight: a doctrine of univocity such as Deleuze's makes it also a matter of indifference whether expressionist language is employed or not; all differences equally express — and so equally dissimulate — being.

Der kleine Mensch kehrt ewig wieder!"), turned away from despair to proclaim his ecstatic wisdom from the mountaintops (". . . denn ich liebe dich, o Ewigkeit! *Denn ich liebe dich, o Ewigkeit!*"),[32] so philosophy must now become a *fröhliche Wissenschaft*, a joyous acceptance of and delight in the whole of being, including all that is ambiguous, aimless, irreconcilable, and aleatory; all that is blameless, ludic, and childlike. It is first and foremost the banishment of the sad passions, the guilt, nostalgia, uncertainty, negativity, and fear that inhibit and palliate the will to power (or force, or desire, or however one names the dynamism that carries life into its fullness); when thought disabuses itself of certain fixations and fruitless distinctions, places itself beyond good and evil, wins surcease from every reactive and resentful motive, and frees itself from its yearning for a lost innocence or purity or presence that never was, and so from its passive and neurasthenic distance from the world, it is able at last to affirm being without fear of transgression, memory of failure, or hope of transcendence; it gains a tragic wisdom that, because it no longer imagines or desires the possibility of escape, can bear all joyously: the eternal return of the same, the storm of difference, the play of absence and presence, sense and nonsense, meaning and madness, creation and destruction, birth and death. Moreover, it can finally begin to *evaluate*, to choose, to make aesthetic discriminations not burdened by a mythic past or an eschatological expectation; it can be creative — in particular, of values — and can enhance and liberate life. Still more splendidly, Zarathustra's terror at the thought of the "small man's" return proves needless; the will disposed to pure affirmation finds that the weak and resentful is precisely that which does not return, for it is utter reactivity, without any intensity proper to itself. When it arrives at this most delightful of truths, thought also arrives at its utmost positivity and purest passion. To cite Deleuze himself,

> There are certainly many dangers in invoking pure differences which have become independent of the negative and liberated from the identical. The greatest danger is that of lapsing into the representations of a beautiful soul: there are only reconcilable and federative differences, far removed from bloody struggles. The beautiful soul says: we are different but not opposed. . . . The *notion of a problem*, which we see linked to that of difference, also seems to nurture the sentiments of the beautiful soul: only problems and questions matter. . . . Nevertheless, we believe that when these problems attain their proper degree of *positivity*, and when difference becomes the object of a corresponding *affirmation*, they release a prior power of ag-

---

32. Taken from *Also Sprach Zarathustra* III, pts. 13 *(Der Genesende)* and 16 *(Die Sieben Siegel; Oder: das Ja-und-Amen-Lied)*. From a certain postmodern perspective, this latter section is the very type of an acceptable hymnody, because its affirmation comes before and after every pathos, reservation, and doubt.

gression and selection which destroys the beautiful soul by depriving it of its very identity and breaking its good will. The problematic and the differential determine struggles or destructions in relation to which those of the negative are only appearances, and the wishes of the beautiful soul are so many mystifications trapped in appearances. The simulacrum is not just a copy, but that which overturns all copies by *also* overturning the models: every thought becomes an aggression.[33]

Thus, for Deleuze, a choice has opened up: the violence of inane consensus or the violence of differential strife, the dialectical captivity of becoming in the myth of negation or the release of becoming by a myth of affirmation whose only practical expression is a war against representation. This means, of course, that to choose wisely is to embrace every freedom but one. Every thought is allowed except the thought that thought may be peaceful, and that only then does it think being truly; every rhetoric is free to unfold itself, but it must also somehow acknowledge that it is necessarily violent by virtue of its rhetoricity; and if it is a rhetoric of peace, it is doubly violent for dissembling its warlike intentions.

The figure of the "beautiful soul," it should also be noted, has perhaps a very particular reference here: something of a recurrent motif in German romantic culture, he visits the pages of Jacobi and (implicitly) Goethe, but makes his most memorable appearance in Hegel's *Phenomenology of Spirit* (¶¶632-71), where he is presented as the very type of conscientious withdrawal; recognizing the irreconcilability of absolute duty and material circumstance, he disappears into his own purity of moral sensibility and conscience; feeling an immediate community with all others and a sense that all wounds can be healed, his morality is devoid of the equilibrium of law, an admirable ethos of tolerance and a limitless willingness to extend forgiveness; so he is also an ineffectual figure, who does not accept the limitations of *Sittlichkeit* and who allows injustice against himself and others to pass without resistance, because his morality — as a morality of the heart — can be expressed only as a passivity transcendent of his responsibilities within the ethical community; in the universality he feels in himself, he knows only the unity of beauty and goodness, a pure divine interiority, empty of determinate content; he refrains from moral judgment and constructive evaluation, does not act, denies himself, and by the ardor of his love withers away. He is a revenant, "ein gestaltloser Dunst, der sich in Luft auflöst" (¶658). He is also, it is arguable, Hegel's Christ:[34] not explicitly called

33. Deleuze, *Difference and Repetition*, xx.

34. Though, it should be mentioned, the more proximate model is probably Novalis; and the figure occurs within the context of a broader denunciation of the sort of ethical purism one associates with the thought of Kant.

such in the *Phenomenology*, but recognizable from an early theological essay Hegel composed on the spirit and fate of Christianity, where a portrait like that of the beautiful soul is also drawn, in the same terms, but as a depiction of Jesus.[35] It is noteworthy, at least in passing, that Deleuze touches upon this figure here, because this is also the only "Christ" Deleuze ever speaks about: a frail, inert, etiolated Christ, a placid, kindly, bovine, Fabian Christ, who withdraws from the storm of being, pines for eternity, God, and the self, and cannot bear the contradiction and strife of becoming, but must gaze upon it through the iridescent veil of infinite reconciliation. And if the beautiful soul in the passage above is, even only in a remote sense, the Deleuzean "Christ," his presence in both Hegel and Deleuze is perhaps an ironic emblem of a deep and essential concord between the two — Christ reconciles Pilate and Herod, after all — because it may well be that this is the only way that Jesus can be grasped within the terms of the totality whose poles Hegel and Deleuze occupy; this is also, incidentally, the Christ of Nietzsche *(vide infra)*. That Hegel (perhaps the most unironic advocate of metaphysical totality), Nietzsche (Deleuze's knight of bad faith, the overman of the antidialectical), and Deleuze himself should all afford the same glimpse of the same figure in the same terms, and that all should dismiss or deride him for his weak, indolent, and naive sweetness before the irreconcilable oppositions of being, is — to say the least — instructive: Christ appears in all these narratives under the form of an impossible possibility (if that), a deliquescent accident within history, because there is no other way to accommodate the aesthetic affront he represents within totality's sublime. The renunciation of power cannot be *a* power unless — as Nietzsche suggests — it is a dissemblance of power; but even Nietzsche finds it impossible to read Christ in this way: his Christ is also a beautiful soul, and he is as one with Hegel and Deleuze in simply denying that such a figure can actually serve as a force within history. As Deleuze writes, "In the circle of Dionysus, Christ will not return; the order of Antichrist chases the other order away."[36] The form of love that Jesus seems to represent, the beauty of his figure within the Christian narrative, could never bear fruit within the being that this totality comprehends, and so must be regarded as the form of withdrawal, negation, that which does not return and cannot be repeated.

One must grasp how deeply this prejudice runs in much postmodern discourse to understand how little this "radicalism" ranges from the metaphysics it

---

35. *Hegel's Early Theological Manuscripts*, trans. T. M. Knox (Chicago: University of Chicago Press, 1948), 234-44; see esp. 236, 239 for language concerning Jesus' "beauty of soul." See also Robert C. Solomon, *In the Spirit of Hegel* (Oxford: Oxford University Press, 1983), 622-25, and Charles Taylor, *Hegel* (Cambridge: Cambridge University Press, 1975), 59-64.

36. Deleuze, *The Logic of Sense*, 301.

denounces; and Deleuze, in his Nietzschean voice, offers the most transparent example of this truth. Deleuze never, anywhere in the course of his philosophical development, escapes the tedious dualism of the active and the reactive, the affirmative and the negative, the creative and the resentful; thus there is no place in his thought for an energy that is neither one nor the other of these things, an energy at once responsive and free, inviting and creating, analogical and expressive. Deleuzean affirmation is always an affirmation of the whole as force, never as gift or charity: not solely because a gift presumes a giver, but because being is *intrinsically* a violence whose intervals are not spaces where charity may be effectively enacted, but merely the shared ruptures between differences. "If it is true that all things reflect a state of forces then power designates the element, or rather the differential relationship, of forces which directly confront one another";[37] nature is an interrelated multiplicity of forces, which are either dominant or dominated.[38] The Nietzschean aesthetic "ethic of joy" that, delighting in multiplicity, creates without reaction, and that affirms life without justifying or redeeming it,[39] must always follow upon destruction; the critical violence of the master must go to the furthermost extremes of a destructive nihilism before it arrives at the moment of conversion and is capable of absolute affirmation; it must suffer the thought of the eternal recurrence before negativity, interiority, and subjectivity are overthrown, forever banishing the resentful ethos of the slave.[40] The perspectivism Deleuze praises in Nietzsche always stands at this point, where there can no longer be a transcendent perspective, but only a perspicacious power to legislate new values according to interests; and without any higher vantage from which evaluation may proceed, by way of universality or laws of resemblance, then evaluation must take distance always as neutral distance, territory to be governed; distance becomes the source of values, and evaluation — as disenchanted creativity — must be active, never reactive, it must be attack, natural aggression, divine wickedness; interpretation must be domination.[41] Here is the heart of Deleuze's philosophy. The true distance of being again opens between the sublime and the beautiful as opposition; this thinking of surfaces subsists upon an aesthetics of the abyss, energy, boundless force, indeterminate instabilities that — through the violence of their ceaseless divergence and convergence within an untold depth of the indistinguishable — give rise to the evanescent shimmering of events and forms; the beautiful — conceived as a staid aesthetics of form, limit, boundary,

37. Deleuze, *Nietzsche and Philosophy,* xi.
38. See Bogue, 20.
39. Deleuze, *Nietzsche and Philosophy,* 17-18.
40. Deleuze, *Nietzsche and Philosophy,* 178.
41. Deleuze, *Nietzsche and Philosophy,* 1-4.

hierarchy, harmony, and accord — becomes simply another manifestation of the essentializing discourse of image and likeness and of the solace of metaphysics, while the sublime — conceived as the turbid immensity of the unrepresentable, a chaotic excess of indeterminacy, strife, incompatible difference, and inchoate energies — is raised up for affirmation, as a divine game of chance and fate, a game whose only rule is the necessity of the casting of the dice (and whose stakes are always the whole). From this sublimity beauty can be extracted, irrelevantly, only as a contraction and a concealment. Metaphysics, in its drive toward totality, classically conceives of the infinite as chaos or negation (or at best a "total" synthesis), and certainly cannot conceive of an infinity that is offered peacefully — without alienation, negation, or deceit — as form. Within this sealed circle, if a form in which peace and the infinite are presented as coinciding should show itself, and offer itself only in the appeal of this harmony, it could appear only as a contradiction or illusion, and must be dismissed as the emptiest of all apparitions: not the beautiful shape of a possible way of being, but only a "beautiful soul."

This Nietzschean contour of the postmodern passes from Deleuze most obviously to Foucault: not only insofar as Foucault's philosophical project, at its most fruitful, emulates the model of Nietzsche's *Genealogy of Morals,* but also insofar as Foucault develops, with such remarkable and persistent historical specificity, one of the principal emphases of Deleuze's study of Nietzsche: that interpretation or evaluation is an act of power, that the will to knowledge expresses a will to power, and that language and discourse are, before all else, forms of power.[42] In Foucault's thought the will to power occupies a position of transcendental authority, prephenomenal, prepersonal, and prehistorical; it is being's own creative energy, life's inherent tendency to repeat itself with ever greater complexity and strength, without requiring the goad or defining limit of the negative. Power is the *ratio* of the world, and it is only a reactive and complacent sensibility that reduces the free play of its energies to the lucidity of intelligible order. Even human history is nothing — as Foucault writes in "Nietzsche, Genealogy, History" — but "a series of subjugations": "In placing present needs at the origin, the metaphysician would convince us of an obscure purpose that seeks its realization at the moment it arises. Genealogy, however, seeks to re-establish the various systems of subjection: not the anticipatory power of meaning, but the hazardous play of dominations."[43] This will is not even aboriginally oriented toward the good of the one willing, much less

---

42. This last emphasis, regarding language, persists to the end of the Deleuzean (or Deleuzo-Guattarian) project, no doubt deepened by the influence of Foucault; see Bogue, 137.

43. Michel Foucault, "Nietzsche, Genealogy, History," in Foucault, *Language, Counter-Memory, Practice,* 139-64, here 148.

67

toward the good as such, but only toward more willing, greater force, an interminable ecstasy of power. There is a violence antecedent to every contingency, history's forms emerge from a struggle of forces, and the course of history comprises merely a concatenation of dominations in which humanity installs its violences.[44] And by "power" Foucault means a ubiquitous, multiform, variable, and inextirpable energy of conquest (a universal prepersonal *libido dominandi*), which ramifies endlessly from extrinsic and "spectacular" violences into innumerable discrete processes of control and subtle mechanisms for subjugating bodies and behaviors;[45] a web of violences reinforcing one another, which all persons suffer and in which all are complicit;[46] and a logic of force, inscribed in history's motion, which expresses itself through an incalculable plurality of agencies, variously but consistently.[47] Thus, says Foucault, the "truth" of any culture or discipline is primarily a style of constraint, a "regime";[48] cultural knowledge is not simply the source, but the effect, of power, always belonging to an interest. In fact, relations of power and subjugation are not invented by such regimes as capitalism, but — always already in place — are merely colonized by systems that variously employ and express them.[49]

A theologian might well be tempted to read Foucault as an unwitting phenomenologist of original sin. After all, he often seems to say no more than what theology already assumes: that the world lies in the grip of thrones, dominions, principalities, authorities, and powers (θρόνοι, κυριότητες, ἀρχαὶ, ἐξουσίαι, δυνάμεις); although to this observation Christian tradition adds the claim that these powers appear as original or as ultimate only within the order that they describe, guard, and govern — which Christ has overcome (Rom. 8:38; Eph. 1:21; 3:10; 6:12; Col. 1:16; 2:15). And when Foucault adopts the model of Jeremy Bentham's panopticon as an exemplary reification of power's movement from more exterior to more interior mechanisms of social constraint (by which it progressively becomes more pervasive and irresistible, as an authority disseminated among and seated within the subjectivities it forms and controls), or when he expresses amazement at the sheer complexity and inventiveness of power, despite the absence of any unifying center of

44. Foucault, "Nietzsche, Genealogy, History," 148-49, 151.

45. See Michel Foucault, *Power/Knowledge: Selected Interviews and Other Writings, 1972-1977*, ed. Colin Gordon, trans. Colin Gordon et al. (New York: Pantheon Books, 1980), 97-99.

46. Foucault, *Power/Knowledge*, 98.

47. See Michel Foucault, *Power, Truth, Strategy*, ed. and trans. Meaghan Morris and Paul Patton (Sydney: Feral, 1979), 60; and Foucault, *The History of Sexuality*, vol. 1, *An Introduction*, trans. Robert Hurley (New York: Pantheon Books, 1978), 94.

48. Foucault, *Power/Knowledge*, 131.

49. Foucault, *Power/Knowledge*, 99-101.

intention or will,[50] he comes perilously close to describing sin, in theological terms. Foucault, though, has no judgment to pass on power per se (it is, of course, life's wellspring), and so he has no use for the notion of sin. And of course, he knows little of Christian theology's conception of sin in its cosmic aspect: its presence not only in the inner precincts of conscience but within the deep structures of human society and history, the way its intentionality precedes the subjectivity to which it gives shape. For him, Christian talk of sin belongs merely to an institutional science of the soul, the confessional's systematic fabrication of a docile "conscience" and self-surveying subjectivity, which now has passed under the still more confining analytic and therapeutic subjugations of the modern "carceral" society, where interiority has become a prison house or torture chamber in which discipline is enforced by its own victim. Still, whatever the limits of Foucault's understanding, he is quite right in thinking that a great gulf is indeed fixed between the Christian story of sin and his of "power": the former still interprets the power of subjugation not as an ontological heuristic, but as privation, utterly negative, never truly creative. Theology begins its reflections in the place where worldly power exerted itself as the absolute violence of crucifixion, but must do so on the side of the crucified: a place where Foucault would certainly see only one force being destroyed by another, and perhaps another more devious force rising from the carnage. Nor is this difference merely that between "mythology" and historical "science": as a critical practice, genealogy may be intended as a deconstruction, through demystification, of all the stable certitudes of the age, but it is of necessity synoptic in its pretensions, systematic in its method, and so almost inevitably metaphysical in its conclusions.

Which yields a few tangential observations. There is an almost embarrassing incompatibility between this "cosmological sublime" and the moral sentiments it is often made to serve. Deleuze, Foucault, and others who adopt language similar to theirs tend to be somewhat oblivious (or indifferent) to the ways their account of the will to power can easily turn into an endorsement of, quite precisely, a *will* to, quite precisely, *power*. Even though there is an impersonal and nonsubjective primordiality to this "will" for Foucault, and even though his philosophical epic is scarcely intended to endue the structures of power he discloses with glamor, still his is an ontology of force whose practical expression can be only one or another instantiation of force (of, that is, an original energy that proceeds outward from itself, encountering only other forces, which it may subdue or to which it must succumb). In fact, for Foucault and Deleuze both, the narrative of force is so pervasive that the political desire for

---

50. See Michel Foucault, *Discipline and Punish: The Birth of the Prison*, trans. Alan Sheridan (New York: Vintage Books, 1979), esp. 195-228, 293-308.

"liberation" becomes more and more idealized in their thought: no longer revolution, which is merely another totalizing expression of power, but only occasional and limited forms of resistance, conceived by Deleuze (and Guattari) in
terms of upsetting "sedentaries" by departing along nomadic "lines of flight"
(from volition to volitation, so to speak), and by Foucault as a Stoical art of
crafting the self (from volition to involution). In either model of freedom — of
the restraint or diversion of the will to power — the Kantian subject, the inviolable individual, is retained, however diminished, concealed, and unacknowledged. This is inevitable: the Kantian myth of the subject's moral freedom is the
last bulwark against totalitarian impulses. The ghost of the subject must still
emerge from one shadowy corner or another to rattle its chains and declare its
right to power, if power is not to be the prerogative of collectivities that do not
depend upon the myth of the individual: the individual will to power must not
be obviated by any more expansive expression of will, but the reason for this remains obscure (probably something along the lines of "fascism is vulgar").
There is a piquant futility in all of this; as much as it preserves the assumptions
of modernity regarding the punctiliar individual, the inalienable power of will,
and freedom as the lifting of constraints from the will, this school of the
postmodern reveals itself as a completion of the project of the Enlightenment,
but insofar as it has dispensed with Kant's unrepresentable but necessary moral
analogy between the transcendental subject and God, it has also brought that
project to its inevitable collapse. "Nietzschean" moralism is a sad absurdity.
True, Nietzsche himself would have found the Nazis vulgar, and he denounced
fashionable anti-Semitism in his day, but there is no way within the
Nietzschean narrative to prevent a renarration of the Reich's mass-murders as
merely careless acts of Aryan exuberance, not resentful but affirmative, natural
gestures, a bit of playful aquiline depredation; and similarly, while Deleuze and
Foucault may resist collective expressions of power, it is difficult to see why they
should, as only a Kantian transcendental subject (that is, one that has not been
serialized) needs to be saved from flowing into greater expressions of force. The
longing for an impossible freedom — the dream of a flight to the exteriority of
nomadic migrations or to the interiority of self-creation — remains as a governing pathos, although it is obviously nothing but a metaphysical nostalgia.

Inevitably, again, there can be no ethos attached to this vision of things
but that of "affirmation." The postmodern condition ultimately renders every
other act of evaluation empty and a bit ludicrous. And affirmation has about it,
at the very least, less self-importance than the anguish of classical "ethics." One
might, for example, cite a passage from the early (more Nietzschean) Derrida,
from his seminal deconstruction of Lévi-Strauss's myth of a natural realm of
intuited presence lost to the *pharmakon* of the sign: "Turned towards the lost or
impossible presence of the absent origin, this structuralist thematic of broken

immediacy is therefore the saddened, *negative,* nostalgic, guilty, Rousseauistic side of the thinking of play whose other side would be the Nietzschean *affirmation,* that is the joyous affirmation of the play of the world and of the innocence of becoming, the affirmation of a world of signs without fault, without truth, and without origin which is offered to an active interpretation."[51] Phrased thus — as a letting be of the sign, the "adventure of the trace," as Derrida then calls it — affirmation seems quite attractive, quite creative, "liberating," and "positive." Advocates of this affirmative ethos, moreover, are as one in denying that it implies an idiotic complacency before everything that occurs; as the setting loose of evaluation and the emancipation of perspectives, it confers responsibility on all to choose with care and with creative gaiety. Not that such claims ultimately make a sheerly willful affirmation of the world any less fantastic or arbitrary: as an act of aesthetic evaluation, if it must first and unhesitatingly affirm the whole, it can be accomplished only upon mountaintops, from an impossibly sublime perspective; but as soon as one enters into history, evaluation becomes an analogical process of ordering desires, and if one insists on entering history by descending from such heights, those desires and that evaluation may be for or of anything, any practice, however noble or barbaric, kind or cruel. It is nonsensical to assert that the "positivity" of affirmation is somehow a bar against the creative *jeu joyeux* of, say, fascism; every conceivable perspective and desire is compatible — by way of whatever rhetorical negotiation — with superabounding affirmation. This is not to deny the serious concern that underlies this entire course of thought: to affirm the whole, ideally, is to free oneself of the debilitating notions that difference is itself only a negation from which truth must be retrieved or by way of which *Geist* returns to itself, that being requires a transcendent "solution" to its ambiguity in order to be justified, or that the world is a unitary process obedient to abstract values outside itself.

Still, it is questionable whether a pure affirmation can ever fail to culminate in one or another of the more robust and pitiless nihilisms unless its inner premises are in fact theological: because only the affirmation that actually creates transcendently is capable of setting difference free without burden, without negation, without reaction; only God's "It is very good" can give difference in the pure positivity of its being: because here affirmation and creation are one. This permits something like eschatological or metaphysical irony to govern the enthusiasm of affirmation: affirmation made in accord with an infinite transcendence, bound by no necessity to the world's mechanisms, can be made of the entirety of being without ever becoming a justification for whatever is simply the case; it is a pure affirmation that nonetheless can judge violence and cruelty not by negation, reaction, or mere moral sensibility, but by the same ab-

---

51. Derrida, *Writing and Difference,* 292.

solute creativity that gives the world freely. From the Christian point of view, infinite perspectives of affirmation open up: not merely perspectives from which catechetically to mimic the divine approbation, but vantages from which different appropriations of it may proceed analogously, through a sharing in God's infinite embrace of creation and through a repetition in thought, word, and deed of the original divine gesture of love. But a Christian understanding of affirmation, then, entirely reverses the logic of the modern or postmodern sublime, by proceeding from a theological account of beauty: a beauty in which a truer sublime (the inexhaustible glory of being) is contained. A philosophy whose concept of affirmation is merely the result of a *reaction* against dialectical negation (thus retaining the narrative of ontological violence that dialectic presumes) cannot ultimately make a morally credible distinction between hospices and death camps (Nietzsche's distaste for both would be virtually identical), between the hymeneal bed and rape, or between peace and war, except through a willful and ever more hyperbolic insistence on certain political preferences no longer susceptible of justification, nor even particularly compelling. Perhaps this is the inevitable condition of all discourse; at some point every tradition is groundless; much postmodern thought is novel simply (and perhaps commendably) in that it allows its *aporiai* to lie so near the surface. Still, there is a price paid to dance on the arm of Dionysus: whereas Christian thought, whose affirmations are of all creation and yet are analogical rather than total, can distinguish more than arbitrarily between two different institutions that, in one sense or another, promote death, by asserting that the hospice — as a structure of charity — participates in being by reflecting the creative love of the triune God while the death camp — being a structure of evil — participates only in nothingness and reflects nothing, the postmodern "wisdom" enjoys no such luxury, but is driven by its better angels to school itself in distaste for what (by its own account) is not intrinsically distasteful; it "knows" that strife is inevitable and not a violation of being, and yet it strives to preserve indefinitely its sense of moral alarm before what is, after all, only another name for being itself: *polemos, Kampf*. . . . Of course, in the end, greater consistency is no evidence of superior vision; between these two myths of affirmation, reason alone cannot adjudicate; rhetoric still must exhort and implore.

3. *The ontological sublime,* or the discourse of the unrepresentable when transposed into an audibly Heideggerian key. The principal elements of this approach to sublimity should by this point be obvious. Ever since Heidegger's discovery of the very premise for a fundamental ontology within phenomenology's "antimetaphysical" collapse of "it is" into "it appears," many a philosopher in the Continental tradition has found it impossible to descry the countenance of being anywhere but in the event of appearance itself, or to imagine

this event except as the "nothing" that "nothings" in the being of beings, the wan nimbus of the *not* that impartially grants, by its advent (or withdrawal), the temporalization of being, the play of finitude's *this* and *that*. So it is that Kant's distinction between the beautiful and the sublime, read through this lens, is often assimilated to the sterile fecundity of the ontico-ontological difference (which is, as with Heidegger, a dialectical difference, whether acknowledged as such or not); indeed, the former is even occasionally treated as a direct precursor of the latter. In the endearingly inane formula of Éliane Escoubas: "[T]he Kantian sublime . . . is a distant and intermediate glimpse of the ontological difference: an intermediate glimpse of the appearing of what appears. Of appearance itself."[52] In the experience of the sublime, on this account, what is intuited (in either the Kantian or common usage of the term) is not the infinite lying *beyond* the sensible manifold (on either the hither or thither side of the theoretical), but simply the eventuation of the difference that gives (and closes off within itself) the world.

The thinker who best effects this metabolism of Kantian aesthetics into Heideggerian ontology is undoubtedly Jean-Luc Nancy; nor has anyone else been as successful in preserving both the aesthetic and ontological intonations within a single style of argument. For Nancy the moment of the sublime awakens reflection to the motion of form's donation from the formless, the arrival of figure's limit from the not-this of "unlimitation."[53] He recognizes that Kant's treatment of the beautiful involves an account of the self's enjoyment of its own powers, one so profound, in fact, as to ascribe to the self a degree of fulfillment in itself formerly found only in God (32); the beautiful, though, is the domain only of limit, border, the place of exchange between the merely agreeable and the truly sublime (33). But when sensibility, in the apprehension of sublimity, accomplishes a passage to the limit itself, representation and presence are called into question by an intimation of what makes them possible: here one gains an experience of "the nothing" that "sets itself off" — which is to say that "[i]n a sense *nothing* sets itself off thus" (35). This is, properly speaking, the experience of "unlimitation": not really, that is, of *the* unlimited (which might mean merely the infinitely ontic, a determinate infinity in excess of what appears), but simply of the unpresentable "there is" of presentation. "[I]t is a matter . . . of the movement of the unlimited, or more exactly, of 'the unlimitation' *(die Unbegrenzheit)* that takes place on the border of the limit, and thus on the border of presentation" (35). In this tearing or cutting away at the margin (36), the limit is "unbordered" so that presentation may occur (37); and the sublime sim-

---

52. Éliane Escoubas, "Kant or the Simplicity of the Sublime," in *Of the Sublime,* 70.

53. See in particular Jean-Luc Nancy, "The Sublime Offering," in *Of the Sublime.* Parenthetical page numbers in the following text are to this essay.

ply is this movement of presentation, this infinite gesture that carries all away into an absence of form (38), this sheer *il y a* or *es gibt* whose motion grants the stability of representation. One discovers presentation "itself" at the limit between figure and elimination, and it is pure limit, beyond which lies nothing else: it is not form, which might yield a sense of the free accord discovered in self-recognition (such as one finds in the beautiful), or in the homogeneous (that is, in the schemata of the understanding), or in the heterogeneous (as with certain dialectical and romantic styles of thought), but simply a limiting and unlimiting (41). It is the gesture that distinguishes form from the formless, and to "see" it is to experience a rapture toward the nothing, and thereby to receive the world as the gift of transience. Here Nancy's language can verge on the mystical: contemplation of the sublime is an offering, a yielding up of thought, an abandonment to a presentation yet to come, and a surrender of the will to determine what comes; this offering at the limit, where the gift of the world is met by the sacrifice of rational ambition, is nothing less than "freedom" (48). The passage beyond self is sublime dispossession, a condition of exposure to the absolute surface — the "writing" — of existence, which relieves thought of the burden of comprehensive theory and liberates the world from the tyranny of a transcendent eternity, and so grants to thought a true "sense of the world."[54] The world is the *open:* it comes as nothing but the arrival and dissolution of its own sense (not *meaning,* that is, as this would signify a grasp of the whole as an ordered, teleological totality); the "world's worlding" is sheer writing, which gives and will give nothing beyond the "thin line" of sense's proposal and disappearance; sheer "painting" or "design," but without vision.[55]

There is, obviously, precious little of Kant in all of this. Nancy even has the audacity to dismiss the rationalist triumphalism of the third Critique's treatment of the sublime as little more than an occasional tone of voice (48). Of course, Kant's text suggests not so much as a tremor of humility before being, but only a sense of awe before the majesty of reason; for him the sublime is not an unconquerable alterity that genuinely disrupts the serene self-regard of reason — being's advent within thought under the form of anxiety or rapture before the nothing — but is thoroughly enfolded within reason, as a singular but brief sojourn within the course of reason's odyssey, a moment of hesitation as

54. For Nancy's best exposition of his philosophy of immanence (or pure existence) — his "deconstruction of Christianity" (to employ his solecism) — see Nancy, *The Sense of the World,* trans. Jeffrey S. Librett (Minneapolis: University of Minnesota Press, 1997). It reads a bit like a gallicized pastiche of Nietzsche and Heidegger at times, and is predictably unrefined in regard to the theological tradition, but it is a thorough and vigorous meditation on an "eventual" ontology.

55. See Jean-Luc Nancy, "De l'écriture: qu'elle ne révèle rien," *Rue Descartes* 10 (Paris: Albin Michel, 1994).

imagination's exhaustion is followed, in an almost immediate syncope, by the exhaustion of nature's utmost power before reason. Nevertheless, Nancy's redaction of Kant displays quite resplendently an entirely modern (and postmodern) prejudice: between the sublime and the beautiful, there is no continuum of eminence, but only the indissoluble bond of dialectical *difference* (not merely opposition); and it is the sublime that "figures" forth being, while the beautiful can speak only of beings. While there is no room in such a scheme for a coincidence of the transcendentals, nonetheless it is the sublime that is the "truth" that permits the beautiful its enchanting untruths — though, of course, Nancy would reject such terms. Within this duality, this necessary and unbreakable *liaison* between irreconcilables, the world comes to pass and passes away — that is, arrives entirely as its passage into nothing. Truth is most assuredly not beauty: neither so the reverse.

4. *The ethical sublime,* or the discourse of the unrepresentable when a more genuinely Kantian vein has been struck: Kantian, that is, only insofar as it concerns a kind of categorical imperative, though certainly not one that emanates from the "moral law within" or the power of reason to legislate for itself. The foremost representative of this "school" of the sublime would surely be Emmanuel Levinas, whose thought is often characterized as a kind of "Jewish" postmodernism, though it might more accurately be described as Manichaean, Orphic, or gnostic.[56] Levinas's importance, it must be noted, lies not in the clarity of his thought (which is, in truth, a prodigy of incoherence), but in the utter purity of his idiom; in his work one encounters a logic of the ethical that other thinkers repeat, but none with such absolutely unalloyed and hyperbolic intensity. It should also be noted that the good opinion that Levinas's work at present enjoys is so great (in large part because it appears apt to satisfy some commendable appetite in certain thinkers in this postmetaphysical age for *some* language of moral responsibility) that it may seem somewhat coarse to observe that it is poor philosophy — the banal tortured into counterfeit profundity, the obviously false propounded as irresistibly true, other forms of thought caricatured and condemned with a vehemence frequently vicious, and a fulminant tone of mystical authority assumed wherever principled argument proves impossible — but, even so, this is my contention; as is the no doubt even coarser assertion that Levinas advances a view of the world that is perhaps a little depraved.

---

56. Gillian Rose has described Levinas's vision as "Buddhist Judaism" in Rose, *Mourning Becomes the Law: Philosophy and Representation* (Cambridge: Cambridge University Press, 1996), 37, and "Judaic Manicheism" in Rose, *Judaism and Modernity: Philosophical Essays* (Oxford: Blackwell, 1993), 43. See also 213. Her judgment is just.

For Levinas the place of the unrepresentable is occupied not by "being," "chaos," or "*différance*," but by the "Other." That which defies presence and representation, that which stands over against what we can grasp within the horizons of our habitual universe of thought and action, that which is sublimely true is the otherness of the other, the alterity that always precedes and escapes the intentionality by which we compose a world according to our own capacities. Moreover, supposedly, the very transcendence of this otherness constitutes a command, an infinite obligation that permits us no respite and excites in us an ethical desire susceptible of no satiation. And it is a command that carries with it an inescapable accusation, one that convicts us of our gross absorption in our own being, our comfortable habitation within the estates of the "Same," whose prospects open only upon the reassuringly familiar; to hear the call of the Other is to know oneself as guilty. Allegedly, it is the possibility of genuine otherness, and its mute but unanswerable interpellation, that Western philosophy (including what Levinas calls "rational theology")[57] has almost always forgotten or striven to suppress, in order to confine the thinkable within the boundaries of the self, its rationality, its native powers, and its possession. Western philosophy is, in the proper sense, an *odyssey*, a venturing forth solely for the sake of an ultimate return; but the ethical, when the alien appeal of the Other interrupts our blissful idyll of self-possession, provokes us to endless Abrahamic pilgrimage, a departure from all that is securely ours, a flight from which we cannot ever return.[58] Hence Levinas's notorious condemnation of Husserlian phenomenology and Heideggerian ontology: the former can imagine the Other only under the form of an "appresentative analogy," which reduces the other to an alter ego, a reflection of the subject's own "egoity";[59] and the latter subordinates all thought to the immanence of Being, which "exposes" or "exhibits" itself in beings, and so within thought. In neither scheme does the Other arrive as other, nor can it require of the self more than the self possesses in itself. The oddity of Levinas's critique, however, is that it never succeeds in making a simple (and one would think obvious) critical distinction between, say, a certain construal of ontology, such as Heidegger's, and being as such;

57. Emmanuel Levinas, "God and Philosophy," in Levinas, *Of God Who Comes to Mind*, trans. Bettina Bergo (Stanford: Stanford University Press, 1998), 56. Needless to say, Levinas has only a very general impression of theological tradition.

58. Emmanuel Levinas, *Totality and Infinity: An Essay on Exteriority*, trans. Alphonso Lingis (Pittsburgh: Duquesne University Press, 1969), 33-35.

59. See Edmund Husserl, *Cartesian Meditations: An Introduction to Phenomenology*, trans. Dorion Cairns (Dordrecht: Kluwer Academic Publishers, 1995), 89-151. Levinas's translation of the *Meditations* (appearing many decades before the original German was published) more or less introduced phenomenology to France; which makes all the more perplexing his rather unsubtle reading of Husserl.

rather, Levinas rejects the philosopher and the subject of his inquiries as one. Levinas simply accepts Heidegger's ontology (to the extent he understands it), assimilates it to all previous metaphysics, and then turns his back on being itself, to pursue the ethical into a region that is "otherwise than being." As early as 1935, in an essay entitled "De l'évasion,"[60] Levinas speaks of Being or existence (which for him are synonymous) as an overwhelming and brutal prison wherein the human spirit languishes, a force whose awful power the spirit cannot overcome, but must instead "evade": not transcend, which would require a power more monstrous still, but elude by way of "excendence," an escape empty of personal will (74). The experience of pure being, writes Levinas (introducing a theme to recur many times in subsequent works), is a confrontation with sheer, bare existence that provokes in one a condition of "nausea" (90).[61] A culture devoted to being, he says, must be "barbarism" (98). In *De l'existence à l'existant* (1947),[62] Levinas states still more explicitly that the good is absolutely beyond being, and there is no access to it save by way of "departure"; existence is an impersonal evil, night, an event without substance;[63] when one encounters the sheer *il y a* of being, denuded of particular beings, the "evil in Being . . . becomes the Evil of Being."[64] True, Levinas elsewhere speaks of the "mute roar" of the *il y a* as an original agitation, provoking the "insomnia" that gives birth to consciousness, wakefulness, moral vigilance;[65] but it is against being and its savagery that one must be vigilant.

All of which accounts for the oddest feature of Levinas's thought: though it ostensibly concerns the Other, such is the severity of its logic that the other — to remain truly other — cannot in any way actually *appear:* neither by way of phenomenology's analogies and reductions, nor by way of any prior understanding of being and beings, nor within the reach of simple recognition (in every case, one remains within the confines of the Same). Rather, alterity is intimated solely in moments of rupture or discontinuity; the otherness that makes demands of us is alien to us, from beyond the totality. Of course, the possibility of knowing something of this otherness must open somewhere within normal

---

60. Published originally in *Recherches Philosophiques*, the essay has been reprinted as Emmanuel Levinas, *De l'évasion* (Montpellier: Fata Morgana, 1982). Parenthetical page numbers in the following text are to this work.

61. It is almost certainly from Levinas that Sartre "borrowed" the theme of the first of his attempts at literature. French existentialism was largely a result of Levinas's introduction of phenomenology into France.

62. In English, Emmanuel Levinas, *Existence and Existents,* trans. Alphonso Lingis (Dordrecht: Kluwer, 1988).

63. Levinas, *Existence and Existents,* 63.

64. Levinas, *Existence and Existents,* 19.

65. Levinas, "God and Philosophy," 58.

experience, even if the Other is not an *object* of experience. In the essay of 1948, "Time and the Other," Levinas discovers the possibility of a transcendence beyond being within the diachrony of our time-bound existence; this is our transcendence toward the Other, who is for us absolute futurity; in fact, nowhere is the other's alterity better suggested than in our encounter with our own death, which befalls us as utter disjunction, utter impossibility: "this precisely indicates that the other is not another myself, participating with me in a common existence. The relationship with the other is not an idyllic and harmonious relationship of communion, or a sympathy through which we put ourselves in the other's place . . . the relationship with the other is a relationship with a Mystery."[66] So alien is the other to my identity that the desire alterity excites is not even a need proper to my being: the Other hollows out a new space in the self.[67] The governing theme of Levinas's best book, *Totality and Infinity* (1961), is that the ethical knows nothing of beings within being: it is an event resistant of all thematization, and can be characterized only as transcendence, infinity, exteriority, God. It arrives, unbidden, and establishes itself in me, despite my incapacity to contain it; it is the idea of the infinite occurring in thought, which (as Descartes noted) awakens one to what is beyond the self.[68] "Relation" with the Other is impossible within the economy of representation or according to the dynamism of natural desire or delight: "Total alterity, in which a being does not refer to enjoyment and presents itself out of itself, does not shine forth in the *form* by which things are given to us";[69] nor can it be seen in "the beautiful, whose essence is indifference, cold splendor, and silence. By the façade the thing which keeps its secret is exposed enclosed in its monumental essence and in its myth, in which it gleams like a splendor but does not deliver itself. If the transcendent cuts across sensibility, if it is openness preeminently, if its vision is the very openness of being, it cuts across the vision of forms and can be stated neither in terms of contemplation nor in terms of practice. It is the face; its revelation is speech."[70] Lest one be misled by Levinas's reference to the "face" and "speech," however, it should be noted how elusive of definition such concepts are in his discourse: he most emphatically means neither the particular features of a unique visage nor the content of anything actually spoken (an immediately visible face or intelligible utterance falls within the Same's pernicious circle). He means the event of otherness (which infinitely disturbs us), and not the shape of the other (which can at most stir cupidity or revulsion). The face is the

66. Emmanuel Levinas, *Time and the Other,* trans. Richard Cohen (Pittsburgh: Duquesne University Press, 1987), 75.

67. Levinas, "God and Philosophy," 59.

68. Levinas, *Totality and Infinity,* 204.

69. Levinas, *Totality and Infinity,* 192.

70. Levinas, *Totality and Infinity,* 193.

divine alterity that lies behind all faces, seen as invisible. In the ethical relation, one must not even notice the color of the other's eyes;[71] the face is "signification," but entirely without context;[72] it enters the world from absolutely beyond,[73] and is seen only in "the gaze of a human being looking at another human precisely as abstract human disengaged from all culture."[74] Or, as Levinas more austerely states it, it is not available to sight at all, but is the place where intention dissolves in "a *for another,* a suffering for his suffering, without light."[75] Ethics is a "relation without relation," a "desire" for the absolutely other, and pure "asymmetry"; its source is a God who is wholly other, infinity without relation to being's totality. God here is the idea of God occurring in me,[76] constituting my subjectivity as the purest passivity, "a passivity more passive than any passivity, like the passivity of trauma" (64), inciting in me a desire without end for the good (67), though he "must remain separated in the Desire": "The Desirable [God] commands me to what is the nondesirable, to the undesirable *par excellence;* to another" (68). This is "Love without Eros" (68), "God-coming-to-mind as the life of God".[77] Like the god of the gnostics, infinitely remote in the inaccessible depths of the *pleroma,* entirely alien to the *"kenoma"* of the demiurge's world, Levinas's God never meets us within the scope afforded by our own being or nature: "God cannot appear as the cause or creator of nature. . . . we could say that God is the other who turns our nature inside out, who calls our ontological will-to-be into question. . . . God does indeed go against nature for He is not of this world."[78] Only such a God, untouched by being and nowhere revealed in its splendors, can yield the good: "when we say that God cannot satisfy our desire, we must add that the insatisfaction is itself sublime! What is a defect in the finite order becomes an excellence in the infinite order. In the infinite order, the absence of God is better than his presence; and the anguish of our concern and searching for God is better than consummation or comfort."[79]

---

71. Emmanuel Levinas, *Ethics and Infinity: Conversations with Philippe Nemo,* trans. Richard Cohen (Pittsburgh: Duquesne University Press, 1985), 85.

72. Levinas, *Ethics and Infinity,* 86.

73. Emmanuel Levinas, "Meaning and Sense," in Levinas, *Basic Philosophical Writings,* ed. Adriaan T. Peperzak et al. (Bloomington and Indianapolis: Indiana University Press, 1996), 50.

74. Levinas, "Meaning and Sense," 58.

75. Emmanuel Levinas, *Otherwise Than Being, or Beyond Essence,* trans. Alphonso Lingis (Dordrecht: Kluwer, 1991), 18.

76. Levinas, "God and Philosophy," 63. The parenthetical page numbers in the following text are to "God and Philosophy."

77. Emmanuel Levinas, "The Old and the New," in *Time and the Other,* 138.

78. From an interview entitled "Ethics of the Infinite," in Richard Kearney, *States of Mind: Dialogues with Contemporary Thinkers* (New York: New York University Press, 1995), 190.

79. "Ethics of the Infinite," 197.

Obviously, from the Levinasian perspective, an "ethics" allied with aesthetics would be monstrous,[80] and an "aesthetic ethics" a contradiction in terms. Nothing of being, no matter how eminently elevated it may be, and certainly not the meretricious glamors of sensible nature, can possess a moral significance. It is true that in Levinas's earlier work he attempts to find some space — perhaps propaedeutic to the ethical — in the goods of nature; he grants if not the actual goodness, at least the "sincerity," of the things we "live from": light, air, shelter, food. These things we enjoy for themselves, as they fill our needs and please us; but still they compose our world of self-concern, and in the moment that this circle of enjoyment is crossed by the Other, it is rendered guilty; desire for the infinite then must summon us into holy exile. *Totality and Infinity* even offers a phenomenology of eros and fecundity,[81] which seems to promise some accommodation with the flesh; but the erotic, for Levinas, is the possibility of the good only in its surrender to what eludes enjoyment. Especially revealing in this regard is this phenomenology's treatment of the figure of the "Woman," who serves as the mute unprotesting threshold of an *exitus* toward a "future not future enough" (the son born in fecundity's "discontinuous time"), a delightful if liminal animality (263) — at once modesty and nudity — who merely offers the occasion of transcendence. Levinas's model of eros is the caress (257-58), which — as opposed to the embrace — opens out upon the true moral realm of "discontinuity" precisely insofar as it *passes over;* not only does it disdain possession, but it becomes a kind of moral contact only when it passes beyond contact to achieve the insensibility of an empty hand, and so embodies the pathos of departure. In any event, even the meager warmth afforded by these feeble heliotropisms soon dissipates from the gelid pages of Levinas's texts; by the time of his second magnum opus, *Otherwise Than Being* (1974), eros has been put wholly to flight. In this (in every sense) terrible book, a host of more violent expressions come to the fore and render his emphasis even more uncompromisingly extreme: the Other's proximity is my "trauma," an "accusation" that "persecutes" me, exploiting my "vulnerability," holding me "hostage," consuming me with "obsession," forcing me to make "expiation" (and so on). Moreover, even the rigors of "relation without relation" are multiplied by the "illeity" of God: an alterity absolutely other than even the otherness of the Other, a transcendence whose sheer infinity of absence is as impersonal as the discord of the *il y a*, introducing a wound or fissure within my subjectivity, tracing itself in the place of the "third" who is yet other than the Other; this tertiary distorts my relation with

80. On this, see the very curious (and silly) essay "Reality and Its Shadow," in *The Levinas Reader,* ed. Seán Hand (Oxford: Blackwell, 1989), 129-43.

81. Levinas, *Totality and Infinity,* 254-85. Parenthetical page numbers in the following text are to this work.

another, bends it toward the absent God and the place of the one outside the circle of acquaintance, converting my motion toward the Other into absolute responsibility for every other, devoid of the affectivity of love or natural benevolence.[82] Otherness now wears the aspect of the "Enigma":[83] an essential withdrawal, an impenetrable hiddenness within all language, where the "Saying" transcends the "Said" in its very utterance.[84] In this impalpable contact or formless encounter, I am addressed by an injunction issuing from an absolute and immemorial past, never present to me in continuous time;[85] I find that even before I am, I am responsible. This address requires the surrender of the *conatus essendi*, the will to persist that is the origin of war;[86] it elects me as its hostage to offer up in "a sacrifice without reserve."[87] In full truthful exposure to the Other — who comes with an ahistorical, eschatological suddenness, though without the offer of eschatological hope — I can answer only with the admission of my debt and submission of my will: "Here I am." Such is my responsibility that even my utter passivity before the Other is something I must expiate:

> This passivity deserves the epithet of complete or absolute only if the persecuted one is liable to answer for the persecutor. The face of the neighbor in its persecuting hatred can by this very malice obsess as something pitiful. . . . To undergo from the other is an absolute patience only if by this from-the-other is already for-the-other. . . . "To tend the cheek to the smiter and to be filled with shame," to demand suffering in the suffering undergone (without producing the act that would be the exposing of the other cheek) is not to draw from suffering some kind of magical redemptive virtue. In the trauma of persecution it is to pass from the outrage undergone to the responsibility for the persecutor, and, in this sense from suffering to expiation for the other.[88]

This "generosity" of the for-the-other, as Levinas often asserts, positively "requires an *ingratitude* of the Other":[89] I must expect and want nothing in return.

There is no need to continue with this digest; but there is much that still should be said. I confess that, with the exception of the obviously barbarous ideologies of this past century, I know of no modern philosophy of "values"

---

82. Levinas, *Otherwise Than Being*, 111-12.

83. The term is introduced in "Énigme et phénomène" (1965): Emmanuel Levinas, "Enigma and Phenomenon," in *Basic Philosophical Writings*, 65-77.

84. Levinas, *Otherwise Than Being*, 23.

85. See Levinas, "God and Philosophy," 68.

86. Levinas, *Otherwise Than Being*, 4.

87. Levinas, *Otherwise Than Being*, 15.

88. Levinas, *Otherwise Than Being*, 111.

89. Levinas, "Meaning and Sense," 49.

more morally hideous than that of Levinas. Behind his convulsive and ostentatious ecstasies of self-denial and self-torture, with all their mournful bombast, one can easily lose sight of an immensely troubling feature of his discourse: it is plainly bizarre for an ethics that begins from a solicitude that the Other not suffer the themes and reductions of the Same to terminate in a language that, quite without compunction, reduces the other to the theme of "persecutor," a sacrificer of hostages, an accuser, a stranger to gratitude. Obviously, Levinas's concern is to safeguard the purity of ethical intention — but this always means only *my* purity. Does this not perhaps serve a somewhat self-aggrandizing moral heroism, a selflessness so hyperbolic that it must ultimately erase everything distinct, desirable, and genuinely *other* in the other in order to preserve itself from the contamination of need, dependency, or hope? Of course, Levinas's Other is not really other at all: without theme, context, contour, identity, the other is always the same, always nothing but the infinite orientation of *my* ethical adventure, my flight of the alone to the alone, secure in my purity of intention. By expecting nothing of the other, wanting nothing, I leave the other behind; and stripped of the dignity of the desirable (or even the visible), the other becomes merely my "occasion." The "null-site" of subjectivity[90] somehow owns a supersensible freedom as irrefrangible as any Kant could imagine. It is hard not to see here something like a triumph of transcendental subjectivity, the Fichtean Ego surpassing the nonego, toward the Absolute: an infinite trajectory, untroubled by a world of shared expectations; or to hear a trace of gnostic hubris in the loneliness of this responsibility before an address from beyond the world's totality, undistracted by the other's identity — or the color of the other's eyes. Of course, this is the peril of any truly "categorical" ethics: an absolutely extreme rhetoric, being always one-half of a contradiction in flight from its necessary antinomy, must comprise its own inversion. However, what makes the spectacle afforded by Levinas's thought — the utter ruin of the whole rationality of love — so disheartening is that it offers not even the consolation of rational coherence. The ethical "relation without relation" that Levinas describes is nonsense: there is no encounter — nor even a trace within an encounter — that is not "thematized," conforming to intentions largely determined by cultural tradition. But even if there were, there would still be no such thing as unthematized responsibility: the claim that obligation erupts from the singularity of an irrecuperable event, indifferent to every context, and from the affront of an alterity whose only appearance is interruption and accusation, is sheer assertion. In truth, given the nature of the abstract event Levinas describes, it might just as well (and just as blamelessly) be taken as a provocation to kill the Other.

90. Levinas, *Otherwise Than Being*, 17-18.

Admittedly, Levinas's ethics is, in part, an attempt to escape the sacrificial delirium of natural or "pagan" sacrality, but, in that he can imagine no (sacramental) way of return to the world, his own sacrifice (of being, of nature) is no less awful. If he did not feel compelled to draw such absolute divisions — between being and the good, light and ethics, joy and obligation, vision and responsibility — but strove instead to liberate all these things from the transcendental empire of self-subsisting subjectivity, all might be well. He might show how what we "live from" can burgeon into the desire to live for others. Instead, in denying this continuity and indeed replacing it with an opposition, he can offer merely his ghastly world-renunciation, a rejection of being as simple elemental strife, and thereby succeeds in destroying the only premises for moral action: analogy, vision, and joy. For only if being is freed from its subordination to the violence of the sacred and the "natural," and received as a gift of the transcendent (and so impossible to contain within any circle of the Same); and only if the other is also received as a gift, seen within the light of being as one who must *be,* and one with whom I wish to share yet more being; then is morality possible, not only as injunction, but as a desire that wakens me to something more than subjectivity. True, following the rigorist model of modern (that is, Kantian) ethics, any excitation of interest destroys the ethical at its source (my perfect freedom — or "passivity"); and if presence and beauty cannot coincide, if the possibility of joy in the other is not also the possibility of ethics, if hunger for the visible cannot also become a hunger for the good, then blindness and alien sublimity must be the (irrational) context of the ethical. In fine, if ethics is pure disinterest, then the good cannot appear as being or phenomenon, or anywhere within the realm of the "theoretical"; but this simply means that disinterest is the wrong formula for the ethical. What, after all, is really more disruptive of simple self-possession, persecution or joy? Joy feeds on what it receives, but rarely on what it establishes; it is a true wakefulness to what I do not ever already possess, and it requires a continuity between what evokes and what is evoked, an analogy that places itself in me. But if my generosity follows upon the persecution I suffer, in reaction to a pathos, then it must have the form of utter contrariety, and must therefore be entirely *my* achievement. Love without eros can be only a subject's victory over the effrontery of the given. For Levinas, the good is so opposed to the ontological that it can have no reality except as a *privatio mali,* prompted into paradoxical "existence" by the aggression of the Other's arrival; the good can only "be" good as the negative of a *substantial* suffering. But only if being and phenomenality are themselves good and continuous with the good is it worthwhile speaking of ethics.

Modern prejudices aside, obligation flows from love or the possibility of love, and love (in both its strength and its indigence) is never entirely devoid of eros. It requires of course humility to acknowledge one's need for the other's response, to allow the "empirical" self its dependency, even if the "transcendental" self must then lose some measure of its purity — enough humility to be awestruck by the beauty of another: this one cannot possess; one needs its otherness to taste of it. An infinite and anonymous alterity, on the other hand, one possesses entirely. An "intentionality" that never crosses the analogical interval between oneself and another need never come to a halt. It is beauty and wonder that bring intention up short and prevent it from traversing the distance of being in indifference; beauty — the sudden splendor of otherness — forbids both absorption in oneself and the "infinitist" orientation of an ethical titan. What startles and provokes is glory, in which one finds a coincidence of strangeness and recognition. Often, seeing the color of another's eyes is the beginning of "responsibility." Of course, it is sadly true that real desire is typically absent, and that, for just this reason, beauty is not always visible; there is always a degree of utopian or eschatological deferral in moral desire; but without love's vital appetite, and the capacity for sympathy it opens, there is no impulse within one that can be cultivated toward a responsibility not consequent simply upon immediate affection or interest. The truly moral alternative to those malign representations by which one often reduces another to the contemptibly familiar is not the superintentional blindness of pure, persecuting obligation (which makes the other convertible with the "evil of being"), but another representation, according to a better order of desire, a more charitable enlargement of one's own desires to encompass the good of another; this is simple moral intelligence. And this is why the hope of reciprocity, of gratitude, is the only true generosity: it is one's consent to behold and be beholden to another (anything less reduces the other to nothing). Certainly a condescending benevolence that seeks to dominate others, that demands extravagant gratitude as its price and continues to demand it in order to hold another captive, is the worst imaginable abuse of moral relation; but the possibility of abuse is itself the reverse of possible *use*.

Could there really be ethics devoid of the will to be, the *conatus essendi*? After all, the desire to be is always in some part a desire to be *with others*, and but for the wish to persist in being and enjoy its goodness — even when one must give it up — one has nothing to extend to another, and no reason to desire being *for another*. Levinas's ethics is perhaps for this very reason stringently minimalist; it proscribes murder and callousness but says nothing about increasing another's joy. A genuinely effective morality, on the other hand, must begin from the capacity for love, and (as, for example, Bernard of Clairvaux understood) the love of self is the beginning of all love, and in a transfigured form is inseparable from its end. Ethics is a social love, born from the preoccupations of the flesh: it is a refinement of want, an education of vision, a revelation within one's innate desires of the beauty present in all otherness (even when deeply hidden). As divertingly dramatic as is the urgent catastrophism of an ethics of the absolutely singular event and of infinite, pitiless obligation, it inverts the order of moral wisdom: by itself, no otherness (especially no unrepresentable otherness), nor all the abysmal suffering in the world, could provoke one moment of love, mercy, or even concern from an isolated self; but once love has been roused, sympathy stirred, or joy evoked, the self begins to be able to bear and struggle against any suffering or evil with a real moral passion. And this love requires an analogy between self and other; as much as Husserl's talk of the alter ego horrifies Levinas, it follows from a simple recognition of the inescapable limits and profound potentials of human experience. Analogy, when all is said and done, is not identity, nor even a special taxonomy; it would in fact be a contradiction of logic to seek to capture another by way of a truly analogical appraisal, because the attempt would necessarily be defeated by the very interval of the analogy itself (which must be the interval of an irreducible difference, as much as of a similitude). The analogical "reduction" is always also a reduction of the same to "another other," a subordination of the self to a likeness to which the self actually belongs and which it cannot encompass; it elevates selves (within the scope being affords) above their isolation, while preserving their differences. To acknowledge a shared participation within a way of being, that is to say, far from "totalizing" being, is to be borne forth from a false sense of sufficiency into the illuminating strangeness of that to which one belongs before one belongs to oneself. No such disruption of the self's sovereignty is provided by Levinasian ethics: without the light of beauty, concrete desire, knowledge, similitude, hope, joy, representation . . . one's sole index of the good must be one's transcendental purity of will. This is why Levinas never actually succeeds in imagining "alterity," but only absolute negation (and nothing comes of nothing). If the infinity of the "Other" could break in upon being as he says, as absolute contrariety, precisely this would mark the self's world as a closed totality; if the good can enter being only over against being, then the ontological fold is sealed upon itself, and two infinities (the elemental *apeiron* and the alien good) sustain one another in their eternal opposition. While this mimics a certain idealist suspicion of appearance (as it does a metaphysical separation of the sensible from the true), it neither frees reflection from the prison of the ego nor provides a grammar for "ethics."

In the end, so much of what Levinas consigns to the realm of totality — reciprocity, a longing for shared happiness, a desire for the other's regard — is what a more compromising moralist would call community; he, though, consciously resists the language of community, out of his anxiety over its many dangers: tribal, national, and racial associations, the authenticity of blood and soil, religious hatred, and so forth. But he so scrupulously purges the ethical of the fruits of being — joy, beauty's "cold splendor," delight, the affectivity of love, even laughter (in short, life) — that it becomes an almost demonic category. Of course, it is the fate of every purely "dialectical" theology or discourse of transcendence to fail to reconcile worldly being with the highest good, and so to reduce the former to something malign and irredeemable; given his point of departure, Levinas can scarcely do other than subject creation to ever more morbid defamations. This is why his ethics occasionally achieves a grim sickliness so profound that it often appears merely to convert some private melancholy into a resentful malice toward all of being. And yet this is a sign of his consistency: if one cannot — must not — *see* the good, but elects to serve it, terror, paradox, despondency, and tragedy compose the "ethical's" inevitable atmosphere.

Not that others have not attempted something like Levinas's ethics in a more moderate voice, most notably Jacques Derrida. The bright hues of the early Derrida's occasional Dionysiac intoxications long ago melted into the somber autumnal chromas of Levinas's unworldliness; now when he speaks of the ethical, even at a critical remove from the Levinasian vocabulary, Derrida does so in a privative mood, in terms of a sublime otherness that can be grasped only as a trace. But as great as has been the evolution from Derrida's earliest sustained treatment of Levinas's thought, "Violence and Metaphysics,"[91] to such recent works as *The Gift of Death*,[92] his understanding of the ethical has actually remained a fixed line that the curve of this development has merely subtended; and it is probably better described in the earlier phase of his work. "Violence and Metaphysics," to take then the best example, is a critique of Levinas's peremptory rejection of phenomenology and ontology, which to Derrida seems an impossible and self-defeating renunciation of philosophy; discourse, says Derrida, though it is always haunted by violence, is still preferable to the mysticism of "infinity," which can be nothing finally but a certain commanding silence that, in finite terms, is itself violence. Speech is history, he argues, and so the only possibility of either violence or the restraint of violence within its least aggressive manifestation: "Metaphysics is *economy*: violence against violence, light against light: philosophy (in general). . . . This becoming is war. This polemic is language itself. Its inscription." And history is "the very movement of transcendence, of the excess over the totality without which no totality would appear as such";[93] only an economy of violence (which philosophy *may* promote) can preserve historical finitude, as this motion of excess, from the discourse either of an infinite plenitude of presence that can impose

91. Jacques Derrida, "Violence and Metaphysics: An Essay on the Thought of Emmanuel Levinas," in *Writing and Difference*, 79-153.

92. Jacques Derrida, *The Gift of Death*, trans. David Wills (Chicago: University of Chicago Press, 1992).

93. Derrida, "Violence and Metaphysics," 117. The parenthetical page references in the following text are to this essay.

only silence or of the finite totality of the Same. It is history's motion alone, always eluding infinity and totality alike, that transcends mere presence; and if the only "transcendence" is history, and not some impossible feat of timeless "infinition," the practice of ontological and phenomenological scrutiny must be undertaken, philosophical reflection must work to moderate the violences of metaphysical totality *and* the violence of history itself. After all, if indeed this excessive motion must, as Hegel saw, be strife, it is still what bears thought and language on toward the other; nor can the otherness of the other be grasped within this motion but through something like Husserl's phenomenological reduction: only the appresentative analogy of the other reveals the otherness of the other, allows the other to elude every victorious assimilation of otherness (123-24). There is indeed a kind of war in all phenomenality, in every transcendental reduction of the other; but its violence is also nonviolence, an opening of relationality within the medium of a necessary economy; history is, after all, an infinite passage through violence, which truth only an infinitist dogmatism ignores (128-30).

Rather than the apocalyptic choice between a totalizing (hierarchical) finite and a totalizing (featureless) infinite, Derrida prefers a Heideggerian thought of being, which at least lets be the other as other, outside the essentializing schemes of a traditional metaphysics. And only a univocal ontology, says Derrida, lets beings be, without falling prey to a metaphysical anxiety for order. Heidegger's Being, after all, is not some primordial substance, but an original withdrawal; it determines itself only in beings, as a history, manifesting itself by hiding itself. Being, thought thus, does not overshadow beings as a higher value; and without some "precomprehension" of being, no history — no *other* — can appear. True, such an ontology does not escape violence; as Derrida says, the Heideggerian account "supposes that war is not an accident which overcomes Being, but rather Being itself. 'Das Sein selber das Strittige ist' *(Brief über den Humanismus . . .)*. A proposition which must not be understood in consonance with Hegelianism: here, negativity has its origin neither in negation, nor in an anxiety of an infinite and primary existent. War, perhaps, is no longer even conceivable as negativity" (144). But if the affirmation of being cannot avoid also "affirming" war, it can still help to limit war as much as possible, by allowing one to think the difference of being from beings, and so to conceive a "responsibility" that "transcends" the epochal totality in which Being is constrained to show (and hide) itself.

> Being is history. . . . Being dissimulates itself in its occurrence, and originally does violence to itself in order to be stated and in order to appear. A Being without violence would be a Being which would occur outside the existent: nothing; nonhistory; nonoccurrence; nonphenomenality. A

speech produced without the least violence would determine nothing, would say nothing, would offer nothing to the other; it would not be *history*, and it would *show* nothing. . . .

. . . according to Levinas, nonviolent language would be a language which would do without the verb *to be*, that is, without predication. Predication is the first violence. . . . nonviolent language, in the final analysis, would be a language of pure invocation, pure adoration, proffering only proper nouns in order to call to the other from afar. In effect such a language would be purified of all *rhetoric*. (147)[94]

In this early essay Derrida and Levinas confront one another from positions at once opposed and mutually sustaining; the distance between one and one's other (and any rhetoric that would cross it) is, for both of them, fraught with inevitable violence; and, for each, the distance is an ethical interval, which must be kept in place lest a far greater violence break loose. Levinas withdraws from being, rejects its mediations, in order to preserve the other from philosophical reduction, while Derrida steps out into space, knowing that, whatever the risks, it is the only path to another. Of the two, Derrida is the more clear-sighted; in terms of simple historical observation, he commands a position of unassailable logic: history has been a passage through violence, and a failure to restrain it, even through a "phenomenological" reduction of the other, has often enough led to the even greater violence of cultural reduction: colonialism, warfare, spoliation, persecution. What Derrida fears in Levinas's language of justice is the violence of an impossible silence (the death that metaphysics is, the retreat from history and so from being), which can do nothing to restrain the ethical violence that occurs in the concrete eventualities of difference; to acknowledge the violence inextricable in every advance toward the other is also to take responsibility for that violence. Derrida does not entirely reject the ethics of Levinas, obviously, but certainly his absolutism; the language of *infinite* alterity is too excessive; the ethical functions (if at all) not simply as a negation of the moral ambiguities of thought, a sublime silence, but must be a violence that restrains, a war upon war, a struggle with the other that also lets the other be.

This position is at once eminently pragmatic and fiercely ethical: as opposed to the vertical force of metaphysics (especially when, as with Hegel, it shows itself to require a cult of Ares) or to the impossible infinity of an ethical alterity, which makes the other a mute, terrifying, and monstrous sublimity, Derrida's desire to direct thought exclusively toward the horizontal violence of being appears to be the wisest way to restrain violence where it most palpably

94. Levinas's reply to this essay, and his protest that what appears in language need not be confined to the limits of language that philosophy describes, is found in "God and Philosophy."

occurs. This is the choice: we are saved from violence by violence, or else by withdrawal (which is death). When Derrida bids Levinas not to withdraw so far or so swiftly, he asks only that Levinas submit his ethics to the necessary violence of phenomenological reduction, of a gathering of otherness out of a hyperbolic infinity into the precincts of the "Same," though still with its credentials as otherness certified, and its "rights" as difference preserved, by a vigilant, restless, roving moral suspicion. This is, without question, the more *responsible* position to take. But it is worth noting that Derrida, once having acknowledged the ethical's conditions, still cannot account for its impulse, especially when he refuses himself the serviceable obscurantism of Levinas's idiom. Hence the tendency of his more recent work to resort to comparable mystifications — "every other is Wholly Other," the "messianic," the "impossible" gift — to lend weight to his ethics; for if being is still only being, and not also the good, then the ethical emanates only from a beyond whose *ratio* never really inhabits being except as the irreducible event of the singular (but again, as with Levinas, why such an event obliges cannot really be said).[95] In recent years, indeed, Derrida has increasingly followed after Levinas in emphasizing the priority of the other's otherness, and like Levinas, understands this otherness in a way that allows no aesthetic quantity to its priority; the other emerges from, or recedes behind, an all but imageless ethical sublime, as a kind of mystical absence of which one receives intuitions, so to speak: the trace of the other evokes me before I am I, before I arrive; but it is a trace only, and its style of evocation is singularly devoid of pleasing conceits (and so, I would argue, of meaning).[96] And no less than Levinas, Derrida finally seeks shelter in empty pronouncements: "Justice in itself, if such a thing exists, outside or beyond law, is not deconstructible. No more than deconstruction, if such a thing exists. Deconstruction is justice."[97] This is not really surprising: a truly "postmodern" ethics must, as it is still modern, retreat from Hegelian *Sittlichkeit* to Kant's categorical imperative; but, as it is nonetheless postmodern, it cannot share Kant's confidence in the power of reason, and so can

95. For a comprehensive treatment of Derrida's "religious" turn, see John Caputo, *The Prayers and Tears of Jacques Derrida: Religion without Religion* (Bloomington and Indianapolis: Indiana University Press, 1997). This is a poor book in many ways, not least because Caputo's *apologia pro Derrida suo* is so ferocious (and often sanctimonious) that the author never pauses to confront the weaknesses of his own arguments or the recklessness with which he employs certain words ("Jewish," "Christian," "religion," for instance); but it provides an exhaustive and accurate survey of its topic.

96. See Jacques Derrida, "'Eating Well,' or the Calculation of the Subject," in *Who Comes after the Subject,* ed. Eduardo Cadara et al. (London, 1991), 96-120.

97. Jacques Derrida, "Force of Law: The 'Mystical Foundation of Authority,'" trans. Mary Quaintance, *Cardozo Law Review* 11 (1990): 957.

recommend at most either the adventure of a negative infinity or the labor of an endless economy (or, apparently, both at once).

Theology can take nothing from either approach to "ethics": it cannot relinquish its faith in the goodness of being, or embrace the magical thinking that supposes that there is such a thing as a singular event that obliges apart from the thematizations of creeds and traditions; as it cannot accept the division between being and the good, or between the good and the beautiful, it can recommend neither "infinition" nor economy, but must continue to pursue its proper rhetoric, without "ethical" disquiet. The desire to limit violence by surrendering being univocally to the testimony of history, without analogical or eschatological tension, is one that has conceded violence an ontological primacy (and the ethical, as a purely voluntarist response to this violence, is contingent on cultural and political forces it would be quixotic to imagine any discourse of reason or restraint could control). If Levinas's ethics would be ideally, as Derrida claims, devoid of rhetoric, and Derrida's style of restraint would be an ethical invigilation of rhetoric, this is in each case because rhetoric — as the inevitable mediation of difference — has been conceived of as originally violent, imperial, dominating (a prejudice somewhat in keeping with a metaphysical distrust of ungoverned speech, but also with the lessons of history). Thus this final narrative of the sublime points this essay back to its initial task: to describe a rhetoric free of violence, an opening of the distance between selves that can span being without negation, privation, or strife, a rhetoric that shows finite difference to belong — before all else — to an infinite display of blessings at peace with one another, whose intervals are places of aesthetic mediation in which difference may be shared under the aspect of gift. This would ideally be a rhetoric, indeed, both predicative and nominative, invocational and evocative, adorational and lyrical, and endlessly rich in inventive transitions, inviting gestures, styles of grace: beauty.

Again, there may well be something arbitrary in these particular classifications of the narrative of the unrepresentable; and one might well wonder if, taken together, they describe anything like a unified vision or ethos. But the presuppositions they share are legion: that beauty belongs solely within the realm of representation, which is the realm of limit, possession, and stability, and as such dissembles and resists what is other than presence; that the "truth" of being, the good, or the giving of the world is what is other than presence, with an absolute qualitative (that is, dialectical) otherness; that the "sublime" is the intimation of this difference, and as such is both the opposite and the condition of the beautiful; and that the "infinite" (as the name for the truth *of* being or *beyond* being) has then no ontic syntax, no participating analogy, and no actual continuity with the world apart from the sublime instance that adumbrates it under the form of radical discontinuity. As beauty yields nothing of ultimate value, but is at most a soporific that deadens intellectual curiosity, heroic affirmation, tragic wisdom, or moral zeal, only the sublime, as an event without restraints, speaks of freedom, creativity, or ethics; the truth of the world is wholly other than the representable present, and so never assumes the harmonious proportions of worldly beauty, submits to the clarity of recognition, or finds its consummation in delight. Thus our second definition of "postmodernity" (the narrative of the sublime) folds back into our first (an "ontology of violence"): if the world takes shape against the veil of the unrepresentable, is indeed given or confirmed in its finitude by this impenetrable negation, then the discrimination of peace from violence is at most a necessary fiction, and occasionally a critical impossibility; as all equally *is,* and power alone sustains the game of the world, violence is already present in all "truth," though all truthlessness too — sadly or joyously — is violence. This story, again, makes all rhetoric an aggression, all beauty in some sense a lie (an opiate, tactical diversion, or necessary respite from the terror of truth), and every exodus an imperial campaign. The desire for an ethical issue from this story is no doubt quite genuine, but probably also quite absurd.

In a sense these four narratives of the sublime necessarily imply and sustain one another; they are facets of a single jewel; even where they appear most directly opposed (in the figures of Deleuze and Levinas), they complete one another. Being's dispensation (along with thought's possibility) is granted by an original difference, an absence that allows presence, an exteriority never belonging to an interior; the world of presence is then born from the temporal violence of absence, order from a more original chaos, peace from discord, and life from death; hence the event of being can be nothing other than the occurrence of the nothing, the oblivion of form that yields form to representation's paralyzing "recollection," and the temporalization or nihilation of being that gives the world its only "sense"; the visible world, therefore, is not the sphere of value, but only of evaluation, the event of finitude that cannot speak of the "excellence" of the good except through its own sacrifice, and the being of the world is not transcendental eminence but immanent dialectic: thus ethics is a principled blindness. Difference, chaos, the event . . . "evasion." This is the "fourfold" or "ring-dance" (to barbarize Heidegger's lovely image) that opens a postmodern world (though one of the dancers keeps his back turned to the "open"); and in the midst of its irreconcilable tensions, an ethos is shaped and sustained: pagan exuberance tempered by gnostic detachment. Even the seemingly outrageous juxtaposition of Deleuze and Levinas — absolute antinomian affirmation of the world and infinite ethical flight from it — proves perfectly logical: pagans and gnostics both assume the iron law of fate to operate here below and violence to be pandemic in the sensible order (the former simply choose to celebrate the terror and bounty of life, while the latter depart for the sheltering pavilions of a distant kingdom). Both these extremes must appear — tragic joy and tragic melancholy — and indeed fortify one another, once the rupture of beauty from the good has followed upon the withdrawal of being behind the veil of the sublime. This is part of the pathology of modernity. For most thinkers who accept the dimensions of such a world, the two extremes constitute a difficult choice or a mad oscillation; between the pagan and gnostic options the scales can dip either way, except in a few cases where the refined passivity and reflective quietude of an old mandarin like Derrida allow them to achieve a tremulous equiponderance. In every case, though, a faith in the transcendent unity of being and the good (along with the expectation that *philokalia,* the love of beauty, is the form desire takes when it rises toward that unity) is unimaginable.

Neither option is particularly admirable from a theological vantage, though either is understandable (the anguishes of modernity are quite antique, in fact); but of the two, it is the one represented by Levinas that is the more alien to theological tradition. Deleuze (like Nietzsche) at least knows how to say of the world, "It is good" — though in a way that to a theologian seems distorted beyond repair — and this is the first wisdom. Levinas, however, despairing of the world, inverts the meaning of all the "biblical" terms he employs absolutely: the God of glory is reduced to a provocative absence, creation to elemental flux, the liberty of love to the bondage of singular obligation. That this vision should be regarded as a sound depiction of the "ethical" is troubling; that it should be called Judaic is infamous. Biblical morality may be born from the Law, but the goodness of creation everywhere exhibits the majesty of the one who gives the Law; and ethics is never severed from the joy of fellowship, of feasts shared or anticipated (ultimately oriented analogically, in feasts and fasts, toward the peace of all creation), or of praise. To anyone whose sensibility is shaped by the Bible, Nietzsche's thought offers a more congenial atmosphere than Levinas's: the former, at least, never forsakes the love of being.

This is one reason for turning, belatedly perhaps, to Nietzsche himself, in whom theology encounters all the most truly daunting challenges to Christianity emanating from antiquity, modernity, or postmodernity expressed with a purity and force quite simply unmatched in any other thinker. He is also undoubtedly the figure who most conspicuously looms on the threshold of postmodernity. In greatest measure it is he who has determined what ethos must govern any philosophy that would convert disenchantment with (or enmity to) all discourses of transcendence into a vigorous and creative style of thinking, without illusion or regret. Being without transcendence or transcendent purpose: this ontology has had no more eloquent and consistent advocate than Nietzsche (nor one in whose rhetoric the confrontation with theology is more explicit). Not that Nietzsche's thought as such has been accepted uncritically by postmodern thinking; Deleuze and Foucault come closest to assuming a Nietzschean position without apparent embarrassment, but even they — in their sober moments — decline to take the rhetoric of the will to power as far as Nietzsche did; of the better part of postmodern thought it may be said that insofar as Nietzsche's metaphysical inclinations are recognized, they are often rejected, and insofar as the more disturbing ethical implications of Nietzsche's writings are acknowledged, they are not embraced. But this is why Nietzsche is often preferable to his epigones: he announced his ontology without deluding himself that it somewhere makes room for an ethics of political or moral "responsibility." He understood both options the epoch "after" Christianity offers: the "pagan" or the "gnostic," exuberance or withdrawal. The former he endued with the name of Dionysus, the latter (unfortunately) with the name of Christ, and he recognized the impossibility of a reconciliation between them: especially one framed in terms of the "ethical." Moreover, Nietzsche's thought is still quite close to theology, in unexpected ways. If nothing else, it was his ardent conviction that the pain of existence must never be thought just cause for a hatred of the world (a maxim at the heart, though Nietzsche denies it, of a Christian sensibility). More importantly, though, his method was evangelical; his ontology appears in his writings only as part of a thoroughgoing assault on Christianity, one conducted rhetorically, diegetically, in terms of aesthetic critique. He confronts theological reflection, therefore, with a polemical challenge, a war of narratives, and in doing so he liberates theology from apologetical dialectic, in which it has no ultimate stake, and calls it again to its proper idiom: a proclamation of the story of peace posed over against the narrative of violence, a hymnody rising up around the form of Christ offered over against the jubilant dithyrambs of Dionysus, the depiction of an eternal beauty advanced over against the depiction of a sempiternal sublime.

III. THE WILL TO POWER

Nietzsche, perhaps, still indicates a future; the scope of his influence on Western thought is, it seems, scarcely beginning to make itself manifest. For Heidegger, of course, Nietzsche was the liminal philosopher, the flash of lightning breaking out in idealism's long, chill twilight, the fatidic Janus who at once, gazing forward, announced the death of metaphysics and, staring back, gave metaphysics its final form. In the eyes of some, however, Heidegger — however well he grasped Nietzsche's epochal significance — still approached him with too ponderous, humorless, and Teutonic a spirit, and so failed to appreciate that Nietzsche's "metaphysics" is a thoroughly ironic and consciously fabricated fable, devised (like Plato's autochthonous myth) to accomplish an end, not discover an origin: Nietzsche should rather, they say, be taken as a liberator, not Janus but a true Dionysus, causing the citadels of metaphysics, faith, and reason to tremble at his passing, summoning free spirits to bacchanal, calling thought to festival and the task of affirmation before the aimless play of being. For Christianity, however, which has heard all of Dionysus's claims before, Nietzsche may well represent an even more momentous turning in the thought of the West, to wit: the appearance at long last of a philosophical adversary whose critique of Christianity appears to be as radical as the *kerygma* it denounces. Nietzsche grasped, even more completely than Celsus (the only other significant pagan critic of the faith), how audacious, impertinent, and absolute was Christianity's subversion of the values of antiquity: thus allowing theology to glimpse something of its own depths in the mirror of his contempt. In short, with Nietzsche the voice of unbelief at last swells to the registers of the voice of faith and so, curiously, does faith honor.

Of course, in its profound gratitude for Nietzsche's enmity, theology must not be so flattered as to forget to respond to his critique, and to do so "genealogically": to show, that is, that Nietzsche's narrative rests upon premises it dissembles, and that this narrative is accounted for and already surpassed within the Christian story. Nietzsche's critique cannot simply be dismissed, much less avoided, because it strikes too near the core of Christian faith and action; it is too cunning in its understanding of the language of Christian morality and hope, and too deft in its use of the quintessentially Christian practices of narration and evangelical exhortation. After all, the Nietzschean attack on the gospel is first and foremost a virtuoso *performance,* a rhetorical tour de force, moving from imaginative historical reconstructions to displays of brilliant psychological portraiture, from a kind of phenomenology of "the natural" to flights of apocalyptic hyperbole; and it calls for a comparable demonstration on theology's part of a capacity for comprehensive and creative renarrations. Unfortunately, the attempt by theologians to engage Nietzsche on his own terms has been rare (if occasionally notable), even though so much of the terrain of the postmodern lies under the ensigns of Nietzsche's Antichrist. Nor can anything so comprehensive as an adequate theological response to Nietzsche be undertaken here; and it obviously lies outside the scope of the present chapter to deal with all of Nietzsche's remarks concerning Christianity, which range from incidental bursts of invective to passages of sustained argument. Thus I shall confine myself to an account of Nietzsche's treatment of, in order, Christian morality and the person of Christ; and to a partial assessment of the force of his critique, its consistency, and its resistance to a reciprocal theological "deconstruction"; I shall address neither the factual accuracy of his interpretations of Christian history nor the limits of his grasp of the spectrum of Christian thought.[98] It is more to the point to recognize in Nietzsche's imaginative probings of the Christian tradition an attempt at narrative subversion; he understood that Christian truth depends first upon a story, and so to meet his critique of Christianity tellingly (so to put it), one must engage it on the field of rhetoric, persuasion, and aesthetic evaluation first, and not that of "historical science" or the discourses of "disinterested" reason.

This is obvious. What strikes one most forcibly in Nietzsche's attack on Christianity is his distaste for Christian life as an aesthetic phenomenon; it is his sensibility, more than his reason, that suffers offense. "Modern men, obtuse to all Christian nomenclature, no longer feel the gruesome superlative that struck a classical taste in the paradoxical formula 'god on the cross.' Never yet and nowhere has there been an equal boldness in inversion, anything as horrible, questioning, and questionable as this formula: it promised a revaluation of all the values of antiquity."[99] Few are the transgressions of good taste and spiritual hygiene that cannot, in his eyes, be laid to Christianity's charge: as the one great curse pronounced on life, its ethos is no more than a perfidious inversion of noble values, an occult strategy of vengeful resentment, and an exaltation of weakness and deformity at the expense of strength and beauty; as the most acute and perverse kind of decadence, its enfeebling creed drains life from this world by directing life's energies toward another, unreal world;[100] as absolute enmity toward life, it is the poor man's Platonism: vulgar idealism, expressed most perfectly as hatred for the life of the flesh. It was in the Christian tradition uniquely, he claims, that

---

98. There can be little doubt that Nietzsche reads Christianity all too often from the perspective of his time and place; even his treatment of Scripture and sources from late antiquity is colored by the still emerging discourse of German liberal Protestantism. One might cite, as examples of the rather exiguous range of his understanding of Christian tradition, his apparent ignorance of any soteriological scheme apart from the satisfaction theory of atonement (a theory he implicitly attributes to ages of Christian culture to whom it would have seemed quite odd), or his obliviousness to the truth that the post-Kantian, Protestant, and very German emphasis on moral interiority is scarcely typical of Christianity's history in general. These hardly constitute significant objections to Nietzsche's project, however, because he was not really particularly interested in attempting an objective historical account of Christianity, or of anything else.

99. Friedrich Nietzsche, *Beyond Good and Evil*, trans. Walter Kaufmann (New York: Vintage Books, 1966), 60, hereafter *BGE*.

100. See, e.g., Friedrich Nietzsche, *The Anti-Christ*, trans. R. J. Hollingdale (New York: Penguin Books, 1968), 155-56, 186, hereafter *AC*; Nietzsche, *Ecce Homo*, trans. Walter Kaufmann and R. J. Hollingdale (New York: Vintage Books, 1969), 334, hereafter *EH*; Nietzsche, *Thus Spoke Zarathustra*, in *The Portable Nietzsche*, ed. and trans. Walter Kaufmann (New York: Viking Penguin, 1954), 140-42, hereafter *Z*.

antinature itself received the highest honors as morality and was fixed over humanity as law and categorical imperative. — To blunder to such an extent, not as individuals, not as a people, but as humanity! — That one taught men to despise the very first instincts of life; that one mendaciously invented a "soul," a "spirit" to ruin the body; that one taught men to experience the presupposition of life, sexuality, as something unclean; that one looks for the evil principle in what is most profoundly necessary for growth, in *severe* self-love (this very word constitutes a slander); that, conversely, one regards the typical signs of decline and contradiction of the instincts, the "selfless," the loss of a center of gravity, "depersonalization" and "neighbor love" (*addiction* to the neighbor) as the higher value — what am I saying? — the *absolute* value! (*EH*, 272)

Christian benevolence is merely part of the pathology of decadence, "irreconcilable with an ascending, Yes-saying life" (*EH*, 328); and the Christian vision of the "other" world is merely a squalid defamation of the world that is, an idealization that derogates the actual, a soothing promise of immortality that thwarts life's proper instincts (*AC*, 118, 155-56).[101] With gaze fixed on this fabulous eternity, eyes averted from the spectacle of the world, how can the Christian fail to find life impure? For Nietzsche, no doctrine could more exquisitely encapsulate the inmost essence of Christian faith than the immaculate conception — whereby the church "has . . . maculated conception" (*AC*, 147). In short, whereas everything beautiful and noble is accomplished through the refinement (the spiritualization) of the passions (of desire, even of cruelty), the church, on account of its inability to transfigure the animal passions through salubrious disciplines, must prescribe instead their extirpation; unable to transform life into ever higher expressions, Christianity is the gospel of castration.[102]

Nietzsche's gift for denunciations of this sort is all but inexhaustible, and in the course of their elaboration, as a kind of concrescence of their inner logic, a contrary form takes shape, a god appropriate to Nietzsche's own special piety; against the figure of the crucified God he poses that of Dionysus, god of indestructible life, ecstasy, joy, and power. The polarity is expressed with particular force and lucidity in one of the notes collected in *The Will to Power*:

101. See Karl Jaspers, *Nietzsche: An Introduction to the Understanding of His Philosophical Activity*, trans. Charles F. Wallraff and Frederick J. Schmitz (Tucson: University of Arizona Press, 1965), 320.

102. Friedrich Nietzsche, *Twilight of the Idols*, trans. R. J. Hollingdale (New York: Penguin Books, 1968), 42, hereafter *TI*. See Arthur C. Danto, *Nietzsche as Philosopher* (New York: Columbia University Press, 1963), 148, and Jacques Derrida, *Spurs: Nietzsche's Styles/Éperons: Les Styles de Nietzsche*, English facing text translated by Barbara Harlow (Chicago: University of Chicago Press, 1983), 90-95.

Dionysus versus the "Crucified": there you have the antithesis. It is *not* a difference in regard to their martyrdom — it is a difference in the meaning of it. Life itself, its eternal fruitfulness and recurrence, creates torment, destruction, the will to annihilation. In the other case, suffering — the "Crucified as the innocent one" — counts as an objection to this life, as a formula for its condemnation. — One will see that the problem is that of the meaning of suffering: whether a Christian meaning or a tragic meaning. In the former case, it is supposed to be the path of a holy existence; in the latter case, being is counted as *holy enough* to justify even a monstrous amount of suffering. The tragic man affirms even the harshest suffering: he is sufficiently strong, rich, and capable of deifying to do so. The Christian denies even the happiest lot on earth: he is sufficiently weak, poor, disinherited to suffer from life in whatever form he meets it. The god on the cross is a curse on life, a signpost to seek redemption from life; Dionysus cut to pieces is a *promise* of life: it will be eternally reborn and return again from destruction.[103]

As Deleuze describes the opposition, Christ's suffering indicts life as unjust, as guilty and deserving of the suffering it endures, as in need of salvation, and as a dark workshop where life itself can be loved only when it is tender, weak, in torment, mutilated; but the suffering of Dionysus *is* the justice of being. Whereas the cross symbolizes contradiction and its solution, Dionysian affirmation lies beyond either contradiction or reconciliation.[104]

Of course, all his vituperative venom would seem merely coarse and childish (and frankly, much of it does anyway) were it not for the extraordinary story Nietzsche tells regarding the way Christian morality overturned the antique order. I shall not recite in detail the account Nietzsche gives in *On the Genealogy of Morals* of Christianity's "slave revolt" in values; it is sufficient to recall his claim that Christian morals are nothing but those values that are inevitable for slaves, the weak, and the ill constituted, somehow grotesquely elevated to the status of universal law[105] and then — through a cunning supplantation of the "aesthetic" values of the nobles by the "moral" values of the herd — imposed upon the strong and healthy.[106] In this slave morality, with its inordinate emphasis on pity, relief from suffering, consolation, and comfort,

---

103. Friedrich Nietzsche, *The Will to Power*, trans. Walter Kaufmann and R. J. Hollingdale (New York: Columbia University Press, 1983), 542-43, hereafter *WP*.

104. Deleuze, *Nietzsche and Philosophy*, 15-16.

105. Friedrich Nietzsche, *On the Genealogy of Morals*, trans. Walter Kaufmann (New York: Vintage Books, 1969), 33-34, hereafter *GM*.

106. See Alexander Nehamas, *Nietzsche: Life as Literature* (Cambridge: Harvard University Press, 1985), 113.

one finds all the symptoms of nihilism and decline consecrated with the holiest names (*AC*, 117-18). And yet, despite having been incubated within the most debile constitutions, Christian values did indeed triumph over the noble values of antiquity, on account of the force, subtlety, and inexhaustible energy of ressentiment, the spite that animates the impotent and incites the mob against its masters. To those whose diseased natures are in the thrall of resentment — who are "neither upright nor naïve nor honest and straightforward," who love dark corners and who are silent, forgetful, humble, self-deprecating, and clever (*GM*, 38-39) — that attainment of which they are most incapable (that is, noble "goodness") must be in fact "evil"; indeed, the Christian image of the Evil One is nothing but a distillation of the instincts of the higher type of man (*AC*, 117). Christian love is really only the flower that adorns the nettles of a very particular Jewish species of hatred, a sublime vengefulness directed against the healthy, strong, and vigorous (*GM*, 35); Judeo-Christian morality is the ingenious creation of an indefatigably aggressive impotence,[107] which transforms itself into an irresistible power: like the power of vermin, indestructible by its atomistic multiplicity, collectivity, smallness, and voracity. Amid Nietzsche's rhapsodic celebrations of his wild, rapacious, thoughtless, generous nobles, one might well lose sight of how brilliantly the *Genealogy* describes the logic, the fearful inventiveness, of the resentful heart; it is here that Nietzsche, with keen precision, strikes one of his surer blows against the church's understanding of itself: he knows well, and savagely exploits, a certain predisposition in Christian thought — perhaps, Nietzsche might argue, a mechanism for preserving itself against critique — to suspect its own motives, to anticipate the discovery of hypocrisy, egoism, and sin in even its seemingly purest motives. For Nietzsche, however, much more is at stake: hypocrisy, impurity of motives — complaints of this nature would serve little purpose of themselves; it is the very content of Christian morality, its intrinsic enmity toward life, that he detests.

> What is good? — All that heightens the feeling of power, the will to power, power itself in man.
> What is bad? — All that proceeds from weakness. (*AC*, 115)

Nurture of the weak, the essence of Christian morality — indeed, preservation of the weak in their weakness — functions only to obviate the process whereby life evaluates, selects, and elects itself (*AC*, 118).

> The weak and ill-constituted shall perish: first principal of *our* philanthropy. And one shall help them to do so.

107. See R. J. Hollingdale, *Nietzsche* (London and Boston: Routledge and Kegan Paul, 1973), 188.

> What is more harmful than any vice? — Active sympathy for the ill-constituted and weak — Christianity. . . . (*AC*, 116)

There can be no more damning accusation, in Nietzsche's eyes, than that Christian values stand in contradiction to natural existence; there should be nature in morality, he protests; one's values should have life's own shape (*TI*, 48). But where nature is weak, there is the church strong, thriving where life is in retreat, amidst illness and decrepitude; Catholicism's ideal is the world as one vast lunatics' asylum (*AC*, 167). It is chiefly the *cruelty* of the Christian creed that Nietzsche decries, its ruthlessness in teaching humanity to despise joy and vital sensuality (*AC*, 131), in further advancing a certain Jewish falsification of nature (*AC*, 134), and above all in seeking to poison and crush the strong.[108] Christianity, simply said, is false to the world (*AC*, 125).

But what exactly, one must pause to ask, is the world, and what precisely is nature? The current emphasis in the academy on Nietzsche's "antiessentialism" and irony often fails to do justice to his equally pronounced inclination toward miraculously broad, but earnest, pronouncements:

> Here we must beware of superficiality and get to the bottom of the matter, resisting all sentimental weakness: life itself is *essentially* appropriation, injury, overpowering of what is alien and weaker; suppression, hardness, imposition of one's own forms, incorporation and at least, at its mildest, exploitation. . . .
>
> . . . life simply *is* will to power. (*BGE*, 203)[109]

The lessons of nature are "agonistic," they enjoin contest and struggle, presuppose injustice, and have no end but ascent, growth, expansion, and ever greater acquisition.[110] Values, though, that require the suppression of this "nature" rather than its spiritualization and the recognition of its necessity in the economy of culture (albeit in refined form), are the unique achievements of the most depraved world-haters: of, that is, priests.[111] Whether or not it is the case (as Karl Jaspers claims it is) that in opposing unconditional nature to unconditional morality, Nietzsche *knowingly* violates his own injunctions against abso-

---

108. See Karl Jaspers, *Nietzsche and Christianity* (Chicago: Henry Regnery, 1967), 37-38.

109. See also *BGE*, 17 (where it is asserted again that life is will to power), 30 (where the necessity is announced that the interpreter of the world be disposed to interpret it not as law, but as a lawless will to power), and 48 (where it is claimed that the world, viewed from the inside and according to its "intelligible character," appears as will to power and nothing else).

110. Friedrich Nietzsche, *The Gay Science*, trans. Walter Kaufmann (New York: Vintage Books, 1974), 292, hereafter *GS*. See Hollingdale, 78-79.

111. Friedrich Nietzsche, *Human, All Too Human*, trans. R. J. Hollingdale (Cambridge: Cambridge University Press, 1986), 117, hereafter *HH*; *BGE*, 158-59; *GM*, 33.

lutes,[112] it is quite beyond dispute that, for him, consonance with nature is the standard against which any morality must be measured. And Christianity, in his eyes, slyly exploited (and became deeply complicit in) the greatest inversion of nature ever visited upon the human animal: the fabrication of the soul.

The very idea of an abiding agent, a stable presence lurking behind the play of action and appearance, can be an invention only of the cunning of the weak, a metonymic knot tied in the warp of language to provide nature's disinherited offspring with terms whereby to reproach the strong nobles who prey upon them. "To demand of strength that it should *not* express itself as strength, that it should *not* be a desire to overcome, a desire to throw down, a desire to become master, a thirst for enemies and resistance and triumphs, is just as absurd as to demand of weakness that it should express itself as strength" (*GM*, 45). As Deleuze phrases the matter, every force — and force is the prior truth of things — goes, if unimpeded, to the limit of its power or desire; nor is force something distinct from its power, which can remain intact when withdrawn from its manifestation, but is like light and the shining of light: one thing.[113] Reactive forces, however, seek to make the active forces themselves reactive by separating the active from what it can do: the triumph of the reactive is always brought about by subtraction or division.[114] True force is desire, creativity, will to power, and so — as Callicles attempted in vain to explain to Socrates[115] — even when the weak and reactive band themselves together to oppose the strong, they do not form a greater power, but still, in order to work their will, must introduce an interruption — an interval of factitious interiority — between active force and what it is capable of accomplishing, because, says Deleuze, "from the point of view of nature concrete force is that which goes to its ultimate consequences, to the limit of power and desire";[116] this force must be displaced by a moral interval, a "subjectivity" that separates it from itself, if it is to be overcome; but "[i]n each case the separation rests on a fiction, on a mystification or a falsification."[117] To Nietzsche it seems clear that the notion of some fixed and punctiliar subjectivity dwelling below the level of will, drive, and affect is mere fantasy, an illusion created by the enticements of grammar: even as it would be an error to imagine the existence of some independent substance called "lightning" apart from the lightning flash. The "natural man" is not undergirded by some invariable substratum of "self," nor is there some naturally present moral interval wherein such a man could reflectively choose to

112. Jaspers, *Nietzsche*, 146.
113. Deleuze, *Nietzsche and Philosophy*, 53, 123.
114. Deleuze, *Nietzsche and Philosophy*, 56-57.
115. In *Gorgias* 481-527.
116. Deleuze, *Nietzsche and Philosophy*, 59.
117. Deleuze, *Nietzsche and Philosophy*, 57.

withdraw from his act, or recoil from his own force; the bird of prey is not free to be a lamb, nor is it accountable — guilty — for being what it is. But Christian faith feeds upon, above all, the phenomenon of "bad conscience," the strange and unnatural internalization of the strong man's most aggressive instincts: the violence that was forced to turn inward upon the self in the very degree to which constraints were placed upon it by the emergence of civilization. As Nietzsche tells the tale, the strong, semibestial men of war whose savageries made the building of civil societies possible were — once immured within political and social order and made subject to the laws and penalties of the state — little better than caged animals yearning for the wild, longing to set free their repressed vitalities. Driven into a suppressed but habitual frenzy, they transformed themselves into adventures and torture chambers, constructing ever greater heights and depths for their inner worlds; and this hypertrophied interiority (which is also the predisposition to "guilt") proved of inestimable value to the church. For Christianity then ingeniously multiplied the sense of guilty indebtedness civilized peoples feel before their ancestor gods to an infinite sum, by devising the monstrous notions of an eternal penance due for sin and a debt before the divine of such magnitude as only God himself, the creditor, could discharge (a payment, made out of "love," that actually binds humanity to God by an equally infinite debt of gratitude) (*GM*, 45-92). Writes Nietzsche, with elegant exactitude, "the priest *rules* through the invention of sin" (*AC*, 166).

The priest *rules*. For all its claims to have abjured violence, the church was from the first, even before it enjoyed political power, a structure of coercion, of in fact the greatest of imaginable tyrannies. Not that the exercise of tyranny, as such, is any indictment in itself. Nietzsche's later writings, after all, espouse a vision of the world as nothing other than the will to power, a cosmic "pathos" constituted from innumerable quanta of force existing in "relations of tension" (*WP*, 338-39),[118] "a monster of energy, without beginning, without end . . . a play of forces," boundlessly fecund, abundant, contradictory, and recurrent, serving no end but its own Dionysian creativity and destructiveness (*WP*, 549-50), of which every efficient force in the world — natural, "moral," or other — is one or another aspect (*BGE*, 47-48). What Nietzsche despises in the particularly Christian expression of this will, however, is its sheer reactivity, its want of creativity, its empty grasping for control, and its pusillanimous longing to still the turbulences of life. Christianity may allow the invalids created by its palliating spirituality certain mild but consoling expressions of power — acts of benevolence, gestures of condescension (*GM*, 135) — but it simultaneously depresses any impulse toward higher forms of life. And while Nietzsche insists

---

118. See also Danto, 218-19.

that the sublimation of the will to power — through sacrifice, discipline, internalization of law — is a necessary moment in power's creative expansion, he sees nothing in Christian asceticism, morality, or priestcraft but a depraved mockery of this sublimation, a dissimulation, a refusal to acknowledge the church's true motives, and an expression of craven ressentiment directed against those possessed of "free spirits."[119] Even if, indeed, all effects are shapes assumed by the incalculably various will to power, even if what one calls will, thought, and act are only artificially isolated moments within a far greater process, one must still recognize Christian faith as the will to power at its most vulgar and debased: power representing itself as the refusal of power, as the negation of strife, as the evangel of perfect peace — only in order to make itself stronger, more terrifying, more invincible.

All very bracing rhetoric. But when one steps back from the flow of Nietzsche's polemic, one becomes uncomfortably aware of a certain stress at the heart of this critique, a fissure of contradiction constantly displacing the center of the Nietzschean narrative to one or the other side (bridged, perhaps, by a furtive irony, which refuses to take too seriously the claims it impregnates); at one and the same time the edifice of "truth" is in the process of being dismantled and erected. One can scarcely deny, to begin with, the appearance of a seemingly unreflective naturalism in Nietzsche's thought, prompting him to employ such words as "life," "instinct," and "nature" with a casual assurance that belies his own acute awareness of the cultural contingency of all "truths"; and one might justly wonder whether the life he celebrates is anything more diverting than the upward thrusting of an empty will, blind and idiotic, to which he has arbitrarily ascribed (in an ebullition of romantic enthusiasm) such qualities as richness, vitality, and creativity. One is often sorely pressed to hear the ironic tone that will indicate to the attentive ear that discreet juncture where an apparently absolutist metaphysics reveals itself as an intentional and exotic feat of fabulation. If Nietzsche's vision of nature — of being — is simply that of the pagan (Heracleitean, Epicurean, etc.) ἀγών κοσμικός, if the "life" of which he speaks is *essentially* appropriation, injury, and overpowering, then of course ontic difference appears in the Nietzschean narrative as opposition and contradiction; indeed, difference is appreciably different precisely in the degree to which each force resists, succumbs to, or vanquishes another force: an ontology of violence in its most elementary form. Not that this is in any sense a startling observation, nor does it somehow tell against Nietzsche's position; it merely renders dubious the antimetaphysical rigor of his arguments. Can any degree of ironic distance make the Nietzschean critique any less "metaphysical" than

119. Friedrich Nietzsche, *Daybreak*, trans. R. J. Hollingdale (Cambridge: Cambridge University Press, 1982), 217-18, hereafter *D*; see also *GS*, 86-88, and Jaspers, *Nietzsche*, 311.

what it attacks? Or, rather, can that critique sustain itself with any force or durability unless it stakes itself upon the "truth" of the narrative it invokes? And is then the nostalgia of Janus, at the last, unconquerable? This is a question probably of more interest in retrospect, from the perspective of Nietzsche's postmodern disciples (those who hope to reject not only metanarratives but narrativity as such, with its "closure" and hierarchy of meaning), than it could ever have been for the man himself. But it is also a question that cannot simply be ignored as a humorless concern with "literal" readings, because even if one grant that Nietzsche is entirely conscious of his doubleness of tone, this in no way alters the truth that in posing an ontology of violence against the Christian narrative, the advantage that Nietzsche seems to have gained turns out to be, ultimately, only as compelling as any other aesthetic preference. There would be no objection to this, of course, if it were not for Nietzsche's habit of treating his preference as a more honest, less resentful, less arbitrary, and more truthful account of reality; Nietzsche's post-Christian counternarrative (which is itself perhaps occasionally tainted by resentment rather than honesty) cannot be denied its power and its appeal, but it should be recognized not simply as critique but as always already another *kerygma*. Between Nietzsche's vision of life as an agon and the Christian vision of life as creation — as a primordial "gift" and "grace" — there is nothing (not even the palpable evidences of "nature red in tooth and claw") that makes either perspective self-evidently more correct than the other. Each sees and accounts for the violence of experience and the beauty of being, but each according to an irreducible mythos and a particular aesthetics. A battle of tastes is being waged by Nietzsche, and the metaphysical appears therein as a necessary element of his narrative's completeness; the difference that is immediately noticeable, however, between the Christian and Nietzschean narrative dynamisms is not that the former is indiscerptibly bound to the metaphysics of identity and presence, but that the latter is simply more disingenuous regarding the metaphysics it advances.

Of course, Nietzsche would hardly be inconvenienced by such a complaint; truth is always a metaphorical pleating within the fabric of language, he might airily reply, a transposition of meaning from one context to another in an endless series of interdependent tropes, an appearance of proximity to "being" achieved by an ever more devious play of semantic remotion;[120] and his strategy, in all good conscience, is one of suasive exhortation: he means only to urge, at times with magnificent indifference to fine distinctions, the forcefulness of his own metaphors. It matters little, for instance, that the rhetorical flourish of his facile equation of Christianity with Platonism is burdened by no

---

120. See Friedrich Nietzsche, "From: 'On Truth and Lie in an Extra-moral Sense,'" in *The Portable Nietzsche,* ed. and trans. Walter Kaufmann (New York: Viking Press, 1954), esp. 46-47.

small measure of philosophical imprecision, so long as his story has the power to persuade. Nonetheless, it is well to note that Christian thought can exculpate itself of this charge with comparable rhetorical aplomb; if nothing else, the metaphysical implication within the aesthetic denunciation is, in this case, difficult to sustain, if for no other reason than the demonstrable (and historically significant) truth that, while Christian thought early on often adopted a "Platonic" language for its theology, it also found itself moved radically to change that language. It is even arguable that Neoplatonism, in the early centuries of the church, had already altered the Platonic ontology in a slightly "Christian" direction[121] by substituting for the merely specular relationship between the apparent world of chaotic materiality and the ideal world it imperfectly imitates a relationship of emanation, such that all being "belongs" to the multiplicity of nous in its contemplation of the One (as Plotinus would say); for Plotinus, after all, "the infinite" (τὸ ἄπειρον) had already ceased to be a term of philosophical opprobrium, a synonym for the indeterminate and formless, and become a term for the positive plenitude of the goodness of the One. In any event, one approaches Plato's realm of the forms through abstraction from the world of particularity and difference, but something had fundamentally changed by the time Christian theologians began to identify their absolute with the infinite, to equate goodness, truth, and beauty with the whole of being itself, and to introduce into their understanding of the Godhead the language of relation, responsiveness, and creativity. Whether or not the "Platonism" patristic theology found congenial to its aims had already begun to unburden itself of the Platonic χωρισμός and to exorcise from itself the specter of a "bad infinity," Christian thought, insofar as it appropriated a Neoplatonic morphology of being, transformed it in accord with its own narrative; what remained then was a formidable collection of concepts and terms, now integrated into a more generous scheme of signification and rendered analogous by another, radically more transcendent analogate. When Christian thought defined the Trinity as a coequal circumincession as opposed to a hierarchy of diminishing divinity, the Neoplatonic story of substantial emanation — and with it, the last trace of an *ontological* space of the simulacral — became meaningless; if the beauty of material existence is not merely the overflow of a self-enclosed, strictly unitary, and entirely spiritual beauty into the confining channels of material deformity, but is the unnecessary, untrammeled, and contingent expression of a divine delight that is always already "differential," created difference is loosed, as univocally good in its creatureliness, though it is analogically imparted; and when Christian thought replaced the identist and substantial analogy Platonism presumed between the world and "God" with a genuinely ontological anal-

---

121. So Milbank (295) thinks.

ogy between creatures who own no substantial claim on being at all and a God who is the utterly transcendent and absolutely immediate actuality of any being's existence, every form of metaphysical reasoning had to be recast. Even the Neoplatonic thought of the infinite as an excess of perfection in a state of divine and monadic simplicity came to be radically surpassed by a Christian account of the infinite (which Gregory of Nyssa first gave coherent shape).[122] To regard creation as the gift of *yet another difference* is not to treat this world as merely a distinct and inferior reality from which one is obliged to flee in order to attain to the absolute, but is rather to see finitude as embraced by and containing the grace of the infinite; for classical Christianity it would perhaps be less proper to speak of "another world" than to say, quite simply, that the world is infinitely greater than one might expect, in one's less reflective moments.[123] Were this not so, Christian tradition would not have been able to sustain the biblical affirmation of creation's goodness, to speak of creation's participation in the good (Frederick Copleston is quite justified in objecting to Nietzsche's habit of describing Christianity in terms proper to Manichaeism),[124] or even to have described creation — including human art and virtue — as belonging to the *gloria Dei*. Christian "truth" is more spacious — it must be — than the "truth" of Platonism; the Christian Logos must be conceived of as containing all of creation and history within itself — without despoiling creation of its differences and reducing ontological contingency to a condition of impoverishment and distortion — and so is, as Karl Jaspers perceptively phrases it, "open to the *alogon*";[125] which is to say, on the one hand, that the world is comprised by God's being and so can be known only in particular perspectives,[126] and on the other, that absolute truth is God himself, who is transcendent of the world and in whom being and the infinite are one, and so cannot be grasped at all save in the series of perspectives that, in themselves, are still apophatically denied to possess any ultimate purchase on the divine. As created being is the analogical

122. See Ekkehard Mühlenberg, *Die Unendlichkeit Gottes bei Gregor von Nyssa: Gregors Kritik am Gottesbegriff der Klassischen Metaphysik* (Göttingen: Vandenhoeck & Ruprecht, 1966); see also below, part 2, I.3.

123. Does "another world" that is truly other enter Christian thought except in the theology of someone like Bultmann, for whom the demolition of the architecture of the antique cosmos, in which the heavenly and earthly were seamlessly joined, leads to the discovery of a truly separate realm of spiritual (or existential) interiority, where faith is enacted not among the concrete contingencies of time but within a secret inner core of time, an inner sanctuary of disembodied illumination? Prior to this turn in modern Protestantism, is not such thought a phenomenon only of gnosticism?

124. Frederick Copleston, *Friedrich Nietzsche, Philosopher of Culture* (London: Search Press, 1975), 137-38.

125. Jaspers, *Nietzsche and Christianity,* 71.

126. Jaspers, *Nietzsche and Christianity,* 72.

expression of the infinite Trinity, it "corresponds" to its source not through an inanition of the simulacral and particular, in order to converge upon the ideal, but by way of its own motion of differential excess, as the expressive rhetoric of an infinitely responsive and differentiating God. Thus it is scarcely clear whether the Christian tradition or the Nietzschean critique is demonstrably more "idealist."

But, again, all this serves to overburden Nietzsche's diatribe with critical scruples; in speaking of Christianity as popular Platonism, Nietzsche is not making a metaphysical or hermeneutical claim; he is simply expressing his repugnance for an ethos that denigrates the senses, strives against the instincts of the flesh, and defers ultimate value to the realm of spiritual "reality" alone: the ethos of "castratism," the cult of death. Nietzsche's Dionysus, by contrast, supposedly unites in himself the strongest impulses of spirituality and sensuality;[127] an emblem of the most pious godlessness, he represents enmity against every faith that distracts life from itself, in all its wasteful, extravagant, contradictory magnificence. (And here, lamentably, Nietzsche's callow apostrophes to "Life" sound notes that will echo down the plangent corridors of a whole century's literature of puerile paganism, from A. C. Swinburne and Havelock Ellis to Gore Vidal.) Still, even within these limits, it is not altogether certain how far Nietzsche's rhetoric can credibly be taken, for however just his condemnation of pious otherworldliness may be — and the church has seen no end of it — it is the unambiguous renunciation of gnosticism, and not the paradoxical renunciation of classical Christianity, that would correspond most nearly to his account. Indeed, no one familiar with late antiquity and the world in which the gospel was first preached can be unaware that a prevailing spirit of otherworldliness had long been moving inexorably through the empire: not only gnosticism, but every variety of etherealizing devotion, mystery religions, Eastern esoterica, mystical Platonisms, and the occult; the contempt for the flesh expressed by Valentinus, Ammonias Saccas, Plotinus, the Mithraic mysteries, or even the sanctimoniously ungroomed Emperor Julian was more bitterly world-weary than any of the exorbitant expressions of spirituality to which the church fell prey. One may agree with Nietzsche that this atmosphere of acosmic and incorporeal religiosity defames the world, and one may acknowledge that it infected every institution and spiritual aspiration of its age, including those of the church; but one should also recognize it as first and foremost a *pagan* phenomenon: a growing awareness, within an increasingly pluralistic and cosmopolitan empire, that the pagan cosmos was a region of strife, in response to which one could adopt only the grammars of empire or spiritual retreat, and an increasingly fashionable tendency to elect the latter. Christianity

127. See Jaspers, *Nietzsche*, 347, 434.

suffered from the contagion in some considerable measure, but was also able to resist it as paganism could not, because it had at its disposal means for renarrating the cosmos from the ground up. But Nietzsche may serve as a reminder that the church did not always entirely free itself from the lingering residue of paganism: its otherworldliness, its inability to see the beauty of creation without succumbing to the pain of being, its terror before a world of violence; the joyous, sacrificial communality and heroic agape of the desert fathers could not entirely resist the invasion of an occasionally exsanguinating spirituality; the model of Simon Stylites and his kind was too eagerly admired by a populace that tended to understand his spiritual achievement in terms of a spectacle, as a feat of impossible endurance and abnegation of the self. But it was also into this crepuscular world of transcendental longings, of a pagan order grown weary of the burden of itself, that the Christian faith came as an evangel promising newness of life, and that in all abundance, preaching creation, divine incarnation, resurrection of the flesh, and the ultimate restoration of heavens and earth: a faith, moreover, whose symbols were not occult sigils, or bull's blood, or the brackish water and coarse fare of the ascetic sage, but the cardinal signs of fellowship, feasting, and joy: bread and wine. There was in such a faith an undeniable assault upon pagan values: a certain very Jewish subversion, a rejoicing in the order of creation as gift and blessing, an inability to grow too weary of the flesh, an abiding sense of the sheer weightiness — *kabod* — of God's glory and the goodness of all that is; but it is a subversion that Nietzsche does not grasp from the perspective of his rather adolescent adoration of pagan harshness, and so his story grows shrill and unbalanced. If Christian culture were simply spiritualist, if it endorsed an ethos like that of the *Corpus Hermeticum* or the libretto of *Parsifal,* Nietzsche's indictments of Christian "castratism" would command great force; but for all the cunning and psychological inventiveness of his genealogy, it fails at every juncture to accommodate the complexity of what he wishes to describe. The orthodox doctrine of creation out of nothingness, and its attendant doctrine of the goodness of creation, led the church (more radically even than Neoplatonism) to deny to evil any ascription of true being, to define it not as an essence or positive force but as mere negation, *reaction,* a privation of the good (στέρησις ἀγαθοῦ), a perversity of the will, an appetite for nonbeing — but no objective thing among things: all things had to be affirmed, and with equal emphasis, as God's good creation.

And surely there is something almost tediously wrong in asserting that Christ's crucifixion has ever figured in Christian tradition as a repudiation, rather than ultimately an affirmation, of the fleshly life Christ was forced to relinquish. "Verily I say unto you, I will drink no more of the fruit of the vine, until that day that I drink it new in the kingdom of God" (Mark 14:25; cf. Matt. 26:29; Luke 22:18) — wine clearly appears here as the perfect and concrete emblem of the beauty of creation and the joy of dwelling at peace in the midst of others: not the wine of Dionysus, which makes fellowship impossible, promising only intoxication, brute absorption into the *turba*, anonymity, and violence, but the wine of the wedding feast at Cana, or of the wedding feast of the Lamb. In fact, if I may be permitted an excursus, it is conceivable that a theological answer to Nietzsche could be developed entirely in terms of the typology of wine. After all, the wine of Dionysus is no doubt of the coarsest vintage, intended to blind with drunkenness rather than enliven whimsy; it is fruit of the same vine with which Dionysus bridged the Euphrates, after flaying alive the king of Damascus, so that he could conquer India for viniculture (so we know from Plutarch, Pausanias, Strabo, Arrian, Diodorus Siculus, and others); and of the same vine for which Lycurgus mistook his son Dryas when driven mad for offending the wild god, causing him to cut Dryas down for "pruning" (as Homer and Apollodorus report); the vine that destroyed the pirates who would not bear Dionysus to Naxos (so say Homer, Apollodorus, and Ovid); it is the wine that inflamed the maenads to rend Pentheus limb from limb, led by his own mother Agave (as Euripides and others record); the wine repeatedly associated with madness, anthropophagy, slaughter, warfare, and rapine (one need consider only the Dionysian cult at Orchomenus — with its ritual act of random murder — and the story of the daughters of Minyas — frenzy, infanticide, cannibalism — from which it sprang). The wine of Christian Scripture, on the other hand, is first and foremost a divine blessing and image of God's bounty (Gen. 27:28; Deut. 7:13; 11:14; Ps. 104:15; Prov. 3:10; Isa. 25:6; 65:8; Jer. 31:12; Joel 2:19-24; 3:18; Amos 9:13-14; Zech. 9:17), and an appropriate thank offering by which to declare Israel's love of God (Exod. 29:40; Lev. 23:13; Num. 15:5-10; 18:12; 28:14; Deut. 14:23; 15:14; 18:4); it is the wine that "cheers the hearts of gods and men" (Judg. 9:13), to be drunk and shared with those for whom nothing is prepared on the day holy to the Lord (Neh. 8:10), the sign of God's renewed covenant with his people (Isa. 55:1-3), the drink of lovers (Song of Sol. 5:1) and the very symbol of love (7:2, 9; 8:2), whose absence is the eventide of all joy (Isa. 24:11); it is, moreover, the wine of agape and the feast of fellowship, in which Christ first vouchsafed a sign of his divinity, in a place of rejoicing, at Cana — a wine of the highest quality — when the kingdom showed itself "out of season" (John 2:3-10); the wine, again, forsaken with all the good things of creation, when Christ went to his death, but promised to be drunk anew at the banquet table of his Father's kingdom, and from which — embittered with myrrh — he was forced to turn his lips when on the cross (Mark 15:23; Matt. 27:34); the wine, finally, whose joy is imparted to the church again, and eternally, with the fire of Pentecost (Acts 2:13), and in which the fellowship of Christ and his flock is reborn with every celebration of the Eucharist. Of course, Nietzsche was a teetotaler and could judge the merit of neither vintage, and so it is perhaps unsurprising that his attempts at oino-theology should betray a somewhat pedestrian palate.

At the very least, though, one might ask of Nietzsche some recognition that the doctrine of resurrection could never be reducible to a simple doctrine of the immortality of the soul, of a spiritual essence yearning for liberation from the prison house of the flesh, but must be an assertion of the belief that from the divine side the world of God's making will be shown to be worthy of his eternal affirmation. Or a recognition that the eschatological vision described by Paul in the eighth chapter of Romans describes the ultimate revelation of God not as a destruction of this world in favor of heaven, but as the world's transfiguration and glorification. And given the most venerable strain of Christian soteriology, which understands Christ's cross and resurrection as the conquest of death and the return of his invincible life, it is questionable how far the terms of Nietzsche's opposition between the mythologies of Christ and Dionysus can credibly be taken; and questionable whether the Deleuzean embroidery upon this typology does not prove a bit threadbare and vulgar: Does the suffering of Christ confirm being's guilt while the suffering of Dionysus proclaims its innocence, or may one exercise some subtlety here and see in the cross and resurrection of Christ the story of life's unjust suffering (that is, the injustice of a violence that crucifies), and of a justice that cries out for the salvation of what lies in bondage, and reveals itself as a deathless love of creation's fullness? This crude dualism, between a suffering that condemns life and another that hallows it, ignores the multivalency of both narratives; or rather, it leaves unquestioned the life Dionysus affirms and entirely fails to see what life is raised up with Christ. Simply said, Dionysus's affirmation is a curse pronounced on life, while Christ's renunciation affirms the whole of creation.

As for Nietzsche's contention, in *On the Genealogy of Morals*, that the idea of a soul, an abiding subjectivity lying behind the actions of the nobles — the ravening birds of prey — was the invention of the imaginations of the weak upon whom the nobles visited their spoliations, and who wished to believe in a moral interval, an intermediate ground between agent and action at which they could direct their reproaches, it is unlikely that it can bear very close scrutiny. Milbank can be credited with the most inspired riposte to this story: no leap of fancy, he observes, is required for the slave to reprehend the master; there is no need for a "metonymic" displacement of moral judgment onto a permanent "self," because within "noble" actions there is always already a metaphoric tension. The wild warrior of primitive, tribal societies did not simply *resemble* the eagle or the lion, but actively imitated them, took them for totems; noble naturality was already a cultural invention, the mimetic piety of man-becoming-eagle. Perhaps, then, the slave has merely seen the truth of metaphor, and so is entirely justified in denying the necessity of noble aggression or the inevitability of life's boisterous violences, and equally justified in choosing another story, woven from a more pastoral tropology, whose grammar depends not upon the romance of strength and acquisition but upon the primordiality of love.[128] Milbank also notes that Nietzsche is little interested in the codes that were already written into heroic society, but imagines the order of that society (rather fantastically) as consisting in the compromises arrived at between powerful men, in the prime of their animal exuberance;[129] and he suggests, further, that another genealogy of subjective interiority might more plausibly locate its origins in the fanatical self-referentiality of heroic culture.[130]

One should probably ask whether the phenomenalistic monism of Nietzsche's account of noble naturality is not still as firmly wedded to a subjective essentialism as Christian thought could ever be. When, after all, one likens the unfettered power and uncomplicated immanence of the noble in his action to the indivisibility of lightning and the lightning flash, the felicity of the image veils a fairly obvious intellectual crudity. Lightning, as it happens, possesses very little in the way of linguistic ambiguity, and any given flash has a very particular and uninvolved history; but one need only consider the linguistic, social, and political complexity of human existence, the historicity and metaphorical provisionality of every human "essence," to recognize in the martial virtues of the noble not simply an original and natural phenomenon, but an effect — and a stage effect, at that. Were the noble warrior simply his own phenomenon, an immediate expression of himself, present to himself in the event of his "unveiling," what would he be other than an egological substance? Where there is no distinction between action and identity, where no moral space intervenes, is this not still the concrete reality of a self, invariable and absolute, the Cartesian ego transposed into a phenomenalist key? A moral interval is characteristic of a metaphysics of the "self" (of a Cartesian soul) presumably because it is thought of as an interval that can be traversed "backwards," in order to find that fixed terminus a quo whence moral action proceeds and so to alight upon a simple substance of self-present identity; the reproaches of the slave are meant to arrive at an agent, to whom actions are exterior and accidental, and in whom there is no division between what he is and how he is: an agency immediately at hand — unwritten — within the interiority of the soul. The inward space of Cartesian reflection still remains an "exterior" apprehension of the manifold, from which thought retreats to fall back upon the indivisible substance of an unquestioned and monadic identity, inseparable from the action of thought. Is it not obvious that his account of the self is just as irredeemably "identitial"

128. Milbank, 287-88.
129. Milbank, 283.
130. Milbank, 290-91.

from the very ease with which Nietzsche can construct analogies of resemblance: lightning, eagles, lions . . . ? A "phenomenalized" substance, a soul brought to the surface of time and space, is still a pristine essence, in which identity vibrates as a single note of absolute presence. And a self that is called "event" rather than "substance" is at least as mythical as an enduring subjectivity. If what one refers to as the subject is in truth a series of happenings rather than a substratum of identity, one still indicates a substance: one that exists as the univocally reiterated moment of self-presence, and as an identifiable sequence of concrete eventuations of identity; it is even a substance to which one may point, a causal and phenomenal insistence, a concatenating presentation of self, neither retaining nor protaining, but whole and complete in its repetition. One catches a hint in Nietzsche's language of the most substantial metaphysical "substance" of all: Did not Augustine, for example, speak of God as being without accidents (*De Trinitate* 5.3), who *is* what he has (*De civitate Dei* 1.10.10.1), and did not Aquinas, in keeping with tradition, deny accidents to God because such constitute the potential of becoming other than what he is (*Summa theologiae* 1.3.6)? What exactly, after all, is the "moral" interval that Christian thought imagines the soul to possess, if not precisely an *interval*, an opening or delay, where will doubles back upon itself or divides, where thought hesitates between identity and difference, where desire pendulates from delight to delight ("delectatio quippe quasi pondus est animae," as Augustine says; "delectatio ergo ordinat animam"),[131] and where the self finds itself always subject to the bearing over (μεταφέρειν) of metaphor? Is not such an "interiority" merely an intensity, an inward fold of an outward surface (to misappropriate Deleuzean terminology), a space of interpretation, where the self's "plot" may be rewritten? One might argue against Nietzsche that only an *essential* self could be immutable and resistant to every renarration. The special pathos of the human is one of ubiquitous metaphor, the condition of being always an interpreted being, never to be traced back to a place prior to culture or language, to a state of nature and simple presence; there is always in the action of the person a formidable absence of the person, an "otherwise" within presence; even the instincts of the flesh, upon which Nietzsche places so great an emphasis, are curiously inadequate in delineating the shape of the human — "totemism" is born with human "nature." In the end, for all his efforts to liberate the subject from the labyrinthine metaphorics of the soul, Nietzsche can at best merely prefer the kinds of animals that the "noble" chose to imitate.

This is of no small concern: part of our current postmetaphysical orthodoxy is the certitude that Christian "theism" and the idea of the self are the two poles of a single onto-theological myth; the subject whose death post-

---

131. Augustine, *De musica* 6.11.29.

modernism announces, who reconstructs the world from its own original position in Descartes's *Meditations,* who is at once the proprietor of Kantian freedom and the hostage of the carceral society's therapeutic scrutiny, supposedly descends from the "subject" that makes its debut in such texts as Augustine's *Confessions* and *De Trinitate* and that allegedly stands at the heart of the Christian narrative as the Archimedean point from which the sublimity of "difference" can be constantly displaced, the citadel of selfhood from which chaos may be held at bay; the self of modernity, so the story goes, is Hellenism's nous or pneuma, enriched by the Christian language of the *imago Dei* and sin, now serving as simultaneously the rational surety of the world and an instrument of social tyranny. This story wants for subtlety.[132] There have been many "selves," many "souls," in the history of the West, describing no continuum but one that is largely semantic; nor does any "postmodern" inclination of thought, inherited from Nietzsche, accomplish anything but the invention of yet another species of subjectivity. It is even questionable that Nietzsche succeeds at being a more radical critic than classical Christian theology of the idea of an invariable spiritual essence; this is not to deny the prominence traditionally enjoyed within Christian culture by talk of the self or soul, nor certainly to deplore it, but from certain vantages within the Christian tradition Nietzsche might appear somewhat retrograde. True, for Nietzsche there is no single self revealed by the creative and interpretive disclosures of the genealogist or the psychologist, but only a mortal, subjective multiplicity, a social organization of drives and affects, habits, qualities, and velleities (*BGE,* 20-21); even the simplest intentionality is a surface, concealing more than it shows, a symptom (*BGE,* 44). In a sense, though, this merely repeats the Platonic metaphor, which makes of the soul a polis, an image of the "truth" that also appears outwardly in the world: a multiplicity whose strife must be vigilantly governed, lest it fall prey to the chaos that lies about on every side (an image serving, for Plato, as simultaneously a psychology and a politics). For Nietzsche, of course, there is obviously no self-sufficient rational faculty — no philosopher-king — to bring the disorder of the self into a uniformly organized and stable commonwealth, but only an endless series of conflicting passions (an Ephesian, rather than an Eleatic, interiority). Yet, predictably, the flight from metaphysics is described metaphysically: intention is a surface, a symptom, because Nietzsche too must find depths within depths, a changeless substrate of anarchic and autotelic will to power that, like Dionysus, is rent into innumerable fragments without ceasing to be one indestructible essence. It is difficult to see, in fact, in precisely

---

132. As an obligingly rudimentary example of this postmodern thematic of the metaphysical self, its place in Christian "onto-theology," and its demise, see Mark C. Taylor, *Erring: A Postmodern A/Theology* (Chicago: University of Chicago Press, 1984), 34-51.

what sense the twin practices of Nietzschean genealogy and Nietzschean psychology do not tend toward a metaphysics of the self that, far from dismantling subjectivity, merely brings it to rest upon a different foundation or "motive." When, for instance (to choose among hundreds of examples), Nietzsche asserts that a popular pious adoration of saints is really only an admiration for the clarity of the saint's expression of the will to power, the intensity with which he manifests our shared desire for dominion (*BGE*, 65), it seems all too obvious that this narrative of power has become an excuse for avoiding the testimony of the surface. One enters here into Nietzsche's confessional, not to be absolved of sinful motives, but to be judged for the hypocrisy of failing to acknowledge them; there is no end of therapeutic terror in this place. Of course, it may well be that the saint fascinates a lust for power every bit as much as he or she convicts hearts of their want of charity; there are many dark and devious motives for many things, as desire is invaded in every quarter by sin; but desire is neither simply sin nor simply will to power. The saint may also evoke a quite blameless response to the type he or she at once embodies and varies; the saint, as an opening upon or interpretation of the form of Christ, may simply draw the gaze of the one who looks on into another radiance, another ambit of vision, a different aesthetic of being, in which one finds some measure of liberation from the self and its baser impulses; many lights and colors play upon the surface of the saint. Nietzsche's apparent subtlety at such points invariably turns out to be surpassingly reductive and rhetorically monochrome: his is a constantly reiterated fiction of a second, inward, inverted gaze, a furtive and feral circumspection *within* each gaze, doubling its intent; he is compelled always to find a second, more interior, more fundamental motive. But if one stays at the surface of things, at least temporarily, and entertains the radical notion that most things are superficial, other perspectives appear: there may be a latent desire for power that the saint stirs into renewed longing, but the saintly form also embraces powerlessness and self-donation, the motion of charity, the love of the neighbor; and one can understand the saint and oneself according to this grammar; the saint's portrait may occupy many frames, and may transfigure the eyes that gaze upon it. Neither what appears in saintliness nor what moves others to admire it can be grasped by so simple and mechanical a psychology as animates Nietzsche's science of the soul. Nietzsche, though, cannot rest content with the ambiguity and richness of the surface; he must imagine instead an interiority of invariable disposition, by which the surface may be uniformly explained: as symbol, symptom, lie. But surfaces are always more complicated than "depths."

What, indeed, is the Christian understanding of the soul? What is the *imago Dei,* and how does it resemble God? There is no entirely adequate answer to such questions, but any of worth will look nothing like the "subject" lost in the ruins of modern metaphysics. For example: the tendency to take Augustine as in some sense the father of the modern subject and the most perfect exemplar of the onto-theologian proceeds from a fairly maladroit exegesis of texts like the *Confessions* and *De Trinitate*, one which finds in their pages simply the story of God and the soul, two discrete substances whose mutual regard insures the meaningfulness of being as a whole. If this reading were essentially correct, one would expect to find in either text Augustine's discovery of a stable subject, an appropriable identity present to itself, a singularity transcendent of time's motion; there would have to be some still point at which, in traversing the inward interval, one finally arrives; but this is precisely what Augustine never discovers. The interiority that opens up in the *Confessions* possesses no center in itself, nor does it depend upon an idea in relation to which it is a shadow tormented by its simulacral drift; instead, it is an infinitely revisable, multiplicit, self-contradictory text, whose creaturely contingency is restless in its longing, founded in nothing, and open to what it cannot own by nature. *Memoria* appears for Augustine — even in this fairly early text, written when the language of Neoplatonism still sprang easily to his lips — not as Platonic anamnesis, but as an open space filled with more music than it can contain, constantly "decentering" itself, transcending itself not toward an idea it grasps or simply "resembles," but toward an infinite it longs for despite its incapacity to contain the infinite; it is an interiority in which every mere "self" is swallowed up by an infinite desire. To cross this "moral" interval is not to transcend the accidental so as to arrive at the substantial, but is rather perpetually to transcend any fixed identity: a transcendence which is always more transcendent, an infinite scope within the self that no self can comprise, and to which the self belongs. The *imago Dei* is not simply a possession of the soul so much as a future, a hope; the self forever displaced and exceeded by its desire for God is a self displaced *toward* an image it never owns as a "substance." Thus, within himself Augustine finds no place to stand, nor does he glimpse above him a higher self, an idea that serves as the ontological treasure stored up for him in heaven, guaranteeing his identity; but he does see a light that embraces him as it shapes him — without need — as a vessel of its glory. Even in *De Trinitate*'s most "metaphysical" moments, the image of God is precisely that which cannot be fixed and cannot lend stability to a unified "ego," because it is a trinitarian image, whose plurality does not *correspond* to "hierarchical" aspects of the soul (this is a Christian, not a Platonic, soul), but rather illuminates the soul as an interdependence of equally present but diverse energies, and so leaves the self in a state of circumvolving multiplicity. The very meaning of the *Confessions*, after all, depends upon an understanding of the particular life, the particular self, as always reinterpretable; the soul is a story that can always be retold, subjected to new grammars, *converted*. The Christian understanding of the soul is, of necessity, dynamic, multifarious, contradictory; no one more profoundly expressed this dynamism than Gregory of Nyssa, for whom the soul could be understood only as an ἐπέκτασις, an always outstretched, open, and changing motion, an infinite exodus from nothingness into God's inexhaustible transcendence (in Kierkegaardian terms, repetition). Theology need feel no pangs of conscience in this matter; for while Nietzsche simply draws a quasi-Platonic picture of the self as polity (or, as the case may be, anarchy), the Christian tradition substitutes for the Platonic soul something still more dynamic: an openness of the "self" before infinite being and infinite novelty.

Really, it matters little whether Nietzsche was still a metaphysician, as Heidegger saw him, or just an irrepressibly mercurial and mischievous ironist, because irony has always been a contour within the metaphysical (what did Plato *believe?*). The will to power is only a story, perhaps, but so is every metaphysics; and even as a story, its plot has often a poignantly dialectical logic. Nietzsche's able advocate, Deleuze, has assured us that "For the speculative element of negation, opposition or contradiction Nietzsche substitutes the practical element of *difference,* the object of affirmation and enjoyment. . . . The empirical feeling of difference, in short hierarchy, is the essential motor of the concept, deeper and more effective than all thought about contradiction."[133] But this is by no means clear. To begin with, one should be suspicious of any "empirical feeling" that stands identifiably prior to the code (the metanarrative) employed to describe it. And while Nietzsche may dispense with such notions as the thing-in-itself or the "soul," he nevertheless clings to an equally naive belief in the essential *event*, the transcendent event of power present in all the universe's finite transactions: hence, a Christian repudiation of power must turn out to be the strategy whereby power assumes an unprecedentedly potent form. The will to power necessarily remains hidden within, and is indeed advanced by, its own negation. This is metaphysics *tout court,* more crudely monistic than Hegel's, and no less dependent on the circular myth of negation. There is, in the Nietzschean cosmos, a perpetual deployment of violence against violence: early on he imagines this in terms of the simple dialectical opposition of Apollo and Dionysus, but soon comes to see Apollonian order as itself a recoil of an original Dionysian violence, a violence that is a creative dynamism and the engine of its own multiplication (thus dialectic and identity emerge from one another). It may be true that Nietzsche has little taste for the grosser manifestations of power (though his views here know their vicissitudes), and it may also be the case that the truly Dionysian will is harsh only in order to create and is most harsh with itself, but this in no way mitigates the violence that sustains this ontology: difference originates always as opposi-

133. Deleuze, *Nietzsche and Philosophy,* 9.

tion, and the genealogist of morals (as Foucault has said) must inevitably discover in history a series of dominations and subjugations (ontology and historicism here run inextricably together). It may be, in fact, that Nietzsche does not intend to be a vulgar monist; the world of his philosophy is not "one thing" — love, hate, war, peace — and cannot be comprehended from any one perspective (*GM*, 118-19). But at the same time, he cannot countenance the suggestion that the Christian exclusion of violence from original or ultimate reality is an intelligible or even honest philosophical position: it must be the querulous dissemblance of the man of ressentiment, there cannot be a repudiation of power immediately transparent to itself because "*This world is the will to power — and nothing besides!*" (*WP*, 550). Difference *cannot* be sustained simply within a relationship of love; there is no perfect openness before the other, nor very much real openness at all except what is left open as a ruse or broken open by force. This is the magisterial metaphysics that for Nietzsche *uniformly* validates the world's multiplicity of values, its always deeper and invariable truth; and he reserves such special acrimony for Christian morality because its language has tried to subvert the game — the agon — that sets the rules of that multiplicity.

Of course, Nietzsche is quite correct: as Celsus understood, Christianity did indeed subvert the language of noble virtue, especially insofar as the latter presupposed the necessity of strife and honored strength for its own sake; Christianity, in its origins, perversely refrained from the celebration of acquisition and dominion. But this much, for all the church's frequent failure to embody the good it proclaims, theology has never sought to hide: when Nietzsche says that every civil state is created and maintained by violence (*GM*, 86-87), or that cruelty lies at the base of society and culture (*GM*, 64-69), he asserts nothing that is not already present in Augustine's account of the *civitas terrena* as a city founded upon violence, indeed upon fratricide (Rome being the paradigm of all secular polities).[134] For Augustine, though, this genealogy of culture remains a thoroughly historical observation; another city can be imagined, enacted, even experienced in the midst of a history alien to it, a history known to the church as sin: originally unnecessary and of a secondary order of reality. For Nietzsche, though, it describes nature's patrimony to humanity, the inexorable advance of the ubiquitous will to power. In the end, what the theologian should probably most deplore in Nietzsche's thought is that it simply is not nearly historicist enough.

However, when all of this has been said, little has been achieved. Once one has demonstrated that Nietzsche proceeds from a fairly foundational set of pre-

---

134. I must cite one of Milbank's more tersely epigrammatic remarks: "*The Genealogy of Morals* is a kind of *Civitas Dei* written back to front" (Milbank, 389).

mises, that he is a metaphysical fabulist and that his metaphysics is circular, one has made only a very small advance against his position. It is true that the element of irony does not make metaphysics less metaphysical, but an irony entirely conscious of itself proves remarkably resistant to any bad conscience; it can slough off the surd of metaphysical assurance without inconveniencing itself or impeding metaphysical invention. To expose the Nietzschean metaphysics is not yet to bring his critique to a halt; one has merely seen behind one of his tricks, grasped the logic of his initial moves, but one has not reached the end of his game, because it is with just this sense of the inadjudicability of contradictory narratives that Nietzsche begins. Here, at least, one must agree with certain contemporary readings of Nietzsche, over against Heidegger's, and recognize the metaphysical moment in Nietzsche as prolegomenal to the aesthetic (and so, finally, as itself aesthetic). Nietzsche has yet to be outstripped in philosophical irreverence, even by his most loyal intellectual heirs, in the matter of "truth's" subservience to evaluation. Nietzsche is engaged principally in identifying an aesthetic disposition, a critical vantage, from which to wage a war of stories; he wishes to overcome the Christian narrative but never imagines he has "proved" it meaningless. This is why one does not confront Nietzsche's full case "against the Crucified" unless one turns to the books of the 1880s, in which the critique of Christianity becomes more obviously an act of artistic imagination. Where Nietzsche is most convincing, and where his treatment of Christianity cannot be *factually* gainsaid, is where he portrays the church's faith as a telling of the tale of being to which he is implacably opposed, in place of which he intends to tell another story. There is nothing facetious in saying that it is as a cutting critic of the Christian aesthetic that Nietzsche is most effective. In general, Christian thought has understood as well as Nietzsche that truth cannot be decided by pure and disinterested reason (as if there were such a thing), but must be allowed to disclose itself as rhetoric, persuasion, narrative form; the evangel makes its appeal to the heart and eye, and has no arguments profounder than the *forma Christi*. Nietzsche's account, apart from its aesthetic challenge, is one the church can either dismiss or even accommodate in its own understanding of itself: any tradition that enjoins constant skepticism regarding its own most basic motives, that insists on an almost merciless cognizance of its own hypocrisies, and that habitually convicts itself of its chronic inability to comply fully (or even meagerly) with the mission given by its "founder" can entertain the possibility that its history has in some sense been a sustained apostasy from itself, a will to vengeance more often than charity (the word "ressentiment" cannot but strike a responsive chord in a Christian conscience). What the church should not be able to abide, though, is a rhetorical assault on the form of Christ (no matter how often it has perpetrated moral assaults of its own), nor can it very well suffer any insinuation that it enjoys no true historical continuity with or access to the life and teachings of Jesus of Nazareth; and these are the strategies that distinguish Nietzsche's line of argument in his most rhetorically brilliant attack on the Christian tradition, *The Anti-Christ.*

Brilliant, that is, but not invincible: Nietzsche's own acuity and subtlety make his task in this text difficult. For while he has no difficulty reading Christian history according to his narrative of the will to power, the figure of Christ remains, for him, somewhat elusive of this story. He mounts, therefore, a two-pronged attack, on the one hand asserting that Christianity as a whole constitutes a contradiction of Christ's actual evangel and, on the other, depicting Christ himself as someone whose teaching was necessarily ineffectual, a supreme decadent, detached from reality and preaching dreams. The immediately obvious weaknesses of *The Anti-Christ* are in many cases those of late nineteenth-century German Protestant biblical scholarship, with which it seems reasonable to suppose Nietzsche had some acquaintance (hence his portrayal of Christ as principally a moral teacher, a gentle soul, proclaiming God's fatherhood and the brotherhood of man, but not as the apocalyptic prophet of the Gospels, or the whip-wielding rabbi driving money changers from the temple, or even really a first-century Jew). But this should not distract one from the more durable aspects of Nietzsche's portraiture, nor from the occasional force of his aesthetic assessment of the figure of Christ in the Gospels. What is most astonishing about *The Anti-Christ* is that Nietzsche makes no attempt therein to argue that the ministry of Jesus can, like the ministry of the Christian church, be treated as a covert strategy of the will to power; if his Jesus is moved in any way by this will, it is only in its most rarefied form: not as a crude desire to dominate, expand, or acquire, but as an overwhelming sense of the presence of eternal bliss in the present moment, of universal reconciliation with God, and of the solidarity of all men in a fraternity of mutual love and forgiveness. Nietzsche never gives the slightest indication that he does not take entirely seriously Christ's own repudiation of power; he seeks only to demonstrate that such a repudiation belonged to a way of life that was incommutable and flawed, blighted at the roots, incapable of entering into history or of changing the conditions of human existence.

Obviously there is something dubious about any attempt to abstract a "historical" Jesus from the New Testament, and to his credit, this is not really Nietzsche's aim; nor is his Jesus any more implausible than that of, say, Harnack. If anything, Nietzsche's reconstruction of the figure of Christ is to be preferred to many others, in that he is at least candid enough to confess how much of an *imaginative* project it is that he has undertaken. "What I am concerned with is the psychological type of the redeemer. For it *could* be contained in the Gospels in spite of the Gospels, however much mutilated and overloaded with foreign traits: as that of Francis of Assisi is contained in the legends about him in spite of the legends" (*AC*, 140-41). This *"could"* is at least some kind of admission of the ultimate impossibility of pursuing such a psychology as a purely "scientific" project. To treat the Gospels as palimpsests, concealing the original text of the historical Jesus, is often to arrogate to oneself considerable license for creating a Jesus amenable to one's purposes; this has long been the special disease of the search for the historical Jesus, and it is certainly the case with Nietzsche; but *The Anti-Christ* does not simply limn a caricature and then make it an object of ridicule. Still, it is just as well to note from the outset that, in the end, Nietzsche's "psychology of the redeemer" must be accounted an imaginative failure, if for no other reason than that it never actually succeeds *at all* in reinterpreting the figure that appears in the text of the Gospels, but becomes instead an incredible feat of hermeneutical intuition; so remote is the portrait Nietzsche draws from the narrated Christ of the Gospels that the texts can be used to very little effect, with the result that his Jesus turns out to be less a subversion of the biblical Jesus than an arbitrary (and rather conventional) construction. Christ, for Nietzsche, remains a point of particular resistance for the narrative of power, as is evident from the extreme inventiveness required of him as he attempts to commensurate and encircle Christ's aesthetic force; and still invention flags, falls far short, exceeded in every direction by the uncanniness of the Christ of the Gospels — and this failure could not be more instructive.

Nietzsche expresses special contempt for Renan's use of such psychological types as the hero or the genius to describe Jesus. One cannot, Nietzsche insists, call heroic a person who preached that evil should not be resisted, who knew only "blessedness in peace, in gentleness, in the *inability* for enmity" (141); "idiot" is the better epithet (perhaps on the model of Prince Myshkin): Christ lived in a sweet delirium, in which a life of eternal love seemed present in each moment, in which all men appeared as equal, the children of God; an inner world of his own creation, one to which he fled principally on account of his excessive sensitivity to touch and abrasion, his morbid dread of reality's sting; his was a child's evangel, an exhortation to simple faith, a devotion to an inner light and an immunity to all concrete realities (29-32, 141-44). Nietzsche rejects as barbarizing falsifications all attributions to Christ of irony, gall, or esprit, and all the nonsensical apostolic dogmas of a "second coming" or "final judgment" (142-43). Jesus was indifferent to dogmatic Judaism and to all formulations of religious orthodoxy; for him the entire world was a language, a system of spiritual symbols (144). This is why Christ's evangel could not possibly survive him:

> such a symbolist *par excellence* stands outside of all religion, all conceptions of divine worship, all history, all natural science, all experience of the world, all acquirements, all politics, all psychology, all books, all art — his "knowl-

edge" is precisely the *pure folly* of the fact *that* anything of this kind exists. . . . he never had reason to deny "the world," he had no notion of the ecclesiastical concept "world." . . . Neither *can* such a doctrine argue: it simply does not understand that other doctrines exist. . . . Where it encounters one it will . . . lament the "blindness" — for it sees the "light" — but it will make no objection. (145)

Christ's good tidings were that all sin and guilt were remitted, all punishment abolished, all separation from God overcome — now, in the present; he taught no system of belief, but only a sense of blessedness, a form of life; "*evangelic practice alone* leads to God, it *is* God!" (146). As the supreme symbolist, able to acknowledge the actuality of only his own inward universe, even his use of such terms as "son of man," "God," or "the kingdom of heaven" was metaphorical, a poetical plying of symbols of eternal "fact" (146). "But it is patently obvious what is alluded to in the symbols 'Father' and 'Son' — not patently obvious to everyone, I grant: in the word 'Son' is expressed the *entry* into the collective feeling of the transfiguration of all things (blessedness), in the word 'Father' *this feeling itself*, the feeling of perfection and eternity" (147). Even death, for such a one, is only a symbol, and Christ's death was a final realization of the life he led (147-48).[135] In short, Nietzsche's Christ is a study in the psychopathology of moral and intellectual angelism. Unfortunately, this figure — though somewhat altered, certainly somewhat more exaggerated, and described with even greater distaste — is at the last boringly familiar: in Nietzsche's Christ, as I have said, one renews acquaintance with Hegel's "beautiful soul."

The church, then, according to Nietzsche, actually represents the absolute opposite of Christ's evangel; "in reality there has been only one Christian, and he died on the Cross" (151). The church was built by staggeringly unimaginative philistines, unable to understand or, certainly, to imitate Christ's life; they transformed their master into a savior, a judge, a rebel against the prevailing social order, the *one* son of God; though Christ's death was itself free of all ressentiment, in the minds of his disciples it became an act of divine vengeance, a revelation of human guilt, and an event of sacrificial propitiation (152-54). Nietzsche especially condemns Paul for his role in this falsification; to Paul he ascribes a positive genius for hatred, and accuses him of inventing the resurrected Christ, the lord of history, and the doctrine of judgment: in order, so the story goes, to extend his sacerdotal tyranny over the herd (155). Only by way of such dogmas could the church inveigle into its fold the impudent dross that became its vast constituency (115-16). Nietzsche's treatment of Paul is, as it happens, easily the weakest, tritest, and most risible portion of *The Anti-Christ*; one

---

135. See also *BGE*, 220.

could scarcely conceive of a diatribe that could succeed better at being at once so unbalanced and so platitudinous. But from the morass of these pages one can still extract the substance of the accusation being made, and it is one with a certain real gravity for Christian thought: that the historical church, far from simply failing to live up to Christ's teachings, contradicts them in every essential feature. This is no simple attack on Christian hypocrisy; not only does the church fail to live up to what it professes, but *that very profession* is diametrically opposed to everything Christ was. Such an accusation carries with it an altogether devastating force — if, that is, one is actually convinced by Nietzsche's portrait of Christ.

It would be fruitless to ask whether Nietzsche's Christ is a psychologically plausible figure (perhaps he is); but as a historical reconstruction he is rather absurd, and more or less unimaginable in terms of Jesus' time and place. It is difficult at first to know what to make of Nietzsche's portrait, chiefly because it describes so singular a pathology in Nietzschean psychology: for the "man of ressentiment" everything is a cause of pain, and so he resents (*EH,* 229-31), but Christ's reaction to reality's afflictions, as Nietzsche imagines him, is neither resentment nor resistance, but an ethereal withdrawal, detachment, and tabescence of the will. This makes no very creative use of the texts; the more one inspects the picture presented, the more it looks like pure invention or a feat of divination more penetrating than any mere hermeneutical method: the Christ of the Gospels possesses simply too much irony and gall for this to be taken as an incidental addition to the memory whose impression was left in the Gospels (so much gall, in fact, as to be the cause of some considerable discomfort to Christians who occasionally wish that this biblical Christ cut a somewhat more domesticated figure — not so feckless as the piscine imbecile Nietzsche describes, of course, but something no more threatening than a social worker, or a community organizer, or ideally a conscientious bourgeois). The oddity of Nietzsche's Christ is how close he comes to a cliché on the one hand and how remote he seems from the texts from which his picture is extracted on the other: he appears in *The Anti-Christ* as a sort of outlandish hybrid between a fin de siècle Parisian decadent, nourished on absinthe and opium, and an autistic child. The implausibility is difficult to exaggerate; the fiction is so thoroughly polemical that all proportion and narrative continuity is lost — an imaginative failure, as I have said. It would seem that, for Nietzsche, the figure of the Gospels remained to the end indomitable: in Christ he encountered a restive, alien, and intractable quality that had to be put at a distance by a combination of invective and extravagant psychological speculation. Admittedly, to deem *The Anti-Christ* an artistic failure is an entirely aesthetic evaluation, but in regard to Nietzsche nothing could be more pertinent. In this work, finally, the form of Christ remains rhetorically untouched (which is what is at issue for Nietzsche:

he is not like Harnack, deluded that he can retrieve something of Christ's historical substance as an objective quantity). To Nietzsche, whose limited psychological phenomenology can accommodate nothing that does not obey the simple taxonomy of active and reactive, Christ can be grasped only as withdrawal, dissolution, spindrift evaporating at the verge of the great ocean of violent energy that is the cosmos; it is inconceivable to him that the lamb brought to slaughter could be also the lion of Judah. But if there is an energy — which Christians call agape — that does not conform to this polarity between active and reactive, dominant or dominated, but is at once creative and responsive, evoking and evoked, and is able to constitute the distance between differences as neither force, nor violence, nor plain univocal heterogeneity, but as an analogical peace, as the gaze of recognition and regard, and as gift; if, in short, Christ represents a model of being that is active in receiving and creative in responding, or in which these things abide within one another, indivisibly, then the Nietzschean cosmos is revealed to be not simply an arbitrary fiction, an aesthetic perspective, but also perhaps — by comparison — a fairly squalid one.

This is, of course, what is at stake in Nietzsche's "psychology of the redeemer," and this is why Jesus must tenant his narrative in just this fashion. The otherness that Nietzsche encountered in Christ, the strangeness and refractoriness to conventional psychology, is openly acknowledged in *The Anti-Christ:* Christ desired no power and suffered from no resentment toward his persecutors — indeed, he loved them. For Nietzsche this means Christ was a dreamer, which is to say a decadent, a creature of perishing life; but then again, perhaps a dreamer might also be creative. A certain degree of detachment from merely "obvious" circumstances, a certain distance and oneiric cast of mind, is required for any creative action; a new practice requires a new imagination of the world. Depending on the "dreamer" or the dream, the oneiric may be a force of historical effect, cultural change, social genesis, or revolution; the oneiric may be that rhetorical excess that reconstitutes understanding and practice, that alters the vision of others; it need not be only an inward and perishing force. A Christian might well acknowledge that Christ was a masterful "symbolist" — the documentary evidence is sufficiently convincing — but precisely in the sense that Christ showed that the world was a text that could be read differently: according to the grammar not of power, but of agape. The Christian contention, then, would be that this "dreamer" could also, in reenvisaging the world, initiate a real historical sequence, a positive if oft-imperiled "new creation." He was a "revolutionary," recasting the very form and reconstituting the very substance of the human in the life he lived in perfect faithfulness. And obviously the church may then regard itself as somehow a partial realization and imperfect enactment of this new creation — this kingdom without coercion — that was made flesh in Christ and is continuously made present in the Spirit.

The church has Christ as its beginning and its end. Nor need any Christian meekly accept the Nietzschean division between what Christ saw and what he did: or rather, what Christ saw and what, in consequence, he did not do. One might even ask if Nietzsche is not engaged throughout *The Anti-Christ* in a strategy of ressentiment, the interposition of a moral interval between Christ (the agent) and the church (his agency), in order — to use Deleuze's happy turn of phrase — to separate Christ's (aesthetic) force from what it can do. A deviousness bred of weakness and a poverty of aesthetic imagination will — so one is reliably informed — inevitably assert itself in this way. In truth, Christ's cleansing of the temple precincts, his creation of a new and holy space within history, can be conceived quite compatibly together with his "symbolic" pronouncements; his injunction to "render unto Caesar" may be regarded not merely as a dreamer's recoil from "reality," but as the active rejection of one order in favor of another, intended to make room for the concrete community of the church and its peculiar practices. For Nietzsche this remains always inconceivable: to allow that the symbolist of the Gospels could be also creative, forceful, imperious, and capable of discrimination and judgment — to allow, that is, that the "idiot" whose rejection of power was final and still free of resentment could genuinely enter into history, or constitute an apprehensible aesthetic form among the many forms cast up by time, or pose against all philosophies of will and power the historical example of a community able to live, however imperfectly and infrequently, by charity rather than force — would give the lie to Nietzsche's own narrative of cosmos and history, his own metaphysics and (more importantly) aesthetics.

Again, there is little but force of rhetoric behind Nietzsche's constant reversion to a pagan vision of the world as perpetual agon, a terrible collusion of chaos and order, which is shaped and controlled through the judicious deployment of various powers, such as "reason" or "the state," or (as is the case with Nietzsche) merely affirmed as wasteful but indestructible creativity. Nietzsche is a pure metaphysician insofar as he cannot endure the "irrational" idea of a freely creative and utterly transcendent love; he thirsts for the soothing fatalism of "necessity." Thus he merely repeats the wisdom of totality, now redoubled and reinvigorated by a critique internal to itself: like Dionysus, totality rends itself apart to give itself new birth; the limbs of Parmenides are reassembled in the form of Heracleitos. If, however, the language of Christ's evangel is taken seriously, for even a moment, a certain salutary trembling must pass through the edifice of totality: it is irreconcilably subversive of all the values of antique virtue and public philosophy, whether guarded by Apollo or animated by Dionysus; it makes every claim to power and to rights not only provisional, not only false, but quite simply absurd. Christians claim that the beauty that appears in Christ, contrary to all judicious taste, abides with and in the poor, the godforsaken, the forgotten, and the lowly, not simply as a sweetening of their lot with bootless sentimentality, or because Christianity cherishes life only when it is weak, perishing, and uncomely, but because Christ — who is the truth of being — in dwelling among and embracing these "slaves," shows them to be luminously beautiful. Can this be believed? To entertain the possibility that such a language could indeed effect the reality it depicts, even if fitfully and failingly, or to imagine that the future that impends upon every instant might lie open to the practice of such a reality, would require a far more radical historicization of thought, a more radical antiessentialism, than Nietzsche's: it would require the belief that nothing in the world so essentially determines the nature of humanity or the scope of the human soul that there is no possibility of being reborn.

Finally, of course, as I have repeatedly insisted, it is taste, rather than historical evidence, that must dictate whether one elects to see Christ as a creator of values or as an impotent decadent. Again, it is Nietzsche's aesthetic evaluation — in this case his preference for the form and allure of noble values over Christ's gospel of love — that remains unassailable. The metaphysical aspects of his critique, which continually float to the surface wherever they are denied, are embarrassing if regarded as anything other than facets of an imaginative narrative, an attempt at a more compelling story, whose appeal is rhetorical, whose logic is figurative, and whose foundation is none. Nietzsche's disdain does not follow from the force of his reasoning; it is that force. Despite which, certain of his postmodern followers all too often allow the metaphysical within Nietzsche to predominate (quite contrary to their intentions) by taking his narrative of being and his distaste together in such a way that the narrative comes to constitute an assumption that functions all the more pervasively for going unacknowledged: the Heracleitean cosmos is taken as, in some sense, an unproblematic and unarguable truth, and the only alternative to totalizing metaphysics (of which, however, it is a very venerable variety). Still, in the case of Nietzsche, it is the aesthetic side to which theology must attend, because this provides the only real challenge to the Christian *kerygma:* one gospel confronts another; Nietzsche's preferences are all. And they are preferences that are scintillatingly well expressed in numerous passages throughout his writings, such as one notable reflection in *The Anti-Christ* upon the kind of persons — the sordid little provincials — one finds everywhere in the New Testament: "Their ambition is laughable: people of *that* sort regurgitating their most private affairs, their stupidities, sorrows, and petty worries, as if the Heart of Being were obliged to concern itself with them; they never grow tired of involving God himself in even the pettiest troubles they have got themselves into. And the appalling taste of this perpetual familiarity with God" (144). In fact, Nietzsche may well be right; there is little in the New Testament, given his tastes, that might favorably compare with Homer — or even with Apuleius. One Gospel story that one can assume, from this quotation, earned Nietzsche's disdain is that of Peter, hearing the cock crow and, remembering his denial of Christ, going apart to weep.[136] Nowhere previously in the literature of antiquity had the tears of a rustic been treated as anything but an object of mirth; certainly to regard them as worthy of attention, as grave or meaningful or tragic or expressive of a profound human grief, could appear only grotesque from the vantage of a classical, noble aesthetic. There was indeed a revolution, a slave revolt, both in those frightfully subversive tears and in the shocking tastelessness of a narrator so indiscreet as to record them, so vulgar as to view them with anything but elevated contempt. And this is where the battle lines, ruefully to say, between Nietzsche's narrative and the Christian narrative have been irrevocably drawn. The most potent reply a Christian can make to Nietzsche's critique is to accuse him of a defect of sensibility — of bad taste. And this, in fact, is the last observation that should be made at this point: Nietzsche had atrocious taste.

IV. THE COVENANT OF LIGHT

According to Empedocles, the cosmos is a minute island of order in the midst of the formless chaos of the universe:[137] an image of being that repeats on a universal scale (so imparting the appearance of ontological necessity to) the reality of the polis. It reflects, as Hans Urs von Balthasar observes, a certain pagan intuition of the cosmos as a fragile armistice preserved among innumerable forces of disruption, besieged on every side by disorder and violence, and threatening to dissolve into meaninglessness; it is a vision of being that is present, for instance, in the Platonic scheme of idea, image, and simulacrum, or in the Aristotelian ethic of moderation, which is meant to arrest and repel the forces of excess that threaten every order, rational, political, moral, or emotional.[138] The cosmos and the city, the city and the soul: this is the golden thread of analogy running through ancient Greek metaphysics; the serene lineaments of rational form are always engaged in a struggle with the tragic depths they comprise and with the turmoil that surrounds them as fate and as the infi-

---

136. See Erich Auerbach, *Mimesis: The Representation of Reality in Western Literature,* trans. Willard R. Trask (Princeton: Princeton University Press, 1953), 40-49; Auerbach finds in this tale a decisive break with the serene proportions of antique heroic or moral narrative: comparing Peter's remorse to the emotional portraiture found in Petronius, Tacitus, Sallust, and others, he sees in Peter "the image of man in the highest and deepest and most tragic sense" (41).

137. Fragment 31 in Diels.

138. See Hans Urs von Balthasar, *Theo-Drama: Theological Dramatic Theory,* vol. 2, *Dramatis Personae: Man in God,* trans. Graham Harrison (San Francisco: Ignatius, 1990), 350-52.

nite. According to Gianni Vattimo, "When Nietzsche speaks of metaphysics as an attempt to *master the real by force*, he does not describe a marginal characteristic of metaphysics but indicates its essence as it is delineated right from the first pages of Aristotle's *Metaphysics*, where knowledge is defined in relation to the *possession of first principles*."[139] Metaphysics in this sense, the articulation of unarguable principles, is always an attempt to still the tumult of existence; it is itself already war against war: finding difference unbearable, only ungovernable strife, it seeks the unmoving foundations of being, there to build. As a science of essences, enabling us to discriminate proper from deficient realizations of those essences, it grants us a natural taxonomy by which to assign everything and everyone (e.g., masters and slaves) their correct places. And historically, the rejection of metaphysical order expresses itself, at most, as a desire to bear the unbearable, to endure ontological strife rather than submit to "totalizing" tyranny, but leaves the most essential metaphysical premises intact. What, for instance, could be more pathetically confined than Deleuze's attempt to defeat Platonism through a simple reversal of the priority of *eidos* and simulacrum, *forma* and *materia*? (One is reminded of Feuerbach's reversal of metaphysical theology, which merely resulted in an equally metaphysical anthropology.) Just as a lapsed Catholic is recognizable from living his entire life as one long, indefinitely sustained gesture of apostasy, the postmodern philosopher is still a philosopher, still a dialectician, still within the city walls of totality; that he longs for the nomad's perilous exile from the polis does little to alter this fact, as this merely confirms the topology of being as either polis or exile.

Which prompts me to repeat the assertion that theology owes Nietzsche a debt: I intend nothing facetious in saying that Nietzsche has bequeathed Christian thought a most beautiful gift, a needed anamnesis of itself — of its strangeness. His critique is a great camera obscura that brings into vivid and concentrated focus the aesthetic scandal of Christianity's origins, the great offense this new faith gave the gods of antiquity, and everything about it that pagan wisdom could neither comprehend nor abide: a God who goes about in the dust of exodus for love of a race intransigent in its particularity; who apparels himself in common human nature, in the form of a servant; who brings good news to those who suffer and victory to those who are as nothing; who dies like a slave and outcast without resistance; who penetrates to the very depths of hell in pursuit of those he loves; and who persists even after death not as a hero lifted up to Olympian glories, but in the company of peasants, breaking bread with them and offering them the solace of his wounds. In recalling theology to the

---

139. Gianni Vattimo, "Towards an Ontology of Decline," in *Recoding Metaphysics: The New Italian Philosophy*, ed. Giovanni Borradori (Evanston, Ill.: Northwestern University Press, 1988), 60.

ungainliness of the gospel, Nietzsche retrieved the gospel from the soporific complacency of modernity (and at a time when and in a land where modernity had gained a commanding advantage over it); this first eruption of the postmodern, which arrived appropriately as a rediscovery of a pagan ontology and aesthetics, reminds theology that against the God declared in Christ, Dionysus and Apollo stand as allies, guarding an enclosed world of chaos and order against the anarchic prodigality of his love. Many of theology's native resources might otherwise have continued to lie largely unexploited. Since Nietzsche was always sufficiently aware that the "death of God" is not something that has simply epochally occurred, but must now be narrated and invented (lest only the "last man" inherit the earth), he always showed enough good manners to confront theology with what is clearly a story, stridently posed against the Christian story. And so theology is reminded that it has — and may boldly tell — another tale: one in which the being of creation is an essential peace, hospitable to all true difference, reflecting the infinite peace of God's triune life in its beauty and diversity. For this recollection of its uniqueness within the world totality describes, and for this provocation to renew the kerygmatic essence of theology, Christian thought would be churlish not to be grateful.

But Nietzsche also reminds theology how great is its rhetorical burden. The story of being that Christianity tells, of creation as a word of peace whose ultimate promise is also peace, looks so very frail standing alongside the imposing figures of "history" and "nature," in their blood-dyed robes, trailing their clouds of contingency, cruelty, and ambiguity; the protological and eschatological tensions within the Christian story leave it vulnerable to the accusation of irresponsible idealism, or of an unwillingness to rein its narrative in when its messianic horizon threatens to engulf the clarity of "realist" thinking in a night of mythical abstraction (theology, not always unaware of this, even occasionally attempts to construct one or another kind of political "realism" of its own, even though this can be accomplished only through a series of tactical apostasies). Nonetheless, the Christian claim is also that this protology and this eschatology do not merely stand outside human history, but enter into it decisively in the resurrection of Christ; the peace of God — the shalom of creation and of the day God declares his rule out of Zion — has a real historical shape and presence, a concrete story, one which has entered into human history as a contrary history, the true story God always tells, in which violence has no place but rather stands under judgment as provisional, willful, needless: nonbeing. The Christian tradition is nothing if not the evangel of this eschatological peace offered in the present moment, as the true form of difference and the style of its transmission: the evangel, that is, of the crucified as the Lord of history, in the perpetual power of the Spirit. Given the enormous scope of such claims, and the recklessness of such promises, theology cannot avoid considering the aesthetics of its rhetoric, and whether its rhetoric can truly reflect the being of the world. For if, of course, distance is an original discord, if the event of difference is both singular and total, then the space between any two beings, despoiled of all analogical light, is a desert, and every embassy of peace that crosses the distance is accompanied by rumors of war; every preference is arbitrary, and so all rhetoric an aggression; the gospel is then a lie. So that "place between" must be narrated as, first and foremost, light and peace, a distance of mediation, dissemination, writing, and rhetoric that is for just that reason a distance of gift, freedom, and beauty *primordially* (however disfigured by sin). And to do this with appropriate vigor and certainty of resolve, theology must go further than even Nietzsche's most stentorian invective reaches, to recover a still more radical sense of its own "perversity," and so a deeper knowledge of its own understanding of infinity, beauty, truth. . . . It must, in short, recover an adequate sense of a certain "Christian interruption."

Nor should it doubt the magnitude of that interruption. When I began this part of my argument with a reference to Milbank's characterization of postmodern thought as, in large part, an "ontology of violence," I did so well aware that this aspect of his thought is often taken, by allies and foes alike, as quite a provocative contention — whether seen as an instance of penetrating deconstruction or of dismal calumny. This, it seems to me, exaggerates both the novelty and the scandal of his remarks. *Of course* all the discourses we typically call "postmodern" are ontologies of violence: they belong to the history of philosophy, which has never, insofar as it has functioned as a self-sufficient and autonomous discipline, been able to think the being of the world except in terms of a certain strife between order and disorder, a certain set of tragic limits to being's expression of itself, and a certain inevitable structure of deceit within the fabric of the finite. Every "metaphysical" ontology presumes that, in some quite original and ultimate way, difference is violence itself, even (indeed, especially) when it is an ontology that thinks it has freed itself of the totalizing tendencies of "onto-theology." There is nothing startling or even blameworthy in this; it is inevitable, given that all philosophy is, by definition, a discourse concerning necessity — not, that is to say, *necessitas* in the theological sense, the utter fittingness with which divine freedom expresses the goodness of its nature in the generosity of its act (being itself the *actus* of all that is); but necessity in the sense of being's finitude, its absolute limitation to the condition of the world in its "worlding," its fatedness. However well a "pure" metaphysics may be able to conceive of ontological dependency, it can never, by its own lights, arrive at the thought of true contingency; even a Heracleitean metaphysics of chance is anything but a philosophy of the freedom of the ontic or of the ontological, but is — as Nietzsche and Deleuze so well understand — a doctrine of the absolute necessity of the being of this world; even the most etherealizing "idealism" can at best conceive of the ultimate as the apex or "absolute" of the totality of beings, the spiritual resolution of all the ambiguities of the immanent, but can never really think in terms of true transcendence. If the ambition of a metaphysics is to deduce from the conditions of the existence of the world the principles of the world — to move, that is, from the "that" of the world to the "what" of its being, or from finitude to its ground — then it must embrace within itself, as an element and indeed principle of being, all that is negative and tragic in the exteriority of existence: pain, alienation, ignorance, strife, death, the recalcitrance of matter, the ineluctability of decay, the inevitability of every order's corruption and dissolution . . . war. . . . And it must meet the sad necessity of these things in a way appropriate to the wisdom it can comprise: acceptance, affirmation, resignation, flight to a higher world, a "rational love of God," a "negation of negation," playfulness, or (as with, say, Sakyamuni, Schopenhauer, or Levinas) one or another form of melancholic or heroic nihilism. Being, in its totality, is a tragic economy, in some sense a structure of sacrifice in which beings suffer incompletion and destruction in order that being may "be." The world and its principles assure one another only through the reciprocal founding of a fulfillment in negation, the completion of finitude in the ultimate mystery of the absolute, and the display of the absolute in the violence of its alienation; the indissoluble dialectic of being and beings is one in which what is preserved is always negated, and vice versa. The land of unlikeness is explicable only in the light of the forms, but where else can the forms shine out from themselves? But it is this very reality — the tragedy of being in its dispensation — that is the secret of philosophy's power; for it can thrive as a deductive enterprise, able to move from the world to the world's principles, only insofar as what is, is what must be; only because being must appear thus, constrained to these manifestations, and only because being must express itself in beings, is metaphysics possible. With these maxims presumed, it is a matter less of discernment than of sensibility or style whether the philosopher will build according to the immense crystalline architectures of the Platonic universe or seek to tear the edifice of idealism apart in a delirious abandonment to the pathos of inescapable immanence; whether he will pursue the adventure of the Concept or wallow in the carnage of "difference"; whether he will while away the hours in a ceaseless discrimination of substances from their accidents or remain in a condition of suspenseful and thoughtful attendance, awaiting the next glimpse being grants of itself through the veil of its "destinal" epochality. Under the regime of necessity, the philosopher is always king.

In this respect theology should, politely, borrow certain things from Heidegger's "history of being." The collapse of metaphysics, the reduction of rationality to technological mastery of the "standing reserve" of nature, subjectivist humanism, the birth, in short, of "nihilism" — all of this did perhaps actually have its first dim stirrings in some primordial turning away from the light toward the things illuminated, a certain forgetfulness of being necessarily implicit within philosophy's very wakefulness to being. Perhaps in some fateful oblivion of the mystery of being's event, the search for being's foundations (the relentless quest for positive truth) commenced, and then proceeded along a path that, in the end, would prove the ruin of all philosophic faith. If nothing else, as I have said, it was from certain elements within "Platonism" — its myth of the tragic loss of eternal vision, its longing for the cold retreat of Pythagorean number and ideal purity, its abhorrence of the formless *apeiron* and the empty *chora* — that all the terms of modernity's or postmodernity's inversion of metaphysics took shape; and nowhere within the long history of this great palindromic progress was the inviolable law of necessity absent. This much, at least, of the "history of nihilism" should be welcomed, as a moment in which Western philosophy achieves a profound awareness of itself, its destined "vocation," and in which it learns to relinquish certain ambitions. It should not be welcomed, though, insofar as it becomes an excuse for an equally metaphysical discourse of "fundamental ontology" or "immanation." More importantly, this history should not be allowed to assume the monolithic unity Heidegger imposed upon it, in his own long and occasionally resentful struggle against the theological resources on which, to the end, his thought drew. For there was, within the history of Western philosophy, in the midst of its achievements and failures, a singular interruption, the arrival of a discourse of truth in which every principle of necessity became subordinate to the higher principle of gratuity. Christian thought, and its long history of metaphysical speculation, did not occur as just another episode in the genealogy of nihilism; it was in fact so profound a disruption of many of the most basic premises of philosophy, and so audacious a rescue of many of philosophy's truths from the impotent embrace of mere metaphysical ambition, that it is doubtful yet that philosophy understands what happened to it, or why now it cannot be anything but an ever more self-tormenting denial of that interruption. The Jewish language of creation — however this may be parodied as a story regarding mere efficient causality or an even greater intensification of the impulse of metaphysical "founding" — in truth introduced into Western thought the radically new idea that an infinite freedom is the "principle" of the world's being, and for the first time opened up the possibility of a genuine reflection upon the "ontico-ontological difference" (to name the question that Heidegger so powerfully invoked, and then spent the remainder of his philosophical career actually evading). And the Christian understanding of God as Trinity, without need of the world even for his determination as difference, relatedness, or manifestation, for the first time confronted Western thought with a genuine discourse of transcendence, of an ontological truth whose "identity" is not completed by any ontic order of descent and ascent. The event of being, for beings, is a gift in an absolute sense, into whose mysteries no *scala naturae* by itself grants us proper entry. And if the world is without necessity (the necessity of system, or "immanence," or total event), but is more originally gratuity (even if it must reflect the goodness of the wellspring of being in that gracious marriage of "essence" and "existence" that creation is), then transcendental reflection may be able to grasp many things, but by its own power it can accomplish neither the limits nor the contents of what is; it is at best a ship adrift when unanchored by the logic of the necessary. If there is no force of fate or negative determination or material limit in the order of being, but only a power of grace, creativity, imagination, and love that gives being freely, whose gift is bound only by the necessity of ontological *convenientia* and concinnity — as a manifestation of the beauty in which creation lives, and moves, and has its being — rather than by that of self-determination, then this misconstrual of the contingent for the necessary constitutes the primal error that renders all merely human philosophy incapable of receiving the real in the limpid truth of its appearing. Or, phrased theologically, it is in this way that even the wisest of philosophies attests to the universal blindness of sin.

And it is for this reason also that theology's interruption of the "history of nihilism" was philosophy's redemption, its healing, the fullest possible deepening of its openness to being, and indeed the infinite increase of its highest eros. Within the environs of Christianity's narrative — of Trinity, creation, and divine incarnation — the language of beauty could not but become even more important, and the dignity of worldly beauty more vital, than had ever been the case in pagan Greek culture or the world it shaped. A God whose very being is love, delight in the glorious radiance of his infinite Image, seen in the boundlessly lovely light of his Spirit, and whose works are then unnecessary but perfectly expressive signs of this delight, fashioned for his pleasure and for the gracious sharing of his joy with creatures for whom he had no need (yet loved even when they were not), is a God of beauty in the fullest imaginable sense. In such a God beauty and the infinite entirely coincide, for the very life of God is one of — to phrase it strangely — infinite form; and when such a God creates, the difference between created beauty and the divine beauty it reflects subsists not in the amphiboly of multiplicity and singularity, shape and simplicity, finitude and indeterminacy, but in the analogy between the determinate particularities of the world and that always greater, supereminent determinacy in whose splendor they participate. Indeed, the event of the world simply is the occurrence of this analogical interval, the space in which beings rise up from nothingness into the light that gives them existence. And this is why theology redeems philosophy, this is how it recovers all of philosophy's most enchanting prospects upon being: precisely by detaching them from the morbid mythology of "grounds," and by resituating them within the space that the analogy between divine and worldly being opens up, setting worldly being free peacefully and preserving it beautifully. Thus, for Christian thought, to know the world truly is achieved not through a positivistic reconstruction of its "sufficient reason," but through an openness before glory, a willingness to orient one's will toward the light of being, and to receive the world as a gift, in response to which the most fully "adequate" discourse of truth is worship, prayer, and rejoicing. Phrased otherwise, the truth of being is "poetic" before it is "rational" — indeed is rational precisely as a result of its supreme poetic coherence and richness of detail — and cannot be truly known if this order is reversed. Beauty is the beginning and end of all true knowledge: really to know anything, one must first love, and having known one must finally delight; only this "corresponds" to the trinitarian love and delight that creates. The truth of being is the whole of being, in its event, groundless, and so in its every detail revelatory of the light that grants it. Heidegger himself, ever the creature of his early theological teaching, came close to realizing this, in his attempts to deliver the language of truth from the confines of every form of positivism, or analytic mastery, or propositional reductionism; but ultimately he proved too forgetful of the radical question of beauty that Christian thought had raised, and so retreated back again along the tenebrous woodland paths of ontological necessity, in search of the "how it is" of the event rather than the "that it is" of the world, seeking a clearing where it never had been (nor ever could be) found.

Of course, Heidegger, like Nietzsche before him, was unable to see that his own revolt against metaphysics was itself really nothing more than a necessary moment in metaphysics' recovery of itself from theology; for, in a sense, philosophy could not receive the gift Christian thought extended to it and remain what it had been — the science of mastery, the interrogation of the "ground" — but neither could it simply ignore Christianity's transformation of its native terms: once the splendor of being had been assumed into Christian *philokalia*, once the light of the world had become part of the discourse of ontological analogy and transcendence, and once the difference between being and beings had entered thought and disrupted every attempt to "deduce" from the world its metaphysical identity, philosophy could not simply reassert itself as an independent project but had to discover a new foundation upon which to build. Henceforth metaphysics, like a king forced to wrap himself in the incognito of a pauper, would have to suffer the most extreme self-divestment before it could reclaim its autonomy. This is the true sense in which theology is part of the history of nihilism: it leaves nothing good behind for philosophy to claim as its own, it steals all the most powerful instruments of philosophical heuristics for its own uses (despoiling the Egyptians, to employ the classic figure), and so makes it inevitable that, in the wake of theology's cultural influence, philosophy must advance itself ever more openly as a struggle against light, an ever more vehement refusal of the generosity of the given. Nihilism is indeed the hidden core or secret vocation of metaphysics — as figures as diverse as Jacobi, Nietzsche, Heidegger, and Vattimo assert — but in the post-Christian age, nothing but that core, that vocation, remains: and so it must become ever less hidden, ever less secret. (Could anything be more illustrative of the simultaneous indigence and ambition of contemporary philosophy than, say, Jean-Luc Nancy's contention that the chief task of thought now is the deconstruction of Christianity?)

And in truth, Western theology made its own, quite substantial contributions to modern "nihilism": when nominalism largely severed the perceptible world from the analogical index of divine transcendence, and thus reduced divine freedom to a kind of ontic voluntarism, and theophany to mere legislation, such that creation and revelation could be imagined only as manifestations of the *will* of a god who is, at most, a supreme being among lesser beings, theology and philosophy alike were surrendered to a kind of elected darkness; and when the nominalists, or those of the *factio occamista* who followed them, succeeded in shattering the unity of faith and reason, and so the compact between theology and philosophy (or as, in an Occamist moment, Luther phrased it, "that whore"), both were rendered blind. In the curious agonies of modernity, once being's beauty, its poetic coherency, no longer enjoyed proper welcome, it became for some (both Catholic and Protestant) more or less axiomatic that faith, to be faith, must be blind; but then reason, to be reason, must be so as well. For theology, of course, this represents an incalculable impoverishment: it contributed to a quite unbiblical dread of the goodness of creation, a misconstrual of divine glory as a supernatural corollary to the majesty of the sheer power of a human monarch, the idolatrous diminution of God to the condition of a composite being — rather than the source of all being — whose acts could, like ours, be indifferently related to his essence, expressing or dissimulating his nature. Revelation, rather than an elevation and glorification of natural knowledge, a Taboric deepening of worldly light till it becomes capable of disclosing its divine source, became a rupture of experience, an alien word, a paradox. Various pietisms and puritanisms could offer no counsel more redemptive than the admonition to look away (for all admiration is mere "lust of the eye"), until the utter imbalance of this revolt against human reason, in all its dialectical extremism, culminated, ironically, in a repetition of Platonism's deepest melancholy (though now no longer wedded to Platonism's levities): despair over our incarceration in the *regio dissimilitudinis*. At a critical moment in cultural history — not that there were not various fateful moves in the history of Western theology that led to it — many Christian thinkers somehow forgot that the incarnation of the Logos, the infinite *ratio* of all that is, reconciles us not only to

God, but to the world, by giving us back a knowledge of creation's goodness, allowing us to see again its essential transparency — even to the point, in Christ, of identity — before God. The covenant of light was broken. God became, progressively, the world's infinite contrary. And this state of theological decline was so precipitous and complete that it even became possible for someone as formidably intelligent as Calvin, without any apparent embarrassment, to regard the fairly lurid portrait of the omnipotent despot of book III of his *Institutes* — who not only ordains the destiny of souls, but in fact predestines the first sin, and so brings the whole drama of creation and redemption to pass (including the eternal perdition of the vast majority of humanity) as a display of his own dread sovereignty — as a proper depiction of the Christian God. One ancient Augustinian misreading of Paul's ruminations upon the mystery of election had, at last, eventuated in fatalism. But whatever the confusions theology subjected itself to at the birth of modernity, Christian thought's betrayal of itself was every bit as grave a diminishment of philosophy; if theology was subjected to the abysmal sublimity of a god of absolute arbitrary will, philosophy was delivered into the hands of his lesser twin, an equally featureless, equally merciless god: the transcendental ego.

The tradition of Christian thought, in radicalizing the eternal beauty of ancient philosophical longing, and in summoning philosophical eros toward a far more transcendent end, left the world groundless in itself and so, in a manner of speaking, gilded the glory of the world with the additional aura of wonderful gratuity and fortuity; the shining — the *phainein* — of the phenomena now belonged to another story, and could no longer provide irrefragable evidence of reason's ability to gain possession of the world's principles. To detach itself from theology, then, and to discover an order of evidences not rendered unstable by the history of its obviously quite successful employment within the discourse of divine transcendence, philosophy had to find for itself another ground. And this could be accomplished only by way of an initial refusal of the world in its immediacy, with all its astonishing allure and terror, and all its insistent apparency; this simple but absolute moment of rejection, inverting the order of truth, moving truth from the world in its appearing to the subject in its perceiving, secured reason's "freedom" perhaps, but also unveiled with extraordinary suddenness that "nihilistic" terminus that Heidegger saw (perhaps fancifully, perhaps not) as having been paradoxically but ineluctably determined in the eidetic science of Platonism. "Now will I close my eyes," writes Descartes, "I will stop up my ears, I will avert my senses from their objects, I will even erase from my consciousness all images of things corporeal; or, at least . . . I will consider them to be empty and false" (*Meditations* III). Surely this austerely principled act of abnegation (or self-mutilation) was, if not the founding gesture of modernity, the supreme crystallization of its unsentimental logic.

Thereafter the trustworthiness of the world could be secured for reflection only within the citadel of subjective certitude, as an act of will.[140] The transcendental turn in philosophy was a turn to instrumental reason as foundation; the truth of the world could no longer be certified by the *phainein* of what gives itself to thought, but only by the adjudications of the hidden artificer of rational order: the ego. Understanding, now indiscerptibly joined to the power of the will to negate and establish, could not now be understanding of a prior givenness, but only a reduction of the exterior to what is answerable to and so manipulable by reason. If philosophy begins in wonder, *thaumazein*, the dazzlement of a gaze lost in the radiance of the given — which provokes vision to ascend into its transcendent splendor, so as to convert wonder into wisdom — it can nonetheless end, it seems, in an anxious retreat from world to self, from wonder to stupefaction, from light to will. Again, it was Christianity's divorce of the light from the myth of necessity that in some sense forced the transcendental option to be made; Christianity's story of transcendent freedom made possible its distorted reflection in a discourse of truth premised upon the subject's rational reconstruction of experience from its own freedom of will; but only a conscious project of immanent reason, independent of any narrative of transcendence that would locate the freedom of truth in the prior givenness of the light, could rescue philosophy from theology's narrative of being as gift. The phenomena had to be made conformable to our gaze, rather than taken as the shining forth of being, provoking our gaze to a rapture beyond itself; wakefulness to transcendence had to be displaced by the "clear-sighted" and disenchanted regime of a controlling scrutiny. When the wakened gaze was transformed into the gaze that establishes, the world could be world only as the *factum* of my intelligence, and the indifferent region of my investigations. The phenomena, when allowed to return, could exist for me only as mensurable quanta; natural light — which has no power to reduce reality to proposition or calculation, but only the power to offer the world to recognition and illumine it as mystery — had no real probative value, but itself was found in need of transcendental certification. And beauty was the very reality that had to be made of no account, diminished to the status of subjective impression or ornamental fancy, deprived of its primordial immediacy and power to rouse thought from its circadian slumber to a prereflective awareness of the mystery and glory of being; the most universally available transcendental had to become the most trivial of the world's quite unquantifiable irrelevancies.

140. This is certainly not a novel genealogy of modern nihilism; it, or something quite like it, is argued in Michael Allen Gillespie, *Nihilism before Nietzsche* (Chicago: University of Chicago Press, 1995), with great energy and to great effect. Not that many aspects of Gillespie's history, and certain of his conclusions, are not very disputable.

True, Descartes himself never intended to seal thought up within an inescapable interiority; he even "discovered" a thought of the infinite that must, he concluded, have been placed in him by God, given its absolute irreconcilability with all finite experience; but in this very discontinuity between empirical knowledge and the concept of the infinite, as he construed them, he gave eloquent expression to the prejudice, by his time quite pervasive, that immanent and transcendent truth are dialectically rather than analogically related, as the former embraces a world of substances that exhaust their meaning in their very finitude while the latter can arrive among these substances only as a self-announcing paradox. God's infinity, in such a scheme, is not truly the infinite — other than every finite thing by being "not other," not another thing, but the possibility and "place" of all things — but merely the negation of finitude, the contrary instance that is nowhere found in my finite cognitions. The thought of the infinite was, from this point on, destined to serve the language of negative determination or subjective autonomy; not only is the infinite beyond seeing, it is without analogous mediation in the seen; no *via eminentiae* can lead from the "what it is" of experience to the "that it is" that gives being to beings and allows them to be seen and thought. A world certified by my founding gaze, and then by God, conceived only as *causa efficiens et causa sui,* can admit the infinite into its calculus only as the indivisible naught that impends upon every real number, the "not-this" that secures every "this" in the poverty of its finite factuality. Inevitably the power of such an "infinite" to disrupt the ordered internal universe of the ego, as it seemed it must for Descartes, could not be sustained; while the distinction between the featureless infinite of the superempirical God and the perceiving ego functioned for Descartes to prove that "I" do not constitute my experience any more primordially than I am constituted by the creative will of a hidden God, it required only the next logically necessary step of distinguishing the empirical ego from the transcendental ego to collapse the distinction between the infinite and subjectivity altogether. This is the singular achievement of Kant. The transcendental project, in its inchoate and insufficiently "critical" form, could escape the circularity of knowledge — the ceaseless and aporetic oscillation of epistemic priority between understanding and experience, between subject and thing — only by positing, beyond empirical ego and empirical data alike, a transcendent cause. But, as Kant certainly saw, this is simply to ground the uncertifiable in the infinitely unascertainable. Nor was it possible for him to retreat to the premodern language of illumination, which would resolve the seeming impossibility of correspondence between perception and the perceived by ascribing their harmony to the supereminent unity in which the poles of experience — phenomena and gaze — already participate; once the possibility of any real evidentiary gravity had been definitively situated within the knowing subject, such a "metaphysics" be-

came a critical impossibility, as it could not be established by the agency of reason in any purely "voluntary" and irreducible sense, but could be seriously en-
tertained as an ultimate answer only by a mind resigned to a condition of active
passivity, a kind of humble surrender to the testimony of a transcendence that,
by definition, cannot be delivered over to the certitudes of an autonomous ego.
And so Kant had no final choice but to arrive at the absolutely metaphysical *decision* to ground the circle of knowledge in a transcendental capacity behind or
within subjectivity; this "transcendental unity of apperception" accompanying
all the representations made available to the empirical ego was, of course, a
metaphysical superaddition to the given, but it was one to which, given the limits of modernity's conjectural range, there was no apparent alternative. Moreover, it assured the subject a transcendence over and mastery of the theoretical,
a supersensible freedom that is, as we have seen, announced in the rupture of
the sublime. In a sense, Kant's "Copernican revolution" might better be called
"Ptolemaic": if Copernicus overthrew the commonsense geocentrism of ancient cosmology by advancing the heliocentric thesis, displacing the center
from "here" to "there," Kant (as an inheritor of the epistemological caesura
such a revolution seems to introduce, more forcibly than Platonism, between
sensibility and verifiable truth) enacted at the transcendental level an entirely
contrary motion, reestablishing the order of knowledge by moving the axis of
truth from the "sun of the good" to the solid, imperturbable *fundamentum
inconcussum* of the *subjectum* (substrate, substance, ground) *transcendentale.*
Now the phenomena would revolve around the unyielding earth of
apperception; again, we would stand at the center.

Perhaps, given the often irreversible forces of historical contingency, all
of this was an unavoidable development in Western philosophy; but purely
from the perspective of philosophical necessity, it was never a critical destiny
for thought as such. Phenomenality, apart from transcendental metaphysics,
need not be seen as, at most, the shimmering veil of the theoretical suspended
between the twin noumenal sublimities of transcendental ego and *Ding an
sich.* Nor need the stability of the "I" be grounded solely in the purity of subjective interiority, rather than in the constancy of the light that forms "me."
And to discover, as Kant did, how much is known before it is known, how
much is presumed a priori in every posterior act of knowledge, is not necessarily to have determined how consciousness constitutes its world — nor, certainly, to have arrived at the vast machinery of the schematism of perception
and the synthesizing energy of imagination — any more than it is to discover
how much of my knowing and how much of the known transcend the consciousness they shape; indeed, such a discovery more properly, with fewer
metaphysical leaps of logic than Kant's epistemology requires, merely declares
again, even more emphatically, that all being and knowing is the work of an ir-

reducible givenness. (Once again, Heidegger almost grasped this, whenever the vulnerable theologian momentarily slipped out of the philosopher's diamantine carapace.) Of course, it is asking too much of transcendental philosophy that it recognize this: what the transcendental ego can understand is so much more limited than the reality visible to the soul. But before modern subjectivity had fully evolved and emerged from the waters, a person was indeed conceived as a living soul, swimming in the deeps, participating in the being of the world, inseparable from the element he or she inhabited and knew; and the soul, rather than the sterile abstraction of an ego, was an entire and unified spiritual and corporeal reality; it was the life and form of the body, encompassing every aspect of human existence, from the nous to the animal functions, uniting reason and sensation, thought and emotion, spirit and flesh, memory and presence, supernatural longing and natural capacity; open before being, a permeable and multiplicit attendance upon the world, it was that in which being showed itself, a logos gathering the light of being into itself, seeing and hearing in the things of the world the logoi of being, allowing them to come to utterance in itself, as words and thought. The soul was the simultaneity of *foro* and *intus,* world and self, faith and understanding. Perhaps such language seems, from the post-Kantian vantage, somewhat less than rigorous; but it certainly requires nothing so elaborate (nor so arbitrary and unconvincing) as the Kantian architectonics of knowledge to sustain it. And what was lost when the soul was forsaken for the self (however one interprets the logic of the move) is the world that the soul could at once dwell in and reflect within itself: the immediate impress of beauty, splendor, otherness both familiar and inviolably other, the desire this provokes, the overwhelming and strangely articulate address of its radiance, its inviting transcendence. In reality, subjective certitude cannot be secured, not because the world is nothing but the aleatory play of opaque signifiers, but because subjective certitude is an irreparably defective model of knowledge; it cannot correspond to or "adequate" a world that is gratuity rather than ground, poetry rather than necessity, rhetoric rather than dialectic. Every act of knowledge is, simultaneously, an act of faith (to draw on Hamann's delightful subversion of Hume); we trust in the world, and so know it, only by entrusting ourselves to what is more than ourselves; our primordial act of faith meets a covenant that has already been made with us, before we could seek it, in the giving of the light. No one can shut his eyes to that splendor, or seal his ears against that music, except as a perverse display of will; then, naturally, knowledge can be recovered again only as an exertion of that same will. But one then has not merely lost the world momentarily, so as to receive it anew as "truth." One has lost the world and its truth altogether, and replaced them with a phantom summoned up out of one's need for a world conformable to the dimensions of one's own power to establish meaning — a world that is nothing but the ceaseless repetition of otherwise meaningless instantiations of that power.[141]

In any event, it was not the destiny of Western thought simply to rest, secure and contented in the citadel of the self, gazing out over its turrets at the picturesque vistas of a world of close horizons and limpid views, purged of metaphysical mystery; the first great convulsion of philosophy's long and violent recoil from its "Christian interruption" culminated in Hegel, who saw that worldly reason would always be in retreat if it could not overcome theology's metaphysical strategies and enfold them within itself, and so who (in modern theology's most annoying irony) went about recovering the rationality of classical trinitarian doctrine from the forgetfulness in which generations of theologians had allowed it to lie, so that he could rethink it, turn it inside out, and bring its strange and disruptive energies under the government of Western metaphysics. This aspect of the history of "nihilism" is too little recognized. Hegel was engaged not only in the venerable metaphysical task of subordinating difference to the Same, nor even only in the impossible task of bringing under speculative control the radical historicality that Christian theology unleashed within the "absolute" (though certainly this), but in an attempt to overcome a final and irreducible difference that Christian thought had imagined within God; the historicization of Spirit functioned not only to "spiritualize" history but to idealize the three-personed God of theology, by making God and history a mutually sustaining and orderly process: idealized history as the unitive measure of God and God as the logic of history; Hegel was out to subdue not only Dionysus, but the Trinity. Indeed, the Dionysian gets considerable free play in Hegel, in the guise of the irrecuperable surd of *mere* particularity, or of the bad infinite, or indeed of the very energy of truth's dialectic ("Das Wahre ist so der bacchantische Taumel," as the preface of the *Phenomenology* notoriously announces, "an dem kein Glied nicht trunken ist" — ¶47): within any metaphysical scheme that aspires to encompass the totality of reality in the inevitability of its logic, Dionysus is in some form a necessary dramatis persona, as the meaningless and chaotic exterior of being, or as its inmost tragic mystery. What Hegel could not abide, though, was the notion either of a God who possesses within himself differentiation, determination, community, joy, and perfection in complete liberty from the world, or of a world left thus devoid of meaning in the ultimate speculative sense of "necessity" and so "reduced" to a

---

141. Perhaps the most immediately suggestive aspect of the huge theological trilogy of Hans Urs von Balthasar is the great reversal it effects — simply in its sequence — of Kant: it entirely inverts the order of the three Critiques, starting from an aesthetics in the light of which practical reason then appears as a dramatic theory, concluding in a treatise on theological reason whose purview has been determined in advance by an account of the priority of divine beauty.

"needless" and thoroughly aesthetic reality: as an unforced, *additional* expression of the love that God enjoys in absolute self-sufficiency. Hegel's trinity is the God of totality, and the Hegelian system is a war of totality against the Christian infinite, against a theology that makes difference and its endless serial particularity good in itself, embraced by a divine boundlessness that is not altered by or involved within a more essential core to history and its tragic probations. Divine infinity, conceived as trinitarian, already differential and determinate, requires no determination *within* being, and so makes of all created being an unnecessary, *excessive* display of its glory precisely by setting difference free in its "aimless" particularity. The Christian infinite is its own exteriority, without need of another, negative exteriority to bring it to fruition; even evil is only a privation, a tergiversation from being, a nothingness given shape by a desire that gives itself shape only as the rejection of love. And without the majestic mythology of necessity governing the realm of the absolute, the comforting pathos of necessity disappears from the realm of history too. The thought of the Christian infinite — in which difference is always difference, beauty always beauty, and in which peace and being are equiprimordial — leaves philosophy bereft of any final power of adjudication over history and history bereft of any inner structure of tragic rationality. Theology disfranchises the philosopher, and exposes Dionysus as a bore.

This is no less an intellectual bereavement for post-Hegelian, "post-metaphysical" forms of philosophy; it is no more unthinkable a state of affairs for Hegel than Heidegger, for instance, whose thought cannot do without the necessity of being's event, its necessary limitation within the dispensations of its epochal sending, its "finitude." The most irenic *Gelassenheit* of the philosopher is still pervaded by the sadness of fate, and must be so: only in letting be what must be, in its mission and its errance, its clarity and duplicity, can the philosopher hear the voice of being "pealing softly" in the "fourfold." And Heidegger's spiritual progeny, however they might amplify his language of the event and the temporality of being, are no less bound to fate's whims. Nancy's certainty of the sealed immanence of world, for example, and of the pure superficiality of the event of "presence," for all its *joie de mourir*, serves only to advance, within the narrow confines still available to "postmetaphysical" reason, a new myth of necessity, a new version of the tragic and dialectical ontology that limits the world to what metaphysical scrutiny can certify. Thus his understanding of Kant's analytic of the sublime as an account of the rupture that occurs at the border of presentation, the play of limitation and unlimitation that yields that anticipated figure to which reason offers itself up: form is the frozen figuration left in the aftermath of an original alienation, and so in its finitude can speak only of itself, and can speak of being only in its annihilation. Once again the event of world and thought can be stated only as sacrifice, as an original economy sustaining order over against (but in dependency on) chaos — but it cannot be conceived as gift, as the donation of form, a radiance that meets us as the gratuity of a still always more eminent splendor that *limits itself*, not out of necessity, but according to the kenotic and ecstatic love of the *bonum summum et splendissimum*. For any truly postmodern discourse the myth must be guarded: there is an invisible excess to be revered, feared, appeased, obeyed, fled to, embraced as energy, resisted ethically — but always dealt with sacrificially. But this brings the argument back to where this part of the book began, and begins to touch upon questions that will be addressed below.

Suffice it to say here that only in having broken from or interrupted the history of Western thought did theology open up the prospect of a peace otherwise unimaginable: one not bought at the price of restraint, or ethical flight, or abstraction, or reduction, or death, or an enervating distrust of vision and speech. The properly Christian thought of difference as harmonizable (not synthesizable), without any residue of inassimilable or tragic contradiction, remains possible (even in this postmodern hour) precisely because the regime of abstract essences was long ago abandoned, the immemorial anxiety regarding the "grounds" of identity was stilled. In the light of Christian reflection, one knows oneself as a creature, an instance of grace, a "groundless" overflow of God's glory; one knows that one does not emanate from the absolute, but rather has been called from nothingness into the infinite — which embraces all manifestations of being as "paratactic" moments in the unfolding discourse of divine splendor, as analogous enunciations of a divine rhetoric, without reducing them to pure, lifeless ideas. Being is not a welter of images from which essences must be wrested in an action of noetic rarefaction on the one hand, nor a chaos of the unthematizable on the other, but is an unmasterable beauty boundless in its variations. Every instance of being, *as this particular being,* equally declares God's glory. In a sense, this is the closest theology comes to the concern for difference in the Deleuzean doctrine of univocity; one might almost speak of a univocity of glory, except that divine glory is an infinite display of analogical differentiation. What one can most definitely say, though, is that there is a final indistinction between being and beauty in this way of thinking. And beauty does not "essentialize" (essences are supremely anaesthetic), but remains always at the surface: in closely wrought details, elaborate devices, suavities of style, immensities and fragilities, grandeurs and graces; it is the "eloquence" of being, which reveals being's gratuity. The only "sublime" in this vision is the sheer illimitability of this eloquence. This is why one can speak here properly of a rhetorical ontology, a story of being which grants neither chaos nor idea priority, but which dissolves both in the freely flowing (and so analogical) "expressionism" of a creative God of love.

And if the Christian infinite is not a formless and indeterminate sublime, over against the finite, that arrests beauty and relegates it to the realm of triviality and deceit, but is actually always the donation of the finite, an eventuation of beauty, a display of gifts, whose being is a peaceful gesture, both creating and crossing the distance, then there is a Christian discourse of being that requires neither the acceptance of war nor the abandonment of history, that eludes all the gods of totality, of the city or the waste. The passage through time may be conceived as the transmission of difference as gift, not the "original violence" that permits the approach to the other, and the mediation of thought and language may be conceived not simply as a reduction of alterity to the Same, but as a charitable venture, in accord with an infinite that reveals itself as beauty, and hence the continuous *enrichment* of difference through peaceful supplementation and discovery. If the infinite is already the beautiful, and beauty really is the manifestation of being's truth, then an infinity of rhetorical adornments, properly ordered, cannot obscure or dissemble that truth; rhetoric alone can "correspond to" or "disclose" the rhetoric of being, so long as its style and the desire that most fundamentally orients its endless deferrals aspire to the charity that gives the world: for then its every "needless" conceit is ever more true. In the Christian narrative of being, there is the possibility of a community of difference where all transitions and intervals may be so understood, so given and so received, as to be a sharing of goods and a setting free; the dynamism of such a being together is that of *epektasis* (the Pauline image, read through Gregory of Nyssa): an outstretched and constantly changing love and progress toward and within the divine infinity, within which all finitude is released in the radiance of its differing — not the opiate beauty of Dionysian dissolution or the static beauty of Apollonian order, but a trinitarian beauty that is motile, various, creative, abundant in signs of peace. The violence of finitude may often be unavoidable, but it is never *necessary*.

Which — to return again to the issue of postmodern "ethics" and its ambiguities, and tensions, and interminable hesitations — is why theology should not worry itself inordinately over certain questions regarding the ego's gnoseological indelicacies, or allow itself to fall prey to certain inhibitions on account of the ego's indiscretion in encountering others and presuming to "know" them. After all, the disagreement between Levinas and Derrida over the ethical implications of phenomenology's appresentative analogy, which in a sense "reduces" the other to an alternate self, in no way weakens their more fundamental agreement on the premise that such an analogy constitutes an original violence, because each still speaks (however he might protest) within the context of an epistemological tradition that understands knowledge as a representation of essences accomplished by the cognitive will of a subjective consciousness. But why place the priority of understanding here, where only a Cartesian ego or a Kantian transcendental subjectivity would be pleased to find it?

This is, if nothing else, inept phenomenology: an epistemology premised on subjective intentionality alone is, at the end of the day, mere "psychologism"; only if one imagines that the appresentative analogy is the achievement of a self-subsistent ego, at once empirical and transcendental, simply returning to itself in its intention, representing the world to itself under the inflexible legislations of the apparatus of perception, and so filtering being through the alien medium of consciousness, is this question of "violence" so terribly pressing. A profounder phenomenology, and a more searching attention to the conditions of knowledge, would not begin from this crudely mechanistic model of thought, or admit into its logic this idea of a magical transaction between world and consciousness. The event of the world and the event of thought cannot be so brutally separated; the self *occurs* as the manifestation of the world, the event of being; all knowledge is indeed intentional, which means, precisely, not only that all thought has an object, but that, as a consequence, thought belongs to being's disclosure of itself. Before the subject can be a conqueror of the other's alterity, then, in what would be a strictly *secondary* moment of violence, the subject is already a recipient and, so, creature of a gift: an aesthetic effect. This is cognition's "phenomenological circle": the intention that "precedes" all perception is also an intention already "invited" by the splendor of concrete form, already awakened by the aesthetic exteriority of otherness, the beauty of the other, which informs intention in the intentional act, shapes and summons it, as an obsecration of a subjectivity that *is* only in being opened — formed — by the light of the other; one's "self" is that "matter" in which beauty impresses itself, that "place" where the light of the other, and of all being, shines, gathered in a reflective surface of incalculably various sensitivity (the physical senses, thought, imagination, anticipation, memory, desire, fear . . .). What is given in any knowledge is not only the "thing known," as delivered over to the "knowing mind," but the entire circle of the event that is being and knowledge (what theology calls the gift of illumination, flowing from the supereminent coincidence of knowledge and being in the Trinity). There is, then, no "ethical" need to leave the other suspended between the superintentional darkness of blind obligation and the imprisoning representations of an imperious ego, unable to show himself or herself. All true otherness appears only under the form of an analogical difference; this, though, does not mean a difference simply dissoluble within the abstraction of resemblance, but rather one sustained in proffering itself — and so becoming itself — according to a shared dwelling in the light that gives being, a common grammar of love and delight, of beauty. This allows the other *to be* and *be other*, to shine, to vary me in my recognition of his or her otherness. And thus the "self" also appears or becomes in this event, as an alternate other, sustained in its difference by an aesthetic analogy of the other's radiant particularity — like in beauty, unlike in beauty; the other being thus received and the self thus fashioned, the phenomenological apperceptive analogy may be regarded as a peaceful supplement that redonates a "self" that is already a gift of the other's beauty. The style of receiving is all, knowing the other as a gift really given, peacefully imparted. This requires no necessary reduction to the Same, but rather eyes to see and ears to hear.

And what one sees and hears, if desire seeks it, is the creature's participation in God, the fountainhead of being. The beauty there in the other, in the otherness of the other, is embraced in an infinity that affords limitless scope for creation's differences within its always fuller harmony, and both one and one's other are intervals, inflections, reciprocally constitutive modulations of the same, shared music of infinite analogical expression, inhabiting the same endlessly various distance of divine glory. The other is not therefore *originally* an idol of thought, but an icon in which the infinite is pleased uniquely to disclose itself. And so the most original apprehension of the other lies in the beauty of rhetoric, which truly reflects the other, because the other really is first and foremost an inflection of a freely self-giving and infinite glory (a divine rhetoric); and because one is oneself such an inflection, given form and scope by the infinite array of differences that otherwise articulate that glory, the mediation between one and one's other — the rhetoric — need not be alienation or reduction, but can be growth, emergence, invocation, and delight: the gesture of peace. One is, to use the imagery of Gregory of Nyssa, a vessel that expands in receiving the infinite *(vide infra)*, which offers itself in an infinitely various series of icons. Being is not simply a bare category indifferently embracing an endless plurality of arbitrary instances; it is the fullness and unity of all determinacy in the Trinity, unfolding its light in the unity and diversity of beings, composing endless and endlessly coinherent variations on an infinite theme (not, that is, a theme to which the whole is somehow reducible, an "essential" meaning, but a theme in the musical sense, which is itself in its display of supplementation, variation, and difference). If being and truth are conceived as already rhetorical, if truth is ultimately aesthetic — a style, a unity of form and message, having no separable essence or content for dialectic to pry loose — then peace may be the true name of being: the distance of the other, crossed by the rhetorical *excess* of the other, may awaken one to the truth of the other as long as one can receive that excess as glory. One could not stand here at a farther remove from the Levinasian understanding of the exteriority of the face, which for him must of necessity be seen as a trace, an effaced face, absent from itself and every context, from all being and all light. The face of the other, for Christian eyes, must of necessity be visible *only* in the peculiarities of its features, and only within an unforeclosable sequence of perspectives and supplementations; it is always an aesthetic event. The other is "placed" within being, within the infinite, not as a mere localized essence, but as a unique and so adequate expression of the infinite. The other has a world, and therefore the world has in him or her a face. This is not to deny the reality of the secret, the inviolable alterity that always transcends the grasp of intention; but it is to suggest that this alterity is expressed and opened, in an always deepening way, by the sheer rhetoric of the other's exteriority, and, moreover, that the "secret" is nothing so empty as the impenetrable enigma of the "wholly other," but is rather the ever greater splendor of the other's participation in God's infinity. The other's interiority is really an inexhaustible openness, an always more eminent phenomenality, an ever fuller reflection of the Trinity's infinitely achieved exteriority. Seen truly, as a living *soul* (the *forma corporis et vita,* to provide the correct definition again) mirroring a light that fills and exceeds it, the other always reveals infinitely more precisely in eluding my grasp, and to cease seeing more is to lose the other. Violence, thus, arises only as a result of a desire not ordered toward the other as love because not directed ultimately toward God's infinity; for only in his light do we truly see.

If it seems that, in using such language, I am merely advocating a return to philosophical naïveté, making a theological virtue out of a truculent impatience with modern thought's critical rigor, and attempting to represent rhapsody as reason, I can say only that it is not until one adequately recognizes the degree of sheer faith that inheres in every employment of reason that one can turn again to recognize what degree of rationality is or is not present in any given act of faith. It is true that I want to defend a theological reappropriation of what I have called the "covenant of light" — a trust in the evidence of the given, an understanding of knowledge as an effect of the eros stirred by the gift of the world's truth — but this is because (among other things) I wish to see modern theology free itself from any superstitious adherence to the arid dogmatisms of transcendental logic (modern or postmodern). What is the noumenal freedom that the sublime adumbrates, or the noumenon that sensibility never reaches, or the "chaosmos" that only a dissonant *sentiendum* announces, or the event that representation occludes, or *différance* — and so on — but an empty concept, an object of simple irrational fideism? To move from the thought that there may be that which exceeds knowing to the conclusion that all knowledge is representation, dissimulating this invisible excess, and that the tragic dialectic between appearance and hiddenness is the event of absolute qualitative contradiction, is to allow one's reflections to be governed by a kind of pure, unreflective religious sentimentality. I believe that what, in part, I mean to advocate is simply a phenomenology liberated from transcendental stricture: beginning from the phenomenological presuppositions that being is what shows itself, and that the event of the phenomenon and the event of perception are inseparable, I wish nonetheless to say that only a transcendental prejudice would dictate in advance that one may not see (or indeed does not see) in the event of manifestation and in the simultaneity of phenomenon and perception a light that exceeds them as an ever more eminent phenomenality: not only the hidden faces of a given object, or the lovely dynamism of visible and invisible in presentation, but the descending incandescence and clarity of the infinite coincidence of all that grants world and knower one to the other. This is not to say that one can simply deduce Christian metaphysics from empirical perception, obviously; but it is to insist that such a metaphysics is scarcely the founding of the visible in the simply invisible, of the immanent in a merely posited transcendence: rather it is a way of seeing that refuses to see more — or less — than what is given. It is a passage to the infinite that does not depart from the beautiful to pass through the paradox of the sublime toward the featureless abyss of an otherness available only to reason, but one that attempts to advance into the beautiful forever, finding the world ever more fully even as one enters into its transcendent truth. To use the language of Maximus the Confessor, it attempts to see in everything its logos: that is, its essential openness to the Logos, to the transcendent light of infinite being — an openness that gives every being its being, an openness "displacing" the nothingness from which every being is called (though, as Maximus would say, only perfect love is capable of such vision). Even if it were not my contention (which it is) that this "metaphysics" is intrinsic to Christianity, and that without it theology cannot be complete and biblical revelation cannot be fully understood, unfolded, or preserved, I would still say that the theologian must always proceed according to the essential attitude of such a "transcending" phenomenology: an initial trust in the goodness and veracity of being, a self-surrendering availability before the testimony of creation (always, of course, embraced within and consummated by an even more essential faith in God revealed in Christ). Why is it, after all, that one can speak meaningfully and intelligibly of beauty, in any instance of experience, though one is not referring to any discrete object alongside the object of attention? How is it that one may say that a thing is beautiful and another recognize the truth or error of the remark, understanding in either case what has been said? It is, I want to say, because beauty — which is no thing among things — is being itself, the movement of being's disclosure, the eloquence by which everything, properly and charitably regarded, says infinitely more than itself. Beauty is the transcendence of being in the gift of the immanent, and so my intendings are never adequate to the fullness of its address, to the ever greater meaning that I do not constitute but that always constitutes me, within my desire. The experience of the beautiful is the sudden intimation of the fortuity of necessity, of the contingency of a thing's integrity; it is an awe that awakens one to the difference of being from beings, of "existence" from "essence," allowing one to see within the very concord, within their difference, of any phenomenon and its event a fittingness that is also grace. This is an original agitation, a discovery not of a sublime "beyond" the beautiful or qualitatively different from beauty, but the sublime within beauty, a surfeit of splendor that demands wonder. One then sees that though the "what it is" of anything is never commensurate to the delightful or terrible truth "that it is," it is always good (though sin and death may distort any object and any vision of it) that this is *this,* and that this *is.* And this mysterious coherence of the wholly fitting and utterly gratuitous urges reflection toward the proportion of their harmony: toward, that is, the infinity where "essence" and "existence" coincide as the ontological peace of both a primordial belonging and an original gift. Thus the experience of beauty is a knowledge of creatureliness and a hunger that can never have done with the things of earth. It is also an insatiable hunger for God. Apart from the language of beauty, then, and all it may allow one to say, theology becomes destitute and fruitless. Only with regard to beauty and the "openness to being" it both answers and provokes, can Christian thought say adequately how it is that the Light that "shineth in darkness" is also "the true Light, which lighteth every man that cometh into the world."

This, of course, is the most crucial issue. Again, Christ (God's full and everlasting Word) is a persuasion, a form — incalculably various in the facets he shows — offered outward to the world as the real shape of creation, the true grammar of being. He stands precariously within human understanding, on the far side of Lessing's ditch, intractable to abstraction, and yet in all his particularity extending himself to human eyes and minds as the way, the truth, and the life. His beauty, if grasped, is the true story of being, told from before the foundations of the world to the end of time. But this means that Christ must have real aesthetic force; he must be able to appear not as a docetic phantom, nor even as only an impossible possibility, but as a real and appealing form of being, a way of dwelling among others, a kind of practice. It is not enough to say Christ "happened": he must be available to vision, as a concrete shape and motion that it is still possible to extend, to compose variations upon, to reappropriate and rearticulate: in Christ, in the practice of Christ as a real style — a real presence — within history, one must be able to taste and see that the Lord is good. As I have argued, totality — pagan, Hegelian, Nietzschean, postmodern — simply cannot grasp Christ as powerful in his powerlessness, cannot interpret him except as an evanescence. But Christ is no beautiful soul; nor does he come to the rescue of *Sittlichkeit* and its ethics of responsible action; he comes as the fire of the infinite, proclaiming another kingdom, another order, a story of being at odds with that of the totality he overcomes. To accept Christ as a real and appearing beauty, capable of assuming and sustaining his shape within time, is to be confronted by the limitations of the aesthetic of totality, its wearisome motifs of the hero, the peasant, and the occasional beautiful soul; the beauty Christ discloses remains invisible to anyone who finds beauty in a violent stilling of violence, in tragic grandeur lifted up above the squalor of creaturely abjection. Christian beauty is also a hidden beauty, prior to all "essentialist" representations, a messianic secret, a *kenosis*. The form of Christ, whose appeal requires a real response, enjoins a love that alone reveals a beauty more primordial — and more prodigally bestowed — than Apollonian armistice. The God who goes to the outermost of being, in the form of a slave, and even past the limits of being into the silence of death, but who then nevertheless — and in just this particular and "slavish" shape — offers himself anew as a radiant and indestructible beauty, forever present in the midst of those who love him, has violated all Apollonian order and, at the same time, left no room for the Dionysian to occupy: the madness, turmoil, chaos, and cruelty of being, the ungovernable violence of the pagan infinite and postmodern sublime, is shown to be falsehood, lying everlastingly under the damnation of the cross, because the infinite that *is* has crossed all the boundaries of totality (even death, its defining horizon) and remained — forever — form. Nietzsche has every right to be appalled. Christian rhetoric, therefore, offers Christ *as* rhetoric, as beauty, but also as presence, mediated aesthetically by an endless parataxis of further "statements" for just that reason all the more present (a presence that *is* rhetoric cannot be estranged from itself or made remote by the interminable deferral of rhetoric, so long as the *style* of its excess is sustained); the church's only task is to enact and offer this form. As the story of Thomas's doubt emphasizes, the resurrection of Christ imparts anew the real presence of this same Jesus of Nazareth, and in the power of the Holy Spirit he draws ever nearer, becomes ever more present, in an ever greater display of the various power of his presence.[142] This is a beauty that does not hover over or beyond history, recalled as privation and hoped for simply as futurity, but pervades time as a music that now even the most frenetic din of violence cannot drown out.

Which brings these pages back, at long last, to the question posed in the introduction: Can the Christian evangel of peace advance itself rhetorically, as beauty, in such a way as to make that peace real? Can the beauty of Christian

---

142. All of this will be argued more fully below, but I should note here my general suspicion of theologies of the presence of Christ in the church that place it under the form of absence or withdrawal, or of the "degree zero of a series," such as one associates with certain of the works of Michel de Certeau or Eberhard Jüngel: see especially Jüngel, "The Effectiveness of Christ Withdrawn: On the Process of Historical Understanding as an Introduction to Christology," in *Theological Essays*, ed. J. B. Webster (Edinburgh: T. & T. Clark, 1989). The "Objective Evidence" section of Balthasar's *The Glory of the Lord: A Theological Aesthetics*, vol. 1, *Seeing the Form*, trans. Erasmo Leiva-Merikakis (San Francisco: Ignatius, 1982), 429-683, is, to my mind, a far better model of Christ's presence in history, in the power of the Spirit, and a far richer reading of the pneumatology of Christ's "valedictory" discourse in John's Gospel.

rhetoric narrate itself in perfect consonance with the story of ontological peace that it advances, or will it fall prey to contradiction? Is the "gift" of evangelical appeal a peaceful gesture, or is it the most devious strategy of power, a violence that dissembles itself in order to persuade for persuasion's sake? Can its gift (eschatological peace really present in time) be given? To this point, I have merely given an abstract précis of an ontological discourse, but I have not as yet unfolded it as belonging to the very rationality of the Christian story, present without contradiction throughout, communicable without betrayal of its essence, and able to survive the incredulities and suspicions of our age.

This is by no means a simple affair; the problem of violence raised by postmodernism's implicit ontology is marvelously manifold in the manner of its appearance: as the wielding of a metaphysical mandate to colonize peoples and inscribe its power in docile bodies; as Socratic dialectic, which cunningly conceals its rhetorical and figural basis and acts out an asymptotic approach to a forever receding line of "rational" truth so as to overcome the other, to steal the ground from beneath and so subdue the other by an "impersonal" appeal to reason; as the power of Hegelian dialectic to absorb otherness into its historical teleology of total gnosis *(Aufhebung* as *Verdauung);* as, again, the Hegelian necessity of negation; as any metaphysical scheme's attempt to incarcerate otherness in the taxonomies of extractable "essences"; as the use of ethical "principles" to legitimate "benign" regimes or measures of restraint; as the unambiguous aggressions of persecution, trial, terror, torture, war, coercion, and retribution; as the mythology of sacrifice and the ascetic suppression of life. Moreover, from the theological vantage, postmodern discourse compounds the issue with its own violences: its tale of being as a cosmic agon, principally, and all the strange ways it recapitulates the evils it denounces: the way in which Deleuze and Guattari, attempting to describe the living of a nonfascist life, reinvent the nihilistic aesthetics of Marinetti or Jünger, or in which Lyotard and Derrida unreflectively revert to a classical liberal narrative of difference whose only real embodiment must be an imposition of certain Western prejudices regarding the limits of meaningful discourse upon all other narratives, or in which Foucault succumbs to his own narrative of power so thoroughly that the only political hope he can enunciate is the rescue of autonomous arbitrary will from collective arbitrary will (which, by his own account, is really impossible), or in which all of them repeat without fail a narrative of being wherein the ethical occurs as an inexplicable nostalgia, and whereby either fascism, unrestrained capitalism, or Stalinism might be just as plausibly advanced. Nor does the postmodern escape the tendency to fashion its own analogy of cosmos, city, and soul: the image of being as force makes political arrangements first and foremost a confluence of powers, not really a possible grammar of accords, and the freedom of the self power unleashed; the univocity of being is an image that portrays difference formally, through the inanition of differential content, and so — by refusing to allow any analogical disruptions of the plane of immanence — inevitably arranges being homogenously, as formally uniform instances of punctiliar difference which must be governed as equally inviolable and equally dangerous quanta of force (that is, a state conceived as a coincidence of individual forces of will is always one or another kind of homogenizing police state, in ways it would require a Foucaultian acuity to enumerate). Confronted by so many mutations of the problem, the need for theology to demonstrate that its rhetoric can span all things without violence, according to a beauty whose appeal is not adventitious to its narrative but present continuously and without contradiction in its every moment, could not be more pronounced.

To be clear on this matter: the critique of the Christian tradition that postmodern discourse inherits from Nietzsche and never abandons is twofold: firstly, Christianity is a "totalizing" discourse that enacts a metaphysical violence against difference, and does so through an evangel of peace that dissembles its appetite for power; and secondly, given that the truth of being (rarely explicitly so called) is differential strife, Christianity is ontologically impossible in its own terms, but must be a rhetoric of conquest straining to fill out the form of an ephemeral dream, a Christ whose renunciation of power makes of him a historical nullity and an aesthetic absence. Theologians who fall to either side of this critique, either by denying the rhetorical essence of theology or by accepting the postmodern vision of being as a violence from which Christ withdraws, but who nevertheless wish to remain apologists for the faith, are condemned on one hand to repeat an ever more metaphysical discourse of dialectical "truth" (which is fruitless), or on the other to become unworldly, even gnosticizing Christians, seeking to imitate the withdrawal of Christ as a flight to an impossible realm beyond history. There is a third way, which accepts the irretrievability of purely dialectical "truth" but still rejects the metaphysical assumptions of postmodernity, and this is the way of theological aesthetics. Persuasion is always intrinsically violent only if there is a truth (power) more basic than what appears in the figural play of language; if being is figural play, and originally peaceful, one may conceive of peaceful persuasion; if beauty is the truth more primordial than strife, then beauty does not dissemble but restores the face of being. And, moreover, if the measure of truth is the correspondence of beings not to fixed ideas but to an infinite beauty whose form is the agape freely shared within the Trinity, known by way of participation, by renewing the gesture of that love, and if truth is the peaceful event of being's limitless difference, as variations on a beauty that infinitely differentiates, rather than an essence toward which dialectic must make an endless selective nisus, then there is no need to answer the Nietzschean critique by any means other than a fuller theological narrative and charitable practice: Christian thought need only show it enucleates a beauty that is anything but incidental, but which is narrated continuously, necessarily, and coherently throughout its story *as rhetoric* and *as peace.*

Within Christian theology there is a thought — a story — of the infinite that is also the thought — the story — of beauty; for pagan philosophy and culture, such a confluence of themes was ultimately unthinkable. Even Plotinian Neoplatonism, which brought the Platonic project to its most delightful completion by imagining infinity as an attribute of the One, was nonetheless compelled to imagine the beauty of form as finally subordinate to a formless and abstract simplicity, devoid of internal relation, diminished by reduction to particularity, polluted by contact with matter's "absolute evil"; nor could later Neoplatonism very comfortably allow that the One was also infinite being, but typically placed being only in the second moment of emanation, not only because the One, if it were also Being, would constitute a bifid form, but because being is always in some sense contaminated by or open to becoming, to movement, and thus is, even in the very splendor of its overflow, also a kind of original contagion, beginning as an almost organic ferment in the noetic realm and ending in the death of matter. Christian thought — whose infinite is triune, whose God became incarnate, and whose account of salvation promises not liberation from, but glorification of, material creation — can never separate the formal particularity of beauty from the infinite it announces, and so tells the tale of being in a way that will forever be a scandal to the Greeks. For their parts, classical "metaphysics" and postmodernism belong to the same story; each, implying or repeating the other, conceives being as a plain upon which forces of meaning and meaninglessness converge in endless war; according to either, being is known in its oppositions, and oppositions must be overcome or affirmed, but in either case as violence: amid the strife of images and the flow of simulacra, shining form appears always only as an abeyance of death, fragile before the convulsions of chaos, and engulfed in fate. There is a specular infinity in mutually defining opposites: Parmenides and Heracleitos gaze into one another's eyes, and the story of being springs up between them; just as two mirrors set before one another prolate their depths indefinitely, repeating an opposition that recedes forever along an illusory corridor without end, seeming to span all horizons and contain all things, the dialectic of Apollo and Dionysus oscillates without resolution between endless repetitions of the same emptiness, the same play of reflection and inversion. But the true infinite lies outside and all about this enclosed universe of strife and shadows; it shows itself as beauty and as light: not totality, nor again chaos, but the music of a triune God. Nietzsche prophesied correctly: what now always lies ahead is a choice between Dionysus (who is also Apollo) and the Crucified: between, that is, the tragic splendor of totality and the inexhaustible beauty of an infinite love.

PART 2

The Beauty of the Infinite

A *Dogmatica Minora*

To speak too freely of *the* Christian narrative, without any more specific frame of reference, is either to grant oneself unlimited license to rove through theological history or to condemn oneself to forty years' wandering. To escape, therefore, both the temptation of the genteel tourist's liberty and the peril of the encyclopedist's interminable exile in the desert of historical particularity, I shall proceed in strict reliance upon the most elementary and binding canon of catholic confession, the Nicene-Constantinopolitan symbol (in its unadulterated Greek form); as the authoritative précis of the faith of catholic orthodoxy, East and West, to which subsequent councils were answerable, it allows a vantage upon the broad main current of the Christian tradition and its canonical interpretation of Scripture, but forbids too unbridled a dash into the hermeneutical open spaces. Further to limit my inquiry, I shall address the creed in four discrete moments: Trinity, creation, salvation, and eschaton. This order, it might be noted, arguably reverses the historical sequence of doctrinal development: it was in the eschatological light of the risen Christ's lordship over history, grasped with such consuming immediacy by the early church, that thought regarding the nature of salvation originally began to achieve any degree of theological clarity; and as a result of its meditation upon the mystery of salvation, the church soon came to an understanding of the roles of the Son and Spirit in creation and to, in the course of time, the doctrine of God's Trinity. The contents of the creed do not constitute simply some system of metaphysical affirmations, but first and foremost a kind of "phenomenology of salvation"; the experience of redemption — of being joined by the Spirit to the Son and through the Son to the Father — was the ground from which the church's doctrinal grammar arose. To begin thus, then, from the creed, is to assume a certain critical distance, without yet presuming to attempt to withdraw to a place of advantage, outside of and no longer responsible to the tradition. This "minor dogmatics" takes the heritage of Nicene and Chalcedonian orthodoxy as the proper environment of its inquiry; any subsequent modification of or retreat from the narrative will be disregarded as local, arbitrary, elective, and aberrant in nature, perhaps conceded the status of a legitimate theologoumenon, but accorded neither authority nor very much attention. This is mere prudence.

Two other observations should be made. The first is that, perhaps on account of some perversity of authorial temperament, this essay in "dogmatic theology" (a term that should indicate a style of theology that does not reduce the faith to a series of discrete propositions) is undertaken by way of a sequence of theses; this is done only to render both orderly and concise a great variety of topics. There is no systematic or deductive sequence to these theses; they constitute a series of interrelated but also somewhat independent interpretive vantages upon the essential matter. I confess that this will be a rather deliberate and often repetitive way of advancing my argument, one that will proceed by steps but will also occasionally double back to reassert a theme with a new resonance and, I hope, greater clarity. Moreover (and this concerns method), I shall make no attempt to construct a critical history of these theological loci; documentation will vary, from section to section, according to the peculiar logic and requirements of each given thesis.

The second observation is that the title I have given this small dogmatics is a condensed statement of my argument. Briefly: to speak of the "infinity of beauty" would call attention to nothing extraordinary; there are many senses in which such a phrase might convey some commonly accepted meaning: as mere romantic hyperbole, as a reference to the indeterminate surplus of suggestiveness inhabiting any beautiful object, as indicating the inexhaustibility of delight or mystery inhering in the experience of beauty, and so on. But to speak of the beauty of the infinite is genuinely to name the Christian difference in aesthetics, a thought of the beautiful inconceivable in the terms available to non-Christian philosophy, ancient and modern alike. In the story the church tells concerning God and his creatures, beauty and infinity both are narrated as nowhere else, in such a way as to show how each belongs to the "grammar" of the other, and how both belong to a common language of delight and peace.

I. TRINITY

---

1. The Christian understanding of beauty emerges not only naturally, but necessarily, from the Christian understanding of God as a *perichoresis* of love, a dynamic coinherence of the three divine persons, whose life is eternally one of shared regard, delight, fellowship, feasting, and joy.

And there came a voice from heaven, saying, Thou art my beloved Son, in whom I am well pleased.

Mark 1:11

And the Holy Ghost descended in a bodily shape like a dove upon him, and a voice came from heaven, which said, Thou art my beloved Son; in thee I am well pleased.

Luke 3:22

Every good gift and every perfect gift is from above, and cometh down from the Father of lights, with whom is no variableness, neither shadow of turning.

James 1:17

This then is the message which we have heard of him, and declare unto you, that God is light, and in him is no darkness at all.

1 John 1:5

i. Divine *Apatheia*

In *Mysterium Salutis* Karl Rahner enunciates a simple formula that should be regarded as axiomatic for all meditation upon the Christian doctrine of God: "The 'economic' trinity is the 'immanent' trinity and the 'immanent' trinity is the 'economic' trinity."[1] The modern return of Western systematic theology to the doctrine of the Trinity — to many eyes the most metaphysical of Christian credenda — has been the result, in point of fact, of a renewed and earnest attention to the particularities of Christian history, the concrete details of the story

---

1. In English: Karl Rahner, *The Trinity,* trans. Joseph Donceel (London: Burns and Oates, 1970), 22.

of Christ and his church, and the scriptural understanding of how God has acted within history for the restoration of the created world. The pathology of liberal Protestant theology's dogmatic wasting disease — of which no symptom could be more acute than the reduction of the doctrine of the Trinity to an appendicitic twinge at the end of Schleiermacher's *The Christian Faith* — was one of progressive and irrepressible abstraction, a moralization and spiritualization of salvation that made of Christ the unique bearer (as opposed to the unique content) of the Christian *kerygma;* and the theological rediscovery of the Trinity has come about precisely because the salvific significance of Christ's historical specificity has been to some considerable degree recovered from the confining prejudices of modern thought. More to the point, what Rahner's maxim describes is the necessary shape of all theological rationality. In Cappadocian theology, for instance, the coessentiality and coequality of the divine persons was defended as the necessary theological interpretation of the economy of salvation, as a truth made manifest in the life, death, and resurrection of Christ and in the mediation of salvation to the believer in the sacraments of the church (witness the arguments of Basil's *On the Holy Spirit* and Gregory the Theologian's *Five Theological Orations*). In the early centuries of Christian thought, the Trinity was gradually apprehended as the mystery truly revealed in God's saving action, and not as a metaphysical secret imparted mystically to the church; it was not until three centuries and more had elapsed, councils had been called, and doctrine had been defined that a text like Augustine's *De Trinitate*, in which the doctrine assumed the aspect of faith's object (as opposed to its explication), was possible: and while such a possibility, in one sense, was the result of a certain ecclesial liberation from the anxiety of dogmatic dispute, in another sense it was arguably the occasion for the inauguration of a certain pattern of theological forgetfulness. Not that there is anything to be deplored in Augustine's magnificent series of intense, brilliant, and theologically necessary theoretical allegories on the doctrine of the Trinity, but it is also the case that to some eyes they are not always obviously wedded to a deeper consideration of the story of atonement. And later theology (Eastern no less than Western) sometimes obeyed the logic of the divorce of the doctrine of God from the story of God's manifestation of himself in history — with occasionally dismal consequences. Trinitarian thought uninformed by the gospel narrative results, inevitably, in an impoverishment of both that thought and that narrative; hence the importance of the affirmation that the Trinity as economic or as immanent is the one God as he truly is, whose every action is proper to and expressive of his divinity.

Two perils, however, attend any attempt to translate Rahner's maxim into fuller theological discourse. The first lies in the temptation to take it as an abolition of any distinction between God's immanence within himself and his gracious presence within history:[2] the way, that is, of one or another sort of theological repristination of Hegel's "trinitarian" logic. This is obviously an impossibly broad designation, and might equally well (and equally misleadingly) be applied to the loose, rhapsodic, paraenetic expostulations of Jürgen Moltmann, or to the vastly more systematic but paradoxically even more incoherent thought of Eberhard Jüngel (with its liberal lashings of late romantic nihilism), or to the more cautious dogmatic projects of Wolfhart Pannenberg or Robert Jenson. Still, Jenson might be said to speak for many when he writes: "To reclaim Hegel's truth for the gospel, we need only a small but drastic amendment: Absolute consciousness finds its own meaning and self in the *one* historical object, Jesus, and *so* posits Jesus' fellows as its fellows and Jesus' world as its world."[3] We flirt here with calamity. If the identity of the immanent Trinity with the economic is taken to mean that history is the theater within which God — as absolute mind, or process, or divine event — finds or determines himself as God, there can be no way of convincingly avoiding the conclusion (however vigorously the theologian might deny the implication) that God depends upon creation to be God and that creation exists by necessity (because of some lack in God), so that God is robbed of his true transcendence and creation of its true gratuity. The God whom Genesis depicts as pronouncing a deliberative "Let us . . ." in creating humanity after his image and as looking on in approbation of his handiwork, which he sees to be good, is the eternal God who is the God he forever is, with or without creation, to whom creation adds absolutely nothing; God does not require creation to "fecundate" his being, nor does he require the pathos of creation to determine his "personality" as though he were some finite subjectivity writ large, whose transcendental Ego were in need of delimitation in an empirical ego; God and creation do not belong to an interdependent history of necessity, because the Trinity is already infinitely sufficient, infinitely "diverse," infinitely at peace; God is good and sovereign and wholly beautiful, and creation is gift, loveliness, pleasure, dignity, and freedom, which is to say that God is possessed of that loveliest (and most widely misunderstood) "attribute," *apatheia*.[4] The absence of creation, the theater of the

2. See John Thompson, *Modern Trinitarian Perspectives* (Oxford: Oxford University Press, 1994), 28-29, concerning the author's apprehensions regarding the danger of collapsing the immanent Trinity into the economic, so making the divine persons (in Thielicke's phrase) "masks of a phenomenal drama."

3. Robert W. Jenson, "The Holy Spirit," in *Christian Dogmatics*, ed. Carl E. Braaten, Robert W. Jenson, and Gerhard O. Forde, 2 vols. (Philadelphia: Fortress, 1984), 2:169.

4. Though this is a matter I shall presently address, I should observe that the widespread impatience among theologians with the language of divine impassibility, always fortified by the prejudice that such a doctrine represents an unreflective "hellenization" of the gospel, has too often served to obscure the real questions at issue, the doctrinal concerns that the teaching of di-

Trinity's economy, would in no way alter how God is God; as Athanasius insists, with or without the world the Father has his Son (*Contra Arianos* 1.18).[5] One might even say — as alarming as it may sound — that God does not even need us to be "our" God; all we are, all we can ever become, is already infinitely and fully present in the inexhaustible beauty, liveliness, and "virtue" of the Logos, where — as the infinitely perfect reflection of the divine essence that flows forth from the Father, fully enjoyed in the light of the Spirit — it is present already as responsiveness and communion; thus God indeed loved us when we were not, and that he then called us to be (Rom. 4:17) and to participate in the being he pours into us is an act of generosity wholly fitting to, but in no way determinative of, his goodness. Indeed, one should even say that all that Jesus of Nazareth was and is the Son of God was and is in the supereminent, *timeless* eternity of his act of being, and would have been and would be with or without a world. This may seem the height of theological austerity, even of hellenization, but it is actually quite the opposite. The freedom of God from ontic determination is the ground of creation's goodness: precisely because creation is uncompelled, unnecessary, and finally other than that dynamic life of coinherent love whereby God is God, it can reveal how God is the God he is; precisely because creation is needless, an object of delight that shares God's love without contributing anything that God does not already possess in infinite eminence, creation reflects the divine life, which is one of delight and fellowship and love; precisely because creation is not part of God, the context of God, or divine, precisely because it is not "substantially" from God, or metaphysically cognate to God's essence, or a pathos of God, is it an analogy of the divine; in being the object of God's love without any cause but the generosity of that love, creation reflects in its beauty that eternal delight that is the divine *perichoresis* and that obeys no necessity but divine love itself. Thus Rahner's (utterly necessary) maxim can serve a genuinely theological end only if taken to mean that the Trinity who is economically revealed is indeed, without remainder (such as some Sabellian singularity prior to all hypostatic identity, or a

---

vine impassibility answers, and the very real philosophical revision — utterly consistent with itself and Scripture — that the teaching underwent in the hands of the greatest of the patristic theologians. For two examples of books in which this sort of misunderstanding, coupled with grave philosophical mistakes, leads to very misguided conclusions, see Joseph M. Hallman, *The Descent of God: Divine Suffering in History and Theology* (Minneapolis: Fortress, 1991), and Paul S. Fiddes, *The Creative Suffering of God* (Oxford: Clarendon, 1988). I treat *apatheia* more fully in D. B. Hart, "No Shadow of Turning: On Divine Impassibility," *Pro Ecclesia* 11 (spring 2002): 184-206. Thomas G. Weinandy, *Does God Suffer?* (Notre Dame: University of Notre Dame, 2000).

5. Athanasius says this because, as he insists, what God is in himself he is toward us. See *Contra Arianos* 2.11; 3.1f.; *Ad Serapion* 1.14-17, 20ff.; 2.2; 3–4.6. I wish to endorse an Athanasian understanding of Rahner's maxim.

fourth divine person, or a nature distinct from the one assumed in the order of relations within the mystery of salvation), the true and everlasting God as he is in himself: for God is not a finite subject, whose will could be other than his being, and so is truly fully himself in all his acts *ad extra,* and the *taxis* of his salvific activity toward us is the same *taxis* that is his triune life. The maxim stands then as a guard against any kind of nominalism on the one hand, and on the other, any tendency to forget that the dogma of the Trinity is required and defined — and permitted — by the narrative of Christ.

But, one might ask, how can the temporal event of God in our midst be the same as God's event to himself in his eternity if so absolute a distinction is drawn between the enarrable contents of history and the "eternal dynamism" of God's immutability, *apatheia,* and perfect fullness? How can the dereliction of Christ, his self-outpouring, truly be the same action as the eternal life of blissful immunity from suffering that classical Christian metaphysics insists upon? These are the questions that largely animate the Hegelianizing project in modern theology, and have long inspired theologians to reject aspects of the tradition that they see as a metaphysical corruption of the Bible's "narrated" God: the distinction between being and becoming, between eternity and time, between the Logos as eternally begotten in the bosom of the Father and the Son of Man begotten "this day" (of course, in truth, it is never a matter of whether such distinctions are to be made, but how to make them, without compromising the narrative of Scripture and the unity of God in Christ). Immutability, impassibility, timelessness — surely, many argue, these relics of an obsolete metaphysics lingered on in Christian theology just as false belief and sinful inclinations linger on in a soul after baptism; and surely they always were fundamentally incompatible with the idea of a God of election and love, who proves himself God through fidelity to his own promises against the horizon of history, who became flesh for us (was this not a change, after all, in God?) and endured the passion of the cross out of pity for us. Have we not seen the wounded heart of God, wounded by our sin in his eternal life, and wounded by it again, even unto death, in the life of the flesh? This is why so much modern theology keenly desires a God who suffers, not simply with us and in our nature, but in his own nature as well; such a God, it is believed, is the living God of Scripture, not the cold abstraction of a God of the philosophers; only such a God would die for us. At its most culpable, the modern appetite for a passible God can reflect simply a sort of self-indulgence and apologetical plaintiveness, a sense that, before God, though we are sinners, we also have a valid perspective, one he must learn to share with us so that he can sympathize with our lot rather than simply judge us; he must be absolved of his transcendence, so to speak, before we can consent to submit to his verdict (and, after all, in this age we are all rather bourgeois about such things and very jealous of our "rights"). At its most commendable, though, this appetite testifies to our capacity for moral rage and perplexity, our inability to believe in a God of perfect power and imperturbable bliss in the wake of the century of death camps, gulags, killing fields, and the fire of nuclear detonations. We long for a companion in pain, a fellow sufferer; we know we have one in Christ; and we refuse to allow any ambiguity — metaphysical, moral, or theological — to rob us of his company. All of this I shall address when I discuss Christology, particularly in section III.2, but I shall make two observations now. First, as valid as all such concerns are in their way, they entirely miss the point: the Christian doctrine of divine *apatheia,* in its developed patristic and medieval form, never concerned an abstract deity ontologically incapable of knowing and loving us; far from representing an irreconcilable contradiction or logical tension within Christian discourse, the juxtaposition of the language of divine *apatheia* with the story of crucified love is precisely what makes the entire narrative of salvation in Christ intelligible. And second, it is an almost agonizing irony that, in our attempts to revise trinitarian doctrine in such a way as to make God comprehensible in the "light" of Auschwitz, invariably we end up describing a God who — it turns out — is actually simply the metaphysical ground of Auschwitz.

Regarding the former remark, more below; regarding the latter, I shall say simply that the problems inherent in a trinitarianism without distinction between God's eternal being and the historical manifestation thereof are as much moral as metaphysical. Consider, for example, the powerful and profound attempt of Robert Jenson to find in the story of Jesus, and all that attaches thereto, an essential narrativity in the identity of God. Jenson, one must immediately say, does not write theodicy and never adds his voice to the querulous choiring of those who want God to absolve himself of his transcendence, and he takes great pains to avoid the obvious traps of "Hegelian" trinitarian theology in general, most especially that of metaphysical "necessity" in the relation of God and world; that, in my estimation, he inevitably fails in this speaks only of the impossible dilemma he creates for himself through his point of departure. In the first volume of his recent *Systematic Theology,*[6] he lays out his understanding of the unity of immanent and economic Trinities with utter clarity: God the Father from eternity has determined that he shall be the God he is in his unique relation to the man Jesus, a relation for which the Spirit — as God's eternally possessed "future" — frees the Father; thus the Father finds his identity as God, along with the Son and Spirit, in the dramatic history of his encounter, in Christ, with the horizon of death (227) and his triumph over it

---

6. Robert W. Jenson, *Systematic Theology,* vol. 1, *The Triune God* (Oxford and New York: Oxford University Press, 1997). Parenthetical page numbers in the following text are to this work.

(219): "his identity must be constituted precisely in the integration of this abandonment. The God of crucifixion and resurrection is one with himself in a moment of supreme dramatic self-transcendence or not at all" (65). God's eternal being, thus, is not to be distinguished from this historical achievement; "he . . . can have no identity except as he meets the temporal end towards which creatures live" (65). God's eternity has a past, present, and future (Father, Son, and Spirit), his eternity is temporal (a view Jenson believes, mistakenly, that he can defend from the theology of Gregory of Nyssa),[7] and he is himself by determining and finding and becoming himself. God is who he is because he has a story, in which he acts, determines his action, and accomplishes his nature. Or, as Jenson also puts it, the Father is like the transcendental Ego seeking its "I," its empirical ego, in the man Jesus, while the Holy Spirit is the freedom that allows this adventure (120):

> [T]he identity that a consciousness has is the Ego that it finds within its field. With creatures, consciousness thereby becomes finite, constrained to the limits of the object by which it identifies itself. The Ego as which the Father finds himself is the Son. But the Son exists not at all for himself and altogether for those for whom the Father intends him. Thus the father's preoccupation with the Son, Jesus' intrusion into the outward flight of the Father's consciousness, does not restrict the Father's consciousness but is rather his consciousness's opening to its universal scope. (220)

So the Trinity is the dramaturgical dance of these distinct moments: the divine "past" and the divine "future" achieving their object in Jesus, who is the creature who is also God precisely in being the focus of this event: "That Christ has the divine nature means that he is one of the three whose mutuality is the divine life, who live the history that God is. That Christ has human nature means that he is one of the many whose mutuality is human life, who live the history that humanity is" (138). Whether Jenson thus avoids imagining God as a kind of collectivity, or as a kind of dialectical tension in which identities subsist as mutually positing, it is difficult to say: when the universal scope of an essentially Hegelian vision of Trinity has been reduced again to the more "subjectivist" emphasis of an earlier transcendental idealism, one set of ambiguities replaces another; but Jenson's intention certainly is to describe a divine unity and divine triplicity that sustain one another without collapsing into a mere metaphysical abstraction, impossibly removed from the earthly identity of Jesus of Nazareth. "The Father is the 'whence' of God's life; the Spirit is the 'whither' of God's life; and we may even say that the Son is that life's specious present. If, then, whence

---

7. See sec. I.3 below.

and whither do not fall apart in God's life, so that this duration is without loss, it is because origin and goal, whence and whither, are indomitably reconciled in the action and suffering of the Son" (218-19). The preexistence of the Son therefore consists in his eternal presence to the Father as God's eternally willed Logos: God has chosen from all ages to unite himself to this man, and, as God *is* his act of choice,[8] he is, as the event of this choice, the man Jesus; "Thus it is the Incarnate Son who is himself his own presupposition in God's eternity" (140). The Son exists in eternity — and is manifest accordingly even in the Old Testament — as an inherent pattern of movement within the divine identity, a momentum toward incarnation (141). Nor are any of the painful particularities of the incarnation exterior to the internal movement of God's identity; the pathos of the Son is related to a pathos within the Father, both of which are taken into the love of the Spirit:

> God the Son suffers all the contingencies and evils recorded in the Gospels, and concludes them by suffering execution. God the Father raises him from the dead; nor do we have reason to think of his act as dispassionately done. So and not otherwise the Father triumphs over suffering. God the Spirit is the sphere of the triumph. And "triumph" is the precise word: the Father and the Spirit take the suffering of the creature who the Son is into the triune life and bring from it the final good of the creature, all other creatures, and of God. So and not otherwise the true God transcends suffering — whatever unknowably might have been. (144)

This last clause, incidentally, refers to an assertion that Jenson makes at two places in his text (65, 141): we must say that God could have been the very God he is without creatures, but we cannot say how.

It is precisely this assertion, however, that calls attention to an instability in Jenson's system: it is simply prima facie false that if God achieves his identity in the manner Jenson describes, he could have been the same God by other means, without the world. The logic of such a proposition can never span the gulf between either and or, because in this case the gulf is absolute: if God *could* be God otherwise, then he already *is* God otherwise; this is who God is, which history can manifest but never determine. If, however, the particular determinations of this history are also determinations of God — as he "chooses" to be God — then there can be no identity of God as *this* God apart from the specific

---

8. A difficult proposition to affirm: it is one thing to say God is his *act,* if one means that he is *actus purus;* but when one speaks of God freely determining himself as God, choosing to be God thus rather than otherwise, one has posited a purely spontaneous force of will logically prior to God's own nature, a purely subjective *arbitrium;* and this can never be resolved again into the simplicity of an identity of act and essence.

contours of *this* history. And the voluntarist caesura that Jenson appears to introduce between God and the history in which God chooses to define himself, as if he were an omnipotent but finite subject logically prior even to his own essence, merely proves the point. If somehow in the abyssal pastness of God's eternity, in its relation to its endless and always already possessed futurity, there is a decision that God's eternal temporality will be unfolded according to the history of Jesus — in his relation to all human and cosmic history — then God's final identity is absolutely and necessarily bound to the conditions he elects (though presumably he could become some other God, even if this leaves one with the very problematic notion that there is already some sort of deliberating identity to the Father prior to the delimiting empirical object in which he "finds" himself). And this also means that God's identity is in some absolute sense inseparable not only from the life and person of Jesus of Nazareth, but from the entire order of contingencies that Jesus inhabits. So when, as above, Jenson speaks of a "small but drastic amendment" to "Hegel's truth," one which will allow us to speak of "absolute consciousness" finding its own "meaning and self in the *one* historical object, Jesus," he is advocating the impossible. Hegel's logic cannot work that way, and the system is not something to be trifled with: it is too well thought out, and one step toward it is complete capitulation. The only way the distinction between being and becoming can be overcome (if it is at all possible or desirable), is by way of a complete collapse of the difference. Being must be identified with the totality of becoming as an "infinite" process. Otherwise one cannot avoid Heidegger's onto-theological critique (and frankly, Heidegger's critique almost certainly holds against the complete system anyway): one is identifying being with a being among beings, one's God is an ontic God who becomes what he is not, possessed of potential, receiving his being from elsewhere — from being. And as a being, he is in some sense finite, divided between being and being *this,* and so cannot be the being of creatures.[9] Admittedly, Jenson borrows Aquinas's definition of God as the perfect coincidence of essence and existence (213-14), but such language is irreconcilable with his trinitarian story (unless, perhaps, he indeed intends to em-

9. See E. L. Mascall, *He Who Is: A Study in Traditional Theism* (London: Longmans, Green, 1945), 112: having argued that while a God who is determined by the world can provide a metaphysical explanation of the course of worldly history, yet can never actually provide an explanation of the sheer "that it is" of the world, Mascall concludes: "nothing less than a strictly infinite God can provide the explanation of the world's existence, and that, in consequence, the world must be, in the fullest sense, contingent and altogether unnecessary to God. Various objections . . . complain that, on such a view, God could not have the intimate interest and concern with his creatures that is manifested in the Christian Religion. . . . while this would certainly be true if God was a finite being, it is not true if God is infinite." I do not believe that this is a logic that theology can intelligibly forsake.

brace the whole of Hegel's logic).[10] Among other things, this means that this God fails the test of Anselm's *id quo maius cogitari nequit:* a standard whose provenance may not exactly be biblical, but whose logic ultimately is, and that is a rule that teaches us to recognize when we are speaking of God and when we are speaking of a god, when we are directing our mind toward the transcendent source of being and when we are fabricating for ourselves a metaphysical myth.

Logically speaking, "absolute consciousness" cannot simply find itself in one object among other objects, even if it includes those other objects secondarily, as its context or ambience, or simply as objects of grace; all other objects, however they are arranged around the unique object of "absolute" attention, are implicated in and indeed determine that object and so the contents of the absolute. Everything that allows Jesus to be who and what he is, all the historical determinations before and after, belong to that identity, as does every condition of cosmic and historical becoming. And this does not cease to be true even of the most tragic historical consequences of the event of God in Christ (but for the coming of the gospel, would the division within covenant history, between Jews and Gentiles, have occurred, would that division have become a division fixed in the heart of the West, and would the Holocaust have come to pass?). This is not simply a matter of God allowing sin to exist and shape history: Jenson's trinitarian theology cannot work unless one posits not only the necessity of evil, but indeed the necessity of the actual history of evil. The first part of this equation Jenson acknowledges; he accepts the "supralapsarian" understanding of the incarnation in its depressing Lutheran and Calvinist form: for God to act in the fashion he does, the conditions that require redemption must be in place, for "the goal of God's path is just what does in fact happen with Jesus the Christ, and sin and evil belong to God's intent precisely — but *only* — as they appear in Christ's victory over them" (73). For God to be the God he has determined that he will be, "a mystery of suffering, of an interplay between created regularities and evil, must belong to the plot of God's history with us and to the character of its crisis and fulfillment" (73-74). The first problem with such a formulation is that, in depicting God as one who in any sense intends sin and evil, it reduces God to a being whose nature is not love (even if at the end of the day he turns out to be loving, having completed his odyssey of self-discovery, for a being can possess love only as an attribute); and one might justifiably wonder if a God who chooses himself so — should one say "dispassion-

10. Jenson seems to limit the meaning of the definition of God to "necessary existence," rather than a problematization of the idea of divine "existence" as such; but what the definition also says is that God is not a being, his *actus* is not limited by *potentia*, he does not choose to be God *thus* or *thus*, he is without ontic determinations, but is ontologically (infinitely) determinate. See also Jenson, *Systematic Theology*, vol. 2, *The Works of God* (Oxford and New York: Oxford University Press, 1999), 35-38.

ately"? — over against the creatures who suffer the adventure of his self-determination should evoke love in return. But the second problem is the other half of the equation mentioned above: if God's identity is constituted in his triumph over evil, then evil belongs eternally to his identity, and his goodness is not goodness as such but a reaction, an activity that requires the goad of evil to come into full being. All of history is the horizon of this drama, and since no analogical interval is allowed to be introduced between God's eternal being as Trinity and God's act as Trinity in time, all of history *is* this identity: every painful death of a child, every casual act of brutality, all war, famine, pestilence, disease, murder . . . all are moments in the identity of God, resonances within the event of his being, aspects of the occurrence of his essence: all of this is the crucible in which God comes into his own elected reality. One risks here converting the Christian God into a god of sacrifice in the ultimate sense, the god of Stoicism or Hegel, in whom the divine identity and the offering made to the divine have been conflated in one great process of arrival and destiny, negation and triumph. And a god forged in such fires as these may evoke fear and awe, but not genuine desire. If, speculatively, Jenson's theology seems to fail Anselm's test, morally it seems to fail the test of Ivan Karamazov: If the universal and final good of all creatures required, as its price, the torture of one little girl, would that be acceptable? And the moral enormity of this calculus is not mitigated if all of creation must suffer the consequences of God's self-determination. Nor can one get around these problems by speaking of God as an infinite identity, in which the finite can participate without determining the final truth of that identity: a genuinely transcendent infinity can assume the finite into itself without altering its own nature, but any "consciousness," however "absolute," that determines itself in a finite object is always a finite consciousness, even if the ultimate synthesis of its identity is, in its totality, "infinite" in the circular Hegelian sense. This can be only the infinite of total repletion, the fullness of ontic determinations in their interrelated discreteness and dialectical "yield"; only thus can being be one with becoming. The God whose identity subsists in time and is achieved upon history's horizon — who is determined by his reaction to the pathos of history — may be a being, or indeed the totality of all beings gathered in the pure depths of ultimate consciousness, but he is not being as such, he is not life and truth and goodness and love and beauty. God belongs to the system of causes, even if he does so as its total rationality; he is an absolute *causa in fieri,* but not a transcendent *causa in esse.* He may include us in his story, but his story will remain both good and evil even if it ends in an ultimate triumph over evil. After all, how can we tell the dancer from the dance? The collapse of the analogical interval between the immanent and economic Trinity, between timeless eternity and the time in which eternity shows itself, has not made God our companion in pain, but simply the truth of our pain and our only *pathetic* hope of rescue; his intimacy with us has not been affirmed at all: only a truly transcendent and "passionless" God can be the fullness of love dwelling within our very being, nearer to us than our inmost parts, but a dialectical Trinity is not transcendent — truly infinite — in this way at all, but only sublime, a metaphysical whole that can comprise us or change us extrinsically, but not transform us within our very being. Were this the trinitarian mystery, we would indeed be unable to speak of God or faith in terms of original or ultimate peace; the postmodern suspicion would prove well founded, for in our story violence would prove necessary, belonging to who God is, and our faith would indeed be metaphysics after all, in the frightening sense: a myth of necessity, of ultimate grounds, a transcendental reconciliation of all contingent suffering in an ultimate structure of meaning, and another invitation to *homo sacer* to yield to his *taedium deitatis* and not only lay down his knife, but erase all faith from his heart.

Of course, Jenson says and intends none of this; but one must ask of him and of every theologian who seeks to make the doctrine of the Trinity the place where time and eternity meet as absolute identity whether, when the logic of their theology is pressed on toward its ultimate implications, it can arrive at any other end. The haste with which we have tried to free ourselves from the constraints placed upon our discourse by classical Christian thought follows from a twofold error of judgment: on the one hand, we have assumed too quickly that we understand how the tradition used the terms it took from Greek philosophy and bent to its purposes; and on the other, we have not sufficiently thought through the implications of the alternatives. A God who can become, who can acquire determinations, who has his future as potential and realizes his future through "dramatic self-transcendence," is not God but a god, a mere supreme being; and regarding the gods, Christianity has always quite properly been identified as atheism. This is doubly true if God is seen as freely determining his identity, as a kind of project, acting as a kind of voluntarist *causa sui*. Theology must, to remain faithful to what it knows of God's transcendence, reject any picture of God that so threatens to become at once both thoroughly mythological and thoroughly metaphysical, and insist upon the classical definitions of impassibility, immutability, and nonsuccessive eternity. This is in no way a contradiction of the story of God as creator and redeemer and consummator of all things: because God is Trinity, eternally, perfectly, without any need of negative probation or finite determination. God does not have to change or suffer in order to love us or show us mercy — he loved us when we were not, and by this very "mercy" created us — and so, as love, he can overcome all suffering. This is true in two related and consequent senses: on the one hand, love is not originally a reaction but is the ontological possibility of every ontic action, the one transcendent act, the primordial generosity that is con-

vertible with being itself, the blissful and desiring *apatheia* that requires no pathos to evoke it, no evil to make it good; and this is so because, on the other
hand, God's infinitely accomplished life of love is that trinitarian movement of
his being that is infinitely determinate — as determinacy toward the other —
and so an indestructible *actus purus* endlessly more dynamic than any mere
motion of change could ever be. In him there is neither variableness nor
shadow of turning because he is wholly free, wholly God as Father, Son, and
Spirit, wholly alive, and wholly love. Even the cross of Christ does not determine the nature of divine love, but rather manifests it, because there is a more
original outpouring of God that — without needing to submit itself to the order of sacrifice that builds crosses — always already surpasses every abyss of
godforsakenness and pain that sin can impose between the world and God: an
outpouring that is in its proper nature indefectible happiness. These are matters to be addressed later,[11] but here I can at least offer a definition of divine
apatheia as trinitarian love: God's impassibility is the utter fullness of an infinite dynamism, the absolutely complete and replete generation of the Son and
procession of the Spirit from the Father, the infinite "drama" of God's joyous
act of self-outpouring — which is his being as God. Within the plenitude of
this motion, no contrary motion can fabricate an interval of negation, because
it is the infinite possibility of every creaturely motion or act; no pathos is possible for God because a pathos is, by definition, a finite instance of change visited
upon a passive subject, actualizing some potential, whereas God's love is pure
positivity and pure activity. His love is an infinite peace and so needs no violence to shape it, no death over which to triumph: if it did, it would never be
ontological peace but only metaphysical armistice. Nor is this some kind of
original unresponsiveness in the divine nature; it is divine beauty, that perfect
joy in the other by which God is God: the Father's *delectatio* in the beauty of his
eternal Image, the Spirit as the light and joy and sweetness of that knowledge.[12]
As Augustine says of the three persons, "In that Trinity is the highest origin of
all things, and the most perfect beauty, and the most blessed delight. Therefore
those three are seen to be mutually determined, and are in themselves infinite";[13] that is, infinitely determined as the living love of the divine persons —
to "one another" — to which infinity no moment of the negative or of becoming or even of "triumph" can give increase. Hence God is love.

11. I must defer my discussion of impassibility in relation to the *kenosis* of the Son and
the cross of Christ till sec. III.2.

12. See Augustine, *De Trinitate* 6.10.11; Gregory of Nyssa, *De anima et resurrectione*, in
Migne, *Patrologia Graeca*, 46:93, 96, hereafter *PG*.

13. *De Trinitate* 6.10.12: "In illa enim Trinitate summa origo est rerum omnium, et
perfectissima pulchritudo, et beatissima delectatio. Itaque illa tria, et ad se invicem determinari
videntur, et in se infinita sunt."

ii. Divine Fellowship

The second peril besetting any interpretation of Rahner's maxim lies in the reverse temptation: to forsake the economic for the immanent Trinity, by allowing some far too thoroughly developed speculative account of the Trinity to determine what in the story of Christ's relation to the Father and the Spirit is or is not genuinely revelation, genuinely trinitarian, and so to blind one to details of that story that do not quite fit into this account. If the economic Trinity is the immanent, such that nothing can be assumed to be *merely* economic (that is, provisional) in the order of the divine action in salvation, then the doctrine of God can never arrive at a speculative closure that would make it any less difficult to master than the story of Jesus itself. A case in point: in Eastern Orthodox tradition the church's celebration of Jesus' baptism by John is called the Feast of the Theophany, because what is revealed in the audible and visible coincidence of the voice of God declaring the Father's pleasure in his Son, the dove descending, and the incarnate Word is nothing less than the Trinity itself, in the fullness of its shared love, its immanent dynamism of distinction and unity. The constellation of figures in this tableau constitutes an icon, a crystallization of the mystery of faith in one perfect image: not, that is, a simple allegory, but a real showing of God, manifesting simultaneously the full drama of salvation and the full order of intradivine relations, revealing them to be not only compatible motions but identical. The descent into the waters, whereby Christ submits to a sanctification of which he has no need, is an image both of the way of the Son into creation, his gracious descent into flesh, time, and space, ultimately into the darkness of death and hell, but also of the way the Son goes forth eternally from the Father, receiving all from the Father and restoring all to him in "selfless" adoration; Christ's emergence from the waters is at once his resurrection, his ascent and return of all creation to the Father as a pure offering, and also his eternal "response" to the Father as the Father's everlasting Word; the descent of the dove is at once the blessing of the Spirit, sent by the Father upon the Son and imparted by the Son to his church as the teacher of all truth, who bears tidings of Christ, but also the Father's eternal gift to the Son of the Spirit, who forever bears joyous tidings of the Son to the Father. This is, in fact, the aspect of this passage in the Gospels that seems most difficult to reconcile with too spare a speculative scheme of trinitarian relations, and that is most easily overlooked: that in declaring himself, even in uttering himself eternally, God both addresses and responds. In Matthew's Gospel, at the baptism of Jesus (as at the transfiguration), the voice of God proclaims the Father's favor; the Son is indicated, declared, offered outward as the Father's true image. In Mark and Luke, however, the Son is directly addressed by the Father's voice, as "thou": "in thee I am well pleased" (was well pleased, εὐδόκησα). And according to Mark, Christ is immediately (εὐθὺς) sent by the Spirit into the desert to pray and fast, to answer and offer himself to the Father. Here where Christ's ministry begins, where his proclamation of God's love is shown to belong to his identity as the eternal utterance of the Father, he not only speaks with the Father's authority but addresses the Father, regards him, responds to him; and the Spirit, witnessing this reciprocity, answers it as well, differently, reflecting and reinflecting it. If the economic Trinity is God in himself, graciously extending the everlasting "dance" of his love to embrace creation in its motion, then one dare not exclude from one's understanding of the Trinity the idea, however mysterious, of a reciprocal Thou. I say this because Rahner himself, in *Mysterium Salutis,* makes such an exclusion; he does allow — with an air of resignation — that the term "Persons" must be retained when talking of the Trinity,[14] but one could still read his model of the trinitarian *taxis* as a set of merely formal relations within the divine essence (109-14), and he clearly denies to the immanent Trinity any "response," any reciprocal Thou (106 n). It is, one must say, a quite rigorous and orthodox reasoning that leads him to his conclusion, but his treatment remains far from satisfactory and must, in the light of his own indispensable maxim, be modified. One must abide the irreducible mystery of God's oneness in the persons' distinctions, of a single and infinitely complete divine utterance that is one precisely as already eminently embracing reciprocity. One obviously must resist the lure of a purely social trinitarianism — which is, if pure, nothing but tritheism — and avoid imagining that the Trinity's "responsiveness" encompasses another utterance, alongside the Father's expression of his essence in the simplicity of the eternal Logos; but still one must acknowledge this distance of address and response, this openness of shared regard.

This issue has become painfully perplexing in recent decades on account of the misguided willingness of many modern theologians to accept, and employ, the distinction that Théodore de Régnon so modestly, but so influentially, claimed to have discovered between Western and Eastern styles of trinitarian theology: the tendency, that is, of Latin thought to proceed from general nature to concrete person (the latter as a mode of the former), so according priority to divine unity, and of Greek thought to proceed from person to nature (the latter as the content of the former), so placing the emphasis first on the plurality of divine persons.[15] There is some minimal truth to this distinction perhaps, at least as regards the very early difference of Alexandrian subordinationism from Roman modalism, but it is more myth than reality, and has served little pur-

---

14. Rahner, 44. The parenthetical page numbers in the following text refer to the ET of Rahner's *Mysterium Salutis,* titled *The Trinity.*

15. Théodore de Régnon, *Études de Théologie Positive sur la Sainte Trinité,* 2 vols. (Paris, 1892), 1:433.

pose in recent years but to feed Eastern polemic and Western insecurity, and to distort the tradition that both share. Just as certain modern Orthodox theologians have occasionally forgotten the complexities of patristic trinitarianism, and have ventured formulae that risk portraying God as plural, so many Western theologians have come to believe that they must choose between "Greek" personalism and "Latin" essentialism. Moreover, in the latter case, certain moves in modern Western dogmatics have, quite apart from the disputes between East and West, made such a choice seem pressing; Karl Barth, for instance, professed a preference for the term "mode of subsistence" (τρόπος ὑπάρξεως) over the more perilous *persona* or πρόσωπον:[16] not, of course, out of some secret Sabellianism, nor certainly out of some discreditable desire to "depersonalize" the living God of Scripture, but out of a very keen sense of the imprecision of the word "person," of the differing connotations of the term ὑπόστασις, and of how far the modern understanding of personality (as isolated, punctiliar, psychic monad) lies from anything that can be said sensibly of God. Nicholas Lash, in a book with the extremely unfortunate title *Believing Three Ways in One God,* pronounces the arguments against continued use of the term "Persons" decisive,[17] and recommends instead the Augustinian category of "subsistent relations": "we *have* relationships," he writes, "God *is* the relations that he has. . . . God, we might say, is relationship without remainder, which we, most certainly, are not."[18] As theology this is sound enough (though I entertain considerable doubts regarding its value as anthropology); Lash is simply obeying the logic of, say, Augustine's prudent rejection of a trinitarian analogy drawn from the relationship of husband, wife, and child (*De Trinitate* 12.5.5–7.12), in favor of more elliptical analogies drawn from the mind's inner complexity. But, one must ask, should not the relationality that, in a sense, "exhausts" the personality of the Trinity be made the starting point for a theological assault on the modern notion of the person? Or for a more "constitutive" account of relationality within human identity? Not to ignore the difference of God from us, but does not the burden and the promise of trinitarian thought lie now in its incompatibility with modernity's understanding of personality, and its ability, consequently, to expose that understanding as a perverse and sinful fiction? Indeed, do we really possess identity apart from relation: Is not even our "purest" interiority reflexive, knowing and loving itself as expression

---

16. Karl Barth, *Church Dogmatics* I/1: *The Doctrine of the Word of God,* trans. G. W. Bromiley (Edinburgh: T. & T. Clark, 1936), 355-68. See also Colin E. Gunton, *The Promise of Trinitarian Theology* (Edinburgh: T. & T. Clark, 1991), 164-66, regarding the author's dissatisfaction with this aspect of Barth's trinitarian terminology.

17. Nicholas Lash, *Believing Three Ways in One God: A Reading of the Apostles' Creed* (Notre Dame, Ind.: University of Notre Dame Press, 1993), 31.

18. Lash, *Believing Three Ways,* 32.

and recognition, engaged with the world of others through *memoria* and desire, inward discourse and outward intention (hence the genius of Augustine's "interior" analogies)?

Without question, Christian thought must not conceive of the Trinity as a federation of three individual centers of consciousness; but still it must do justice to the biblical God; and the language routinely offered as alternatives to the term "persons" invariably fails to reflect the immediacy, livingness, and concreteness of the scriptural portrayal of God, either in the Old Testament or in the New. John's accounts of the prayers of Christ — heard as addresses to the Father, but also clearly as a response to the Father's mission of the Son — are resonant with both an intimacy and a distinction of voices, of places of address, that make "persons," for all its inadequacy, an indispensable word. Surely, preferable to despair over the possibility of making theological sense of the term "divine persons" in an age when the common concept of personality has been shaped by so vast an assortment of discourses — philosophical, psychological, social, anthropological, etc. — is the course taken by a number of modern Orthodox theologians (in particular, Vladimir Lossky): to take the language of trinitarian dogma as an imperative to think the concept of the person anew, from above, in a distinctively Christian way.[19] As Aquinas avers, whatsoever is said truly of God is said truly of God alone, only analogously of creatures; and it is precisely because the term "persons," when applied to the divine *perichoresis*, is governed entirely by the language of relations (the divine σχέσεις, upon which Gregory the Theologian placed such emphasis)[20] that theology is obliged to call the modern image of the person into question. As Régnon argues in his study, the self-inclination and self-possession of the human person account for all the vicious tendencies of sin: "orgueil, ambition, jalousie, avarice; toutes passions se résumant en seul mot: *égoïsme*" — but such tendencies become recognizable as sin only in being brought into the light of that "divine person" whose "egoism" consists in his relatedness, his self-giving, and all of whose Father's "I-ness" is expressed in the gift of his substance, poured forth into the Son.[21] For Pavel Florensky the language of divine persons — and here he strikes a vein far richer, and far more faithful to the "economic" trinitarian dynamism of atonement, than that represented by the mere exclusion of a reciprocal Thou from the thought of God — is one of self-oblation, according to which each "I" in God is also "not I" but rather Thou; for the di-

19. See, for example, Vladimir Lossky, "The Theological Notion of the Human Person," in Lossky, *In the Image and Likeness of God* (Crestwood, N.Y.: St. Vladimir's Seminary Press, 1974), 111-23.

20. See *Orations* 23.8-11; 29.2-16; 30.19f.; 31.9-16; 42.15f.

21. Régnon, 1:67-69.

vine circumincession is always a relationality of "self"-renunciation in favor of
— an opening out to — the other.[22] It is thus that God in himself is, as Hilary
was fond of observing, never solitary.[23] One might even say that, in God, divine
"substantiality" is the "effect" of this distance of address and response, this
event of love that is personal by being prior to every self, this gift of self-offering
that has already been made before any self can stand apart, individual, isolate;
God *is* as the differing modalities of replete love (to speak like Richard of St.
Victor), whose relatedness is his substance.[24] And the revelation of this infinite
condition of person-as-gift, "before" every "I," is a revelation also of what the
only true meaning of person is, even when applied to creatures. Certainly the
essence of salvation is that souls and bodies should be drawn into the dynamism of the trinitarian life, as the Spirit integrates them into the coinherence,
the *sobornost,* of the body of Christ, where one becomes a true — that is, selfless
— person: a person in communion. The sanctification bestowed by God's
Spirit is also a light cast upon humanity, as it stands within Christ, the one true
man: a light that shows the isolated self to be a trace only, the effaced emblem of
a forgotten gift, given before the self is a self, before the I has arrived.[25]

Certainly, here especially, one must be acutely conscious of the analogical
interval within the word "person" when applied both to God and creatures, and
always recall that the moral and ontological categories in which human personality subsists are appropriate only to the finite and composite; the relationality
of human persons, however essential it may be, remains a multiple reality,
which must be described now in social terms, now in psychological, now in
metaphysical; it is infinitely remote from that perfect indwelling, reciprocal
"containment," transparency, recurrence, and absolute "giving way" that is the
meaning of the word περιχώρησις or *circumincessio.* For if we forget this interval, we not only risk lapsing into either a collectivist or solipsistic reduction of
human relationality — exclusively outward or inward — but we are likely to
adopt either a tritheistic or a unitarian idiom when speaking of God. Our being
is synthetic and bounded; just as the dynamic inseparability but incommensurability in us of essence and existence is an ineffably distant analogy of the
dynamic identity of essence and existence in God, the constant pendulation be-

22. Pavel Florensky, "Der Pfeiler und die Grundfeste der Wahrheit," in *Östliches
Christentum,* vol. 2, *Philosophie* (Munich, 1925), 62.

23. See Hilary, *De Trinitate* 4.21; 6.12-19; 7.3-8, 39; 8.52.

24. See Richard of St. Victor, *De Trinitate* 3.14; Gregory the Theologian, *Orations* 18.42;
22.4.

25. See Vladimir Lossky, *The Mystical Theology of the Eastern Church* (Cambridge and
London: James Clarke, 1957), 114-95; see also Grigorios Larentzakis, "Trinitärischer
Kirchenverständnis," in *Trinität: Aktuelle Perspektiven der Theologie,* ed. Wilhelm Breuning
(Freiburg: Herder, 1984).

tween inner and outer that constitutes our identities is an ineffably distant analogy of that boundless bright diaphaneity of coinherence in which the exteriority of relations and interiority of identity in God are one, each person wholly reflecting and containing and indwelling the other. Because for us personality is synthetic, composite, successive, and finite, we are related always in some sense "over against," in a fragmentary way, and to be with others always involves for us a kind of death, the limit of our being. Of course, Christian faith teaches that God can transform our death into life, our limits into the charity of *kenosis,* and that our dwelling in him will be an ever greater dwelling of him in us, and so all of us in one another; still, while we can enjoy this openness of personality by way of participation in God's infinity, we will never know that infinity as identical with our essences. In God, the "inwardness" of the other is the inwardness of each person, the "outwardness" of the other is each person's outwardness and manifestation. It is precisely here that the artificial distinction between "Greek" and "Latin" theology has worked the most injurious mischief, by prompting many to rush to one end or the other of a scale that must be kept in balance. One must say, at once, that the divine simplicity is the result of the self-giving transparency and openness of infinite persons, but also that the distinction of the persons within the one God is the result of the infinite simplicity of the divine essence. In the words of Gregory of Nyssa, "the divine nature exceeds each [finite] good, and the good is wholly beloved by the good, and thus it follows that when it looks upon itself it desires what it possesses and possesses what it desires, and receives nothing from outside itself. . . . the life of that transcendent nature is love, in that the beautiful is entirely lovable to those who recognize it (and God does recognize it), and so this recognition becomes love, because the object of his recognition is in its nature beautiful."[26] Or as Augustine writes, making utterly evident the trinitarian presuppositions in such language,

> [T]he Son is from the Father, so as both to be and to be coeternal with the Father. For if the image perfectly fills the measure of him whose image it is, then it is coequal to its source. . . . He has, in regard to this image, employed the name "form" on account, I believe, of its beauty, wherein there is at once such harmony, and prime equality, and prime similitude, in no way discordant, in no measure unequal, and in no part dissimilar, but wholly answering to the identity of the one whose image it is. . . . Wherefore that

26. Gregory, *De anima et resurrectione,* in *PG,* 46:93-96: Ἐπεὶ δὲ οὖν παντὸς ἀγαθοῦ ἐπέκεινα ἡ θεία φύσις, τὸ δὲ ἀγαθὸν ἀγαθῷ φίλον πάντως, διὰ τοῦτο ἑαυτὴν βλέπουσα καὶ ὃ ἔχει, θέλει, καὶ ὃ θέλει, ἔχει, οὐδὲν τῶν ἔξωθεν εἰς ἑαυτὴν δεχομένη. . . . ἥ τε γὰρ ζωὴ τῆς ἄνω φύσεως ἀγάπη ἐστίν, ἐπειδὴ τὸ καλὸν ἀγαπητὸν πάντως ἐστὶ τοῖς γινώσκουσι (γινώσκει δε ἑαυτὸ τὸ θεῖον), ἡ δὲ γνῶσις ἀγάπη γίνεται, διότι καλόν ἐστι φύσει τὸ γινωσκόμενον.

ineffable conjunction of the Father and his image is never without fruition, without love, without rejoicing. Hence that love, delight, felicity or beatitude, if any human voice can worthily say it, is called by him, in brief, use, and is in the Trinity the Holy Spirit, not begotten, but of the begetter and begotten alike the very sweetness, filling all creatures, according to their capacities, with his bountiful superabundance and excessiveness.[27]

How is it that such a God is one? It is because each divine person, in the circle of God's knowledge and love of his own goodness (which is both wisdom and charity), is a "face," a "capture," of the divine essence that is — as must be, given the simplicity and infinity of God — always wholly God, in the full depth of his "personality." This is why the language of *tropos hyparxeos*, applied to God, cannot displace that of person but only confirm it: for any "mode of subsistence" of the infinite being of God must be an infinite mode, a way whereby God is entirely, "personally" God. God is never less than wholly God. Just as the Father is the plenitude of divine goodness, in whom inhere both his Word (manifestation, form) and Gift (the life in which the Word goes forth, light in which he is seen, joy in which he is known, generosity wherewith he is bestowed), so in the Son the depth of the paternal *arche* and the boundless light of and delight in wisdom also inhere, and in the Spirit the plenitude of paternal being and filial form inhere in the "mode" of accomplished love. Each person is fully gathered and reflected in the mode of the other: as other, as community and unity at once. Here, in the mystery of divine infinity, one finds, necessarily, a perfect coincidence of the languages of "subsistent relations" and of "divine persons." And so it is correct to seek trinitarian *vestigia* both in the multiplicit singularity of the soul, which subsists in memory, understanding, will, and so forth, and also in the communal implications of each of us in one another, in the threefold structure of love, within which circle we together, as the event of shared love, constitute (however poorly or sinfully) the human "essence." We waver between these two analogical orders at an infinite distance from their supereminent truth, in that distance that all the created intervals of our being show forth; and of course, the orders are not separate: knowledge and love of neighbor fulfill the soul's velleity

27. Augustine, *De Trinitate* 6.10.11: "Imago enim si perfecte implet illud cuius imago est, ipsa coaequatur ei, non illud imagini suae. In qua imagine speciem nominavit, credo, propter pulchritudinem, ubi iam est tanta congruentia, et prima aequalitas, et prima similitudo, nulla in re dissidens, et nullo modo inaequalis, et nulla ex parte dissimilis, sed ad identidem respondens ei cuius imago est. . . . Ille igitur ineffabilis quidam complexus patris et imaginis non est sine perfruitione, sine charitate, sine gaudio. Illa ergo dilectio, delectatio, felicitas vel beatitudo, si tamen aliqua humana voce digne dicitur, usus ab illo appellatus est breviter, et est in trinitate spiritus sanctus, non genitus, sed genitoris genitique suavitas, ingenti largitate atque ubertate perfundens omnes creaturas pro captu earum. . . ."

toward the world, and so grant each of us that internally constituted "self" that exists only through an engagement with a world of others; but that engagement is possible only in that the structure of interiority is already "othered" and "othering," in distinct moments of consciousness' inherence in itself. In the simultaneity of these two ways of analogy it becomes possible — with immeasurable inadequacy — to speak of the trinitarian God who is love.

iii. Divine Joy

All of which, at last, brings me back to the theophany at the Jordan: it is here, at Christ's baptism, that the Father, within the economy of salvation, clearly speaks his Word; here God declares himself, and the Father's everlasting utterance of the Son becomes discernible; and the form of his utterance is a declaration of pleasure. Is it an excessively literal reading of Rahner's maxim to say that the Word of God is thus shown to be also the joy of God, that the Son is spoken *in* being the Father's delight? For surely the approbation, the εὐδοκία, of the Father expressed here is also his eternal χαρμονή, his τέρψις. If this theophany reveals God as *perichoresis,* it also shows him to be the God whose life of reciprocal "giving way" and "containing" (χωρεῖν) is also a kind of "dancing" (χορεύειν), and the God who is τερψίχορος, delighting in the dance. When Scripture says God is love, after all, this is certainly not some vague sentiment concerning the presence of God in our emotions, but describes the life of God, the dynamism of his substance, the distance and the dance: the unity of coinherence, but also the interval of appraisal, address, recognition, and pleasure. And if the descent of the dove at Christ's baptism reveals that every act of God, as Basil says, "is inaugurated by the Father, effected by the Son, and perfected by the Holy Spirit" (*De Spiritu Sancto* 16.38), it reveals also that God's love is always entirely sufficient in itself: as the third, who receives and returns the love of Father and Son, and so witnesses, enjoys, and perfects it, the Spirit is also the one in whom that love most manifestly opens out as sheer delight, generosity, and desire for the other.

There is a long, predominantly Western tradition of speaking of the Spirit as the *vinculum caritatis* between Father and Son, which — if it is taken to mean that in the divine life the indiscerptibility of love and knowledge is such that God's generation and procession enfold one another, the Spirit acting as the bond of love between Father and Son, the Son as bond of knowledge between Father and Spirit, the Father being the source of both — is a good and even necessary term. But it can also be misleading, in various ways: as Orthodox theologians occasionally worry, it can give the appearance that the Spirit is not as irreducibly "personal" as Father and Son; if made too rigid, it impairs our understanding of God as a triune coinherence, whose shared love is the being God is and not merely the action proper to one hypostasis (as though Father and Son were persons in an anthropomorphic sense, distinguishable from the act of their love, which would be intermediate between them); it can make the Trinity seem like a totality, a mechanism composed of parts or a synthesis accomplished in distinct and successive moments, rather than the God who is infinite, incomposite, and yet differing, wholly God as Father, as Son, and as Holy Spirit; it might almost be taken as an explanation of "how God works," each person of the Trinity occupying some discrete position and function in the metaphysical constitution of God. Correctly understood, however, it does none of this; and it depicts the Spirit as not simply the love of Father and Son, but also everlastingly the differentiation of that love, the third term, the outward, "straying," prodigal second intonation of that love. Because God is Spirit, as much as he is Father or Son, the love of Father and Son is forever, in utterance and response, also differently inflected, renewed, restored, as plenitude. God, in being Father and Son, is not the reflex of God, the reiteration at an infinite distance (which would merely be the distance of totality) of the Father's identity, the polarity of an omnipotent Narcissus and his shadow, because he is also Spirit, a perpetual "divergence" of that mutual love toward yet another; the harmony of Father and Son is not the absolute music of an undifferentiated noise, but the open, diverse, and complete polyphony of Father, Son, and Spirit. The Father's entire being, which he possesses in his paternal depth, is always also both filial — manifest, known, imparted — and spiritual — loved, enjoyed, perfected — and this event of God's knowledge and joy is the divine essence — exteriority, happiness, communion — in its infinite unity. The Spirit is not only the bond of love, but also the one who always breaks the bonds of self-love, the person who from eternity assures that divine love has no single, stable center, no isolated "self": as Dumitru Staniloae says, the Spirit is that other in whom Father and Son meet "again," in the commonality of their love *for another*.[28] In this way the Holy Spirit indeed perfects the love of God, immanently and economically: immanently, completing it *as* love, deepening it in his "excessive" difference, the further sharing of love, beyond what would be contained in mere mutuality; and economically, by being the differentiation and perfection of divine love "outward," whereby, graciously, it opens out to address freely (and so to constitute) the otherness of creation, and invest it with boundless difference, endless inflections of divine

28. Dumitru Staniloae, *Theology and the Church*, trans. Robert Barringer (Crestwood, N.Y.: St. Vladimir's Seminary Press, 1980), 93-94. See also Richard of St. Victor, *De Trinitate* 3.19, on how the love of just two persons would be an isolated and polarized love that must disappear into itself, and how therefore true love always seeks a third to share that love.

glory. It may seem here that these pages are wandering from argument into rhapsody, but it is necessary to establish the proper trinitarian diction for all that is to follow.

Necessary because a distinctively Christian understanding of beauty is contained in trinitarian theology, whose nature is intimated with exquisite brevity in the words of the Father at Christ's baptism. The most elementary statement of theological aesthetics is that God is beautiful: not only that God is beauty or the essence and archetype of beauty, nor even only that God is the highest beauty, but that, as Gregory the Theologian says, God is beauty *and* also beautiful, whose radiance shines upon and is reflected in his creatures (*Oration* 28.30-31). As Dionysius insists, we should not distinguish between God as beauty and as infinitely beautiful, the splendor that gathers all things toward and into itself (*De divinis nominibus* 4.7). The beauty of God is not simply "ideal": it is not remote, cold, characterless, or abstract, nor merely absolute, unitary, and formless. It is the beauty of which the psalmist speaks when he exclaims, "I shall be sated, upon awaking, in beholding thy form *(temuna)*" (17:15), and praises the savor, the sweetness *(noam)* of the Lord (27:4). "For how great is his goodness," Zechariah says, "and how great is his beauty *(yofi)*" (9:17). God's beauty is delight and the object of delight, the shared gaze of love that belongs to the persons of the Trinity; it is what God beholds, what the Father sees and rejoices in in the Son, in the sweetness of the Spirit, what Son and Spirit find delightful in one another, because as Son and Spirit of the Father they share his knowledge and love as persons. This cannot be emphasized enough: the Christian God, who is infinite, is also infinitely *formosus,* the supereminent fullness of all form, transcendently determinate, always possessed of his Logos. True beauty is not the idea of the beautiful, a static archetype in the "mind" of God, but is an infinite "music," drama, art, completed in — but never "bounded" by — the termless dynamism of the Trinity's life; God is boundless, and so is never a boundary; his music possesses the richness of every transition, interval, measure, variation — all dancing and delight. And because he is beautiful, being abounds with difference: shape, variety, manifold relation. Beauty is the distinction of the different, the otherness of the other, the true form of distance. And the Holy Spirit who perfects the divine love, so that it is not only reflective but also evocative — calling out to yet another as pure delight, outgoing, both uncompelled and unlimited — also makes the divine joy open to the otherness of what is not divine, of creation, without estranging it from its divine "logic"; and the Spirit communicates difference as primordially the gift of beauty, because his difference within the Trinity is the happiness that perfects desire, the fulfillment of love; for the Spirit comes to rest in the Son, there finding all the joy he seeks, reinflecting the distance between Father and Son not just as bare cognizance, but as delight, the whole rapture of the divine essence.

Jonathan Edwards calls the Spirit the beautifier, the one in whom the happiness of God overflows and is perfected precisely *as* overflowing, and so the one who bestows radiance, shape, clarity, and enticing splendor upon what God creates and embraces in the superabundance of his love.[29] And this beauty is the form of all creaturely truth; thus no other can be known as other apart from recognition and love, analogy and desire. Delight in beauty "corresponds"; joy in beauty, when it is truly joy, reflects the way in which God utters himself, and utters creation, in the Spirit's light; joy repeats, in some sense, the gesture that gives being to beings, and alone grants knowledge of being as original peace.

---

2. The Christian understanding of difference and distance is shaped by the doctrine of the Trinity, where theology finds that the true form of difference is peace, of distance beauty.

In the beginning was the Word, and the Word was with God, and the Word was God.

John 1:1

I and my Father are one.

John 10:30

But when the Comforter is come, whom I will send unto you from the Father, even the Spirit of truth, which proceedeth from the Father, he shall testify of me.

John 15:26

Holy Father, keep through thine own name those whom thou hast given me, that they may be one, as we are.

John 17:11

That they all may be one; as thou, Father, art in me, and I in thee, that they also may be one in us: that the world may believe that thou hast

29. See Jonathan Edwards, *Miscellanies*, in *The Philosophy of Jonathan Edwards*, from his private notebooks, ed. Harvey G. Townsend (Westport, Conn.: Greenwood Press, 1972), 260; and *Essay on the Trinity* (New York: Scribner's, 1903), 108. Edwards's attribution to the Spirit of a special role as beautifier is taken up by Patrick Sherry in his *Spirit and Beauty: An Introduction to Theological Aesthetics* (Oxford: Clarendon, 1992).

sent me. And the glory which thou gavest me I have given them; that
they may be one, even as we are one: I in them, and thou in me, that
they may be made perfect in one; and that the world may know that
thou hast sent me, and hast loved them, as thou hast loved me.

John 17:21-23

i. Divine Difference

Another way of receiving Rahner's maxim is to look not only at the narrative
sequence of the Gospels, with its mysterious intertwinings of the actions of the
divine persons in the ministry, death, resurrection, and ascension of Christ, but
also at the experience of creaturely integration into the corporate identity of
the church. As has been said, Basil of Caesarea was able to fill out the doctrine
of the Trinity in his *De Spiritu Sancto* by calling attention to the presence of the
Spirit in every aspect of the Christian's redemption — completing it, perfecting
it — so that to deny the divinity of the Spirit would be to deny the efficacy of
one's own baptism: as only God can join us to God (which is what salvation is),
the Spirit who unites us to the Son (who bears us up to the Father) must be
God.[30] Perhaps then one should look back, from the vantage of the
pneumatologically accomplished reality of salvation (participation in the
church), at what the Spirit has made of sinful humanity, the better to grasp how
the economic Trinity is known to us. If the Spirit completes the economic action of salvation by sustaining the church in the interval of eschatological suspense between Christ's resurrection and return, then it is in the light of how the
Spirit refashions humanity after the likeness of God in Christ that Christian
thought begins to see the fullness of the mystery imparted in salvation: the
Spirit completes the image of God — just as he completes the Trinity's life immanently — and this is (or should be) made visible in the corporate and
common life of the church. One is, at least, encouraged by the verses cited immediately above to see in the communality and interdependency of the church,
the peaceful participation of Christians in one body, a true if vastly inexact image of how God is forever a God dwelling in and with, a God who truly takes
delight and is truly at peace; the unity of the church somehow reflects the way
in which God is one: "that they may be one, even as we are one: I in them, and
thou in me." Original unity is original "reciprocity." This is perhaps a fairly ele-

---

30. Though, of course, it is Gregory the Theologian, in *The Five Theological Orations*,
who explicitly speaks of the Spirit as "God" and "homoousion" (*Oration* 31.10). Basil's argument
certainly requires this affirmation, but — whether from wise discretion or from an unwillingness to say more than Scripture or the Nicene symbol — he nowhere uses the words.

mentary theological observation, but it throws into relief the strangeness of Christian language, its willingness to place difference at the origin; if indeed the thought of difference is the imperative of philosophy liberated from idealism and metaphysical nostalgia, we may inquire whether the postmodern thought of difference is genuinely more radical (or simply more "diremptive") than what trinitarian theology already implies.

Of course, to talk of difference in terms of the Trinity must necessarily inspire distrust: Is this not just another metaphysics of the one and the many, an attempt to subdue difference by "grounding" it in a transcendent substance or ideal structure of differentiation as such? But this is a somewhat tedious — if perhaps inevitable — question, and one moreover that altogether misses what is genuinely of interest in the matter. Theologically there is no value in speculation about ideal or metaphysical *causes* of difference, ontic or ontological; the triune *perichoresis* of God is not a *substance* in which difference is grounded in its principles or in which it achieves the unity of a higher synthesis, even if God is the fullness and actuality of all that is; rather, the truly unexpected implication of trinitarian dogma is that Christian thought has no metaphysics of the one and the many, the same and the different, because that is a polarity that has no place in the Christian narrative. Whereas, for instance, the One of Plotinus eventuates in difference by way of conversion and remotion, the benign ontological apostasy that erupts from the *theoria* of Nous, for Christian thought difference does not *eventuate* at all, but is; Christianity has no tale to tell of a division or distinction within being between a transcendental unity and a material multiplicity that achieves — in the tension between them and in the speculative convertibility of one with the other — the coherence of totality, but knows only differentiation and the music of unity, the infinite music of the three persons giving and receiving and giving anew. Created difference "corresponds" to God, is analogous to the divine life, precisely in differing from God; this is the Christian thought of divine transcendence, of a God who is made inconceivably near in — whose glory is ubiquitously proclaimed by — creation's infinity of difference from God, its free, departing, serial excess of otherness. Theology speaks of nothing if it speaks taxonomically of the one and the many, because difference as revealed in the trinitarian economy precedes this static and mutually conditioning opposition; the motion of divine love shows self-contained singularity to be a fiction of thought, for even in the "instant" of origin there is the otherness of manifestation: knowledge and love. Ἐν ἀρχῇ ἦν ὁ λόγος: God is always articulate, an address, given over in the image that repeats and yet repeats at a distance and is borne over into yet another open intonation; God, one might presume to say, is God in supplementation, repetition, variation; and yet the one God. There is nothing theologically objectionable in, say, Deleuze's desire to speak of difference first and last, or his repeated insistence that there is nothing more "true" than difference; for Christian thought, what is objection-able is his *metaphysical* certitude that difference is purely singular, tautological, an ontic violence in the instant of its rupture. The triune God is not that which negates — or is unveiled through negating — difference; he has no dialectical relation to the world nor any metaphysical "function" in maintaining the total-ity of being. He is not the high who stands over against the low, but is the infi-nite act of distance that gives high and low a place. As the God who gives a dif-ference that is more than merely negative and that opens out analogically from the "theme" he imparts (the theme of free differentiation, oriented in love to-ward the other and all), he shows that difference is — still more radically, more originally — peace and joy. This is a thought of difference that lies outside any "metaphysical" scheme (Hegelian or Deleuzean, for instance), an ontology without need of determinate negation *and* without any inherent tendency to-ward opposition or rupture: in neither sense need it ever cross the interval of the negative. Nor is there any negation or alienation in the relation of God to creation: the latter is but a further address, another modulation of the way in which he utters himself, in that which is infinitely different from him and which is — and for this very reason — his tabernacle and the manifestation of his beauty.[31] When Derrida asks if God is the name that already opens ontolog-ical difference,[32] the virtue of his question exceeds the prejudices that prompt it; he means to ask a thoroughly philosophical question, which presumes al-ready to understand the nature of the difference that "the divine" brings into view; but the trinitarian name of difference is one that makes the ontological difference of which Derrida speaks — the constraint whereby beings are shown in the erasure of being — merely another fable concerning the totality of the one and the many.

Christian thought stands outside the opposition that is presumed within either a metaphysics of ontological hypotaxis (such as any idealism describes) or a metaphysics of ontological rupture (such as postmodernism professes); it knows only the beauty of being's parataxis, its open, free, serial, and irreducible declaration of glory; it grasps being neither as an immobile synthesis that stands over against and sublates every utterance, nor as the sheer cacophony of aleatory violence, but as rhetoric, the outward address and proclamation of the God who has eternally spoken, who speaks, and who will speak, the God who "others" himself in himself and contains and surrenders otherness as infinite music, infinite discourse. As a "metaphysics" of creation, it rejects every claim

31. See Hans Urs von Balthasar, *The Glory of the Lord: A Theological Aesthetics,* vol. 1, *Seeing the Form,* trans. Erasmo Leiva-Merikakis (San Francisco: Ignatius, 1982), 506-7.

32. Jacques Derrida, *Writing and Difference,* trans. Alan Bass (Chicago: University of Chi-cago Press, 1978), 149.

regarding the identist "substance" that "underlies" plurality (call it the One, the Concept, *différance*). Indeed, the very concept of substance, of οὐσία, is so transformed by its assumption into trinitarian doctrine as to make immeasurably more complex any talk of discrete or immutable "essences." When, for instance, Gregory the Theologian insists that the thought of God's oneness must immediately be accompanied by the thought of the Three (*Oratio* 40.41), he is noting that God is not secondarily Trinity; indeed, rather than liken the Trinity — in the venerable and plausible style of other early Christian writers — to the sun and its rays (a "total" unity, that is, that manifests itself in distinct and derivative moments), Gregory adopts the remarkable and vaguely disorienting image of three suns, whose light is one shared yet also somehow severally imparted radiance of love (*Oratio* 31.32). God, in short, is not a hierarchy of prior essence and posterior manifestation, indeterminate being and then paradoxical expression, but is always already expression, already Word and Likeness; to speak of his *ousia* is not to speak of an underlying undifferentiated substrate (a divine ὑποκείμενον), but to name the gift of love, the glorious movement of the divine persons, who forever "set forth" and "converge." Thus God is the distance of the infinite, the *actus* of all distance. It is crucially important that the peculiarity of trinitarian thought be grasped here. Orthodox trinitarianism, as it came to be articulated, far from simply absorbing into theology the speculative grammar of the circumambient philosophical culture, overcame the language of metaphysical order to which Christian thought might easily have succumbed, and in so doing arrived, for the first time in Greek thought, at a genuine concept of divine transcendence. In the fourth century the Cappadocians, in their struggle against the *pneumatomachoi,* made it clear that the elaborate but explanatory metaphysical hierarchies of Alexandrian speculation (whether Christian, Jewish, pagan, or gnostic), those diminishing degrees of economically reduced divinity by which the inaccessible and divine "height" of reality was thought to be joined to lower reality, were alien to genuine Christian trinitarianism, and that the Christian God is at once infinitely more transcendent of and, in consequence, infinitely nearer to (within the very being of) finite reality than was the inaccessible God of antique metaphysics, the supreme being set apart on being's summit, the fixed hook from which the cosmos dangled. The three persons are not economic accommodations of a supreme ontic principle with inferior reality, but are rather all equally present in every divine action (Basil, *De Spiritu Sancto* 16.38), each wholly God, even as they differ. Because (as the divine economy reveals) the persons of the Trinity are one action of mission and fulfillment, immanently and economically, Christian theology discovered it could not account for what the Areopagite calls τὸ τῆς οὐσίας διάφορον (*De ecclesiastica hierarchia* 4.3.1), being's differentiation, in terms of a system of substances mediating a supreme substance confined within its supernality. The Plotinian descent from unity to plurality was displaced by God's *perichoresis* as unity and difference, and the tragicomic ambiguity of emanated finitude was displaced by the joy of God's immanently diverse fullness and of finitude's gratuity. Only when the chain of necessity was thus broken, the hierarchy of hypostases between the absolute and the contingent replaced by the analogical interval between trinitarian infinity and the gift of created glory, could God be understood as being in its transcendence, free of ontic determination, wholly transcendent and immediately present, transcendent (free) of even the "transcendence" imaginable within classical metaphysics. Thus theology can speak of being as rhetoric, and see in the surface of being a kind of intelligible discourse — not one concerning the scale of bare substances, but a doxological discourse, an open declaration of God's glory, by which the God who differentiates speaks his beauty in the groundless play of form and action, the free movement of diversity, artistry, and unnecessary grace. The occurrence of difference as difference, as the reverberation of variation in the very event of difference, expresses — not dialectically, but aesthetically — the superabounding joy, delight, regard, and response that is God's life. At its infinite analogical remove, created being (both in forms and accidents) belongs to God's utterance of himself, and as God is infinite, comprising in his *perichoresis* the full scope of all difference, variation, and response, it is precisely creation's departure from God that approximates God, its setting forth as that which is not God that is its return to God, its reception of the gift of being that is its restoration of the gift to God.

ii. Divine Perfection

If difference is not simply departure from an origin, but lies at the origin and is the origin (as the prologue of John's Gospel attests), then the divine *ousia* is neither indeterminacy nor monad.[33] Fatherhood, as Athanasius remarks, is not a mere property of God, for God is Father in himself (*De decretis* 22). In the eternal generation of the Son, according to Bonaventure, the Father eternally frames his Eternal Art (Bonaventure's name for the Son), who is both the likeness of the Father and the fullness of all God can do and does, and from whom all things receive their beauty, their shining measures of differentiation.[34] In the life of God, already, there is "language" — icon and *semeion* — but neither negation nor sublation. In the light of this thought of difference — before and

33. See T. F. Torrance, *The Trinitarian Faith* (Edinburgh: T. & T. Clark, 1993), 311.
34. See especially Bonaventure's *Commentaries on Peter Lombard's Sentences* I: d.6, a.u., q.3, resp.; see also *Breviloquium* 1.8 and *Collationes in Hexaemeron* 1.13.

containing all *ousia* — even such a "postmetaphysical" construal of ontological difference as the late Heidegger's concern with the *Austrag* between being and beings, the passing over from concealment to unconcealment and the opening of being in the occlusion and effacement of being, appears to be still too dependent upon dialectic, still — even in its atelic, "eschatological" indifference to all dialectical process — too fixated upon the diastole and systole between being and beings, and still too metaphysical in its tale of how being suffers the violence of erasure even in the "event of appropriation" *(Ereignis)*. Because God is Trinity, beings "pass over" from (or, rather, receive) being peacefully, for the motion of the distance is the movement of what moves, what gives: the divine persons who have being as that gift that passes from each to the other. For God is infinite *as* Trinity, not only transcendent of all boundaries but also, therefore, never a boundary to himself: never totality or system or process, but always already complete and always venturing forth across every boundary. And if the Spirit is God who differs yet again, an "unexpected" further inflection of God's utterance of himself, so that difference is never merely the reflex of the Same but the fullness of reply, in all the richness and dilatory excess of the language of love, then the Spirit eternally remodulates the divine distance, opens a futurity (to speak in terms of extreme analogical remoteness) to the Father and Son, a "still more" in the music of divine address, awaited and possessed. The Spirit's "perfection" of the divine life and act, as that movement of desire and love that finds all its delight in the splendor of the Son, is also the movement of the Father's creative will, which finds in the Son that inexhaustible fullness of actuality and grace by which the Spirit gives being to beings in endless diversity. As Rahner says, in the saving action of the economic Trinity, the real hypostatic idioms are displayed,[35] and the Spirit's idiom is one of variation within difference. This is why, incidentally, Augustine is essentially correct in the shape he gives to his trinitarian analogies; when he finds a *vestigium trinitatis,* for instance, in the threefold dynamism of the act of love (lover-beloved-love itself) or of the soul's embrace of reality (memory-understanding-will), he calls attention to the way in which the acts of God are one, but with the unity of a fullness that can properly express itself in being's rich and varied surface, because it has its unity in a third term that is openness as such. God is not, in brief, the sublime One of Neoplatonism, but the Trinity: not simply "sublime," that is, but beautiful.[36]

The reality of the difference of the Spirit's difference from the Son's difference is traditionally expressed as the distinction between generation and procession: which, as John of Damascus says, one may know are distinct with-

---

35. Rahner, *The Trinity,* 24-33.
36. See Symeon the New Theologian, *Hymns of Divine Love* 24 and 31.

out knowing how (*De fide orthodoxa* 1.8). Neither enjoys priority over the other, any more than priority is assigned between knowledge and love: each is given by and made full in the other. In the economy of salvation, one sees that the Son receives from the Father the power to impart the Spirit, that the Spirit receives from the Father the power to communicate the Son, that the Son and Spirit are both sent and sending (the Spirit sending Christ into the world, the waters, the desert, the Son sending the Spirit upon the disciples), that all give, receive, restore, and rejoice — to, from, and with one another — and that, again as John of Damascus says, the Holy Spirit is always between the Father and Son (1.13), occupying the distance of paternal and filial intimacy differently, abiding in and "rephrasing" it. The Spirit is, as a common patristic usage has it, the light wherein the Son is seen, and the Father is seen in the Son;[37] the Spirit "interprets" the Logos, bears tidings (ἑρμηνεύειν) of the Son before the Father, shows the Son to the world, proclaims the Father in the Son. He is the light of creation, the radiance of the Word's splendor, and the light of the transfiguration, granting us a vision of the Father's depths in the beauty of the Son, and in the Son's mystical body. Dumitru Staniloae calls Vladimir Lossky somewhat to task for his inordinate stress upon the distinction between the Son's action to unify and the Spirit's action to confer particularity within the church;[38] and of course, to allow such a scheme to become too rigid would be again to succumb to an impulse to "arrange" God into separate functions or moments; but given that in the economy the Son saves persons by embracing them within the corporate identity of his body while the Spirit imparts the Son in an endless diversity of settings and draws creatures in an always peculiar fashion into that identity (each, of course, in and by the other), perhaps something here is revealed concerning the immanent trinitarian *taxis.* In the Spirit the infinite richness that passes from Father to Son is also the infinite openness of the divine distance, the endless articulation of the inexhaustible content of the Father's very likeness in the Son. There is a danger here, perhaps, of sounding like Plotinus, as though the Father were the One from whom difference departs in successive stages of noetic contemplation and psychic dissemination. But, again, the Trinity is not a Neoplatonic dégringolade of the divine into lower orders of being, or a monad progressively distorted into multiplicity; at the source, and as the source, is divine difference, a shared giving and receiving that is the divine life. God is the event of his circumincession, in which he has graciously made room for beings. God is the divine interval of love's superabundance, of life, of the gift. In God is no inward, unrelated gaze, no stillness prior to relation, or suspended in dialectical relation to otherness; his gaze holds another ever in re-

37. See Symeon the New Theologian, 11.
38. Staniloae, 39.

gard, for he is his own other. In that fullness, descent and departure are not secondary movements, nor separate phases within a metaphysical totality, but are God's one life of joy. And to say that the Spirit inflects the distance between Father and Son differently is to say that in every "moment" of that distance there is a difference, an aesthetic surfeit in its phrasing; each "extractable" interval is measured differently. Thus God utters himself with a fullness of rhetorical effect, an endless range of response, embellishment, invention. And as the Spirit is always between Father and Son, and proceeds through the Son, and as the Son is begotten in the Spirit, and as Son and Spirit are always with the Father, each person donating and redonating himself and the other, one may speak of God as always somehow, even in the immediacy of his love, his own mediation, deferral, icon. As the Son is the true image of the Father, faithfully reflecting him in infinite distance, and as the Spirit forever "prismates" the radiance of God's image into all the beautiful measures of that distance, one may speak of God as a God who is, in himself, always somehow analogous; the coincidence in God of mediacy and immediacy, image and difference, is the "proportion" that makes every finite interval a possible disclosure — a tabernacle — of God's truth. And as God's utterance of himself is thus always opening into numberless variations, intonations, ornamentations, and delights, it is, so to speak, perlocutionary, always rhetorical; indeed, God's life is — one is emboldened to say — rhetoric.

But one must pause here to make an obvious observation: to talk thus of distance, difference, language, icon, mediation, and so forth is to speak at an analogical remove whose proportion is still that between the infinite and the finite, between which (logic seems to dictate) there is no real proportion. Even if God's infinity is plenitude rather than the fallow *chora* or sterile "nothing" of a more immanentist ontology (infinite place rather than primordial displacement), still all the riches of God are, by virtue of his simplicity, wholly convertible with his essence. For the finite to reflect or "reach" the infinite, though, must there not necessarily be a double negation, a reduction of the finite from concrete difference to abstract identity and a reduction of the infinite to determinate negation? Or if not, can the "proportion" of divine difference be anything but absolute difference, the tragic distance of the "Wholly Other" that merely, under the name of God, introduces metaphysical melancholy into theology and reduces God to a being placed over against the world? To answer these problems we need to consider the distinctively Christian understanding of the infinite — to which end I now turn to the first (and still the greatest) Christian thinker of divine infinity, Gregory of Nyssa. For Gregory God is to be understood first as τὸ ἀνέλπιστον κάλλος, an unanticipated beauty, longed for but without certain hope, and so evoking desperation (*In canticum canticorum* 12): a God "seen" only by the infinite inflaming of desire (2), whose savor draws one on into ever greater dimensions of his glory, so that one is always at the beginning of one's pilgrimage toward him, always discovering and entering into greater dimensions of his beauty (8). This is so because God is always beyond and still above the beyond (ἐπέκεινα, ὑπὲρ ἐπέκεινα) (*In ecclesiasten* 7), but also because God abides in absolute intimacy with creation as the infinite of surpassing fullness, whose beauty embraces and exceeds all that is.

---

3. In the Christian God, the infinite is seen to be beautiful and so capable of being traversed by way of the beautiful.

And [Moses] said, I beseech thee, shew me thy glory. And [God] said, I will make all my goodness pass before thee. . . . And he said, Thou canst not see my face: for there shall no man see me, and live. And the LORD *said, Behold, there is a place by me, and thou shalt stand upon a rock: And it shall come to pass, while my glory passeth by, that I will put thee in a clift of the rock, and will cover thee with my hand while I pass by: And I will take away mine hand, and thou shalt see my back parts: but my face shall not be seen.*

Exod. 33:18-23

We may speak much, and yet come short: wherefore in sum, he is all.

Sir. 43:27

Jesus answered them, Is it not written in your law, I said, Ye are gods? If he called them gods, unto whom the word of God came, and the scripture cannot be broken; say ye of him, whom the Father hath sanctified, and sent into the world, Thou blasphemest; because I said, I am the Son of God?

John 10:34-36

Brethren, I count not myself to have apprehended: but this one thing I do, forgetting those things which are behind, and reaching forth unto those things which are before, I press toward the mark for the prize of the high calling of God in Christ Jesus.

Phil. 3:13-14

*But we all, with open face beholding as in a glass the glory of the Lord,
are changed into the same image from glory to glory, even as by the
Spirit of the Lord.*

2 Cor. 3:18

*Whereby are given unto us exceeding great and precious promises: that
by these ye might be partakers of the divine nature, having escaped the
corruption that is in the world through lust.*

2 Pet. 1:4

i. Desire's Flight

Our words cannot encompass God, for he exceeds all his works; thus Jesus ben
Sirach is moved to his most striking utterance: τὸ πᾶν ἐστίν αὐτός. This is not
an assertion of some variety of pantheism, surely, much less any other metaphysics of "the all"; no book of the Bible manifests a firmer grasp both of God's
transcendence and of his indwelling glory. God is all, but not the whole, not the
closed circle of totality; he contains and exceeds, gives creation its breadth of
difference, but at the same time infinitely transcends his gift. Yet divine transcendence is not just the distance of an infinite remoteness, nor the abstract infinity of being's empty supremacy over beings. It is not only possible but necessary to reckon God's transcendence by moving continuously from the vision of
beauty within the created order — its quantities and proportions and diversi-
ties — to the praise of God's embracing infinity; for not only is God qualitatively infinite, over against the ceaseless ebb and flow of finitude, but he is the
dynamic God who (so to speak) quantitatively surpasses the whole of being's
glory, as its supereminent plenitude, whose radiant beauty is truly declared in
creation's swift and shifting play of forms and distances. How it could be that
God is at once transcendent, no being among beings, but also infinitely rich in
being's splendors, outstripping creation in his concrete and determinate fullness, was in a sense the singular concern of Gregory of Nyssa; and his ingenious
appropriation of Paul's language of straining or stretching out toward the fullness of Christ provided him with a term (ἐπεκτεινόμενος, ἐπεκτείναι,
ἐπέκτασις) for advancing, against the static hierarchies of conventional metaphysics, a genuinely dynamic ontology, and with it a new conception of what
constitutes the relation between the divine archetype and its created image. He
succeeded in imagining an infinite that is, while boundless, still supremely aesthetic: not a formless sublime exceeding and annihilating the beautiful, but an
endless display of beauty, surpassing the beautiful as the ever more beautiful,
imparting beauty to beings from its own depth of loveliness; and he succeeded

also in describing with extraordinary originality the force of creaturely desire, as it ventures forth to encounter ontological infinity (to which it aspires) not as a qualitative dialectical negation, nor as a privation of the aesthetic, but as divine "excess," grasped in its very transcendence under the form of the soul's own superabounding joy and longing. Hence the power of his thought still to remind theology that nowhere in the Christian understanding of being is there to be found the distance of the pagan *apeiron* or the postmodern sublime, and that violence is always only the refusal of that intimacy in deferral, that mediation, that is the true form of all distance: that the beautiful, that is, is not an enfeebling, deceptive, or violent stilling of the prior tumult of being, but is itself the grammar and element of an infinite motion, able to traverse all of being without illusion or strife.

According to Gregory, creation is in its every aspect a movement. Words such as τροπή and κίνησις retain distinctly opprobrious connotations in the more "Platonizing" climate of, say, Origen's thought, but for Gregory change is simply constitutive of created nature; creation is itself (Gregory employing the traditional argument) a conversion from the darkness of nonbeing toward the light of God, a kind of ontological heliotropism.[39] As utter contingency, it is pure mutability, a motion from moment to moment, place to place, not only in creatures' incessant peregrinations but within their very identities (*De anima et resurrectione;*[40] *PG*, 46:141B-C); the created dies every moment, writes Gregory, to be reborn the next (*In canticum canticorum* 12;[41] *GNO*, 6:351); if it ceased to change, it would cease to exist (*De hominis opificio* 13;[42] *PG*, 44:165A-C). Each person, he says, is a nation — someone new at every instant, from conception to death (*DAR* 141C-D) — and the whole of humanity is an unfolding "series," a successive realization of the creative word (the first Adam) that God uttered in making humanity in his image: an image that exists only in the fullness of these different articulations taken altogether.[43] To be human is to be an "act," thor-

---

39. See M. Canévet, "Nature du mal et économie du salut chez Grégoire de Nysse," *Revue des sciences philosophiques et théologiques* 56 (1968): 87; and Jean Daniélou, "La colombe et la ténèbre dans la mystique Byzantine ancienne," *Eranos-Jahrbuch* (1954): 53.

40. Hereafter *DAR*. Though so far I have cosseted my lethargy by citing ancient texts only by their divisions, in the case of Gregory this practice will be suspended. The edition cited will be the *Gregorii Nysseni Opera (GNO)* of Werner Jaeger et al.; works not yet included there will be cited from the Migne *Patrologia Graeca (PG)*.

41. Hereafter *ICC*.

42. Hereafter *DHO*.

43. See Hans Urs von Balthasar, *Presence and Thought: An Essay on the Religious Philosophy of Gregory of Nyssa* (San Francisco: Ignatius, 1995), 50-52, for a brief treatment of this "diastematic" view of human nature as a spiritual plenitude serially filled out in the unfolding of time and space. To this aspect of Gregory's thought I shall turn when I discuss eschatology, but I shall remark here that nothing could be more misleading than to take this as simple ideal-

oughly dynamic (in either one's sensible or intelligible aspect), in transit, without center in oneself, borne away or driven toward what lies beyond. Desire is the energy of our movement, and so of our being. It may draw one toward the good — which is boundless and allows for endless pilgrimage within itself — or toward evil — which is nothing but a parasitic and umbratile privation of the good, an abyss mimicking the true infinite; but in either case one moves, one changes: all is traversal. In each instant the self departs from itself, in ecstasy or repetition, urged on by a longing for an elusive beauty (*Oratio catechetica* 221;[44] *GNO* 3.4: 55-56). The soul is forever seeking to take its fill of the world's endless play of becoming (*De beatitudinibus* 4;[45] *GNO* 7.2: 121) and, still unsated, to pass beyond the boundaries of the world altogether, toward the supreme beauty (*DHO* 12: 161C-164A). As that which moves, becomes, is reborn or repeated, human nature's perfection (τελειότης) is nothing but this endless desire for beauty and more beauty, this hunger for God (*De vita Moysis* 1.10;[46] *GNO* 8.1: 4-5).

The reason such language is not mere poetical fancy is that it appears in the context of a broader theological understanding of divine infinity, which lends it some considerable degree of theoretical cogency. It is the principal thesis of Ekkehard Mühlenberg's *Die Unendlichkeit Gottes bei Gregor von Nyssa* that Gregory was the first "Greek" thinker either to attribute to God, or develop a philosophical description of, positive infinity. Whether this is entirely true or not, it is certainly the case that few philosophers or theologians before Gregory were willing to describe the divine as τὸ ἀόριστον: neither Plato nor Aristotle ascribed "infinity" to absolute reality, as for both the infinite was merely the indeterminate, formless, and irrational; Origen argued that were God infinite, he would be without definition and would, in consequence, be incomprehensible even to himself (*De principiis* 2.9.1). As Mühlenberg writes, "Trotz aller negativen Theologie wird der Grieche niemals behaupten, daß Gott an sich selbst ohne Grenze oder Begriff wäre. Gott könnte dann nicht mehr gedacht sein und also nicht das Denken selbst, der Reine Geist, sein."[47] Yet Gregory broke

---

ism, Platonist, Philonian, Hegelian, or other, or again as some metaphysics of process; while Gregory's language is part Plato, part the Stoa, he arrives at a place rather removed from the caves of the one or the colonnades of the other.

44. Hereafter *OC;* while citing the *GNO* edition, I include the traditional chapter divisions that it does not preserve.

45. Hereafter *DB.*

46. Hereafter *DVM;* while citing pages from the *GNO* edition, I include the chapter divisions used in the Sources chrétiennes edition: Grégoire de Nysse, *La Vie de Moïse, ou Traité de la Perfection en Matière de Vertu,* ed. and trans. Jean Daniélou, S.J. (Paris: Les Éditions du Cerf, 1968); which divisions are preserved in the only English translation.

47. Ekkehard Mühlenberg, *Die Unendlichkeit Gottes bei Gregor von Nyssa: Gregors Kritik am Gottesbegriff der Klassischen Metaphysik* (Göttingen: Vandenhoeck & Ruprecht, 1966), 103.

with this wisdom. Mühlenberg suggests that Gregory was able to do so because he reasoned (at least implicitly) that God can comprehend himself on account of divine wisdom's intrinsic boundlessness.[48] This may be true, but one should also recall that for Gregory God is not only infinite, but Trinity, whose self-knowledge is an entirely "adequate" — equally infinite — Logos, toward which he is utterly — equally infinitely — inclined in the movement of his Spirit.

And it is the trinitarian shape of Gregory's thought that makes all the difference. After all, one who hesitates to accept Mühlenberg's high estimate of Gregory's originality might wish a closer comparison to Plotinus, who did speak of the One as infinite;[49] according to W. Norris Clarke, at least, this is not mere apophasis: by "infinite" Plotinus means, inter alia, limitless plenitude as well as simplicity, absolute power as well as absolute rest.[50] Plotinus even asserts, as does Gregory, that love for the One must be infinite because its object is (*Enneads* 6.7.32). The infinity of Plotinus's One, then, is no longer mere indeterminacy, as it was for earlier Greek philosophy, but rather the indeterminate but positive wellspring of all of being's virtues, possessing those virtues in an indefinite (and so limitless) condition of perfection and simplicity. Yet, as near and occasionally congenial to Gregory's thought as Plotinus's seems, the infinity of the One still belongs to a metaphysics of the whole, a discourse of necessity; it is the metaphysical reverse of the realm of difference, its abstract and formless "essence," at once its opposite and its substance, the absolute distinction and absolute unity of being and beings. The infinite, then, is the ground of the finite precisely in that it is "limited" by its incapacity for the finite; the One's virtues are "positive" only insofar as they negate, and so uphold, the world. Thus Plotinus's thought comprises, if only implicitly, a kind of diremption and recuperation: the ambiguous drama of *egressus* and *regressus,* a fortunate fall followed by a desolate recovery. As the world's dialectical counter, its "credit" or "treasury," sustaining its totality, the One is of necessity the eternal oblivion of the here below; it is not mindful of us, and shows itself to us only in the fragmentation of its light, shattered in the prism of Nous, dimly reflected by Psyche in the darkness of matter. So the bounty of being is pervaded by a tragic truth: the diffusiveness of the good is sustained only by the absolute inexpressiveness of its ultimate principle. But Gregory is a Christian, and so he must think of God's infinity as a love that gives without need, rather than the unresponsive speculative completion of the

48. Mühlenberg, 139-40.

49. See *Enneads* 5.5.6-11; 6.7.18, 32. See also W. R. Inge, *The Philosophy of Plotinus,* 2 vols. (London: Longman and Co., 1918), 2:116-18.

50. W. Norris Clarke, "Infinity in Plotinus: A Reply," *Gregorianum* 40 (1959): 76, 90-91; see also Clarke, "The Limitation of Act by Potency: Aristotelianism or Neoplatonism?" in Clarke, *Explorations in Metaphysics: Being, God, Person* (Notre Dame, Ind.: University of Notre Dame Press, 1994), 75-79.

world's necessity; as Trinity, the divine *apeiron* is already determinate, different, related, and sufficient; it freely creates and wholly exceeds the world, being neither the world's emanative substance nor its dialectical consummation. Whereas the One spends its inexhaustible power in a ceaseless disinterested overflow into being, the Christian God creates out of that agape that is the life of the Trinity: God not only gives being to difference, but elects each thing in its particularity, is turned toward it and regards it, and takes it back to himself without despoiling it of its difference. Thus no mere metaphysical prescinsion from multiplicity can lead thought up to being's highest truth. To pass from the vision of the world to the *theoria* of the divine is not simply to move from appearance to reality, from multiplicity to singularity, but rather to find the entirety of the world in all its irreducible diversity to be an analogical expression (at a distance, in a different register) of the dynamism and differentiation that God is. The "here below" is at once more remote from and much nearer to its divine source in Christian thought: though created, no part of God's essence, nor an outward diffusion of God, it "corresponds" to God in ways that the thought of Plotinus could never allow. Difference within being, that is, corresponds precisely *as difference* to the truth of divine differentiation. Thus the energy of desire drawing creation to God is not a recoil back from finitude, toward an unexplicated and disinterested simplicity whose "eyes" are forever averted from the play of being and its deficiencies, but answers — *corresponds to* — God's call to what he fashions for himself, and what is in itself nothing but an ontic ecstasy ex nihilo and *in infinitum.* The relationship, then, of our desire for beauty to the eternal source of beauty is not grounded in a prior identity, even though it subsists upon creation's participation in God; our desire does not subserve a return to the stillness of our proper being: it is our being.

ii. Changeless Beauty

What Gregory understands "infinity" to mean when predicated of God, however, is very much (at least on the face of it) what Plotinus understood it to mean in regard to the One: incomprehensibility, absolute power, simplicity, eternity. God is uncircumscribable (ἀπερίληπτον), elusive of every finite concept or act, boundless, arriving at no terminus: in Gregory's idiom, "that which cannot be passed beyond" (ἀδιεξίτητον) (*Contra Eunomium* 3.7;[51] *GNO*, 2:226).[52] God is

---

51. Hereafter *CE*.

52. See *In Ecclesiasten* 7 (hereafter *IE*), *GNO*, 5:412; see also Charles Kannengieser, "L'infinité divine chez Grégoire de Nysse," *Revue des sciences philosophiques et théologiques* 55 (1967): 59.

the perfect completeness of what he is; the boundaries of bounty, power, life, wisdom, goodness are set only where their contraries are encountered (*CE* 1; *GNO*, 1:71-73; *DVM* 1.5: 3), but God is without opposition, as he is beyond nonbeing or negation, transcendent of all composition or antinomy; it is in this sense of utter fullness, principally, that God is called simple.[53] To say, moreover, that he is eternal is to say not only that he is without beginning or end, but that he is without extension or succession at all (*CE* 3.7: 226-27); the divine nature knows no past or future, no sequence, but is like an endless ocean of eternity (*CE* 1: 133-34); it is not time, though time flows from it (*CE* 1: 135). Gregory in fact uses the absence of temporal interval in God as a cardinal argument for the co-equality (*CE* 1: 133-40, 196-98), indeed co-infinity (*CE* 1: 120-21), of the Son and Spirit with the Father. Extension, whether of time or of space, belongs exclusively to the created order and distinguishes it from the unimaginable infinity of God, who contains beginning and end at once in his timeless embrace (*CE* 1: 133-36; *CE* 3.6: 198-99).[54] This is hardly an extraordinary aspect of Gregory's thought, but it must be kept in view nonetheless, inasmuch as the difference between creaturely diachrony and divine eternity is also, for Gregory, the condition that makes union between the creature and God possible. The insuperable ontological difference between creation and God — between the dynamism of finitude and an infinite that is eternally dynamic — is simultaneously an implication of the infinite in the finite, a partaking by the finite of that which it does not own, but within which it moves — not dialectically, abstractively, or merely theoretically — but through its own endless growth in the good things of God (*ICC* 6: 173-74). Creation's "series," its ἀκολουθία *(vide infra)*, is at an infinite distance from the "order" and "succession" of the divine *taxis* (*CE* 2; *GNO*, 1:245-46), but that distance is born of God's boundlessness: the Trinity's perfect act of difference also opens the possibility of the "ontico-ontological difference," as the space of the gift of analogous being, imparted to contingent beings who, then, receive this gift as the movement of an ontic deferral. God's transcendence is not absence, that is, but an actual excessiveness; it is, from the side of the contingent, the impossibility of the finite ever coming to contain or exhaust the infinite; the

53. See *ICC* 5: 157-60; see also Mühlenberg, 121-22.

54. One must reject Jenson's claim that "the infinity that according to Gregory is God's deity is *temporal* infinity" (*Systematic Theology*, 2:216), a view he takes from Mühlenberg (106-11); while Gregory succeeded better than his predecessors in describing divine eternity in terms of a fullness that all the ages cannot exhaust, this remains coherent only because of the absolutely inviolable analogical distinction he draws between time and the trinitarian eternity that makes time possible. He is in fact quite severe toward those who would introduce intervals of time into the divine nature (*CE* 1: 196-98). See D. L. Balás, "Eternity and Time in Gregory of Nyssa's *Contra Eunomium*," in *Gregor von Nyssa und die Philosophie*, ed. H. Dörrie, M. Attenburger, and U. Schramm (Leiden: E. J. Brill, 1976), 146-47.

soul must participate in it successively or endlessly traverse it, "outstretched" by a desire without surcease, an "infinition" of love; but God pervades all things, and all is present to his infinite life (*OC* 32: 79). Because the difference between God and creation is not a simple metaphysical distinction between reality and appearance, but the analogical distance between two ways of apprehending the infinite — God being the infinite, creatures embracing it in an endless sequence of finite instances — the soul's ascent to God is not a departure from, but an endless venture into, difference. The distance between God and creation is not alienation, nor the Platonic *chorismos* or scale of being, but the original ontological act of distance by which every ontic interval subsists, given to be crossed but not overcome, at once God's utter transcendence and utter proximity; for while the finite belongs to the infinite, the converse cannot be so, except through an *epektasis* toward more of the good, which can be possessed only ecstatically: possessed, that is, in dispossession.

Within this original gift of distance, however, desire can fabricate intervals of apostasy: attempts to achieve a distance from distance. As evil, for Gregory, in keeping with venerable metaphysical wisdom, is that purely privative nothingness that lies outside creation's motion toward God, it never stands in relation to the infinite but is always an impossible attempt at an ending, a constant breaking of the waves of being upon an uninhabitable shore, the ceaseless cessation of time. The creature, however, is called to an endless attendance upon and successive growth within God's light, never lapsing into that nothingness, and yet never transcending the conditions of finitude. In the thought of Hegel, to take the most obvious counterexample — the most metaphysical account imaginable, that is, of the identity of infinity and particularity — being posits itself by negation, by its own convertibility with nonbeing, "solving" itself through the synthesis of being and nonbeing in becoming; the negative interval of dialectical opposition is thus the inner mechanism of change and the unity of being's "history." But in Gregory's thought becoming requires no probation by nothingness, no sacrificial economy of contradiction and sublation: movement within what is, within the good, is eternal, because negation is neither the necessary condition of difference nor the source of its fecundity; difference can be forever remodulated *as difference* through the interminable analogical interrelatedness of finite existence because God's plenitude of determinacy is both truly transcendent of the ontic play of this and not this, and truly Trinity. The soul, whose inmost truth is *trope* and *kinesis,* is for that very reason open to this infinite that expresses itself in the sequences of creation's purely positive and "fitting" supplements, its variations on the theme of divine glory. Creation, says Gregory, is a symphonic and rhythmic complication of diversity, of motion and rest, a song praising God, the true, primordial, archetypal music, in which human nature can glimpse itself as in a mirror (*In inscriptiones*

Psalmorum 1.3;[55] *GNO,* 5:30-33). We are music moved to music: finitude is not a condition of violence, a wounding of the universal syncopated by the holocaust of the particular; and so there is no ontological warrant for violence, only a causal one, an aberrant series, born of a perverse desire, turned from the light of the infinite toward nothingness — which determines nothing. Creation is, as its first word, a partaking in the inexhaustible goodness of God; and its ceaseless flow of light and shadow, constancy and change, mirrors both the "music" of God's ordering words and the incomprehensibility of his changeless nature (*CE* 2: 245-51, 261-62), while the restless soul, immersed in the spectacle of God's glory, is drawn without break beyond the world to the source of its beauty, to embrace the infinite (*DB* 4: 121; *DHO* 12: 161-64).

This last, obviously, is impossible in bare ontico-ontological terms; but God fashioned humanity to be a vessel of his glory, which for Gregory means nothing less than a living communion of the finite with the infinite, without the former being lost in the latter. In the end, as it turns out, creaturely mutability itself proves to be at once the way of difference from God and the way of union with God. To begin with, change is a means of release from sin; that same changeableness that grants us the liberty to turn toward evil allows us also to recover the measure of divine harmony and to become an ever shifting shape of the good, a peaceful cadence of change that, in its ceaseless departure from itself, establishes the good within itself as the theme upon which it endlessly elaborates (*IIP* 1.7: 43-51); and the good is infinitely various in its intonations. For creatures, who cannot statically comprehend the infinite, progress in the good is, Gregory observes, the most beautiful work of change, and an inability to change would be a penalty (*De perfectione;*[56] *GNO* 8.1: 212-14). We are pure movement, but whoever can "contain" this ceaseless dynamism on all sides, so to speak, through the practice of virtue, can turn it into a movement that is entirely "upward," into an ever greater acquisition of the good (*De virginitate;*[57] *GNO* 8.1: 280-81; *DVM* 2.243: 118). In this way the changeable puts on changeless beauty. Gregory's great exemplar of the virtuous soul is Moses: though he is filled to overflowing, says Gregory, he always thirsts for more of God's beauty, "not according to his own capacity, but according to God's real being"; and such is the action of every soul that loves beauty: drawn on forever by a desire enkindled always anew by the beauty that lies beyond the beauty already possessed, receiving the visible as an image of God's transcendent loveliness, but longing all the more to enjoy that beauty face-to-face, the soul experiences ceaseless delight precisely in that its desire can know no final satiety (*DVM*

55. Hereafter *IIP.*
56. Hereafter *DP.*
57. Hereafter *DV.*

2.230-32: 114). As God is infinite, while evil's nothingness lies "outside" the infinite altogether, desire for the good can expand forever without passage through negation (*DVM* 2.237-38: 116); and so the true vision of God is never to arrive at desire's end (*DVM* 2.239: 116).

Gregory speaks of spiritual progress principally in terms of virtue, but by this he means more than either the prudent restraint of sinful nature or the active pursuit of morality; for virtue has no being outside the plenitude of God's goodness. Whereas the perfection of things sensible, says Gregory, lies in their limitations, the perfection of virtue is its very limitlessness (*DVM* 1.5-6: 3-4): this because it is the presence of the infinite God; and every excellence within the soul is nothing less than a participation in God's fullness[58] — again, not as a fixed property or substance, and not according to the soul's own capacity, but only through its ecstasy. Still, when Gregory speaks of a "growth" in glory, he really means a transformation of the soul into something other. "In all the endless ages, the one running to you becomes greater, more exalted, ever growing in proportion to his ascent through the good" (*ICC* 8: 246). Gregory likens the soul partaking of divine blessings to a vessel endlessly expanding as it receives what flows into it inexhaustibly; participation in the good, he says, makes the participant ever more capacious and receptive of beauty, for it is a growth into the goods of which God is the fount; so no limit can be set, either to what the soul pursues or to the soul's ascent (*DAR* 105B-C). Though the infinite cannot be circumscribed or "grasped," desire never ceases to expand in its constant motion toward the fullness of the good (*DVM* 2.238: 116); it stretches out toward infinity, as if, *per impossibile,* to comprise it; and by an endless successiveness, by sempiternity, the soul is joined to eternity. Without venturing into the more obscure regions of Gregory's thinking on time, suffice it to say here that he regards everything created, material or otherwise, as existing in a state of succession that distinguishes it from God, though he ascribes the quotidian pains and severer limitations of cosmic time to sin's effect upon the world; and he imagines salvation as involving a liberation from the inconstancies of sinful time (the tension between progress and regress, birth and death), but never a liberation from mutability as such. Salvation must ultimately consist, rather, in a transition to a changeableness unburdened by sin and death, a perpetual tending forward, an endlessly greater apprehension of divine glory by creatures who "kinetically" experience the peace of God, and finitely live in his infinity (*De mortuis;*[59] *GNO,* 9:34-39).

Some disagreement exists among scholars as to whether Gregory should then be classified as a mystical or moral theologian, but such a distinction, one

58. See Balás, 68-69.
59. Hereafter *DM.*

suspects, would have been unintelligible to him. This question is really of interest only if one fundamentally misunderstands the nature of either mystical or moral theology, or both, but it calls attention to certain "gnoseological" issues raised by Gregory's theology (issues that become, inevitably, ontological as well). The human mind, unable to transcend time or form any coherent concept of a reality that is not composite and extended, can enjoy no direct knowledge of the divine infinity, as Gregory explicitly states (*IE* 7: 412). Some, taking this as their point of departure, have raised objections to the traditional view of scholars like Jean Daniélou that Gregory's spiritual treatises concern mystical union with God; Gregory's sense of God's absolute transcendence, the argument runs, precludes the idea of union. This is certainly Mühlenberg's contention.[60] C. W. MacLeod agrees that God's infinity, as Gregory conceives it, forbids any embrace by the creature, any *unio mystica:* Gregory's God is utterly inaccessible, and Gregory's spirituality is concerned not with knowledge but with virtue; participation in God is simply continuous assimilation to him, the soul following always behind, experiencing God's presence not in the way of the Dionysian mystic, but in its tirelessly faithful incomprehension.[61] And R. E. Heine insists that for Gregory God is so wholly beyond comprehension, direct intuition, or presence as to make union impossible.[62] Leaving aside the vexatious question of whether such authors have entirely understood the traditional theology of *unio mystica* (they have not), one can grant that for the most part this is all more or less indisputable; but it constitutes only half the truth. Moreover, one may certainly stipulate that Gregory's treatises have nothing to do with the practice of ascetical mysticism as a "noetic" discipline, as distinct from the practical life of Christian virtue; but not only does his thought in no way preclude the mystical (at least not when the tradition of contemplative prayer is approached with fewer preconceptions than these scholars exhibit), it definitely invokes the mystical. Unless one understands that the pursuit of virtue is not, for Gregory, simple "ethics," but the acquisition of God, and that moral and mystical knowledge differ not in kind but only in intensity,[63] one reads him in modern (even perhaps Kantian) terms; and frankly, if one reads a text like *In canticum canticorum* without recognizing that its language of the "wound of love," of the advance of knowledge under the form of unknowing eros, and of nuptial intimacy describes a genuine and ever deepening union between God

---

60. Mühlenberg, 147.

61. C. W. MacLeod, "Allegory and Mysticism in Origen and Gregory of Nyssa," *Journal of Theological Studies,* n.s., 22 (1971): 365-72; MacLeod, "Analysis, a Study in Ancient Mysticism," *Journal of Theological Studies,* n.s., 21 (1970): 52.

62. R. E. Heine, *Perfection in the Virtuous Life,* Patristic Monograph 2 (Philadelphia, 1976), 109-14.

63. As Gregory remarks, "ἀγάπη strained to greater intensity is called ἔρως." *ICC* 13: 383.

and the soul, one is rather resisting the obvious. Gregory's grasp of the radical ontological disparity between God and creation is balanced by his understanding of the union of God with creation in the economy of salvation; and thus he means what he says when he calls the practice of virtue participation *in* God and the presence of God to the soul: he means, in a word, deification.

As it happens, this too is an issue of contention. One of the most misleading features of Mühlenberg's book is its anachronistically austere vision of human sanctification. He observes, correctly, that for Gregory the perpetual dissatisfaction of the soul in its flight toward God testifies not to any innate capacity for the infinite on the soul's part, but only to the unattainability of the divine being. The soul's progress is a continuous partaking of the good, inspired by love of the ever invisible God — a love whose boundlessness flows entirely from God's infinity. And so, Mühlenberg concludes, talk of the soul's ecstasy in Gregory's theology is no different from talk of moral exodus, and signifies only that the soul is always at the beginning of its pilgrimage; but human limits cannot be overstepped, and the soul cannot be deified insofar as it cannot become infinite.[64] Moreover, Mühlenberg argues, Christology provides no qualifications to this, as Christ's humanity, having been assumed immediately into the divine life from God's side, is transcendent of the conditions of the rest of humanity, and so alone enjoys union with God. And so when Gregory claims that creaturely growth in the good will be eternal, he means simply (so the argument continues) that every obstacle of sin will have fallen away. When in the course of his commentary on the Song of Songs Gregory speaks of the mingling of the soul with the divine (observes Mühlenberg), he refers only to the human nature of Christ; where he turns to talk of the soul's yearning for the beauty of her bridegroom, he no longer speaks of a union πρὸς τὸ θεῖον, but only in the comparative: πρὸς τὸ θειότερον or πρὸς τὸ κρεῖττον (162-65). Again, as the soul's progress is endless, it can never arrive at deification (203). Mühlenberg even makes a point of distinguishing the theology of Gregory of Nyssa from that of Gregory the Theologian; the latter, he claims, may speak of divine infinity and perpetual progress (*Orations* 38.7; 28.12), but what he means is that the soul's aim is to comprehend the whole Godhead, which it is able somehow to grasp (". . . ὅλου θεοῦ χωρητικοὶ καὶ μόνου, τοῦτο γὰρ τελείωσις, πρὸς ἣν σπεύδομεν" — *Oration* 30.6); but human divinization, claims Mühlenberg, is something to which Gregory of Nyssa's theology is implacably opposed (169-70).

Without belaboring the issue, it should be said that Mühlenberg has drawn this final distinction in the wrong place, and so exaggerated it. Certainly

---

64. Mühlenberg, 147-62. Parenthetical page numbers in the rest of this paragraph refer to Mühlenberg.

the Theologian occasionally speaks more boldly than does the younger Gregory about our ultimate knowledge of God (e.g., *Oration* 38.17), though then only in order to make sense of Paul's language of knowing "even as I am known"; but aside from certain lapses of caution, his writings clearly preserve a sense of the difference of our souls from that "end whereto we hasten." This, though, is a secondary concern; more to the point here is the imbalance that Mühlenberg introduces into Gregory of Nyssa's theology. It is certainly so that Gregory is circumspect when speaking of human deification, and often does so in specific reference to the incarnation; but Mühlenberg still separates him quite incredibly from the theological environment of his time. The truth is that Gregory, who like his contemporaries saw redemption as God assuming human nature in order to join it to the divine nature, merely pursued with more rigorous logic the implications of such an account; the entire thrust of the theology of eternal progress is precisely to show how it is possible to speak intelligibly of deification, despite the ontological distance between God and creation: by showing that it is not an uncrossable abyss but a genuine distance, reconciled and yet preserved in the incarnate Logos, crossed from the divine side so that it may be crossed forever from the side of the creature; and by showing that the God who is infinite, for this reason, cannot be made absent by any distance. Certainly no suggestion could be more implausible than that Gregory limits the divinizing effects of the incarnation to Christ's humanity alone, for the simple reason that Gregory's understanding of salvation is that creation has been rescued from sin and death by the divinity that Christ has introduced into the entirety of the common human nature (*In illud: Tunc et ipse filius*;[65] *GNO* 3.2: 14, 20-21; *Antirrheticus*; *GNO* 3.1: 160-61), and has made available to all through his life, death, and resurrection; it would, in fact, be impossible to coax any other soteriology out of Gregory's writings.[66] There can be no ontological or natural continuity of identity between the created and the divine in Gregory's thought, granted, but as Balás writes, "this rejection of an 'intermediary' *(meson)* is actually the presupposition of his well-developed theology of the 'Mediator' *(mesitēs)*: the incarnate Logos, truly God and truly man, assuming humanity ('man') not by necessity of nature but out of free *philanthrōpia*."[67] And as Mediator, Christ will admit humanity, Gregory says, "to participation in divinity" (*DP* 205); the saved soul is raised out of its own nature to dwell fully in the Holy Spirit (*Adversus Macedonianos*;[68] *GNO* 3.1: 98), and God becomes ever more present to the soul through Christ in the Holy Spirit (*In sanctam Pentecosten;*

---

65. Hereafter *IITIF.*
66. See *OC* 35: 86; 37: 97-98; see also below.
67. Balás, 52.
68. Hereafter *AM.*

GNO 10.2: 288-89; *DM* 45-48), who is the glory that the Son had with the Father before the world existed, God's own bond of unity (*IITIF* 21-22; *ICC* 15: 466-68), the light that draws us into the Trinity's own "circle of glory" (*AM* 64-65). The blessings of the incarnation are infinite, for God is infinite; the partaking of those blessings must be eternal because, though opening ever more to God, the soul can never reach a satiety *in itself* of the endless good; but the future life will be a real taking on of the divine, an enlarging of the soul's capacity (*CE* 1: 112) beyond the superabundance already attained, always only to find that the fullness of that in which it participates still infinitely exceeds and beckons it. This is, that is to say, a real acquisition of the good, not merely a continual apprehension of each new "good," as though the instances of virtue were a series of points all equidistant from another point (God) at an impossible distance.

Thus God comes to dwell in the soul and the soul migrates into God (*ICC* 6: 178-79), being eternally lifted into an ever greater participation in God himself (*ICC* 8: 246). Mühlenberg comes perilously close to thinking of divine infinity as though it were an "object" that simply happens to be "infinite" and therefore ungraspable, but this reduces the relation — the ontological difference — between the infinite and finite to incoherence: for if the infinite can thus be opposed to the finite, it is itself, in the end, only finite, and in consequence merely the negation of the finite, and finitude too is a negation, one that remains for the creature firmly and constitutively in place. Gregory's concept of God would be, for all intents and purposes, the same as Plotinus's of the One: a sad love for what cannot love, a hopeless reaching out toward a self-enclosed power that forbids communion. Indeed, Gregory's vision of God would be more austere still, inasmuch as for Plotinus one can at least achieve union with the One through the sacrifice of one's finite particularity. But clearly Mühlenberg is wrong. It is implicit to the logic of Gregory's thought that the immediacy of God to the soul, within his very incomprehensibility, is a necessary corollary of his transcendence: were God merely "objectively" incomprehensible, rather than the ontological movement of hiddenness and revelation within us, he would be only another being, in one sense absolutely beyond us, but in another sense — speculatively — entirely conceivable. Thus the extraordinary union of the soul with God (deification) is the creature's perfection, within the existential movements of will and thought, of a natural union of the creature with God in the ontological movement of divine transcendence and creaturely contingency. The reification of the infinite, like the reification of "being," can only transform the distance between infinite and finite (as between being and beings) into a *chorismos* between "things," but Gregory sees this distance as also, by virtue of this ontological difference, genuine participation, measured out in the measures of the moving soul. In the most elementary sense, as God is himself goodness and life (essence and "attributes" being one in him), his infinite plenitude is the real "content" of creaturely growth; as the soul is capable of capacity, to put it awkwardly, of being "extended" always beyond what it is, toward the unattainability of the, so to speak, whole infinity, it is the ever greater receptivity that is the subject of growth[69] — that is born into subjectivity through repetition forward. It is thus that Gregory speaks of the perfection of human nature as a growth without achievable limit (*DVM* 1.10: 4-5): because it is growth in the presence of the infinite. Moreover, this presence is an infinite deferral, but not the deferral of absence, alienation, or violence; it is delight, blessings, ceaseless approach, endless rapture. Gregory depicts the state of the soul that has passed beyond the possibility of relapse into sin as pure succession, pure repetition, divided no longer between memory and hope, past and future (*CE* 1: 136; *DAR* 93B): it will be a sheer futurity in which the soul, "forgetful" of what has gone before because the previous state has been subsumed into the ever greater reality of the "present," will still remain intent upon the yet greater beauty that lies ahead (*ICC* 12: 366). This is, indeed, an account of exodus, but also of (in the sense common to all patristic theology) deification: "when the bridegroom calls to the soul," writes Gregory, "she is refashioned into the yet more divine and, by a beneficent change, changed from her glory to one still more exalted" (*ICC* 8: 253); for whosoever "thirsts for participation in God (διψῇ τῆς τοῦ θεοῦ μετουσίας)" drinks of the divine fountain without ever being sated, because this fountain "transforms into itself the one who takes it in (πρὸς ἑαυτὴν μεταποιεῖ τὸν ἁψάμενον) and endows him with a share of its own power" (*IIP* 1.5: 39-40).

iii. The Mirror of the Infinite

Any talk of knowledge of the divine must involve a measure of paradox. Gregory quite explicitly rejects the notion that the creature could ever attain to a knowledge, a θεωρία, of the divine essence, and says the mind's only access to the invisible and incomprehensible is through its yearning; and yet also, therein, one sees God (*DVM* 2.163: 87). Perpetual progress in the divine is a θεωρία τῶν ἀθεωρήτων (*ICC* 11: 326): a contemplation of the inconceivable, a vision of the invisible. It is a progress both in darkness and in light, a seeing mediated by a constant receiving of gifts, signs, images, and beauties; as such, it is a knowledge of God that is not really "epistemic," in the sense of a discursive "science" of the divine "essence."[70] Gregory speaks of David going out of himself to *see* the divine beauty that no creature can behold, even while remaining entirely

---

69. See *CE* 3.6: 211-12; *OC* 8: 243-48.
70. See *CE* 3.5: 165; *DB* 7: 150.

unable to say how he has seen it (*ICC* 10: 307-11). Such vision is granted by the analogy of beauty, the likeness to divine splendor that one achieves in oneself through participating ever more fully in the beauty of God's light; one whose heart rises up out of evil toward God comes to see, in oneself, the image of the divine nature in its own beauty, like the sun reflected in an immaculate mirror; divinity is this purity, this beauty, and is all the virtues, and if these be in one, then God truly dwells within one (*DB* 6: 140-44). Each person is "a free, a living mirror" (*ICC* 15: 440), whose entire interior dynamism should become this perfect surface, till no separation between "depth" and "surface" remains, no distinction between an inner and "spiritual" apprehension of God and an extrinsic, "aesthetic" conformity to the divine image (*DP* 212). In this state, every dualism, especially that between flesh and spirit, is overcome, so that "the manifest exterior is within the hidden interior, the hidden interior within the manifest exterior" (*DB* 7: 160-61). One becomes a sign, entirely, an inflection and reflection at a distance of the divine glory, a deferral of God's presence that is simultaneously a real embrace of his infinity, an impression of God that is also another emphasis, another expression.[71] Indeed, as one is changed in the light of the Spirit, the mirror of the soul comes to be bathed in a kind of chiastic radiance, so that the trinitarian *taxis* — the glory of the Father streaming forth through the Son to the Spirit — is reflected in an ascent of that sanctifying light from the more "exterior" to the more "interior" moments of the soul: the light the Spirit instills in us rises from our acts and practices, upward to the speech (λόγος) they put into action, and from there into the mind, which is the soul's principle (ἀρχὴ), until there is a "harmony of the hidden man with the manifest" (*DP* 210-12), and our "return" to ourselves becomes a kind of specular reflex of God's own return to himself (from the Spirit, through the Son, to the Father) within his eternal circle of glory.[72] And this movement of the invisible and the visible, each in the other, is possible for the finite soul because it is a movement first "within" God's infinity. There are, after all, two distinct though consequent senses in which one may speak of the invisibility of God: there is, on the one hand, the sheer infinity of the divine nature, which — flowing from the Father — is the common *proprium* of the divine persons, who as one forever exceed and excite our souls' most extravagant ecstasies; and there is, on the other hand, that invisibility of the Father within the trinitarian *taxis* that is altogether convertible with (or, rather, "converted in") the "visibility" or manifestation of the Logos to the Father and the "visibility" or illumination of the Spirit for the Father (*DP* 188-89). The infinity, and so inaccessibility, of God is known

71. See Balthasar, *Presence and Thought*, 115-16, 121-29.
72. Cf. also *AM* 105-7. See D. B. Hart, "The Mirror of the Infinite: Gregory of Nyssa on the *Vestigia Trinitatis*," *Modern Theology* (October 2002).

to us in both aspects, and it is only because the former invisibility (divine transcendence) proceeds from the latter (the plenitude of the paternal *arche* within
the trinitarian structure of manifestation, of self-outpouring love and self-
knowing wisdom) that the restless mutability of our nature can become, by
grace, a way of mediation between the infinite and the finite. We can mirror the
infinite because the infinite, within itself, is entirely mirroring of itself, the Father's incomprehensible majesty being eternally united to the coequal "splendor of his glory," his "form" and "impress," in seeing whom one has seen the Father; we can become images of God that shine with his beauty because the
Father always has his image in his Son, bright with the light of his Spirit, and so
is never without form and loveliness (*DP* 188-89). Yet this would all still be impossible, in the calculus of infinite and finite, if not for that second order of divine hiddenness: God's transcendence, in the full ontological sense, allows God
to be simultaneously inapprehensible to the soul and yet present to the soul as a
creature never could be — within its very being.

Here again, the gnoseological question proves to be ontological as well —
though Gregory's ontology is difficult to summarize on account of his somewhat unsystematic use of terms like *ousia* and *physis*. Certainly, for Gregory the
mystery of salvation is deification, and Psalm 82:6 and John 10:34-35 clearly allow that the creature can come to be called a *theos*, but at the same time Gregory would never allow that the created could come to participate in the divine
ousia, the being of God as God; Scripture speaks, though, of creaturely participation in the divine nature (2 Pet. 1:14). For Gregory, to put it simply, the divine
nature consists in those things proper to God (his "attributes"), which are graciously imparted to his creatures and of which we may gain some knowledge,
while his *ousia* is that whereby God is God, to which these "attributes" belong
not as accidents (God having no accidents) but as essence, and which lies beyond all creaturely comprehension (*DP* 188). This is quite conventional metaphysical terminology, of course; but the matter of greatest importance here is
the distinction thus preserved between the God who possesses — who *is* — the
fullness of the divine and the creature who participates in the divine: for the latter there must always be — even within its relation to its own essence — a real
distinction between subject and object, motion and motion's aim, ecstasy and
form, participation and "substance." This is the nature of contingency, its essential act of "repetition," its need to participate in even its own essence.[73] Just
this difference from God, however, this need of the created always to partake of
its own nature, this dyadic oscillation running through its grasp of its own
form and "perfection," makes possible its participation in and union with, in
the economy of its finitude, the infinite God. God is present within the very

73. See *CE* 1: 95.

abiding "ontico-ontological" difference, as the being, and so infinite expanse, of that difference. To quote Jean Daniélou, "La possibilité de ce progrès perpétuel est lié chez Grégoire à sa doctrine de la transcendence divine, comme absence totale de limite. La perfection de l'esprit sera conçue comme participation à cette illimitation."[74] God, obviously, is not participable as matter is, in parts, but arrives within the confines of created being without ceasing to be infinite; called upon to accommodate the infinite, the finite must — the alternative being either God's absolute absence or, perhaps, the soul's annihilation — become ever more open, ever greater and more capacious (*CE* 1: 112); and creaturely mutability allows for this. Exactly how God is present to the creature remains ineffable for Gregory, and whether the fourteenth-century Palamite distinction between God's essence and energies would have found favor with him is an open question.[75] "Presence" is probably as much as need be said: the parousia of what belongs to the divine *ousia*. This is merely the language of the ontological difference: the soul's relation to God — the relation of the contingent to the infinite, of becoming to He Who Is — is not the relation between two things, "this" and "that"; and there need never be for the creature a hard and fast division between the ontological and existential: created nature, ever changing, is what happens to it, and so is ever more divine because the Holy Spirit acts upon it — fashioning the mutable fabric of finite being into the motile beauty of the divine image.

Again, Mühlenberg is correct in saying that, for Gregory, the creature cannot become infinite, but when he asserts that the soul's eternal progress is an effect *only* of the divine infinity, and not of any capacity innate to the soul, he makes a maxim out of what for Gregory is only one side of a paradox. The soul of course has no effective ability to become infinite, but does have the capacity infinitely to become; though ever finite, it is, one might say, teleologically

---

74. Jean Daniélou, *L'Être et le Temps chez Grégoire de Nysse* (Leiden, 1970), 105.

75. Gregory himself appears to reject any "realism" regarding the divine energies (*CE* 1: 87), but Palamas is able to draw on language of Gregory's, and I am not at all convinced that Palamas ever intended to suggest a *real* distinction between God's essence and energies; nor am I even confident that the energies should be seen as anything other than sanctifying grace by which the Holy Spirit makes the Trinity really present to creatures. I take the distinction to mean only that God's transcendence is such that he is free to be the God he is even in the realm of creaturely finitude, without estrangement from himself and without the creature being admitted thus to an unmediated vision of the divine essence. For accounts of Palamism that link it directly to Cappadocian theology, see M. Canévet, "St. Grégoire de Nysse," in *Dictionnaire de Spiritualité* VI, col. 1007-8; G. Habra, "The Sources of the Doctrine of Gregory Palamas on the Divine Energies," *Eastern Churches Quarterly* (1957-58): 244-52, 294-303, 338-47. For accounts of Palamism as an apostasy from Cappadocian thought, see E. von Ivanka, "Palamismus und Vatertradition," in *L'Église et les Églises*, vol. 2 (Chevretogne, 1955), 29-46; Ivanka, "Zur hesychastischen Lichtvision," *Kairos* (1971): 81-95.

infinite, even as it is perfected in the imperfection of endless traversal; and while it cannot overstep the line between Creator and creature, this is never a fixed line. For Gregory, all humanity is transfigured in Christ, and is saved through its endless transformation into what God brings near; the human soul, assumed into Christ, is a *theion* striving ever after the *theioteron,* seeking the uncontainable plenitude of God. The eternity of change that Gregory understands as the substance of salvation will not be, then, the back of a fugitive God perpetually withdrawing into an infinite distance while the soul lags doggedly and indefatigably behind. For while God is, in a very real sense, at an infinite distance from the creature, in another sense, by virtue of his transcendence, he is that distance: that cannot be, but must be, and throughout eternity is being, traversed. All distance belongs to that intratrinitarian event that gives being to all things. And the divine image is not then some distant facsimile of God: the soul's virtue is God's own overflowing goodness within it. This is the dynamism of the image, the true nature of the sign: in its deferral and difference from what it indicates, in its constant motion of difference, it may yet be the form of presence (a trinitarian truth, clearly). This is also the dynamism of salvation: God in Christ assumes human finitude into himself without despoiling it of its finitude, while the creature, unable to assume the infinite into itself fully, nonetheless forever stretches out toward that as its end. In a sense the soul is related to the unity of God through its own multiplicity; the divine nature does not, says Gregory, possess truly distinct attributes, but is only thus expressed to the created mind that reaches out toward it (*CE* 2: 364-65). There is perhaps an echo here of the Plotinian notion that Nous contemplates the One under the aspect of plurality, though the One possesses its infinitely fertile virtues in a state of undifferentiated simplicity; but in the context of trinitarian theology, and within a scheme not of emanation but of creation, the analogy between the divine unity and creation's multiplicity can no longer be conceived as the analogy between the purity of undistorted light and its diffusion into the iridescence of being, but must be understood as an analogy between the fullness of being and its *expression* in the diversity of beings. Finite reality is an image of that complex simplicity that obtains in the Trinity: the love of the Father for the Son, of each for the Spirit; the fullness of difference in the Logos, who is already image and response, within the Spirit's enlivening splendor. And so when the soul is adapted to the diversity of perfections it perceives in the divine life, it becomes an ever clearer expression, a visible and living sign of God. The creature's extension in time becomes an endless commentary, an endless series of particular perspectives, on God's unextended eternity, which is always already expressible beauty (for the Father always has his form and splendor). The ontological difference itself is thus not dialectical, any more than it is identist; it is the interval of an expressive analogy, between God's infinite beauty and the motion by which finitude is beautiful. There is no room in such thought for the formless sublime, chaos, the probation of negation, the positivity of nonbeing, or the abolition of beauty; there is room only for a peaceful dynamism in which God's glory is declared by distance, and by the traversal of distance.

As it happens, this line of reasoning in part accounts for Gregory's notorious universalism (based on premises so very different from Origen's). Every creature that can see and contemplate is drawn irresistibly, from its creation, toward God's beauty, turning from it only through spiritual blindness. As the soul is fashioned in the image of that beauty, its very being is an eros for the perfect goodness of God; and so long as it is deficient in the good, it can neither cease to conceive a desire for a greater indwelling of the limitless beauty its deepest nature craves — and in which it can arrive at no final satiety — nor halt its progress into eternity (*CE* 1: 285-87). The salvation of all souls is inevitable because each soul is a changing image of the infinite God; the dynamism of the soul has only God's absolute, changeless fullness as its source and end, and God's eternity as its element. Salvation, for Gregory, is simply that same act — but made perfect in Christ — by which God rouses us each moment from nonbeing, as a pure stirring of love, seeking union with him. In its endless pilgrimage toward God, the creature is always being created anew (*ICC* 6: 174), always entering into that one act by which God gives being to beings; coming from God, then, and going to God are one and the same thing. Within the core of Gregory's "creationist" metaphysics, a scheme of *egressus* and *regressus* is retained, but is drawn into a unity: the single gesture of the ontological difference, God's creative *actus* constituting its ontic expression as a pilgrimage into the infinite, a journey from nothingness into God's beauty, forever. The "ontico-ontological difference" is a gift that is its own return, and is itself also the unity of what it differentiates. If, then, the finite is joined to the infinite by being drawn always out of its limitations, evil — which is finitude itself, the nothingness and formlessness of a self-positing sublime — must pass away; confronted by the infinite in Christ, it cannot persist. There is no dark underside to God's infinity, no shadow subsistence of evil, no dialectical and coterminous current of the negative; the creature's free progress must ultimately move beyond evil, for in being joined to God's endlessness, and in being in itself endless mutability, the soul cannot be contained within the bounds of evil's pure negation. Evil is, says Gregory, like a cone of shadow cast out weakly into a universe of light (which is how the geocentric cosmology of late antiquity conceived of night); the moving soul cannot but pass beyond it into the infinite good (*DHO* 21: 201B-4A). Moreover, for Gregory there are not separate species of evil — sin, suffering, death, hell — but only the single fact of that which strives against the will of God in creation, a limitation absurdly opposing itself to his limitlessness, and so the "failure" of God to save all creation would appear, in Gregory's eyes, to involve an impossible dualism: the notion of an eternal hell, of an endless godlessness parallel to the endlessness of God, would involve the logical nonsense of a dual eternity, an eternity that is not God (*IIP* 2.8: 100-101). Gregory's universalism, though, is a subordinate issue; what is of interest here is the light it casts on Gregory's larger vision. That is to say, Gregory's understanding of the infinite never dissolves into abstraction: infinity is God alone, in his fullness, in whom all richness, beauty, motion, and life already dwell, without violence, negation, diremption, or the sacrifice of the particular. "Philosophy" — eidetic *theoria,* dialectical idealism, postmodernism — stands upon another vision of the infinite; but Gregory's story is of an infinite already beautiful, already full of form and love and election, and so of a progress that can always be from good to good, glory to glory, according to an orientation that peacefully passes from each instance to the next, according to the true grammar of difference, without need of any interval of the negative, or of the refining clarity of death.

iv. Infinite Peace

While neither denying nor regretting that Gregory spoke the philosophical lingua franca of his time — "Platonic" and Stoic — I must make one observation: to say that in Gregory's thought it is one thing to come from God and to go to God is not simply to speak in terms of a Neoplatonic diastole and systole of being. It is a trinitarian affirmation first, a recognition that God is in himself a gift of distance; and for the creature, it means that the way of finitude is not one of departure from and return to an ideal purity, but one of contingent participation and implication in the infinite expression of God's love, a progress not of ideal reduction but of glorification, endless "musical" enrichment. There is no ontological *regressus* in the thought of Gregory, but rather a moral "return" of the soul to God that is necessarily a real taking on of the divine. And creation is an expression of the divine that is not merely noetic, in the Neoplatonic sense, which can be reflectively reduced to a formless truth, but aesthetic: its measures, proportions, differences, and deferrals are fitting to the theme they express, irreducibly, because that theme is difference and its beauty. Thus the truth of being is grasped by the soul not merely noetically, according to a scheme of essences, but aesthetically, in the soul's most "superficial" elations, its desire finding in creation's visible beauty a true image of the God after whom the soul yearns (*DVM* 2.231: 114). One moves in God's infinity only if one moves upon surfaces. To be raised up eternally into glory, to be deified, is to traverse every series of being in such a way as to see God's beauty expressed in each, in endless variety. Sin, violence, cruelty, egoism, and despair are the discords that disrupt the surface, but always as privation, a failure of love; they are no part of being's deep music, but only shrill alarms and barren phrasings, apostasies from music altogether. Evil, for all its ineradicable ubiquity, is always originally an absence, a shadow, a false reply, and all violence falls within the interval of a harmony not taken up, within which the true form of being is forgotten, misconstrued, distorted, and belied. This is not to imagine being as a music without dissonances, but as one without ultimate discords for the soul that turns its motion toward God's all-embracing eternal order of love, seeking to recover the theme of this love and articulate it anew forever.

It is for this reason that one may say that Gregory's thought points toward a remarkably original understanding of image and sign. As Gregory's is an ontology not of emanation but of creation, his understanding of the image as such is properly one of expression rather than of mere dissemination: the image *in its condition as image* expresses how God is God. Not by dissolution into a higher essence, but by an analogical correspondence of its created structure of difference and mediation to the God whose inner life is one of differentiation and mediation, the image expresses the truth of distance, of the God who is Trinity. All creation declares God's glory, and so should be understood not simply according to a logic of substances, but first as a free and flowing succession of *semeia,* within which "substances" are constituted as the relative stability of the "notes" or "moments" that the whole discourse (the Logos) calls forth; being, as a kind of cogent rhetoric, is the aesthetic surface of shared implications and complications whose very needless excess expresses the nature of divine love. Rather than a strong distinction between sign and substance, then, one should perhaps speak of "substantial signs" or of "semeiotic substances." Perhaps one can read Gregory in something like (and against) the way Deleuze reads Leibniz. In Deleuze's *The Fold,* the monadology of Leibniz is transformed into a "nomadology": the accord of every series in a preestablished harmony is recast as the divergence of every series into (in a phrase borrowed from Pierre Boulez) a "polyphony of polyphonies";[76] and the implication of all things in the monad's unique perspective becomes the folding and unfolding continuity in disjunction of surfaces, and the truth (or truths) of infinitely many perspectives. Deleuze, being a thinker of what he calls the "neo-Baroque" — the atonal, the sublime — has really no use for Leibniz's ontological "harmonics"; but for Christian thought the infinite and form can and must be thought together, not in the interest of some banal cosmic optimism, but because the measure of difference is primordially peace, a music whose periods, intervals, refrains, and variants can together (even when incorporating dissonances) hymn God's

76. Gilles Deleuze, *The Fold: Leibniz and the Baroque,* trans. Tom Conley (Minneapolis: University of Minnesota Press, 1992), 82.

glory. Embracing neither the austere moral calculus of Leibniz's determinism nor certainly Deleuze's adolescent fascination with sheer divergence and aleatory digression, one can yet conceive of an infinite, "ontological" music that eminently contains all transitions and intervals together, in which any series may digress without ever passing beyond reconciliation, beyond the reach of musical mediations that might restore it to the measures of that original peace that allows it to move at all (this is, of course, to speak eschatologically). Here again one must invoke the ontological difference, and with it the difference between the infinite music of the Trinity and the finite harmonies and discords of our fallen song. A "baroque" Gregory, so to speak, is one whose understanding of the divine image as perfected only in ceaseless motion completes an understanding of creation as a continuous unfolding (*akolouthia*, to use Gregory's word) of a marvelous "fabric" expressive of God's transcendent abundance. In the case of Gregory, for whom the soul (somewhat like Leibniz's monad) can in a sense mirror the whole of being's display, it becomes possible to see the image not as simply the naked eidetic correspondence of *eikon* and archetype, but as dynamic correspondence by way of likeness and difference, or likeness as difference. Here one has dispensed with any concept of a malign ontological interval between *eikon* and simulacrum, as the mystery of the image is not simply its inner approximation to an invariable anonymous essence, but its "superficial" arrangement of the signs it comprehends. The soul is an image of God in its traversal of all the *semeia* of being, within an infinite that always bestows itself in concrete instances of beauty, *kabod,* and so is an image by "reflecting" the whole infinite series in itself: inflecting the infinite and being inflected by it and all its interdependent positionings, by being always in motion, impelled by love, finding its proximity to God only in the endless music of this deferral. This is the soul's steadfastness in the good, changelessly beautiful amid change, drinking in an inexhaustible beauty. Only in Christ, of course, has this ordering of the finite toward the infinite perfectly occurred; only here is the true image of God and the true form of the creature entirely given; but the Holy Spirit is able always to bring all natures into conformity with that love, to reconcile them to the infinite according to the salvation Christ has wrought, and to fashion in them anew the beauty for which they were created.

In any event, this reading of Gregory (as a theologian of divine expression and exposition, rather than of either mere mystic flight or inviolable divine remoteness) calls attention to a salient detail of his thought: for him there can be no distinction drawn between a "bad" infinite (interminability, endlessness of a series, perpetual addition) and a good infinite (reconciliation of finitude's contradictions in a higher synthesis), not because the distinction is new with Hegel (in Platonism's separation of image from simulacrum it is already implicit), but because Gregory has overcome the idealist separation of truth from difference.

There is reconciliation in the realm of the finite, for Gregory, precisely by way of interminability, excess and *egressus,* a deferment that *is* progress, upon the plane of "immanence"; and the reconciliation at which one arrives (or is forever arriving) is not an abstraction that merely enervates contradiction, but in fact occurs by way of the "bad" infinite: it does not extract a higher "truth" from a dialectically "necessary" opposition, but rather discovers the "tonal" median (Christian "virtue") that allows contradiction to be reshaped as counterpoint, and finds the wider scope of musical coinherence where differences are revealed as unique modulations of the same infinite theme. Everything has an unforeclosable disseminative seriality implicit within it, and any series (as opposed to the stability of an unalterable substance) can be mediated into consonance with every other series, not dialectically, but by a shared measure of peace, by the charity that makes way. Primordially and eschatologically, this is the true form of being, discoverable even amid discords that fabricate series of their own, intonations of nonbeing, irredeemable magnitudes of noise; for in the light of Christ, following after him, limitless possibilities of peace appear to view. God's transcendence is the supereminent fullness of all blessings, which gives analogical expression to itself in creation: God sets it at a distance — and so it is created — but is himself the infinite distance that measures out all its differences within the abundant harmony of trinitarian peace. As Trinity, his is always somehow a determinate infinity, so that each thing's determinateness is actually an advance "quantitatively" toward the fullness of the infinite he is; but each thing is also always at that qualitative distance that makes it free, determinate, finite, pleasure, and gift. Indeed, the infinite qualitative difference is, in a sense, an effect of the infinite quantitative distance: not, that is, because God is simply the coincidence of every series (in a pantheistic sense), but because he is the infinite in which every series moves, and lives, and has its being. For Gregory, therefore, the always remaining infinity is not simply the interval between created and divine natures (statically conceived), but is the ever new infinity of the ever present God in distance, and the infinite dynamism of one nature being transformed toward another. This is so because divine infinity is that infinity, full of form, that belongs to the Trinity, whose unity is also a differentiating love. For Gregory, God's presence to the creature is real, not as what is present to hand but as the time of infinite traversal. And this is so, without need of the mechanism of the negative, because God is the infinite who is ever more, of beauty and of peace.

4. The infinite is beautiful because God is Trinity; and because all being belongs to God's infinity, a Christian ontology appears and properly belongs within a theological aesthetics.

And Laban said, This heap is a witness between me and thee this day. Therefore was the name of it called Galeed; and [of the pillar] Mizpah; for he said, The LORD watch between me and thee, when we are absent one from another. If thou shalt afflict my daughters, or if thou shalt take other wives beside my daughters, no man is with us; see, God is witness betwixt me and thee. And Laban said to Jacob, Behold this heap, and behold this pillar, which I have cast betwixt me and thee; this heap be witness, and this pillar be witness, that I will not pass over this heap to thee, and that thou shalt not pass over this heap and this pillar unto me, for harm. The God of Abraham, and the God of Nahor, the God of their father, judge betwixt us.

Gen. 31:48-53

And God said unto Moses, I AM THAT I AM: and he said, Thus shalt thou say unto the children of Israel, I AM hath sent me unto you.

Exod. 3:14

But will God indeed dwell on the earth? Behold, the heaven and heaven of heavens cannot contain thee; how much less this house that I have builded?

1 Kings 8:27

In the year that king Uzziah died I saw also the Lord sitting upon a throne, high and lifted up, and his train filled the temple. Above it stood the seraphims: each one had six wings; with twain he covered his face, and with twain he covered his feet, and with twain he did fly. And one cried unto another, and said, Holy, holy, holy, is the LORD of hosts: the whole earth is full of his glory. And the posts of the door moved at the voice of him that cried, and the house was filled with smoke.

Isa. 6:1-4

For in him we live, and move, and have our being.

Acts 17:28

And he is before all things, and in him all things consisted.

Col. 1:17

i. God and Being

The God of Israel is not a local God; he does not inhabit only a particular temenos, even one coextensive with the entire universe; even the heaven of heavens cannot contain him. Yet he is the God who elects Israel as his bride, who tabernacles among his people, whose *shekhinah* abides in his temple; the God who is all does indeed, as he chooses, dwell upon the earth. The same God who infinitely exceeds all things addresses Moses out of the burning bush to proclaim himself: *"Ehyeh asher Ehyeh,"* "I am that I am," or rather, "I will be what (where, when) I will be." The infinite God declares his freedom to appear, to act, to be in the midst of that which his infinity comprises; he is the infinite who is not merely boundlessly "sublime" but who — by virtue of being beautiful — goes where he will. All things that are dwell in the glory of God, and yet the glory of God becomes visible as a beauty among the world's beauties (Exod. 16:10; 24:16; 29:43; Num. 14:22; Deut. 5:24; 1 Kings 8:10f.; 2 Chron. 7:1-3; Ps. 97:6); when besought by Moses to show his glory, God answers, "I will make all my goodness (beauty, *tub*) pass before thee, and I will proclaim the name of the LORD before thee" (Exod. 33:18-19). This is the liberty of a God who is infinite but never without name or form *(temuna)*: Moses beholds "the form of the LORD" (Num. 12:8). "Indeed," writes Hans Urs von Balthasar, "this double movement corresponds to the very being of God, who is both unique and infinitely determined in himself, and the one who includes all things in his embrace."[77] When Laban erects the heap of stones called Galeed (cairn of witness) and the pillar called Mizpah (watchpost), he invokes the witness not of a God who guards boundaries but of a God transcendent of all boundaries, holding worldly distance within his more original distance, a God who inhabits and contains every interval, holding the place (in both ontological and moral terms) of "justice." To pass the pillar of Mizpah to do harm to another is not to transgress the borders of a ruling numen, and so to offend against him, but is to pass before the gaze of the God who keeps every region in his power, who is the God of Abraham and of Nahor. As the God whose infinity is triune, "determinate," *determined toward* the other, he transcends every limit — transcends even the dialectic of finite and infinite, which has served so loyally, in so many metaphysical epochs, to

77. Hans Urs von Balthasar, *The Glory of the Lord: A Theological Aesthetics*, vol. 7, *Theology: The New Covenant*, trans. Brian McNeil (San Francisco: Ignatius, 1989), 137.

sustain the fruitful *chorismos* between objective form and indetermination, presence and absence. But the God of Scripture is infinite precisely as the God who loves and acts, and who can be loved in turn: infinite precisely because he will be what and where he will be.

What, though, does this mean? What has been said *regarding being* — and with what measure of coherence — when one has said that God is the "infinitely determinate" source of all being, the eternal "I am"? This is not a question to be evaded by a fideistic recoil to some destructive (and largely modern) division between "biblical" and "philosophical" theology; theology that refuses to address questions of ontology can never be more than a mythology, and so must remain quite deplorably defenseless against serious philosophical criticism. More importantly, the question of being, for theology, has been made peculiarly acute in the modern age, given that a great deal of philosophy and theology now floats in the broad wake of Heidegger's "onto-theological" critique. To speak of being theologically is inevitably to resort to the language of participation — every alternative being ultimately incoherent — which Heideggerian orthodoxy forbids as a misunderstanding of being as perduring presence, an oblivion of the quiet mystery of being's sheer "presencing"; and, after all, the Heideggerian idiom is so damnably seductive, especially the late Heidegger's ever more pronounced affectation of a "pagan" patois, which allows him to portray the mystery of being not with the lineaments of some rigid transcendental structure of categories and causes, but as, for instance, the "fourfold" tension of heaven and earth, gods and mortals, wherein being is disclosed and yet hidden in the event of its disclosure. But Christian theology is obliged to speak of being as the infinite "distance" of God and of beings as an endless variety of expressive and participatory modes of glory: which would make the difference between beings and being not the oscillation between manifestation and hiddenness, but the difference between the display of the infinite (the economy of the hidden and the manifest within creation) and being as infinite display (the transcendent coincidence of hiddenness and manifestation within God), or the difference between the musical moment — which is never simply presence as such, but an inflection of retention and protention — and the infinite music, music itself, that is accomplished in God. Admittedly, this last metaphor does look suspiciously like a discourse of whole and parts, but it is meant to suggest an "expressionist" ontology that (unlike that of Spinoza) is analogical, not univocal: beings express God's infinite being by being other than God, not as the negation or occlusion of that being, but by bearing testimony to the richness and glory of the infinite they traverse, as moments of distance opened within God's transcendent act of distance. Time, successiveness, in such a vision, cannot be regarded as the "nihilation" through which being is exposed in its destruction, but must be understood rather as the ecstatic movement of the finite in its "disclosing" traversal of the infinite, and as the fruitful synthesis of finite existence and finite essence in the energy of becoming. This is, quite confessedly, a language of plenitude: the analogy between God's life as the joyous coincidence of all the riches of his infinite being and all the peace of his utterly simple fullness on the one hand, and creation as an expression of the richness of the infinite in a condition of radical contingency on the other. And, one must add, this analogy holds only insofar as beings comprise within their "essences" each a persisting interval of incommensurability that is the created likeness of the infinite ontological interval between God and them. That is to say, a creature's likeness to God, posed between the pure ontic ecstasy of its participation in being ex nihilo and the infinite ontological plenitude of God's being *in se* (between, one might say, its intrinsic nothingness and God's supereminent "no-thing-ness"), cannot simply take the form of a homonymy of "attributes" applied to two discrete substances, but must consist, radically, in the rhythm of the creature's difference from God, its likeness to his unlikeness, under the form of a dynamic synthesis of distinct moments of being that, in God, coincide in simple and infinite identity: by being distinguished in itself between what it is and that it is, between "essence" and the force of becoming, between its creaturely particularity and the infinite distance it traverses. In no other way can a being be *a being* — that is, a finite act of existence. God is not so divided; and yet, because he is Trinity, and because therefore his being is also the gift that is always being given determinatively to the other, and so is never simply undifferentiated presence, he is also the God who can be *within* his infinite distance, who is at liberty therein, who is infinite and yet also infinitely *formosus*, and who can consequently make all his beauty pass before the eyes of Moses, even as Moses passes before him in endless pilgrimage.

In truth, there is no compelling reason given by Heidegger — however confidently he claimed, and his disciples claim, the contrary — for abandoning the traditional theological understanding of the ontological difference. The evident difference between being and beings shows us that being is no particular thing, that beings might be otherwise than they are. Moreover, there is no way of thinking being and beings together — no account of a fittingness or analogy between being and beings as the beings they are — within the closed circle of this difference except in terms of sheer identity or sheer negation, either of which is a metaphysics of the totality.[78] But one may instead see the difference as indicating, within the unity of every being, an analogy pointing to the God in whom being and being determinate (or of being Who He Is) are not divided,

---

78. See Hans Urs von Balthasar, *The Glory of the Lord: A Theological Aesthetics*, vol. 5, *The Realm of Metaphysics in the Modern Age*, trans. Oliver Davies, Andrew Louth, Brian McNeil, John Saward, and Rowan Williams (San Francisco: Ignatius, 1991), 449.

the God who can give difference not simply as manifestations and obscurations of being, but as gracious declarations of the infinite distance to which the being of beings belongs. "Ipsum esse absolute consideratum infinitum est," remarks Thomas Aquinas, "nam ab infinitis et infinitis modis participari possibile est" (*Summa contra Gentiles* 1.43). This is so because the created *esse* in which the creature participates itself (while being absolute) does not, strictly speaking, "exist" or "subsist" (*De potentia Dei* 1.1). Is this just a metaphysics of presence, another way of thinking being as substance, *ousia*, foundation? Does it fail to think the ontological difference? Or the event of that difference? In truth, every attempt to talk of being is a metaphorical labor; the Heideggerian tendency to treat every philosophical discourse save Heidegger's as irredeemably metaphorical, as "forgetful" of what Heidegger has recalled, is symptomatic of a dogmatism that never interrogates its own presuppositions regarding the trajectory a philosophical thought of being must take; the conviction that "onto-theology" understands being simply in terms of "causes" and "grounds" — without any analogical latitude being granted such terms — is reductive, to say the very least, and disingenuous insofar as it is a conviction oblivious to how easily deconstructible Heidegger's own metaphors are.

We should do well, I think, to consider precisely what claim either the early Heidegger's "fundamental ontology" or the later Heidegger's "thoughtful speaking" makes upon theology, and whether in fact either truly represents something "beyond" metaphysics. More precisely, we should ask whether the mature Heidegger's increasingly intense concern not just for the ontico-ontological difference as such but for the opening or event or *"Austrag"* of that difference genuinely places his thought at an appreciable and commanding remove from metaphysical "forgetfulness," or whether in fact it merely brings forgetfulness to its most radical expression. After all, as I have said above, the early Heidegger's crossing of the threshold from phenomenology to ontology was made possible by the phenomenological collapse of any meaningful distinction between "it is" and "it appears"; and while this might seem to be a sign of critical scruple and scientific rigor, it is also most certainly a move that remains, at some level, metaphysical, even conjectural, and that too quickly hardens the transcendental vantage of post-Kantian epistemology into an inviolable dogma (though this, Heidegger later sought to escape). Moreover, Heidegger was forced at first to argue toward the legitimacy of any ontology at all, and had to do so only in terms that the phenomenological realm of inference (the economy of appearance and hiddenness) comprises: hence, being could not be thought outside of the closed circle of what appears — and does not appear. Not that he saw this only as a limitation (though perhaps he genuinely understood it as a critical discipline); he certainly also saw in it the occasion of a play for power. In the notorious essay of

1927, "Phänomenologie und Theologie,"[79] he made the boldest attempt in the history of modern philosophy to seize back from theology the high ground of "metaphysics": discourse on being. It was in this essay that he attempted to reduce theology, ever so gently, to the status of an "ontic science," a discourse regarding the special comportment of faith toward the cross of Christ, an analytic of "Christianness." He had, obviously, a late scholastic and Lutheran tradition of theology to draw on here (not to mention much modern Protestant thought), which was all too hospitable to false demarcations between the spheres of philosophy and theology, but in truth Heidegger's guiding concern was philosophy's hegemony. Again, as I argued in part 1, modern philosophy's special melancholy is its need to escape theology's fuller and more coherent account of all the topoi of classical reason; and the modern philosopher who does not simply want to abandon the concerns of the great tradition, in the Anglo-American analytic manner, but who feels compelled still to speak of the whole of reality, must forsake many metaphysical ambitions precisely so as to pursue the ultimate metaphysical ambition of "deducing" the nature of being in abstraction from all "revelation" or "illumination." In this early essay, Heidegger's audacity is quite astonishing: he makes a space for theology that, by any just measure, is no more than the space of a pathology, of a psychological fixation played out purely "locally," precisely so as to steal from theology that language of being and beings (which he will later thematize as the ontico-ontological difference) that only arrived for human reflection when the doctrine of creation assumed, but altered, antique metaphysics. And while Heidegger claims that in discriminating between the spheres of faith and critical reflection he is not placing them in rivalry to one another, or granting one priority over the other (ontic and ontological concerns, or empirical and theoretical investigations, belonging to entirely different orders of truth), this is manifestly a lie: the philosopher, for example, is able to see that the theologian's special language of sin falls under the more original, ontological determination of Dasein's guilt (Schuld), and thus the analysis of guilt can clarify and correct the concept of sin, but never the reverse (W, 64/P, 51-52); after all, Heidegger assures us, "there is no such thing as a Christian philosophy" (W, 66/P, 53).

The problem, though, that should be immediately evident is that Heidegger's philosophy, precisely because it seeks to begin from a position unassailably removed from theology, possesses no resources for talking about being *in its difference*. By forsaking reason's necessarily ecstatic movement toward

79. In Martin Heidegger, *Wegmarken* (hereafter *W*), in *Gesamtausgabe* 9 (Frankfurt am Main: Vittorio Klosterman, 1976); in English, *Pathmarks* (Cambridge: Cambridge University Press, 1998), hereafter *P*.

a horizon continuous with and yet transcending the scope of experience, in order instead to capture being's truth within the horizon of *Dasein*'s grasp of the world, Heidegger merely condemns himself to wallowing endlessly in the ontic process of becoming and passing away, within which he arbitrarily isolates certain *"existentiell"* structures of experience in order to assign them a heuristic, "existential" significance, pointing toward the mystery of being; and thus his every assertion regarding being, however exhaustively it may be preceded by a phenomenological treatment of being-in-the-world, ultimately has the character of a feat of divination. This is really why *Being and Time* was never completed: the project is impossible. The beguiling but ultimately hopeless shape of the early Heidegger's thought is nowhere more evident than in 1929's "Was ist Metaphysik?" As powerful as is this essay's treatment of the "nothing" that, when grasped, makes us aware of beings qua beings (makes us grasp, i.e., that beings *are*), its treatment of, say, boredom or of, more determinatively, anxiety as a *Stimmung* that enjoys a privileged ontological probity (*W,* 110-12/*P,* 87-88) is, again, arbitrary and consequently a mystification. Moreover, while anxiety might make one conscious that what is, is set over against the nothing, to cross from this apprehension of ontic contingency (which is how theological tradition would describe it) to any conclusion concerning being as such involves either taking leave of the entire ontic economy of existence and nonexistence (which means, transcending finite determination) or mistaking this economy for the sole truth of being (which leaves the real question of being, as distinct from all beings, unaddressed); Heidegger pursues the latter course. That is to say, no matter which fundamental mood — boredom, anxiety, joy, wonder — reveals to us the strangeness of existence, its sheer fortuity, the kind of "nothing" that opens up within this experience is merely the opposite of existence; to suggest, then, a convertibility of the "nothing" and "being," as Heidegger does (following a glittering concatenation of wild assertions: being is what shows beings as beings, the nothing discloses to us that beings are beings, thus in the being of being the nothing nothings . . .), is simply to avoid the issue. This nothing (which, in this clearly dialectical scheme, is the nonexistence of beings) can open for us a perspective on being only if being is to be conceived as the opposite of the existence of whatever is; this is not only an empty notion, but in fact in no proper sense opens an ontological perspective on anything at all: being, if it is really to be grasped in its *difference* from all beings, however much a sense of that difference may be granted by the ontic oscillation between existence and nonexistence, cannot be opposite of anything at all[80] — it is set over against neither existence nor nonexistence within finite reality, but is the "is" both of "it is" and of "it is not," and so the difference between the two cannot describe the

---

80. See Maximus the Confessor, *The Chapters on Love* 3.65.

difference of being from both. The simple opposition of "is" and "is not," being an ontic play of limitation and contradiction, is not an ontological determination, but is merely what raises the ontological question in the first place. Thus to confuse being with nonexistence, which is the only kind of "nothing" that anxiety can reveal, is as gross a species of *Seinsvergessenheit* as to confuse being with simple existence; one is merely choosing, between the ontic "this" (which is "not nothing") and the ontic "not this," to identify being with the latter (which really, though, is only a moment within the determination of finite "essences"). It is true that the difference between beings and nonbeing reveals to us, if we are attentive, that being is not a being among beings; but by the same token, if we do not succumb to the temptation of dialectic, it should also reveal to us that being is as mysteriously beyond nonbeing as beyond everything that is. It is the very synthesis within beings of what they are and that they are (and hence of what they are not) that makes it impossible to say, within terms of ontic process, how to speak of being. Again, Leibniz inquires, how is it that there are beings at all, and not much rather nothing? And he is unlikely to be satisfied by some murky confusion of being with the nothing, as the question might just as well be asked thus: What permits beings and nonbeing to be distinct from one another, such that beings are the beings they are while nothing remains nothing *(ex quo nihil fieri potest)?* How can this setting apart *be?*

Which is a question that, pursued far enough, makes one wonder whether Heidegger's greatest claim to the mantle of antimetaphysical prophet — his treatment of the temporalization of being, with its attendant diagnosis of onto-theology's confusion of being with enduring presence — may rest not simply on an oversimplified history of Western thought (which it certainly does), but on a very basic logical mistake. To determine if this is so, however, one should consider the later Heidegger, who after his celebrated *Kehre* supposedly turned his eyes from *Dasein* to *Sein* (from what vantage who can say), and increasingly to the *es gibt* of the event that grants the ontico-ontological difference to each age of thought, under the form of forgetfulness. In Heidegger's work before this fateful turning, one is occasionally told, one might mistake the being of which Heidegger speaks as some version of *esse commune,* the sheer existence that all beings share and that is nothing apart from beings, but Heidegger's later work makes clear that this is not the case. John Caputo, in his *Heidegger and Aquinas,* argues that *esse commune* has, as its only counterpart in Heidegger's thought, the "beingness" of beings, the abstract fact of existence, which is not what Heidegger means by *Sein.*[81] This is both true and false; yes, Heidegger means more than the "existence" of "existents" when he speaks of being; but neverthe-

---

81. John Caputo, *Heidegger and Aquinas: An Essay on Overcoming Metaphysics* (New York: Fordham University Press, 1982), 143.

less, he also confines the thought of being to a finite economy of "presencing" that is nothing but the process of "beingness," or the way beings exist in their "existingness" as long as they exist, and thus his ontology can never be more than a reflection upon how beings appear within this economy, the very being of which still remains uninterrogated (why is there an economy of existence at all, and not much rather nothing?). Nor is this problem mitigated by Heidegger's fabled *Ereignis*. As Caputo points out, Heidegger was increasingly willing to grant that all metaphysics possesses some sense of the ontological difference as such — else there would be no philosophy — but what metaphysics habitually fails to think, he still argued, was the distance of the difference between being and beings:[82] thus being and beings are locked within a circle of mutual grounding (that pernicious "double founding" of onto-theology: beings in being, being in the supreme being), while never a thought is given to the mysterious eventfulness of their passing over, one to the other, and their setting apart. All is rigid presence, substance, structure, but the utter givenness of the *Anwesen* of beings — their arrival in the light of being, their tremulous lingering, their passing away again into concealment — goes unremarked in its peaceful, continuous silence. This is clearest in 1959's *Identität und Differenz*, where Heidegger takes two "steps back" away from beings: one goes only as far as the difference of being from beings, which metaphysics knows and thematizes by fashioning some generalized model of a characteristic proper to beings; but the second step goes farther, into the more primordial differing of the difference, the *"Austrag"* *(auseinander-zueinander-tragen)* that gives being and beings to one another and that grants each epoch the possibility of its forgetful thinking of the ontological difference.[83] This appropriating event *(Ereignis)* is not to be confused with creation, according to Heidegger, as it is a letting-be-seen, not a causal making, an *actus*;[84] it is the more original giving, that hides itself — withdraws itself — in order to give. That is, it gives the process of ἀλήθεια or φύσις, the surging up and whiling of beings in being's juncture. As Heidegger's essay of 1946, "Der Spruch des Anaximander," explains, the juncture falls between two absences, two concealments: the future "to-come" and the past "having-been."[85] This is where the differing occurs, this is the twofold absence it holds apart so as to allow presence its whiling (*H*, 355). What is present is not some substance forced between absent substances, but "presences" only in allowing itself to belong to the absent (*H*, 357); and in this order

---

82. Caputo, *Heidegger and Aquinas*, 155-56.

83. Martin Heidegger, *Identität und Differenz* (Pfullingen: Gunther Neske, 1957), 65.

84. A word, frankly, that Heidegger reads with stunning vulgarity; see Caputo, *Heidegger and Aquinas*, 169.

85. In Martin Heidegger, *Holzwege* (hereafter *H*), in *Gesamtausgabe* 5 (1977), 334-36.

of being and beings, we glimpse something of the essence of tragedy (*H*, 357-58). In a 1950 footnote added to the text, Heidegger makes so bold as to say that the discrimination *(Unter-Schied)* of which he is here speaking "is infinitely distinct *(unendlich verschieden)* from being, which remains the being *of* beings" (*H*, 364 n. d). The event may also be called Logos, a word that for Heidegger most truly means a "laying-out that gathers together":[86] Logos gathers all destining *(Shicken)* to itself, keeping each being, whether absent or present, "in its place and on its way," and by its assembling "secures all things in the all," sending each into its own (*VA*, 226-27). This then is the final form of Heidegger's temporalization of being: being and beings are given to one another in the event that always opens the juncture between them by opening it as a juncture between the arrival of the concealed future and departure of the concealed past, allowing beings to waver into presence, perdure, and waver into nothing; it is a passage from nothing to nothing, surmounted by a mysterious noncausal, "vertical" event that gathers and apportions and sustains the finite economy of nihilation, and which, as Logos, occurs for us in language, and then finally in the thoughtful hearing of language — not so much of what it says, as of its gathering saying of the world in its "worlding." Hence the order of those sonorous, incantatory sentences at the end of "Brief über den Humanismus": as clouds are the clouds of the sky — allowing it to be seen, distinctly, as sky, even in obscuring it — so language is the language of being; and, as the vast dark earth is scarcely scored by the inconspicuous furrows drawn in it by the farmer's plow, so thought is a humble turning of the surface of language, whose immensity it scarcely touches (*W*, 364/*P*, 276).

All of which is extremely alluring, in an autumnal, late romantic way. Certainly, one must also say, Heidegger's diagnosis of nihilism — developing as it does Nietzsche's brilliant reading of the "death of God" as the inevitable terminus of all Western philosophical "positivisms" — is a precious ornament of twentieth-century philosophy (if only as a critique of *modern* philosophy), as is his attempt to reunite the idea of truth to the full presence of what is, and so free it from the barren, and also ultimately nihilistic, equation of truth with sufficient reason or positive ground. However, like Nietzsche before him, his historical vision was far more limited than he seemed to realize, and his own philosophy was far more "fated" by the tradition he was trying to "retrieve" than even he appreciated. Heidegger, coming at the twilit cusp of philosophy's final abandonment of the Christian intellectual tradition, was able to gaze across the chasm of theology, now largely lost in shadows, to the remote dawn of philosophy on its far side, and to construct a genealogy of nihilism that was both bril-

---

86. Martin Heidegger, "Logos (Heraklit, Fragment 50)," in *Vorträge und Aufsätze* (hereafter *VA*), *Gesamtausgabe* 7 (2000).

liantly illuminative of much of the great level plain he surveyed and abysmally oblivious of how deep theology's "interruption" of that plain was; and, for this very reason, even as he felt free to ask again, unabashed, the question of being, he himself could do nothing but bring that nihilism to something very like its consummation. He could ask the question, that is, because the forgetfulness of its meaning had become so entirely complete; which yields the curious irony that the philosopher whose idiom was the most robustly and indefatigably "ontological" ever was also the one whose entire career was marked by a failure to ask — or even quite to grasp what it would mean to ask — the question of being. One must reiterate that Heidegger never genuinely considers being as truly *ontologically* different from beings; even when he speaks of his *Ereignis*, he is merely attempting thereby to seal the event of the world within its own immanent happening, its process; but this is in every sense an ontic process only, over which the question of being's difference continues to hover. How is it that becoming is? — which is not the question Heidegger asks. In his words,

> whatever has its essence in arrival and departure we would like to call becoming and perishing, which is to say, transience, and therefore not being; for we have long been accustomed to opposing being to becoming, as if becoming were a nothingness and did not even belong to being, which one habitually understands only as sheer perdurance. If, though, becoming *is*, then we must think being so essentially that it not only comprises becoming in some empty concept, but that, rather, being ontologically *(seinsmäßig)* supports and characterizes becoming (γένεσις-φθορά) in its essence. (*H*, 343)

The flaws in the reasoning in this paragraph, as in the entire project from which it emanates, are fairly elementary. For one thing, it is a confusion of issues to say that "metaphysics," in distinguishing between becoming and being, thereby treats becoming a kind of nothingness; rather, traditionally, and quite logically, Western thought has recognized that it is becoming's obvious reality, and its inability to account for itself, that turns thought toward being's difference from all that has being. Then there is the oddity of the paragraph's central argument: "if becoming *is* . . ."; to risk an unpardonable flippancy, by the same token we might say that being has always been characterized as something altogether different from bananas — *but if bananas are* . . . In either case, it is the "is" of becoming or the "are" of bananas that remains imponderable, and simply collapsing the subject into its verb advances our cause not a step. The notion that being has, throughout metaphysical history, been characterized, with lumpen simplemindedness, as sheer enduring presence is so religiously asserted by Heideggerians that one is almost loath to enter the lists against it. Yes, eternity

— as timelessness — has long figured in Western thinking of what is other than all beings, but three things must be kept in mind: first, a sense of the difference between timelessness and substantial perdurance was not lost upon all the philosophers of antiquity, pagan, Jewish, or Christian, nor should it be on us; second, the prejudice of metaphysical tradition that becoming is not being may at times appear as a crude distinction between what changes and a great changeless substance, but it more properly arises from the realization that nothing in the ontic play of existence and nonexistence (not even becoming, or the process of "disclosure") is its own "is," which cannot be some thing that becomes, that has an other, or that contains potential; and third, as a term of negation, "eternity" is an absolutely necessary moment in prescinding from beings to being, the alternative to which is utter nonsense. For Heidegger the pathology of metaphysics is its incorrigible tendency to fix upon some characteristic of beings in general and from that distill a name for being, and then to treat beings as imitations or instances or reflections of that original, supreme, enduring thing. The most interesting observation one can make about this is that Heidegger himself does precisely what he condemns: he brings the great inversion of modern thought, its "Ptolemaic revolution," to its conclusion by simply taking the ontic characteristic of temporal change, of becoming and transiency, generalizing it as the process of hiddenness and unhiddenness, and making of it a name (or many names) for being — thereby mistaking that process for the ontological difference, and so treating being as nothing but a reflection of our own "beingness." Over this syncope of being and beings, then, he erects an arch of fate, of μοῖρα, which apportions finite things to their placement and displacement in a cycle of endless immanence,[87] and thus confirms beings in their potentiality (their nothingness) as the "ground" of being.[88] In scholastic terms, Heidegger merely elevates possibility over actuality — but he still has not touched the essential mystery: Why is it that either possibility or actuality *is?* What is the "is" of "it is possible"?

Here we arrive at the crucial issue. Caputo ends his treatment of Aquinas and Heidegger by trying to reconcile the two thinkers in a "dimension of depth," beyond Aquinas's metaphysics, in the mystical dimension of his thought; but Caputo never considers whether we might move beyond Heidegger's "metaphysics," and the book ends on an astonishingly depressing note: "possibility is always higher than actuality, *sicut Martinus dicit.*"[89] Caputo accepts Heidegger's claim that Thomas's language of *actus* and *actualitas* reflects a thoroughly "Roman" distortion of Aristotle's *energeia*, one emanating from a

---

87. See Martin Heidegger, "Moira (Parmenides, Fragment VIII, 34-41)," in *VA,* 235-61.
88. See 1930's "Vom Wesen des Grundes," in *W,* 123-75.
89. Caputo, *Heidegger and Aquinas,* 284.

culture of fabrication, technology, conquest, and power, whose governing "motif" was one of efficient causality. I, for one, find no virtue in this argument; I think Thomas more than adequately discriminates between a crudely univocal use of the language of cause or act and his properly analogical use, and I most certainly deny that *actus* is philologically, semantically, or historically bound to the connotations Heidegger assigns it (Heidegger was never quite the classicist he liked to pretend he was). Perhaps if Heidegger's knowledge of Christian thought had ever extended further back, in any significant way, to the patristic sources of the tradition, and he had not tended to think toward the earlier tradition (if at all) only "backwards" from later, modern developments, his treatment of the term would not have been so extraordinarily primitive (apparently he had some sense that Greek patristic thought was somewhat more elusive of his "onto-theological" critique than late scholasticism, but it was an awareness without much scope). So, now that Gilson and others who so enormously exaggerated Thomas's originality no longer dominate Thomist scholarship, we may certainly, if we wish, retreat from Thomas's exquisitely refined terminology to earlier moments in the continuous tradition of Christian ontology that he was interpreting — to the Cappadocians, or Augustine, or Maximus, above all to Dionysius the Areopagite — and choose some other word: *energeia*, "plenitude," "light," "the Good," etc. Could Heidegger have read Dionysius or Maximus, speaking of God as the fullness of being, "leading" (to use the Dionysian term) beings into being, or as the light that shines in and on all things and draws them to himself, or as the infinite source of beauty that "excites" the "eros" of beings out of their nonbeing, and interpreted this simply as a discourse of double founding, a mere causal economy between a supreme thing and derivative things? Could he have encountered Dionysius's language of the divine ecstasy that calls forth and meets our ecstasy, and so gives being to beings, or of the Good's supereminent "no-thing-ness," and treated this too as a form of ontic causality infinitely magnified, without significant analogical ambiguity? The reason such questions are as pointless as they are unanswerable is that Heidegger's commitment to his own metaphysics of process, epochality, language, and "thought" (to, that is, his diluted and suppressed Hegelianism) was absolute, and was irreconcilable with any discourse of transcendence; his was an entirely "immanent ontology" — a thing that is, as he says of "Christian philosophy," a "square circle." So let us continue to speak of actuality.

What would it mean really to elevate possibility over actuality? Could this quite obvious ontic truth — that what is possible is in some sense in surfeit of what is, in the present moment, actual — really be an ontological truth as well? To be precise: no, of course not. Heidegger's process of *Anwesen*, like any economy of finite determination, consists in a dialectic between "this" and "not this," a setting off of what is from all that might be, that has been, that will be —

all that is concealed, potential, all that *is* not. But such a dialectic would remain an inert impossibility, a nonevent, never coming to pass at all, if the difference between possible and actual were not preceded by and enfolded within a prior actuality. The nothing cannot magically pass from itself into something; *fieri* cannot precede *esse*. Heidegger sensed this well enough to find it necessary to make a distinction between the event and what eventuates, but perversely refused to acknowledge the transcendent plenitude of "realized" being to which the event must lead thought. To speak of this transcendent act, which infinitely and simply is all that the possible might possibly be, as merely some cause, some efficient power, is worse than absurd. Christian thought from the time of Gregory of Nyssa, Dionysius, and Maximus had developed an ontology of the infinite (drawing on Plotinus's thought, while freeing it from its metaphysical identism) which Aquinas, in the West, brought to a particularly lucid expression: being is not to be thought of in terms of either essences or their finite existence; the "infinite," which for Aristotle named only the inchoate potentiality of matter apart from the limit of form, now names the fullness of being, *esse*, which is the transcendent actuality of essence and existence alike; being differs from beings, to speak analogously, as does truth from anything true. We are far beyond any naive essentialism here.[90] This language of participation, however much one may wish to resist it, cannot (except as a display of doctrinaire cant) plausibly be called onto-theology. Moreover, if one properly grasps how different this thought of *actus* is from all thoughts of the general characteristics of beings, how radically indeed it opens up the thought of the distinction between being as being and beings as beings, one must see that it is a thought that makes every ontic economy thinkable: for while, in the realm of the ontic, the possible is in some sense a wellspring of the actual, this necessarily finite order requires a kind of conceptual inversion, which renders its logic infinite, if one is to think of being as such, for even possibility — whether one conceives it as abstract forms or simply concealed temporal *"ecstases"* — must first *be*. If this seems like an argument toward necessary being, or toward Aquinas's claim that the distance between existence and nonexistence is infinite — well, indeed it is; but one must also recall that "necessary" here does not mean a first cause in the ontic sense, but the transcendent "possibility of possibility" (which must be infinite actuality). Anyway, even to think of possibility as "higher" than actuality is covertly to think of it as actual, as having a more "eminent" being, which must be forced into definite manifestation, an indeterminacy that must be distributed into temporal determinacy by the apportioning hand of fate. Obviously in Heidegger's thought the no-thing-ness of being has not been conceived

90. Gilson is of great help here as regards many of the metaphysical issues here at stake, despite the effect of his mono-Thomism on his historiography.

of as an infinite purity from all limit, but as a mirror inversion of ontic presence in the ontic absence of past and future, so the withholding of being in beings is not, in his vision, the qualitative transcendence of the infinite, but a kind of restrained immensity of "thereness," the absolute com-presence of the totality deferred into temporality. Indeed, this is not a thought of *esse commune,* but only because it has failed to rise from the dialectic of existence and nonexistence to a thought of simple existence as such, and so certainly has not gone beyond that to the thought of being as such. When Heidegger, then, having failed to think toward being's real difference, differentiates his *Ereignis* "infinitely" from all being, it can serve only as the metaphysical seal of immanence, another version of absolute negation as an absolute confirmation of the totality. After all, every mere metaphysics thinks the difference of being from beings in terms of the necessity of the ontic, and so fails to see how it thus clings to a mythology of the ontic. Only the thought of being's infinite act, neither determined in beings nor lacking anything in their absence, thinks the difference as belonging first to being, not beings (thinks it, that is, from the place of a gift received). Only a theological ontology can really reconcile possibility and actuality to one another conceptually in such a way as to make the passing over of each into the other conceivable as the peaceful event of being in beings.

One must credit Heidegger, however, with one singular achievement: he indeed rescued a kind of pagan thinking from its Christian oblivion, and endued it with both intellectual respectability and ornate charm, despite its fundamental incoherence. He recovered a truly tragic ontology from the buried ruins of antique philosophy, or (to name it according to its more primordial logic) a truly sacrificial ontology. Heidegger would dismiss as a Platonist servility before the "look" of things the desire to ask the question of the transcendentals — the sublime unity that traverses every series, every moment in every series, every part of every moment, *in infinitum,* or the splendor of form, or the truthful abiding of each thing in its proper essence, etc. — and he certainly has no room in his thought for the developed Plotinian or far more developed Christian tendency to see the transcendentals as flowing from an infinite fullness of being pure of all beings. Although such a question and such a thought certainly reach out to the being of things, and the difference of being from beings, far more profoundly and cogently than does Heidegger's language of ἀλήθεια, both the question and the thought are essentially subversive of Heidegger's absolute immanentism. If one were to ask, within the Heideggerian universe, how it is that all things are unities within change, how order and thought and beauty are one and yet utterly distinct, how the world and perception are inseparably joined in a circle of love and knowledge, and so on, one would ultimately be able to answer only that the world appears thus because it must so appear: for being to be in beings, for it to be manifest, it must be forced (or "nihilated," or "destroyed") into the limits of the ontic, its power must be wrested into the juncture as definite and limited forms of wavering perdurance, *Welt* must be torn from the depths of *Erde*, the thing must gather into a unity from the four regions in order to be set off against being's nothingness; so the truth that a thing is and is this thing is the necessary result of a reduction of the nothing to something, the effect of fate's apportionment of the open. This, of course, does not actually answer the question of being; it merely states with a metaphysical peremptoriness that so it must be, without ever making conceivable how it could be so. And so it is that Heidegger indeed brings metaphysics back to a kind of pre-Socratic immersion in φύσις. The image of being as a closed and finite order of placement and displacement, life and death, presided over by the empty determinations of inviolable fate, is the ontology that most purely flows from a certain aboriginal pagan vision of being as sacrifice: as order won through strife, as an economy of destruction and renewal, as totality closed in upon itself. It is an ontology that has no horizon but beings, and so can do no more than abstract from nature and violence and transience to a sublime, dark reservoir of ontic possibility, and to an inescapable structure of arising and perishing.

Here then we might venture a genealogy of nihilism somewhat different from Heidegger's. Heidegger's second step back from metaphysics is not into a more original distinction than the ontico-ontological difference, but merely away from the infinite into the finite, so as to complete metaphysics' decline as a descent into a passive self-sealing immanence, reflecting the world's transitoriness to itself in the fixed, anonymous mirror of the "event." According to Heidegger, being has reached its eschaton, the most extreme limit of its decline, its fated gathering to its ultimate essence (*H*, 327), thought's moment of greatest "risk" in the time of the technological *Gestell* and of realized nihilism;[91] but having achieved this the vantage of ultimate extremity, thought can now look back over the history of *Seinsvergessenheit*, understand what has brought us to this moment, glimpse that flash of light that illuminated being in thought's "first beginning," and prepare ourselves, with a certain pious *Gelassenheit*, for another beginning. In a sense he is right: philosophy, as an independent enterprise of critical reason, is at the point of collapse; Christian thought's interruption and rescue of Western metaphysics has been followed by a revolt of reason whose ultimate form cannot now be anything but nihilism made transparent to itself; so Heidegger, the last metaphysician (or the first of the last metaphysicians), who can see the shape of nihilism but who — as that increasingly otiose thing, a philosopher — cannot step back from this destiny, instead attempts to

91. See Martin Heidegger, "Die Kehre," in Heidegger, *Die Technik und die Kehre* (Pfullingen: Neske, 1962).

press through it to a resignation that somehow "anticipates" and so overcomes nihilism, and that thus returns to metaphysics' origin. However, again because his move is the final reactive agitation of a revolt, the thought of being available to him is still nihilistic, still a finite ontic economy, stripped even of the soothing mirages of modern metaphysics: *Geist,* ego, positivity, etc. Ultimately Heidegger must return to an oblivion of being as profound as his own, the pre-Socratic inability to separate wonder at being from brutish awe before nature and fate, part and whole, becoming and totality — that is, the pre-Platonic indistinction between being and sacrifice. Western thought had attempted to rise from this superstitious subjugation to the world's mere event: Plato and Aristotle, however imperfectly, were both shaken by that effulgent moment of wonder that can free reflection from mere animal dread — the one could not quite transcend the irresoluble tension between change and changeless essences, the other the immanent dialectic of finite form and unrealized potency, and neither could overcome the still "sacrificial" economy of finitude, but both stood within an opening in Western thought that theology could transform into a genuine openness before the transcendent God. Original Stoicism was a step back, in some ways, toward the vision of the universe as sheer fated economy, an order of placement and displacement, as well as a precocious step toward "eschatological" nihilism, the consummation of the sacrificial vision in a cosmic mythology of eternally repeated *ecpyroses,* of the entire universe as an eternal sacrificial pyre; but even Stoicism was profoundly marked by a kind of wonder before the imperishable goodness of the world's being, and soon drew water from other philosophical streams to enliven its metaphysics. Late antiquity, in its syncretism, opened the Platonic tradition yet further to a possibility beyond the metaphysics of the totality, and Christian thought, with its Jewish doctrine of creation, shattered the totality altogether and, for the first time ever, caught sight of being's splendid otherness, within the immediacy of its mysterious presence — within the gratuity of the gift. The history of nihilism is the history of the forgetfulness of this gift, this true thought of being, a history which reaches a terminal, yet interminable, form in Heidegger's quasi-Stoic treatment of time, his "poetic" irrationalism, his spilled Hegelianism, his refusal of all ontological analogy, his absolutely "ontologized" inability to think being. Here the ambiguous Platonic wakefulness to wonder is submerged again into brute passivity, the full Christian awakening is entirely purged from memory, and philosophy becomes a crepuscular pathos, a twilit meditation upon its own death. Within the world of thought though, it seems worth noting, as in the physical world, twilight comes about not because the sun (or sun of the Good) is setting, but only because the world is itself turning away into its own shadow.

I confess, I do not believe in Heidegger's other "turning," his famous

Kehre: the more "objective" tone of the later philosophy aside, there is an essentially transcendental perspective in all of his thought which refuses — not so much, probably, from critical scruple as from a sense of what territory it is over which thought can still plausibly assert its sovereignty — to look beyond its gaze, to see both the horizon of its natural scope and also the more original (more transcendent) distance that makes that horizon possible (despite his claims to the contrary). Obviously there was a turn from the language of "authenticity" and "resolve" toward that of destined historical epochs, but this probably had more to do with Heidegger's political depravity than anything else: the later language has a certain exculpatory impersonality about it that an impenitent old Nazi might have good cause to embrace. So one can quite legitimately return to the earlier point of departure and ask if even phenomenological rigor requires thought to remain in the difference between existents and nothingness, or at best to step away from this opposition and then circle back to it from the vantage of the appropriating event. If we are to choose a *Stimmung* for our investigations that might open our view beyond beings to being, why not rather wonder, or even eros? Anxiety, after all, has no more claim to ontological probity, simply because of its vacuity in regard to particular objects, than do moods that encompass and yet somehow exceed their objects, to rise toward a fullness that might account both for the splendor of particular things and for the inexplicably still greater hunger that they animate. Anxiety's inward retreat reveals far less than the outward abandon of desire. Perhaps love's appetite, excited by beauty, sublimity, or simple "thereness," always presses on toward the wellspring, the supereminent plenitude in which unity, beauty, goodness, truth, knowledge, and desire belong to one another; and perhaps what comes "disclosingly" to pass in such a mood is the open splendor of being's self-donation in beings, an infinite act at once gathering or holding all things together in transcendent peace and prismating its infinite determinacy in an endless diversity of finite combinations of transcendental moments. This is not a fanciful suggestion: one's disposition to see more than one sees is determined by intentions (both of the simple eidetic variety and of the hermeneutically richer linguistic and cultural variety), and it is folly to imagine that the nothingness opened up in dread is less "metaphysical" or "onto-theological," or more obvious, than the no-thing-ness of being considered as transcendent fullness of determinacy. Moreover, the "ontologically erotic" gaze, which loves and desires being, is more attentive to the actual constituting truth of what is seen than is the anxious awareness of the nothingness that coyly flutters behind the seen; love sees the mystery of a thing's fortuity, its persistence within a unity that is "transfinite," its immediacy and alterity, its splendor within its own "essence," its intelligibility, and the way it in itself holds together the multiplicity of these transcendental aspects as a realized unity amid, and in still greater unity with, difference and change. Such a gaze sees that the being of things is to be sought in the abiding source in which anything participates; love's vision knows moments of enchantment, in which it achieves a recognition of the inescapable persistence of being's peaceful, sustaining light (infinitely different from both the violence of time and nature or the stillness of any ultimate ground) as a "gratuitous necessity" — which then compels thought to risk a conjecture toward the infinite. Such a gaze, that is, sees being as an infinite font of manifestation, showing itself in the existence and essences of things, kenotically allowing (without alienation from its own diffusive goodness) the arrival in itself of what is intrinsically nothing in itself: the pure ontic ecstasy of contingent beings; the gaze of love sees that it must pass beyond the ontic play of negativity and positivity, until ontic negation is inverted and revealed to be the effect of a prior plenitude. When Heidegger calls being "eschatological," he does so in a milkily Hegelian way, and so the word's meaning for him remains suspended between the historico-dialectical and the existential; but it can be made into a genuinely ontological claim: for finite beings every moment is eschaton, each instant is an arising of all that is from nothing (not from the concealed, nor from some ultimate ground, but from nothing at all) into the infinite, a birth into its absolute end; each moment is a call, a judgment, across the ontically impossible distance between nonexistence and existence, by which beings are "adjudged" with an ontological justice, and brought to their ultimate encounter with being — because for beings, in their becoming, being is absolute futurity. Finite being is an eros in its very essence, an ecstasy beyond itself, toward that infinity of beauty that declares itself both as transcendent mystery and as glorious immediacy.

ii. God beyond Being

It should be obvious enough, one would think, that Heidegger's project is inimical to the classical Christian idea of God as the source of being, or of being as originally his good gift, and is one whose occasional allure for theologians intent upon dissolving the intractable historicality of Christian thought into the reefless flood of ontology could scarcely be more dreadful in its consequences. At the very least, one should not hesitate to grant that, for those seduced by the old *Förster's* siren warbling, a theological aesthetics is an impossibility: the thought of being for such persons becomes the thought that forbids the God of Scripture his form and splendor, his appearing beauty, his freedom to be what he will be; the divine can figure only either as a continuous negation, withdrawal, absence, or nothingness (insofar as the divine is an ontological category) or as a poetical site within the ontical deployment of the *Geviert* (insofar as the divine is a region of being or an ontic symbol). Nevertheless, many are the modern theologians for whom the Christian "aesthetics of the infinite" has been rendered inconceivable or meaningless because — having mistaken Heidegger's account of metaphysics for something far more penetrating and profound than it is — they believe they must altogether divorce the thought of God from that of being (than which, in this view of things, nothing could be more indigent and empty). If, moreover, one is persuaded by Heidegger's diagnosis of onto-theology, and yet one still does not wish to think of God in mythological fashion, as a being among beings, then one must choose between the only two ways available for discriminating being from God: the nihilist and the dualist (which, ultimately, prove to share much in common). One could, perhaps, adduce no better specimen of the former way of proceeding than a brief article by Robert Scharlemann called "The Being of God When God Is Not Being God."[92] As a historical essay on Western metaphysical or religious thought, one should immediately note, its judgments are deeply confused: it is presumed, throughout the text, that something blandly called "theism," whose nature and history can be described in the most general and uniform terms, and whose end it is now possible to recognize in the wake of the Enlightenment, can be meaningfully ascribed to every century of Christian thought prior to late modernity. Scharlemann's deconstruction of this "theism," as far as it goes, is entirely correct, but his notion that it is possible to think God not as a being among beings, at least correctly, only after the Enlightenment is a little silly. It is not even seriously arguable that what Scharlemann calls theism was ever a *theological* current prior to the deism of Enlightenment religion or the moral God of Kant. To think of God as a supreme being among lesser beings in the fashion Scharlemann has in mind requires a profoundly modern concept of what beings are: objective, unitary instantiations, not "participating" in being but standing forth as punctiliar substances, devoid of analogical tension within themselves, and as discrete "entities" embraced within the empty and abstract category of being or — more properly — existence. "Theism," as Scharlemann describes it, is imaginable only within the context of a "univocal" account of being (but theology did not begin after Suárez); the tradition of Christian metaphysics has for the most part rarely made room for a "general" concept of being (not even, *pace* the "radically orthodox," in the thought of Scotus), or for a "theism" that unreflectively comprises God and the creatures together within the broader category of being. To put it very indelicately, Scharlemann's treatment of traditional Christian metaphysics is surprisingly inept.

92. Robert Scharlemann, "The Being of God When God Is Not Being God: Deconstructing the History of Theism," in *Deconstruction and Theology*, ed. Thomas J. J. Altizer et al. (New York: Crossroad, 1982), 79-108.

Putting all this aside, though, it is Scharlemann's own constructive argument that interests me: he starts from the thought that "the world is the being of God when God is not being deity, or the being of God in the time of not being." At the end of theism's picture of the world, it is possible, he avers, to reconsider the division between created and uncreated, to take creation into the doctrine of the Trinity: which doctrine can be understood as describing a God who incorporates otherness from himself in his own being, but also as allowing time into the being of God, by distinguishing when God is not being God.[93] Throughout its history, claims Scharlemann, theology has thought of God as being itself, as supreme being, or as uncreated being, but what has been left unthought is being as such (90-91). Just as one "can confuse being with a supreme genus or the highest being[,] one can confuse deity with a supreme 'I,' or an unconditional subject"; but the "symbol" of God's otherness is the "I am" of Jesus in his worldly end (91): God is, to put it simply, the otherness that is invoked and indicated in each "I," and creation is the being of God as not God. Scharlemann rejects the *analogia entis* and language of the creature's participation in God (the entity's participation in being), for failing to think the difference between God and being; God is not being, he asserts, because participation in being is not participation in God: nongodly being is outside of God (94-95). (The argument's logic here becomes a little decrepit, and clearly begs the very question it proposes to address — what, pray tell, is "nongodly" being?) At one juncture Scharlemann invokes Anselm's "definition" of God as that than which a greater cannot be thought, which he takes implicitly to exclude "the theistic picture of God, self, and world," as this (he claims) portrays being as comprehending both God and that which is not God, such that the whole of being appears as quantitatively greater than God; so, taken to its ineluctable end, Anselm's definition must come to embrace the negations of atheism (96-97). He then suggests that the word "God" in a sense refers to language and that God is what language means: "God" means sign-of or pointer-to, in the sense of "not-I" or "not-this"; "God means the negative that can be instantiated upon any object and any subject by the saying of the word" (101-2). And as "God" refers to that otherness manifested upon every object or subject, the word "God" is the reality of God (102). "God is around only as the absence to which the divine name testifies," as the God who has gone for the "good reason" called freedom; in each "I am" the God who has gone is presented; God is the annunciation of an otherness now rendered visible after the Enlightenment (102-3). When God is thought, he concludes, as the supreme being, being as such goes unthought; all that is considered is an infinite or uncreated or divine being in

---

93. Scharlemann, 90. The parenthetical numbers in the following text refer to Scharlemann's essay.

contrast to the finite, an infinite therefore delimited by the finite, shown to be finite itself, and exceeded by being as a whole; but if being as such is thought, the God of theism is shown to be no God at all (106-7).

Scharlemann's argument is every bit as unrefined and convoluted as my summary suggests, but it is nonetheless fascinating, in that it demonstrates with remarkable clarity that Heidegger's approach to ontology is impotent to understand theology, in that it is, in itself, nothing but the final expression of a modern philosophical forgetfulness of theology's vision of being. Scharlemann's final fillip regarding the finite and the infinite makes this painfully obvious: the sort of opposition of finite and infinite being he describes is a danger only for a truly univocal ontology, or for the sort of dialectical theology such an ontology permits. In truth, it is only the ontology of infinite being that can elude the dialectic that Scharlemann so deplores (a dialectic which might be called "hyperousiological," but whose flawed logic Scharlemann's own "anousiological" dialectic merely repeats, while reducing God yet further to — let us be frank — absolutely nothing at all). The tradition that speaks of God as infinite being and creatures as finite beings that exist through participation is one that has thought through the genuinely qualitative difference between being and beings, and between the infinite and the finite, far more thoroughly than Scharlemann, who merely presumes a univocal ontology and blithely projects it back over a tradition to which it is alien and which it is not able to illuminate. Take for instance Scharlemann's treatment of what he imagines to be theology's *analogia entis* between God and creatures: on his account the *analogia* consists in a discrimination between creatures and God as two kinds of existents, who subsist in the shared abstract quality "being," of which creatures are finite instances and God is the sole "infinite" instance. Scharlemann, for what it is worth, correctly points out that such an analogy leaves being in a state of vacuous and ungraspable imprecision, and can serve only to obscure the way God is near to creatures (94); but this aperçu, for all that it is an obvious truism, has all but no relevance to theological tradition. The problem is that the *analogia entis* has simply, in Scharlemann's account, become indistinguishable from a sort of "univocal analogy" (which can only be an analogy of attribution, between a quality in finite and infinite form, rather than an analogy of being), such as one might derive from the teachings of Locke or Wolff. But the *analogia entis* (in its developed form) does not concern a *grasp* of being at all; rather it introduces an analogical interval into being itself, because it has already grasped that the God Who Is is nonetheless no being among beings. Because the ontological difference has been thought (which in Christian thought begins, correctly, from the thought of creaturely contingency, the whylessness of the creature's being), the thought that finite being might have been different from what it is (and so is different from the original actuality that grants it) is conceivable. Thus theology can imagine an analogy between an *esse* that is participated in by what subsists, without diminution or constriction, and a transcendent act of being that is also subsistence: the life of God. Being itself is different in God, because God is not a being, yet is; he does not belong to being, but is being, and yet subsists. If from a Heideggerian vantage this idea of an *actus essendi subsistens* is merely "onto-theologic," a conception of God as an entity, this is only because the thought of subsistence will always appear to be the thought of an "entity" when one has not allowed for the analogical interval that is introduced into subsistence as such by the *analogia*. Thus, inevitably, being is only a metaphysical abstraction for Scharlemann, a formless and empty purity — and this raises a question.

Certainly one of the more absurd moments in Scharlemann's argument is his suggestion that "theism" fails the test of Anselm's *id quo maius cogitari nequit*, because theism makes being "quantitatively" greater than God. Again, this is true enough if the "theist" operates (consciously or not) within a univocal understanding of being; but it is simply an empty accusation when directed at a tradition that sees being as itself riven by an irreducible analogy. What warrant is there, that is to say, for attempting to rescue God from the lowly station of a mere being, quantitatively inferior to being as such, by setting the divine over against both the ontic determinacy of beings and the ontological indeterminacy of "being as such," unless a metaphysical decision has been reached in advance that being is abstract and univocal? For Heidegger, obviously, no less than for Hegel, all determinacy must be regarded as a posterior concretion, a negation (or "nihilation"), for otherwise being has been objectified as an entity. Yet what if being — as first and foremost the life of the God who is Trinity and, as such, always a gift that is shared, determined toward another — is not the most pure, the most abstract, the most empty, but the most concrete, the most determinate, the most beautiful? Or if what is imparted analogically to creatures is a being always already determined toward otherness, always already form and light and beauty? What if, in the very calculus of infinite determinacy, being is set off qualitatively from beings not as empty indetermination, but as ontological plenitude, supereminently exceeding beings? This is an aesthetic and an ontological question at once, and — still more importantly — a theological question: Does the thought that God is not a being among beings necessarily forbid the thought of a dynamic, acting, self-revealing God, as evidently Scharlemann believes it must? Is such a thought merely unreflective "theism," an idolatrous diminution of God? Is the venerable tradition of speaking of God as the one in whom essence and being are one a forgetting of being as such, or is the question of being as such a forgetting of God? To repair again to that very unfashionable estaminet, "necessary being," if being is not plenitude — the original fullness of a determinately infinite act —

then there can be no finite beings, neither actually nor possibly (for nothing, to be precise, *is* possible). Scharlemann himself invokes the Hegelian distinction between the bad infinite and the infinite of reconciliation, between an infinite defined in opposition to the finite and an infinite that is really the negation of the oppositions of finitude (the negation of negation), while still distinguishing between this infinite and God (95-96). Yet this latter distinction (like Heidegger's distinction between φύσις and the *Ereignis*) merely redoubles an economy by sealing it from within; and so Scharlemann's "God" is a banality: the bare negation that sets free, invoked upon every object or subject, the absence displayed as the "otherwise" of every "I am." Just as for Hegel pure being is convertible with nothingness and becomes determinate *(Dasein)* in actively negating nothingness, so for Scharlemann the freedom of creaturely being consists in that unmasterable negation that the word "God" indicates, the otherness of God in the time of not being; God is a negation in perpetual advent, the not-God of creaturely being's autonomy and difference, the God whose absence is the grace of existence.

If though one is not moved to embrace the notion that finite being *is* only through a prior negation, an opposition that defines it, and if one has not set out from an understanding of being as abstract and empty prior to negation, such language as Scharlemann adopts in regard to God looks like a sicklier version of dialectical idealism. Indeed, talk of "negation" (rather than simply "limitation" or "finitude") has a formidable power of mystification in it. There is, though, a purely positive account of finite being, as the analogical expression of a positive and determinate infinite act of being. The terminations, transitions, and intervals that define finite being are not determining negations, but are the effects of a coinherent "musical" expression in which each moment is not "opposed" or "negated" by what differs from it, or by being as such, or by God, but is "extended," "deepened" in the scope of its participation in the infinite. Nor is the ontological difference a kind of negation — in fact, if one thinks about it, the notion that it could be depends on a desperate confusion of the ontic and the ontological; rather, it is the expressive play of being, whose infinity *is* expression. This is not to deny that there is a kind of "relative negativity" in the oscillation within finite being between existence and nonexistence, and between "this" and "not this"; but in this oscillation nothing is actually negated: for beings are ex nihilo and so even their limits are positively emergent over against, literally, nothing at all; and being as such, in God, is infinite eminence, concretely transcending and embracing the existent and nonexistent both in its infinite act, and is negated by neither. As God pours forth the abundance of his being, kenotically, in beings — in finite instances of his determinacy, in finite intensities of those "transcendentals" that are convertible with his essence — he remains the purely positive act of what, in finite experience, has the form of a synthesis between positivity and negativity: both these poles participate in and analogically manifest the transcendent coincidence in God of his perfect trinitarian "I am" and the "not-any-being" of his infinite essence. Here theology can turn a benign gaze on Deleuze's concern for the positivity of being and its expression, even as it rejects his ontologically barren discourse of "immanence." God is, as Nicholas of Cusa says, the most concrete and determinate, the *coincidentia oppositorum* (which should not be taken dialectically): he embraces all ontological "opposites" not as oppositions or negations, but as series that, extended into his peace, belong together and unfold into the same music. Such a thought is surely free of every confining fideism regarding substances, and truly introduces the dynamism of successiveness — seriality or repetition — into the philosophy of being; it is a thought that conceives "determination" not as the issue of the negative, but as first and foremost difference, in the concreteness of its differing (after all, negation's logic is one of identity).

This, in the end, is the most vexing aspect of so many theological negotiations with the critique of metaphysics: they do not take into proper account the language of being that opens up in the doctrine of the Trinity, and advert to the doctrine (if at all) only in its Hegelian form, as a doctrine regarding the being of the world. By preserving the absolute idealist distinction between quantitative and qualitative infinity (rather than seeing both as participating in the same transcendent act) and the notion of the probation of the negative (even in its Heideggerian and supposedly nondialectical form), Scharlemann still remains too much a dialectical metaphysician; this leads him to treat God's transcendence as a dialectical counter to the world, and according to a dialectic of absence at that. Here, though, Gregory of Nyssa grasped the genuinely Christian difference long ago: he overcame this division of infinities, which is a division implicit in Platonism, and in every pure idealism from Plato's to Hegel's. More to the point, Gregory was able to think of finite difference as genuine *difference*. Whereas Scharlemann conceives of the freedom of finite being in terms of God-as-negation, so that there must always be within the finite a tension that is also inevitably the negation of its own particularity (in a "univocal" ontology, beings "say being" always in the same way, and so in the privative mood), Gregory's thought allows for an infinite in which the particularity of difference occurs as the free and open expression of the God who is, and so in which every being, uniquely, "says more" of God's infinite Word. This is the primordial analogy. The God who is infinite and no being among beings is also the personal God of election and incarnation, the dynamic, living, and creative God he is, precisely because being is not a genus whereunder God as "a being" might be subsumed, but is the act through which beings are given form by the God who is never without form and beauty. The acts of God are not "symbols" of the "history" of God's advent as absence, but actions of the God who comprehends being, who abides in the interval while embracing all that falls on either side. God is always "being God," transcendent and yet present as the one who is and shows himself, indifferent to metaphysical demarcations between transcendence and immanence, infinity and finitude, being and beings: precisely because God transcends and makes possible these categories, in their being, he inhabits them simultaneously without contradiction. It is Scharlemann — as is inevitable when a univocal ontology forces one into a dialectical thicket — who has made of God a "thing" that must be "not-deity" in order to be also "the being of deity," a dialectical syncope of the negative in every moment of the rhythm of difference. He takes exception to a scheme that confines God within the univocity of being, but confirms being *as univocity* by simply extracting God from being altogether and then, paradoxically, objectifying him as determinative negation.

For a trinitarian theology, in command of its proper analogical ontology, God is not touched or limited by the ontological difference, not because he is simply beyond being altogether or because he comprises being and nonbeing (or God and not-God), but because, inasmuch as he is the *actus* of all beings, the "fold" of the ontological difference is unfolded in him from the first: and so he exceeds this difference in creation, makes it his mystery or the occasion of the showing of his mystery. God's "ever greater" lies not in his "negative transcendence" but in being the trinitarian context of being and the truth of being as always determined, always differing, such that nonbeing is truly for him — as it cannot entirely be for the creature — nothing at all. Thus, utterly contrary to Scharlemann's eccentric usage, Anselm's definition of God should be read in terms of Gregory's understanding of the infinite. The God who is shows his glory not as the nimbus of otherness that dwells like a phantom glamor about all finite things, the absence that indeterminately determines them, but as quantity, *kabod*. All that is, finitely apprehended (which is to say aesthetically, as a continuous series of objects appearing in distance, to be ordered according to a style of desire that corresponds to God's infinite love), fills the distance as light, approach, proximity, and peace, because God gives his beauty an expression and a weight that can be traversed. God exceeds beings as the ever greater, the more beautiful, radiant, and full of form, and so the ontological difference cannot limit what is said of him: for it is merely the contingency of that quantity, its freedom as expression, bounty, and gift (which is what being always already is). The Trinity exceeds being, not like a Neoplatonic monad dwelling beyond being, but by comprising being in the essential act of triune love. In that living unity, difference is without need of departure from the One to the many, without need of blossoming from the indeterminate into its negation in form, but subsists within the interval opened by God's infinite "self-determination" in the other. As Gregory Palamas says: "When he spoke to Moses, God said not

'I am Essence,' but rather 'I am that I am.' Consequently, He Who Is is not produced by essence, but essence comes about from He Who Is; for He Who Is embraces all of being in himself" (*Triads in Defense of the Holy Hesychasts* 3.2.12).
Augustine is surely right when he speaks of the supreme form and loveliness of
the triune God, and of God as the *forma infabricata* who imparts to everything
its *species,* its countenance and beauty. And Nicholas of Cusa is also surely right
to speak of the Trinity as the unity and essence of beauty on the grounds that
the beauty of the Trinity is not only beheld and desired, but also beholds and
desires (*Excitationes* 6): for neither unity nor the infinite is ever without form.
God embraces all of finitude without negation, alienation, fall, or constriction;
as Gregory understood, one does not turn from finite being when one turns toward God's infinity: the whole fabric of being is woven in infinite light, its entire terrain belongs to the infinite distance in which God exceeds and is present
to creation. All of being is the place of return, the way of the creature's progress
from glory to glory, through the folding and unfolding of an infinite that is always quantitative, even in its qualitative distance. God's infinite is weighty, and
within it God is approached through the pilgrimage of quantity, the ecstasy of
epektasis. There is only one "mechanism" of determination: the eternal priority
of form — of image, of very likeness — and infinity as an infinite texture of
harmonious supplementation; it is this boundlessness of the "bad" infinite that
God called good in the beginning.[94]

A more promising "post-Heideggerian" theology than Scharlemann's,
perhaps, is that of Jean-Luc Marion. The book by which English readers generally best know him, *God without Being,* is concerned in large part with
Heidegger's ontology, which for Marion is simply a discourse of totality, one
that excludes the Christian God precisely because it subordinates the thought
of God to the thought of being. His way of resolving the matter, however, is
largely to concede Heidegger's account of the ontological difference, and then
to elevate "Love" over "being" as the proper name of God;[95] he even (though he
has in recent years retracted this part of his argument) takes Aquinas to task for
privileging *esse* among the divine names, and reads Aquinas much as Levinas
reads Heidegger. Marion places his own emphasis on the distance between God
and creation, the distance of the gift, God's liberty over the ontological difference and his ability to cross all of being as the God who is God with or without
being: "Only love does not have to be. And [God] loves without being" (138).
The problem with Marion's approach is that, while it begins quite appropriately

---

94. See Gregory, *In Christi resurrectionem* 3.
95. Jean-Luc Marion, *God without Being: Hors-Texte,* trans. Thomas A. Carlson (Chicago:
University of Chicago Press, 1995), 61-138. Parenthetical page numbers in the following text are
to this work.

from the thought of God's distance from creation as the distance of a gift, it makes that distance objective, too much like the distance between two "things": this has the twofold effect of converting that distance into something like the interval of an absence — a *chorismos* — on the one hand, while depriving creation of its proper share in divine goodness, its real and indefectible beauty — its power to declare God's glory — on the other. The latter issue comes to the fore in Marion's altogether remarkable treatment of vanity (108-38): he writes quite profoundly of the ennui that afflicts one who gazes upon the world without seeing it as the gift of God's love, and of the emptiness that one thus finds in all things; beauty is present only where there has been love, but only vanity where the light of love has not fallen. As John Milbank remarks, however, in the course of a generally perceptive critique of Marion's thought, "the vanity of the world outside the light of divine grace is not a thesis concerning an ultimate indifference to the world's content. . . . for the world seen in the light of divine grace is the world seen as that light."[96] Marion fails to make John of Damascus's distinction: that God is infinitely distant from all things οὐ τόπῳ ἀλλὰ φύσει (*De fide orthodoxa* 1.13). As a result, Marion nearly falls prey to that paradox whereby the most radical kind of transcendence becomes in fact a radical kind of immanence: by seeming to place God at an objective distance, Marion seems almost to place God within the scope of finite differential distance; God is somewhere else. This ultimately has the consequence of reducing God to a being after all, set over against the totality of beings, for he and the world must be embraced then within a neutral distance, an abstract "being"; God's being (or beyond-being-ness) must be construed as peculiar to him in a way that makes it simply other than creation's being, and so (as Scharlemann might remark) finite. Transcendence is thus portrayed as absence from created being, over an interval indifferent to God and alien to the divine, which God must cross in order to love. This brings us back toward a negative dialectic in which the affirmation of being's *diaphora* is possible only by simultaneously showing them to be *adiaphora.* If God's "beyond" becomes the punctiliar and abstract otherness, like that of the One, rather than the perichoretic "context" of difference, the most fundamentally biblical affirmation of Christian thought is ignored: that it is the differences of creation that are very good and that, *as differences,* declare God. Whereas Marion is correct to turn from the consideration of being (as a univocal category) to the distance that gives being (the distance of the gift), he fails to think that distance as God's transcendent act of being, which is always one of self-outpouring love: for God's is the only distance wherein the play of being and beings can unfold. Being is always already light, form, beauty — be-

---

96. John Milbank, "Can a Gift Be Given? Prolegomena to a Future Trinitarian Metaphysic," *Modern Theology* 11, no. 1 (1995): 134.

cause God, who is beautiful, is the source of all being, God *is* as Trinity. Marion at times seems prone to an almost Marcionite tendency to alienate God from creation on the one hand, and toward a Levinasian tendency to make the discourse of the divine an acosmic, anaesthetic discourse on the other; happily, the means for avoiding either tendency are provided already by Marion's understanding of the icon (7-24).

Even here, though, there are problems. Marion's intention is to elevate the "iconic" gaze of God, which enters being from beyond the totality, over the "idolatrous" aspiration of the finite gaze, which marks the (sacred) limit of the totality from within itself. Taken to an extreme (as it sometimes seems it is in Marion's thought), such a distinction draws a demarcation between revelation and natural thought, desire, or reverence that brings one rather too near to the incoherent catastrophism of dialectical theology. To the degree that Marion reduces the iconic liberty of the divine to a gaze that seems to emanate from an invisible sublimity merely outside the fold of ontological difference, he lapses into dualism. Insofar, however, as God's gaze, for Marion, belongs indeed to an icon, his thought shows the way past this peril. The point Marion goes to some lengths to make is that whereas the idol is the product of an objective gaze (a defatigation of vision, where the gaze comes to rest upon the "first visible," having ceased to transpierce all things), and whereas the idol thus confines the divine to the measure of the human gaze, to a visibility that is also secretly the brilliant, mirrored reflection of the human countenance (9-15), the icon provokes vision, summons it to the place where the visible is penetrated by the invisible. The icon shows an infinite gaze: not one simply set at a distance but one which draws vision into itself, which gives distance; and shows that along with the original *ousia* there is already the hypostasis (an eminently trinitarian thought) whose gaze infinitely deepens the visible, transforming the creature, saturating the creature with glory. It is the hypostasis, by holding us in an infinite gaze, that permits us to pass beyond the mirror of our idolatry into its eyes, because it shows us a face — which is also to say that every face is an icon (17-22). The reason I would want to endorse this line of discourse (despite its occasional deficiencies, a tendency to subordinate the aesthetic particularity of the icon to the invisibility of its gaze, or to make it sound as if the icon contravenes being itself, rather than our idolatrous ontologies) is that it beautifully expresses the genuinely Christian understanding of how the finite and the infinite are related. The icon is an instance of an infinite regard that is also openly seen — that acts and reveals itself — within the finite; the icon is an aesthetic instance that is also still — and in a sense, for that very reason — infinite; its glory saturates the visible without ceasing to be the gaze that both comprehends us at a distance and draws us into itself as distance. One must simply emphasize, somewhat over against Marion's own rhetoric, that the distance given by the gaze is none other than the distance of created things, the distance in which the icon is *seen:* that the divine distance embraces the distance of creation from God, making creation itself the radiance of divine glory. All of this is conceivable, for theology, because of the priority (which the icon declares) of hypostasis, this coincidence of the aesthetic and the infinite — this liberty of God to be in his infinite distance as the God he is, this eternal beauty *of* distance, and this transcendence of the aesthetic over the thought of "being as such" — that is the uniquely Christian story of the infinite, the uniquely trinitarian thought of beauty.

In the end, where Marion is right regarding our vision of being (insofar as he starts from a phenomenologist's vantage) is in saying that love is necessary first, before beauty can be seen, for love is that essential "mood" that intends the world as beauty and can so receive it (this much we must admit: anyone suffering a profound grief, in which love's joy has been transformed into sorrow, knows how utterly oppressive and imprisoning seems the brute immensity of the world, its unforgiving impersonality, its callous grandeur and vapidity, its hideous persistence . . .). Where Marion errs obviously is in surrendering being to Heideggerian poverty, stripping it of its infinitely actual splendor and power and grace, by failing to see that love is in fact ontological, and reveals beauty as the world's truth: love is the original act that makes beings to be, and so the being of beings *is* beauty, is light. When fallen vision — the victim of despair, anger, envy, anxiety, rapacity, avarice — ascends from these inessential moods to the perspicacity of charity's *oculus simplex,* it *sees* being. To the degree that Marion's language of the icon points to this truth, it carries his thought toward a truly trinitarian ontology, and toward an understanding of the relation between being and the good immeasurably to be preferred to the Levinasian language of the "face": to see the other as an icon, that is, far from imprisoning the other in one's prior thematism, is to discover in the other's sheer, "superficial" splendor an irreplaceable gathering or intensity of the infinite, intrinsically lovable, a unique gift of being's infinitely desirable beauty. Still, Marion's approach, at least in *God without Being,* is instructive; set alongside Scharlemann's sterile project, it makes us see that anousiological and hyperousiological discourse share certain of the same defects: both subordinate the divine and the worldly to a kind of dialectic, setting God over against finite being. In either case, world and God are reduced to one or the other end of a polarity — world ever more wholly the Same and God ever more wholly Other — embraced within the still greater reality of the "whole"; in either case, that is, thought has been confined within a metaphysics of the totality, the world has been left bereft of its self-transcending eros, its transcendental ecstasies, and God has been denied the glory of his infinitely rich, living, and beautiful being. To put it simply, neither anousiology nor hyperousiology takes us beyond metaphysical grounding or (if one wishes to employ the term) onto-theology; we must, if the escape from metaphysics in this malign sense is truly our aim, resort to the language (contrary to all postmodern wisdom) of ontological analogy.

iii. *Analogia Entis*

I use the term "analogy of being" as shorthand for the tradition of Christian metaphysics that, developing from the time of the New Testament through the patristic and medieval periods, succeeded in uniting a metaphysics of participation to the biblical doctrine of creation, within the framework of trinitarian dogma, and in so doing made it possible for the first time in Western thought to contemplate both the utter difference of being from beings and the nature of true transcendence. Most of the details of such an ontology have already, in much of the preceding, been described, and so I shall add only a few elaborations (and it has all been said incomparably better by that most biblical of theologians, Dionysius, in *The Divine Names*); and I should note that, in choosing the term *analogia entis,* I am using it in the very particular sense it was given in the last century by the remarkable Erich Przywara.[97] It is, one must acknowledge, a controversial turn of phrase among some Christian thinkers: Karl Barth's notorious, fairly barbarous rejection of the *analogia entis* as the invention of antichrist, and the principle reason for not becoming Roman Catholic,[98] was directed at Przywara's book — a verdict that, frankly, speaks only of Barth's failure to understand Przywara. Whether one takes Barth's pronouncement, as Jüngel and others have done, as a reaction against the remoteness from God that so empty a concept as "being" actually suggests[99] or, rather more correctly in all likelihood, as a rejection of what Barth took to be a form of natural theology, it is ultimately nothing but an example of inane (and cruel) invective. Nor does Barth's later acceptance of the "principle" of analogy, in the etiolated but more "dramatic" form of an *analogia relationis,* improve the picture, as this more "existential" proportion between God's act and our response, without the correct ontological grammar to support it, has the very effect he so dreaded: it reduces God to the status of a mere being, in some sense on a level with us. To state the matter simply, the analogy of being does not analogize God and crea-

---

97. See Erich Przywara, *Analogia Entis: Metaphysik* (Einsiedeln: Johannes-Verlag, 1962).

98. Karl Barth, *Church Dogmatics* I/1, *The Doctrine of the Word of God,* trans. G. W. Bromiley (Edinburgh: T. & T. Clark, 1975), xiii.

99. See Eberhard Jüngel, *God as the Mystery of the World,* trans. Darrell L. Guder (Edinburgh: T. & T. Clark, 1983), 282. For Jüngel's own treatment of analogy and his own preference for analogy based on the advent of God's Word, see 261-98.

tures under the more general category of being, but is the analogization of being in the difference between God and creatures; it is as subversive of the notion
of a general and univocal category of being as of the equally "totalizing" notion
of ontological equivocity, and thus belongs to neither pole of the dialectic intrinsic to metaphysical totality: the savage equivalence of univocity and
equivocity, Apollo and Dionysus, pure identity and pure difference (neither of
which can open a vantage upon being in its transcendence). For precisely this
reason, the *analogia entis* is quite incompatible with any naive "natural theology": if being is univocal, then a direct analogy from essences to "God" (as the
supreme substance) is conceivable, but if the primary analogy is one of being,
then an infinite analogical interval has been introduced between God and creatures, even as it is affirmed that God is truly declared in creation (for God is,
again, infinitely determinate and is himself the distance — the act of distance
— of the analogical interval). Thus the *analogia entis* renders any simple
"essentialist" analogy impossible. Conversely, though, the rejection of the analogy, far from preserving God's transcendence, actually serves only to objectify
God idolatrously as a sublime absence or contradiction: one is left with a duality that inevitably makes of God and creation a dialectical opposition, thus subordinating God to being after all (but this argument we have already re-
hearsed). Moreover, apart from the *analogia entis,* the very concept of
revelation is a contradiction: only insofar as creaturely being is analogous to divine being, and proper to God's nature, can God show himself as God, rather
than in alienation from himself; there would be no revelation otherwise, only
legislation, emanating from an ontic god separated from us by an impossible
distance, or perhaps the ghostly call of the gnostic's stranger god. Certainly
creatures cannot ascend by way of discrete "essences" to a grasp of God, but
creatures still belong to God's infinity; to deny this is to be left in the intellectually sterile condition of the religious dualist, who can affirm God's glory only
through the negation of worldly beauty. Rejection of the analogy of being,
properly understood, is a denial that creation is an act of grace that really expresses God's love, rather than a moment of alienation or dialectical negation;
it is a rejection, that is, of Acts 17:28, and ultimately of Genesis 1:1 (and everything that follows from it). If rejection of the *analogia entis* were in some sense
the very core of Protestant theology, as Barth believed, one would still be
obliged to observe that it is also the invention of antichrist, and so would have
to be accounted the most compelling reason for not becoming a Protestant.

But, really, how should one understand the analogy? One should begin
from the recognition that God is the being of all things, beyond all finite determination, negation, and dialectic not as the infinite "naught" against which all
things are set off (for this is still dialectical and so finite), but as the infinite
plenitude of the transcendent act in which all determinacy participates. Again,

this is to say that both existence and nonexistence in the realm of the ontic — both "position" and negation — equally require this act in order to be. Nor is it enough to see this transcendent movement of being, yielding being to both the "is" and the "is not," as a primordial convertibility of being and nothingness in need of the tragic solution of the finite — Hegel's "becoming," Heidegger's "temporalization," Derrida's *différance* — as this very convertibility would already be an ontic opposition within the absolute, a finite, intrinsic indetermination subordinate to its own limits and still requiring an ontological explanation of the prior act of simplicity in which its unresolved, essential contradiction must participate in order to constitute a unity (in order, that is, to be). Being, simply said, cannot be reduced to beings or negated by them; it plays peacefully in the expressive iridescence of its welcoming light, in the intricate weaving of the transcendentals, even in the transcendental moments of "this" and "not this," which speak of God's simple, triune infinity: his coincidence within himself of determinacy ("I am that I am," "Thou art my beloved Son") and "no-thing-ness" ("Wherefore he is all," "In him we live, and move, and have our being"). And the analogy, most importantly, should be seen as an affirmation of God as Trinity: as the source of all being, and yet the living God of creation, redemption, and deathless love; it is the metaphysical expression of the realization that the very difference of creatures from God — their integrity as the beings they are, their ontological "freedom" — is a manifestation of how God is one God. The analogy of being begins from the belief that being always already differs, within the very act of its simplicity, without any moment of alienation or diremption; to be is to be manifest; to know and love, to be known and loved — all of this is the one act, wherein there is no "essence" unexpressed, no contradiction awaiting resolution. Thus the analogy always stands beyond the twin poles of the metaphysics of the necessary: negation and identity; it reveals that purely dialectical and purely "identist" systems are ultimately the same, imprisoning God and world within an economy of the absolute, sharing a reciprocal identity. If God is thought either as total substance or total absence, foundation or negation, "ground of Being" or static "Wholly Other," God appears merely as the world's highest principle rather than its transcendent source and end (this is why I say the only way of speaking of God beyond the categories of "metaphysics," in the malign sense, must be analogy).

This is the ultimate speculative context in which I want to advance the claim for Gregory of Nyssa's treatment of the infinity of God and of creaturely *epektasis:* the analogy of being — the actual movement of analogization, of our likeness to God within an always greater unlikeness — is the event of our existence as endless becoming; and this means that becoming is to be thought, for Christians, without resort to the tragic wisdom of any metaphysical epoch ("Platonism's" melancholy distaste for time, change, and distance, despite their necessity, or Hegel's dialectic, or Heidegger's resolve, or any other style of thought that can think becoming only "backwards" from death). Both our being and our essence always exceed the moment of our existence, lying before us as gratuity and futurity, mediated to us only in the splendid eros and terror of our *in fieri*, because finite existence — far from being the dialectical labor of an original contradiction — is a pure gift, grounded in no original substance, wavering from nothingness into the openness of God's self-outpouring infinity, persisting in a condition of absolute fragility and fortuity, impossible in itself, and so actual beyond itself. Becoming is an ecstasy, and nothing besides; it is indeed a constant tension — between what a thing is and what it is not, between its past and its future, between interior and exterior, and so on — but it is not originally a violent departure from the stability of an original essence. Our being is simply the rapture of arrival, and while its contours are always necessarily defined by the shadows of the "no longer" and the "not yet," it is only secondarily, because of sin, that these become for us sources of a tragic anxiety (mourning for the lost, lust for the unattained) rather than faith, hope, and love ("remembrance" of our true end, eros for God's infinity, the love of all things in God). Creation is always, in every moment, liberation, a freedom in which the possibilities of loving all things in the love of God or of turning to things from God both present themselves, and in which, consequently, we are judged. The event of our being is already emancipation from metaphysical necessity, the ontic ecstasy of the ex nihilo, prayer, worship, awakening, a displacement of nothingness by openness, a reflex of light; and our response to this original, ontological vocation can be only, in any moment, acceptance or rejection (which means we experience God's gift as either election or dereliction). However, even though becoming is thus a kind of "crisis," especially for sinful creatures, it is most originally peace, birth, and life. Gregory's language of *epektasis* perfectly describes an ontology that has broken with every myth of metaphysical pedigree: creaturely becoming, in its original and ultimate truth, departs from no ground but simply hastens to an end, and so need neither suffer the gravity of memory, the anamnesis of the immemorial principle, nor be driven on by tragic anxiety; the exterior is not exile, but emergence into God's manifestation (his Logos). As Maximus the Confessor says, our end is our beginning, our logoi are found in God's Logos, we come to be in God, by participation *(Ambiguum VII)*.[100] That which is most interior to us, "essence," is the most exterior: we become what we are by finitely traversing the infinitely accomplished "exteriority" of the Trinity, appropriating what is "ours" only through an original surrender of every ground. Nature and essence exceed our grasp, and our hunger for the Good above us is our feeding upon being, our ontological "de-

100. See esp. *PG*, 91:1077C-1080C.

light" (rather than the morbid self-embrace of our own substance or foundation). This primordial ecstasy never needs to fold back upon itself in a dialectical recovery of "self" from "other" or "anamnesis" from the phenomena; our perpetual oscillation, within the event of our being, between actuality and possibility, our striving toward our "essence," is our participation in God's own convertibility with his own act of love and knowledge. God is the infinity of being in which every essence comes to be, the abyss of subsistent beauty into which every existence is outstretched.

Or, to phrase the matter differently, the analogy of being is an emancipation from the tragedy of identity, which is the inmost truth of every metaphysics or theology (whether dialectical and dualist or idealist and monist) that fails to think being analogically. Because the analogy subsists not between discrete substances sheltered alike under the canopy of being — between "my" essence, to which existence is somehow superadded, and God's essence, which possesses existence simply as a necessary attribute — but between the entire act of my being and the transcendent act of being in which it participates, the event of my existence, in its totality, is revealed as good and true and beautiful in its very particularity. Being, considered either as the truth of essence (the transcendental determinations that are imparted and mediated to us throughout time in the event of our existence, as continuously we become what we are) or of existence (the gratuitous event of our participation in being as what we are is called, every moment, into unmerited being), is one perfect act of self-manifesting love in God, while in us it is a dynamic synthesis of the incommensurable "what" and "that" of our being. Thus our likeness to God, which is all that makes us to be (to share in the Logos's eternal standing forth, in the light of the Spirit, as the likeness of the Father's being), is, in the difference between finite and infinite, always embraced in a greater unlikeness — and this is the difference that lets us be. When the difference between being and beings remains unthought or forgotten, and so the analogy between being and beings, this interval is collapsed: the most eminent truth of our being is inverted to the ground of the I, and from this springs all the grandeur, melancholy, and cruel impotence of metaphysics in its "nihilistic vocation." When metaphysics is premised upon an analogy of identity, or on a continuity of identity between what one is and the eternal "I am," "I know," "I see," or "I will," it does not matter if one's grammar is monist or dualist; all reality subsists in the interval between two vanishing points: the supreme principle or substance and the bare, featureless, unchanging essence of "my" most proper "self." This is even true of the noblest achievement of Western metaphysics, Neoplatonism, when left unredeemed by theology: for if the truth of things is their pristine likeness in substance (in positive ground) to the ultimate ground, then all difference is not only accidental but false (though perhaps probatively false); to arrive at truth one must suffer the tragic annihilation of the immanent, a merciless reduction of the exterior to an interior so absolute as to have no outward contour; the calculus of identity is absolute zero, the destitution of all form. The reduction of truth to identity (no less than its reduction to absolute alterity) is already nihilism, and ultimately must reveal itself as such: the most high is the infinitely desolate, the most true is the nothing. Thus, again sounding the Nietzschean alarm, we can say that the abolition of truth as a value was always already secretly inaugurated in the search for truth as positive ground. The elations of Neoplatonism are so very instructive here because they are so transparently wedded to the pathos of philosophy in the West, in its every epoch: the interval discriminating the most high from the here below is the tragic moment of exteriority, alienation, "proof," which allows a distance for reflection, *theoria*, anamnesis . . . but from there to here every movement is one of division, reduction, contamination, and oblivion, and every converse movement, from here to there, is an inversion of the same "benign" impoverishment — reduction, decortication of the world, oblivion of the flesh, flight from time, a journey of the alone to the alone. Here, as nowhere else in the tradition, one encounters both the sweetest ecstasy and most abysmal horror of the experience of truth as perfect self-recognition: the dynamism of truth is destruction, laying waste to being's adornments, erasing the world from the space between the vanishing point of the One and the vanishing point of the nous, in their empty correspondence. This is why the tragic "dualism" haunting Platonism could give rise so naturally to the tragic "monism" of Plotinus — for dialectic and identism are finally the same (which is why the postmodern dread of eternity and recognition in no way escapes the melancholy of Platonism's dread of "dissemination": the ontological vision of both is equally fixed in the same self-torturing dialectic of Same and Other). The doctrine of creation, however, in saying that all things live, move, and are in God not because they add to God or can in any way determine his essence, but as gracious expressions of the plenitude of his being, knowledge, and love, frees metaphysics from any nihilistic destiny: the *maior dissimilitudo* of the ontological analogy means that the *similitudo* between God and creatures, rather than dwelling in a thing's flawed likeness to some higher essence, distorted in the mirror of space and time, subsists rather in that synthesis of transcendental moments and particular event that constitutes each thing in its being. Each actuality, in its difference, shows forth God's actuality in its fullness. Indeed, the "greater unlikeness" in the proportion of the analogy means that the "likeness" in the analogy is ever greater the more fully anything is what it is, the more it grows into the measure of its difference, the more profoundly it drinks from the transcendent moments that compose it and allows all its modes of disclosure to speak of God's infinite goodness. Thus the *analogia entis* is supremely aesthetic: all beings, in their intrinsic nothingness, become what they are in drawing on an infinite wellspring of determinacy, particularity, and actuality. As opposed to the analogy of identity, which finds truth in the ever less particular emptiness of an essential singularity, the analogy of being finds truth in the ever greater particularity of each thing as it enters ever more into the infinite that gives it being.[101] There is also, it is almost needless to say, a far greater intimacy between God and creatures granted by the *analogia entis* than by identist thought: the most high principle does not stand over against us (if secretly within us) across the distance of a hierarchy of lesser metaphysical principles, but is present within the very act of each moment of the particular; the infinite nearness of the *interior intimo meo* is given precisely in the infinite transcendence of the *superior summo meo* (who is *non aliud*).

The analogy also allows one to see the difference between being and beings, and the "withdrawal" that permits beings to stand forth from being — which involves, obviously, a seeming "constriction," "occlusion," and "withholding" of being — not as negation or nihilation but as *kenosis*. For anything to appear, it is true, there must be a more general hiddenness: the unseen sides of an object that, in being hidden, allow a distinct form to emerge from "total" presence, the obscuration of everything the object shields from view, the hiddenness of past and future that allows the object to disclose itself out of its temporal "ecstases," and indeed the invisibility of being itself, its deferral of its absoluteness in its gracious giving way to the finite; but it makes all the difference in the world whether one sees this movement of hiddenness within manifestation in terms of an original negation or in terms of that perfect self-outpouring that is itself the original movement of plenitude, of full manifestation. After all, if the continuity between being and beings is not univocal but truly analogical, being must not be conceived in an ontic fashion — as, say, a great reservoir of possibility that must be apportioned by the "nothinging" of the nothing — but is a transcendent act that is full in being utterly "exposed"; it is the immediate act of being sustaining the entire circle of manifestation in the realm of the ontic, granting actuality equally to visibility and invisibility, presence and absence, and allowing both to share in its own resplendent, self-manifesting, self-knowing, self-loving *apatheia* and bounty. Being cannot be negated by the negative, for the entire economy of manifestation is its good gift; there can be no strife, no original violence, between being and beings, because, as Maximus says, it is impossible for the infinite to be on the same level as the

---

101. Thomas Aquinas writes that "veritas fundatur in esse rei magis quam in ipsa quidditate": this means, he argues, that the "adequation" that truth is consists in an assimilation of the intellect to the *esse* of any given thing, whereby it accepts each thing as it is (*In I Sent.*, D. 19, q. 5, a. 1, *solutio*). This is an elegantly succinct formulation — truth is the fullness, not the impoverishment, of a thing's modes of being; judgments are true if one accepts beings as beings in the fullness of their determinations.

finite that shares in it *(Ambiguum VII)*,[102] for beings know nonexistence as the contrary of their existence (which is participated being), while being itself is beyond contrariety altogether (*Centuries on Love* 3:27-29). Ontological analogy instructs the pure eye how to see what it sees as the gracious *kenosis* of the supereminent in the finite, and as the simultaneous exaltation of the finite in the peaceful coincidence of all its transcendental moments; it teaches vision to see that coincidence not as the savage blaze of "total light," a substance that is rent asunder in the plurality of existence, but as the embracing unity that allows the finite the space to be. But for the analogy, one might fail to see that in the very "hanging together" of the moments of experience there is a prior act of grace in which unity and difference both subsist (as if, in a crudely structuralist way, one were to see language as consisting *only* in the differential placing of signs and lexemes, but fail to note how a prior unity shows itself in the very "ontological" pertinacity of language's structure);[103] one might not see that the great sea of possibility that is fitfully actualized as "world" is still infinitely distinct from the actuality — the unity — that allows the possible to be. In short, the analogy instructs us to see the world as creation, as God pouring himself inexhaustibly forth as the place — the *chora* — of the not-God, of the as-nothing, giving distance to beings in the infinite distance of the Father's self-outpouring in his eternal "manifestation" and image: the lamb slain from the foundation of the world, always raised up by the Spirit. This is why consideration of the *analogia entis* concludes this long meditation on trinitarian doctrine: the Father forever sees and infinitely loves the whole depth of his being in the Son, illumined as responsive love in the fullness of the Spirit, and in the always determinate infinity of his triune being God begets all the riches of being — all that all things might ever be — in the image and light of his essence; and thus God himself is already his own analogy, his own infinite otherness and perfect likeness. All things — all the words of being — speak of God because they shine within his eternal Word. This trinitarian distance is that "open" in which the tree springs up from the earth, the stars turn in the sky, the sea swells, all living things are born and grow, angels raise their everlasting hymnody; because this is the true interval of difference, every metaphysics that does not grasp the analogy of being is a Tower of Babel, attempting to mount up to the supreme principle rather than dwelling in and giving voice to the prodigality of the gift. It is

102. See esp. *PG*, 91:1081.

103. One cannot, of course, take the route of the transcendental tradition and simply ascribe the unity of experience to the synthesizing activity of the transcendental Ego, as the question of the transcendental Ego's *being* (and so unity) will still assert itself, and the Ego will itself be so abstracted from any ontic particularity as to become simply another form of the same "ontico-phenomenological problem": How is it that what is, is — that is, shows itself, and stands forth?

the simple, infinite movement of analogy that constitutes everything that is as a being, oscillating between essence and existence and receiving both from beyond itself, and that makes everything already participate in the return of the gift, the offering of all things by the Spirit up into the Father's plenitude of being, in the Son. By the analogy, each thing comes to be as pure event, owning no substance, made free from nothingness by the unmerited grace of *being* other than God, participating in the mystery of God's power to receive all in giving all away — the mystery, that is, of the truth that God is love.

II. CREATION

1. God's gracious action in creation belongs from the first to that delight, pleasure, and regard that the Trinity enjoys from eternity, as an outward and unnecessary expression of that love; and thus creation must be received before all else as gift and as beauty.

And God saw every thing that he had made, and, behold, it was very good. And the evening and the morning were the sixth day.

Gen. 1:31

Where wast thou when I laid the foundations of the earth? . . . When the morning stars sang together, and all the sons of God shouted for joy?

Job 38:4, 7

Let the heavens rejoice, and let the earth be glad; let the sea roar, and the fulness thereof. Let the field be joyful, and all that is therein: then shall all the trees of the wood rejoice Before the Lord.

Ps. 96:11-13

Then I was by him, as one brought up with him: and I was daily his delight, rejoicing always before him; Rejoicing in the habitable part of his earth; and my delights were with the sons of men.

Prov. 8:30-31

So shall my word be that goeth forth out of my mouth: it shall not re-
turn unto me void, but it shall accomplish that which I please, and it
shall prosper in the thing whereto I sent it.

Isa. 55:11

I beseech thee, my son, look upon the heaven and the earth, and all
that is therein, and consider that God made them of things that were
not; and so was mankind made likewise.

2 Macc. 7:28

Through faith we understand that the worlds were framed by the word
of God, so that things which are seen were not made of things which do
appear.

Heb. 11:3

Thou art worthy, O Lord, to receive glory and honour and power: for
thou hast created all things, and for thy pleasure they are and were
created.

Rev. 4:11

i. *Analogia Delectationis*

The difference between being and beings, when understood in a Christian
fashion, is also (within the sphere of the ontic) the difference between beings
and nonbeing; it is the condition of absolute contingency that defines
creaturely existence. Every finite being is groundless, without any original or
ultimate essence in itself, a moment of unoccasioned fortuity, always awakening from nothing and always enfolding within itself a nocturnal interval of
nothingness, an interior oblivion that is at the same time the space of what
Augustine called *memoria*, the place where our souls open out upon the prospect of that wise and loving light that illuminates them from without. Of
course, to speak of memory is to speak only of the creature's "recollection" of
being without foundation, of being always placed at a distance from what gives
being, in the place of one who has been called and who can now only answer.
Memory, thus conceived, is at one with a forgetfulness; as opposed to the Platonic anamnesis, which is an escape from the forgetfulness imposed upon the
soul by the flesh, it is before all else the memory of flesh, the memory that
"dust thou art, and unto dust shalt thou return" (Gen. 3:19). One arrives in being not from some other place, not from some prior state of bliss or
pleromatic glory, but always as one summoned from nothingness, framed by

grace, receiving all while meriting nothing. It is just this play between memory and forgetting, this simultaneous radical dependency upon and incomprehension of God's being, that is the knowledge of one's creatureliness. And nothing more concisely expresses God's transcendence over the fold of ontological contingency than what 2 Maccabees says of created things: ὅτι ἐκ οὐκ ὄντων ἐποίησεν αὐτά ὁ θεός. The very first verse of Genesis sets Jewish and Christian thought apart from any metaphysics that conceives of an eidetic or substantial continuity — as a necessity — between being's source and the event of worldly being, between ground and manifestation, and sets it apart also from sheer myth (the primordial form of metaphysics), which generally describes some cosmic sacrifice, or cosmic venery, or effluence of divine substance to account for the being of the world.

The Bible makes no such claims, but depicts creation at once as a kind of deliberative invention ("Let us make . . .") and, consequently, as a kind of play, a kind of artistry for the sake of artistry. This is expressed with exquisite delicacy by the figure of Wisdom in the book of Proverbs, at play like a small child before the eyes of God, as his delight in all his works; and expressed equally gracefully by the image of the stars singing and the angels rejoicing at creation in the book of Job. For this reason, inevitably, when Christian thought comes to speak of God as being, or of an analogy between creation and the God who gives it, it involves a subversion of many metaphysical concepts of being, a displacement of many an *eidos* by the *eikon* that is like God only in differing freely (and infinitely) from God. Christian talk of an analogy between the being of creatures and the being of God is something like speaking of the irreducible difference and yet declarative relationship between the being of a work of art and the creative being of the artist (which is not, surely, an arbitrary relationship, any more than it is "necessary"). No one ever displayed a profounder incomprehension of this analogy than Heidegger, as is especially obvious from his general impatience with what he took to be a medieval objectification of being as the concrete *factum* of creation, a product present at hand. In truth, the motif of creation as a divine handiwork is not an analogy simply between a producer and a "product," but between the creative delight and freedom of the artist and the expressive freedom of the shapes that are crafted by that delight, between the divine love that precedes every object of love and the *Anwesen* (so to speak) of those things that bear witness to that love by the simple letting be that brings them forth in radiant and limpid form. Again, the analogy is a disjunction and a difference, while also being the interval of creation's participation in the being that God gives as his gift: creation tells of God's glory precisely because it is needless, an expression of a love always directed toward another. The being of the creator differs in being imparted outward to creation, almost as (to use the same unsatisfactory comparison) the being of the artist differs in the otherness of his work, which participates in the artist's own essential act of being, know-ing, and loving. It is thus that I speak of created being as an expressive analogy, or as an analogical expression. The analogy lies in no static hierarchy of es-sences, no mysterious grounding of the soul's substance in the divine sub-stance, but in the delight that calls out to — and so gives being to — difference, and in the love that evokes and responds: in, that is, beauty.

Creation's being is God's pleasure, creation's beauty God's glory; beauty reveals the shining of an uncreated light, a Taboric effulgence, upon all things, a *claritas* that discloses the lineaments of what it infuses and shows them to be the firm outlines of that weight, that *kabod*, that proclaims God's splendor; it is the coincidence of forms upon the surface of being and the infinite depths of divine light of which all form partakes.[104] God thus gives particularity to differ-ence, gives form, radiance, and gravity; all the things that differ are the weight of glory, are glory itself, the bounteousness of God's goodness standing "out-side" itself. Creation thus is without foundations; it attends God, possessing no essence apart from its character as a free and open utterance within the infinity of his self-utterance. In creation God, who is never without his Word, neverthe-less utters himself "outward" to that which has being only because God's ad-dress can never be without reply (Isa. 55:11). In the strictest sense theology can use a term like *ousia* of God alone,[105] and then always as determined, by the perichoretic dynamism of the Trinity, as *ousia* in transit, so to speak, the per-petual handing over in love of all that the Father is to the Son and Spirit, and the perpetual restoration of this gift. Creation is only a splendor that hangs upon that life of love and knowledge, and only by grace; it is first and foremost a surface, a shining fabric of glory, whose inmost truth is its aesthetic corre-spondence to the beauty of divine love, as it is eternally expressed by the Trin-ity: a sacramental order of light. Alexander of Hales claims that the beauty of the divine lies in the order of relation of the three divine persons (*Summa theologica* I, inq. i, tract. 3, q.3, art. 2, ad 2), and Augustine says the beauty of cre-ation is a proclamation of divine beauty (*De civitate Dei* 2.4.2), while Hilary speaks of the God who is all beauty and who is reflected in the beauty of his cre-ation (*De Trinitate* 1.6-7);[106] and this beauty of the Trinity, this orderliness of God's *perichoresis*, is the very movement of delight, of the divine persons within one other, and so the analogy that lies between worldly and divine beauty is a kind of *analogia delectationis*. The delightfulness of created things expresses the

104. See Francesca Aran Murphy, *Christ and the Form of Beauty* (Edinburgh: T. & T. Clark, 1995), 52-53, 142.

105. See T. F. Torrance's remarks on the theological terminology of Athanasius in Torrance, 310-11.

106. See also *De vera religione* 52-54, and *Confessions* 11.4.

delightfulness of God's infinite distance. For Christian thought, then, delight is the premise of any sound epistemology: it is delight that constitutes creation, and so only delight can comprehend it, see it aright, understand its grammar. Only in loving creation's beauty — only in seeing that creation truly is beauty — does one apprehend what creation is.

Writing of the theology of Bonaventure, regarding the analogy between the numerical proportions of worldly beauty and the unity of the Trinity, Hans Urs von Balthasar remarks that "this tendency of what is created to reveal the divine points back to the power of God the Word to express himself — and so it points back to the pleasure of the creator; and the Word itself points back to the relationship of expression within the Godhead, to the Father's joy in begetting."[107] Creation, as an "aesthetic" expression of trinitarian love, is always already grace in the fullest sense: it is that "gracefulness" that reveals the nature of divine "graciousness." Indeed, God's affirmations of the goodness of his creation in the first chapter of Genesis can be taken as indicating first and foremost an aesthetic evaluation rather than a simply moral one; it is only with sin that the goodness of creation must be conceptually separated into solitary transcendental categories, and only with sin that creation is seen to possess a distinct ethical axis. One might almost say that the separable category of the moral is an intrusion upon the aesthetic joy that is the upwelling source of creaturely existence, as is a separate category of truth once the paradisal experience of divine love in the blameless beauty of creation is lost. Thomas Traherne writes, in his *Centuries:*

> Can you be Holy without accomplishing the end for which you are created? Can you be Divine unless you be Holy? Can you accomplish the end for which you were created, unless you be Righteous, unless you be just in rendering to Things their due esteem? All things were made to be yours, and you were made to prize them according to their value: which is your office and duty, the end for which you were created, and the means whereby you enjoy. The end for which you were created, is that by prizing all that God hath done, you may enjoy yourself and Him in Blessedness. (1:12)[108]

---

107. Hans Urs von Balthasar, *The Glory of the Lord: A Theological Aesthetics,* vol. 2, *Studies in Theological Style: Clerical Styles,* trans. Andrew Louth, Francis McDonagh, and Brian McNeil (San Francisco: Ignatius, 1984), 345. Here again one should invoke Balthasar's great reversal, so to call it: his upending of the Kantian critical sequence so that no practice of pure rationality is conceivable apart from the aesthetic and then dramatic involvement of the creature in the trinitarian economy of creation and salvation.

108. Citations and page references in the text are taken from the 1908 Dobell edition of *Centuries of Meditations,* reissued in its modernized form under the more correct title *Centuries* by A. R. Mowbray and Co. (Oxford, 1985).

And:

> To conceive aright and to enjoy the world, is to conceive the Holy Ghost, and to see his Love: which is the Mind of the Father. And this more pleaseth Him than many Worlds, could we create as fair and great as this. For when you are once acquainted with the world, you will find the goodness and wisdom of God so manifest therein, that it was impossible another, or better should be made. Which being made to be enjoyed, nothing can please or serve Him more, than the Soul that enjoys it. For the Soul doth accomplish the end of His desire in Creating it. (1:10)

Hamann lamented the dire effects of the fruit of the tree of knowledge, in causing humanity to prefer speculative concepts over poetic enjoyment as the principal way of grasping the truth of things;[109] for him, to a degree perhaps unparalleled in Christian thought, the true knowledge of God in creation — the true analogy — lay in a childlike rapture before the concrete and poetic creativity of God, in the task of translating the language of that creativity, and in the rearticulation of that language in poetic invention. In the experience of beauty, even now, we recover, in some measure and at some moments, this paradisal theme. Nicholas of Cusa remarks that eternal wisdom is tasted in everything savored, eternal pleasure felt in all things pleasurable, eternal beauty beheld in all that is beautiful, and eternal desire experienced in everything desired (*Idiota de sapientia* 1); he even claims that a man who sees a beautiful woman, and is agitated by the sight of her, gives glory thus to God and admires God's infinite beauty (*Excitationes* 7). And Augustine says delight is the weight in the soul that causes it to tend toward or away from the love of God, according to how it orders the heart in regard to the beauty of God's creation (*De musica* 6.10.29). None of this is to say that the soul can gain access to an immediate intuition of the divine form in the fabric of creation, unclouded by sin, untroubled by the misery of earthly life; what is at issue is a hermeneutics of creation, a theological embrace of creation as a divine word precisely in its aesthetic excessiveness, its unforced beauty. Inasmuch as *creation* is not the overflow of some ungovernable perturbation of the divine substance, or a tenebrous collusion of ideal

---

109. See Johann Georg Hamann, *Briefwechsel,* ed. Walter Ziesemer and Arthur Henkel, 7 vols. (Wiesbaden: Inselverlag, 1955-79), 5:265 ("Kein Genuß ergrübelt sich — und alle Dinge folglich auch das *Ens entium* ist zum Genuß da, und nicht zur Speculation. Durch den Baum der Erkenntnis wird uns der Baum des Lebens entzogen — und sollt uns dieser nicht lieber seyn, wie jener — immer dem Beyspiel des alten Adams folgen, als [uns] an seinem Exempel spiegeln — keine Kinder werden, wie der ⟨Gottes Sohn⟩, neue Adam Fleisch und Blut an- und das Kreuz auf sich genommen") and 6:492 ("Durch den Baum der Erkenntnis, werden wir der Frucht des Lebens beraubt, und jener ist kein Mittel zum Genuß dieses letzten *Endzwecks* und *Anfangs*").

form and chaotic matter, but purely an expression of the superabundant joy and agape of the Trinity, joy and love are its only grammar and its only ground; one therefore must learn a certain orientation, a certain charity and a certain awe, and even a certain style of delectation to see in what sense creation tells of God and to grasp the nature of creation's inmost (which is to say, most superficial) truth. Creation is a new emphasis in the divine dialect of triune love, whose full, perfect, and infinitely diverse expression is God's eternal Word.

This also means that the things of the senses cannot of themselves distract from God. All the things of earth, in being very good, declare God, and it is only by the mediation of their boundless display that the declaration of God may be heard and seen. In themselves they have no essences apart from the divine delight that crafts them: they are an array of proportions, an ordering or felicitous parataxis of *semeia,* and so have nothing in themselves by which they might divert attention from the God who gives them, no specific gravity, no weight apart from the weight of glory. Only a corrupt desire that longs to possess the things of the world as inert property, for violent or egoistic ends, so disorders the sensible world as to draw it away from the God that sensible reality properly declares; such a desire has not fallen prey to a lesser or impure beauty, but has rather lost sight of corporeal, material, and temporal beauty *as* beauty, and so has placed it in bondage. Of course, theology has suffered, historically, from a variety of etherealizing susceptibilities: the occasional dualistic tensions within a small portion of patristic metaphysics, or Zwingli's spectral theology of the sacraments, or the Calvinist mysticism of bare and unadorned worship (which idolatrously mistakes God for some object that can be lost among other objects), and other tendencies to imagine that the soul is purified by being extracted from the life of the senses or that God is glorified by the inanition of the world. On the one hand, such thinking confines God and world to a relationship of totality, an oscillation between wealth and impoverishment, ideal and shadow, truth and falsehood, rather than recognizing the world as the free expression of the infinite's all-embracing abundance of light. On the other hand, and more grievously, such thinking offends simply by being unbiblical, insufficiently chastened or inspired by the doctrine of the incarnation, and unable to grasp that the trinitarian God is already full of fellowship, joy, and glory, and requires no sacrifice of worldly love — no commerce of totality — to make his glory replete; the world adds nothing to the triune God, either by being affirmed or by being denied, but only by being affirmed in love does it bear witness to God. Thus to come to see the world as beauty is the moral education of desire, the redemption of vision; it is in the cultivation of delight that charity is born, and in the cultivation of charity that delight becomes possible. In learning to see the world as beauty, one learns the measure of a love that receives all things not to hold onto, not "for me," but as beautiful in their own splendor;

and in learning the measure of charity, which lets what is be in its otherness, one's vision of the world becomes open to its beauty, and is deepened toward that infinity of beauty that comprises it.

If this all appears to be waxing either too assertively dogmatic or too buoyantly rhapsodic, it is only in order to return again to that cardinal axiom of any Christian theological aesthetics: that creation is without necessity. The Christian God is never a God of abstract subjectivity, an unexplicated simplicity requiring an "exterior" medium of determination, because God is Trinity, who explicates himself, utters himself, and responds eternally, and has all fellowship, exposition, and beauty in perfect sufficiency; and so creation can never be "necessary" for him. Of course, one would not want to suggest that the freedom of God in creating is merely the spontaneous, deliberative liberty of a finite subject, which would make God's nature a slave of his will; true freedom — ontological freedom or *apatheia* — is the perfect and unimpeded fullness with which the divine nature is itself, with which God is God (just as true human freedom is the fulfillment of our nature in its union with God's goodness). Thus we can say that, for God, there might just as well have been no creation (for creation adds nothing to God, but only participates in him), but assert nevertheless that creation is "necessary" in another, aesthetic sense: it has been from eternity fitting to God's goodness to be a loving creator, manifesting his trinitarian love in creatures. No statement could be more demeaning of God's transcendence than the conjecture of Duns Scotus that God *could*, should he wish it, create a world entirely alien to his own nature (as though God were a limited subject possessed of a limited nature). But no statement could more thoroughly confine God to a metaphysical totality (or, as it happens, more thoroughly deprive creation of its expressive freedom) than Hegel's "ohne Welt ist Gott nicht Gott."[110] The divine desire that constitutes created being ventures "beyond" the trinitarian dance only because that desire always possesses the generosity that gives difference, the beauty that declares itself. Hegel's Idea goes forth from a poverty of immanent reflection, not from an interior beauty, and goes into its opposite, into nothingness (with which, in a sense, it is convertible). The beautiful, then, as the sign of God's freedom and sovereignty, has no primary role in Hegel's thought; beauty can figure in the system only secondarily, through the metabolism of negation. To see created being as in any sense a metaphysical necessity for God is inevitably to see it as issuing from the sublime, as determining, articulating, negating, or "beautifying" what in itself lacks determination, adequate expression, sufficient delight, or true beauty; creation as the wholly good (which is to say, primordially beautiful) expression of the good (which is also to say, beautiful) God can be grasped only as radical nonnecessity. The Christian God never goes out into his "oppo-

110. G. F. W. Hegel, *Begriff der Religion* (Leipzig, 1925), 148.

site" because the entire motion of condescension — creation, covenant, incarnation — is already contained in the perichoretic motion of the Trinity: in the eternal going forth of the Son, the everlasting spiration of the Spirit, the eternal restoration of all things to the Father. Thus God, even in the midst of what is not God, is always the God who wants for nothing, who goes forth into what he freely loves and chooses: creation, Israel, the church. Creation, *as* creation, is free, unforced, apportioned, elected, known, and loved by God, and so is most originally an aesthetic moment to the divine, and a moment of peace; no defining violence of negation, no unexpressed potential in the divine nature brings the world to pass. And this is the special glory of creation: whereas Hegel sought to discover in worldly being the dignity of divine necessity, Christian theology ascribes to creation the still higher dignity of delight. Creation is good in itself, so good as to be pleasing to the infinite God even though he has no need of it; it is never a determinative play between negation and indifference, a vacillation between meaning and mere particularity. Because, for Christian thought, creation is a free and expressive display whose every detail declares God's glory, and not an odyssey of divine self-determination, particularity is affirmed; and as there is no meaningful distinction between "essence" and exposition in created things — because creation is groundless, hanging upon God as an iridescence of his glory — there is nothing more basic than creation's superficial sequences of beauty, and nothing to be "rescued" from particularity by that dialectical redoubling whereby what negates is in turn negated. And it is the absence of necessity that truly tells of God, that "corresponds" to the God who is always abundant in delight, fellowship, and love.[111]

The absence of a necessity interior to the divine, moreover — perhaps to state the obvious — can be meaningfully asserted only if it be also acknowledged that there is nothing in the way of an exterior necessity that could evoke creation from God; that is to say that creation is not an act of overcoming, an act of conquest, a necessary assertion of divine power over against darkness, chaos, or nothingness. The myth of chaos, of course, exercises a powerful fascination for theology, as much for its moral as its cosmological implications, and there is certainly some biblical language upon which one can draw to support such a picture; but when such language is taken so literally that it obscures the difference between God's transcendent act of giving being to what is not and the oscillating play of finitude's forms and forces within creation (especially fallen creation), it can become the most malign of mythic narratives. That be-

---

111. That God is not compelled to create, and is indeed free not to create at all, is a commonplace of patristic theology; see, for example, Irenaeus, *Adversus haereses* 2.10.4; Athanasius, *Contra Arianos* 3.59-62; Gregory the Theologian, *Oration* 29.6. See also Lossky, *Mystical Theology*, 45.

ing is always a collusion of order and disorder, or the fragile alliance of form and a refractory material substrate, or a struggle between stabilizing hierarchies of political, emotional, or rational force and the indeterminate and convulsive forces of nature, the self, or matter is in one sense or another the mythos of pagan philosophy and culture, of many "reactionary" and "progressive" rationalisms alike, and of a certain style of postmodern romance — again, it is the tale of the endless contest and mutual dependency of Apollo and Dionysus (each of whom has his partisans). But it is an idea fundamentally at odds with the biblical narrative of creation. Even the waste and darkness (the *tohu* and *bohu*) of Genesis 1:2 is the creature of God (Gen. 1:1): not an autonomous, intractable, and formless matter subdued and shaped by the imposition of form, but only the dormant fallow of creation waiting for God to bring it graciously to foison. The image of creation as a conquest of chaos has recurred often enough in Christian thought, just as sin has often been regarded as the reincursion upon the world of the chaos or nothingness God overthrows in the act of creation; one sees it, for example, in various currents of medieval and Renaissance Platonism (in, say, the twelfth-century school of Chartres, especially as formulated by Bernard of Chartres or Bernardus Sylvestris, or in Renaissance hexaemeral epic, from du Bartas to Milton). But the peril of the image, to risk again stating the obvious, is that it can veil the freedom and unconstrained joy of the God who expresses himself in creating and in loving what he creates. The doctrine of *creatio ex nihilo* speaks of a God who gives of his bounty, not a God at war with darkness, and if the radical nature of this doctrine is not appreciated, God and creation cannot be thought except in terms of totality, and a totality of violence at that. This is the chief problem with Barth's treatment of Genesis 1, which suggests that creation is somehow prized from chaos, and that God must then actively preserve creation against a chaos that somehow abides as its other side.[112] But creation's other side is, quite simply, nothing at all; creation is, in its entirety, the shining surface that it shows to God, the intervals and instances of beauty, in its light and darkness, that endlessly declare his glory in their diverging and converging lines, developments, and transitions.

No theologian evinces a keener sense of creation as pure surface (to return predictably to my chief protagonist) than Gregory of Nyssa: creation for him *is* only as the answer of light to light: apart from this, there is no world to speak of at all. This is true even of "material" nature: Gregory, like Basil before him, in various places denies that the world even possesses any material substrate apart from the intelligible acts that constitute its perceptible qualities; the world of bodies is a confluence of "thoughts," "bare concepts," "words," noetic

112. See Karl Barth, *Church Dogmatics,* III/1, *The Doctrine of Creation,* trans. J. W. Edwards, O. Bussey, and Harold Knight (Edinburgh: T. & T. Clark, 1958), 102-10.

"potentialities" (*In Hexaemeron; PG,* 44:68-72; *DAR* 124; *DHO* 24: 212-13), proceeding from the divine nature; its *esse,* one might almost say, is *percipi;* the phenomenal realm is not, says Gregory, formed from any underlying matter, for "the divine will is the matter and substance of created things (ὕλη καὶ οὐσία τῶν δημιουργημάτων)" (*ΙΙΤΙF; GNO* 2.2: 11), the "matter, form (κατασκευὴ), and power (δύναμις) of the world" (*De vita Gregorii Thaumaturgi; GNO* 10.1: 24); the here below, it seems, is like a mirror without a tain, a depth that is pure surface, and a surface composed entirely of the light it reflects. This is a far more coherent vision of the world's relation to God's knowledge and love of his own goodness than that of, for instance, Eberhard Jüngel, who says (with a certain mythopoetic brashness) that God must overcome nothingness by relating himself to it creatively.[113] But nothingness does not challenge God, it is not some "thing" with which God becomes creatively involved; he passes nothingness by without regard, it is literally nothing to him, it has no part to play in the way by which he is God or in his desire to create. Nothing is what is overcome, indeed, but this is to say that there is no original overcoming. There is only the text, the song, of creation, which is unfolded continuously, its infinite openness telling of the infinite God. God's triumph is always already complete; it lies in his being the God he is in eternity, always infinitely "going forth" from and "possessing" himself. Creation is not a conquest of the abyss. The myth of chaos is the mythos of the sublime, the legend of Dionysus, the cultic legitimation of every warlike state; but creation is a gift contained by God's infinity, passed between the persons of the Trinity, within which infinite distance all its intervals of difference participate. Moreover, it is only within these intervals of beauty that the sublime — as delay, intensity, dissonance, immensity — occurs at all. The expressive beauty of creation conceals no chaotic depth, but only embraces intensities and complications of surface; and even the most tragic of circumstances points to no deep and abiding truth, but only to disorders and derangements of the surface, wounds to be healed. There is no chaos, but only a will toward chaos, and the violence it inflicts upon being.[114]

---

113. Jüngel, *God as the Mystery,* 223.

114. The perennial appeal of the idea of chaos is reflected in the science of "chaos" that became so fashionable in the last decade. However, as all the literature attests, this is not a science of *chaos* at all, at least not as that word has classically been understood. Rather than the entirely formless, atelic, uniform, and impotent immensity of chaos, this science is concerned with a special kind of indeterminacy; and even here it is an indeterminacy that is radically formal, set free in its indeterminacy by the very wealth of determinative sequences it comprises. Properly speaking, it is a science of difference, and what it successively discloses is an endless richness of levels of harmony, magnificent complexities, series of fractal analogy, forever diverging, and yet always recapitulating and varying that from which they diverge. There is, in short, a sort of baroque interminability of exposition in the fabric of things.

ii. The Gift

If creation is not to be conceived as the overcoming of something that *must* be overcome in order for creation to be at all, then it must be conceived as gift. This should, obviously, be an unproblematic assertion, but the meaning, indeed the possibility, of the giving of "the gift" has become something of an issue in Continental philosophy, and has recently been subjected to a tortuous consideration by Derrida, whose conclusions on the matter fall somewhat along the lines that the idea of the gift is incoherent except (to some limited and still ambiguous degree) in the terms of a kind of ontological nihilism (by which I mean a species of Heideggerian "nihilationism").[115] The currently fashionable form of the question, especially in French intellectual circles, began its life as a theme within certain anthropological and social studies, most notably Marcel Mauss's *The Gift;*[116] the role of the gift in tribal societies, and so in society in general, has been so thoroughly reduced, in successive interpretations, to a contractual mechanism, a token of power, a calculus of indebtedness, a contest between "men of substance," and a circulation of credit, that the very notion of beneficence has been in large part displaced by the image of society as a machine that functions by way of a coercive economy of symbolic exchange. After all, as the origin of contract, the gift always carries with it the burden of a reciprocal obligation, a debt that is often dissembled by the conventions of generosity and gratitude. Not that Mauss's understanding of the issue was anywhere so bleak; he rather sensibly saw the (nonidentical) reciprocity of gift giving as the primordial basis of moral community; but such a temperate view of the matter, with its patience for the ambiguity of mixed motives, and lacking the thrilling corrosiveness of the Marxist soupçon, obviously had little chance of being absorbed into the moral grammar of chic academic radicalism. The most influential formulation of the gift as a practice whose principal function is to secure a debt of obligation is perhaps that of Pierre Bordieu, who distinguishes the gift from other "obliging" institutions by two principal features: difference and delay. A gift that is *exactly* reciprocated is a gift that is returned, rejected, and a debt of gratitude that is immediately discharged is shown to be an unwelcome, formal obligation, and in either case the response is a tautologous return of the same, a violence, like a blow instantly returned.[117] A gift differs from other forms of exchange not because it "generously" demands nothing in return, but

---

115. See Jacques Derrida, *Given Time*, vol. 1, *Counterfeit Money*, trans. Peggy Kamuf (Chicago: University of Chicago Press, 1991).

116. Marcel Mauss, *The Gift*, trans. W. D. Halls (London and New York: Routledge, 1990).

117. See Pierre Bordieu, *Outline of a Theory of Practice*, trans. Richard Nice (Cambridge: Cambridge University Press, 1977), 1-30; see also Milbank, "Can a Gift?" 125.

solely by the style of return it elicits; and so it is only by obligation (albeit a particular fashion of obligation) that the gift is recognizable as a gift that has been given and received. To Derrida, for whom the thought of the gift is both indispensable and contradictory, this means that a gift cannot be given or received without falling into the circular exchanges of indebtedness; the disinterestedness of the gift (which for him constitutes its gratuity) is impossible because of the social economy within which the gift must appear. Derrida is fanatically uncompromising on this point: even if the gift is given with no expectation of tangible return, it still cannot be truly a gift, because the gift elicits recognition of the giver, and even the intention to give requires a recognition by the giver that he or she is a giver;[118] the gift, given or intended, carries with it a credit of glory. And, as Derrida writes, "There is no more gift as soon as the other *receives* — and even if she refuses the gift that she has perceived or recognized as gift. As soon as she keeps for the gift the signification of gift, she loses it, there is no more *gift*. Consequently, if there is no gift, there is no gift, but if there is gift held or beheld *as* gift by the other, once again there is no gift; in any case the gift does not *exist* and does not *present* itself. If it presents itself, it no longer presents itself" (14-15). Subjectivity as such is incompatible with the gift (24), and so the gift acts within the circle of intentionality as an impossibility that the circle manifests only by obscuring. Derrida even calls into question the "generosity" in Marion's language of the pure "gift" or "call" that precedes and exceeds the circle of being's economy (which is itself problematic for theology, given Marion's own needless wariness regarding the impurity of "ontological" interest),[119] for does not the call, Derrida wonders, circle back to the name and truth of the "father" in a circle of economy that cancels the gift (52)? The only gift, for Derrida, that can be given is no gift at all: given without intention to no one whom it can oblige, it must be the gift of nothing. The ontological import of this line of reflection is that in the end the only gift is the radical nongift of time, the present moment, that is nothing at all but the nihilating passage of time from futureto past, the dissolution of being in its manifestation as temporality: the gift is the *es gibt* of being, or the empty yielding of the *chora*, the effect of nothing (123), the pure giving of nothing (the present) to no one, whose delay is endlessly deferred toward that difference — that reciprocation of the gift — that can never be given, never owed, never desired. The gift is no gift: the *present* that is not (a) present. The significance of this for theology would seem to be that if ever this *es gibt* is supplanted by "it is given," a totalizing discourse

---

118. Derrida, *Given Time,* 13-14. Parenthetical page numbers in the following text are to this work.

119. See the brilliant but flawed *Etant donné: Essai d'une phenomenologie de la donation* (Paris: Presses Universitaires de France, 1997).

of power and indebtedness — of credit and obligation — has taken shape; talk of a God who creates from the beneficence of his love is a self-defeating metaphor. Derrida does, though, have his own use for the figure of the gift: it acts for him as the impossible horizon of exchange, the utterly self-annihilating gift of the immemorial event, the primum mobile that — running contrary to the cycle of exchange, of intention and recognition — sets that cycle in motion. The gift is the effaced gesture of being's absence or lack, devoid of generosity, remembrance, or gratitude, and is so the purest forgetfulness and purest donation (147).

There is no need to rehearse again my opinion of the particular ontology behind all of this; I should like instead simply to interrogate the moral grammar that informs the argument. The altogether doctrinaire premise that goes unexamined in such reflections, after all, is a moral one: that purity *of intention* is what assures the gratuity of the gift, and that that purity is assured by complete disinterest, defying recognition and reciprocation alike. One does not like to imagine that Derrida has uncritically succumbed to a Kantian (or, for that matter, Kierkegaardian) rigorism that requires an absolute distinction of duty from desire; but then why must the thought of the gift be confined to so narrow a moral definition of gratuity or of selflessness, purged of desire? And should it be? When Derrida explicitly eschews the motif of solar superabundance, the Nietzschean metaphor of the gift (162), he nevertheless chooses to take the image of time's gift — being's nihilating outpouring — as his image of the ethical; he even invokes the Platonic Good, the inexhaustible giver that gives from beyond presence, from beyond being (161). There is an odd confluence of themes in all of this: the diffusive generosity of the Good allied to the moral rigorism of Kantian ethics, combined with the gnostic emphasis of Levinas on a privative narrative of the ethical, an extraontological and extraphenomenological priority of ethical donation. Again, on this last, *scripsi quod scripsi.* But I must remark that it seems clear that the inhuman extremism of a Kantian dogmatism regarding ethical disinterestedness has burdened Derrida with a definition of the gift that is simply a category mistake. Why, after all, put any emphasis on purity of intention when considering the gift unless one assumes in some sense the priority of a subjectivity that possesses a moral identity prior to the complex exchanges of moral practices, of gift and gratitude? Or, if one has not assumed such a subjectivity, why allow the idea of the gift no wider ambit than is provided by this myth of the punctiliar self whose ethical integrity consists in a kind of self-sufficient responsibility before an ethical sublime? John Milbank, in his extremely useful essay on this entire issue, quite correctly suggests that it may be redundant to assume that there is anything that *is* apart from its ability to give itself, apart from the expressive invention of identity in the extrinsic economies of donation and restoration; and that it is presumptuous to assume that the gift cannot be the inventive and expressive gratuity of a truly creative giver, whose involvement in the gift is more than the perpetual recirculation of power and debt.[120] Indeed, is it not simply correct to say that the good that is done or the gift that is given is itself the good, and the secondary and reflexive attempt to find a "deeper" index of moral intention by which to measure the deed or the gift relies on a myth of autonomous, self-founding subjective interiority that cannot substantiate itself? Derrida really never elevates his thinking of the gift out of the duality of the most unrefined kind of account of phenomenological intention-ality, as if the question must be determined by the model of a preexisting tran-scendental ego whose noesis receives the gift as a noema, meaning that the al-ways prior intention is the work of a pure subject while the always posterior object is simply the discrete aim of this intention (but surely it is the entire circle of intention and world that is given, as that utterly gratuitous blaze of illumina-tion that opens up between distinct moments of being whose ultimate actuality is one shared transcendent act of truth). Nor is it only Derrida's concern for pu-rity of intention that partakes of a certain Enlightenment mythology; there seems also to be an unspoken solicitude for the recipient of the gift, that other subject whose indivisible interior freedom would somehow be compromised by the imposition of any exterior obligation or debt (except the direct injunction of the ethical). But none of these terms constitutes the inevitable moral grammar of giving, especially not if the gift is, before all else, that which gives the recipient: if, that is, one is constituted by the gift one receives, both by what it is and by how one receives it. After all, there is no reason why it is more correct to say that the gift forces a return than to say that the gift allows or even liberates a response, and so is the occasion of communion. One's self is perhaps nothing but the gift of the other's otherness, defined by what one receives from the other and by what style of receiving one adopts: received as gift or as burden, eliciting de-lighted response or merely guilty indebtedness (or ingratitude), the gift is the oc-casion of the self, the event of a self, and to consider first the self that is obligated by — rather than the self that is born in — the gift is to invert the order of what is given and what restored. One becomes a "person," one might say, analogous to the divine persons, only insofar as one is the determinate recipient of a gift; one is a person always in the evocation of a response. The gift is given, even if the self that intends and the self that is bound by obligation exist together in a relation-ship that is not purely "ethical"; it is in the priority of the gift that a giver is born into the measure of charity and a recipient is born into the measure of delight and gratitude, because God has given out of a charity and a joy that is perfect in the shared life of the Trinity, and in him desire and selfless charity are one and the same. The division of the ethical from desire and the good from the beautiful

---

120. Milbank, "Can a Gift?" 120-21, 132.

is imaginable only in terms of an atomistic individuality that, by definition, cannot participate in the gift; this is the individuality that theology is obliged to deny.

Milbank is surely right to deplore in this sort of rigorism regarding the gift the echo of a certain theological current that has so severed agape from eros as to reduce the former to a sterile, almost suicidal expenditure of love,[121] most notably (and most disastrously) represented by the work of Anders Nygren.[122] This (utterly Kantian) current so exaggerates the selflessness of divine love as effectively to evacuate the image of God of all those qualities of delight, desire, jealousy, and regard that Scripture ascribes to him. Such a separation of loves receives perhaps its appropriate parody in the image of an endless and disinterested outpouring of nothing toward nothingness. But in what sense, precisely, is an agape purified of eros distinguishable from hate? Or utter indifference? In what sense is the bounty of such a love distinguishable from the disposal of the superfluous? Would there not be something demonic in a love without enchantment, without a desire for the other, a longing to dwell with and be recognized by the other? In truth, there is already something extremely strange in Derrida's argument against the language of the metaphysics of plenitude and the generosity of the Good, and for a discourse of the poverty and "nothinging" of being, on the basis of a presumed incompatibility between charity and eros (how, after all, unless one accepts a metaphysics of supereminence, can one move so easily from moral to ontological categories?), that I am not entirely certain that the dewy opalescence of Derrida's celebrity has not blinded many readers to the feebleness of his reasoning here. But, from the standpoint of Christian thought, the most questionable aspect of Derrida's account of the gift is not so much its "nihilist" contour as the ethical purism that underlies it, the rigid definition of gratuity that prevents him from assaying a somewhat less dogmatic and inflexible interpretation of exchange. The emaciated agape that gives without reserve but also without desire of return can never be anything but the energy of an absolute debt, the superincumbent burden that exacts from being an impossible, infinite return; but if divine agape is generous in another sense, if it is actually *charitable* by giving way to otherness, by desiring the other dearly enough to give in a way that liberates the other even as it "binds" the other — by desiring the other, that is, as the very impulse of charity, and thereby relieving the other of any debt of pure and disinterested return — then the idea of the gift may yet prove resistant to too astringent an ethical purism. Truly, only when a giver desires a return, and indeed in some sense desires back the gift itself, can a gift be given as something other than sheer debt; only the

121. Milbank, "Can a Gift?" 132.
122. Anders Nygren, *Agape and Eros,* trans. Philip S. Watson (London: SPCK, 1982).

liberating gesture of a gift given out of desire is one that cannot morally coerce another, and so can reveal the prior, aneconomic rationality of giving that escapes every calculation. Absolute "selfless" gratuity, which will not submit to reciprocation, is pure power; but interested exchange — even though sin inevitably corrupts all exchange with the shadow of coercion and greed — is not simply an economy over against which the impossible gift stands as a dialectical counter, but is able rather to manifest a more primordial free gesture (free because it seeks a return and so is not simply "necessary") that underlies and ultimately exceeds any economy. In simple human terms, a love that is inseparable from an interest in the other is always more commendable, more truly selfless, than the airless purity of disinterested expenditure, because it recognizes the otherness and delights in the splendor of the other. The Christian thought of God's creative agape has nothing to do with the sublime and sublimely disinterested abyss of the One, but belongs to the thought of the Trinity: it is a love always of recognition and delight, desiring all and giving all at once, giving to receive and receiving to give, generous not in thoughtlessly squandering itself, but in truly wanting the other. Thus the "ethical" must belong, for theology, to an aesthetics of desire: of gratuity, grace, pleasure, eros, and interest at once. A Christian ethics cannot help but concern itself with the cultivation of desire, with learning to desire the other because the other is truly desirable, because every other is truly beautiful; the moral task is to love because one truly sees and to see because one truly loves: to educate vision to see the glory of *this particular one*. The wish of Levinasians, by contrast, to free the other of "my" intentionality, only reduces the other to an anonymous opacity, a mere formal instance of an infinite alterity that impends upon, but cannot inhabit, the sphere of the gaze. But the most *moral* of labors is that of being moved to love by the infinite particularity of the other, to desire the aesthetic unrepeatability of the other, and to be drawn out into a distance determined by and shared with the other; the ethical lies in awakening to the reality of the beauty that God shapes in his image, over a shared distance. This is the trinitarian grammar of the good; upon the gracious distance of this original aesthetics of love, the ethical as an independent and prior category, unlearned in desire, can only intrude. Love is capable of an *epektasis* toward the truly desirable, a stretching out that is not a backward speculative return to metaphysical identity or moral withdrawal into subjective probity, but a "return" always to the outwardness of the gift, an ecstasy able to claim the other as beloved and desired in a trinitarian way: possession by way of dispossession, gratification of desire through the discovery of another. Such a desire is the only blessing worth receiving, because it extends desire and love even to those who think themselves undesired and unloved, and because it remembers and calls back those who would otherwise be forgotten.

A love that is at once agape and eros can never be reduced to the calculation of indebtedness, because the claim the gift makes upon the recipient is already "presumptuous": it is already an entreaty to consent to be loved and to love in return. Thus the obligation of gratitude is also a burden charitably assumed, a response that — because it is desired — can never simply be owed. Rather than the gift being a dissimulation of debt and power, perhaps all economies of debt and power sinfully mask the original language of love that is born of the gift; perhaps the exchange of desire and delight, the charitable longing for the other made tangible in the exchange of signs of regard, is the prior truth of the gift, as it is given perfectly, by God; there is no compelling reason (save prejudice) to assume the opposite. Then it would follow that the gift is no gift, but only bondage to an inaccessible and so absolute benefactor, precisely if it is not a sign of interest. And this also means that true generosity liberates from debt because it must, to declare true interest, give again. This is the unanticipated strangeness of the divine economy of the gift: the giving of the gift and the return of the gift are accomplished at once, and then assured by further giving. Indeed, one might add to Bordieu's two reflexive definitions of the gift — difference and delay — a third definition: the gift is recognizable, apart from other economies of exchange, because it can and must be given again. For a number of reasons: firstly, because a gift given once and once only, without any prior or posterior supplement, is indistinguishable from the formal discharge of a customary obligation, an indifferently imparted token deserving no response, an impertinent attempt to obligate another, an accident, or an aborted overture to a genuine act of generosity, and so declares neither interest nor generosity; secondly, unlike the repeated practice of giving that belongs to a strictly defined system of exchanged benefits (such as paying one's rent), the gift is shown to be a gift because it can be repeated even in the absence of an "appropriate" or clearly defined response, because, that is, it insistently declares even an unwelcome or unreciprocated love or regard, despite discouragement or excessive delay; thirdly, because a gift is hermeneutically impenetrable if it occurs only once, in an instant, and so must always be given both as promise and as substance, and again as memory, and then again as repetition, ad infinitum (much as the gift of an engagement ring is no gift without the endlessly renewed and endlessly varied giving of the substance of the giver, out of desire and delight). And it is precisely this interminable and ungovernable giving again that lifts the gift out of all calculable and ethically categorizable systems of debt: the entreaty of a gift declaring love — say flowers — may evince some form of obligation from the recipient, but at the same time obliges the giver to show that the entreaty is real, that its impulse is steadfast and at the same time various, that it perseveres and at the same time can express itself in many ways. Because the sign of the gift is manifestly a sign of interest, desiring a return of signs also declaring interest, there is no prior ethical purity or singularity to which the return of the gift must answer, but only the shared medium of dependency, longing, generosity, and charity whereby love is simultaneously expressed and created by the exchange of signs. Though, indeed, the giver must not *presume* gratitude, he would be cruel (Prometheanly cruel) not to desire it. And of course, but for the continued exchange of signs over a long and undefined period, regard is never fully or truly declared; the still more fundamental delay of the gift lies not in the singular interval between *this* gift and *that* response, but the delay of any final, immediate, and total expression of the interest given form by this ceaseless language of love, this constant giving and receiving, throughout time. Indeed, as the trinitarian economy of salvation reveals, God gives again even the gift cast away, and indeed gives the response that those who have received the gift can no longer make; this is not the economy of an infinite multiplication of indebtedness, as Nietzsche claimed, but an infinite "economy" in which debt cannot be calculated because remission from debt is given before any debt can become a stabilizing power of obligation. The gift of creation draws the creature from the first into the language of address and response that is the trinitarian life, in which the response is always given for the other, on behalf of the other, and always received as something not simply required but longed for, requested, besought. By the gift being given again, debt is not infinitely multiplied (the "debt," as Anselm points out, is already infinite), but is revealed to be itself the gift discovered anew, revealed as a *felix culpa* even as it is discharged. And in the giving of the gift distance is given and sustained, by way of repetition and reclaiming: the distance that mediates, that allows one to see and desire the other, that allows the other to be truly and irreducibly other, and that may be crossed.

Ultimately for Christian thought the gift cannot be conceived apart from trinitarian dogma.[123] To believe in the possibility of the gift within the immanent exchanges of finite existence is to believe in the possibility of analogy, the possibility that what is given can be received differently and restored, without alienation from itself and without the entire dynamism of exchange being reduced to a single uniform reality like the circulation of power and debt. To believe that the gift can cross distance, make absence into a living and traversable distance, and so give distance is to believe that at the surface of being, in its semeiological and metaphoric supplementarity, there can be a real sequence of impartation and restoration, a real and inventive expression of love, a real paratactic enrichment of and so exposition of the gift, and that no narrative of

---

123. For a recent attempt to rescue the thought of the gift from Derrida's rigorist distinction between the extravagance of the gift and the economy of exchange according to trinitarian doctrine, see Stephen H. Webb, *The Gifting God: A Trinitarian Ethics of Excess* (Oxford: Oxford University Press, 1996).

depths (no metaphysics of power, no metanarrative of exchange) can account for its prodigal and gracious excesses. It is to believe that surfaces are "profounder" than "depths." Or rather, dependent upon the trinitarian narrative, Christian thought is prohibited from imagining a depth that is determinative of or more authoritative than the incalculably various exposition of the surface, the manifold and interminable richness of the language of exchange. In the Trinity the gift is entire, and entirely "exposed": the Father gives himself to the Son, and again to the Spirit, and the Son offers everything up to the Father in the Spirit, and the Spirit returns all to the Father through the Son, eternally. Love of, the gift to, and delight in the other is one infinite dynamism of giving and receiving, in which desire at once beholds and donates the other. And creation is always already implicated in this giving of the gift because it is — in being inaugurated by the Father, effected by the Son, and perfected by the Spirit — already a gift shared among the persons of the Trinity, in transit, a word spoken by God in his Word and articulated in endless sequences of difference by the Spirit and offered back to the Father. Creation is a gift already given and already restored, that is received back even as it is given, constituted by divine desire and pleasing to God in its constitution. The Trinity, in a sense, is the "economy" of the gift, from which individual instances of ethical subjectivity cannot be extracted. God has no simple subjectivity to guard, nor any that can accumulate credit; God is God in and only in the giving of the gift, in the establishing of "personality" in the extravagant giving away of his wealth — his *ousia* — and in the always delighted receiving of all his wealth, substance, essence, and life. As, in its every eventuation, a repetition of the motion of the gift that is the divine life, creation is an effect of desire, and its beauty is that which reveals the divine agape and the divine eros to be one and the same. Creation is, before all else, given by God to God, and only then — through the pneumatological generosity of the trinitarian life — given to creatures: a gift that *is* only so long as it is given back, passed on, received and imparted not as a possession but always as grace. This is indeed a "circle" — the infinite circle of divine love — and for that very reason capable of a true gift: one that draws creatures into a circle upon which they have no natural "right" to intrude. And if creatures participate in God's language of love — in this erotic charity of the gift — simply by being creatures, it is all but impossible for them not also to give, not to extend signs of love to others, not to donate themselves entirely to the economy of agape; the gift must be actively withheld not to be given. Such is sin: suppression of the gift, so that distance becomes absence, without substance, without presence; for presence and substance are the effects of a certain style of transmission, a certain charitable measuring out of all the intervals of created being, and when sin corrupts the language of giving, the gift is lost. In God, though, nothing is lost, and the substance of hope lies in the knowledge that God has given — and will give — again.

iii. Desire's Power

This is also to say that, for Christian thought, the true creativity of desire must be inseparable from charity. I say this with an eye to that other current within postmodern discourse, the Nietzschean analytic of desire, and of its positivity and creativity, especially as developed in the work of Deleuze — a current that may seem to run contrary to the Levinasian or Derridean language of the "ethical" but which in fact merely mirrors its surreptitious and dreary subjectivism. In his earlier phase, particularly in *Nietzsche and Philosophy*, Deleuze speaks primarily of power, or the will to power, which measures itself out, increases itself, spontaneously extends itself for the purpose of delight, without need of the negative influence of pain to stir it into action;[124] in later works the language of power is gradually displaced by that of desire, but this reflects no appreciable change in emphasis: desire, for Deleuze, is power, and delight is always somehow an aggression. A delight evoked by the adventitious event of the beautiful would be, for Deleuze, a passive and reactive sentiment, and nothing more. For him, therefore, desire is an eruptive "singularity," a creative force that posits what it wants and destroys and creates in order to attain it; though it does forge real connections between singularities and across series, desire is without telos, and it has its specific "perfection" within itself; it is an *energeia* (which is a force emanating from within itself) rather than a kinesis (which is "Platonic," a mimetic force of attraction). Desire proceeds not from lack, that is, but from an interior richness of disruptive and productive power.[125]

Without dwelling overlong on this matter, it would be wise to note (for the purpose of further advancing our story) the theological alternative. Certainly the Christian way of describing desire and its creativity cannot possibly be confined to the narrow interstice lying between active and reactive passions. Created things must always move, and "desire" is the proper name for the force of movement (τῆς κατ᾽ ἔφεσιν κινήσεως τὴν δύναμιν, as Maximus says),[126] but desire must be conceived as neither simply lack nor energy, neither poverty nor wealth, but as a simultaneous power of giving and receiving, creating and being drawn, inventing and thereby finding the object of desire. In God desire both evokes and is evoked; it is one act that for us can be grasped only by analogy to that constant dynamism within our being that comprises the distinct but inseparable moments of interior energy and exterior splendor. In the life of the

124. Gilles Deleuze, *Nietzsche and Philosophy*, trans. Hugh Tomlinson (New York: Columbia University Press, 1983), 59, 206.

125. See especially Gilles Deleuze and Félix Guattari, *Capitalism and Schizophrenia: Anti-Oedipus*, trans. Robert Hurley, Mark Seem, and Helen R. Lane (New York: Viking Press, 1983), 10-36.

126. *Liber Ambiguorum* VII (*PG*, 91:1069B-C).

Trinity, the other is given by desire and also calls forth desire; God is both address and response, gift and appealing radiance. And it is of this love that both ventures forth and is drawn out that creation is a rephrasing, an "object" of divine delight precisely in being a gift of divine love, shining within the infinitely accomplished joy — the *apatheia* — of the Trinity; and so creation is imparted to creatures also as the desirable and the delightful, as something that can be truly seen only through a certain creative volition toward it, and as something that always evokes from creatures more than their creative intentionality would be adequate to provide. Both lack and plenitude, poverty and wealth, abide in such longing: nothing can be entirely possessed nor anything entirely lost. Invention and fortuity, creativity and responsiveness, power and powerlessness cannot be discriminated into the sealed categories of what acts and what reacts, what evokes or is evoked; the dynamism of desire is entire only in the mutual play of donation and restoration, which is our participation in the "intellect" and "will" — the Logos and Spirit — of the Father, the outpouring and offering up of God's fullness, the gift and (with all "delay" and difference, but without division or privation) its return. Really, it is banal to limit the creativity of desire to some model of Dionysian *energeia,* jealously guarded against any hint of mimetic kinesis (and this latter, consequently, reduced to a pusillanimous pathos), and doubly banal to insist that desire must be defined in terms determined either by its "object" or its "subject" rather than by a more primordial belonging together of beloved and lover, "thing" and "sign," world and soul. Desire is creative when it is directed not only toward a particular *quid,* but toward a certain radiance, a certain ordination and ordonnance of all things, a certain rhythm that places all things in peaceful sequences of donation and redonation; desire creates in finding proportions of peace. This is the secret of true art, which both speaks and receives the world in one integral movement of generosity and gratitude. And if desire belongs most properly not to some tension between *eidos* and simulacrum, nor to a spontaneous and autotelic force of pure volition, but concerns itself more properly with the gravity and ordering of every series, sin is a desire that proceeds according to a false or violent ordering: an orientation not toward an evil object (within creation, no object is inherently evil), nor even toward the gravity of any particular object, but toward that which is, quite literally, exorbitant, outside every series of God's *kabod* and creative love. Sin is the repetition of an absence, whose logic is suppression, aversion, and privation. But creative desire seeks a greater fullness of the splendor of being's whole display, creation's beauty in all its depth, by taking up the "theme" that God states in creation, elaborating upon it, and devising measures of accord.

To revisit briefly, then, a theme already touched upon: it is in terms of this divine delight that gives being and also regards it, desires it, that theology may speak of the affirmation of being, because such delight belongs to a very particular kind of distance. The Nietzschean strain in the postmodern — found in differing quantities in Deleuze, Foucault, Derrida, Lyotard, and a host of others — invariably terminates in a kind of jubilant delirium, a joyous passion that can affirm the play of the world in all its prodigal wastefulness, without resentment and despite all suffering; this is the only ethos of which a univocal or Dionysian narrative of being is capable, its highest possible value. As I have complained, though, the affirmation of being in general affirms nothing in particular; an absolute generality of being may assure the absolute difference of particularity, but this is also to say its absolute indifference (such is the irony of the absolute); and, as I have also complained, this language of Dionysian affirmation marks only the finest distinction in feeling, an arbitrary judgment pronounced upon the whole of things, without any scope of analogical discrimination. As much as Deleuze and others may invoke the Nietzschean talk of evaluation (that is, the creation of values through aesthetic judgment), affirmation must still be univocal — must still be of the whole — in order to be any sort of affirmation at all, as Nietzsche well understood. The eventuation of *chronos* upon the aleatory point of *aion*, the *es gibt* of being, the eternal return (or what you will) is that moment where election and rejection, affirmation and the curse, are one and the same. Deleuze, in particular, so insists on being's "necessity" — so that no "outward" context, no transcendental contours or exteriors, can determine the value of what is — that no distance is possible for this judgment; in such a scheme, affirmation concerns not the content of particular differences but only difference as such, which is a kind of indivisible universal. When being is so sealed off against analogy, it can be grasped only as a totality, a contained Heracleitean flow, an economy of violence. Inevitably the game of Dionysus is one in which the stakes are all and nothing simultaneously, one that can be played with equal elation and indifference in a summer meadow or a death camp. Dionysus may be, as Deleuze often remarks, πολυγηθής,[127] god of many joys, but he is also πολυφθόρος, a baneful and destructive god, ἀνθρωπορραίστης,[128] the one who rends men asunder, the god who delights in the sword and the spilling of blood.[129] Dionysus is the god who measures himself to become greater, more sublime, and is consequently the god who must destroy, who must be cruel, to find his measure; he is the god who is torn apart, and so the god who is served and affirmed when Pentheus is torn apart. But the Christian affirmation of creation, which is no less an affirmation

---

127. See Hesiod, *Works and Days* 614; Pindar, fragment 153.2.

128. Aelian, *Various History* 12.34: a name that recalls the Dionysiac practice of human immolation through dismemberment, as reported by Porphyry, *De abstinentia* 2.55.

129. *Orphic Hymn* 45.3.

of all things, proceeds from a different understanding of being. Because God creates for his pleasure, without need, he does so at a distance of appraisal and approbation, an aesthetic distance; this is also the distance of judgment, of election and rejection, from which God pronounces creation good with an "ontological justice" that also, at the same time, condemns much that occurs among creatures. It is not simply difference as such upon which God bestows his approbation, but the content of what differs, the particularity of each thing, the creature's place in the analogical discourse that creation is. Dionysus is a god who cavorts among corpses, and thus affirms all things; the God who creates for his delight and out of love pursues his lost even into the depths of hell, and thus affirms all things. The play of Dionysus is nothing like the play of Wisdom before the throne of God; the latter rejoices in a gift that, once given, is desired back by the giver (which is to say a true gift, a gift of boundless worth, given to the other, in trust that the other will respond). Nietzschean postmodernism's "affirmation" might just as well be the oblivion of the One of Plotinus, turned unrelatedly inward (*Enneads* 6.8.17), or of Aristotle's Prime Mover; Dionysus cannot be concerned — in the midst of being's wanton and extravagant play — with lost sheep. The God of the Bible, however, turns to face creation from the first, in making it, and then in calling it good; he gives creation at a distance, and continues to regard it, continues to await its response, its repetition of the gift, and in this way opens the distance of critique, judgment, and redemption. Because being's differences are affirmed in their particularity, because God elects *just these* differences, and delights in them, and desires them for himself, he does not merely consign difference to fate, to the irretrievable flow of time, but also acts to liberate what he makes from sin and death: this is his infinite "it is good."

This is to say, simply enough, that God regards creation in its beauty, and simultaneously that God is transcendent. Because God's distance from creation is analogous to the distance of the divine life, because the God who differentiates differs yet again in being the distance of that which is not God but which expresses his glory — because he pours out his distance again as the only *chora* of those who had no being — God creates a world good in its very distinction from the divine; and thus its goodness is perfectly aesthetic. Only what is set at a distance, one might say, is in any sense good or beautiful (indeed, as one current of Byzantine reflection would have it, hell is nothing but the absolute proximity of God's glory without the interval of the gift: God's glory encountered as sublimity rather than beauty).[130] When Deleuze writes that "The idea of posi-

130. See Maximus, *Quaestiones ad Thalassium* 59 (*PG*, 90:609A-B), on the eschatological encounter of all persons with the kingdom of God, either according to grace or apart from grace; see also Lossky, *Mystical Theology*, 178-79, 234-35; and see my remarks on eschatology below.

tive distance belongs to topology and to the surface. It excludes all depth and all elevation, which would restore the negative and identity,"[131] he means to exclude not only the Hegelian myth of determining negation but every form of transcendence, which he quaintly assumes must always concern itself with negation and identity. But clearly another sort of transcendence is implied by the Christian dogma of God's free creation: neither that of the Platonic exemplar, in the eminent hierarchy of resemblance, nor that of the Hegelian Concept, presiding emptily over the diremptive dialectics of *Geist,* nor that of the emanative abyss of the One. The transcendence of Being over beings — of God over creatures — is such that the very otherness of the transcendent is the intimate actuality of everything in its particularity. Because of his insistence upon the singularity of "substance" (the univocity of being), Deleuze never succeeds at thinking difference as radically as Christian thought does in thinking creation; for only as a kind of expressive rhetoric, analogically removed from every continuity of "substance," is difference real, open to ranges of truly free complexity. Deleuze — the case of Deleuze — grandly illustrates the paradox of attempting to think difference within the confines of a thoroughgoing and univocal immanentism: the thought of difference inevitably becomes indistinguishable from the most absolutist variety of monism (what Hegel would call Spinozan emanationism, though Deleuze prefers the term "immanation"). Difference as such, for Deleuze, is uniform, tautological, capable of no dynamism but violence, devoid of any analogical orderings that would give the particular shape and content of what differs any meaning, or that could liberate that shape or that content from a false or destructive series. Deleuze would have it no other way. But for Christian thought it is God's transcendence that alone allows difference to differ, that permits a common thematic medium between different series, that gives them their ability to elaborate upon and embellish one another, and that looks upon, loves, and elects what differs. Because creation is "not God" in that time when God is most surely God — as the creative God of triune love — a distinction may be made between being (which is the glory of God) and the structures of sin, without thereby succumbing to the metaphysical temptation to reduce all difference to untruth. It is the style of impartation — not simply the "essence" of what is given — that determines the goodness of the gift. And to the transcendent God no detail of what is given is dispensable, nor any necessary; and so he is able at once to affirm and judge, to pronounce all things good and to condemn evil, without contradiction. It is as the transcendent God that he blesses difference in its immanence.

131. Gilles Deleuze, *The Logic of Sense,* trans. Mark Lester (New York: Columbia University Press, 1990), 173.

2. As God is Trinity, in whom all difference is possessed as perfect peace and unity, the divine life might be described as infinite music, and creation too might be described as a music whose intervals, transitions, and phrases are embraced within God's eternal, triune polyphony.

Sing unto the LORD, all the earth; shew forth from day to day his salvation. Declare his glory among the heathen; his marvellous works among all nations. . . . Let the heavens be glad, and let the earth rejoice: and let men say among the nations, The LORD reigneth. Let the sea roar, and the fulness thereof: let the fields rejoice, and all that is therein. Then shall the trees of the wood sing out at the presence of the LORD, because he cometh to judge the earth.

1 Chron. 17:23-24, 31-33

One thing have I desired of the LORD, that will I seek after; that I may dwell in the house of the LORD all the days of my life, to behold the beauty of the LORD, and to inquire in his temple. For in the time of trouble he shall hide me in his pavilion: in the secret of his tabernacle shall he hide me; he shall set me up upon a rock. And now shall mine head be lifted up above mine enemies round about me: therefore will I offer in his tabernacle sacrifices of joy; I will sing, yea, I will sing praises unto the LORD.

Ps. 27:4-6

By him therefore let us offer the sacrifice of praise to God continually, that is, the fruit of our lips giving thanks to his name.

Heb. 13:15

And a voice came out of the throne, saying, Praise our God, all ye his servants, and ye that fear him, both small and great. And I heard as it were the voice of a great multitude, and as the voice of many waters, and as the voice of mighty thunderings, saying, Alleluia: for the Lord God omnipotent reigneth. Let us be glad and rejoice, and give honour to him: for the marriage of the Lamb is come, and his wife hath made herself ready.

Rev. 19:5-7

i. The Divine Theme

According to Gregory of Nyssa, creation is a wonderfully wrought hymn to the power of the Almighty: the order of the universe is a kind of musical harmony, richly and multifariously toned, guided by an inward rhythm and accord, pervaded by an essential "symphony"; the melody and cadence of the cosmic elements in their intermingling sing of God's glory, as does the interrelation of motion and rest within created things; and in this sympathy of all things one with the other, music in its truest and most perfect form is bodied forth (*IIP* 1.3: 30-33). The idea of a *musica mundana* or *harmonia mundi* is an ancient one, found in pagan philosophy, from Pythagoreanism to Neoplatonism, and in numerous patristic sources. It exercised a rare fascination for Renaissance and baroque theology, philosophy, and art (as evidenced in, for example, Luis de León's great ode to God's harmony in creation). There are abundant biblical reasons, quite apart from the influences of pagan philosophy, for Christians to speak of the *harmonia mundi:* in Scripture creation rejoices in God, proclaims his glory, sings before him; the pleasing conceits of pagan cosmology aside, theology has all the warrant it needs for speaking of creation as a divine composition, a magnificent music, whose measures and refrains rise up to the pleasure and the glory of God.[132] Augustine, reflecting on the transience of created things, suggests that the beauty of the world, like that of a poem (declaimed, of course, by a rhapsode), lies in its transitions (*De vera religione* 21.40-43); and at one point he argues that the beauty of the cosmos can no more be grasped by creatures than can the beauty of a poem by the discrete syllables that must pass away in order to bring it about (*De musica* 6.11.30). Admittedly, such language can easily lapse into a quite conventional philosophical resignation, willing to absolve the world of its suffering and despair on account of the aesthetic necessity for splashes of poignant contrast within creation's chiaroscuro. The truly interesting feature of Augustine's thought on the matter, though, is his way of

---

132. The image of a cosmic harmony, or of creation as music, recurs often enough in the tradition of Western literature that a comprehensive catalogue of citations is quite impossible; one might call attention, however, to Plato's *Republic* 10.617b-c, Aristotle's *Metaphysics* 14.6, the book of Wisdom 19:18, Macrobius's *In somnium Scipionis* 2.1-4, Clement of Alexandria's *Protrepticus* 1.5, Gregory of Nyssa's *De occursu Domini* 1.422, Isidore of Seville's *Etymologiae* 3.17, and Boethius's *De institutione musica* 1.2; and given the particular favor the image enjoyed during the Renaissance and early baroque, one might also mention the *Orchestra* of Sir John Davies, the *Davideis* of Abraham Cowley, Henry Vaughan's "The Morning Watch," Crashaw's *Sospetto d'Herode* 26.6 and *The Teare* 1.141, Milton's *Arcades* 72-73, his second *Prolusion,* and *Paradise Lost* 3.579 and 5.178, Dryden's *A Song for St. Cecilia's Day,* and Martin Fotherby's *Atheomastix* 2.12.4; and one should, of course, make mention of certain lines from Shakespeare (such as *The Merchant of Venice* 5.1.60-65) and Henry Purcell's exquisitely beautiful *Ode on St. Cecilia's Day* of 1692, set to words by Nicholas Brady; examples are numberless.

relating the soul — as a rhythmic sequence, a repetition that retains the memory of what has gone before — to the rhythms of creation: virtue is, he argues (very like Gregory), the establishment of the soul's proper rhythm (*De quantitate animae* 55); and the soul that is virtuous is one that turns its rhythms (or numbers, *numeri*) not to the domination of others, but to their benefit (*De musica* 6.14.45). Augustine is not entirely original here (there are Stoic precedents for such language), but his treatment of the theme does exemplify one palpable shift from the pagan to the Christian understanding of world harmony. As Leo Spitzer, in his magisterial *Classical and Christian Ideas of World Harmony*, remarks, "According to the Pythagoreans, it was cosmic order which was identifiable with music; according to the Christian philosophers, it was love. And in the *ordo amoris* of Augustine we have evidently a blend of the Pagan and the Christian themes: henceforth 'order' is love."[133] Such a change in emphasis was natural: for Christian dogma all beauty and order belong eminently to the order of the trinitarian relations, and so have no basis profounder than love.

Here, it seems to me, is the chief appeal of this tradition: the image of cosmic music is an especially happy way of describing the analogy of creation to the trinitarian life. Creation is not, that is, a music that explicates some prior and undifferentiated content within the divine, nor the composite order that is, of necessity, imposed upon some intractable substrate so as to bring it into imperfect conformity with an ideal harmony; it is simply another expression or inflection of the music that eternally belongs to God, to the dance and difference, address and response, of the Trinity. Lyotard, inheritor that he is of the metaphysical myth of chaos, imagines divinely heard music as white noise, "collapsed" sound, a singularity that must explode in order to become music at all, in order for difference to escape from the Same.[134] Between that singularity and the violence of its differentiation there is no middle term: again, the aesthetics of the beautiful is preceded and superseded by the aesthetics of the sublime, which is an aesthetics of the formless.[135] Deleuze sees all cosmic order as the dialectical residue of an absolute disorder: milieus (vibratory blocks of space-time) and rhythm, he says, are born of chaos, all milieus (which are characterized by the periodic repetition of their "directional components") open out into chaos, and the retort and riposte of milieus to chaos is rhythm.[136] A

133. Leo Spitzer, *Classical and Christian Ideas of World Harmony: Prolegomena to an Interpretation of the Word "Stimmung"* (Baltimore: Johns Hopkins University Press, 1963), 19-20.

134. Jean-François Lyotard, *The Inhuman* (Stanford: Stanford University Press, 1988), 162-63.

135. Lyotard, *The Inhuman*, 33.

136. Gilles Deleuze and Félix Guattari, *A Thousand Plateaus*, trans. Brian Massumi (Minneapolis: University of Minnesota Press, 1987), 313.

Dionysian rhythm, that is to say, embraced within the incessant drumbeat of being's *unica vox* as it repeats itself endlessly, from whose beat difference erupts as a perpetual divergence; and even if Dionysus allows the odd irenic caesura in his dance — the occasional beautiful sequence — it constitutes only a slackening of a tempo, a momentary paralysis of his limbs, a reflective interval that still never arrests the underlying beat of difference. Theology, though, starting from the Christian narrative of creation out of nothingness, effected by the power and love of the God who is Trinity, might well inquire whether rhythm could not be the prior truth of things, and chaos only an illusion, the effect of a certain convulsive or discordant beat, the repetition of a sinful series. It may well be that each and every "essence" subsists upon its own interior repetition, like the return — always varied, stated with a new beat and a different harmony — of the phrase from Monsieur Vinteuil's sonata that haunts the narrator of Proust's *À la recherche du temps perdu* for many years, and equally true that difference and repetition are the only forces of essence;[137] but does the distribution of difference occur always in the stress between a formless chaos and the invariable beat of the dance of Dionysus, or is the rhythm or music of being already sufficiently various in itself, already differentiated into analogical complexities, and already sufficiently flexible to liberate difference endlessly? Is the music of being that of Dionysus, or is it something more like infinite counterpoint, a music like Bach's? If the trinitarian life is always already one of infinite musical richness, "heard" by God in its fullness, in the inexhaustible variety of its phrasings and harmonies, and if creation is a complementary music, an endless sequence of variations upon the theme of God's eternal love, then there is no aboriginal sublime that surpasses the moment of the beautiful; rather, the sublime appears as a particularly intense serial display of beauty, a particularly weighty manifestation of God's glory (but all terror may be turned into praise). Or there is the fabricated sublimity of evil, the immense discords of sin that disrupt charity's unfolding, derange every series, and resist every analogical path of recovery of the divine theme. Being as God gives it, though, is originally nothing but degrees of splendor, hierarchies of beauty; creation *is* divine glory, told anew, and so its aesthetic variety is nothing but the differing modes and degrees with which participated being is imparted. Creation's rhythm is analogical, not the interminable monotony of the "univocal" event, and so becomes ever more actual as its complexity and beauty increase in intensity — as, that is, it participates more fully in the richness of God's infinite "form."

In a sense, the postmodern myth of the chaotic sublime is merely the current form of a rather conventional metaphysical myth of aboriginal purity. In

137. Gilles Deleuze, *Proust and Signs*, trans. Richard Howard (New York: G. Braziller, 1972), 48.

Of Grammatology, Derrida calls attention to Rousseau's distaste for overly elaborate musical forms and his conviction that a polyphonic plurality of lines represents a corruption and degradation of melody — for melody, Rousseau believed, was born in simple song, the pristine clarity of a single voice.[138] As Derrida observes, this is all part of Rousseau's nostalgia for a lost condition of natural innocence, the immediacy of the direct address, before all writing, the clarity of the true voice: the same yearning after the pure and immediate that Derrida elsewhere calls the reign of the inner ear, the belief in an oracular inwardness to hearing, a purer apprehension filtered from the contaminations of polyphony or polysemy.[139] The romance of the unwritten, the longing for immediate presence, which for Derrida constitutes the metaphysical impulse par excellence, is classically expressed in terms of a remembered paradise, a state of natural innocence, or a pure and undiluted beauty forsaken. One could equally well say, however, that it is this same romance of immediacy that the postmodern analytic of the sublime transcribes into its harsh, Dionysian key. It is instructive, for instance, that the aesthetic model to which Lyotard often adverts in his treatment of the sublime is abstract expressionism, which he appears to find uniquely suited to "representing" the unrepresentable; but there is a profound irony in this. No less than a forced and insipid classicism, abstract expressionism belongs to the tradition of Rousseauian romanticism; it presumes to "express" the artist's creative temper as an immediate presence, or attempts an immediate communication of a certain inchoate pathos, an energy or ferment. The emotional and aesthetic tumult of a purely abstract expressionist canvas merely crystallizes a certain myth of the ego as pure sensibility, pure "force" and "energy" (and all those other vacuous abstractions favored by Pollock's apologists). What is this, if not a radical discourse of presence, of an intuition of the unintuitable (like the psychotic catatonia that Deleuze and Guattari treat as an immediate intuition of the chaotic depth of being)? Is not such an aesthetics also a nostalgia for an unwritten immediacy? If the sublime of romanticism and postmodernism alike manifests itself as formless force, it is still a sublime whose nature has somehow thereby been grasped, as that which is *ultimately* unharmonizable in difference.[140] But, again, how can an entirely immanent perspective determine how the unrepresentable sublime "looks" or "sounds"? What if abstraction can itself all too easily become conventional, invariable, confining, and trite, incapable of any imaginative departures or ex-

138. Jacques Derrida, *Of Grammatology,* trans. Gayatri Chakravorty Spivak (Baltimore: Johns Hopkins University Press, 1974), 195-200.

139. Jacques Derrida, *Margins of Philosophy,* trans. Alan Bass (Chicago: University of Chicago Press, 1982), xvii.

140. Lyotard, *The Inhuman,* 4.

pressive quantities, while real "expression" is always a sequence of interrelated differences, analogies, icons, styles of mediation? The question of taste aside, it may just as well be representational art — whether that of Giotto or Francis Bacon — that offers a greater vantage upon being's "sublimities," precisely because it shows being as the repetition of analogies, representations, signs, mediations, and differences, harmonized in an incalculable complexity; perhaps the "true sublime" is seen in Vermeer's luminous vacancies or Titian's fabulous azures, where it appears as radiance, mystery, attendant upon form. Perhaps the true sublime is endless mediacy, endless and beautiful deferral. Similarly, Deleuze (commendably uninterested in abstract expressionism), in trying to transcribe the sensibility of the baroque into that of the aleatory and atonal (which he should do more to distinguish from one another), fails to account for the oddity that all aleatory music is more or less the same, precisely because it emancipates difference in the form of a digression that must scrupulously avoid not only the patterns of tonality but every transmission of structure; one is confronted here by an aesthetics that renders the difference of each note from every other absolutely indifferent, because the effect of an aleatory straying proves remarkably and tediously uniform, varying only in degrees of intensity. The difference that Deleuze's aesthetics of being celebrates is rather like the difference of one suburban shopping mall from another; it has nothing to do with the anfractuous effusions of baroque ornamentation, but inevitably proves to be merely the formal distinctness of interchangeable ciphers; and here Deleuze betrays his own insights regarding difference and repetition. Repetition is impossible without, at least, a serial analogy of one moment to the next, a thematic motif upon which elaborations can be worked, a first gesture; and difference can emerge only from this ramifying power of analogy. As Schönberg realized, in moving from atonal music to the twelve-tone row, the differentiation of the particular musical moment is achieved through just this analogical divergence, in the course of a thematic transmission within a tonic structure, whereas an oceanic totality always threatens to engulf difference when the atonal dissolves into the merely aleatory. Can there be real difference that does not arise within a thematic motion? Can there be a theme that is not also already a changing, disseminative diversity? And is the language of the sublime that postmodernism often adopts not then a new version of romantic Sturm und Drang, indeed the last gasp of romanticism?

Honestly, it is difficult to be convinced by a discourse of difference and distance that attempts at the same time to be a discourse of Heracleitean flux, because there is no distance in the flux: all dimensions are consumed before they arise. This is the "totality" in the aleatory: every moment of repetition is a singularity that entirely (or, if one prefers, virtually) contains the shape of the whole, a Leibnizian monad that is no longer in any meaningful sense a "perspective" on the whole, because the whole is a sublime, unmediated, absolute presence. For Christian thought, on the other hand, true distance is given in an event, a motion, that is transcendent: a pure prolation in which all patterns are "anticipated," in an infinitely fulfilled way that allows for every possibility; it even makes space for the possibilities of discord, while also always providing, out of its analogical bounty, ways of return, of unwinding the coils of sin, of healing the wounds of violence (the Holy Spirit is a supremely inventive composer). It is transcendence, the divine distance, with its analogical scope, that prevents presence from being totality, and this distance is the original "thematism" — the transcendent act of music — that makes real difference possible: repetition can occur only within a thematism that differentiates repetition from what it repeats, and yet allows it to be, quite precisely, repetition. This "first difference" is the ontological difference, the primordial analogical disproportion between God's infinite transcendence and finite becoming that is the act of creation. This difference is itself the theme, present in every moment of the ontic, that inaugurates all the variations of finitude; and as this difference is a movement of grace within the triune act of divine being, all the variations that follow from it testify to the Trinity (in their being, form, and particular splendor). If for Lyotard the sublime (conceived as the unpresentable) must be the starting point of modern aesthetics,[141] beauty remains the still more original point of departure for a Christian aesthetics, because the sheer interminability of beauty's serial display can always overtake every invariable sublimity, and submit it to the analogy of beauty. The beautiful surpasses the sublime because beauty is capable of endless intricacy, and so is able to "present" anything; and the sublime, whether as an effect of immensity or disorder, still never ceases to belong to an infinite display that, from another vantage, may be grasped in its beauty (and, within this display, other perspectives are never wanting). The quantity of beauty always appears in a distance that is the distance of God, and seen thus, it appears as glory, weight, splendor. And the ordering of desire toward the infinite God allows creatures to see all the differences of creation not only as proximate mediations of divine glory, but also as mediated goods in and of themselves: for it is God who differentiates, places, and discloses, God who, as Dionysius says, keeps all elements in their separateness and their harmony (*Divine Names* 8.7). An infinite gravity — an infinite *kabod*, an infinitely determinate beauty — embraces and gives weight to the rhythms of creation. In God, then, lies the infinite horizon of the beautiful, its always greater spaciousness, the splendor of a boundless freedom that shows it-

141. Jean-François Lyotard, *The Postmodern Explained: Correspondence, 1982-1985,* trans. Don Berry, Bernadette Maher, Julian Pefanis, Virginia Spate, and Morgan Thomas (Minneapolis: University of Minnesota Press, 1992), 10-11.

self in the for-itself of beauty; hence the end of desire for the beautiful lies nowhere in the totality of things but in the act that lets them be, which lies beyond the serener horizons of phenomenology and hermeneutics, the topology of the one and the grammar of the other, the hierarchy and hypotaxis of both. This is why beauty's sudden extravagance and excess is uncontainable, and more uncontrollable than the sublime, more dynamic, while the sublime (however conceived) is at most a moment of seemingly formless stress and restiveness within a greater energy, appearing as such on account of its essentially *weaker* grasp of being's infinite determinacy and beauty.

The great problem with a philosopher of chaos like Deleuze, with his insistence upon the internal spontaneity and eruptive force of the energy of difference, is that he fails to be sufficiently superficial: he fails to attend to the way in which difference concretely occurs, in sequences of positionings, interdependencies, and analogies that make room for one another. One might best characterize the properly Christian understanding of being as polyphony or counterpoint: having received its theme of divine love from God, the true measure of being is expressed in the restoration of that theme, in the response that submits that theme to variation and offers it back in an indefinitely prolonged and varied response (guided by the Spirit's power of modulation). There is no substance to creation apart from these variations on God's outpourings of infinite love; all the themes of creation depart from the first theme that is mysteriously unfolded in the Trinity, forever complete and forever calling forth new intonations, new styles of accompaniment and response. The circular, "synthetic," and pleromatic grandeur of the Hegelian infinite and the chaotic, univocal, and unharmonizable flux of the postmodern infinite are equally dreary; but the Christian infinite, free of the mechanical hypotaxis of the one and the boring boisterousness of the other, yields a profuse and irreducible parataxis, a boundless flood of beauties, beyond synthesis, but utterly open to analogy, complexity, variations, and refrains. Within such an infinite, the Spirit's power to redeem discordant lines is one not of higher resolution but of reorientation, a restoration of each line's scope of harmonic openness to every other line. It is the promise of Christian faith that, eschatologically, the music of all creation will be restored not as a totality in which all the discords of evil necessarily participated, but as an accomplished harmony from which all such discords, along with their false profundities, have been exorcised by way of innumerable "tonal" (or pneumatological) reconciliations. This is the sense in which theology should continue to speak of the world in terms of a *harmonia mundi,* a *musica mundana,* or the song of creation.

A cautionary note, though, must be sounded when speaking of creation's "theme," at least at present. Derrida has expressed his impatience with any attempt to interpret texts according to "themes," stable meanings that somehow mysteriously abide throughout the full play of the text's signification; one does not escape the "Platonism" of treating a text as mere referential mimesis, he admonishes, by turning to themes and ideas, but simply arrives at a worse Platonism: one goes from Plato to Hegel, from mere mimetic doubling to totalizing system.[142] To avoid misunderstanding, therefore, let me stipulate that creation can never be understood, in Christian thought, simply as a text that conceals a more fundamental set of abstract meanings, to which all its particularities can be reduced; when I use the word "theme" here, I mean it in its strictly musical sense, to indicate a phrase or motif, a point of departure, which is neither more true nor less complex than the series of variations to which it gives rise. The "theme" of creation is the gift of the whole, committed to limitless possibilities, open to immeasurable ranges of divergence and convergence, consonance and dissonance (which always allows for the possibility of discord), and unpredictable modulations that at once restore and restate that theme. The theme is present in all its modifications, for once it is given it is recuperated throughout, not as a return of the Same but as gratitude, as a new giving of the gift, as what is remembered and as what, consequently, is invented. The truth of the theme is found in its unfolding, forever. God's glory is an infinite "thematism" whose beauty and variety can never be exhausted, and as the richness of creation traverses the distance of God's infinite music, the theme is always being given back. Because God imparts the theme, it is not simply unitary and epic but obeys a trinitarian logic: it yields to a contrapuntal multiplicity allowing for the unfolding of endlessly many differing phrases, new accords, "explicating" the "complication" of divine music. The theme is not an idea but a concrete figural substance, an insistence and recurrence, a contour of joy, a donation. In short, it is a "thematism of the surface," not a thematic "content" more essential than created difference: a style of articulation, a way of ordering desire and apprehending the "shape" of being, its proportions, dimensions, and rhythms. Being is a surface of supplementarity, an expressive fabric forever filling itself out into ever greater adornments of the divine love, a porrection of the gifts of the Holy Spirit, to creation and, thereby, to the Father.

ii. Divine Counterpoint

Bach is the greatest of Christian theologians, the most inspired witness to the *ordo amoris* in the fabric of being; not only is no other composer capable of more freely developing lines or of more elaborate structures of tonal media-

142. Jacques Derrida, *Dissemination,* trans. Barbara Johnson (Chicago: University of Chicago Press, 1981), 205-7.

tion (wheresoever the line goes, Bach is there also), but no one as compellingly demonstrates that the infinite is beauty and that beauty is infinite. It is in Bach's music, as nowhere else, that the potential boundlessness of thematic development becomes manifest: how a theme can unfold inexorably through difference, while remaining continuous in each moment of repetition, upon a potentially infinite surface of varied repetition. And it is a very particular kind of infinity that is at issue, for which there is really no other adequate aesthetic model: Wagner's "infinite" melody (so called) consists not in unmasterable variations but in the governing logic of motivic recurrences; Wagner's greatest achievements might almost be said to make audible a quintessentially Hegelian logic, in a music pervaded by the most voluptuous and luxuriant kind of metaphysical nostalgia, the "infinity" of its unbroken melodic flow being of the most synthetic variety, rationalized (or sublated) by an abstractable system of leitmotivs. Is any music more fated than that magnificent arch spanning the course from Siegfried's funeral processional to Brünnhilde's immolation and the conflagration of the gods in *Götterdämmerung?* In Bach's music, though, motion is absolute, and all thematic content is submitted to the irreducible disseminations that fill it out: each note is an unforced, unnecessary, and yet wholly fitting supplement, even when the fittingness is deferred across massive dissonances by way of the most intricate contrapuntal mediations. Nor are dissonances final, or ever tragic: they are birth pangs, awaiting the glory to be disclosed in their reconciliations — their stretti and recapitulations. Bach's is the ultimate Christian music; it reflects as no other human artifact ever has or could the Christian vision of creation. Take for example the *Goldberg Variations,* in which a simple aria from the *Anna Magdalena Notenbüchlein* is stated, only to be displaced by a majestic sequence of thirty variations composed not upon it, but upon its bass line (a simple descent from the tonic to the dominant, G to D, scarcely material sufficient for a lesser talent), and in which every third variation is a perfect canon (the canonic refrain being lengthened at each juncture, so that the final two are canons upon the octave and upon the ninth). When at the end of this glittering, shifting, and varied series the aria is restated, it can no longer be heard apart from the memory of all the variations in which it has been reimagined: it has acquired a richness, an untold profundity, of light and darkness, joy and melancholy, levity and gravity; it *is* all its ornamentation and change. Or consider the massive, shatteringly profound *Ciaccona* at the end of the second Unaccompanied Violin Partita, whose initial theme is no more than four bars long, a bass phrase of absolute simplicity that is successively reborn in sixty-four variations, passing from the minor, through the major, and back to the minor again, arriving at a restatement (with a few chromatic adornments at the end) that, again, contains all the motion, variety, and grandeur of what has gone before. One could imagine no better illustration of the nature of creation's "theme."[143]

Creation's form — a departing theme, submitted to innumerable variations and then restored, immeasurably enriched — is too lively and splendid to be reduced to the helotry in which, for instance, the Hegelian epic of *Geist* would confine it: no ideal and accomplished music, no final resolution beyond the "negations" of music, brings creation to a "fulfilled" silence; Christian eschatology promises only more and greater harmony, whose developments, embellishments, and movement never end and never "return" to a state more original than music. The analogy between God's and Bach's handiworks is audible chiefly in Bach's limitless capacity to develop separate lines into extraordinary intricacies of contrapuntal complication, without ever sacrificing the "peace," the measures of accord, by which the music is governed. This is especially evident, of course, in the great fugues, particularly of the later years: a double, triple, or even quadruple fugue is never too dense for Bach's invention to comprise, to open up into ever more unexpected resolutions, nor does a plurality of subjects ever prove resistant to augmented, diminished, or inverted combinations. Perhaps the most exquisite examples of this inventiveness are to be found in the second book of the *Well-Tempered Clavier* and in the *Art of the Fugue,* but one might look anywhere in his oeuvre: the very lovely Fugue in F Major (BWV 540), for instance, in which the two contrasted subjects come together in a third part where they appear together in five different intervals, until they arrive at the magnificent conclusion in which the treble restates the fugue's original motif; or, to take an example particularly appropriate to theological concerns, the great Prelude and Fugue in E-flat Major, Bach's "trinitarian" fugue, which is actually constructed from three fugues on three different subjects and in three different time signatures, the first (the "paternal") fugue's subject appearing in each of the other two in a rhythmically varied form, "generating" the second fugue and crossing, by way of a stretto, to the third. This is the pneumatological dynamism in Bach's music, so to speak, the grace that always finds measures of reconciliation that preserve variety; and so this is how it offers an aesthetic analogy to the work of the Spirit in creation, his power to unfold the theme God imparts in creation into

143. In something like the same terms, one could mount a theological defense of allegory, in the narrative sense. Often maligned as a pointless exercise in doubling a tale, whose significance evaporates when the veil of the allegorical narrative is drawn back to disclose the story it imitates, allegory might more charitably be taken as commentary by way of variation; the very style and order by which one tale reflects the lineaments of another in its own dimensions creates a new perspective upon and deepens the original narrative. This is what one might call interpretation through reciprocal poiesis. (And all creation could be said to constitute an allegory upon the story of divine love, the infinite and completed tale of the Trinity.)

ever more profuse and elaborate developments, and to overcome every discordant series.

Of course, from the vantage of a radically immanentist discourse, especially one such as Deleuze's, it is just this pneumatology that makes the analogy suspect: surely the Spirit, thus invoked, is a metaphysical mechanism, whose function is to delimit, rationalize, and unify all divergent series in some kind of *Aufhebung*. Such is a suspicion perhaps impossible finally to dispel, but for Christian thought, it is worth saying, the unity that the Spirit offers is of a radically *inventive* kind: he is the *creator Spiritus* who brings about the terms he unifies, as the open exposition and wholly aesthetic expression of his love, the whole fullness of whose work is its only "meaning." His presence is most definitely not the dialectical Ariadne's thread that is unwound through, and leads back out of, the labyrinth of history; he redeems creation's many lines not through negation or sublation, but by a musical accumulation, a restoration through further development and invention. Because God is Trinity, and creation a song shared among the Persons, God is the context in which the polyphony of being is raised up, in which even silenced voices are preserved, and promised a restored share in creation's hymnody. As God is the "place" of what differs, all distance belongs to God's distance, all true creaturely intervals are "proportions" and "analogies" of his infinite interval, all created music participates in his infinite music. The one voice with which God pronounces creation good is also the "irisating" voice of election, an address and a vocation that necessarily "analogizes" being, evoking from it its endless response, its polyphony; and so good is the theme imparted in creation that God desires it back, in the same generous measure with which it is given, sustained in its goodness as a beauty of which, still, only God is capable. The Holy Spirit, as the perfection of God's love, the differing yet again of divine differentiation, and the delightful, outgoing, unbounded power of the divine life, always brings out of creation its "depth" of differentiation, calls forth the radiance of being's surface, causes difference to differ most profoundly within itself, and lends to all the inflections of the divine gift a vibrancy and particularity beyond any merely formal differentiation. As the third person, the superabundance of divine love, the for-itself, fullness, and joy of that love, he bestows a harmony that can never be anything but a free, "superfluous," wholly fitting sequence of further developments. The Spirit is eternally turning the face of creation to the Father by conforming it to the Son, and thus creation is beautiful, and a gift restored.

Being is itself uneven for creatures, susceptible of a greater or lesser apprehension, recollection, and recovery of its theme; being itself is something lost in the privative measures of sin and progressively recovered in receiving anew the measure of charity. It is the music of harmonious differentiation, which is infinitely fulfilled in the trinitarian *perichoresis*, and which, in creation, can be lost, forsaken, or belied. In sin, all intervals become disordered; desire is directed no longer toward the infinite horizon of this unfolding music, but seeks to introduce its own caesurae into being, to enclose itself, to possess itself as force rather than as a participation in creation's polyphonic intricacies. Still, just as Christian thought cannot think of distance as the effect of the "simulacral" deficiencies of space and time (truth lies nowhere but in the proper ordering of "simulacral" transitions, and the only untruth is sin), neither can it entertain the Deleuzo-Nietzschean notion that distance is merely the differential element of each force.[144] Distance is the gift of trinitarian charity, address and response, regard and donation, pouring its richness into created "numbers." Creation is a diaphoral economy, an unending action of communication, and there are innumerable levels of beauty within its intervals: degrees of interiority and exteriority, folds, intense arrays of specular surfaces and, then again, interludes of shadow or limpidity; but what is enfolded, ultimately, is that thematic or analogical content that mediates one interval to another. The vibration of difference between two persons, say, does not reflect the areas of simulacral deviation of both from an inert ideal, but unique stylings, modulations, and variations upon the gift; and it is all these variations that, taken together and ordered by love, constitute the divine image, as Gregory of Nyssa *(vide infra)* argued. Placed within musical reach of one another, all the limits of creaturely being — physical, temporal, linguistic, and so forth — mark the places where transitions are possible, where charity can be enacted and the gift imparted. Because of the ontological difference that truly matters — that between the God who is the distance of difference and creatures that appear in distance — it is always possible to fabricate the most radical kind of interiority, a distance from distance, a boundary of inwardness sustained by a constant turning away in pride; but, if open in love to the ever more manifold exteriority of creation, every interiority folds and unfolds into infinite music.

If all creaturely being subsists upon repetition in difference, then the being of any creature is more than the particularity of a substance that can be extracted from the entire sequence of repetition. Every creature, in its terrible fragility, is perfected in a radically unfounded condition of dependency (upon God) and interdependency (with all creation), and the human soul is a particularly rich contour of the surface of being, a particularly deeply folded interval, enclosing a more nocturnal interiority than other folds, a richer capacity to reflect otherness, a specular "profundity"; but this inwardness is a detail of the aesthetic whole of creation, not an isolated enclave that exists prior to or apart from the aesthetic, linguistic, and communal occasion of its folding. As I have mentioned above, it is commonly assumed in postmodern discourse that

144. Deleuze, *Nietzsche and Philosophy*, 6.

Christian morality and metaphysics is responsible for the emergence of the Cartesian ego, the modern subject that both suffers and "wills" the mechanisms of social power that confine it, and there is some slight truth to this. Again, however, there is no seamless genealogy that unites Augustine to Descartes, or John Locke, or any other of the proponents of the modern myth of punctiliar individuality. It is certainly true that Augustine explored and "invented" spiritual interiority in a richness and detail, and with a subtlety and ingenuity, for which there were few precedents, but this interiority is only another interval, a plangent space, a more deeply woven fabric, in which the sound and shape of divine love resounds with particular sonorities or effoliates into particularly sinuous patterns. As John of the Cross says, it is the special proportion that God's "infinite voice" assumes in each soul, its special range of resonance (*The Spiritual Canticle* §14 & 15.10-11). When Augustine looks inward to *memoria*, he does not find an unshakable ground of subjectivity, or an unmoving center of identity, but a vertiginous prospect upon the infinite. *Memoria* does not simply recollect, in the fashion of the Platonic anamnesis, but contains what the mind is inadequate to harbor (*Confessions* 10.8.15); it is the mind's opening upon the mystery of time and the summons of eternity, a multiplicit unity, whereby we remember, understand, and love (10.8.19). The image of God lies in its very plurality, its irreducibility to a simple substance, because it is an *imago Trinitatis* (*De civitate Dei* 19.21-24). *Memoria* is a depth of reflective knowledge (*De Trinitate* 15.15.24), but not the spiritual catenation between divine substance and a discrete finite substance, resting firmly upon its own changeless noetic foundation. This is the only possible Christian narrative of the "self": that the inmost interiority proves, at the last, to be simply the most capacious openness before time and eternity. *Memoria,* indeed, is nothing apart from the creaturely course of repetition: it is the capacity of the soul that retains the pattern and impulse of what has gone before while still anticipating what lies ahead. As Augustine says, drawing on a rich Christian tradition of ascetic self-scrutiny, sin is a motion or series continually digressing from the order of charity, which the soul is powerless to bring to a halt because memory retains the soul's habitual pattern of movement (rhythm, cadence, ordering) and impresses it upon each succeeding moment (*De musica* 6.5.14). For Christian thought, as much as for Deleuze (indeed, more so), interiority is the deeply folded inside of an outside surface, and as such always folds and unfolds, encloses and discloses the surface of things.

I might add that if this is what it is to be a creature, if one possesses not even oneself except as a gift of and project for the surface of being, then there is nowhere but in the aesthetic richness of this surface that one may find — or serve — another. That hyper-Kantian postmodern moralism that I have already so roundly excoriated is, to my mind, most thoroughly irrational and even offensive in seeing ethical desire as lying in an impossible renunciation of desire, a "guilty" response to the absolute exteriority of the other (to which it remains totally inadequate). For a discourse caught in the trammels of a simplistic discourse of Same and Other, the only index of the authenticity of a self's "hunger for the good" is the pathology of the unhappy consciousness, and the only index of the authenticity of an ethical practice lies in the cruel peremptoriness with which that consciousness is forbidden the resolution and solace of a circuitous return to the self. If, though, we dispense with this mythology of a discrete interiority attempting to work the good over against the impenetrable enigma of a discrete exteriority, we can throw off the burdensome nonsense of an ethics of absolute obligation and imagine desire for the good in Gregory of Nyssa's terms instead: a desire that corresponds to a determinate infinity of superabounding beauty, of that presence in deferral that eludes and invites longing, and opens up all things to love; the inappropriable otherness of the other may be conceived as infinite then precisely because the other belongs to an infinite aesthetic order, a boundless horizon of varying perspectives and ceaseless supplementation, to which every I also belongs. Thus I find my "self" only in finding my "other" (and vice versa) in the splendor of the infinite. Within the unfolding music of creation the other appears as a particular figural intensity, an irreplaceable interval, a unique positioning whose infinite "scope" is nothing other than that music, that infinite distance of creation's paratactic display that endlessly "extends" the placing of the other and is expressed in and "advanced" by that placing. In the "sounding together" of our intervals and phrasings, within the harmony of the good, we possess the analogical medium that permits us to know and to be known, to be obligated, shamed, enticed, blessed, and forgiven. Whereas the infinity that Levinas glimpses in the face of the other is a negative infinity, Christian thought is called to find in the other one whose displacement would be of infinite gravity because the other is an indispensable moment in a positive infinity; when the other is lost, all music is forsaken. The voice and face of the other, the infinity revealed therein, is always aesthetic. The thought of the postmodern sublime — if it can be thought — cannot wake one to the music of the other; it is in the shining multiplicity of things that the other appears as divine delight, as belonging *here,* dwelling in the midst of *these things.* The face is a beauty that opens to an infinite that is beautiful; it reveals the desirability and inviolability and aesthetic necessity of the other; it is the beauty that humbles the one who looks on by showing that the other is the delight of God, and the music of his rejoicing.

3. As God utters himself eternally in his Word, and possesses all the fullness of address and response, and as creation belongs to God's utterance of himself (as a further articulation, at an analogical remove, of the abundant "eloquence" of divine love), creation may be grasped by theology as language.

And God said, Let there be light: and there was light.

Gen. 1:3

The heavens declare the glory of God; and the firmament sheweth his handiwork. Day unto day uttereth speech, and night unto night sheweth knowledge. There is no speech nor language, where their voice is not heard. Their line is gone out through all the earth, and their words to the end of the world.

Ps. 19:1-4

For as the rain cometh down, and the snow from heaven, and returneth not thither, but watereth the earth, and maketh it bring forth and bud, that it may give seed to the sower, and bread to the eater: So shall my word be that goeth forth out of my mouth: it shall not return unto me void, but it shall accomplish that which I please, and it shall prosper in the thing whereto I sent it.

Isa. 55:10-11

Thou hast ordered all things in measure and number and weight.

Wis. 11:20

Surely vain are all men by nature, who are ignorant of God, and could not out of the good things that are seen know him that is: neither by considering the works did they acknowledge the workmaster: But deemed either fire, or wind, or the swift air, or the circle of the stars, or the violent water, or the lights of heaven, to be the gods which govern the world. With whose beauty if they being delighted took them to be gods: let them know how much better the Lord of them is: for the first author of beauty hath created them. But if they were astonished at their power and virtue, let them understand by them, how much mightier he is that made them. For by the greatness and beauty of the creatures proportionably the maker of them is seen.

Wis. 13:1-5

He filleth all things with his wisdom, as Phison and as Tigris in the time of the new fruits. He maketh the understanding to abound like Euphrates, and as Jordan in the time of harvest. He maketh the doctrine of knowledge appear as the light, and as Geon in the time of vintage. The first man knew her not perfectly: no more shall the last find her out. For her thoughts are more than the sea, and her counsels profounder than the great deep.

Sir. 24:25-29

We may speak much, and yet come short: wherefore in sum, he is all. How shall we be able to magnify him? For he is great above all his works. The Lord is terrible and very great, and marvellous is his power. When ye glorify the Lord, exalt him as much as ye can; for even yet will he far exceed: and when ye exalt him, put forth all your strength, and be not weary; for ye can never go far enough.

Sir. 43:27-30

In the beginning was the Word, and the Word was with God, and the Word was God.

John 1:1

For the invisible things of him from the creation of the world are clearly seen, being understood by the things that are made, even his eternal power and Godhead; so that they are without excuse: Because that, when they knew God, they glorified him not as God, neither were thankful; but became vain in their imaginations, and their foolish heart was darkened.

Rom. 1:20-21

For this cause I bow my knees unto the Father of our Lord Jesus Christ, Of whom all fatherhood in heaven and earth is named.

Eph. 3:14-15

I am Alpha and Omega, the beginning and the end, the first and the last.

Rev. 22:13

i. Divine Expression

God names himself the Alpha and Omega of things, their beginning and ending: not the truth that simply lies fixedly beyond the vagrant syllables of being, the silence that surrounds or prescinds from the discourse of finitude, but himself the first and last word, the fullness of speech. God is, so to speak, infinite discourse, full of the perfect utterance of his Word and the limitless variety of the Spirit's "reply." Here, in the most elementary terms, is Christian metaphysics: God speaks God, and creation occurs within that speaking, as a rhetorical embellishment, a needless ornament. According to Augustine, God fashions sensible things in order to signify himself (*De Trinitate* 3.4.10); he speaks creation, and so language is a light in which creation is made visible (*De Genesi ad litteram* 1.2.6–5.11). Says Dionysius, one may name God from creatures because all creatures are contained in him from eternity (*The Divine Names* 1.1.6). Maximus the Confessor says, in his seventh *Ambiguum* (and elsewhere), that the creative logoi of all things dwell in the Logos, and within the economy of creation — its "indivisible difference" and "unconfused particularity" — the Logos resounds in the differentiation and diversity of all things. Nor are the logoi of things simply anonymous "universals": all beings, in their particularity, subsist within the creative *ratio* of the divine language as "eternal" locutions. For Bonaventure creation speaks of God in its every aspect, in its "origo, magnitudo, multitudo, pulchritudo, plenitudo, operatio, ordo . . ." (*Itinerarium mentis ad Deum* 1.14). Nicholas of Cusa, in *De filiatione Dei*, speaks of the sensible world as a legible book, a great voice in which God's Word reverberates, a manifold language spoken by the Father, through the Son, and in the Spirit who fills all things; and the infinite God, Nicholas often maintains, shows himself in the infinity of signs — or "mirrors" — within creation (*Compendium* 8). According to Berkeley, the inmost truth of sensible things is their semeiotic character, their participation in the divine language (*Alciphron* 4.7-15). Hamann, in his *Aesthetica in nuce*, speaks of God as the "mighty orator" and the "poet at the beginning of days,"[145] and in his *Ritter von Rosenkreuz* describes the paradisal state as one in which every created thing was a living word, communicating God's energies to all the senses (*SW* 3:32). And one cannot exaggerate the prevalence of the idea of the *liber naturae* in Christian tradition.[146] It is not, then,

---

145. J. G. Hamann, *Sämtliche Werke: Historische-Kritische Ausgabe (SW)*, ed. Josef Nadler, 6 vols. (Vienna, 1949-57), 2:200-206.

146. Recently John Milbank has used this entire tradition to revise language concerning substances in theology, to do away with too absolute a distinction between *res* and *signum*, and to demonstrate the inseparability of the language of *ousia*, within theology, from language of dynamic expression. See Milbank, "The Linguistic Turn as a Theological Turn," in Milbank, *The Word Made Strange* (Oxford: Blackwell, 1997), 84-120.

very outlandish to say that for Christian theology the world is "spoken"; that there is no reality or truth prior to language; that there is no species of intelligibility that wholly escapes the logic of poetic analogy, metaphor, and deferral; that all is utterance; and that, to borrow a phrase, *il n'y a pas de hors-texte.*

If, though, one is indeed to colonize Derrida's most notorious oracle for theology, and with him deny the reality of any "metatext" (in the sense of the extratextual), one may as well also grant that to say that creation is spoken is also to say that it is written — a texture of semeiotic deferral. Lest it be suspected that my hidden motive for speaking of creation as language is a desire to argue for a metaphysical hierarchy of correspondences, a symbolic economy between the world's "outer" and "inner" texts, I should say that, for biblical reasons, the world can be imagined as a realm of divine *semeia* only in a principally "rhetorical" sense: the *liber naturae* is a text of majestic lucidity, whose exquisite and terrible intricacies are stylistic, not hermetic; the world is not a vast system of auguries and "symbols," merely pointing away from itself to a realm of rational or magical essences. Scripture attests to God speaking his glory in creation, not his arcana; the invisible things of him are clearly seen. It is as a kind of poetry that the discourse of being is revelatory, as endless sequences of beautiful turns of phrase, and the proper response to this language — the reply that properly grasps, interprets, and corresponds to the truth of creation — is doxology. The Word comprehends all words transcendently, not as a great silence destitute of speech, but as the fullness of utterance, a "sounding silence" of utter plenitude, the Father's entire depth expressed in the agile radiance of the Spirit. As all talk of "substance" is most properly deferred to God, and then as the "effect" of the infinite discourse that God is, creation should be seen as a kind of miraculous wordplay, a brilliant persiflage within the "logic" of the Trinity, demonstrating the inexhaustible richness of God's Word in the endless diversity of its combinations. To speak of the book of nature is not even to invite speculation regarding the possibility of a natural theology, or of a rational deduction of divine truth or first principles from the evidences of nature. Theology has always affirmed the reality of a natural order and natural law, certainly, while also acknowledging that sin both obscures that order and weakens our grasp of it; but in a world fashioned within the splendor of divine glory, no law or proportion or way of nature is discernible apart from a prior education of sensibility and comportment, or from a training in subtle appreciation, dignified enthusiasm, and robust *oratio obliqua.* Even the passage from Romans 1 so often invoked in defense of natural law theory is concerned principally with the immediacy of God's glory, the manifest declaration of his Godhead in creation; what is deplored in those who fail to glorify God is, so to speak, an inadequate aesthetic response, a failure to appreciate the magnitude and ubiquity of the divine address, a deficiency of taste and gratitude. Thus theologians need not agonize over banal postmodern denunciations of Christianity's supposed negation of all signifiers in a "transcendental signified," or of theology's alleged fear of "difference" and its mythology of an aboriginal fall from the purity of silent immediacy. The effect of sin, for Christian thought, is not that deferral and dissemination have displaced an immediate voice and presence, a more than Edenic intimacy with God, but only that this interminable dissemination cannot be received as the always differing presence — the analogy — of God. The gift of creation, its expression of divine love, is not immediacy, but an inexhaustible thematism of the mediate; the gift lies in just this "impurity," this deferred presence, the ceremonious delay of a rhetorical gesture, which enjoins a rhetorical response: a sacrifice of praise.

To speak of creation as "expression," I must note, is to invoke a very particular tradition of reflection, taking in certain currents of Renaissance Neoplatonism (Jewish and Christian), German *Sprachphilosophie,* as well as (so says Deleuze) Spinoza and Leibniz. Expressionism in philosophy, to borrow the English title of Deleuze's study, is a tradition of reflection on the one and the many, the unfolding or explication of the one in the many, the implication in the many of the one, and God as the complication of all nature. For Deleuze, whose special enthusiasm is reserved for the Spinozan variety of expressionism, being is "singular" and expression is univocal, neither emanating from nor resembling any principle, but only disclosing the immanent "modes" of being;[147] in *The Fold* he describes expressionism in terms of the aesthetics of the baroque, in which every object is "lost" in its explication, every thought accomplished in its exposition, and the world is seen as an endless sequence of inflections, events, foldings, and unfoldings: this vision of reality, in which a thing's content cannot be distinguished from the rhetoric of its exposition, but *is* only insofar as it is "invented" or expressed, serves for Deleuze as the model of unitary being, each of whose immanent modulations implicates the whole, as each digresses from singularity to singularity. When I speak of creation as expression, however, it has nothing whatsoever to do with the question of the one and the many as such; the coincidence in Christian thought of the doctrines of the Trinity and of creation ex nihilo renders that question a matter of indifference (for both the unity and the multiplicity of finite reality are contingent, and participate in an act in which unity and multiplicity are the same). While it is certainly desirable to say that in creation no hard division can be drawn between essence and exposition, and even that within the trinitarian *perichoresis* God is never an indeterminate ground of pure divinity, prior to or apart from the utterance of his Word and breathing forth of his Spirit, still God and world do not

---

147. Gilles Deleuze, *Expressionism in Philosophy: Spinoza,* trans. Martin Joughin (New York: Zone Books, 1990), 167-80.

constitute between them a single order of content and explication, and so one can properly speak only of "analogical expression." Deleuze would be appalled: for him the demarcation between analogical and expressivist thought is absolute and inviolable, certain as he is that the spontaneous, explicative expressivity of being can only be rendered impotent and empty by the application of analogical schemes of resemblance (again, this is all Deleuze imagines analogy to be). Expression, for him, must admit of no interval, either of likeness or unlikeness: it is its own truth.

I want to say precisely the opposite: what is first expressive in creation is the analogical interval between God and the creature, inasmuch as its rhetorical surfeit expresses the delight and freedom that God is. Creation's words are analogous to God's eternal utterance of himself because in their restless dynamism of essence and exposition, or content and expression, they reflect under the form of a finite and complex synthesis the perfect and simple convertibility in God of essence and expression, *ousia* and *perichoresis*. That is, I am expressed in words and deeds, not as a hidden substance that my words merely signify, but as the event and mutable constancy of the ceaseless supplementation and deferral whereby I am at once disclosed, discovered, and invented; and even here there are analogical intervals, moments of delay or suspense, between what has been expressed and what will supplement it, between my words and the "self" to which my words refer, between one word and the next, and I in a sense am all these intervals — these analogical disjunctions within continuity — taken together. But God expresses himself entirely as God, in the infinitely accomplished act of triune love. Precisely because God does not come to or discover or achieve himself in and through creation but simply declares his glory therein, we find God in and through creation as the generous source and end whose goodness shines upon the surface of every sign. It is this (to Deleuze) contradictory notion of a transcendent origination of being's expressivity that allows for real difference, a real "digressionism," whose truth is its unfolding. An "expression" bound entirely to its own immanent force expresses nothing but its own expression — expresses, that is, precisely nothing, repeats nothing (this, for Deleuze, is precisely why it is "free"). True expression, though, even when no real or absolute distinction is drawn between it and the content it discloses, is possible only if there is that movement that allows it to differ, to be at once a new word and an act of disclosure. There must be an original difference that precedes each finite utterance, that frees each word from every "ground"; becoming is set in motion by its ontological differentiation from the transcendent actuality in which it participates, beings differ from moment to moment and from other beings because they first differ infinitely from being, and finite expression is set free by its difference from the transcendent act of God's utterance. This is the difference that allows every sign to be simply what it is, with no secret inner fold, and yet to speak in and with all other signs. The irreducible synthesis of the sign — the tension within it between the self-manifestation of transcendent truth in which it participates and the insufficiency of its own finite essence — is what causes each sign to "seek" its supplement, to become what it is (its meaning), to surrender its own ground to another sign so that in language's differing the ever greater difference of the divine utterance can show itself. To see creation thus, as an expressive surface reflecting God, endlessly folding and unfolding, implicating and explicating, is perhaps to replace the Kantian caesura between the phenomenal and the noumenal with the dynamic traversal of God's distance, but it is not to discern a continuity without analogical interval between God's knowledge of himself and his "reprise" of that knowledge in what he creates. God is the supreme rhetorician. As opposed to the mechanistic monism of Spinozan expression, Christian thought makes room for the thought of expression as deferral, as writing, transcription, mediation, and dissemination; it is the divine distance from (this transcendent presence to) creation that makes the world an inflection of the eternal Torah, the writing that the Logos comprises as difference.

ii. Divine Rhetoric

If creation's language does not consist simply in a direct correspondence between *this sign* and *that meaning,* but in its ever various enunciation of glory, then its character as divine address is revealed in (for want of a better term) its style. Erich Auerbach and others have noted that the originality of Augustine's prose lies in its departure from the immobile architectonic intricacy and monumental hypotaxis of classical rhetoric to the fluid, motile, and supple transitions of parataxis (simple sentences joined by the most elementary copula of all, the word "and"); I find it tempting to take this as a metaphor for the transition from a pagan to a Christian view of being, for that revolution in sensibility that, at the speculative level, prompted the church, in its development of trinitarian theology, to reject the intricate hierarchies of metaphysical mediations between the world and its ultimate principle, offered by various late antique Platonisms, in favor of a discourse of true transcendence, of God as wholly present in each moment of created reality, as the very energy of its being. Creation, for all its natural and supernatural hierarchies of transcendental truth, is not a static integration of superordinate and subordinate parts in a structure that, as a whole, achieves metaphysical completion, with God at its highest pinnacle; nor is the language of creation governed by an ideal meaning that consigns whatever is "inessential" in its locutions to the realm of the simulacral or adiaphoral; creation obeys the grammar not of the total but of the infinite (or, so to put it, the "bad" infinite that God calls good). Nothing that truly is, is an "inessential" or accidental locution: each instance of difference tells of God's glory, differently, as another rhetorical embellishment. Divine love extends itself as a boundless display of gifts; and as creation is the expressive analogy of this love rather than a direct emanative exposition, the mind does not attain to the "truth" of things through an *ascensus* toward the true voice prior to creation's rhetoric, but through an apprehension of divine glory now, already, in the material "differend," in the moment, in the reflection and echo of the divine declaration of creation's goodness and God's love. One "remembers" by hearing more, perceiving creation's beauty in the ever more eminent eloquence toward which all created signs stretch out, and to fail to hear leaves one without excuse. The language of creation leads nowhere but onward into the infinite distance that gives creation: the Spirit who brings all things into conformity with the divine Word is not the Spirit who sublates, but a pillar of fire or of cloud, illumination or darkness, the nomadic *nomos* who leads always on into the bounty of creation, to a beauty revealed by grace as the grammar of all things, the destination of infinitely many wanderings.

So long, then, as God's expression in creation is thought of analogically, one may justly employ Nicholas of Cusa's famous dictum: "Deus ergo est omnia complicans, in hoc quod omnia in eo; est omnia explicans, in hoc quia ipse in omnibus" (*De docta ignorantia* 2.3). The Logos is not — like the Nous of Plotinus — the prism of the one, the moon in whose opaline pallor the light of the sun acquires shades and nuances; as the eternal utterance of the Father, the Son contains not just the abstract, anonymous essences of things, but the whole rhetoric, the entire display, of infinitely many differences. He contains them, moreover, as the perfect rhetoric of love, which dissimulates nothing, knows no violence or alienation from its source, and expresses all things; he comprises a limitless "economy," a dissemination of signs without reserve, declaring love, proclaiming peace and glory. Which is to say that God's utterance of himself, articulated anew in creation, is present to creation always as deferred referral, the fullness of the infinite that can be "spoken" by creation only in the ceaseless parataxis of things, the *epektasis* of one sign to the next, the "slippage" of meaning. Such is the nature of God's infinity that immediacy and mediation are the same in him. Hence, one should waste little time dispensing with Derrida's accusation that the entire tradition of Western (indeed, human) thought obeys a metaphysical nostalgia for immediate presence, and so seeks to overcome the signifier's restless, indefinite referral to other signifiers, meaning's lack of respite or finality, the economy of difference, the Dionysian riot of being that cannot be reduced to the stillness of a serene spectacle;[148] it is impossible to

148. See Derrida, *Writing and Difference*, 24-26.

take seriously a pathologist of the metaphysical disease who insists in trading in such coarse simplifications. It is Derrida who has raised the specter of some sort of opposition between *total* presence and *total* absence, and so it is unsurprising that he is then able not only to diagnose it but to undertake its exorcism. Has anyone, though, ever thought of presence as absolute immediacy, apart from a few genuine monists of the *advaita* variety, like Śankara or Meister Eckehart? Derrida is altogether too certain that he has found the ideal model of metaphysical nostalgia in Rousseau's distress over the "decline" of music from simple melody, to harmony, and then (most depraved of all) to counterpoint, which causes sincerity and emotive inflection to be lost in the calculus of intervals.[149] The longing for the lost voice, the true father, the immediate address: doubtless, no religious or speculative system is utterly devoid of such a hunger for the absolutely pure; but it would do no harm to make a few distinctions.

To begin with, Christian teaching, certainly, does not describe a perfect and self-present divine address or Word that is then diminished, alienated from itself, or lost in the indefinite deferral of being's "writing." Between the infinite plenitude of God's Word and the flowing measures of creation's loquacity, the relation is one of grace: of analogy. One must at least insist on the difference between Rousseau's sentimental attachment to insipid and unaccompanied monody and, say, Hamann's praise of God as the poet at the beginning of days: the difference between the God whose image and service is the unadorned half note and earnest vibrato and the God who delights in — because he is — polyphony. In this book's introduction I accused Derrida of a structuralist's indifference to narrative particularities, and I repeat the charge: he does not pay a moment's attention to what theology says, but simply imposes upon it his tidy set of binary oppositions. When, for instance, he takes as an example of the Western prejudice against writing's deferrals the regret of John Chrysostom that we must repair to the written word because, sinners that we are, we do not bear the inscriptions of the Holy Spirit upon our souls,[150] he appears to have missed a fairly crucial feature of the metaphor: John does not desire an end to writing, but simply a better text; he laments the fact that the text of the self is not written in accord with the love of the Spirit, that there is a separation of "interiority" from the exteriority of God's gift of created freedom and the law of charity, that the text must be recovered from our sinful desire to write ourselves, to be perfectly present and sufficient to ourselves. Far from giving voice to a pathetic yearning for the unwritten, John cries out for a more radical textuality, converting mind and flesh into the book of the Spirit: would that Christ were the most deeply inscribed text in us, that the grammar governing

149. Derrida, *Of Grammatology*, 199.
150. Derrida, *Writing and Difference*, 11.

our articulations of ourselves and making us "present" were of another style. "Writing" is not sin; but sin takes away a style, a creative play of intervals; it loses a theme, it transforms text into "my" substance. God, though, creates a "rhetorical" world, its "substance" entirely "exposed," at the surface. Creation is "excess," an analogy of the "exceedingness" of the Father's gift of his being to the Son and Spirit.

God's speech in creation does not, then, invite a speculative nisus toward silence — the silence of pure knowing or of absolute saying — but doxology, an overabundance of words, hymnody, prayer, and then, within this discipline of gratitude and liturgy, a speculative discourse obedient to the gratuity of existence and the transcendence of its source, or a contemplative silence whose secret is not poverty but plenitude. God's address may even be given as law, as command and prohibition, but always to establish thereby a grammar of adoring response. God's is a language of love, it never expresses itself in hierarchies of abstract "meaning" or becomes "taxonomic" (except, perhaps, in the way the voice from the whirlwind names God's wonders before the stricken Job, or in the way the Song of Songs praises every aspect of the beloved). This is why theology must find itself on the side of "rhetoric" over against that of "dialectic," crudely defined, or at least recognize their inseparability. One should not separate in God's *Verbum* the traits of *sermo* and of *ratio;* one should, though, insist that the two meanings inhere in one another for Christian thought in a way that pagan philosophy could not imagine (for even if Middle Platonism recognized in the divine logos both the rational structure of reality and the self-manifestation of the divine in a derivative principle, it could not understand the supreme "logic" unifying these concepts: God as self-outpouring love). Human language, which is a further implication within the linguisticality of creation, a particularly responsive and vagrant intensity thereof, can never achieve its truth by abstraction from the free play of supplementation, of doxological excess, the power to bless and curse, name and lie, respond in love or demur in anger. Dialectic and "analysis" are sterile illusions apart from a prior aesthetic education of desire that prepares the soul to make of its words offerings to the Word (in the highest form, offerings of divine names). Indeed, the very idea of an "analytic" philosophy is a hopeless one: in attempting to reduce every "synthetic" proposition to one or more analytic truths, self-evidently and even tautologously correct, one makes the mistake of imagining that truth for finite beings is ever anything but synthetic: just as being is granted to beings by an act that transcends the conditions of finitude, so truth inhabits words that in themselves can never be adequate to the fullness of what they express; thus all real philosophy must include the motion of conjecture toward that transcendent horizon that shows itself yet hides itself in beings, and the animating logic of such conjecture must be one of contemplation and praise. I am not arguing for mere jubilant irrationalism here, and one certainly can insist upon the doxological rationality of theological discourse without succumbing to the postmodern mysticism of the aleatory: because creation is indeed divine address, and because every intonation of its discourse can be reconciled with the theme that God imparts in creating, the world is not simply a Dionysian festival of endlessly many signifiers, opaque to one another, spilling over one another in wasteful and extravagant play; its significations are infinitely susceptible of analogy, they are transparent before one another, they can be arranged into rational orderings of desire and delight that "correspond" to the rational ordination of divine love that gives them, before which their transparency is transformed into sheer incandescence. As opposed to the boring univocities of Dionysus, the monotonous beat of his dithyrambs, and the chaotic romp of uniform and punctiliar instances of difference, the prosody of creation is fluid, varied, inventive, and always able to unfold into glorious complexities of living verse. Prior to every rhetoric of power, every coercive discourse, every dissimulation and violent persuasion, is a rhetoric that is peace.

To return then to a persistent theme (and to this book's initial question), if this talk of creation's rhetoric is at all illuminative, then it provides a way of understanding how obligation before the other, and even the very possibility of the other, can be expressed and enacted rhetorically, and yet without violence. In the terms of that seemingly irresoluble tension between Levinasian hyperbole regarding infinite alterity and Derrida's resigned acceptance of the impossibility of ethics without the violence of rhetoric, metaphor, and interrogation,[151] the premise that rhetoric must be, in some degree, violence is always either openly asserted or broadly implied. For Levinas the distance between one and one's other must be dark, an oblivion of the world, because "metaphysical" or ethical truth is possible only in the context of a superabounding indigence, and the only truly ethical discourse lies in an unworldly Saying prior to every said, present in the said only as the trace, as the apophatic sediment of a language of paradox.[152] For Derrida the said, which of necessity fragments, dispels, and distorts the Saying, is the only way whereby the other is reached, and so even in the ethical there must be an economy of violence, of violence against violence. But we may assert that there is an element other than darkness or violence in which the other is encountered, in which the mediations that pass from one to one's other can indeed invoke and evoke the other without the "Same" assailing the other's otherness. Prior to the Saying that obliges there is the infinite of the said, a determinate word of peace, which loves: there is a gift of light that may be given, one

---

151. See Derrida, *Writing and Difference*, 29-30.
152. See Emmanuel Levinas, *Otherwise Than Being, or Beyond Essence*, trans. Alphonso Lingis (Dordrecht: Kluwer, 1991), 140-51.

to another, because it corresponds to and participates in and is nourished by the infinite rhetoric of God's trinitarian discourse of love. The other arises in the very excess of being's rhetoric, and has the shape of a rhetorical appeal: not the violence of a reduction, an interrogative excavation of the other out of the infinite, but a certain kind of generous style that, participating in the theme of divine love that gives both one and one's other, makes room for analogous and creative responses; a certain rhetorical form, a gesture, that by its gratuity, excess, and beauty displaces every phenomenology or ontology that cannot venture beyond the conditions of the transcendental ego. The other is known *as other* not in the silence of immediacy or identity, nor in the darkness of infinite alterity, but in the free and boundlessly beautiful rhetoric of a shared infinite. The rhetoric of the other evokes my representations, which — so long as they are governed by charity — can take the form of peaceful replies. The rhetorical display that is given across the divine distance, in which the other figures as a unique "turn of phrase" (as does the I), means that there is always, in every moment of difference, a mediating rhetoric of love that offers infinite scope for reconciliation, return, gestures of peace. One need only attune one's words to the Word who speaks all things, and who is himself spoken from all eternity.

iii. *Analogia Verbi*

The analogy between God and creation, so the book of Wisdom seems to suggest, is not one between the here below and the far above, between lesser and greater powers, human and divine forces within the order of being; all of creation is the sign of God's power in its very want of divinity, in the failure of even its greatest beauty and splendor to attain to the majesty of God. The proportion — the analogy — that created things declare is that of an ever greater distance from God, even in God's expression of himself in creation; the proportions of created things, their orders of magnitude, quantity, and beauty, tell of an infinite proportion — an infinite interval — of ever yet greater magnitude, "quantity," and beauty. God differs infinitely from created beauty not by being utterly alien to it, but by being infinitely more beautiful. And for this reason the language of analogy functions within theology not as some presumptuous grasping after the "essences" of things, nor as a discourse that establishes a hierarchy within totality, but as a fruitful coincidence of the incommensurable within deferral; it is concerned with the ordering of language, the ways in which language crosses distance, mediates its measures, makes its interstices into suitable images of how it is with God. Analogical reasoning must be understood, before all else, as a dynamic movement of thought toward the "whole infinity" of God; its essential impetus is a desire that wills the downfall of all mere concepts when they encounter the persistent interval within analogy — because that interval is analogy's power. Theology's analogical speech should be understood as *epektasis:* language, drawn on by the beauty of the Word who is the distance containing all the words of creation, traverses the analogical interval between God and creation (of which God himself is the distance), between creation's proportions and the proportion of peace that belongs to God's infinity; and so there can be no end to the progress of language toward God — so long as it is governed by the measure of charity revealed in Christ — nor any "comprehensive" portrayal of the interval. The understanding of analogy I want to defend here, I should then add, has little to do with analogy's epistemological status, with what objective knowledge or discursive "facts" one might acquire regarding substances or regarding God, the "supreme substance," through a rational movement from finite to infinite being. In contrast to more traditional (and perhaps more substantial) discussions of analogy, I want to consider principally how analogy (as a linguistic event) constitutes, for Christian thought, a true (and so peaceful) rhetorical style.

Aquinas, in the *prima pars* of the *Summa theologiae,* says certain words by which Scripture refers to God are employed metaphorically, their proper reference being to created things, while other words refer to God properly, though their mode of signification applies only to creatures (1.13.3), and that what is said of creatures and of God is said neither univocally nor equivocally but analogically (1.13.5). This, brief though it be, is a sufficiently exhaustive account of the varieties of analogy; what is crucial to note, however, is that in either form — improper or proper reference, metaphor or "description" — these analogies are placed by Aquinas, following Dionysius, under the topic of the names of God, not within a discussion of divine attributes. This is a distinction that could not be more important. There is a vast difference between the theological enunciation of the "divine names" and the philosophical enumeration of the "attributes of deity," which is nothing less than the difference between two ontologies: between a metaphysics of participation, according to which all things are embraced in the supereminent source of all their transcendental perfections, and a "univocal" ontology that understands being as nothing but the bare category of existence, under which all substances (God no less than creatures) are severally placed. The former permits the practice of theological nomination — speculative, liturgical, metaphorical — because, even in positing an infinite qualitative difference and disproportion between God's simplicity and creaturely multiplicity, it allows for a continuity of eminence between creation's transcendental moments and the transcendent wellspring from which they flow; thus one may in some sense name God from creatures, even though the truth of those names is infinitely beyond the capacity of finite reason properly to grasp. As for the latter ontology, it would certainly seem to offer thought a more obvious and substantial form of analogy: a direct and proportionate similitude (albeit in finite and infinite instances) between attributes inhering in discrete beings. It would seem, indeed, that the metaphysics of participation, precisely insofar as it regards God not as a being but as the source and ultimate truth of all beings, opens an abyss between God and creatures that neither thought nor language can traverse without losing its moorings in human understanding. A more univocal ontology, though, allows the meanings of our attributions to remain intact, even with the addition of the further attribute "infinite." A classic example would be Locke's formula for arriving at a rational understanding of God: we begin from various simple ideas derived from finite reality and appropriate to God, which we then multiply by infinity and combine to fashion for ourselves the complex idea of a supreme being (*An Essay concerning Human Understanding*, bk. 11.23, §33). A more guarded and austere example would be that of Kant, who allowed that analogy might be used of God, but only insofar as it remains rhetorical and quadratically proportional (a:b::c:d), and does not take the form of a simple comparison between two discrete things, or between two things in relation to a third thing held in common[153] (which sounds quite reasonable till one grasps how utterly vacuous the knowledge of this proportion is without the ontological participation of one of the two sets in the other). The problem, though, with any practice of identifying the divine attributes univocally, as "features" of the divine "substance" in much the same way as they are features of created substances (even in the agnostic Kantian form of proportionality), is that the God thus described is a logical nonsense: a being among beings, possessing the properties of his nature in a composite way, as aspects of his nature rather than as names ultimately convertible with one another in the simplicity of his transcendent essence, whose being and nature are then in some sense distinct from one another, who receives his being from being as such and so is less than being, who (even if he is changeless and eternal) in some sense becomes the being he is by partaking of that prior unity (existence) that allows his nature to persist as the composite reality it is, a God whose being has nonexistence as its opposite. . . . This God is a myth, an idol, and one we can believe in and speak of only so long as we have forgotten the difference between being and beings.

So, following Aquinas's scheme, we should note that the more direct form of theological analogy, that of proper predication, which offers up to God such names as "good" and "true" and "beautiful," does indeed obey a certain proportional logic (for we can never speak of God by comparing his "substance" to "our substances") that is sustained by an ontology of participation — not, ob-

---

153. Immanuel Kant, *Prolegomena to Any Metaphysics That Will Be Able to Present Itself as a Science*, trans. P. G. Lucas (Manchester, 1962), 121-28.

viously, of God and creatures in a tertium quid but of creatures in God. As we know ourselves through the possession of "properties" (which is what, for a finite being, such things as goodness, truth, or beauty are), and through certain properties consonant with love can come to know the original logoi of our natures, by which we are called into being and toward which we are outstretched, so from this synthetic movement of becoming (or failing to become) what we are we fashion proportional analogies of the infinite "proportion" of God's perfect self-knowledge in his Logos, and of the coincidence in his simplicity of all he is and "has." This is permitted to us, and this knowledge can show itself in our thoughts and words even as it exceeds both, because our logoi are eternally embraced in God's Logos. Of the more indirect, improper, and metaphoric way of naming God, we should say that for what it lacks in strict "propriety" it often more than compensates by its suggestive, poetic, and conceptual force, its capacity for enriching thought and language through a fertile and evocative mingling of ambiguity and clarity. Some metaphors are more fruitful than others precisely because they are more irreducible to simple proportional logic, and have a more singular kind of impenetrability that endows them with a peculiar power of gathering and distributing other metaphors within their semantic range; Paul Ricoeur calls these "root metaphors":

> [W]ithin the Hebraic tradition God is called King, Father, Husband, Lord, Shepherd, and Judge as well as Rock, Fortress, Redeemer, and Suffering Servant. The network engenders what we can call root metaphors, metaphors which, on the one hand, have the power to bring together the partial metaphors borrowed from the diverse fields of our experience and thereby to assure them a kind of equilibrium. On the other hand, they have the ability to engender a conceptual diversity, I mean, an unlimited number of potential interpretations at a conceptual level. Root metaphors assemble and scatter. They assemble subordinate images together, and they scatter concepts at a higher level.[154]

For Ricoeur root metaphors occupy a liminal position between the realm of semantic intelligibility and the realm of symbols, which he sees as being grounded in presemantic life, at the "dividing line between *bios* and *logos*";[155] the symbol — an image that, in being interpreted, reveals the world's articulacy — represents the capacity (so perceived by sacral orders of discourse) of the cosmos to signify.[156] Ricoeur is surely correct that there is a certain metaphori-

---

154. Paul Ricoeur, *Interpretation Theory: Discourse and the Surplus of Meaning* (Fort Worth: Texas Christian University Press, 1976), 64.

155. Ricoeur, *Interpretation Theory,* 59.

156. Ricoeur, *Interpretation Theory,* 62.

cal "depth" or intensity within language that, at particular points within a given discourse, governs, gathers, deploys, and enriches subordinate ranges of somewhat less expressive metaphors; and this depth or intensity is, in every instance, the effect of a certain impenetrability, or of a simultaneous impenetrability and suggestive figural fullness that always evokes — but is never exhausted by — the supplementation of other "fitting" expressions. A phrase such as, for instance, "God is love" — which is neither exactly predicative nor uncomplicatedly metaphoric — provides within the context of the discourse to which it belongs a moment of extreme semeiotic resistance, the richness of an irreducibility that calls out for a constant energy of addition and deferral, an eruption of analogical additions proportionate to and determined by its intensity. To say this differently, the "successful" theological metaphor is one that is not analytic, but is, so to speak, a kind of synthetic a priori: it says more than can be said, it is somehow logically prior to all its efficient causes — or rather, it exhibits its final cause first. Theological locutions like "the church is the bride of Christ," for instance, or "Christ is the temple and the glory" occur at a point of extreme, inspissated, and indissoluble intensity, which gathers together diverse aspects of a whole textual, liturgical, moral, and speculative tradition in a phrase or image that defies complete translation into another equivalent phrase or image. Hence such a metaphor reveals its meaning by way of its inexhaustibly fecund resistance to final analysis, by which it continues to generate newer and more elaborate metaphorical and hermeneutical locutions (we know "bride of Christ" or "Christ the bridegroom" to be meaningful from all our inherited usages within the tradition, but we can express our understanding of its truth only by speaking of the nuptial bond of God and Israel, of the mystic's experience of the dart of love, of the mother of God as the true type of humanity and of the church, of Hosea's marriage, of the "marriage" of divine and human in the incarnate Word and in the divinized creature, of Christ in the wedding chamber of the heart, of the miracle of Cana, of the wedding feast of the Lamb, of the indwelling of divine glory in Israel, of marriage as sacrament rather than contract, and so on in infinitum). I am tempted to wax Heideggerian and say that such a metaphor (like the poetic speaking of being) is where a gathering logos gathers in such a way as to disclose the belonging together of what otherwise would be left in oblivion, and so thereby allows "being" (or rather, the tradition) to show itself thus or thus.

Here, obviously, one is assuming that the movement of analogy occurs within a prior movement of transcendent truth, which sustains the tradition and makes it live. One could obviously see, in this poetic fluidity, not a radiant richness emanating from a final cause, but — like a good Nietzschean — merely the absence of any identical origin, making all truth nothing but an illusion sustained by the movement of untruth, of the "metaphoricity" that "bears over" experience into thoughts, thoughts into words, and words into other words, without *arche* or telos; rather than seeing this "bearing over" and this "grounding" of metaphors in other metaphors as a manifestation of being itself as always "borne over" (the Father poured out in the Son and Spirit, the Logos pouring itself out in logoi and gathering all logoi in itself), one could see the inescapable "dissemination" of words as merely the impossibility of true reference. We should recall, again, that it is the possibility of all analogy whatsoever (not merely formal metaphysics) that is called into question by postmodern critique. While theologians may at times entertain doubts concerning the possibility of an analogy between divine and created being, Derrida's acute sense of the interminable supplementarity and divagation of language renders the thought of analogy (conceived as a scale of similitudes) dangerous and vapid, while prophets of "energy" like Deleuze and Foucault insist upon the impossibility of subjecting anything to the "hierarchical" discourses of analogy, which they see as irredeemably concerned with negation and determination and with all the metaphysical fixities that confine difference within the scaffolding of the Same. As Deleuze writes, "analogy has always been a theological vision, not a philosophical one, adapted to the forms of God, the world, and the self."[157] Seen thus, analogical predication is the very form of metaphysical violence, disrupting being's "necessity," its singularity, rendering reactive or negative the determinative sequences of being, and reducing finite determination to the mere numerical distinction of one thing from another. Foucault's denunciation of every metaphysical campaign against difference is as uncompromising as it is imprecise: the scale of similitudes, of resemblances and representations, is, he claims, the prison house in which difference can only languish and waste away:

> Good sense is the world's most effective agent of division in its recognitions, its establishment of equivalences, its sensitivity to gaps, its gauging of distances, as it assimilates and separates. And it is good sense that reigns in the philosophy of representation. Let us pervert good sense and allow thought to play outside the ordered table of resemblances; then it will appear as the vertical dimension of intensities, because intensity, well before its gradation by representation, is in itself pure difference: difference that displaces and repeats itself, that contracts and expands; a singular point that constricts and slackens the indefinite repetitions in an acute event.[158]

157. Deleuze, *The Logic of Sense*, 179-80.
158. Michel Foucault, *Language, Counter-Memory, Practice: Selected Essays and Interviews*, ed. Donald F. Bouchard, trans. Donald F. Bouchard and Sherry Simon (Ithaca, N.Y.: Cornell University Press, 1977), 183.

Hence good sense can conceive of difference in only a posterior sense, as the issue of the negative: "For difference to exist, it was necessary to divide the 'same' through contradiction, to limit its infinite identity through non-being, to transform its positivity which operates without specific determinations through the negative. Given the priority of similarity, difference could arise only through these mediations."[159] Thus, cast in the form of dialectic, the traditional philosophical affirmation of difference aids only in the recuperation of identity.[160]

This is all very exhilarating and "revolutionary," no doubt, even if only in an ineffectual academic way, and even if the absolute elevation of difference and intensity over similitude and stability is as intellectually stultifying and crude as its reverse; but it says nothing (and knows nothing) about the theological tradition of trying to understand the venture of analogical language out across the distance of an analogical ontology. Theological analogy is not the art of representational hierarchy, but in fact functions subversively of stable classifications and orders of resemblance; far from founding discourse in hierarchies of representation, indeed, it merely records and responds to the gratuity of God's "outward" impartation of his life of love, his life of difference *as* love. God is God always in giving the gift freely, without need of scales of essences to certify the "meaningfulness" of his expression. The assumption that pervades every postmodern critique of analogy is that its discourse concerns a preanalogical or metaphysical substance, which is only secondarily irisated into difference, and whose unity is recuperable through resemblance. Theological analogy, however, as I have argued, concerns nothing but the original analogousness of being. As analogy (even when conceived according to the creature's participation in God) is a proportion (rather than a medium shared between two things), there is always an analogical interval that separates and unites its "objects"; and this is its peculiar beauty and elusiveness. A proportion is neither an essence nor a negation; analogy is that form of discourse that is apophatic and cataphatic at once, that does not so much offer an epistemic advance upon a property as govern ignorance joyously and convert it into wisdom (not absolute comprehension). Analogy is a proportional aesthetics, which converts the world into a grammar of doxology and so reveals the true style of its sequences; it is an education of language and of vision, such that the "words" of being can be apprehended as glory, gift, and thanksgiving. The intelligibility of analogy, of course, is always dependent upon and reducible to further semantic supplementation, but this proves no hindrance to its practice, because analogy is a motion within and according to the infinite, an attempt to portray the in-

159. Foucault, *Language, Counter-Memory, Practice*, 184.
160. Foucault, *Language, Counter-Memory, Practice*, 185.

terval of love that is the life of the Father speaking and knowing himself in the Son and Spirit, an attempt to discover finite intervals in words whose peculiar terms make them "proportionate" to that infinite interval opened in God's Word.

For Christian thought, creation is always in a sense analogous, always something "handed over," metaphorical, telling of God precisely in its distance and difference from God: a divine semeiology directed toward the God who comprises all signs in the infinity of his determinacy. In theological terms it does not matter whether the practice of analogy wears the aspect of a proportional comparison that obviously leaves open the interval between its terms, an exemplarist discourse regarding created reflections of the divine or *vestigia Trinitatis,* or a mere rhetorical device likening one order of being to another for suasive effect, because in every case the Christian narrative fixes analogy's proportions within an infinite (not a total) hierarchy of mediations, which can never become a taxonomic index of the world or an economy of epistemic correspondences. Analogy is the art of discovering rhetorical consonances of one thing with another, a metaphorical joining of separate sequences of meaning, and thus "corresponds" to the infinite rhetoric of God; it is to discover in the implication of every created thing with every other the way in which all things are images and gifts of an infinite glory, when they are seen according to an ordering of desire that accommodates and assumes the essential gesture of divine grace, the love of and desire for God and creation that somehow imitates the way God loves and desires God, and loves and desires creation in God. And to speak more truly, more beautifully of God is to participate with ever greater pertinacity in the plenitude of God's utterance of himself in his Word. In its inventiveness the good analogy discloses the artistry of God's eternal Logos; it combines the world's symbols, and transcendental moments, and subtle or grand gestures in an utterance whose truth is its capacity to direct thought and desire toward the supereminent plenitude that is the ultimate truth of every created quality or form, and to manifest the belonging together of all things gathered in the splendor of God's beauty.

Consider, for instance, the thought of Bonaventure, on the face of it an unambiguous discourse of essences, an exemplarist "deduction" of the metaphysical sympathies between created things and their divine archetypes. Certainly the *Itinerarium mentis ad Deum* describes the mind's elevation from created images to a contemplation of the divine mystery they signify, which certainly involves a motion of reduction and abstraction (2.6), an ascent from the temporal to the eternal. As Balthasar says, "the reservation which characterises Augustine as much as Denys when they speak of the revelation and communication of the Trinity to the world disappears, and the Trinity is not (as for Denys) the absolutely separated and unknowable, nor (as for Augustine) is everything in the world that speaks of the divine Persons mere appropriation. Rather, the Trinity is truly revealed in its overflow into the world (in creation and the Incarnation of Christ), and shows itself thereby to be the a priori ground of everything that exists in the world."[161] And yet, still, the principal term of the analogy between the Trinity and the world is aesthetic: the sensual apprehension of and delight in beauty leads to a sharing in that authentic delectation that belongs to the Trinity, in whose measures the creature participates through grace (*Itinerarium* 2.1-8). In greeting creatures in an attitude of admiration and delight, and in seeing them in the light of the incarnate Son who is the direct manifestation of the Father's beauty, one comes to taste of the Father's delight in giving expression to his beauty in his eternal Word and in the Spirit's articulation of all the words that the divine Word comprises. For Bonaventure, following the grand tradition, God has the power to express himself openly in what is not God, without alienation from his nature, because he always already perfectly expresses himself in the Son, and in the Son gives expression to everything that is or is possible.[162] The *rationes aeternae* of all things belong to the Word, the *Ars aeterna* (as Bonaventure calls him),[163] who expresses entirely the Father's beauty (*Collationes in Hexaemeron* 12.5-11), who is the Father's very likeness and self-knowledge (*Breviloquium* 1.3). In the begetting of the Word, every other word is spoken; and in the giving of the Gift (the Spirit) every other gift is given (*Itinerarium* 6.2). Thus, as Balthasar remarks, "In contrast to the scarcely considered upwards-tending *analogia entis,* there is a very strong downwards-tending analogy: the eternal Word of expression knows better and says better what each thing wants to say than the thing itself knows."[164] In the Eternal Art, all things are produced, preserved, sustained, and distinguished one from another (*Itinerarium* 2.9), and the words that dwell in the Word are infinite in number (*Commentary on the Sentences* I, 35, art. unicus, 4-5). Here, as it happens, as with Maximus, one encounters a certain fruitful indistinction between the eternal "reasons" of things and their finite instantiations: if, after all, the words of creation are *infinite* in quantity, there is no need to think of them simply as "ideas" at all, at least not in the sense of abstract and general categories in which particular instances participate. Rather, the supreme rhetoric of God's Word merely contains, in the fullness of its free and accomplished expression, the entire scope of difference, every being both in its purest possibility and its most proper actuality, the whole rhetoric of creation unmuted by sin. The Word is not the idea that underlies or overshadows

---

161. Balthasar, *Glory of the Lord,* 2:261.
162. See Balthasar, *Glory of the Lord,* 2:352.
163. See especially *Itinerarium* 1.3.
164. Balthasar, *Glory of the Lord,* 2:294.

particularity, toward which thought ascends by way of an immolation of the particular, but the infinite "place" in which difference is set free, the infinite rhetoric that allows the boundless speech of being to sound forth. And if the Word comprises an infinity of possibility, then all finite expression is free, open, unnecessary, an elected style of address, a poetic invention. God is indeed the supreme rhetorician, artist (*Commentary on Luke* 12.39), or craftsman (*Itinerarium* 1.9), whose power, wisdom, and goodness radiate from all created things (1.10) and are seen in all creation's weights, measures, and proportions (I.I 1). Thus every creature is a *vestigium* of divine beauty (2.11-12),[165] in ways too marvelous to calculate or "reduce"; even as the senses of the spirit delight in the sheer variety and abundance of the fruits of paradise, the soul finds in the Word a mirror containing the beauty of all form and light and a book containing all things inscribed by God, the supreme artisan (*Lignum vitae* 12.46).[166] The primordial analogy, then, between God and world is the analogy of beauty, of delight, artistry, even as creation's rational coherence speaks of the eternal *ratio* of God; the "essences" of things do not simply converge upon the divine essence to lose themselves therein, but rather find themselves in God, as free expressions of love and delight, dwelling together in infinite peace, together hymning the glory of their creator. It is the overwhelming immensity and variety of created beauty, the sheer eloquence with which creation proclaims divine glory, that "corresponds" to God (*Itinerarium* 1.15). Created *vestigia* are divine locutions in an endless and bewildering array of different inflections; and from their beauty one receives an image of, share in, and impulse toward that delight that belongs to God.[167] As Bonaventure insists, likeness of the creature to God is not a *similitudo univocationis sive participationis* (that is, participation of God and creature alike in some third term), because there is no univocal category to which God and creatures both belong, but a *similitudo imitationis et expressionis* (*Commentary on the Sentences* 1, 35, art. unicus, conclusio); the creature imitates and expresses God, as every rhetorical excess expresses the rhetorician.

165. Created things "sunt vestigia, simulachra et spectacula nobis ad contemplandum deum proposita et signa divinitus data."

166. See Balthasar, *Glory of the Lord*, 2:333.

167. See especially *Itinerarium* 2.8: "Secundum hunc modum species delectans ut speciosa, suavis et salubris insinuat, quod illa prima specie est prima speciositas et suavitas et salubritas, in qua est summa proportionalitas et aequalitas ad generantem; in qua est virtus non per fantasma, sed per veritatem apprehensionis illabens; in qua est impressio salvans et sufficiens et omnem apprehendentis indigentiam expellens. Si ergo 'delectatio est coniunctio convenientis cum conveniente' [Augustine, *De vera religione* 18.35ff.]; et solius dei similitudo tenet rationem summe *speciosi, suavis* et salubris; *et* unitur secundum veritatem et secundum pulchritudinem replentem omnem capacitatem: manifeste videri potest, quod in solo deo est fontalis et vera delectatio, et quod ad ipsam ex omnibus delectationibus manducimur requirendam."

Bonaventure's is a metaphysical language, certainly, but not a discourse of the totality. The motion of any *merely* metaphysical *ascensus* must be, by definition, one of progressive abstraction (and some may think Bonaventure's language occasionally strays in this direction), pressing not only toward the diaphaneity of particular things but ultimately toward their dissolution: an anamnesis of the there above that is, necessarily, an amnesia of the here below. Bonaventure's ontology, however, "ascends" to the contemplation of God always by way of the profusion of being's infinite array of *differentia,* through a ceaseless progress in love; it does not abandon the phenomena, or subject them to a noumenal inversion to their hidden ground, but in obedience to their beauty follows them on into the ever more eminent phenomenality from which they descend and within which they are enfolded: the limitless *phainein* of the Logos. The infinite is an endless river of divine beauty, a ceaseless overflow of distinct delights, blessings, names, differences, and forms. For Bonaventure the great danger that besets a mind unschooled in praise is an oblivion of being in the contemplation of beings (*Itinerarium* 5.3-4), or a "naturalistic" tendency to take the world as directed toward itself (as, that is, a totality), rather than as oriented toward the infinite beauty of God (*Collationes in Hexaemeron* 12.15), in which it lives, moves, and is; but this means not that we should avert our eyes from beings, but that we should hear them as they speak of more than themselves, and should speak of them in and toward God.

That is, if God speaks the world, the world speaks of God, always saying more than merely world, and we speak licitly of God in and through the world: we name God from beings, even as we know that he, in his inaccessible mystery, alone knows the "meaning" of his names; all fatherhood in heaven and on earth is named of him. Thus, for example, the Father's love of the Son may be likened proportionately to a human parent's love for a child not simply as a convenient anthropomorphic fiction, but because creation is a real participatory expression of that eternal love that is always being born in the Father's giving of the Son, the Son's response to the Father, the witness and rejoicing of the Spirit. In every case, though, exemplarist or otherwise, analogy remains a "disjunctive synthesis" (to misappropriate Deleuze's terminology), which reconciles precisely by preserving the distance between the things reconciled. Because analogy is the felicitous coincidence of the apophatic and the cataphatic, its most appropriate form is doxological; it "clarifies" language about God not by reducing it to principles of simple similitude, but by making it more complex, more abundant and polyphonic, richer, deeper, fuller, according to the grammar of praise; it offers all words back up to the Word, who sets them free. Analogy saves apophasis from assuming the form of a mere systematic privation of attributes, a mystical ascent toward annihilation in the divine silence, and saves cataphasis from becoming an absolute pronouncement that attempts to reduce God to a principle or object; analogy is that lambent interval between the two dreamt-of poles of totalizing metaphysics. The apophatic impulse, especially, if unchecked by the inconclusiveness of analogy, becomes merely a flight from signs rather than a humble sense of their incompleteness and an awareness also of their rhetorical surfeit — that excess of signification that surpasses stable concepts. Between the desert of absolute apophaticism and the immobile hypotaxis of absolute cataphaticism stands the infinity, the unmasterable parataxis, of analogy, at home in an endless state of provisionality and promise. Analogy differs and defers, as a style of rejoicing, as a licit and yet infinitely insufficient act of predication, and as an aesthetic and moral reply to the divine address. Understood thus, the rhetorical, proportional, and exemplary are one: a rhetoric of peace, a "portrayal" of the infinite.

In a sense, theological analogy reflects the very logic of language's deferrals in such a way as to disclose their original peacefulness. If, as Roman Jakobson suggests, language can be understood as a tension between metaphor and metonymy (a distinction that cannot be regarded as absolute),[168] then analogy is simply the inmost logic of language made visible: it is at once the language of likeness and of proportion, of exemplarity (moving "metaphorically" from one frame of reference to another) and of particularity (remaining "metonymically" fixed in its context of reference). In its exemplary and metaphoric motion, analogy undertakes its quantitative *epektasis* toward God's beauty, while in its proportional and metonymic rootedness in the separate realms of discourse it spans, it preserves at every moment the interval of qualitative difference that separates the analogand from its analogate. If metaphor passes from one frame of meaning to another in order to achieve a proportion between discrete realms of meaning and imagery while metonymy remains situated within the more immediately referential interdependency of the syntagma in which it occurs, it is the interval of analogy — the interval between proportions that is also the interval to be traversed between two orders of signification — that constitutes language's ubiquitous tension; and when analogy passes from one context of reference to another (thus completing the motion of metaphor), and so simultaneously deepens and enriches the language by which the object of reference is described in either context (thus intensifying the rootedness of metonymy), it shows itself to be, at its best, a creative and reconciling practice, the gesture of peace, the inventive artistry of love. When it makes its metaphoric leap from one order of discourse to another while still

---

168. For a convenient summary of the distinction (in the context of a discussion of aphasia), see Roman Jakobson and Morris Halle, *Fundamentals of Language* (Paris: Mouton, 1971), 90-96.

preserving its proportionate placement in the discourse from which it emanates, it shows itself to be language's second difference, its pneumatological and outgoing power, which liberates difference as particularity, form, content, richness, and transparency rather than as univocal rupture and singularity; by crossing categories of meaning without simply disrupting the content — the context and coherency — of those categories (though some order of desirable disruption must occur), analogy releases an ever greater depth of particularity, a thematic plangency within the object of analogy that can be brought to hearing only by the "disjunctive synthesis" that casts one order of meaning in the light of another, that discovers resonances shared across irreducible intervals of difference.

Every sign (not just the root metaphor) is in a sense opaque, incapable of referential closure or of exhaustive exposition in other sequences of signification; but from the perspective of analogical thought, this very opacity can be seen as a fruitful resistance to reduction, a refractory or restive gravity that continually yields to further supplementation and reveals the entire parataxis of being's signs to be, potentially at least, an array of charitable donations, a motion of peace and abundance. Within the world of signs — within a world that is signification — opacity is transparency, insufficiency is the energy of adequation; the sign's resistance constitutes the transparency of being's surface, the openness of the horizon, the vision of what lies always ahead or what fills the distance. It is the relative fixity but manifest incompleteness of the metonymic that looses the endless serial divergence of metaphor. In a sense the inadequacy of the sign is like the *skandalon* of the text of Scripture, which for Origen was the provocation to allegorical interpretation and deeper devotion; desire is excited by the shortfall — the insufficiency — of the referent. An immense promise lies in the scandal of the sign, and gives rise to that allegorical metabolism by which one thing, through poetic conjunction, retells another thing, and is conversely retold by it; and both things shift in meaning, by way of this paratactic enrichment; and all things can be extended into an infinite context of meaning, to tell of the boundlessly expressive God. The sign's "ontic" insufficiency shows forth the "ontological" majesty to which it aspires. It is the Logos that renders all logoi provisional, unfulfilled, and yet boundless in their scope of meaning; it is the infinite analogical interval that sends the language of theology (and all language) upon its endless pilgrimage. Whatever is revealed of God disrupts — that is, renders analogical — what might otherwise be mistaken for stable and abiding categories: language concerning God's Fatherhood, for instance, delivers language concerning human fatherhood into a condition of perpetual provisionality.

According to Levinas, "God's" divinity cannot be given shape within language, within the world's chain of signification, but the trace of his transcendence can be expressed in the hyperbolic superlatives of language.[169] Divine transcendence can give discourse its structure, but cannot be made manifest in the sequences of correspondence or correlation that language is, because nothing within the said can or could correspond to a divine that is otherwise than being. This is Levinas's story: divine transcendence, in its infinity, is an impossible presence — which is also to say absence — that presses upon every instance of the said, always outside and over against the successiveness, referrals, and deferrals of language. There is, though, a better way of naming God's transcendence: it is that absolute excess expressed in the interminable supplementarity of language, as the infinity that comprehends and surpasses the entirety of the said, the concrete and determinate infinity that quantitatively exceeds all the sequences of spoken meaning, the utterance that infinitely comprises and outstrips all the finite utterances of being. It is not the trace that is both lost and recalled in the abandonment of language, but the very deferral of language itself that is the real and manifest presence of the transcendent, of the infinite God who always says infinitely more — who is the act of utterance never effaced by, but rather made manifest in, the finite utterances of creation (had we but ears to hear). Derrida, in discussing Heidegger's understanding of the trace of the ontological difference in the text of Western metaphysics (which is again the trace of what somehow stands before and apart from the textuality in which it is manifest), remarks that "The trace is not a presence but is rather the simulacrum of a presence that dislocates, displaces, and refers beyond itself. The trace has, properly speaking, no place, for effacement belongs to the very structure of the trace. Effacement must always be able to overtake the trace; otherwise it would not be a trace but an indestructible and monumental substance."[170] This describes the logic of the trace quite well, whether one is discussing the trace of being or of difference, the trace of the infinite, the trace that is the absence of presence or presence of absence, and so forth; in every case language, textuality, phenomenality is sealed off against an impossible immediacy of reference or presence. The trace lingers as an indication of that untraversable, unanalogizable interval (or rather, abyss) between the diachronic deferrals of the said (which is expressive of only other sequences of restless signification) and the synchronic totality of "monumental substance" (which *is* not, but which is forever "metaphysically" invoked); it is the tension between speech and a silence whose original withdrawal is the possibility of speech. But perhaps, setting out from the discourse of analogy (especially as it

---

169. Emmanuel Levinas, *Collected Philosophical Papers,* ed. and trans. Alphonso Lingis (The Hague: Nijhoff, 1987), 62.

170. Jacques Derrida, *Speech and Phenomena, and Other Essays on Husserl's Theory of Signs,* trans. David B. Allison (Evanston, Ill.: Northwestern University Press, 1972), 156.

might be reinterpreted in terms of Gregory of Nyssa's account of divine infinity), this last residue of the tension of metaphysics (even of metaphysics in dissolution) can be overcome; perhaps the qualitative infinity of a saying pure of any contamination by the said, which can insinuate itself into the termless infinite — the "bad" or quantitative infinite — only as the effaced trace of what is forsaken in the event of being, should be set aside, in either its dialectical or "nihilist" form, in favor of an analogical dynamism that surpasses this distinction altogether, an infinite movement of signs whose possibility lies in the continuity, across the distance of an ever greater unlikeness, between finite words and the *actus* of all saying and meaning, which speaks all things within its simple fullness. Analogy collapses the distinction of infinities (a distinction that, however deconstructed, cannot but depend upon some form of idealism), and so allows theology to think of deferral as the gift of presence, or presence as giving itself through supplementarity; in the analogical, final meaning is deferred to the witness of all difference, which is the witness of the determinate infinite that expresses itself there.

For Christian thought, then, analogy is not a discourse that recovers a lost or obscured identity; it does not discover a likeness that has been made unlike through the defatigation, palliation, or enervation of emanation; nor does it restore or repristinate a likeness made corrupt by its decline into materiality; nor does it disclose the ground of a metaphysical homonymy between the transcendent and the immanent, a dialectical drama of negation and determination. Certainly the analogical never offers an epistemic grasp of the divine, such that God comes to occupy a more and more stable place in a taxonomy of concepts. Insofar as analogy describes the way in which creation manifests the God who gives being, difference is the first term of the likeness, and speaks of the trinitarian God who always has distance and difference. And so analogy widens the interval of difference even as it closes it, asserts an ever greater dissimilitude embracing every similitude. Such is the nature of the ontological difference that analogy identifies: the God whose "infinite form" comprises all distance is himself the distance, the interval, between God and creation. God's infinite otherness comprehends all creation's likenesses. Theological analogy, proceeding from an *analogia entis,* does not identify substances within a hierarchy of substance, but succeeds as analogy precisely in its rhetorical excessiveness: not simply its hyperbolic intimation of an unsayable otherness, but its power to eventuate in ever greater ranges of supplementation, ever more elaborate and intricate metaphorical inventions. Analogy — as the dynamism by which language preserves and crosses the interval of the metaphoric and metonymic, the apophatic and cataphatic, the qualitative and quantitative infinite — is that infinitely open rhetoric that is still always exceeded by, and is always reaching out toward, the plenitude of the truth into which the Holy Spirit leads, the divine

utterance by which God is God. It instructs in a style, a way of speaking; it cultivates a vision; it is an experience of "being led into all truth"; it culminates —
or rather, abides — in faith: it is the receiving of words. In this way one's grammar is converted, one enters ever more into divine rhetoric and divine music:
one is conformed to Christ by assuming, and being assumed by, the language of
God's revelation. If analogy gives way to a language of frozen essences, of metaphysical correspondences, or of simple systems of substance, and so becomes
idolatrous and seeks to still the interminable deferrals of language, it fails not
through overreaching but through poverty, through an aesthetic deficiency, a
want of ingenuity. Indeed, insofar as analogy "corresponds" to its analogate
(the triune God), it does so through a certain restless inability to arrive at a depiction of the God who is infinitely different. The transcendence of God releases an endless sequence of utterances, each elaborating upon the other and
each rendering the other provisional, not because divine transcendence stands
over against language as the inexpressible, but because it infinitely exceeds every finite expression, comprehends it, and beckons it onward. In this way analogy recovers not a thing, not a substance, but corresponds to the gift of being
— the free, poetic utterance of creation — by imitating the gesture of the gift,
by replying to creation's rhetoric with something of the same poetic energy of
love, devotion, and delight. In assuring that difference does not become indifferent, does not disappear behind the griseous veil of ontological univocity,
analogy shows itself to be a diligent craft that discovers within its very contingency and inadequacy a *new* intonation of that truth that can always be recovered, because it is a truth that is a certain style of articulation, invention, and
appropriation, that is always open and always yielding to what is eminently
greater than itself. In its constant, mobile departure from tautology, analogy allows all things to reflect, answer, invoke, and shed a radiance upon all other
things, so that being's full display becomes visible as created light. Embraced by
the infinity of the divine utterance, governed by the words imparted by Scripture and according to the inventive grace of the Spirit, the words of analogy return to God precisely in venturing out into creation.

"Finality" of reference, then, is not the proper aim of analogical predication, except in an eschatologically and even infinitely delayed sense. Whenever
theological discourse sets out from a simple analogy — say that between the
love shared by husband and wife and the love shared by the persons of the Trinity, or that between human delight in beauty and God's delight in creation, or
that between God's mercy and a rushing stream — it engages in a style of language that is incapable of sustaining itself except through the constant refinement of its terms, which can be pursued only by way of further acts of analogy.
We need not pretend ever to escape the "text." As Augustine remarks, every
word is defined by only another word, or by a gesture that is still only another

sign (*De magistro* 2). Analogy is the linguistic practice that acknowledges and obeys this dynamism while also making manifest the eros for the infinite that stirs souls to become articulate, and to reflect upon their words. Because it introduces an analogical interval (which cannot, by definition, be reduced to "literal" correspondence, even when God is the "literal" reference) into every discourse of theological meaning, the practice of analogy never converts the signified into a stable "identity." This is why the epistemological yield of analogy cannot be isolated in merely conceptual categories, however much it may evoke and require them *in via;* it is as a semantic *practice* that analogy first corresponds to divine truth, and therein it acquires its epistemological function, inasmuch as knowledge is a practice, a kind of making, and analogy is a practice of praise, a refinement of the language of adoration, a chastening and setting free of tongues. In this way alone can language — which is deferral, metaphor's fruitful departure from and return to metonymy — faithfully reflect the language of the God who is always "imaged," who is his own "analogy": for analogy sees that the interminable semantic slippage of language is not simply devolution into the flux of ontological univocity, the perpetual play of the trace, the disappearance of presence in the making present of things, but the gesture of donation, the thematic variation and elaboration that is the very form of presence, the immediacy of the mediate, set free by the God who is his own mediation, his own response. In the yielding of each thing to each other, all becomes incandescently beautiful. Analogy follows the path of creative ordination and illimitable differentiation by which the Spirit is always perfecting creation: not through imposing upon it a simple unitary order of correspondences, but through creating ever more elaborate implications of complexity, ever more unanticipated resolutions, ever more ingenious and inventive harmonies — God's difference showing itself in the indefatigability of this ecstasy of naming, this venturing out across the divine distance. The always greater dissimilitude that encloses — or rather, exceeds — each of analogy's similitudes is the infinite trinitarian distance that one is still "quantitatively" traversing even when one seems to have found rest and strength in a clear likeness — like a wanderer who rests by a pool only to become enchanted by the limpidity with which he sees himself and the sky above reflected in its waters — and which therefore urges one to rise, depart again, and go on "from strength to strength." The "ever greater" of this unlikeness must not be mistaken for a dialectical tension or a contradiction within the analogy that simply erases (or sublates) what the analogy posits. This would be the cataphatic and apophatic oscillation of a purely adventurous mysticism whose terminus ad quem would be simply a "knowing" silence, an end to words, rather than their consummation. Rather it is a quantitative ever-greater that reveals the nature of the qualitative ever-greater as infinite fullness. The *maior dissimilitudo* is an infinite intensity, a living interval, manifestly crossed in Christ: not *aufgehoben* or held in fruitful tension, but always already a single discourse of boundless difference, one music, infinitely expressed in the trinitarian *perichoresis* and unfolded in creation, and in which the creature takes part not through dialectical negation but through an endless and joyous *epektasis*.

The traditional definition of analogy, which makes God the prime analogate who is the proper subject of the analogical predication, could be mistaken for the most ponderous kind of foundational discourse, a kind of talk concerning the inward fold of the sign — a concept or signified, embedded in universal "truth" — were it not the case that analogy is incapable of providing any concept that is, strictly speaking, conceivable; the face of the sign, turned toward God, yields further signs, their faces similarly averted from earthly eyes. What analogy does in deferring all proper predication to God is to multiply the inappropriability and opacity of the sign — its transcendence or excess — to infinity; meaning that it can never be free of or incapable of further supplementation. Analogy is a discourse of truth that has disabused itself of the notion that truth is a thing only to be grasped; truth is a dynamic donation, a splendor shared by the God who is always declaring his love in the gift of his *ousia*, within which splendor infinite progress is possible: knowledge that knows also the ever greater unknowing that calls it forth and onward. Analogy subsists upon the pursuit of the more beautiful, fitting, and unanticipated, and so speaks of a God of infinite beauty, harmony, and novelty; the analogical (in its metaphorical restlessness and predicative insufficiency) is the language of love drawing the lover onward, an ecstasy, always drinking in more of the infinite. Insofar as its motion of deferral is governed by charity and the language of praise, it is an *epektasis* of language toward and in the Word, a motion that, in traversing all the *semeia* of being and in always discovering new measures of accord and new styles of rejoicing, thematizes the infinite as beauty and as peace. And this thematization of the infinite — which then "corresponds" to the rhetoric of God in creation and redemption — is the highest piety, the sacrifice of praise, the utterance of the names of God.

But of course, all this talk of analogy is an abstraction if considered apart from the form of Jesus of Nazareth. As Bonaventure insists, the soul could never, in its condition of sin, reason its way from the things of the world to the beauty of God: only because the eternal truth assumed human form and became a ladder restoring the broken ladder of Adam, can the soul enter into and delight in the glory that creation makes manifest (*Itinerarium* 4.2). It is Christ, the Logos and measure of all things, who calls analogy forth, who shows the proportions, forms, and bounty of creation in their truest light. If not for Christ, analogical practice would dissolve into a shapeless and insubstantial parataxis (in the worst sense: catalectic, anacoluthic, arbitrary); it could apprehend, ultimately, only the sublime interminability of things, rather than the beauty that pervades and embraces them. In the time of sin, God himself, who imparts the theme of creation, must give the theme again, must himself restate his supreme rhetoric: which comes now in the form of a servant.

III. SALVATION

1. Salvation occurs by way of recapitulation, the restoration of the human image in Christ, the eternal image of the Father after whom humanity was created in the beginning; thus salvation consists in the recovery of a concrete form, and in the restoration of an original beauty.

Now is the judgment of this world: now shall the prince of this world be cast out. And I, if I be lifted up from the earth, will draw all men unto me.

John 12:31-32

Jesus cried and said, He that believeth on me, believeth not on me, but on him that sent me. And he that seeth me seeth him that sent me.

John 12:44-45

But be of good cheer; I have overcome the world.

John 16:33

Therefore as by the offence of one judgment came upon all men to condemnation; even so by the righteousness of one the free gift came upon all men unto justification of life. For as by one man's disobedience many were made sinners, so by the obedience of one shall many be made righteous.

Rom. 5:18-19

But now is Christ risen from the dead, and become the firstfruits of them that slept. For since by man came death, by man came also the resurrection of the dead. For as in Adam all die, even so in Christ shall all be made alive. But every man in his own order: Christ the firstfruits; afterward they that are Christ's at his coming. Then cometh the end, when he shall have delivered up the kingdom to God, even the Father; when he shall have put down all rule and all authority and power. For he must reign, till he hath put all enemies under his feet. The last enemy that shall be destroyed is death. For he hath put all things under his feet. But when he saith all things are put under him, it is manifest that he is excepted, which did put all things under him. And when all things shall be subdued unto him, then shall the Son also himself be subject unto him that put all things under him, that God may be all in all.

1 Cor. 15:20-28

And hath put all things under his feet, and gave him to be the head over all things to the church, which is his body, the fulness of him that filleth all in all.

Eph. 1:22-23

Let this mind be in you, which was also in Jesus Christ: Who, being in the form of God, thought it not robbery to be equal with God: But made himself of no reputation, and took upon him the form of a servant, and was made in the likeness of men: And being found in fashion as a man, he humbled himself, and became obedient unto death, even the death of the cross.

Phil. 2:5-8

Who is the image of the invisible God, the firstborn of every creature: For by him were all things created, that are in heaven, and that are in earth, visible and invisible, whether they be thrones, or dominions, or principalities, or powers: all things were created by him, and for him: And he is before all things, and by him all things consist.

Col. 1:15-17

Who now rejoice in my sufferings for you, and fill up that which is behind of the afflictions of Christ in my flesh for his body's sake, which is the church.

Col. 1:24

For here we have no continuing city, but we seek one to come.

Heb. 13:14

i. The Form of Distance

To speak of Christ as God's supreme rhetoric, as a way of understanding his character as the eternal Word and express image of the Father, is also to call attention to the "rhetoricity" of his earthly career: for, despite the "messianic secret" of his mission, there is nothing occult in his teaching, nor do his mysteries seal a hidden deposit of cryptadia to which admission can be gained, by a special few, only through trial, initiation, and a secret gnosis. Christian initiation consists only in instruction in what is openly proclaimed by the church (which refers to what is made utterly manifest in the person and life of Jesus of Nazareth) and in sacramental integration into the community that constitutes Christ's body. One speaks of the hiddenness of the Son's Godhead in the flesh of Jesus, but one does not mean by this anything like the cunning concealments of a gnostic savior: it is the very flesh of Jesus that reveals the nature of his divinity — the essential condescension of divine love — and it is by way of his flesh that his divinity is imparted to others, in the breaking of his body. Christ is called God, is indeed God the Son, and so is not a symbol of God, a mere signifier indicating God, or simply a messenger of God; his continuity with the Father is one of much more radical aesthetic immediacy: he, uniquely, is the very form of God; in him sign and significance are one. As the supreme rhetoric of the Father, therefore, the form of Christ contains and exceeds the whole range of attribution and praise brought to bear upon it; and this is so precisely because it has no docetic surface. There is no failure of correspondence between how Christ appears and the truth he reveals: he is not an impalpable and unworldly redeemer, a ladder for souls, rising up out of the quagmires of flesh and time, but the Lord who saves precisely because he can be grasped, precisely because of his concrete particularity, his real and appearing beauty, which draws others on into history, into the contingencies and particularities of time, into the concrete community of the church. He embodies a real and imitable practice, a style of being that conforms to the beauty of divine love, but that is also a way of worldly godliness; he is no beautiful soul. As the supreme beauty, the *perpulchrum*, Christ — as Bonaventure says — is the measure of all beauty, who restores beauty to what has become formless through sin and death, makes the beautiful yet more beautiful, and makes the exceedingly beautiful more beautiful still (*Collationes in Hexaemeron* 1.34). It may be so, as Michel de Certeau asserts, that Christ offers "a style of existence that 'allows' for a certain kind of creativity and that opens a new series of experiences," but he does so not as the "degree zero of a series," to use the same author's phrase, an absent event, an energy of withdrawal;[171] he

---

171. Michel de Certeau, "Autorités Chrétiennes et Structures Sociales," in *La Faiblesse de Croire* (Paris: Editions du Seuil, 1987), 111-12.

does so as the Logos who comprises — even in his historical particularity — the fullness of every expression to which his form gives rise, the truth of every beauty consequent upon his beauty.

The Logos of Christian thought, that is, is not a synthesis arrived at by way of history's "process," but is at once infinite, surpassing and encompassing the whole of history, and indissolubly particular, situated within the contingencies and complexities of history. The logos of any systematic metaphysics, or of any postmodern flight from metaphysics (which sustains itself by extending indefinitely the moment of metaphysics' death), lives its circumscribed life on the respectable bank of Lessing's ditch, from which it can view the tumult of history with only a removed and dispassionate mien; its discourse is one of abstraction. But, in Christian thought, the "transcendent" vantage that takes in all things is that provided by a particular first-century Jew. It is in the life of Jesus, lived to the end and vindicated in the resurrection, that the measure of the world is given. And while the form of Christ is at once the perfect repetition and fulfillment of the form of creation, Christ comes into a world that has constructed its own totality, its own orders of thrones, dominions, principalities, and powers, and must cast them down — and do so by means of that very historical shape that constitutes his identity as Jesus of Nazareth. Even theology's most ambitious christological predications emerge from the historical event of Jesus; it is, one could say, the very metonymic restiveness of the form of Christ, its implication in an immense range of historical specificities, that yields such endless and endlessly fruitful sequences of metaphorical and speculative commentary, his impenetrability, "opacity," and quite concrete otherness that provide that profound resistance (which is also a profound analogical "generosity") that allows for limitlessly many perspectives upon, variations of, and appropriations of the form he offers to the world: words of praise, theologoumena, the lives of those whose sanctity is an interpretation and expression of who he is, the corporate practices of love and forgiveness that the church (at least ideally) fosters, the sharing again and again of his eucharistic presence, and all the many ways in which the force of Christ's presence in history is extended and expounded and recognized. Christ is the perfect proportion, the complete Word of the God who is always his own analogy; he is the infinite Word whose analogical scope releases — and so contains — an infinite sequence of words. There is in Christ, always already, an alterity and an excess that passes beyond every limitation, every division between the "immanent" and "transcendent," every "excessive" style of predication, even to the point that the word "God" proves necessary to the exposition of his form. And thus Christ — in his incarnation, life, and resurrection, and in the linguistic and aesthetic radiance that shines out from him — reveals the essential truth concerning God's infinity: its determinacy, dynamism, and power to cross every boundary.

Christ expresses, therefore, a trinitarian mystery that can only seem, from the perspective of a human history largely governed by force and falsity, a paradox. The form of Christ inhabits at once a province of shadows and a region of glorious light, he is at once nocturnally and diurnally beautiful, his is simultaneously a way of abasement and a way of exaltation. And these two ways are one: not a before and after, but a venturing forth from and return to the Father that is one motion, one life, one dramatic action that overcomes totality's defining horizon — death — not through reconciliation with the limits it marks but through an infinite act of *kenosis* and glorification that transgresses it, passes it by as though it were nothing. The motion of Christ's life is not one of temporary concealment and dramatic unveiling, diremption and synthesis, or alienation and reconciliation; all trinitarian theology depends upon the belief that Christ's *kenosis* is not a moment of separation, a descent from some otherworldly *pleroma* into a condition of estrangement, but a manifestation of the one eternal act by which God is God. The story of the Son's incarnation, life, death, and resurrection is not the story of a divine masquerade, of a king who goes forth in self-divestment — like the incognito king in *Henry V* visiting the camps at night, or like the duke in *Measure for Measure* going about Vienna appareled as a friar — simply to return, by way of some great Platonic or Hegelian circuit, to the estate he has abandoned, nor is it a story like that of the protagonist in *The Song of the Pearl,* losing himself in the far country and then finding his true self again only in his return to his distant demesne. The Son goes forth because going forth is always already who he is as God, because all wealth and all poverty are already encompassed in his eternal life of receiving and pouring out, his infinitely accomplished bliss and love, his *apatheia;* and so he is hidden in being manifest and manifest in being hidden: he is the God he is in his very divestment and in his glory, both at once, as the same thing, inseparably. Because God is Trinity, and always gives and goes forth toward the other, he is never simply the king who sits immobile at the center of being, deploying his powers; he is not the onto-theos ruling over being's empire, its totality. As the Gospel of John makes clear, Christ's crucifixion is also his glorification; it is in being lifted up upon the cross that he draws the world to himself. Even in Christ's dereliction, God's infinity is made manifest: in the agony of Gethsemane, Christ's prayers express a distance from the Father that is also a pure intimacy (for God is that distance); his distance from the Father, which both recapitulates and overcomes humanity's sinful estrangement from God, reveals the intratrinitarian distance. In going into the region of death, which lies over against God in enmity toward him and his creation, Christ shows that the divine infinity surpasses all separations; and in the resurrection he shows that the Son traverses the infinite as the infinite gift, never ceasing to be form: the "excess" of his infinity remains beauty, even as it spills over and erases boundaries.

Hence, in his going forth, the Son is always drawing near to the Father (such is the trinitarian distance, in which there can be no exile): the Father is always sending the Spirit upon the Son and the Spirit is always bearing tidings of the Son to the Father; and even in his return to the Father the Son is always imparted outward, always sending the Spirit, always being given by the Spirit as sacrament and community. This means that the form of God revealed in the form of Christ is recognizable not only in the singularity of Jesus, but in how his particularity is a style of distance: God is made manifest in the interval opened by the divine persons, and so is seen in the coincidence in Christ's life of obedience and grace and grandeur and lowliness, in all their mystery. The greater the freedom of the Son's journey, the more profound the difference spanned and the farther the distance traversed, the more surely is God God. No worldly measure of glory is equal to what is here revealed. God's power is manifest most profoundly in the Son's *kenosis* because God's power is the infinite peace of an eternal venture of love, the divine ecstasy whose fullness is the joy of an eternal self-outpouring. Thus the divine has no proper "place," belongs to no hierarchy within totality; it is the infinite context of every place, the distance whose original grammar is love, prior to every division between high and low, supernatural and natural, transcendent and immanent. A purely idealist metaphysics of the beautiful (such as, say, Plotinus's) can point in only one direction, away from the world toward the simple and transcendent source of all beauty; but Christian thought, with its trinitarian premise, must follow the path of beauty outward into the world, even into states of privation. Christian thought does not simply ascend to the beautiful, but finds the beautiful in the entire scope of the divine life, even as it proceeds "downward" into utter inanition: God ventures even into the godless, and still his beauty is there, still offered as gift, delight, and love.

A caution, though: the attempt to interpret the truth of God's beauty in abasement can assume a vulgar and unreflective form, especially in this age of fashionable nihilism. Witness Don Cupitt: "[T]he God of Christianity is a God who in Christ becomes human and in the [S]pirit becomes the endless interrelatedness of everything. The doctrine of the Trinity secularizes and enhistoricizes God, disperses God into the flux of the world."[172] This is of course the familiar strategy of that style of impoverished Hegelianism that one associates with "death of God" theologies, such as Thomas Altizer's, which has been assumed into so many attempts to write a "postmodern theology"; it treats trinitarian theology as eventuating inexorably in the exhaustion of talk

---

172. Don Cupitt, "Unsystematic Ethics and Politics," in *Shadow of Spirit: Postmodernism and Religion*, ed. Philippa Berry and Andrew Wernick (London and New York: Routledge, 1992), 155.

concerning God's transcendence, the death of onto-theology, a "joyous" and "sacramental" embrace of finitude. There is nothing extraordinary or original in Cupitt's remark; I quote him, however, not as a novelty, but as illustrative of a pathology. One can quickly set aside the bleak and ghastly suggestion that the Spirit is just another name for the univocity of being — for, that is, the indifferent relatedness of all things (would this include, one almost dreads to ask, the relation, say, between Jews and Nazis?) — but one should pause long enough to note that it demonstrates again how thoroughly dependent upon a conventional metaphysical vision of the transcendent and immanent "postmetaphysical" approaches to the doctrine of the Trinity generally are. Like Nietzsche's madman, announcing God's death and wondering "Who gave us the sponge to wipe away the entire horizon?"[173] the "atheologian" has always already mistaken the God of Christian tradition for one whose transcendence provides the world with its horizon, who defines the limits of being, and who guards the boundaries of totality. To mistake the trinitarian dynamism of the cross for the simple defatigation of transcendence is possible only if one understands the relation between divine transcendence and creaturely immanence in the very terms — a mere opposition between highest principle and world — that the Christian doctrines of creation and Trinity first overcame. The triune God is infinite, transcendently infinite, because the motion of the divine *perichoresis* eternally transcends not only the immanent order of creaturely being but "transcendence" as such; in the trinitarian motion of begetting and procession, wisdom and love, God has always overcome every such horizon, passed beyond every border, by way of a greater transcendence — one that embraces, transfigures, and comprises the immanent in itself. For Christian thought, it is equally impossible either to view the world as being sustained by the tension between immanent and transcendent or to view it as sealed off into a self-contained and yet interminable immanence; it has already cast aside the categories that all such styles of thought presume. The story of Jesus of Nazareth belongs eternally to the life of God because there is no contradiction or tension between the course of the Son into the world — into flesh and time, past the very limits of creaturely being into the darkness of death and hell, past even death into the glorious life of the resurrection — and the eternal being of the Son as God; from eternity God is the boundless, the *apeiron*, who exceeds all these limits, but as form, inasmuch as being — the being of God and then the being of creatures too — is itself nothing but a movement of self-outpouring, manifestation, an act of abasement and exaltation in the single gesture of the gift. In the life, death, and resurrection of Christ, the whole trinitarian mystery

173. Friedrich Nietzsche, *The Gay Science*, trans. Walter Kaufmann (New York: Vintage Books, 1974), 181.

is revealed as an infinite overcoming of every totality, entire and sufficient, a life of fullest love, not requiring the supplement of created time but embracing time nonetheless in its infinite motion. The transcendence of God, far from consisting in a cold and dialectical immunity from the distance of the immanent, consists in his having eternally crossed the immanent in the one proper motion of his triune identity: for the world belongs already to the expressive generosity of the Father in his Word and Spirit, and lives and moves and is in him.

However, the salvific power of the incarnation lies not simply in its revelation of God's form, but in its restoration of the human form, humanity's resumption — in Christ — of the divine image. In Christ God brings about a return of the gift he has given in creation by himself giving it again, anew, according to that trinitarian dynamism in which donation and restoration are one; Christ effects a recapitulation, an ἀνακεφαλαίωσις, that refashions the human after its ancient beauty and thus restores it to the Father. As the Logos who is at once the very likeness of the Father and the true measure of creation, without contradiction, the Son is himself, in a sense, the ontological analogy between God and creation, the Word that comprises and permits endlessly many words, the infinite measure who allows all the measures and proportions of creation to speak of God, as instances of his glory; but as a man he is this analogy in the form of a dramatic action that restores the measure that has been forsaken. Because the true story of the world has been lost in the seemingly endless epic of sin, Christ must retell — in the entire motion and content of his life, lived both toward the Father and for his fellows — the tale from the beginning. Says Athanasius, the Logos became flesh in order to reestablish the original pattern after which the human form was crafted in the beginning, and to impress anew upon creation the beauty of the divine image (*De incarnatione* 11–16). No theologian (except perhaps Paul) placed more explicit emphasis on the theme of salvation through recapitulation than did Irenaeus. One can, admittedly, easily mistake the Irenaean language of *anakephalaiosis* for a decorative exercise in typology, a quaint and picturesque but unsophisticated soteriology (salvation by motif); but, in fact, Irenaeus describes with extraordinary felicity the necessary logic of all Christian soteriology. It is because Christ's life effects a narrative reversal, which unwinds the story of sin and death and reinaugurates the story that God tells from before the foundation of the world — the story of the creation he wills, freely, in his eternal counsels — that Christ's life effects an ontological restoration of creation's goodness; it is because the rhetoric of his form restores the order of divine rhetoric that creation properly is that created being is redeemed in him. True, Irenaeus's account does begin as though it were merely a typological meditation, contrasting the disobedience of Eve with the obedience of Mary, the one's credulity before the serpent and the other's receptivity before the angel of the annunciation (*Adversus haereses* 5.19.1-2); but it soon becomes evident that this fits into a deeply considered understanding of God's saving action in Christ. First and foremost, Christ recapitulates humanity's struggle against evil, and in so doing achieves the victory that humanity could not (5.21.1); he who is from the beginning the head of all things recapitulates the human entirely, in the shape and substance of a whole life lived for the Father, never lapsing into sin, never yielding to the temptation to turn from God, enacting in every instant the divine figure of the human (5.21.1-3). Thus, as Paul says, the disobedience of Adam, which brings death into the world, is undone by Christ's obedience unto death (5.23.2). We are very far here from any kind of vulgar idealism: human "nature" is not a concrete universal that, simply through the metabolism of the incarnation, is divinized. Humanity does indeed possess a true form, a proper nature, but it is one that is also essentially a communal coinherence, as well as a real act, a motion, the entire dramatic fullness of a life. Each person is "narrated" by and "narrates" that nature, and each inevitably repeats the pattern of sin that disfigures it; but Christ, in the entire shape of his life, renarrates it according to its original pattern. Thus, correctly, the ontological, the typological, and the moral accounts of salvation are one for Irenaeus.

It is because the motion of his life thus reinstates the true pattern of the human, one should add, that Christ is brought to the cross. In entering into a world that has fallen under the power of principalities whose rule is violence and lies, the true human pattern (the Logos) can appear only as a form crucified, which the world can grasp only as contrariety. Nonetheless, it is a real form, it assumes palpable shape within time, it can be beheld, imitated, obeyed, and adored; in Christ a real reversal has occurred, within historical experience, a real and visible beauty has cast its light upon the figure of sinful humanity and revealed it to be a false image, an apostasy of the soul from its own beauty. And in the resurrection, what is bestowed by this narrative reversal is shown to be a beauty that is inextinguishable, the beauty that is desired, willed, and claimed back to himself by the Father, the form that he will not suffer to see corruption or to be banished from the world of vision, flesh, and life. The resurrection — far from liberating Christ's otherworldly essence from the servile form in which it has hitherto been hidden — vindicates and imparts again the whole substance of Christ's earthly life, the shape of its particularity, which is, precisely in its humble and slavish form, an overcoming of earthly powers. His is a pattern that sinful history cannot accommodate (which is why pagan critics from Celsus to Nietzsche can find no way properly to account for the figure of Christ or for the force of his presence in time), but this is not to say that he must in consequence withdraw from history; rather, he initiates a real counterhistory, a new practice and new form of life that is —

as it happens — the true story of the world. Thus the recapitulation of humanity in Christ — resurrected humanity — has all the particularity and variety of a concrete historical act: it is a practice, a style of transmission, susceptible of variation, analogical imitation, extension, and elaboration. The hiddenness of God in Christ, Christ's messianic secret, is nevertheless an open and unconcealed shape of existence; it can be followed on through the contingencies of time and can, when seen in Easter's light, be recognized as complete diaphaneity: Christ's moment of most absolute particularity — the absolute dereliction of the cross — is the moment in which the glory of God, his power to be where and when he will be, is displayed before the eyes of the world. When the full course of Christ's life is completed and is raised up by the Father, his "hiddenness" is shown to be a different kind of substantial presence, one that *is* only in being handed over in love, surrendered, and given anew; thus his "hiddenness" is in fact that openness with which his presence is embodied in the church's practices, the exchange of signs of peace, the sacramental transparency of the community of the body of Christ. The church exists in order to become the counterhistory, nature restored, the alternative way of being that Christ opens up: the way of return. It is in this sense, principally, that the Word assumes human nature (as Irenaeus understood): by entering into the corporate identity of the body of the old Adam, the body of death, to raise all humanity up again in his body of glory.

ii. Christ the Sign

The recapitulation of creation in Christ occurs within the one creative utterance of God in his eternal Word; Christ can redeem the world, and restore it to its own nature by uniting it to his, because as Logos he is eternally the source, place, and end of all creation's logoi. This truth is not merely a metaphysical one, though; no less than the appearance of the human form's divine *ratio* within time, the appearance of the eternal Word among the words of creation has a concrete historical shape. The incarnation is the Father's supreme rhetorical gesture, in which all he says in creation is given its perfect emphasis. This is particularly evident in the Gospel accounts of Christ's miracles: the healing of infirmities, the raising of the dead, the feeding of the hungry, even the transformation of water into wine. These are not acts that manipulate or negate the order of creation in order to achieve an astounding effect; in them the goodness of creation is reaffirmed, its peace is restored: they repeat God's gift of creation by imparting joy in the good things of the world — food and wine, fellowship and rejoicing, life and vision and health — to those in whom such joy is lacking. Christ's miracles — as do all the aspects of his life and ministry — constitute a *semeiosis* (John's Gospel, in fact, calls them *semeia*) that restores the original *semeiosis* of the world, the language of divine glory, and that reorients all the signs of creation toward the everlasting sign of God who walks among them. As Augustine remarks, Christ's miracles are not intended merely to provoke amazement; to the person able to read them as signs they are simply true, a discourse of God's truth, a text adorned by the particularly lovely illuminations of the writer, but a text nonetheless (*Sermon* 98.3). Mere marvels — mere tricks or θαύματα — could never be woven into the greater narrative, either of Christ's nature as God's express likeness or of creation in Christ, because such marvels always constitute an interruption, inducing not only awe but confusion; the *semeia* of Christ, however, are transparently acts of lordship and love, and testify to Christ's nature as the creative Word who can command and restore all the words of creation.

Which means, conversely, that all the signs of created being may, without contradiction, speak of him: there is a limitless array of ways in which creation's words may be employed in service to the Word who has spoken them all eternally within the infinity of his "ever greater." Every declaration of Christ (such as the church's confession of faith in him), consequent upon the declaration of divine love that he is, is an attempt to express the glory that is visible as the "other side" of his way of abasement, the Taboric splendor that breaks from his form in an endless series of signs. No claim regarding Christ can be excessive; everything that the Christian tradition says or attempts to say about him can be, at most, a joyous but inadequate attempt to span the infinity of the sign that he is: an *epektasis* of words, in and toward the Word. One might well advert here again to Ricoeur's notion of "root metaphors": by analogy to those moments within language where a special "depth" or power shows itself, one might say that the form of Christ constitutes a moment of unique semeiotic intensity, resistance, and inexhaustibility that corresponds to the boundless fecundity of the Logos; and this richness and impenetrability are due in part to the intractable historicality and particularity of that form, its character as an event among events, irreducible to synopses and systems. The figure of Christ accrues more figures, it yields ever more "excessive" statements in regard to itself, positively requiring the supplementations of Christian dogmatics, various kinds of piety and ecclesial practice, and the formulae of Christian philosophy. This is the analogical and poetical eruption that follows from the aesthetic power of Christ's presence, the inevitable exposition of the style of lordship — the measure of glory — that he embodies, never having said enough until it has said "God" — which is the very impossibility of ever having said enough. And still Jesus of Nazareth, the Father's Logos, beckons language on.

There really is no other instance of a figure like Christ, in whom attributions of such extravagance and details of such mundane particularity not only coincide, but indeed inhere in one another: the story of Christ is immovably fixed within a social and historical context of absolute specificity, apart from which there is no path of salvation. His history is his universality; his humanity is appropriate to his divinity. The infinite motion by which God is God is made manifest in the way of Jesus into the world; God's glory is revealed in the dereliction of the cross; the economy of salvation is the presence in history of the trinitarian *perichoresis*. For this reason there is in Christian thought regarding Jesus a marvelous simultaneity of the "high" and "low," the infinite and finite, the dogmatic and the historical; trinitarian doctrine is not something rescued from the contingencies of Christ's historical existence, but something discovered there — entirely manifest — and nowhere else. Christ's *kenosis* is not diremption but expression, the very shape of God's eternal life; and so, in Christ, the infinite and finite abide together in a new and endlessly variable perspective, upon the unique axis of his temporal career. Insofar as the infinity of the Word made manifest in Christ is rooted in the "metonymic" restiveness of Jesus' finite historical form, all the metaphoric elaborations upon his form that this infinity comprises are still concretely governed by the very particular and unsubstitutable style of his life, and obey the grammar established in his own ordering of creation's signs, his reordering of human desire, his manner of articulating himself as God's eternal utterance. In its resistance to every universalizing reduction, every assault upon its particularity, the figure of Christ sets free an interminable sequence of analogies; and this is itself a sign of his divinity. It is not the case that every form virtually contains an endlessly various effect (the sheer defatigation of the aesthetic force of almost any form in the disseminations of language is inevitable), but the form of Christ uniquely comprehends and exceeds an infinite range of expressions without ceasing to be the particular form it is. If the Word of God comprises not simply the ideas of things but the entire range of being's differing utterances, this is grasped by theological reflection in the rhetorical and figurative radiance that breaks from the form of the incarnate Word; that he contains all words — that he is the true measure of creation, the form that reveals the pleasure of the Father in all his works, and the shape of what is pleasing to the Father — is made clear by the boundlessness of the analogical response he enfolds in the perfect intensity of his form. If creation is an address, a divine discourse of glory, comprised as a paratactic infinity within God's eternal Logos, then the sign that Christ is, in its boundless ramifying fecundity, constitutes the analogy that perfectly corresponds to the truth of the world — and so restores to the world its truth. This is the aesthetic substance of the incarnation, the way in which the analogical interval — the infinite distance — between God and his creatures is shown to be entirely traversed in the incarnation.

To speak thus is again to call attention to the utter difference between the *kenosis* of the infinite and the "negation" of the absolute, between the *power* of the infinite to manifest itself in one instance of the finite and the *need* of the absolute to suffer determination or diminishment in the contingent in order to achieve manifestation. John Caputo (following Derrida) castigates as yet another expression of metaphysics the hermeneutical ploy of subordinating the disseminations of textuality to one or another "thematicism," especially one that defines the finitude of every expression over against an infinity of meaning that no expression can exhaust; the notion of an undifferentiated infinite that simply underlies the finite and contains its divergences belongs to a totalizing dialectic of the infinite and finite, he says, one that seeks to still the undialectical "in-finity" of dissemination, the play without boundaries that obeys no syntax of total intelligibility.[174] This may serve as a rebuke to one or another magisterial philosophical hermeneutics, but I trust it is just such a subsumption of finitude in the infinite that is subverted by the thought of Jesus of Nazareth as the divine Logos, comprising all words; in that Christ is *just this* particular rabbi, this particular life, this particular way of abasement and exaltation, he is not the underlying truth of every discourse as such, the metalinguistic context of all language that assures the openness of every horizon of meaning to every other, the dialectic reconciling all terms. Rather, as Word he comes as a word among words, a discourse among discourses, a particular rhetoric that stands at odds with many of the rhetorics of the world; as the living infinite that passes by every boundary as form, Christ's dramatic and formal concreteness comprehends all the signs of creation by reordering them according to his own form, his own series, his own practice and history. Which is to say his kingdom is not of this world, that the thrones and principalities and dominions that preside over the world often speak a language inimical to the language of creation — the discourse of the gift — and must be overcome by the language that Christ instaurates in himself. No division can finally be drawn between the style of God's address in Christ and the content of what it reveals; and it is a style of being that stands contrary to many of the fashions of the world, its romances of power, its hierarchies of truths, its prudential violences and narratives of rights, rules, and possessions. He is the *ratio* of all things, but is also a word of contradiction, a sword of division. He is not just the absolute truth to which all things, through dialectical labor, may be reduced, nor the shapeless plenitude of a truth toward which all discourse makes an asymptotic approach and with which all "meaningful" discourse is ultimately concerned; the Logos is that infinite distance in which all things participate, but to which all things may attest only insofar as they are conformed to the measure of charity that Christ reveals

---

174. John Caputo, *Radical Hermeneutics: Repetition, Deconstruction, and the Hermeneutic Project* (Bloomington and Indianapolis: Indiana University Press, 1987), 149-50.

as the true *form* of the infinite. The labor, then, whose issue is truth is not first that of dialectic, but that of repentance. Even in "recapitulating" humanity in himself, Christ does not simply effect a "reduction" to an "essential" original, but opens up a new series, a real historical sequence and practical style, which permits endlessly various articulations (what theology calls the communion of saints). This is the limitless motion of *anakephalaiosis,* the way in which the form of Christ renarrates the human form entirely, and in which his particularity at once claims and sets free every other, in the power of the Holy Spirit, who binds all things together in love and releases all things into their particularity in peace.

iii. "What Is Truth?"

If Christ, the eternal Word, is the Father's "supreme rhetoric," then the truth of his evangel is of a very particular kind. As soon as one ventures appreciably past the bounds of logic's most unadorned and uncontroversial claims (and sometimes before one gets that far), one finds that what is called truth is usually a consensus wrested from diversity amid a war of persuasions, the victor's crown of laurels laid upon the brow of whichever dialectical antagonist has better (for the time being) succeeded in rendering invisible his argument's own ambiguities and contradictions (has better, that is, concealed the more purely rhetorical moments of his argument in the folds of his apparently unanswerable "logic"); and into the tumult of history Christ comes as a persuasion among persuasions, a Word made entirely flesh, entirely form, whose appeal lies wholly at the surface. Moreover, the figure of Christ would seem to be at a considerable disadvantage in this fray, standing as it does apart from all those truths that hold most potent sway over history: as Origen says, its rhetoric is one of peace, not advancing itself under the aegis of power or affluence or prestige, but surrendering itself in the form of a servant.[175] The address of God in Christ, the *kerygma* of his form, is transparently rhetorical — it commands no other power over minds — for it calls out for devotion to this man, in all his indigent particularity, his humility, his strange beauty and abiding mystery. This is why God's Word can be received in human history only under the aspect of contrariety: not because the Word of God stands dialectically over against creaturely finitude as such, but simply because the words of creation (though they belong primordially to the peace and expressive beauty of God's Word) lie in subjugation to the rhetoric of power, the glamor of violence, and a certain language of abstract and universal truth, by whose rationality every hierarchy within total-

---

175. See *Contra Celsum* 1.30. Cf. the anonymous *Epistle to Diognetus* 7.3-5.

ity justifies and sustains its regime. A rhetoric of truth that is so openly rhetoric — whose entire gesture is that of a gift committed to others, and whose form is at once so humble and so compelling, so slavish and so forthright in its proclamation of things hidden from the foundation of the world — must inevitably stand as an offense against truths that profess to subsist upon "disinterested" dialectic alone, or array themselves in the trappings of social authority, or advance their claims over others with arms and instruments of juridical terror. Thus the truth of a world order enslaved to sin and death inevitably must marshal all its "dialectical" resources to resist this rhetoric; the truth of the "god of this world" must crucify the truth of God's Word.

Nowhere is this clearer than in the account in John's Gospel of the dialogue between Christ and Pilate (John 18:28–19:12). Nietzsche, predictably, thought Pilate got the better of this exchange, that his "What is truth?" represents the only moment of genuine nobility in the New Testament, and that Pilate, as a dramatis persona of the Gospel, should be read as a canny and incisive ironist, who cannot help but be unimpressed by all of Christ's impudent talk of a kingdom not of this world, and of the truth to which he bears witness;[176] for Nietzsche, jesting Pilate has seen around the illusion informing all claims of truth, every metaphysical, religious, moral, or dialectical discourse alike. But, then again, Pilate's question is itself supremely dialectical, supremely Socratic: confronted by a claim of truth, by a rhetorical gesture that invites recognition from the one addressed but that makes no argument for itself apart from this invitation, Pilate seeks to deflect its force by averting his gaze from the truth placed before his eyes to an abstract question concerning the truth of truth. Jesus, though, has made no assertion to the effect that he is *true,* that he is appealing to "truth" in the abstract, but has said rather that he is himself the truth he offers and bears witness to; he has already answered Pilate's question, as it happens, and Pilate has simply maneuvered away from the unsettling claim Christ makes upon him.[177] And again, when Christ has been scourged and mocked, Pilate seeks one last time to force Christ to provide some account of himself,

---

176. See Friedrich Nietzsche, *The Anti-Christ,* trans. R. J. Hollingdale (New York: Penguin Books, 1968), esp. 162.

177. Perhaps no theologian has ever better understood the character of God's revelation in Christ as rhetorical rapture, rather than dialectical emprise, than Augustine: "Hoc enim scriptus est: *Quoniam deus lux est,* non quomodo isti oculi vident, sed quomodo videt cor cum audit, veritas est. Noli quaerere quid sit veritas; statim enim se opponent caligines imaginum corporalium et nubila phantasmatum et perturbabunt serenitatem quae primo ictu diluxit tibi cum dicerem, veritas. Ecce in ipso primo ictu qua velut coruscatione perstringeris cum dicitur veritas mane si potes; sed non potes. Relaberis in ista solita et terrena. Quo tandem pondere, quaeso, relaberis nisi sordium contractarum cupiditatis visco et peregrinationis erroribus?" (*De Trinitate* 8.2.3).

some pedigree — "Whence art thou?" — that might lend authority to, or at least make explicable, the extraordinary claims he makes for himself; Pilate strives to dispel the power of the rhetoric that stands before him, crowned with thorns, and at the last can only pronounce the one truth he himself knows — "knowest thou not that I have power to crucify thee?" — and can then only bring that truth to pass, even in a kind of helplessness, by handing Christ over to death. Rather than the noble ironist, then, Pilate is simply a purblind reactionary: Jesus has already subverted the order of truth to which Pilate subscribes, and Pilate has no choice but to act to restore it. Christ's, however, is a truth that is only made more manifest in being suppressed; its gesture is that of the gift, which is given even in being rejected; and so, on the cross, Christ makes the sheer violence that underlies the economies of worldly truth transparent to itself, and opens up a different order of truth, a different story, one told anew and with ever greater power every time violence is employed to silence it.

The gesture by which God's Word is offered in time, for this reason, is one that none of the immanent distinctions of the totality can bring to a halt. All worldly understandings of truth and untruth, of the power to govern the disseminations of language and the differing of difference, are inadequate to comprehend or quell the rhetoric of this particular life. Nothing can abate or exceed this discourse of infinite peace that is reborn in martyrdom, that becomes most glorious and most illuminating in being suppressed, that unveils the arbitrary and unfounded nature of the violences it opposes precisely by enduring those violences with inexhaustible love; and this power of God's supreme rhetoric to exceed every word spoken, for or against it, is revealed in the resurrection, when the Father vindicates Christ over against all those orders of prudential and rational truth that have brought him to the cross. If the Father receives his Son crucified as a gift offered up by the Son on behalf of the humanity he has recapitulated in himself, the resurrection is the restoration yet again of the gift, with "difference and delay"; as the disciples who encounter the risen Christ on the road to Emmaus discover, Christ can now no longer be recognized merely as an available and objective datum, a simple given, but must be received entirely as a *donum*, as gift, in the breaking of bread, in the offer of fellowship given anew even when the hope of all fellowship seems to have been extinguished. Even so, in Christ's resurrection it is precisely the concrete form of Jesus, in its proper beauty, that God desires and calls back. Christ's life is not transformed by the cross into a symbol of "religious truth," his form does not melt into a comforting abstraction, because he himself is the only truth, the only way, the only life, and must return as he ever was — sharing food and fellowship with those he loves — if indeed his truth is the truth of God. The resurrection vindicates the aesthetic particularity of truth over against the violences that seek to reduce particularity to nothingness, over against all economies of abstract wisdom, political, philosophical, social, or religious. After the crucifixion, which is the final word — the final proof — pronounced by the powers of the age in defense of their rule and the final argument whereby the totality claims for itself foundations as old as the world, the resurrection suddenly reveals the form of Christ to possess an infinite power of expression, which the final word of the totality can do nothing to silence, or even to anticipate: the power of this world's "final" word is exhausted even as God's Word is only just beginning to be pronounced with absolute clarity. Here, where time is redeemed by the inexplicable occurrence of the eschatological horizon of history as an event within history, the boundless rhetoric set free by the risen Lord reveals and restores the measure given creation before the foundation of the world, before all foundations as such, in the infinite beauty of God's eternal utterance: Christ is seen now as the Lord of all truth, whose Spirit possesses the power always to make present again the form of God that Christ reveals.

The resurrection, then, is God's ultimate offense against the principalities, thrones, and dominions, his transgression of the limits they so jealously preserve, his declaration of himself as the God who at once exceeds all things and yet dwells in the midst of all, as judge; the resurrection testifies to the God who is *apeiron* and who thus crosses all boundaries without ceasing to be form and life and beauty. The Father sends the Spirit upon the Son even in hell, and (as the classic Byzantine Paschal icon so well depicts) Christ breaks the doors of hell asunder, releasing an unmasterable radiance of escape; innumerable ways of peace open up because death is no longer that absolute boundary that necessitates the guarding of all lesser boundaries in a self-sustaining economy of violence. The rhetoric of peace — the analogical ramification of Christ's presence — is now subject to no prudential, tactical, or rational restraints. In a sense the resurrection is an aporia of the language of the powers, a sudden interruption of the story they tell, and the beginning of an entirely new telling of the story of the world; this is perhaps nowhere more powerfully expressed than at the end of Mark, especially if the Gospel is read as ending at the eighth verse of chapter sixteen, when the empty tomb reduces the women come to anoint Christ's body to speechlessness, an amazed inability to say what has been seen or heard. The tomb, after all, is the symbol par excellence of metaphysical totality and of the mythos of cosmic violence: it is terminus and boundary, marking the limit not only between life and death but between being and nonbeing, flesh and soul, cosmos and chaos, history and myth, meaning and meaninglessness, the physical and the spiritual, the clean and the unclean, time and eternity, polis and exile, subject and object; it is, in short, an absolute taxonomic index of the world as enclosed totality; for if every limit is a kind of death, then limit is also the power of life — so long as it is preserved. But it is just this limit that Christ, respecting no boundaries, crosses in absolute freedom. Christ's resurrection, insofar as its cardinal sign is an empty tomb, is quite the opposite of every form of gnostic consolation, every scheme of salvation that merely surrenders creation to the rule of the powers while offering emancipation from the world and its travails; the form of Christ, the way of salvation, never relinquishes its real historical weight, its beauty — its *kabod*. The empty tomb assures us that Christ's postresurrection appearances are something other than mere visions — visions often wander back across the *peras* that the tomb marks — because the *peras* has itself been abolished. The resurrection is a transgression of the categories of truth governing the world, precisely because it is an aesthetic event, eyes and hands can tell it, time comprehends it, it has shape and quantity and splendor, it allows scrutiny and contemplation and astonishment, it intrudes and invites and seizes up with its strangeness and its beauty. Henceforth Christ is a word that cannot be silenced; he can always lay his hand upon another and say, "I am he that liveth, and was dead; and, behold, I am alive for evermore" (Rev. 1:18).

As Bonaventure puts it, the beauty of Christ, which had withered in the passion, blossoms again in the resurrection in order to become the beauty of all (*Lignum vitae* 9.34). And it is a beauty that can really be *seen*, that inhabits the sphere of the creaturely gaze, that even in being prismated into innumerable imperfect expressions throughout time still makes its appeal to eye and heart and invites imitation, appropriation, reexpression. As ever, though, to speak of vision or of visible beauty (or of anything too obviously healthy) is to invite a certain kind of postmodern suspicion — in this case, one concerning "ophthalmocentric" discourse, the mystifying and "objectifying" habit of approaching questions of epistemology, ethics, or metaphysics according to the "metaphorics" of sight. The stabilizing regime of representation, the essentializing tendencies of even the most restrained kind of phenomenology, the invariable subjectivism of every singular and unironized perspective — all of the vices of "metaphysics" are nourished (supposedly) by the privileged position accorded to vision in the history of Western thought. Whether what is at issue is the metaphor of turning one's gaze upward to the sun of the good, the language of eidetic consciousness and the *Wesensschau* of things, the clinical scrutiny that confines its objects to rigid classifications and subjects them to the tyranny of observation, or any of the other taxonomizing, analogizing, or totalizing discourses of reference and representation, the imagery of sight — and particularly clear sight — has historically confined difference within what Martin Jay, in an essay on Foucault, has called "the empire of the gaze."[178] For Foucault in

---

178. Martin Jay, "In the Empire of the Gaze: Foucault and the Denigration of Vision in Twentieth-Century French Thought," in *Foucault: A Critical Reader*, ed. David Couzens Hoy (Oxford: Blackwell, 1986), 175-204. See Jay, *Downcast Eyes: The Denigration of Vision in Twentieth-Century French Thought* (Berkeley: University of California Press, 1994).

particular, the imagery of vision as the measure of truth culminates in the carceral society and its panoptic logic of both social centralization and the individual's own perpetual inward surveillance — for while power begins in spectacle, it becomes most pervasive in the form of the interior gaze of the self-policing subject of modernity[179] (a variant, certainly, of Heidegger's genealogy of nihilism as having been born in eidetic *theoria*). Of course, Foucault longs not so much for the heady freedom of absolute blindness as for a more disruptive optics, a more deceptive, ironic, and clastic ordering of the visible. Perhaps there is some truth in his genealogy, at least, given the ease with which talk of visibility or clarity becomes talk of "obvious" truth, and truth becomes a rationale for power; but, if so, it is well for theology, when confronted by the inextinguishable visibility implicit in the resurrection of Jesus, to remember that the necessity of *seeing* the truth in Christ — far from representing another mutation of the alleged ophthalmocentric regime of "metaphysics" — is a call to an altogether novel order of visibility, a uniquely "Christian optics" that radically reorients vision and alters every perspective, every effect of light, every serene arrangement of the high and the low, the transcendent and the immanent, the beautiful and the unsightly. Plato may have sought to avert his eyes from the bright simulacral spectacle of the world to a more superlunary light, or Bentham may have sought to assume the godlike vantage of a panoptic centrality that would subject all of difference to a single indefatigable and dispassionate scrutiny, but Christian thought is obliged by the particularity of Christ's beauty to move into an entirely different ambit of vision, where one cannot so easily distinguish the above from the below, the godlike from the slavish; Christians are bidden to see in Christ at once the true form of God and the true shape of humanity, and to believe that the Father sees with pleasure his own very likeness in Jesus of Nazareth, even him crucified, and furthermore, consents to view all of humanity as gathered into the beauty of his Son. The divine and the human appear here at once, the very infinity of God is made visible in the brokenness of Christ on the cross, and the deepest depravity of the human heart is grasped only in the light of the risen Lord. No simple metaphysics, nor

---

179. See Michel Foucault, *Discipline and Punish: The Birth of the Prison,* trans. Alan Sheridan (New York: Vintage Books, 1979), 227: "The ideal point of penalty today would be an indefinite discipline: an interrogation without end, an investigation that would be extended without limit to a meticulous and ever more analytical observation, a judgement that would at the same time be the constitution of a file that was never closed, the calculated leniency of a penalty that would be interlaced with the ruthless curiosity of an examination, a procedure that would be at the same time the permanent measure of a gap in relation to an inaccessible norm and the asymptotic movement that strives to meet in infinity." Endless scrutiny, then, detached at the last from every idealism, becomes now a clinical terror, a scientism more terrible than a more "essentialist" species of metaphysics could possibly engender.

any simple concept of the human, can account for the form to which Christian devotion is perpetually turned; nor can anyone who assumes that the truth offered in Christ has the character of a "stabilizing" representation of God or humanity appreciate the delicate inversions and sudden prismatic effusions of this new and very disturbing "Christian optics."

What is at issue here is a species of vision that breaks down the rigid lineaments of a world that interprets itself principally according to the brilliant glamor and spectacle of power, the stable arrangement of all things in hierarchies of meaning and authority, or the rational measures of social order and civic prestige: a way of seeing that lights its way with no facile certitudes concerning the place of God above or of the human below, the orderly architecture of the cosmos and its immanent economies of power and truth, or the opposition of the finite and the infinite. It is a way of seeing that must be learned, because it alters every perspective upon things; and to learn it properly one must be conformed to what one sees. Vision here is inseparable, even indistinguishable, from practice: faith, which is the form this Christian optics must take, lies in the surrender of one's actions to the form of Christ, its measure and proportion, its way of inhabiting the distance. And from the divine side as well, according to theological tradition, the act through which the Father sees the Son and all persons in the Son also effects a change: it justifies and sanctifies, it makes all things pleasing to the Father, it reconciles humanity to God. It is this power of conversion, of optical inversion, by which the form of Christ measures the world anew; in its light, all the orderings of secular power and meaning are exposed, even reversed: the first becomes last, the mighty are put down from their seats and the lowly exalted, the hungry are filled with good things while the rich are sent empty away, the stone rejected by the builder becomes the head of the corner. In raising up this particular form, this particular presence, God judges the visible orders of the world, subjects them to a new and intense radiance that pierces all the trappings and beguilements of power; a murdered slave is the eternal Word of the Father, whom the Father vindicates and makes victorious, and is the supreme rhetoric that unveils the squalor and deceits of the rhetoric of violence. The scale of the reversal cannot be exaggerated: when Jesus stands before Pilate for the last time, beaten, derided, robed in purple and crowned with thorns, he must seem, from the vantage of all the noble wisdom of the empire and the age (which wisdom Nietzsche sought to resuscitate), merely absurd, a ridiculous figure prating incomprehensibly of an otherworldly kingdom and some undefined truth, obviously mad, oblivious of the lowliness of his state and of the magnitude of the powers into whose hands he has been delivered. But in the light of the resurrection, from the perspective of Christianity's inverted order of vision, the mockery now redounds upon all kings and emperors, whose finery and symbols of status are revealed to be nothing more than rags and brambles beside the majesty of God's Son, beside this servile shape in which God displays his infinite power to be where he will be; all the rulers of the earth cannot begin to surpass in grandeur this beauty of the God who ventures forth to make even the dust his glory. There is a special Christian humor here, a special kind of Christian irreverence: in Rome the emperor is now as nothing, a garment draped over the shoulders of a slave and then cast aside. Christianity is indeed a creed for slaves, but in neither the subtle Hegelian nor the crude Nietzschean sense: in contrast to Hegel and Nietzsche — to dialectic and diatribe alike — Christian faith speaks of the slave as God's glory, the one who lies farthest out in the far country, to whom tidings of joy are sent from before the foundation of the world, and from whom the free and infinite God cannot be separated by any distance, certainly not that between the high and low, because he is the distance of all things. Indeed, the beauty of God reveals itself with its most incandescent intensity among those who suffer, who are as children, who are powerless, because — for all they lack — the ultimate privation of violence often has not entered into them, for the simple reason that they do not occupy the position of coercive force. Not that the weak are not sinners, or that spite and cruelty cannot make even of weakness a weapon, but nevertheless, the weakness of sinners is the strength of God, and when he dwells among the suffering, God is most truly known as the God he is.

iv. The Practice of the Form

The soul, as Anselm laments, is rendered obtuse by sin, unable to see the beauty of God, to hear his harmony, to perceive his fragrance, to taste his sweetness, though God imparts some measure of his loveliness to all created things and makes it manifest in them (*Proslogium* 17). It is this divine beauty that becomes visible again in Christ. And yet, even so, the ancient beauty of creation that recrudesces in Christ remains for now a word among words, no less delicate as a historical actuality than any other, no less subject to distortion, corruption, or the forgetfulness of those to whom it has been entrusted. That the power of the Spirit to communicate this beauty anew is infinite is an article of faith; that human beings resist the Spirit with indefatigable ingenuity is the lesson of history. God's is a beauty that can be seen from innumerable perspectives — such is the splendor of Christ's truth — but also a beauty more often hidden in the involutions and elaborate inventions of sin. God's election of creation in Christ is an "aesthetic" action, which expresses the Father's pleasure in the Son, and the response of the church can be only "aesthetic" as well: that is to say, Christ bequeaths the church neither simple ethical principles nor "facts" of heaven, but a way of being in the world, a form that must be answered "gracefully." Only insofar as it attends to the very real practical task that the form of Christ imposes may theology affirm that Christ is, as Augustine says, the wellspring of all beauty (*De diversis quaestionibus octoginta tribus* 23). There is no autonomous sphere of "ethics" within Christian thought, no simple index of duties to be discharged; the translation of the narrative of Christ into practice must proceed as an imaginative reappropriation of that narrative, a correspondence by way of variation, and requires a feeling for — and capacity to "perform" — the shape of Christ's life. To see the glory of Christ in the soul as in a mirror, to be transformed into that same image from glory to glory by the Spirit (2 Cor. 3:18), is to return always again to this finite form and attempt, amid the contingencies of time, to express it anew, to allow Christ to be formed within the church and within Christians (Gal. 4:19). Even in the strength of the Spirit there is a terrible fragility to the beauty that the form of Christ restores to creation, because it can be imparted only as a gift, which may be rejected: its infinite character is expressible only in being committed to others, to the tradition that bears forward the gesture of Christ's presence, entrusted to the Spirit's power to repeat the gift across time. As Gregory the Theologian remarks, insofar as Christ recapitulates humanity in himself and in his body, the disobedience of his members comes to be attributed to him (*Oration* 30.5); as the one whose form, in its particularity, is raised up by the Father, Christ is handed over to the history that he inaugurates. The church is a real unfolding of Christ's presence, a melismatic extension (so to speak) of the theme he imparts, an *epektasis* toward the fullness of his form; but while the church's every utterance, gift, or response, every act of worship, charity, or art (however poor) may belong to the fullness of that music, a certain accompanying discord — an apostasy from the form of Christ — undeniably burdens each hour. Still, the music remains audible. Christ, according to Deleuze, is the one who is not repeated, who does not return in the circle of antichrist; he is a beautiful soul and, as such, an evanescence; he possesses none of the cosmic perenniality of Dionysus, none of the protean plasticity of Baphomet. Any honest appraisal of the event of Christ in history, however, makes obvious the vacuity of such remarks: Christ is repeated endlessly, in the circle of the church, in boundless variety, and unfolds his presence as Word in the unmasterable excess of his historical and aesthetic effect. That the presence of Christ in time possesses an eschatological scope — that he is the eternal Word whose story is the true story of the world — is also an article of faith; that such is his identity can be demonstrated only through the practice of that identity, as his body traverses the interval of time, supplying what is still lacking in Christ's sufferings, striving after the fullness that Christ always invites and already exceeds.

This means, incidentally, that the church cannot conceive of itself as an institution within a larger society, as a pillar of society, culture, and civic order, or as a spiritual association that commands an allegiance simply in addition to the allegiance its members owe the powers of the wider world. The church is no less (as Origen knew) than a politics, a society, another country, a new pattern of communal being meant not so much to complement the civic constitution of secular society as to displace it. If Christ is risen, if this particular form is the infinite Word of the Father and the substance of salvation, then the church has no excuse for surrendering the horizon of history to the forces of "secularity," or for allowing itself to become a mere element within, or function of, secular order. Christ's pattern has been handed over and entrusted to the church as a project; he does not hover above history as an eschatological tension, a withdrawn possibility, an absence, or only a memory, but enters into history precisely in the degree that the church makes his story the essence of its practices. The church, then, as a pilgrimage, whose light and motile transit through time is recognized as an intrusion upon the cultural property of the secular world, should often appear as a transgression of the social order; at other times it should judge social order good and necessary; but in either case it should act only from the vantage of the kingdom. The church itself is (insofar as it is the church) a fabric of endlessly various ramifications and effoliations of Christ's beauty, unfolding between two parousiai, and can enjoy continuity with the form of Christ only so far as it resists the world's every attempt to reduce it to the status of a secondary affiliation. And this is a difficult matter indeed, for Christians are instructed by Scripture to comply with legitimate authority, but also to live according to the justice of the kingdom even now, in the midst of history, and the passage between these two commands must at times prove very narrow indeed. The normal politics of power (or of, to be more precise, the powers) is a politics of chaos and the inhibition thereof; it understands justice in terms of an immediate and hence tautologous reciprocity (in terms, that is, of violence). But the politics of the church can understand justice only according to a disruption of such reciprocity — bearing one another's burdens, forgiving even the debt truly owed, seeking reconciliation rather than due retribution — and so typically should seek to reorder reciprocity after the fashion of the gift, as a differentiation and delay (and a giving again) that distorts the "Same" of violence into the music of forgiveness. Moreover, the church makes of itself a gnostic mystery cult if it mistakes this politics for a spiritual hygiene practiced only within the walls of the basilica — a kind of rite practiced for the sake of personal purity — and does not rather make it intrude upon the world about it. This is the visible beauty of the form of Christ in his mystical body: a beauty not posed over against the world merely as a gnostic or even eschatological *critique*, but offered to the world as a real *evangel*. The maxim that guided the early church's evolving understanding of the doctrine of incarnation was that whatever is not assumed by Christ is not saved; and this may be extended to mean that whatever aspect of the human world is not assumed into the narrative of Christ has not been recapitulated by him, and so still lies in bondage.

The obvious implication of such language is that there really is small room in theology for political "realism" of the sort advocated by Reinhold Niebuhr, which chooses to accommodate itself to the "tragic" limits of history on the grounds that the church of Christ (not only his kingdom) is not of this world, and that Jesus — in his perfectionism and strictly "interpersonal" morality — could not understand the harsher conditions or more insoluble perplexities of political existence[180] (between the Christ of Nietzsche and the Christ of Niebuhr the difference is not spacious). A less obvious implication to many, however, but one that seems to me to follow every bit as ineluctably, is that there is also small room in theology for that passive collaboration with evil that often only flatters itself with the name of "pacifism." However primary the path of nonviolence is for the Christian, the peace of God's kingdom is exhaustively described in Scripture, and it is the peace of a concrete condition of justice; it is neither the private practice of an "ethical" individual, jealous of his own moral purity, nor the special and quaint regime of a separatist community that stands aloof from (in ill-concealed contempt for) its "Constantinian" brethren. Where the justice of the kingdom is not present, and cannot be made present without any exercise of force, the self-adoring inaction of those who would meet the reality of, say, black smoke billowing from the chimneys of death camps with songs of protest is simply violence by other means, and does not speak of God's kingdom, and does not grant its practitioners the privilege of viewing themselves as more faithful members of Christ's body than those who struggle against evil in the world of flesh and blood where evil works. This is why I say that the path of obedience is anything but easy or clear: in either case — that of the realist who resigns himself to the impossibility of justice in human affairs, and so lends his hand to prudential acts of violence, and that of the pacifist who presumes that the history of sinful humanity is too corrupt for any struggle to be just or in the service of peace, and so dares obscenely to choose martyrdom for others — the style of thought is not Christian but gnostic, informed by so profound a despair over the world that God became incarnate in, and so absolute a division between history and eternity, that Christ's presence in time is reduced to a nullity and the church to pre-

---

180. This is, mirabile dictu, Niebuhr's customary reasoning, nowhere advanced with greater clarity or brevity than in *An Interpretation of Christian Ethics* (New York: Harper and Bros., 1935). Many would argue that Niebuhr wrote better-developed or more carefully considered texts (the author himself, for one), and that he in fact disavowed many aspects of this book; but, frankly, Niebuhr's later, longer texts never fundamentally altered the import of his earlier works, but only allowed him to indulge in more ponderous forms of exposition (which had the unintended consequence in some cases of allowing him far too much room to display his shortcomings as a philosopher).

cious historical marginality. But the church must be resigned to nothing: it must act not out of realism or purism, but — in defiance of both — out of a passionate and even militant commitment to the truth of the kingdom, in excess of prudence and in pursuit of a peace more tangible than personal or communal "guiltlessness." The justice of God — the peace of God — can be found and fought for in the heart of history, for the kingdom has already come — the tomb is empty — and will come again; the battle has been won, and we must seek to prepare the earth for a victory that has already claimed us as its spoils. However, the practical consequences of such words cannot here be described exhaustively, even if such description lay in my power; peace above all is served by peace: against personal offense we are still bidden to turn the other cheek, and against every evil to strive as far as possible without using coercive force, and to limit all coercion as far as is possible without allowing peacefulness to degenerate into that sentimental passivity that serves as one of evil's most effective instruments. Christ wielded the whip only when the corruption of God's people had contaminated the very heart of the community, and the secret of his authority to do so was revealed only when he bore without hatred the lashes of the whip wielded by the power of the pagan state.

To conclude, then: Christian morality is a labor of vision — to see the form of Christ, to see all creation as having been recapitulated in him, and to see in all other persons the possibility of discerning and adoring Christ's form in a new fashion. Again, this puts Christian morality at odds with the moral precepts of even the most fiercely principled of postmodern "ethics" (or rather, late modern Kantian ethics). To see otherness as making an infinite moral demand, to understand singularity as possessing an infinite moral gravity and so as making a claim prior to every magisterial metaphysics, phenomenology, or ontology, and to heed the call of justice as issuing from the infinite darkness of the high and holy is the concern not only of Levinas but of (in a moderated and somewhat distanced, but in no way less earnest, fashion) Derrida, and of such thinkers as Lyotard and John Caputo. That every other is infinitely other constitutes what Caputo calls the "myth of justice,"[181] the moral fable that lifts the immediate moral claim of the particular out of the sphere of the universal. Such is the form that an ethics must take in the wake of the death of every metanarrative, and as such, it must (as has been copiously said) subsist upon a privation of the aesthetic; the myth of justice is the myth of a voice from on high, but a voice that is always transcendent of words; it is a myth of terrible darkness, numinous excess, but certainly not of beauty (that font of idolatry). Writes Levinas, "[E]thics is an optics. But it is a 'vision' without image, bereft of

181. John Caputo, *Demythologizing Heidegger* (Bloomington and Indianapolis: Indiana University Press, 1993), 189-92.

the synoptic and totalizing objectifying virtues of vision, a relation or an intentionality of a wholly different type."[182] I have already made clear above, in part 1, why I think such an ethics is impossible, and such language pernicious. Simply enough, apart from the prior "thematizations" of particular traditions of discourse, and without an object of vision, an "image," to subject to these thematizations, "ethics" has no other, can recognize nothing, can experience no event of "obligation." Ethics is an aesthetics: an optics, that is, in an unequivocal sense, an order of seeing that obeys a *story* of being according to which the other is delineated with the radiant proportions of the other, who elicits the infinite regard of God and compels an infinite awe and even love from the one who looks on (an awe that is, necessarily, a recognition of the other's beauty as other). The secret of the ethical is that it is a certain aesthetic convention, a certain kind of aesthetic theme. The "infinition" of thought before the face of the other occurs only as the result of a certain account of the visible; there is no call of the ethical apart from perspectives opened upon the surface of being, stories that not only open the possibility of a desire for the infinite of the other but also describe practices that fill out the shape of obligation. And a failure to acknowledge as much makes the "myth of justice" worse than incredible — indeed, mythological in the most odious way. The capacity to see the other as other, to hear the other as the call of duty, is something that is taught; vision obeys the aesthetics that forms it. And it is only inasmuch as the other appears within an aesthetic ordering of vision that "arranges" the infinite as beauty — that places the other within the infinite as a unique instance and inflection of the beautiful — that the other is recognized as the object of an infinite regard. It is because the other is infinitely placed, within an infinite (that is) that does not end in the indeterminate, that the other exceeds every "totalizing" representation, every syntaxis of high and low, noble and base, worthy and worthless. There can be no final or taxonomic perspective on the other, because the other belongs to an infinity of perspectives, an unending "vista" of the beautiful. For Christian thought it is Christ who thematizes the other as infinite, who reorders the surface of being according to a beauty that allows every other to be seen no longer within the enclosure of totality, but as the very glory of God; it is Christ who at once disrupts the hierarchy of representations belonging to a world conceived as power and instates, in himself, another order of seeing, a motion of the beautiful that goes even into the abyss as form and light; he — the form of God, the form of a slave — is an infinite thematism, embracing the lowest and the highest within himself. This is the new Christian optics, the way of seeing the other in Christ, that diverts attention from the stable representations of secular order

182. Emmanuel Levinas, *Totality and Infinity: An Essay on Exteriority*, trans. Alphonso Lingis (Pittsburgh: Duquesne University Press, 1969), 23.

to the suffering, to the nameless, to the captive and the outcast, even to the dead. Only thus is it possible to extend analogically the language of God as "Wholly Other" to every other, because the other is seen within and by way of Christ, as the beauty of the infinite, the shape of God's desire and object of his love, the splendor of his glory. Everything Nietzsche deplored about Christianity — its enervating compassion for life at its most debile and deformed, the Gospels' infuriating and debased aesthetic, which finds beauty precisely where a discriminating and noble eye finds only squalor and decadence — is in fact the expression of an order of vision that cannot be confined within the canons of taste prescribed by myths of power and eminence, because it obeys the aesthetics of an infinite that surpasses every sinful ordering, every totality, as form, as indeed the form of peace: an order of vision that thematizes the infinite according to the gaze of recognition and delight, which finds in every other the glory of the transcendent other, and which cannot turn away from the other because it has learned to see in the other the beauty of the crucified. Because the God who goes to his death in the form of a slave breaks open hearts, every face becomes an icon: a beauty that is infinite. If the knowledge of the light of the glory of God is given in the face of Jesus (2 Cor. 4:6), it is a knowledge that allows every other face to be seen in the light of that glory.

---

2. In Christ, totality's economy of violence is overcome by the infinity of God's peace, inasmuch as one order of sacrifice is overcome by another: sacrifice as the immolation of the beautiful is displaced by a sacrifice whose offering is one of infinite beauty.

To what purpose is the multitude of your sacrifices unto me? saith the LORD: I am full of the burnt offerings of rams, and the fat of fed beasts; and I delight not in the blood of bullocks, or of lambs, or of he goats. When ye come to appear before me, who hath required this at your hand, to tread my courts? Bring no more vain oblations; incense is an abomination unto me; the new moons and sabbaths, the calling of assemblies, I cannot away with; it is iniquity, even the solemn meeting. Your new moons and your appointed feasts my soul hateth: they are a trouble unto me; I am weary to bear them. And when ye spread forth your hands, I will hide mine eyes from you: yea, when ye make many prayers, I will not hear: your hands are full of blood. Wash you, make you clean; put away the evil of your doings from before mine eyes;

cease to do evil; learn to do well; seek judgment, relieve the oppressed, judge the fatherless, plead for the widow.

Isa. 1:11-17

Why seek ye the living among the dead? He is not here, but is risen.

Luke 24:5-6

I came forth from the Father, and am come into the world: again, I leave the world, and go to the Father.

John 16:28

Jesus saith unto her, Mary. She turned herself, and saith unto him, Rabboni; which is to say, Master. Jesus saith unto her, Touch me not; for I am not yet ascended to my Father: but go to my brethren, and say unto them, I ascend unto my Father, and your Father; and to my God, and your God.

John 20:16-17

For it pleased the Father that in him should all fulness dwell; and, having made peace through the blood of his cross, by him to reconcile all things unto himself; by him, I say, whether they be things in earth, or things in heaven.

Col. 1:19-20

For if the blood of bulls and of goats, and the ashes of an heifer sprinkling the unclean, sanctifieth to the purifying of the flesh: How much more shall the blood of Christ, who through the eternal Spirit offered himself without spot to God, purge your conscience from dead works to serve the living God?

Heb. 9:13-14

For the bodies of those beasts, whose blood is brought into the sanctuary by the high priest for sin, are burned without the camp. Wherefore Jesus also, that he might sanctify the people with his own blood, suffered without the gate. Let us go forth therefore unto him without the camp, bearing his reproach. For here have we no continuing city, but seek one to come. By him therefore let us offer the sacrifice of praise to God continually, that is, the fruit of our lips giving thanks to his name. But to do good and to communicate forget not: for with such sacrifices God is well pleased.

Heb. 13:11-16

i. The Economy of Violence

Totality is, of necessity, an economy, a circulation of substance, credit, power, and debt, a closed cycle of violence, a perpetual oscillation between order and chaos, form and indeterminacy. The myth of the cosmos as a precarious equilibrium of countervailing forces, an island of order amidst an infinite ocean of violent energy — which is also the myth of the polis or of the empire — belongs principally to a sacral order that seeks to contain nature's violence within the stabilizing forms of a more orderly kind of violence: the sheer waste and destructiveness of the cosmos must be held at bay and controlled, by a motion at once apotropaic — repelling chaos by appeasing its chthonian energies and rationalizing them in structures of Apollonian order — and economic — recuperating what is lost or sacrificed in the form of a transcendent credit, a numinous power reinforcing the regime that sacrifice serves. One could argue, in fact, that all pagan order was just such an order of sacrifice, a system of exclusion, which mactated the singular so as to recover the serener forms of the universal, making a holocaust even of the desirable and the beautiful as an appeasement of the formlessness besetting the fragile order of cosmos and city from every quarter. Perhaps, more boldly, one might say that all secular order as such subsists upon sacrifice, upon the calculus of an economy of violence, and preserves the stability of its closed cycle of exchange by rescuing the good of society from the superfluity of what society cannot assimilate — by, that is, converting the inassimilable (the criminal, the surplus of wealth, the impure, cosmic violence itself) into *ousia,* incorruptible wealth, the source and substance of every social order; secular society sustains itself by practicing limited violences that contain and somewhat subdue the limitless violences of being. This is certainly the contention of Augustine in *The City of God:* that the peace of the earthly city is merely martial order (14.1-9), that its virtues are the virtues of empire and violence (19.4-27), that its founding is an original murder (3.6-14) and its stability a violent inhibition of chaos (15.5-6). Rome is born in fratricide, when Romulus slays Remus for leaping over the boundary — the *peras* — that Romulus has drawn in the sand; thus the earthly city is the domain of the brother who slays; but the church belongs to the city of the brother who is slain, of Abel rather than Cain (15.2). As opposed, then, to the blood-steeped sacrifices that so delight the gods of the pagan world (3.14), the sacrifice Christians offer is one merely of love (10.5). For Christian thought, the pattern of sin, endlessly repeated, is to take creation not as a gift but as a violence — either the violence of order or the violence of chaos — an aboriginal strife that must be governed; for to take violence as inescapable is to make of violence a moral and a civic duty. This is the sacrificial logic that theology is called upon to reject: the commerce of the totality, which is overcome by the infinite gesture of Christ's sacrifice.

Can, though, sacrifice defeat sacrifice? Is not the cross of Christ another myth of peace won through violence, of chaos and death subdued by a propitiatory offering, and of, indeed (as Nietzsche said), the infinite multiplication of debt rather than its discharge? One would obviously wish to say not, but one must also have a care that, in making one's argument, one does not fail to account for the element of oblation in the story of salvation. A salutary example, both for good and ill, of how delicate a matter it is to argue against the idea of the cross as divine violence is René Girard; no one else has made so great an issue of the difference between the death of Christ and the death of the "sacrificial" victim. Girard's most extensive treatment of propitiatory exclusion is found in *The Scapegoat,* where he draws an absolute distinction between the mythology that dictates that religions make room, on ritual occasions, for disorder in subordination to order and those biblical narratives that tell their story from the perspective of the victims of both that disorder and that order.[183] Mythologies, according to Girard, generally reflect the thinking of the class of persecutors; and "[s]trong in their righteousness, and convinced that their victim is truly guilty, persecutors have no reason to be troubled" (104). Not that persecutors are always creatures of malice; more often than not they are guardians of the public weal, whose prudence prevents violence from erupting into riot, warfare, or internecine strife. Their sacrificial economics is simply the art of responsible politics. Of Caiaphas's remark that it is better that one die than that the nation perish, for instance, Girard writes: "Caiaphas is stating the . . . political reason . . . for the scapegoat: to limit violence as much as possible but to turn to it, if necessary, as a last resort to avoid an even greater violence. Caiaphas is the incarnation of politics at its best, not its worst. No one has ever been a better politician" (113). And so, "Caiaphas is the perfect sacrificer who puts victims to death to save those who live. By reminding us of this John emphasizes that every real cultural *decision* has a sacrificial character (*decidere,* remember, is to cut the victim's throat) that refers back to an unrevealed effect of the scapegoat, the sacred type of representation of persecution" (114). For Girard this means that theologians who speak of Christ's death (at least in its salvific function) as a sacrifice "once more make sacred the violence that has been divested of its sacred character by the Gospel text" (126); and in so doing they lose sight of the evangel that truly sets free: "The good news is that scapegoats can no longer save men, the persecutors' accounts of their persecutions are no longer valid, and truth shines into dark places. God is not violent, the true God has nothing to do with violence, and he speaks to us not through dis-

---

183. René Girard, *The Scapegoat,* trans. Yvonne Freccero (Baltimore: Johns Hopkins University Press, 1986), 79 and 101. Parenthetical page numbers in the following text are to this work.

tant intermediaries but directly. The Son he sends us is one with him. The King-dom of God is at hand" (189). In *Things Hidden Since the Foundation of the World* Girard goes so far as to advocate a "non-sacrificial reading of the gospel text": the Bible from the beginning seeks to unwind the narrative of sacrifice, he says, taking the side of Abel against Cain, whose violence is indeed the founding of cities;[184] the crucifixion is, thus, in no sense a sacrifice (180); for the notion of divine violence is no part of the Gospel story (189). Girard sees the profound logic of Scripture, as a whole, as lying in its constant movement away from the mythology of sacrifice (205-6), even as the presence of sacrificial and exclusionary themes causes currents of contradiction to run through its text: he contrasts (to the former's discredit) the stories of humanity's expulsion from Eden and that of John's prologue, which speaks of God's exclusion by a violent world (274-76); and he does not hesitate to take the book of Hebrews to task for trafficking in sacrificial motifs and for, in consequence, implicating God in the persecution of the victim (227-31).

That Girard's arguments suffer from an occasional want of subtlety scarcely needs be said; in particular, his failure adequately to distinguish differ-ent senses of sacrifice from one another leads him all too often to treat the his-tory of Israel's faith as a stark opposition between a sacrificial cult and a pro-phetic tradition that has rejected sacrifice, causing him in consequence to overlook the manifold meanings inherent in Israel's many sacrificial practices, the dependency of the prophetic tradition upon the language of sacrifice, and the ways in which the life and death of Christ are received in Christian thought as perfecting God's covenant with Israel — even insofar as that covenant in-volves sacrifice. If Christ's death overcomes a certain sacrificial order, it also ful-fills one. Still, Girard's observations must not be casually dismissed: it would obviously be repellent, for instance, for a Christian theologian to make of the crucifixion a kind of justification for capital punishment; but within a certain understanding of sacrifice, the immolation of the *hostia* and the execution of the criminal belong to the same motion of exclusion, the same inhibition of chaos, the same economic gesture; and this is a distinction that cannot be ig-nored. If the language of sacrifice in Christian thought did properly refer to an economy of exchange, such that God were *appeased* in the slaughter of a victim and his wrath were simply *averted* by way of a prudential violence of which he *approved* (and who can deny that many Christians have imagined their faith in just these terms?), then indeed the Christian God would be a God of violence, and the Christian evangel of peace would simply dissemble another economy

184. René Girard, *Things Hidden Since the Foundation of the World*, trans. Stephen Bann and Michael Metteer (Stanford: Stanford University Press, 1978), 146-48. Parenthetical page numbers in the remainder of this paragraph are to this work.

of violence and debt — one that, in fact (Nietzsche winning the field), has been monstrously magnified. Here, as nowhere else, this book's initial question proves most perilous to ask: Does the language of sacrifice within Christian thought, inextirpable from Scripture, make of the gospel a tale that defeats itself in the telling, the beauty of whose rhetoric proves in the end to be another — and particularly meretricious — variant of the glamor of violence? And this is by no means an easy question to answer: contrary to Girard's contention, the presence of sacrificial language in the New Testament is so deeply constitutive of Christian soteriology (even in its overcoming of sacrificial models of cosmic order) that it cannot simply be dispelled by drawing a firm demarcation between the site of the persecutor and the site of the victim, between the place of eminence and the place of abjection. Girard is right to make this distinction, of course, and even right to do so with a degree of prophetic fervor; but the dangers of his method are many: he risks leaving Israel behind and so, in consequence, the world.

The Christian story of salvation concerns not the descent of some gnostic savior bearing tidings of an alien God, but the covenant that God makes with Israel and the covenant he makes, consequently, with all flesh; it is in the history of Israel that God tells of his love for creation and unfolds the true story of the world he elects; it is in his people, the Jews, that God instates an order of infinite giving that responds to the infinity of his gift in creating, and that stands apart from the hierarchies of worldly power. It is only in fulfilling — indeed, in being the substance of — this covenant that Christ makes the story that God tells concerning creation triumph over the false and violent stories that sinful humanity tells of the world. Girard's treatment of the matter, however, in its most extreme moments, makes out the salvific motion of Christ's life to be almost purely negative, a motion of alienation, running dialectically against history. Not that this is Girard's intention: he intends that the story of the victim be recognized as a true story and one that must be liberated from the narratives of the persecutor; but the effect of his account of salvation is that Christ comes to look almost like a Marcionite savior, who does not so much inaugurate the liberating history of God with us as describe a path of flight from time. Rather than the form that stands in the midst of creation to declare the true shape of creation, Christ looks suspiciously like a figure who saves simply by pointing beyond every economy — and every world; but society is exchange, giving and taking, even in some sense sacrificing one thing for another, offering one thing up for another. Does Christ then offer a new order of exchange and sacrifice, or is he simply the abnegation of human solidarity, a revolutionary outcry that forever interrupts the story of the world but tells no story of its own? Is salvation merely the liberation of souls from the bondage of the world? Again, Girard intends to say no such thing; but where, in the world, does the victim have a story of his own? The answer, for Christian thought, must begin with Israel, apart from which one cannot grasp the way of being that Christ embodies and that the Father vindicates at Easter; it is in Israel's many orders of sacrifice that sacrifice (conceived as an economy of violence) begins to be undone. Girard, however, fails to see the richness, multivalency, and ambiguity inherent in the language of sacrifice in Jewish and Christian thought; he fails to grasp, in particular, the conversion theology effects of the story of wrath into the story of mercy, or how it replaces the myth of sacrifice as economy with the narrative of sacrifice as a ceaseless outpouring of gift and restoration in an infinite motion exceeding every economy. The sacrifice that Christian theology upholds is inseparable from the gift: it underwrites not the stabilizing regime of prudential violence, but the destabilizing extravagance of giving and giving again, of declaring love and delight in the exchange of signs of peace, outside of every calculation of debt or power. The gift of the covenant — which in a sense implores Israel to respond — belongs to the Trinity's eternal "discourse" of love, which eternally "invites" and offers regard and recognition; it precedes and exceeds, then, every economy of power, because all "credit" is already given and exhausted, because the love it declares and invokes is prior to, and the premise of, all that is given.

There are many sacrificial moments in Israel's response to God, of course, and so Israel's cultic practices cannot be reduced to one essential thing univocally termed "sacrifice." There are indeed practices of violence and exclusion, but also practices of sanctification and reconciliation, thanksgiving and adoration. Before all else, though, sacrifice is a *qurban,* a drawing nigh, an approach in love to the God who graciously approaches his people in love. If there are currents of stress in the history of Israel's cult, they do not run between the idea of sacrifice as such and a prophetic rejection of sacrifice, but between different ways of understanding the motion of sacrifice that Israel is, the gift it makes of itself — of its body — to the God who gives it its being and its name. For Christian thought this gift is perfectly made in the life and body of Jesus, with unique finality, but in such a way that all that Israel is, is borne up to the Father, and with it the world. The God of Israel is explicitly a God who requires nothing, who elects and sanctifies as he will, who creates out of the bounty of his love; and for this reason Israel's sacrifice is already in a sense a violation of sacrificial economy, a failure to "contribute" to cosmic order, an offering of thanksgiving to a God who gives out of love of what he gives, and who — far from profiting from the holocaust of the particular — fulfills "sacrifice" by giving the gift again, in excess of what is "required"; this Ezekiel learns in the valley of dry bones. The gift God gives is infinitely given; it does not obey the economy of *ousia,* of circulation and indifferent exchange; God will not suffer to see it absorbed into the cosmic drama of death and regeneration, violence and the fruit of violence. Jesus' devoted gift of himself — the motion of his whole life lived in love toward the Father — entirely fulfills the sacrificial narrative of Israel. The cross itself, of course, is of pagan origin, and so the crucifixion in itself expresses perfectly the sacrificial logic of the secular order; but it is on the side of Christ — the beauty of his particularity, the gesture of *his* sacrifice — that the Father passes judgment, against the sacrificial order that builds crosses. On Golgotha a certain pagan sacrificial analogy between the order of the cosmos and political order — a mimesis of the violence of the sublime, an endless recapitulation of power's war against power — gives way to an iconic analogy between the eternal giving and receiving of the Trinity and creation's character as gift. Within the context of trinitarian dogma, it is possible to think of sacrifice (conceived as gift rather than debt) as the free expression of a love desired of Israel by God, and so not simply owed in any elementary economic sense: a gift given because the graciousness of the gift already received draws forth a response of love and gratitude. That the gift is prior to debt, moreover, and prior to any stabilizing economy of violence, is shown in the resurrection: God's balances are not righted by an act of immolation, the debt is not discharged by the destruction of the victim and his transformation into credit; rather, God simply continues to give, freely, inexhaustibly, regardless of rejection. God gives and forgives; he fore-gives and gives again. There is no calculable economy in this trinitarian discourse of love, to which creation is graciously admitted. There is only the gift and the restoration of the gift, the love that the gift declares, the motion of a giving that is infinite, which comprehends every sacrifice made according to love, and which overcomes every sacrifice made for the sake of power.

The economy of sacrifice, obviously, in some sense seeks to preserve what is given up, by sublimating it, storing it in a transcendent treasury; its motion is one of *Aufhebung,* death overcoming death by the universalization (which is also to say erasure) of the particular. Israel's sacrifice, though — Israel as sacrifice — restores a gift, but preserves no abstract credit as the residue of its holocaust; and while this sacrifice often takes the form of a rite procuring absolution, it does not serve a stable system of debt, but rather forces Israel to recognize itself as a gift to be restored, an address to be answered. To put it differently, Israel, for all the multiplicity of its cultus, "fails" to imagine an economy of sacrifice that neatly closes off the cosmos in a cycle of strict equivalence and indemnity, and so rationalizes loss as a higher kind of gain. This is evident from the beginning of Israel's story, in the binding of Isaac: a sacrifice, that is, that does not effect a limited transaction with the sublime, in the interest of founding or preserving a city, but that happens apart from and before every city; the offering of Isaac can serve no economy, because all of Israel slumbers in his loins, because he is the child of Sarah's dotage who cannot be replaced, because he is the whole promise and substance of God's covenant; he is manifestly, in his particularity, infinitely other. He is the entire gift, returned before the gift has been truly given; but then God, who is not a God of the indeterminate sublime, feeding upon the destruction of the beautiful, but a God of determinate beauty and love, gives the gift again, will not allow the gift to be rendered up into the absolute, will not permit the infinite motion of the gift to be transformed into the closed circle of sacrificial economics. Henceforth Israel is doubly given, and can know itself only as gift, imparted by God and offered ceaselessly back to God, in the infinity of love's exchange. And so the logic of Israel's offering — a perpetual drawing nigh to the God who approaches in love, a continuous *epektasis* after the *temuna* of God — eventuates not in a mythology of sublation, of transcendental credit, but in a cry for eschatological justice. Emboldened by its long history of intimacy with God, suffering persecution far past equanimous endurance, and absorbed in the logic of the gift, late Second Temple Judaism has the audacity to desire and demand back what is given, still in the form of the gift, and not as a higher and indeterminate spiritual reserve, just as God himself desires and demands back the beauty of the gift he gives, not in the abstract form of a debt discharged but in the concrete form of a love declared. The gift remains gift. The rule of economy is that what is sacrificed is recuperable as something else, something desired or needed. This is, after all, the grand Indo-European mythology of sacrifice: the universe — gods and mortals alike — as a great cycle of feeding, nourished on death, preserving life through a system of balanced transactions. There is clearly an essential nihilism in this economy: tragic resignation followed by prudent salvage, for order's sake. But the gift is another thing: it is the refusal of prudential transaction, it is by nature exorbitant and somehow sweetly jealous of its own worth; it has, that is, the shape of love — I want you, I give to you, I cannot bear to lose you. Hence Israel does not turn toward the eternal heights of the numinous to recuperate its "investment," but toward the eschatological horizon to find the gift restored as it was given: it cries out for vindication of the just, for the return of the murdered, for resurrection. This violates all sound economics; Israel resists the reduction of the commodity to its exchange value; it is willing to exceed the contained system of cosmic exchanges, and its regularities, so long as it is not forced to relinquish the gift except as gift, to be given again; it calls upon justice, which is to say the infinite, rather than the fiduciary equivalences of totality. As it longs for the infinite of the other — which is the just measure of the other — Israel forsakes economic recuperation for the rescue of the particular, of every particular; its longing is for the "bad" infinite, which can be made subordinate to no economy at all. This is the infinite excess of God's gift: that it will not cease to be gift and become value.[185]

185. See *Liturgy and Tradition: Theological Reflections of Alexander Schmemann*, ed. Thomas Fisch (Crestwood, N.Y.: St. Vladimir's Seminary Press, 1990), 129-30.

Thus Israel is — and ever more clearly becomes — an extravagant order of sacrifice, which makes no effort to sustain the totality of cosmic order; its longings stretch beyond every visible boundary. When the sacrifice of Israel ceases to be understood as a sacrifice of praise — which means, of an entire life offered back to God, in accordance with his justice — and is seen only as a ritual dangerously similar to a pagan appeasement of the cosmos, prophetic voices rise to its rebuke; but they do this out of faithfulness to the sacrifice that God most truly desires (a broken and contrite heart), not out of disdain for sacrifice. For Christian thought the true order of sacrifice is that which corresponds to the motion of the divine *perichoresis,* the Father's giving of the Son, the Son's execution of all the Father is and wills, the Spirit's eternal offering back up of the gift in endless variety, each person receiving from and giving to each other in infinite love. The pagan or secular sacrificial regime obeys the logic of the boundary, the "justice" of demarcations, the blow with which Romulus slays Remus; the sacrifice that Christ is obeys the life of the God who is *apeiron, aperilepton,* boundless, impossible to "leap over," but crossing every boundary in absolute freedom to declare his love. God is then the God who transgresses the bounds of totality, who violates the contained power of every *temenos,* and whose motion in time must therefore call forth totality's most "natural" gesture: crucifixion. From a pagan perspective the cross is a sacrifice in the "proper" sense: destruction of the agent of social instability in the interests of social order, and the surrender of the particular to the universal; but the shape of Christ's life, its constant motion of love, forgiveness, and righteous judgment, seems (from this same perspective) no sacrifice at all, but merely an uneconomizable force of disorder, an inversion of rank and judicious measure. The God who proceeds as he will, who crosses boundaries and respects no order — law, commerce, empire, class, nations, dominions, markets, death — except the order of love (the only infinite order), is a Word that disrupts the narratives that sustain the world as a reserve, a controlled expenditure, and a recuperation of power. It is expedient that such a Word be silenced, lest the nation perish.

This is why the cross of Christ should be seen not simply as *a* sacrifice, but as the convergence of two radically opposed orders of sacrifice. It is pure crisis, a confrontation between worlds, the raising up of one out of the grip of the other. Within Israel's history the most important practice of sacrifice is ultimately confined to the temple in Jerusalem alone, and this is entirely appropriate: Israel's offering does not express a sacrificial logic simply inherent in being, practicable in any setting, for purposes of auspication or haruspication or private benefit, but is the single action of God's people, the extraordinary motion of Israel's ceaseless exodus toward God, to whom all being belongs, peacefully, and who therefore has no need for it to be portioned to him in an economy of violence. It is this same motion toward God that is made perfect in the life of Christ, in the gift he makes of himself to the Father by the entirety of who he is. The crucifixion is what happens to this sacrifice, even its seal and perfect accomplishment, but not as such its event; the cross is the response of political power to Christ's self-oblation, which is the entire kenotic and faithful unfolding of his mission. There is a double motion in the crucifixion, of gift and immolation: Christ giving himself to God in the entirety of his life lived toward the Father, unto death, and the violence of worldly power folding back upon this motion in an attempt to contain it. The cross marks the place where the totality, in its most naked manifestation as political terror, attempts to overcome infinity — for the infinite, when it invades totality, does so as a kind of anarchy, prodigal in love and uncompromising in judgment — but the cross ultimately fails to put an end to the motion of Christ's life, to the infinity of his gift. Thus one order of sacrifice is raised up, the other cast down, reduced to a kind of futility; and thus we are freed from servitude to the absolute. The sacrificial economy of totality, in the end, can repeat only a single gesture: it has the power to crucify; but the sacrificial self-outpouring of the infinite cannot be brought to an end by crucifixion, because it continues to be the gift it is even in surrendering itself to the violences of the world. Its motion is repeated, unabated, even in being suppressed; even the cross, Rome's most "persuasive" image of terror, is conquered and becomes a far more persuasive image of love. The only force, in fact, that profane power possesses is that very violence that creates martyrs and, in a sense, calls forth the church; power ends in powerlessness at the boundaries it guards, and so finds itself impotent against a God who makes powerlessness the place of his bounty; violence shows itself to be inherently finite and exhausts itself upon the infinity of the gift. Christ's life of love, forgiveness, and devotion is revealed as God's infinite Word, his rhetoric; it violates totality, and totality in turn cannot silence this rhetoric that is most eloquent in being handed over to death. The motion of the gift precedes and exceeds every motion of exclusion; even the traitor's handing over of Christ to death is contained and surpassed by Christ's handing over of himself to the Father.

To speak of divine "excess," I should add, is simply another way of speaking of God's *apatheia*; in either case, I mean the utter fullness of God's joy, the perfect boundlessness of his love, glory, beauty, wisdom, and being, his everlasting immunity to every limitation, finite determination, force of change, peril, sorrow, or need, the trinitarian plenitude of the essential "venture" — the Father's manifestation and love of his goodness in the Son and Spirit — of the divine life; and apart from an unambiguous affirmation of just this classical definition of the divine nature — and most particularly an affirmation of the impassibility of the divine nature of the incarnate Word — no theological sense can be made of the language of Christ's sacrifice that does not, on the one hand,

make of Christian belief a philosophically incoherent farrago of myth and sentimentality and, on the other, implicate the Christian God in evil. I have already,
above, advanced most of my arguments in this matter, but I want to revisit the
issue here only to bring out the absolute centrality of the doctrine of *apatheia* to
Christology, and so to the Christian understanding of Christ's death on the
cross. It is well to remember, after all, that in Christian tradition the teaching of
divine impassibility is not simply apophatic, a limit placed upon our language, a
pious refusal to attempt trespass upon God's majesty in his light inaccessible, but
is in fact very much part of the ground of Christian hope, central to the positive
message of the evangel, not simply an austere negation of thought but a real
promise of joy in God. God's *apatheia* is that infinite refuge from all violence
and suffering that is the heart's rest, the deathless glory for which creation was
shaped in the beginning as its tabernacle, which in Christ has been joined indivisibly to our nature, and which will achieve its perfect indwelling in creation in
the final divinization of all the heirs of glory and the transfiguration of the cosmos. It is also well to remember that, for Christian thought, divine impassibility
is the effect of the fullness of trinitarian charity, rather than a purely negative attribute logically implied by the thought of divine simplicity and bodilessness,
and so is properly synonymous with "infinite love" — for love, even for creatures, is not primordially a reaction, but the possibility of every action, the act
that makes all else actual; it is purely positive, sufficient in itself, without the
need of any galvanism of the negative to be fully active, vital, and creative.[186]
That said, for Christian tradition, no less than for pagan metaphysics, to speak of
God's impassibility is to assert that the divine nature is in itself immutable and
immune to suffering, that God is impervious to any force — any pathos or affect
— external to his nature, and that he is incapable of experiencing shifting emotions within himself. And this is why the teaching has become as scandalous to
many modern ears as was the other side of the same mystery — that the immortal and changeless God had entered into time and space, had lived a human life,
suffered in the flesh, and died a human death — to the ears of antiquity.

Clearly those who want to reject the language of divine immutability and
impassibility, misguided though they be, generally want only to do justice to the
Word's incarnation and crucifixion: it seems simply obvious, after all, that here
we must be talking about a change within the being of God, and of a suffering

186. John of Damascus, for instance, draws a very strict distinction between a pathos and
an "energy" or act (such as charity): the former is a movement of the soul provoked by something alien and external to it; but the latter is a "drastic" movement, a positive power that is
moved of itself in its own nature (*De fide orthodoxa* 2.23). Thomas Aquinas says love, enjoyment, and delight are qualitatively different from anger and sadness, as the latter are privative
states, passive and reactive, whereas the former are originally one act of freedom and intellect
and subsist wholly in God as a purely "intellectual appetite" (*Summa theologiae* 1.20.1a).

endured by God, and so in both cases of a capacity endemic to his nature. From the vantage of the cross, how can the traditional metaphysical attributions of divine transcendence not appear to obscure a clear understanding of who God has shown himself to be? What does it profit one to assert, along with Cyril of Alexandria, that Christ "was in the crucified body appropriating the sufferings of the flesh to himself impassibly"?[187] Or, with Melito of Sardis, that "the impassible suffered"?[188] How can one avoid the sort of "contradictions" that litter the christological treatises of Cyril, for instance, who insisted with more fervor and ferocity than any other theologian of the early church upon the absolute unity of Christ, the perfect simplicity of the identity of the incarnate Logos in all his acts, and yet who apparently felt bound by metaphysical commitments with which this unity seems incompatible? "When the only-begotten Word of God became a human being, he did so not by discarding his being as God, but by remaining, within the assumption of the flesh, that which he was. For the nature of the Word is immutable and unalterable, and can suffer no shadow of change."[189] Rather than trading in paradoxes, why not lay down our metaphysics at the foot of the cross? The truth is, however, that we err when we read such phrases principally as paradoxes; they are actually intended as formulae for explaining, quite lucidly, the biblical story of our salvation in Christ. To begin with, the denial that the incarnation of Christ is a change in God's nature is not a denial that it is a real act of the living God, really coming to partake of our nature, nor certainly is it an attempt to evade the truth that, as the Second Council of Constantinople put it, "one of the Trinity suffered in the flesh."[190] The divine person of the Logos — the only hypostasis to which the humanity of Jesus belongs — has really, through his humanity, suffered every extreme of human dereliction and pain and has truly tasted of death. What the Fathers were anxious to reject, however, was any suggestion that God becoming human was an act of divine self-alienation, an actual μετάβασις εἰς ἄλλο γένος, a transformation into a reality essentially contrary to what God eternally is: for this would mean that God must negate himself as God to become human — which would be to say God did not become human. Hence, a strict distinction must be

187. Cyril, *Third Epistle to Nestorius* (*Ep.* 16) 6, in Cyril of Alexandria, *Select Letters*, ed. and trans. Lionel R. Wickham (Oxford: Clarendon, 1983), 20: τὰ τῆς ἰδίας σαρκὸς ἀπαθῶς οἰκειούμενος πάθη.

188. Melito, frag. 13.15, in *Méliton de Sardes, Sur la Pâque et Fragments*, ed. and trans. Othmar Perler (Paris: Les Éditions du Cerf, 1966), 238: "impassibilis patitur. . . ."

189. Cyril, *Homiliae diversae* 2, PG, 77:985-89: γέγονε δὲ ἄνθρωπος ὁ μονογενὴς τοῦ Θεοῦ Λόγος, οὐκ ἀποβεβληκὼς τὸ εἶναι Θεὸς, ἀλλ᾽ ἐν προσλήψει σαρκὸς μεμενηκὼς, ὅπερ ἦν. Ἄτρεπτος γάρ ἐστι καὶ ἀναλλοίωσις ἡ τοῦ Λόγου φύσις, καὶ οὐκ οἶδε παθεῖν τροπῆς ἀποσκίασμα.

190. Anathema 10.

drawn between the idea of divine change and that of divine *kenosis*. When Scripture says "the Logos became flesh," says Cyril, the word "became" signifies not any change in God but only the act of self-divesting love whereby God the Son emptied himself of his glory, while preserving his immutable and impassible nature intact.[191] God did not, he says (here following Athanasius),[192] alter or abandon his nature in any way, but freely appropriated the weakness and poverty of our nature for the work of redemption.[193] And Augustine makes precisely the same distinction: "When he accepted the form of a slave, he accepted time. Did he therefore change? Was he diminished? Was he sent into exile? Did he fall into defect? Certainly not. What then does it mean, 'he emptied himself, taking the form of a slave?' It means he is said to have emptied himself out by accepting the inferior, not by degenerating from equality."[194] This may appear at first to be a distinction without a difference, but it is in fact a quite logical and necessary clarification of terms, which can be justified on many grounds. For one thing, the absolute qualitative disproportion between infinite and finite allows for the infinite to appropriate and accommodate the finite without ceasing to be infinite; as all the perfections that compose a creature as what it is have their infinite and full reality in God, then the self-emptying of God in his creature is not a passage from what he is to what he is not, but a gracious condescension by which the infinite is pleased truly to disclose and express itself in one instance of the finite. Indeed, in this sense, to say God does not change in the incarnation is almost a tautology: God is not some thing that can be transformed into another thing, but is the being of everything, to which all that is always already properly belongs; there is no change of nature needed for the fullness of being to assume — even through self-impoverishment — *a being as the dwelling place of its mystery and glory.* Moreover, as human being is nothing at all in itself but the image and likeness of God, then the perfect dwelling of the eternal image and likeness of God — the Logos — in the one man who perfectly expresses and lives out what it is to be human, is in no sense an alien act for God. The act by which the form of God appears in the form of a slave is the act by which the infinite divine image shows itself in the finite divine image: this then is not a change, but a manifestation, of who God is. And finally,

191. Cyril, ΟΤΙ ΕΙΣ Ο ΧΡΙΣΤΟΣ (hereafter *EX*), in Cyrille d'Alexandrie, *Deux Dialogues Christologiques*, ed. G. M. de Durand (Paris: Les Éditions du Cerf, 1964), 312-16.

192. Athanasius, *Epistola ad Epictetum; PG*, 26:1064.

193. Cyril, *Scholia de incarnatione unigeniti; PG*, 75:1374; see also the *Third Epistle to Nestorius 3, Select Letters*, 16.

194. Augustine, *Enarrationes in Psalmos* 74.5, Corpus Christianorum, Series Latina 39:1028: "Sicut formam servi accepit, ita et tempus accepit. Demutatus est ergo? deminutus est? exilior redditus? in defectum lapsus? Absit. Quid ergo *semetipsam exinanivit, formam servi accipiens?* Exinanisse se dictus est accipiendo inferiorem, non degenerando ab aequali."

and most crucially, the very action of *kenosis* is not a new act for God, because God's eternal being is, in some sense, *kenosis:* the self-outpouring of the Father in the Son, in the joy of the Spirit. Thus Christ's incarnation, far from dissembling his eternal nature, exhibits not only his particular *proprium* as the Son and the splendor of the Father's likeness, but thereby also the nature of the whole trinitarian *taxis*. On the cross we see this joyous self-donation *sub contrario,* certainly, but not *in alieno.* For God to pour himself out, then, as the man Jesus, is not a venture outside the trinitarian life of indestructible love, but in fact quite the reverse: it is the act by which creation is seized up into the sheer invincible pertinacity of that love, which reaches down to gather us into its triune motion.

This means that in Christ God has made peace with us because he, as God, is peace; and this is why theology must defend its discourse against interpretations of the cross as a revelation of God as our "fellow sufferer": for only a God who is immune to suffering in his proper nature — who is in himself peace and love, without the tutelage of terror, or anxiety, or the refining fire of death — can be said to be in no way culpable for or implicated in worldly suffering; only he is innocent, only he is goodness, love, and holiness, only he can save. The mystery of redemption is the perfection of the "drawing nigh" of God's indwelling and transforming glory, the drawing nigh of "all flesh" to the tabernacle of the presence. In Christ that perfection is achieved, for here the fitful and inconstant nature of the first Adam is brought into intimate contact with the constancy of the divine nature of the last Adam. Indeed, it is fair to say that it is in this sense — before any other — that salvation is a matter of exchange for many of the Fathers. It is the transaction, that is, the *admirabile commercium* of divine and human natures, that occurs in the incarnation of the Word, the miraculous reconciliation of God and humanity that simply is the very *communicatio idiomatum* of Jesus' identity, and that opens out to embrace us within its mystery in the death and resurrection of Christ when, as Cyril says, he accomplishes in himself the exchange of our slavery for his glory (*EX* 366-68) and, having assumed our sufferings, liberates us from them through his unconquerable life.[195] The great Alexandrians, especially, tended to see salvation in terms of the atonement offering of Israel, whose central action was the bearing of the blood of the sacrifice — the blood of the people, as it were, dead in sin — into the Holy of Holies, where it came into contact with the deathless indwelling glory of God, and so Israel was purified of its sins and made alive by God himself, the fountain of life. Just so, Athanasius[196] and Cyril like to speak

195. See Cyril, *Apologeticus pro XII Capitibus contra Orientales,* XII Anathematismus, *PG,* 76:337-80.

196. See *Epistola ad Epictetum* 10, *PG,* 26:1068.

of Christ's body as the temple wherein this immortal glory encounters our humanity, and by a divinizing contact, makes it live eternally. Following Hebrews 10:19-20, Cyril speaks of the veil of Christ's flesh — like the temple veil that hid the Holy of Holies — concealing the transcendence and exceeding glory of the Logos (*EX* 456), so allowing Christ "both to suffer in the flesh and not to suffer in his Godhead (for he was at once himself both God and human)," and thus show through the resurrection "that he is mightier than death and corruption: as God he is life and the giver of life, and raised up his own temple" (474-76).[197] And this is in fact the consummation of the miraculous commerce that occurs in Christ: the perfection of our nature in Christ's resurrection body, a body entirely divinized and so entirely without pain — a body no longer the creature of pain, but a body of love, a pure mirror of a body, reflecting without any shadow of sadness the light that God pours graciously down upon it.

This, then, is the sacrifice of Christ — this is its infinite extravagance and its essential peace. The saving exchange that occurs for us in the incarnate Word is perfectly expressed for Cyril in John 20:17, when the risen Christ says, "I am going to my Father and your Father; to my God and your God"; for here we see how the Son's Father by nature has become our Father by grace, precisely because our God by nature has become his God through condescension (334-36). Indeed, for Cyril, whenever Christ calls upon his Father as "my God," he does so on our behalf and in our place: especially in the cry of dereliction from the cross (442-44). And this is our salvation: for when the infinite outpouring of the Father in the Son, in the joy of the Spirit, enters our reality, the *apatheia* of God's eternally dynamic and replete life of love consumes every pathos in its ardor; even the ultimate extreme of the *kenosis* of the Son in time — crucifixion — is embraced within and overcome by the everlasting *kenosis* of the divine life. Because divine *apatheia* is the infinite interval of the going forth of the Son from the Father in the light of the Spirit, every interval of estrangement we fabricate between ourselves and God — sin, ignorance, death itself — is always already exceeded in him: God has always gone infinitely further in his own being as the God of self-outpouring charity than we can venture in our attempts to escape him, and our most abysmal sin is as nothing to the abyss of divine love. And as the Word possesses this trinitarian impassibility in his eternal nature, and so as God cannot change or suffer, as a man he can suffer all things, bear any wound — indeed, bear it more fully than any other could, in absolute depth — not as wrath or defeat but as an act of saving love: as Easter. And while God's everlasting outpouring, which is for him a life of infinite joy, in assuming the

---

197. . . . καὶ τὸ σαρκὶ μὲν ἐλέσθαι παθεῖν, θεότητι δὲ μὴ παθεῖν — ἦν γὰρ ‹ὁ αὐτὸς› Θεός το ὁμοῦ ἄνθρωπος. . . . Ὅτι γάρ ἐστι θανάτου κρείττων καὶ φθορᾶς, ζωὴ καὶ ζωοποιὸς ὑπάρχων ὡς Θεός, μεμαρτύρηκεν ἡ ἀνάστασις· ἐγήγερκε γὰρ τὸν ἑαυτοῦ ναόν.

intervals of our estrangement from God, appears for us now under the form of tragic pain and loss, the joy is the original and ultimate truth of who he is, is boundless, and cannot be interrupted — and so conquers all our sorrow; he is already higher than the vaulted heavens of the gods and lower than the most abysmal deeps of hell — as bliss, as love; our abandonment of God, and the abandonment of the Son and of every soul in death, is always already surpassed by the sheer abandon with which the Father begets and breathes forth his being. And the terrible distance of Christ's cry of human dereliction, despair, and utter godforsakenness — "My God, my God, why hast thou forsaken me?" — is enfolded within and overcome by the ever greater distance and always indissoluble unity of God's triune love: "Father, into thy hands I commend my spirit."

ii. A Gift Exceeding Every Debt

The question that this approach to the Christian language of sacrifice begs, however, is whether it does not conveniently evade the question of violence at the expense of fidelity to the tradition; after all, the notion that Christ's death constitutes an appeasement of divine wrath against sin figures more than marginally in the history of Christian reflection upon salvation, especially in the West. Is it not the case, one might at least ask, that the theology of atonement has usually involved some sense that the death of Christ is required by the Father as a transaction that accomplishes reconciliation, and has therefore made God complicit in the violence of sacrifice? The locus classicus of the "substitution theory" of atonement is, of course, the *Cur Deus Homo* of Anselm, the first systematic treatment of salvation exclusively in terms of restitution, of a satisfaction of the debt incurred in sin. Certainly Anselm has often been seen as occupying a very particular position in dogmatic history, and has often, in consequence, been viewed (by champions and detractors alike) as the most representative theologian of atonement as punitive recompense. If one is to reconsider the presence of violence in Christian sacrificial themes, and not do so with quite the peremptory disregard for tradition that Girard evinces, it would be disingenuous (to say the least) to ignore not only Anselm's influence but the claim his theology makes upon Christian thought as an interpretation of the New Testament — and a powerful one at that.

Among his theological critics, as it happens, Anselm has long been the victim of his own clarity: he cuts a conveniently epochal figure because he is identifiably a distinctive product of the early Western Middle Ages, because in arguing for the "necessity" of a certain picture of redemption he seems to adumbrate the distinctively Western theological method of following centuries, and because his is so recognizably a *theory* of atonement and hence so easy to abstract, simplify, formulate, and assess. The argument of *Cur Deus Homo* is easily read as an uncomplicated series of rational steps that lead, according to the assumptions implicit within them, to a rigidly rational conclusion regarding the "juridical" necessity of Christ's sacrificial death: an argument that, far from resisting summary, seems to invite it. Every rational creature is created to partake of beatitude in God, Anselm asserts, in return for which the creature owes God perfect obedience, by withholding which humanity offends infinitely against the divine honor and merits death. Inasmuch as humanity has sinned against God, to God's "dishonor," God's honor demands that humanity restore what it has taken away, and indeed give more than it has taken, in order to make satisfaction for its offense; otherwise humanity must suffer the penalty prescribed. Nor can God merely remit the penalty, as it would contradict his own lordship and righteousness were he to allow sin to pass with impunity and thereby raise injustice to a level like his own (transcendent of the rule of any higher law), erasing the distinction between good and evil (in the latter's favor), and creating division within his own immutably righteous will; and so, by way of restitution or punishment, satisfaction or damnation, humanity shall restore the divine honor and the ordered beauty of the created universe. But humanity possesses nothing by which it might satisfy divine justice; as it is God himself against whom the gravity of every transgression is measured, the slightest sin is an infinite offense, calling for an infinite and "more than infinite" restitution. However, it is also contrary to God's goodness and honor that his gracious purpose in creation should come to nothing and that he should abandon his creature to destruction. One is called for, then, who can of his own render to God a payment that surpasses in worth all things under God; but this is possible for God alone; and yet satisfaction must be made by one of the race of Adam. And so, that the divine righteousness remain inviolate, the beauty of creation be preserved, and the divine purpose be fulfilled, the God-man must come, in order to make satisfaction on humanity's behalf: a high Chalcedonian Christology is a "necessity" for understanding how God has resolved this apparent *impasse* between his justice and mercy. Christ as a man owes God his perfect obedience, which he gladly proffers, but as a sinless man he does not owe God his death; when Christ voluntarily surrenders his infinitely precious life for God's honor, and the Father accepts it, the superabundance of its worth calls forth some gracious recompense from God's justice. But Christ, being also God, wants for nothing; and so, lest God's righteousness be defeated by the injustice of no recompense being given, the benefits of Christ's death pass on to those on whom Christ would bestow them. God's infinite honor being more than infinitely satisfied, humanity's debt before God is remitted and humanity receives the grace of salvation, in such measure as persons approach God in Christ's name and live righteously.

This, at least, is Harnack's account of *Cur Deus Homo* in a somewhat too cursory passage in his *Dogmengeschichte;*[198] and perhaps Anselm would have himself regarded it a fair précis of his position. Certainly there are elements in Anselm's theology that invite reduction to a simple economic model of atonement: a model, moreover, that attempts the impossible task of calculating the exchange value of counterposed infinities, thus threatening to obscure the fact that the only infinity at issue is that of God, who cannot be divided against himself. But Anselm's argument, thus denuded of every nuance and ambiguity that enriches the text from which it is drawn, is susceptible of every casual misconstrual the theological mind can devise; it becomes indeed a theological "theory," removed from any larger theological narrative, unable to defend itself by reference to the specific concerns that prompted it or the historical context in which it was situated. For Harnack, as for Albrecht Ritschl before him, Anselm's significance resided in precisely this perceived bare linearity of his thought; for both, Anselm was something genuinely new, a theologian who formulated a "theory of atonement" as distinct from the crude "schemes of salvation" characteristic of patristic thought. In *Die christliche Lehre von der Rechtfertigung und Versöhnung,* Ritschl clearly reserved the exalted words of his book's title for the period commencing with Abelard and Anselm; patristic theology was concerned, at most, with *Erlösung.* "Atonement" language, simply said, is an improvement over the language of earlier ages insofar as it depicts redemption as an objective transaction between the Father and the Son, rather than as the grossly mythic drama of divine descent and rescue, and insofar as it concerns itself with "moral" rather than "physical" reconciliation of the human and the divine. Imperfect, indeed occasionally deplorable (especially where it appears to suggest an opposition between God's mercy and God's justice), Anselm's soteriology is still an important first step toward more considered theories. The mixed verdict of liberal Protestant dogmatics upon Anselm's work is best expressed by Harnack: Anselm's language, he says, is little more than an extension of the logic of Western Catholicism's penitential system, and so concerns itself principally with the placation of God's wrath; the limits of the penitential system confine his theory to the model of a *legal* transaction between Father and Son, rather than one of real reconciliation; nowhere does it show how the opposition of wills between God and humanity is overcome.[199] Harnack recognizes that Anselm's is not exactly a theory of salvation through penal suffering, but this he does not lay to the latter's credit (69). He does com-

198. In English: Adolf von Harnack, *History of Dogma,* trans. Neil Buchanan, 7 vols. bound as 4 (Gloucester, Mass.: Peter Smith, 1976), 6:54-67.

199. Harnack, 6:68. The parenthetical page numbers in the following text are to Harnack's *History of Dogma,* vol. 6.

mend Anselm for disabusing theology of such elements of primitive Christian thought as the notions of a ransom paid to the devil and a "physical" salvation accomplished primarily in the incarnation; and in seeing guilt, rather than death, as that which Christ chiefly overcomes, Anselm further distances himself from the barbarisms of patristic thought (69-70). In the end, though, Harnack sees Anselm's theory as both unbalanced, limiting the work of atonement to Christ's humanity (73), and uncomforting, offering no final assurance of justi-fication to the individual Christian, who must still strive after righteousness to attain beatitude (68-69). It is interesting to note, however, that already, even when viewed in so uncompromising a light, Anselm's argument begins to slip free from a Girardian critique of sacrificial soteriologies: Harnack, in fact, chides Anselm for failing to enunciate a clear theory of penal suffering, for in-deed subverting such a theory, and for failing to see the necessity of *innocent* suffering in particular (one of the most grotesque aspects of Harnack's own theology) and the necessity of not only Christ's obedience but his death (69, 73). This is quite instructive.

Nor is it only liberal Protestant scholarship that has taken Anselm to task for the deficiencies (real or perceived) in his argument; one might cite the much more theologically conservative Lutheran Gustaf Aulén or the Russian Orthodox Vladimir Lossky as examples of theologians whose reservations re-garding Anselm's theory were, if anything, far more pronounced than those of Ritschl or Harnack. Of course, it is rather peculiar that Aulén, who rebelled with such vehemence against German liberal Protestant scholarship, and who rejected its silly characterization of patristic soteriology as merely "physical," should have so unquestioningly embraced the interpretation of Anselm with which that scholarship supplied him. Nevertheless, in his most famous work on the matter, *Christus Victor,*[200] he dismisses Anselm's project without qualm as a radical break from the patristic narrative that Aulén himself champions; he too argues that, in Anselm's theory, it is Christ's humanity that is the true agent of atonement, which (to his mind) places the theory at odds with the Pauline, pa-tristic, and (genuine) Lutheran view of Christ's saving work as a unified divine campaign against sin, death, and the devil; and he too deplores Anselm's sup-posed opposition of justice to mercy, and takes his language as little more than a monstrous exaggeration of penitential discourse. For Aulén the rejection of any "Anselmian" contour in soteriology is a necessary preliminary step in the Western recovery of the "correct" or "classic" view of the atonement, according to which salvation is the result of a single, continuous divine action, a descent into the deepest abyss of human estrangement in order to vanquish death, the

---

200. Gustaf Aulén, *Christus Victor: An Historical Study of the Three Main Types of the Idea of the Atonement,* trans. A. G. Herbert (London: SPCK, 1953).

powers of this world, sin, and wrath, and so to raise humanity up to everlasting life. In the classic view of atonement, says Aulén, talk of sacrifice is intentionally ambiguous; as Gregory the Theologian says, Christ's death is not a ransom paid to the devil but a sacrifice the Father receives from the Son "by economy," solely for sanctification and because divine justice requires that Christ alone should overcome the tyrants that hold humanity captive (*Oration* 45.22). Thus Christ's sacrifice is an internal relation of the divine will, not an extrinsic exchange of expiatory death and forensic merit.

Lossky shares many of Aulén's concerns; while not indulging in many of the latter's broad brush-strokes, he paints perhaps the most damning portrait of Anselm's theory of all.[201] While hardly unaware that Anselm's language is not without some precedent in patristic theology, he still sees it as an incalculable impoverishment of that theology, a decortication of all the richness of the traditional narrative, leaving nothing behind but the single unadorned theme of "redemption." Lossky takes offense at the scandal of a book putatively explaining the incarnation, but without reference to divinization, victory over hell, or the role of the Holy Spirit; and at Anselm's apparent reduction of the resurrection and ascension to a simple happy ending, and of salvation to a change not in human nature but only in the divine attitude toward humanity. Salvation, so conceived, is little more than a drama enacted between an infinitely offended God and a humanity unable to satisfy the demands of his vindictive wrath. Much to be preferred is the ambiguity, richness, and narrative complexity of a text like Athanasius's *De incarnatione verbi Dei*, which allows the story of salvation a greater range of colors, of soteriological models, all narrative in character, and all prohibiting one another from assuming the character of a single, definitive, and exhaustively rational account of atonement.

One should ask, though, whether the actual text of *Cur Deus Homo* has not been lost to view, behind the welter of adverse judgments brought to bear upon it. To begin with, it is not clear that Anselm's language simply reflects the practice of penance and its attendant logic of making reparation to God for particular sins. Penitential discipline provides Anselm a certain grammar, obviously, but his argument is at the same time one that subverts the logic of that discipline, and would seem in fact to reorient it entirely. If every sin is intrinsically an infinite offense, and all penance then technically "unsatisfactory," and if the superabundant benefit of Christ's sacrifice alone remits guilt, penitential practice is both contained and overcome by Christ's redeeming act; if grace, then, allows for a penitential return of the sinner, it does so solely because

---

201. See Vladimir Lossky, "Redemption and Deification," in Lossky, *In the Image and Likeness of God*, ed. John H. Erickson and Thomas E. Bird (Crestwood, N.Y.: St. Vladimir's Seminary Press, 1974), 97-110.

prayerful humility is the fitting form of a redeemed life, and because this way of return is the very promise and substance of salvation for one concerning whom the entire question of satisfaction — in the sense of this impossible "restitution" for sin — has been infinitely deferred, through superabounding mercy. In one stroke Anselm has done away with the notion that penitential practice is a punitive discipline intended to satisfy God's wrath, and shown it to be simply a thankful piety that responds to (and is the result of) an unmerited and transforming grace. A somewhat different story is being told about divine justice — one, frankly, that would be unintelligible if Anselm were, as Harnack claims, unconcerned with actual reconciliation. It is not Anselm, after all, who makes a categorical distinction between his "theory of atonement" proper and such remarks as he makes concerning the appropriation of salvation by those who approach God humbly, contritely, placing their faith in Christ. To Harnack this can only mean that no one can be certain of grace; whether this is evidence of certain Lutheran qualms, on Harnack's part, regarding works righteousness or of a failure to imagine the church as the place where the real experience of salvation is lived out, it is a judgment that blinds him to the link between the vocation of humankind to a prayerful and penitent faith and the overcoming of the sinful human will in Christ's human life of obedience to the Father. In rendering to God the love humanity owes God, but withholds, and by bearing the weight of sin's consequences, and by showing on the cross that the triumph of justice over sin is also the triumph of humility over pride, Christ provides humanity both with a model of obedience and with the assurance that it can always return to God, despite its inability to satisfy divine justice, because it is sustained by the grace of Christ's gift. To cling to Christ in faith, the turn to prayer is required; as one asks for forgiveness, so must one forgive; and one's prayer comes to participate in the satisfaction Christ has made on one's behalf (*Cur Deus Homo* 1.19). Because the rule of God's justice is forgiveness, the charitable practices of the church Christ has redeemed are necessary for a humanity re-created after its original nature.

Of course, the claim that such a scheme is immeasurably remote from patristic soteriology has as its premise — in the cases of Ritschl and Harnack — the peculiar belief that, in the Greek "physical" view of salvation, it is the incarnation in and of itself that saves, wondrously imparting divine energy to human nature as a whole; but this is to ignore a fairly vital feature of patristic thought: that, insofar as the Word's incarnation restores human nature, it is through establishing a new creation to which humanity is admitted by way of Christ's conquest of sin and death and through human integration into the corporate identity of his mystical body. For Aulén and Lossky, on the other hand, the discontinuity with patristic tradition lies in a failure on Anselm's part to give an adequate account of God's action in Christ to overthrow death and the devil and to restore human nature in his resurrection. But, granting that the inflection of Anselm's language is scarcely "Greek," the closer the attention one pays Anselm's argument, the harder it becomes to locate the exact point at which he supposedly breaks from patristic orthodoxy. The divine action follows the same course as in the "classic" model: human sin having disrupted the order of God's good creation, and humanity having been handed over to death and the devil's rule, God enters into a condition of estrangement and slavery to set humanity free. As Anselm asserts, humanity was placed between God and the devil to vanquish the latter for the honor of the former (1.22); and as the fall constituted a victory for the devil, to God's dishonor, so the satisfaction effected by Christ serves God's honor inasmuch as it is a victory over the devil. This is, surely, a variant of a *Christus victor* soteriology, and one that makes questionable every hasty assumption regarding what Anselm means by "satisfaction." Formidable linguistic shifts aside, Anselm's is not a new narrative of salvation. In truth, this facile distinction between a patristic soteriology concerned exclusively with the rescue of humanity from death and a theory of atonement concerned exclusively with remission from guilt — the distinction, that is, between "physical" and "moral" theories — is supportable, if at all, only in terms of emphasis and imagery; Athanasius, Gregory of Nyssa, and John of Damascus (to name a few) were no less conscious than Anselm of the guilt overcome by Christ on the cross, nor he any less concerned than they with the Son's campaign against death's dominion. Indeed, in *Cur Deus Homo* the matter of guilt is somewhat recused: it is guilt that is set aside, made of no account by Christ's grace, so that the power of death should be overcome without violence to divine justice. From very early on in the text (1.6-7) Anselm is engaged in answering a single question: If the rights of the devil (who is himself infinitely indebted to God) over humanity are not really "rights" in any true sense (a position of the purest patristic pedigree), why must the overthrow of death proceed in the fashion that it does? For God could have reclaimed his creatures by force, if all that were at issue were the devil's prerogatives (1.7), but for Anselm the true issue is God's own righteousness. From which unfolds Anselm's story of the "necessity" — the inner coherence — of the action of the God-man. And it is explicitly not a story about a substitutionary sacrifice offered as a simple restitution for human guilt (1.8), but concerns, rather, the triumph over death, the devil, and sin accomplished in Christ's voluntary self-donation to the Father, which the Father receives (as Gregory the Theologian would say) "by economy," so that its benefits might redound to those with whom Christ has assumed solidarity.

On this reading it is difficult to sustain the objection that Anselm has made Christ's humanity the sole reconciling agency in salvation, and reduced the role of Christ's divinity to that of a kind of commodity, the infinite value bartered for human forgiveness. This strangely Nestorian reading of Anselm's

Christology is closely bound to the complaint that Anselm has posed divine justice over against divine mercy, making out the latter to be unobtainable until the demands of the former have been satisfied. In such criticisms it is as if the project (indeed the title) of Anselm's work has been willfully ignored; because, in Anselm's scheme, it is the divine Word who at every juncture fulfills divine justice and offers himself up. What is overlooked is how essentially trinitarian the structure of Anselm's story is. As it can be shown *remoto Christo* that sinful humanity cannot of itself make satisfaction to God, that the God who is always *maius* than whatever can be thought can be reached or sufficed only by God, and that God's goodness cannot suffer defeat, there must be a saving initiative from God's side, and there must already be within the terms of God's changeless righteousness that dynamism that overcomes any apparent incommensurability of mercy and justice. The appearance of such an opposition is the result not only of finite human reason, but of sin: only in the rejection of God's creative mercy is his justice experienced as wrath and dereliction. But the idea of a triune God in whom there exists the "highest concord of justice and mercy" forbids so simple an opposition; and it is because this concord is the truth of a dynamic and living God, in whom the motion of donation and redonation, obedience and love, is already one, that a way of return can be opened for humanity;[202] a return unimaginable in terms of a "monadic" God, the immutability of whose justice could be known only in the awful sublimity of damnation. God is already always an infinite venturing forth and return, an action of reconciliation, response, and accord, in which any opposition of goods is already overcome by the work of deathless love. And while the suffering and humiliation that Christ endures do not belong to his divinity (*Cur Deus Homo* 1.8), and the violence that befalls him belongs in no way to the eternal motion of his divine filiation, it is necessary — fitting — that it is the divine Son who becomes a man and lives out a life of human obedience to God (2.9), as it reflects the Word's eternal motion of love toward the Father, returning to him the superabundance of the "initial" gift of himself — a motion in whose beauty humanity is allowed to partake through the condescension of the incarnation. As Christ says in the Gospel of John, "Therefore doth my Father love me, because I lay down my life, that I might take it again" (10:17); but this love is not merely a consequence of Christ's sacrifice, because this laying down of all he is belongs already to the motion of the Trinity, to the divine love, as its filial intonation. And so Christ does not effect a mere posterior reconciliation of justice and mercy: they do not constitute a dialectical opposition sublated in the act of atonement. Nor do they possess only a mysterious and transcendent unity in God's unsearchable depths, leaving to the human

---

202. On the notion of obedience in the trinitarian *perichoresis*, see Karl Barth, *Church Dogmatics* IV/1, trans. G. W. Bromiley (Edinburgh: T. & T. Clark, 1956), 203-9.

vantage merely the appearance of one relenting before the pressure of the other. In the God-man, within human history, God's justice and mercy are shown to be one thing, one action, life, and being. When humanity fails to take up the creature's side of the covenant, the righteousness that condemns is also the love that restores by surmounting even the obstacle of human disobedience and lawful subjection to death, to take up the human side on humanity's behalf. The divine address and human response are both present in the Word made flesh, just as God's honor and God's condescension are revealed in a single life handed over to the Father. It is the human understanding of justice and honor that proves inadequate, while the unbroken trinitarian action of God in every aspect of salvation testifies to a divine justice whose inner mystery is infinite mercy.

In the end Lossky's critique of *Cur Deus Homo,* by virtue of its brevity and frank simplicity, is the most telling. He oversimplifies Anselm's position frightfully, he concerns himself more with Anselm's exaggerated emphasis of one soteriological motif than with the actual structure of Anselm's argument, and his objections largely reflect many of the suspicions that pass back and forth between Eastern and Western theology (most especially the Orthodox distrust of "juridical" categories of thought); but he is quite correct to be suspicious of a narrative of the atonement that, for instance, says so little about the resurrection and its place in the "necessity" of the incarnation. But while one may prefer the richer narrative complexity of a text like Athanasius's *De incarnatione,* one should also acknowledge that, for Anselm, it is just this complexity that is not desirable. Anselm is already situated in the tradition of Christian discourse, he already knows that Christ has recapitulated human nature in himself and conquered evil on our behalf; it is from this narrative that Anselm has undertaken a (by no means final or exclusive) reduction of the tale, in order better to grasp the inner necessity of its sacrificial logic. He pauses for one critical moment, to contemplate the cross as the grave inner meaning (or inevitability) of God's condescension. If Anselm's account appears to leave the resurrection as a mere coda (which indeed is a failing), it also corrects a certain occasional aporia in patristic thought, insofar as the latter often fails to say how the resurrection vindicates — rather than merely reverses — Christ's self-oblation. Easter is the triumph not of an indestructible and otherworldly savior, but of the entire motion of Christ's sacrificial life of devotion to the Father; the overthrow of death and the devil is accomplished by the peaceful self-donation of one whose life fulfills entirely the vocation of humanity to offer itself in love to the God who gives all things in love. Moreover, Anselm's reading of the cross would be impossible except in the light of Easter, inasmuch as he obviously understands Christ's sacrifice to be, at the last, aneconomic (Christ's death purchases nothing, but his obedience calls forth a blessing), and so his reading is clearly governed by his knowledge that the Father does not retain the "price" paid by Christ's blood, as a ransom (in the human sense of a tribute ceded in exchange for favor or benefit), but raises Christ freely, according to a justice that surpasses retributive equivalence. As for the absence of any clear ontological dimension in Anselm's account of atonement, of any clear talk of the change wrought in human nature by salvation to balance out its more "fiduciary" terms, one might remark that Anselm already writes from within the precincts of the church's pneumatological life; certainly patristic theology never suggests that the transformation of human nature occurs anywhere else: the newly refashioned human nature established in the incarnation is found nowhere apart from the social reality of the church, whose practices of love and forgiveness are already the new life of the sanctified.

Of course, Lossky's most basic complaint against *Cur Deus Homo* is simply that it draws an inappropriate and distasteful picture of God, by attributing to him such unsavory characteristics as an ability to take infinite offense at an insult to his honor, a vindictive desire for a correspondingly infinite restitution, the need for a juridical recompense to appease his wrath; he objects to the idea of a God who requires the violence of sacrifice to restore his order. But this impression of Anselm's argument depends upon a fairly cavalier inattention to a wealth of details. One, for instance, of considerable importance, is a certain ambiguity present in the very word "honor": what Anselm takes it to mean is susceptible of debate, but it certainly does not refer to an infinite reserve of divine pride that prevents God from forgiving unreservedly. If Anselm's usage in any way reflects the jurisprudence and ethos of early medieval feudalism, it is as well to observe that in that context "honor" certainly signified more than a sense either of one's personal dignity or of one's social position, but referred also (and more fundamentally perhaps) to the principle underlying the rather fragile governance of an entire social and economic order, sustained through the exchange of shared benefits and pledged loyalties; one's honor lay not only in the obeisance one received, but in the social covenant one upheld and to which one was obliged (ideally, at any rate). In any event, one need not look beyond the text to see that, for Anselm, God's honor is inseparable from his goodness, which imparts life and harmonious order to creation, the rejection of which is necessarily death; as the source of all creation's beauty and order, it is the righteousness that cannot contradict itself or will anything amiss; it is justice, not wrath, and its manifestation is the *rectitudo* of God's universal government, its rightness and moral beauty. One might also note how little there is in Anselm concerning expiation or reparation, except in the sense of the reparation of a nature deprived of its original beauty and dignity.[203] Nor indeed is

---

203. For a treatment of Anselm's theory of the atonement that brings out this point with particular clarity and beauty, see Michel Corbin, *Prière et Raison de la Foi* (Paris: Les Éditions du Cerf, 1992), 207-328.

there any suggestion made that God is appeased by the "penal" death of Christ (Harnack is right on this score, though chillingly wrong about its implications). Anselm certainly depicts Christ's sacrifice as an offering that somehow "secures" forgiveness by satisfying the demands of divine righteousness, on our behalf; but how far does this really depart from the accounts offered by Anselm's more remote precursors? When Lossky points to a thinker like Athanasius, in order to call attention to the divergence of Anselm's model from its patristic predecessors, even while acknowledging the presence of many of the themes of *Cur Deus Homo* in Athanasius's thought, the irony is peculiarly keen. At one juncture in *De incarnatione*, Athanasius, lamenting the loss of humanity's original beauty in the fall, argues that redemption was necessitated by God's ἀγαθότης (consistency, righteousness, honor, glory), which requires the maintenance and execution of his twin decrees that, on the one hand, humanity will share in the divine life and that, on the other, death must fall upon the transgressors of holy law; to prevent the second decree from defeating the first, guilt must be removed from humanity through the exhaustion of the power of death in Christ's sacrifice (7.1-4). The hold death had on us was just, says Athanasius, and it would be monstrous were God's decree that sin shall merit death to prove false (6.2-3); but it would be unworthy of God's goodness were he to let his handiwork come to nothing (6.4-10). Nor could God simply accept our repentance as just recompense for our offense, as repentance would neither suffice to guard God's integrity nor serve to restore our wounded nature (8.3). In his body, then, Christ exhausts the wrath of the law (8.4; 10.5) and renders satisfaction for our debt (9.1-3). Already present in Athanasius's theology is the very story whose inner shape Anselm will, in a moment of intense critical reflection, attempt to grasp as necessity. Far from an arbitrary arrangement of jurisprudential transactions calculated to effect a kind of forensic reconciliation between humanity and God, the atonement as *Cur Deus Homo* depicts it is an assumption of solidarity with us by an infinitely merciful God in order to fulfill in us that beatitude intended in our creation (2.1), by accomplishing on our behalf what, in our impotence to do good and in his unwillingness to employ unjust means (1.12), could never otherwise have been brought to pass.

If, as I say, Anselm has occasionally been the victim of his own clarity of thought, it is nevertheless the case that it is a clarity frequently concealing an essential paradoxicality: God's order is preserved through his own assumption of the conditions of estrangement; his mercy is imparted in the acceptance of Christ's voluntary death; the highest law of God's inviolable justice is boundless mercy; God's sovereignty necessitates his condescension; the goodness that condemns the sinner requires that sin be forgiven. This is not because Anselm sees God as divided against himself: rather, he has come to see Christ's sacrifice not as an economic gesture (meant to insure the stability of a universe founded on unyielding laws of equivalence and retribution), but as belonging instead to the infinite motion of God's love, in which justice and mercy are one and can never be divided one from the other; he has recognized Christ's act as an infinite motion toward the Father, belonging to the mystery of the Trinity, and simply surpassing all the arrangements of debt and violence by which a sinful humanity seeks to calculate its "justice." Consequently, the only "necessity" Anselm demonstrates in the drama of salvation is a kind of inward intelligibility to the mind grasped by faith. Indeed, in the end Anselm merely restates the oldest patristic model of atonement of all: recapitulation. Granted, he rejects simple typological recapitulation, the correspondence of motifs shared by the narratives of the first and last Adam (1.3-4; 2.9), but he is still concerned with recapitulation in essentially the same sense as is Irenaeus: Christ takes up the human story and tells it correctly, by giving the correct answer to God's summons; in his life and death he renarrates humanity according to its true pattern of loving obedience, humility, and charity, thus showing all human stories of righteousness, honor, and justice to be tales of violence, falsehood, and death; and in allowing all of humanity to be resituated through his death within the retelling of their story, Christ restores them to communion with the God of infinite love who created them for his pleasure. And when Christ recapitulates humanity, he shows the gravity and terror inherent in posing that form over against the violence of the world of sin; he "satisfies" all the requirements of that form by living out his obedience to the Father under the conditions imposed by a sinful order of power, which conditions require his death. It must not be overlooked that for Anselm it is not Christ's *suffering* as such that is redemptive (the suffering merely repeats sin's endlessly repeated and essential gesture), but rather his innocence; he recapitulates humanity by passing through all the violences of sin and death, rendering to God the obedience that is his due, and so transforms the event of his death into an occasion of infinite blessings for those to whom death is condign. Christ's death does not even effect a change in God's attitude toward humanity; God's attitude never alters: he desires the salvation of his creatures, and will not abandon them even to their own cruelties.

Even here, then, in the text that most notoriously expounds the sacrificial logic of atonement, the idea of sacrifice is subverted from within: as the story of Christ's sacrifice belongs not to an economy of credit and exchange but to the trinitarian motion of love, it is given entirely as gift — a gift given when it should not have needed to be given again, by God, at a price that *we* imposed upon *him*. As an entirely divine action, Christ's sacrifice merely draws creation back into the eternal motion of divine love, for which it was fashioned. The violence that befalls Christ belongs to our sacrificial order of justice, an order overcome by his sacrifice, which is one of peace; for though totality seeks to convert

Christ into an abstract credit, in order to preserve itself as an enclosed circle of stable exchange between the life of the particular transgressor and the universal dispensation of civic stability, the donation that Christ makes of himself draws creation into God's eternal "offering" of himself in the life of the Trinity. And simply by continuing to be the God he is, and through the sheer "redundancy" of the good that flows from the infinite gesture of his love — which is a generosity in excess of all calculable economy — God undoes the sacrificial logic of totality; his gift remains gift to the end, despite all our efforts to convert it into debt. This is the infinite gesture that traverses and judges totality, the love that defeats economy. This is the unanticipated grace of Easter. Whether one chooses to follow after Nietzsche and see the redundancy of Christ's merit, inasmuch as it avails for salvation, as an infinite multiplication of debt, depends upon one's prejudices regarding giving and indebtedness — which is prior to the other, which dissembles the other. As for Anselm, though, the primordiality of the gift is the truth of Christ's paschal donation: the gift God gives in creation continues to be given again, ever more fully, in defiance of all rejection, economy, violence, and indifference; there is no division between justice and mercy in God, on Anselm's account, because both belong already to the giving of this gift — which precedes, exceeds, and annuls all debt:

> The mercy of God, which seemed to you to be lost when we were considering God's justice and humanity's sin, we find now to be so great and so in accord with justice, that neither a greater nor a more just can be thought. For what possibly could be understood to be more merciful than that God the Father should say to the sinner — damned to eternal torment and having no means whereby to redeem himself — "Take my Only-begotten and offer him for yourself"; and that the Son should himself should say, "Take me and redeem yourself"? For thus they speak, when they call us and lead us to Christian faith. What indeed were more just than that he — to whom is given a price exceeding every debt, if only given with the love that he is truly owed — should put aside every debt? (2.20)[204]

---

204. "Misericordiam vero dei quae tibi perire videbatur, cum iustitiam dei et peccatum hominis considerabamus, tam magnam tamque concordem iustitiae invenimus, ut nec maior nec iustior cogitari possit. Nempe quid misericordius intelligi valet, quam cum peccatori tormentis aeternis damnato et unde se redimat non habenti deus pater dicit: accipe unigenitum meum et da pro te; et ipse filius: tolle me et redime te? Quasi enim hoc dicunt, quando nos ad Christianam fidem vocant et trahunt. Quid etiam iustius, quam ut ille cui datur pretium maius omni debito, si debito datur affectu, dimittat omne debitum?"

iii. The Consolations of Tragedy, the Terrors of Easter

In distinguishing between two orders of sacrifice, which converge in the death of Christ, I am also calling attention to the difference between two distinct and even opposed "aesthetic" orders. The sacrificial regime of the totality, its economy of violence, which again and again hands the radiant particularity of form over to its destruction so that the equilibrium between order and indeterminacy might be preserved, can offer a concept of the beautiful whose only terms are a certain grandeur and a certain pathos that, together, bedizen the dynamisms of sacrificial violence with a kind of aesthetic necessity and moral symmetry; this is to say, the beauty of the totality is a tragic beauty. If the self-donation of Christ is indeed, by contrast, God's supreme rhetoric, whose beauty draws persons into the narrative God unfolds in Christ and his church, and if the beauty of this rhetoric must also belong to an aesthetic order that does not dissemble violence or array it in the glamor of power, then the beauty of Christ's sacrifice must be distinguished from the beauty of tragedy. But in making this distinction one will find that tragic beauty differs from the beauty of Christ's sacrifice not on account of its greater appearance of gravity, but as a result of its failure to take suffering seriously enough. One must here cut somewhat across the grain of current theological fashion: in the Christian West, in recent decades, how well a theologian appears to appreciate the "tragic depths" of the story of atonement (or, at least, how grave a theologian's voice becomes at certain appropriate junctures in that story) has become for many an index of his "seriousness." Theology has acquired a taste for tragedy, perhaps commendably at the end of an unbearably tragic century. In Catholic circles the most impressive example of this is Balthasar's celebrated "theology of Holy Saturday," with its broad rejection of the traditional triumphalistic imagery of hell's harrowing (a rejection, mercifully, that is progressively moderated in successive volumes of his *Theodramatik*). Protestant thought has perhaps produced no romances quite so grimly magnificent as Balthasar's Christ of the cadavers, but it can boast the ghastly Wagnerian opulence of Jüngel's cult of *Verwesung* and the dark, late romantic coloratura of his unwholesome theological *Liebestod*. It is among British theologians, though (two of whom I shall presently consider), that tragedy as such (or "tragic consciousness") seems to have acquired a certain dogmatic and moral authority. To many, these days, it seems certain that a kind of tragic logic must henceforth prove decisive for theology's meditations on the inextirpable evil and misery of finite existence, the desolation of Christ on the cross, and the relation between the two; how else, after all, can theology avoid banality, bland optimism, an idiot complacency impervious to the horror of human suffering or the magnitude of Christ's sacrifice, and a craven circumvention of the *via crucis*? Inevitably, when this issue is discussed, the Holocaust is introduced as evidence of the need for a "tragic theology." Obviously theologians who argue in this fashion are motivated by the highest moral concerns, and their views cannot easily be dismissed; in some provisional sense they are correct; but in a more ultimate sense they are catastrophically wrong, and for reasons quite opposite of what one might suppose: every tragic wisdom is in fact far too comforting adequately to grasp what has occurred in Christ; and insofar as any theology remains "tragic," it also remains sunk in the very triviality and optimism that the radiance of Easter ought to dispel. Moreover, a tragic theology inevitably gravitates toward that same perfidious "realism" against which I have already inveighed; it can scarcely, at the last, inspire any ethos but one that hovers disquietingly between resignation and masochism (or even sadism). Most importantly, though, it is thoroughly unbiblical — worse, it veils the true biblical narrative (and its provocations) behind the glamorous but ultimately empty allure of an alien and sacrificial spectacle. Simply said, tragic theology lacks theological depth.

This is more obvious in some cases than in others. Especially distressing are those instances when a "suffering God" theology, of the sort I have described above, is cast in its most "pathetic," emotive form (as encountered, say, in the pastoral training offered by many seminaries): at its very worst, this style of thought goes some way toward erasing the distinction, between God and humanity, of who requires pardon of whom. This can be — I intend no easy ridicule — an extremely tempting way of thinking about the cross of Christ, a salve to every wound, a soothing psychological medicament if ever there was one; however, in this context the pro forma moral outrage expressed over the evils of history can often serve to conceal a far more emotionally earnest outrage over the disaffections of the self. "My" hunger for a suffering God — for a fellow sufferer, a companion in pain — can as often as not be a desire for a God who does not offend me with his lordly impassibility or threaten utterly to strip me of what I, in the indigence and incurvation of my longings, cling to as defining who I am: the pain I suffer, the wrongs I have borne, my culpability, admittedly, but a culpability also explicable by my constant condition of personal duress. True, I desire to be forgiven (or, at any rate, excused), but not simply on account of Christ, but on account also of the validity of my complaints and my sense of being ill-used. Thus I want to see the cross as a necessity not only for me but for God: salvation involves a change in God, who is apparently finite and egoistic, like me, who can *learn* to pity more, to enter into deeper fellowship, to come down from his gilded halls, to discover that he needs to be more forgiving and to see things from my perspective too. He *helps* me, then, but does not fully convict me, and he allows me space for my recovery of myself. The cross, one might say, was good for him, if unpleasant, for now he understands me, accepts me, and so I can accept him. The heresy in such thinking is obvious, but not necessarily the moral cruelty: for, in pursuit of my own plaint and chary of anything that might weaken my sense of being aggrieved, I actually do an immense disservice to those for whose genuine suffering I deceive myself that I am principally concerned. Do those who know true and hopeless suffering really long for and need a companion in pain, or a savior? The latter, certainly, for when suffering is so real that personality cannot persist intact, even in the contemptibly reduced form of mere ego, and one's fixations upon one's own significance and upon the disappointments of one's private history are rendered obviously empty, then one knows that suffering is only suffering and nothing more: it is not creative, it does not inspire love but destroys it, it makes the soul into an abyss of anger, misery, and longing for release. Often, sinful creatures that we are, our pity is wakened by pain — ours or others' — but this is not because pain taught us pity (how could it?); rather the power of love was there already, dormant, but prior to every "negative" prompting, and were it not for sin the power of love would not have to cross the interval of suffering.

In any event, happily, the theologians of the ancient and medieval church had the wisdom and strength not to desire such a miserable, imperfect, shadowy god, but to long rather for a God of superabounding and eternal might, life, joy without any trace of pain, the inexhaustible fountainhead of life and light and beauty, a God of infinite ontological health. They were clearly capable, that is, of an ascetic passion that could cultivate real charity by making them seek a well-being and a truth outside their own affections and disaffections and vanities, and so they understood the gospel of divine *apatheia* as revealed in Christ; and they knew that pain — like resentment, ignorance, or cruelty — is essentially parasitic, a privation of being, capable of enriching or perfecting nothing; they thirsted for the wine of divinity, not the bitter lees of their own indignation. Then again, they did not arrive so late in the history of nihilism as we have, they were not as fragile and devoted to therapy, they were not so very near to the "last man." This, at least, is my darker, more sinister, uncomfortably Nietzschean take on tragic theology: it is, in part at least, a creature of our postromantic twilight, an opiate for our age of decline, a result of the triumph of the Narcissi (accomplished in all the arts of self-torture and self-pity). However, there is that other, more morally serious and selfless form of tragic theology, as I have hinted, which attempts to make its uncertain way in the darkness of history, through the ashes of the death camps and over the icy wastes of the gulags — to which I shall devote my attention now. Even so, I believe (and shall endeavor to show) that even this graver, less emotional, more theologically astringent species of tragic consciousness will fail finally to dislodge the self from its sovereignty, but will prove to be the totality's last seduction, the most narcotic metaphysical solace of all.

None of what I say, let me quickly stipulate, is intended as a rejection of tragedy as such (as a dramatic or narrative practice), but only as a critique, from a certain theological vantage, of the sacrificial logic from which Attic tragedy, in particular, sprang and according to which, as a rule, tragedy is still read. There is, of course, an obvious contrast to be drawn between tragedy and the Gospel narratives, with which I am not much concerned, as it is mostly false; George Steiner describes it well:

> Christianity is an anti-tragic vision of the world. . . . Christianity offers to man an assurance of final certitude and repose in God. He leads the soul toward justice and resurrection. The Passion of Christ is an event of unutterable grief, but it is also a cipher through which is revealed the love of God for man. In the dark light of Christ's suffering, original sin is shown to have been a joyous error *(felix culpa)*. Through it humanity shall be restored to a condition far more exalted than was Adam's innocence. . . . Being a threshold to the eternal, the death of a Christian hero can be an occasion for sorrow but not for tragedy. . . . Real tragedy can occur only where the tormented soul believes that there is no time left for God's forgiveness.[205]

The darkness of Good Friday is somewhat dispelled by the radiance of Easter, it cannot be denied; whether this fact should be taken as reducing the moral weight of the gospel to a kind of bland cosmic optimism, however, is a question of a different order. If this is indeed the opposition between tragedy and gospel, the onus clearly falls upon the latter to justify its claims in contrast to those of an art whose vision appears to penetrate more deeply than any other into the terror, suffering, and ignorance of the human condition. After all, tragedy does not encourage; it offers no promise and seems heroically devoid of mystification; it may endow its protagonist with a certain tragic grandeur, but only one that ends in the embral glow of his or her holocaust. Even when, as in *Hippolytus* or *The Eumenides*, the action does not end in utter despair, the import of tragedy remains the same: humanity cannot liberate itself from evil, the adversity of fate, human injustice, or divine malice, but can at best reach an accommodation with the forces that torment it.[206] Nor does tragedy pretend to penetrate the mystery of evil, moral or natural; there is an inscrutable inevitability in the malignity of things that human freedom, far from averting, can only serve. Nor does that evil prove at the last to serve the ends of justice; once loosed, it is majestically promiscuous in its destructiveness, indifferent to innocence, preserving no right proportion between cause and effect, between transgression and retribution.[207]

205. George Steiner, *The Death of Tragedy* (London: Faber and Faber, 1961), 331-32.
206. See Nathan Scott, *The Broken Center: Studies in the Theological Horizon of Modern Literature* (New Haven: Yale University Press, 1966), 133.
207. See Steiner, 9.

The real source of the tragic as such, and its animating rationale, is an unrelieved sense of the indeterminacy of moral meaning, or of moral responsibility; the logic of Attic tragedy consists largely in the constant deferral of moral intelligibility toward the sublimity of a purely cosmic horizon. No play serves as a better example of this than *Antigone,* in which the calamity that overtakes the heroine arises out of a welter of impossible moral resolutions, an insoluble conflict between the substantial goods of familial piety (a sacred obligation) and the civil duties of kingship (a holy office): Antigone, as a woman bound to the cult of the chthonian gods (gods of the dead, so of the family and household), and Creon, as a man and king bound to the law of Apollo (god of the city), may both make their appeals to Zeus, who holds the scales of fate and justice, because both are adhering to a path of holy obligation. The play's disturbing implication is that this conflict, far from being the result merely of profane impulses or moral ignorance (and thus susceptible of religious mediation), emerges in fact from the realm of the sacred. Attic tragedy often locates evil in no particular place, but in a tension between human culpability and divine malice: Oedipus, for instance, recognizes in his fate both the divine guile contributing to his unwitting criminality and the inevitability of the divine justice that overtakes him (in which, as king and interpreter of the city's curse, he is necessarily complicit); in *The Persians* the arrogance of Xerxes is no more or less to blame for his defeat than the divine deception that prompted his actions. This is a moral tension at least as old as the Homeric concept of ἄτη.

But the dialectic between personal culpability and divine malice scarcely exhausts the scope of Greek tragedy's moral ambiguity. In *The Bacchae* Dionysus is a force at once sacred and demonic (this is, in fact, a pointless distinction), the violation of whose mysteries or temenos is indeed a sin but is also practically a civic virtue; Pentheus is destroyed because he resists the orgiastic, chaotic powers of the natural order, but it is only insofar as the cruel, capricious, destructive energies of the Dionysian are resisted that the polis is preserved against the dark forces, however numinous, that lie outside the city walls. Dionysus represents not a random instance of divine malice, but a force residing in the divine that is intrinsically violent; the power of the sacred, from which the city draws its sustenance and to which it must make oblations, is that same power that threatens at every moment to engulf the city in chaos and violence. Indeed, when Dionysus is reproached for the excessive harshness of his judgment upon the polis, condemning it to destruction, the god merely replies that the city's end was decreed by fate, thus indicating that the gods themselves are bound by certain evil necessities, that in fact the tragic is older than the gods. This is why, within the terms of Attic tragedy, the nature of evil is somewhat easier to define than are its origins: it is a force innate to the cosmos itself, a natural energy, a concrete curse or pollution, transmissible, formidable, and morally indifferent; like every natural force, it is under the sway of fate, but is not as such a contradiction of divine order, inasmuch as the gods themselves are subject to the immutable verities of the αἰώνιος κόσμος. Thus one can conceive of evil as a kind of contamination or disease, which can be passed from one person to another, or from one generation to the next. One's understanding of the action of *The Oresteia*, for instance, is limited if one knows only of Clytemnestra's crimes and Agamemnon's noisome character; within these limits the drama looks like a tragedy only of personality (and so very modern); but an Athenian of the age of Aeschylus would have known also (as the play itself shows) of the curse brooding over the house of Atreus. It was Atreus, after all, who violated holy law and fed the children of his brother Thyestes to their father as a savage jest. But, then again, Atreus was the son of Pelops, who was himself served as food at a banquet by his father Tantalus (fortunately, however, to gods, capable of restoring Pelops to life); Atreus was perhaps doomed to recapitulate his house's ancestral crime. And to defer part of the blame onto Tantalus is one step from locating the provenance of sin *in illo tempore*. As a purely aetiological query, the question *unde hoc malum?* is as unanswerable as the question "whence this world?" because being is always already disruption, an eternal order of force. If evil's origin is never isolable within the fabric of being, however, its nature is rather more clear: in the case of the *Oresteia*, in particular, it is a specific kind of contagion pullulating through one house, compelling parents and children to spill one another's blood (Agamemnon consented to the sacrifice of Iphigenia, as well) and threatening to spill over into the community before it is "cured" in *The Eumenides*. Nor should the nature of divine intervention here be misunderstood; Francesca Murphy speaks of Athena as a "humanizing" figure at the end of the *Oresteia*;[208] but in truth, one might just as accurately say she merely represents the violence of "justice" made beautiful and engaging; she restrains and domesticates the furies, perhaps, but also retains their services for the purposes of civic stability. Whether evil and guilt are associated with the divine or demonic (which is not, again, a Greek distinction), individual sin or natural impulse, blood or the city, its reality is that of an objective aspect of the world, more ancient than the laws of gods or mortals, an energy that erupts into quotidian experience or abides for a time with a person, a family, a city, or a people, against which other powers can be marshaled but which nothing can deracinate from existence. One never really finds in Attic tragedy what Helen Gardner calls the *mysterium iniquitatis*,[209] the depthless malevolence that animates Iago or Goneril and Regan; this view of evil emerges in the drama of Christian culture. In Athenian tragedy

208. Murphy, 155.
209. Helen Gardner, *Religion and Literature* (London: Faber and Faber, 1971), 49.

evil is located never simply in a malign will, but always in objective *events:* violations (intentional or not) of sacred boundaries, actions resulting from moral blindness or divine guile, "chance" occurrences that reveal evil's transcendence of even divine law, and processes of nature or fate.

There really is no proper response on the part of the protagonist of Attic tragedy to his or her fate, his or her guilt (again, a rather too modern distinction). When Oedipus sees his error, the end is already clear; action or inaction may slightly mitigate the effects of the curse but cannot avert his destiny; either to acknowledge his guilt or to rail against the terrible immensity of evil would amount to much the same thing. Objective forces have been set in motion, have been in motion since well before his appearance within the story, and his guilt is just one aspect of a process that includes and exceeds his finite actions; his consciousness of his fault leads nowhere but to blindness. One must, then, proceed with extreme caution when speaking of "tragic wisdom" or the power of tragedy to illuminate the human condition. According to George Steiner, "Man is ennobled by the vengeful spite or injustice of the gods. It does not make him innocent, but it hallows him as if he had passed through flame. Hence there is in the final moments of great tragedy, whether Greek or Shakespearean or neo-classic, a fusion of grief and joy, of lament over the fall of man and rejoicing in the resurrection of the spirit."[210] This may indeed be the attractive force of the tragic (though, if so, it is curious that it can be expressed only in Christian terms). There is undoubted appeal in Paul Ricoeur's discussion of a wisdom available to the spectator of tragedy, who is invited to stand in the place of the chorus, engaged in but at a contemplative distance from the spectacle's terror.[211] But even here one wonders what the yield of such wisdom really is: what the chorus always ultimately achieves is, in truth, emotional exhaustion; it foresees or fails to, it warns, it dreads, it ululates, but the only "wisdom" arrived at from the choral vantage is a state of resignation before the invincible violence of being. Of course, one may see this emotional depletion as a serene despair from which a chastened, demystified hope might later arise; and here the question of the particular poetic and ritual form of tragedy may legitimately be raised. Much might be made of the structure and context of Attic tragedy, its central place in the Dionysian festival, with its celebrations of fertility and satyriasis. Certainly Nietzsche, in *The Birth of Tragedy*, took tragedy's Bacchanalian occasion as justification for claiming that tragedy's inmost meaning is the eternal joyousness of life. A theologian might even be tempted to think of the sacred festivities surrounding tragedy as a sort of "paschal" mediation between despair and hope, turning

---

210. Steiner, 10.

211. Paul Ricoeur, *The Symbolism of Evil*, trans. Emerson Buchanan (Boston: Beacon Press, 1967), 231.

the terror of life's dark passages into a source of renewed communal and cultic life. But, then again, whereas the resurrection of Christ in a sense breaks the bonds of the social order that crucifies, so as to inaugurate a new history, a new city, whose story is told along the infinite axis of divine peace, the religious dynamism of Attic tragedy has the form of a closed circle; it reinforces the civic order it puts into question, by placing that order within a context of cosmic violence that demonstrates not only the limits but the necessity of the city's regime. If one too quickly embraces the idea of tragedy as a chastening and refining passage from despair to hope, on account of the Dionysian celebrations that occasioned it, one misses altogether the apotropaic nature of these celebrations: behind Athenian dramaturgy lay memories of the promiscuous cruelty and antinomianism of the god who came out of the Libyan wastes to shake the pillars of the city, and the hope that, if this devastating force could be contained within Apollonian forms and propitiated through a ritual carnival mimicking its disorder, perhaps the polis could for another year maintain its precarious peace against a world that is essentially a realm of countervailing violences. This is far more basic to tragedy than Aristotle's civilized appropriation of tragedy for the civic virtues of mercy and reverence (ἔλεος and φόβος). The form, context, and substance of Attic tragedy underwrite a particular narrative mythos, which depicts violence as the aboriginal continuity between the natural and moral worlds, and the human community as a besieged citadel preserving itself in part through the tribute it pays to the powers that threaten it.

Can there be, then, such a thing as a "tragic theology"? Perhaps no theologian of the twentieth century was more insistent than D. M. MacKinnon that Christian theology heed the testimony of great tragedy, if for no other reason than that the narrative particularities of tragedy might help protect Christian language from the inveiglements of too comprehensive a metaphysical optimism regarding the mystery of evil. "Revelation is not in a charade," he trenchantly observes at one point, "but in an agony, with flesh racked with pain, and human consciousness lost in a sense of the meaninglessness of the world."[212] Christian theology must remain implacably opposed to any species of superficial cosmic optimism, and dare not presume to know any universal significance in its evangel that does not start from the sheer waste of Christ's failure.[213] A theology chastened by tragedy would not blithely separate the language of Christ as Logos from a genuine *theologia crucis*, MacKinnon believes,

212. D. M. MacKinnon, *The Resurrection: A Dialogue Arising from Broadcasts by G. W. H. Lampe and D. M. MacKinnon*, ed. William Purcell (London: A. R. Mowbray, 1966), 67; see also 109-10.

213. Donald M. MacKinnon, *Borderlands of Theology and Other Essays*, ed. George W. Roberts and Donovan E. Smucker (Philadelphia and New York: Lippincott, 1968), 92-93, 102-3.

would not forget that whatever is meant by the assertion that "God is revealed in Christ" can be grasped only in the darkness of Gethsemane, only in the godforsakenness of the cross. Moreover, a "tragic theology" might see with some real clarity the moral ambiguity inherent in all finitude and contingency, even within salvation history; MacKinnon goes so far as to argue that even Christ's decision to follow his Father's will all the way to the cross may in historical terms have entailed consequences of incalculable horror, ranging from the suicide of Judas to the Holocaust.[214] And so he suggests that the story of the crucifixion be read as in some sense a tragic drama.[215] The recognition that God revealed himself most truly in Christ's frailty, dereliction, and death, that his majesty is seen where Jesus is rejected and condemned, may then prevent Christians from averting their eyes from the sufferings of the godforsaken, the oppressed, the accursed. Most crucially, reading the Gospels as in some sense tragic forbids Christians the comfort of any facile diminution of the gravity of Christ's suffering, as if the resurrection constituted some kind of dramatic peripety, a delayed descent from the cross, rather than the raising up of Christ's entire life — including his way to the cross — on the far side of death, and an affirmation of his endurance to the end in loving obedience to the Father.[216] "'Come down from the cross and we will believe.' Many Christians have joined in this cry; many continue indeed to make it their own, even when they pay lip service to the gospel of the Resurrection. But it is only in the light of the Resurrection that those Christians can learn rather to say with understanding the profound words of Pascal, that Christ will indeed be in agony unto the end of the world."[217] All Christian hope depends upon the understanding that the events of Easter do not negate — but vindicate — the events of Good Friday;[218] because it is this understanding alone that allows Christians to find the Word of God present always with them even in Gethsemane, where they lie broken, in exile, impotent to effect their own rescue from the dark forces that pour in upon them. Any species of Easter faith that cannot speak of God in the darkness of the garden must ultimately be eclipsed by that darkness; Christian hope is possible only insofar as Christians do not imagine they possess a perspective from which the terror of the agony of Gethsemane can be explained away. One cannot deny the power of MacKinnon's argument. After all, the gallows of Judas and the gallows of Jesus differ chiefly in that the former is morally intelligible; but it is the latter that is the place of Christian faith and hope.

214. MacKinnon, *Borderlands of Theology,* 103.
215. MacKinnon, *Borderlands of Theology,* 100.
216. MacKinnon, *The Resurrection,* 64-65.
217. MacKinnon, *Borderlands of Theology,* 96.
218. MacKinnon, *Borderlands of Theology,* 96.

Nicholas Lash follows after MacKinnon in his concern that theology subject itself to the refining fire of tragic consciousness. For him, one might say, tragedy serves to forestall deontology or moral certitude, to prohibit any glib assurances or any inclinations toward an unreflective triumphalism, to force Christians always to turn their attention to the moral ambiguity of the particular. Most importantly of all, the tragic contour of the Gospel narrative roots hope in the concrete contingencies of finite existence: "To understand Calvary as the place where *God* died is to understand all other places of death as Calvary."[219] Though, even here Lash allows a defiant, even revolutionary intonation to invade his language, however chastened it may be by its exposure to the tragic:

> The focal point of both memory and hope is Gethsemane and Calvary. It was *there* that God died, and resurrection began. To understand all places of darkness and death to be that garden and that hilltop is, therefore, to refuse to give the last word to all that entombs the body and the mind of man. Jesus taught us to address the darkness as "Father." But we only learn appropriately to do so at the place where he did it. It is only there, at the heart of darkness, that we are enabled and entitled to pray: "All shall be well and all shall be well and all manner of thing shall be well."[220]

For Lash, indeed, the lessons of the tragic must enter more deeply into theological reflection than even MacKinnon contemplates; rather than merely insisting that the resurrection be seen as vindicating the event of the crucifixion, he more or less collapses Easter into Good Friday in such a way that the former takes on the character of simply a second perspective upon the latter, a speculative return to the cross, its most inward meaning. At a rather extraordinary juncture in one essay, in the course of arguing (very poorly) that "belief in resurrection is compatible with disbelief in life 'after' death,"[221] Lash suggests the following interpretation of the story of Christ's resurrection:

> Supposing that, in death, in dying, Jesus discovers that his whole history, and every moment in that history, far from slipping away, ephemeral, into nonexistence, *stands,* eternally — and stands by the transfigured reality and significance which belongs to it from the standpoint of God's eternal light? And supposing that, having gone to the furthest limits of the far country and discovered himself *there* (and not somewhere else) to be at home with

219. Nicholas Lash, *Theology on Dover Beach* (London: Darton, Longman and Todd, 1979), 214.

220. Lash, *Theology on Dover Beach*, 215.

221. Nicholas Lash, *Theology on the Way to Emmaus* (London: SCM Press, 1986), 165.

his Father, he is able, in the gift of his Spirit, to share that discovery with us?[222]

This, it must be conceded, seems indeed to be a *theologia crucis* that has subjected itself to the scrutiny of tragic consciousness; it has, apparently, disabused itself of the universalizing pretensions of metaphysics, the temptation to submerge the particular in the universal or to turn from the demands of the present;[223] it has assumed tragedy's character as spectacle rather than speculation.[224]

One is moved to wonder, though, whether these attempts at a tragic theology accomplish what they mean to. One might ask whether MacKinnon in particular has not so much read the story of the crucifixion in the light of Attic tragedy as read tragedy in Christian terms. And while Lash might be said to have taken the lessons of tragedy to heart, one wonders if he has not somewhat misconstrued the true import of those lessons. And one should perhaps ask of both whether they have properly considered the cultic origins of Attic tragedy, or the ontological and metaphysical premises that make the tragic anything but a remedy to "universalizing" pretensions. It is one thing to be impressed, as MacKinnon is, by Attic tragedy's depictions of the moral ambiguities that ring the protagonist about, but this should be qualified by the recognition that these are ambiguities often caused by the cultic structures of the polis (though this fact may be mythically dissembled), whose resolution, consequently, is sacrificial. These irresoluble contradictions within moral order belong often to a civic order of injustice, which tragedy dissimulates by displacing the responsibility for civic violence to a metaphysical horizon of cosmic violence; the sacrificial structure of the polis is presented as the sacrificial order of the world. Perhaps, however, it is just this mythos — this pagan metanarrative of ontological violence — that the Christian narrative has from its beginning rejected, and against which it must pose itself as an alternative wisdom. Greek tragedy, as a gnosis, a vision of truth, is a particularly alluring feature of a particular linguistic economy, a narrative of being according to which the cosmos is primordially a conflict of irreconcilable forces, embraced within the overarching violence of fate; and the wisdom it imparts is one of accommodation, resignation before the unsynthesizable abyss of being, a willingness on the part of the spectator to turn back toward the polis as a refuge from the turmoils of a hostile universe, reconciled to its regime and its prudential violences, its martial logic. This is the opiate of tragic consciousness, its place in a sacrificial econ-

222. Lash, *Theology on the Way,* 178.
223. Lash, *Theology on the Way,* 180.
224. See Ricoeur, *The Symbolism of Evil,* 212.

omy, its power to stabilize civic order through a brief but enchanting dalliance with the powers that both sustain and threaten that order. Tragedy is never a revolutionary art form: its peculiar artistry lies in making it appear as if the polis has been momentarily invaded by the world's circumambient chaos (which it has repelled), even though everything that occurs in the course of the drama is contained within the rigid lineaments of Apollonian order. Its dramatic effect, that is, arises from the cataclysm it seems to portend; and its special enchantment lies in making its very orderly metaphysics of violence seem disordered and mysterious; but it is purest speculative stability. All is Apollo, to invert Schelling's and Nietzsche's formula; Dionysus is the bright and pitiless glare of reason and prudence.

Tragedy might well represent the most pronounced instance in Greek religion of that mystification of violence that sustains the sacred order of pagan society,[225] the consecration of social violence as a restraint of cosmic violence, natural and divine. This is why it cannot preserve moral thought against the lure of ideology, but can only preserve a particular ideology against critique: its salubrious disenchantment is meant to mesmerize us with necessity's dark majesty. It is here, first and foremost, that the Christian narrative proves resistant to a tragic reading: theology must insist upon "historicizing" evil, treating it as the superscribed text of a palimpsest, obscuring the aboriginal goodness of creation; Christian thought, which conceives of difference within being as primordially an ordination of peace, capable of being sustained within unforeclosable complications of harmony, radically resituates all things (even, ultimately, pain, alienation, and death) within its greater story of creation and redemption, and so can never reconcile itself to any wisdom whose premise is the ontological necessity of violence. The Christian story always begins beyond the city walls, in the place of the negated exterior, but finds that place to be not simply a region of indomitable strife but a realm of beauty, even of peace. This is not the logic of the tragic. In the plays of Euripides someone often dies on behalf of the polis, heroically (which is also to say sacrificially); and it is just this gesture of exclusion, reappropriated by the polis under the form of a heroic *decision* that affirms the order of society, that is the very core of the tragic. But from the vantage of Christian thought, the motion of exclusion, when demystified, is shown to subserve a sacrificial regime whose mechanisms are justified only by way of just this heroic mythology: in the light of Easter, which is the Father's verdict in favor of the crucified and his condemnation of the powers that crucify, Christ can finally be seen only as dying against the pagan polis, as the one the city kills and the Father raises up in defiance of civilization's most essential economic

225. See René Girard, *Violence and the Sacred*, trans. Patrick Gregory (Baltimore: Johns Hopkins University Press, 1977), esp. 68-168.

gesture. Nor is Christ excluded like Oedipus, as the one who purifies society by venturing forth into the abyss, in the interests of society; he dies as a criminal, forcibly excluded, and his resurrection forever associates the divine with the realm of the excluded, the "impure," the waste. Christ suffered without the gate. The resurrection unsettles (indeed, irreparably disrupts) the analogy between cosmic and civic violence; it shows Christ's self-donation to be an infinite motion, indifferent to the boundary between polis and chaos; it "untells" the tale by which power sustains and justifies itself, breaks open the closed circle of exchange and sublation, overcomes totality through the sheer exceedingness of an infinite that is beauty.

Nothing quite so idealizes (and so misrepresents) the nature of Attic tragedy as the claim that it puts thought on guard against the allure of the universal, that it recalls attention from the horizon of absolute meaning to the demands of the particular. The more closely one considers its occasion, the more difficult it becomes to accept the notion that Attic tragedy subordinates speculation to spectacle, or that spectacle can be so easily distinguished from speculation. There is a dangerous imprecision, for instance, in George Steiner's assertion that tragedy ennobles its protagonist; tragedy, in the classical tradition, was possible only for those who were already noble (one would never encounter in Attic tragedy the suffering children who evoked such terror and despair from Dostoyevsky). Only persons already possessed of a special splendor, a glory that shines most brightly in the flames of its own destruction, can make the violence of "fate" seem beautiful; it is the particular protagonist who ennobles the tragic, ennobles violence. Tragedy universalizes the form of the splendid hero: and even so, he is excluded, pushed to the margins; his suffering cannot inaugurate a new *civitas,* but only restores the balance of the old order; he ventures into the void, and so affirms once again that beyond the city walls there is only void. But Christ, who suffers outside the gate, makes of his death an act of inclusion that begins the world anew; his resurrection erases the boundary between city and waste, life and death, pure and impure, exclusion and inclusion, by simply passing these distinctions by in his infinite motion toward the Father. Nowhere now is exile, nor any place a sublimity beyond all beauty. The tragic hero, however, dwells always in that penumbral region between the beautiful and the sublime, guarding the boundaries of both: he preserves the order of beauty (the order of nobility) of the antique world and serves as well to intensify the numinous glamor — the mystery and terror — of the sublime, of fate, death, chaos, and cosmic or divine malice. But, as has been said, the Gospels prove at the last irreconcilably subversive of this aesthetic; Peter's grief over his denial of Christ marks an irrevocable departure from the staid representations of antique order, and announces from the beginning Christianity's tendency to "spill" the tragic out, to overturn the lovely vessel that appeared so splendid standing upright on the dionysia, at the unmoving center of the polis. If *any* suffering is worthy of attention, if divine solace is intended for such as *these* (to recall Nietzsche's declarations of repugnance), then tragedy as such is evacuated of its sacred function: it is no longer a ritual mediation between city and cosmos, nor can it be taken uncritically in its depictions of a special greatness enmeshed in the toils of "fate," its tales of a unique δόξα that makes glamorous the violences that afflict it. Tragedy is not, in its origins, an art of disenchantment; it does not disabuse the spectators of their mythic expectations or universalizing inclinations by bringing vision back from the horizon of the absolute to the particularity of suffering; as Nietzsche understood, only the god suffers.

This is why theologians must not embrace MacKinnon's suggestion that the crucifixion be read as a kind of tragic drama, in the hope that tragedy's concern for the irresoluble contradictions of the particular might put theology on guard against any metaphysical solace that would ease Christian discomfort before the terror and desolation of the cross: metaphysical solace is precisely what the tragic is. It turns attention not toward the one who suffers, but to the sublime backdrop against which the drama is played out; it assures the spectator that this is how things are, this is the constitution of the universe, and that justice is strife; tragic wisdom is the wisdom of resignation and consent, a wisdom that is too prudent to rebel against what is fixed in the very fabric of being, and that refuses to suffer inordinately, enraged by death or resentful of civic order. Tragedy legitimates a particular regime of law, violence, and war: it teaches that μοῖρα places and displaces us, and so leads us to a serene and chastened acceptance of where we are placed and how we are displaced; tragedy resists every motion outward, beyond the sentineled frontier, and reinforces the stable foundation of the totality. Christianity, however, feeds upon a different wisdom, a defiant, Jewish wisdom that insists upon an act of affirmation far removed from the resigned serenity of tragic consciousness: insanely, perhaps, it enjoins a love of creation that will not be reconciled to the loss of what is created but enacts a double motion, an affirmation of the goodness of what is and an expectation of action by God to rescue this wholly good creation from the violences that enslave it. A recognition of the true universality of suffering, of its endless particularity and the infinite gravity of its every instance (no matter how base the sufferer), is a Jewish, not an Attic, accomplishment, and it leads inevitably to a prophetic outcry, a call for a reconciliation that is also redemption, a demand for divine justice; Israel is always — and always ever more — in rebellion against the wisdom of totality. The wisdom of Israel — expressed in the added ending to the book of Job, or in Ezekiel's vision of the valley of dry bones — lies in its growing awareness that God is the God of justice and election, and that his goodness and the goodness of creation can be affirmed only through faith in a future that overcomes all endings; this is the wisdom of an outcry, which begins as a low and plaintive threnody, arrives at its first astonished dramatic peak in the *aqedah,* and then acquires confidence, even audacity, until it can say that God is God only if he confirms his glory in resurrection. And for Christian faith the only true tragic wisdom is that there is no final wisdom in the tragic; Christianity was set against tragic wisdom from the first; far from failing to glimpse behind evil a transcendent horizon, a chthonian depth, Christian thought has simply always denied that such a horizon or such a depth belongs to being in any but a contingent fashion. The cross dispelled the seductions of the tragic by revealing an infinite gulf between the God of creation and the power of death (a gulf, that is, that is not spanned by sacrifice), by emptying the tragic of its heroic pathos and false beauty, and — most importantly — by opening out into a resurrection that reveals love as the source and end of creation. It is from Israel that Christianity learns the grammar of charity, its passionate commitment to creation and its revulsion before injustice, rather than resignation before the magnitude of evil. Christian love erupts from the empty tomb, and so must always be in rebellion against all tragic "profundities."

Such considerations call even more severely into question Lash's reading of the story of Easter as the communication, by the power of the Spirit, of Christ's experience of transcendent "meaningfulness" in the midst of his sacrifice, his sense of the significance of his whole life as standing eternally in God's light. There is, before all else, a moral danger in Lash making of Easter a secondary, speculative vantage upon what happened at Golgotha: it comes perilously close to placing his reading on the side of the pagan order of sacrifice and of its wisdom regarding the crucifixion (regarding every crucifixion). One should, first and foremost, be troubled by the way this reading makes knowledge and spiritual comfort the fruit of an annihilation of finite form; every theoretical recasting of violence is a mactation, a sacrifice in the most elementary propitiatory sense. It requires a certain very refined, altogether exquisite sensibility to grasp the crucifixion in just this fashion: one must step back from the act of murder itself, enacting the partial withdrawal of *theoria,* to that place where truth never simply happens (as difference, as irreducible historical particularity), but where "Truth" is intuited as a total light, something recollected. Such a reading invites not only Kierkegaard's critique of contemplation's aristocratic indolence,[226] but the still more solvent critiques of both Nietzsche and Marx. On Lash's reading the crucifixion becomes a spectacle in the Hegelian sense — with its convertibility between death and life, negation and spirit, death and wisdom — which means it is "true" only insofar as it has a speculative inner fold: the spectacle is always a speculum, the mirror whose specular reflex allows

---

226. Søren Kierkegaard, *Repetition,* in vol. 6 of *Kierkegaard's Writings,* ed. and trans. Howard Hong and Edna Hong (Princeton: Princeton University Press, 1983), 315.

the self a contemplation of itself, a return to the self; and thus the crucifixion constitutes an act of speculation in the economic sense as well, which secures a return of the investment made in the surrender of the particular.[227] Lash's is a reading that follows the contour of sacrifice, that in fact completes and becomes "theoretically" complicit in the violence of the crucifixion — the suppression of the difference (the particular gift) that Christ is — by its theoretical return to "the Same." It obeys the logic of every cross, every judicious and prudent deployment of violence: from the holocaust of the particular, one can always pluck an ember of meaningfulness, a stabilizing "message" that makes of the sacrifice itself a good (or necessary) thing; an interior and golden light can always be rescued from the ashes of the other in the interests of *my* hope. The moment of *theoria,* after all, is always the consummation of sacrifice: that which is negated (Jesus of Nazareth, in this case) is purely negated; but Christ's *death* becomes exemplarily human, and makes death itself meaningful. This story of Christ's inner illumination at the heart of darkness, imparted to the church as a saving truth according to the metaphor of resurrection, somehow legitimates that darkness, its permanence; salvation does not so much take shape in history as in a kind of speculative heroism, which reconciles itself to the finality of loss (but only the loss of the particular). Again, how very Hegelian: at the apex of wisdom sacrifice is made absolute; consciousness devours the flesh of the finite and spews out the bones. What Lash calls resurrection, really, is what it would be comforting to believe is the end of every well-lived — every heroic — life; it is the consolation that is won whenever thought is willing to make this simple sacrificial gesture. In order, however, that the self (or *Geist*) should continue to glimpse itself in a glass darkly, the adiaphoral must be allowed to evaporate, those evanescent things at the margin — flesh, blood, and breath — must vanish in the shadows; but a metaphysical consolation — one may choose to call it "hope" — has been recovered. This brings Christian reflection on the crucifixion only as far as Attic tragedy ever reached. According to Lash, Christ has taught us to call the darkness "Father"; but if it is the *darkness* that is so addressed (the same darkness into which the tragic hero always disappears), it remains uncertain that anyone but Apollo has been served. Far from preventing theology from taking Easter as a peripety of Good Friday (which is Lash's avowed intention), he has made the resurrection into an all the more irreversible speculative peripety; the crucifixion becomes a Hegelian mai-

227. On Hegel's treatment of sacrificial spectacle as a speculative contemplation of death (and as an "economic" recuperation of the waste of negativity and death), see Georges Bataille, "Hegel, la mort et le sacrifice," *Deucalion* 5 (1955): 38: in English, "Hegel, Death, and Sacrifice," in *The Bataille Reader,* ed. Fred Botting and Scott Wilson (Oxford: Blackwell, 1997); and see Derrida's treatment of Bataille's "antieconomic" reading of Hegel in "From Restricted to General Economy: A Hegelianism without Reserve," in *Writing and Difference,* 251-77.

eutic, a necessary moment in the awakening of a more universal gnosis. But by what warrant can theology make the injustice of a legal murder a source of interior solace?

If this seems an excessively harsh reading of Lash's argument, it should be stressed that the question of violence is raised in regard to Christian rhetoric nowhere more crucially than here: if the resurrection in any way is seen to confirm, complete, or eternalize the crucifixion (rather than vindicate the crucified over against a world order that crucifies and mystifies its violences by way of a myth of chaos), then indeed Christianity offers only the same old tragic wisdom, allies itself with the sacrificial economy of totality, and dissembles beneath the beauty of its evangel the sublimity of cosmic violence. A tragic reading of the resurrection makes it repeat the crucifixion, in order to repeat the self, to afford the self a mirror in which to glimpse the shape of its own meaning. Paradoxically, it is that Stoic interiority that Lash ascribes to Christ on the cross that transforms the crucifixion into an extrinsic spectacle, surcharged with meaning, a tableau whose significance resides in itself, a vision that evokes contemplation. But theology is not permitted to make the cross a place of enlightenment, or to allow it its "spectacular" singularity, because the resurrection occurs as yet another event, in excess of the totality death bounds, and so upsets the tragic balance of the scene and leaves it in a state of dramatic undecidability: Is it a kind of ending or beginning? Does Christ on the cross affect history or succumb to history's violences? Where can the cross be aesthetically placed, how can it be seen, when the blinding radiance of the next historical event (where Christ's history would seem to have been exhausted) has so radically altered its deployment of shadows and light? Easter forces Christian reflection out of the depths of speculative solace and back to the surface of history. Christ's resurrection transgresses the orderly metaphysics that makes negation a tragic or dialectical moment; for theology, then, the θέαμα of the crucifixion is never translated into contemplative repose (self, "meaningfulness," *eleos* and *phobos, Geist*), because the serenity of every tragic representation has been disrupted by a sudden, unanticipated, inassimilable declaration of divine glory. Any attempt to reinterpret the resurrection as the speculative inner fold of the crucifixion is also an attempt to moderate the aesthetic affront of Easter, so that the crucifixion may still subserve a return to the self and the Same; but within the Gospel narratives themselves Christ's resurrection is seen as calling us not to ourselves but beyond; the beauty that Christian thought proclaims exceeds both Apollonian harmony and Dionysian affirmation: it is more than classical, Jewish rather than pagan, an unmasterable affirmation. Tragedy demands that the hero venture into an indeterminate infinite, disappear into the sublime absolute, in order to preserve the determinate but fragile arrangements of the polis; Jesus passes beyond the boundaries of the totality but then returns, still as form and radiance and beauty, by an infinite motion, revealing the infinite already to be form and radiance and beauty. The resurrection is uncontainable; it happens outside of all prudent expectations, all rational desires and limited loves, all metaphysical, aesthetic, or religious schemes. If this is not an essential affirmation of theology, it simply recapitulates the totality's idea of beauty and remains complicit in the violence it pretends to transcend: its gospel of peace in fact can give shape to neither peace nor justice.

The God of Israel is not a tragic God, but a God of love and election, a God who loves the beauty of the particular and who therefore does not allow the life of Christ — insofar as it is a life that ends in murder and the silence of death — to stand in his eternal light; even if from his eternal vantage the entire shape of Christ's life is supremely beautiful and worthy of lifting up into himself, he is not a speculative God, not a God who speculates, whose eternal light abstracts from the worldly horror of Christ's murder the transcendent beauty of Christ's life considered as a finished totality — a well-wrought urn. God's gift in Christ is put to death, and must be given again — called back to the surface of things — if it is truly any gift at all. To phrase the matter differently, it is possible to approach the crucifixion as Lash does only if one would dare to make the same move in regard to those who died in the Holocaust, only if one is willing to identify the death camps also as places where, far out in the far country, the Father was found, and leave it at that: only if one can reconcile oneself in this way to the finality of every death accomplished there. If one cannot make this move, however, then Lash's reading must be rejected: rather than a Christian optics, it is an optical trick, a trick with mirrors. Christian thought is obliged to remain bound to Israel's cry for eschatological justice; the Jewish "unhappy consciousness," knowing the contingency of finite existence but refusing to submerge the beauty of the beloved in the indeterminate flux of "nature's" chaos, continues to have the mad audacity to desire back what is lost, not as inward consolation, but in the concrete exteriority of the gift. After the violence of crucifixion (which is the last drama totality can enact, its final word, its boundary), the resurrection is aesthetically (which is to say, historically) another thing; he who was dead is — literally — not dead now; this is an act of rebellion. It is not the beauty of the cross, but of the one crucified, that is rescued at Easter; God's judgment vindicates Christ, his obedience unto death, but not the crucifixion.

If tragedy seeks to recuperate what is lost in death by making the particular instance of death an occasion for the disclosure of the god, then the Christian story stands starkly opposed to tragedy precisely because it views the death of the beloved with far greater gravity and cannot rest content with tragedy's economic optimism, its certainty regarding the credit stored up in the absolute. Christ is God as a particular man, who only in returning exceeds the limit set by death; he exceeds also the *economy* of death, though, by failing to become an abstract security reserved within an abstract infinite, and reveals the infinite to be instead endlessly determinate, boundlessly beautiful, serving no economy at all, but embracing all things. Dionysus may reassemble his torn limbs, but only because he is one in being divided, he is violence, he lives in the death of the particular; Christ, however, is a rabbi, is indeed God as a rabbi, and so is obliterated — becomes no one — unless the Father who speaks him speaks him anew as the illimitable rhetoric and form and appeal of the gift. The resurrection, then, shows the way to no truth within us (existential, tragic, Dionysian, or what have you), but declares anew, with the newest inflection, the glory of God in the beauty of his creatures, and in such a way as to leave us no self-knowledge at all; our story has been interrupted, our tragic narrative of self-recovery overturned. Christ was raised, and so the cross (every cross) is shown to be meaningless in itself; God is not there, and goes there only as the one who violates its boundaries, who disrupts the "hypotaxis" of the totality with the aneconomic "parataxis" of the beautiful, the anarchy (but not chaos) of the infinite. Theology is forbidden to extract any metaphysical comfort from the cross because the violence of crucifixion has been demystified; the crucifixion must not be subjected to the sacrificial logic of speculation, as it is, say, in any "death of God" theology (which recuperates the meaning of this death as the abolition of divine transcendence), or in any theology that makes of the cross a necessary moment for God, a taking into himself of suffering and death (which attributes to suffering and death a primordial autonomy, with which God is obliged to come to terms),[228] because Easter unsettles every hermeneutics of death, every attempt to make death a place of meaning. Rather than seeing the resurrection as a speculative (that is, dialectical) tension that eternalizes the cross, theology must recognize it as a reversal of the narrative of violence that makes crucifixion seem meaningful. In the self-oblation of Christ (which is the entire motion of his life) God indeed comprehends suffering and death, but only as a finite darkness exceeded — and conquered — by an infinite light; God's infinity embraces death by passing it by as though it is nothing at all and by making it henceforth a place of broken limits.

Again, to insist upon a nontragic reading of the cross and of resurrection is to remain faithful to Israel's cry for justice. The only way to avoid the violence of making Christ the object of a speculative sacrifice, in the interest of metaphysical solace, is by affirming that the resurrection occurs apart from the crucifixion, after the crucifixion, in time, and that it therefore vindicates not the cross but the Jew who died there. Only thus is thought prevented from com-

---

228. See Eberhard Jüngel, "Das Sein Jesus Christi als Ereignis der Versöhnung Gottes mit einer gottlosen Welt: Die Hingabe des Gekreuzigten," *Evangelische Theologie* 38 (1978): 517.

pleting the violence of Good Friday by converting it into a speculative Good Friday. Easter unveils the violence of history, its absolute ungodliness, its want of any transcendent meaning; the meaninglessness and tyranny of death is made absolutely clear in the Father *having* to raise the Son for the sake of his love. It is just here that the Christian narrative is seen to depart from the tragic narrative not on account of the latter's "nihilism," but on account of its comforting "optimism." The solemnity and self-importance of Attic tragedy — its magnificent bathos, the protagonist's striving after the sublime — touches upon a very real kind of pain, a suffering that comes in the wake of shattered expectations or hopes, a sense of rage before the indifference of fate or the inexorability of divine "justice" or malice, and a final resignation before the unalterable structures of the universe. But the doctrine of the resurrection opens up another, still deeper kind of pain: it requires of faith something even more terrible than submission before the violence of being and acceptance of fate, and forbids faith the consolations of tragic wisdom; it places all hope and all consolation upon the insane expectation that what is lost will be given back, not as a heroic wisdom (death has been robbed of its tragic beauty) but as the gift it always was. The finality of Christ's death on the cross — which, left to itself, could be so soothing to us, in the somber glow of our wisdom and tragedy's pathos — has been unceremoniously undone, and we are suddenly denied the consolations of pity and reverence, resignation and recognition, and are thrown out upon the turbid seas of boundless hope and boundless hunger. Now that tragedy's hypnotic illusions have been pierced, and we can no longer imagine that there is an order of necessity and a corresponding order of wisdom that make evil explicable and so tolerable, the satiety of tragic knowledge has been stolen from us; for God has shockingly overturned and inverted all the sober verities by which we measure the nature of the world, our common lot, and our place in the order of things. Whether God is then to be rebuked for a certain dramatic vulgarity each of us may judge; but there is henceforth no turning back from this reversal, this peripety, the undoing of which is, precisely, tergiversation — apostasy. We are thus, by the very hope we are given, conducted into the deepest imaginable range of pain, for we may cling now only to an "impossible" hope rather than to some dark but clarifying vision of necessity. In this condition we cannot profit from the tutelage of Attic tragedy, as it is a condition that comprises at once a torment more hellish and abyssal than the suffering of even the most glorious protagonist and a joy far vaster than any evoked by the drama of nature's indestructibility and exuberance and of the city's awesome stability. The dramatic dimensions of the trinitarian drama of the cross and empty tomb are too immense to be played out upon the dionysia. One must now confront loss without the comfort of a speculative return to the self; the tragic speculum is shattered by resurrection, and faith is made to see in every death only the meaningless and hopeless destruction of the beloved, the injustice that consumes the other, and hope henceforth must consist in a rebellion against tragic wisdom, against the logic of totality, and in a desire for the other in the other's beauty once again. Between life and death there is no longer any reconciling gesture, any profitable commerce; the death of the other affords one no illuminating spectacle, but cries out instead for redemption — offers no glimpse into the mystery of fate that would allow one to arrive at serenity or the peace of a wise pathos, but constitutes a permanent derangement of the surface, something rent in the fabric of being. In the light of Easter, the singularity of suffering is no longer tragic (which is to say, ennobling), but merely horrible, mad, everlastingly unjust; it is the irruption of *thanatos* into God's good creation. We are bereft of the ability to see in death the wanton play of Dionysus, the suffering and joy of sempiternal nature, and can see now only the face of the one who is lost.[229] This is a failure of judicious order, to be sure, an impossible longing that will not submit to the exchange values of economy; but once this longing has been evoked, Attic tragedy can never seem quite so profound again: it can say only that *this* is how things are, fate consumes its children, but some die majestically, numinously, and in the light of their immolation we find ourselves able to bear the unbearable. The truly unbearable, though, has been hidden from view: the sheer contingency of evil, the injustice that destroys what is beautiful, the absolute, irrecuperable loss of the beloved. And this, at the last, is why theology must take leave of the tragic: the Jews who died in the Holocaust, to return to that, did not die like the protagonists of Attic tragedy, but as Christ did; they were not splendid figures undone by fate, destroyed (though with a sullen magnificence) by the way things are — the mythical — but were the anonymous victims of political violence. None of the mystifications of tragic consciousness should be allowed to intrude here, no talk of a conflict of divine necessities or natural forces should divert attention from the truth that these

---

229. If one wanted to consider the difference that is wrought on tragedy by Christian culture, one might reflect upon the case of *King Lear*. Were *Lear* an Attic tragedy, it might well end upon the heath, at the height of the protagonist's madness and at the point of his greatest and most demonic (that is, ennobling) despair, where he arrives at a final exhaustion of passion. Certainly there would not be the strange and beautiful reunion with Cordelia, overbrimming with imagery of resurrection and talk of forgiveness, because this scene of reconciliation (which strains after an eschatological hope) makes the subsequent death of Cordelia more terrible than anything in Attic tragedy: precisely because the spectator has been granted a glimpse of the joy that tragic wisdom is impotent to adumbrate — the restoration of the beloved — the death that follows is seen to be absolutely without meaning, without beauty, imparting no wisdom, resistant to all assimilation into any metaphysical scheme of intelligibility or solace. It is noteworthy, as well, that Shakespeare returned again and again to this motif of the daughter lost and restored again, in the "problem plays" or "romances" — in *Pericles*, *Cymbeline*, and (most movingly) *The Winter's Tale* — but always now with the "resurrection" placed at the end.

lives were unmade by the quite contingent political arrangements of an unjust order, and by the demonic cruelty of human sin. Their deaths were without meaning, beauty, or grandeur.

In the light of Easter, all the sacrifices totality makes are seen to be meaningless, an offense before God, disclosing no deeper truths about being; the system of sacrifice is a tautology, a practice that justifies itself through further practice; but what the totality is willing to sacrifice on behalf of metaphysical solace is what God raises up. Because of the resurrection, it is impossible to be reconciled to coercive or natural violence, to ascribe its origins to fate or cosmic order, to employ it prudentially; as difficult as it may be to accept, all violence, all death, stands under judgment as that which God has and will overcome. The resurrection defies all human expectations, but especially insofar as it deprives thought of the consolations of the tragic. Violating the limit toward which all totality builds, by erasing the distinction (and the interdependency) between order and chaos, it leaves no space for limited accommodations with death, political prudence, or resignation before the sheer power of worldly regimes. And as futile as it may seem to affect so defiant and rebellious a tone against death itself — indeed, to revolt against death — this is the burden of the Christian narrative; that such a revolution is not hopeless, though, has been shown within time, at the empty tomb, and its ultimate vindication is the only promise upon which Christian hope may feed. Only in the light of this impossible desire for the one who is lost, this insane expectation of a restoration of the gift, and this faith in what is revealed at Easter is it *morally* possible for Christian thought to regard the interval between oneself and the lost beloved as potentially an inflection of divine rejoicing, a distance of peace: not by way of some sublation of the beloved, nor according to the serene proportions of tragic wisdom, but by way of the Holy Spirit's ingenuity in resurrection, his ability to sustain the theme of God's love (the gift given) over the most dissonant passages, now under the form of hope. And so, again, theology turns away from tragedy's mystification of violence, its awe before the sublimity and inevitability of violence, and back toward Israel's cry for eschatological justice. The resurrection of Christ is now an insuperable obstacle within the fabric of history that tragic wisdom cannot overvault, a concrete, aesthetic scandal whose irreducible sign is an empty tomb, which now marks a boundary beyond which God has passed in Christ without allowing the beauty of his gift to be consumed by the indeterminate, and beyond which — consequently — human reflection can no longer pretend to venture on its own: every speculative, tragic, abstract, or sacrificial appropriation of death, as an occasion or horizon of meaning (as in itself meaning, or meaningful as the death of the other), has been surpassed by an infinite gesture, by the disorienting rhetoric of the empty tomb, by the radiance of the resurrection, and by the palpable wounds of the crucified.

IV. ESCHATON

Christian eschatology affirms the goodness of created difference, reveals divine truth to be inseparable from beauty, and exposes the totality as false and marked with a damnable finitude.

And he shall judge among the nations, and shall rebuke many people: and they shall beat their swords into plowshares, and their spears into pruninghooks: nation shall not lift up sword against nation, neither shall they learn war any more.

Isa. 2:4

And the glory of the LORD shall be revealed, and all flesh shall see it together: for the mouth of the LORD hath spoken it.

Isa. 40:5

For, behold, I create new heavens and a new earth: and the former shall not be remembered, nor come into mind. But be ye glad and rejoice for ever in that which I create: for, behold, I create Jerusalem a rejoicing, and her people a joy. And I will rejoice in Jerusalem, and joy in my people: and the voice of weeping shall be no more heard in her, nor the voice of crying. . . . The wolf and the lamb shall feed together, and the lion shall eat straw like the bullock: and dust shall be the serpent's meat. They shall not hurt nor destroy in all my holy mountain, saith the LORD.

Isa. 65:17-19, 25

For I know their works and their thoughts: it shall come, that I will gather all nations and all tongues; and they shall come, and see my glory.

Isa. 66:18

The hand of the LORD was upon me, and carried me out in the spirit of the LORD, and set me down in the midst of the valley which was full of bones, and caused me to pass by them round about: and, behold, there were very many in the open valley; and, lo, they were very dry. And he said unto me, Son of man, can these bones live? And I answered, O Lord GOD, thou knowest.

Ezek. 37:1-3

When the Son of man shall come in his glory, and all the holy angels with him, then shall he sit upon the throne of his glory: And before him shall be gathered all nations: and he shall separate them one from another, as a shepherd divideth his sheep from the goats: And he shall set the sheep on his right hand, but the goats on the left.

Matt. 25:31-33

But if the Spirit of him that raised up Jesus from the dead dwell in you, he that raised up Christ from the dead shall also quicken your mortal bodies by his Spirit that dwelleth in you.

Rom. 8:11

Because the creature itself also shall be delivered from the bondage of corruption into the glorious liberty of the children of God. For we know that the whole creation groaneth and travaileth in pain together until now.

Rom. 8:21-22

Behold, I shew you a mystery; we shall not all sleep, but we shall all be changed, in a moment, in the twinkling of an eye, at the last trump: for the trumpet shall sound, and the dead shall be raised incorruptible, and we shall be changed.

1 Cor. 15:51-52

And I heard a great voice out of heaven saying, Behold, the tabernacle of God is with men, and he will dwell with them, and they shall be his people, and God himself shall be with them, and be their God. And God shall wipe away all tears from their eyes; and there shall be no more death, neither sorrow, nor crying, neither shall there be any more pain: for the former things are passed away. And he that sat upon the throne said, Behold, I make all things new.

Rev. 21:3-5

i. Time's Surface, Eternity's Light

The kingdom of God, the Gospels assert, is adventitious to history: it comes suddenly, like a thief in the night, and so fulfills no immanent process, consummates none of our grand projects, reaps no harvest from history's "dialectic." Only thus does it complete all things. And in the light of an eschaton that has already, in the resurrection of Christ, been made visible within history, the eschatological interruption of time (which breaks open every discourse of meaning or power that pretends to self-sufficiency) is seen to press upon each moment within time, an ironic syncopation that unsettles the stern and steady beat of history, a word of judgment falling across all of our immanent "Truths," whether of power, privilege, or destiny. History, as a strictly causal sequence, has no salvific power, reflects no universal or providential order, has no metaphysical yield. In a sense the eschatological liberates time from the burden of history, allows time a purely "aesthetic" character, an unnecessary, free, rhetorical graciousness; time is seen to be a declaration of divine glory, rather than a divine or human or ideal labor that achieves its end through an inevitable but ennobling (or at any rate, enlightening) strife. The kingdom repeats the gift that is always being given in time, and so in no way completes the logic of human history; history's probationary darkness — its Sabbatarian suspense — is due to privation, not process. In the paschal light of the kingdom, the household, the city, the entire epic of civilization are denuded of the glamor of "necessity." History's ceaseless strife can be construed in neither a Hegelian nor a Heideggerian fashion, neither as diremption nor as nihilation, neither as the epic of *Geist* nor as the nonteleological temporal dispensation of being. The eschaton shows that eternity, for creatures, is futurity and that existence is "repetition," and so shows time to be a fabric of glory, and so makes its surface shine. Time indeed is emancipated, not only from the myth of anamnesis, the recollection of immutable forms by eternal selves, nor only from the myth of the history of *Geist,* which abandons transient selves to oblivion in pursuit of its "spiritual" logic, but also from the equally static myth of Heracleitean flux, which imprisons time in the perpetual recurrence of the univocal "event": as the eschatological interruption of the kingdom is not of this world, and so constitutes an affirmation of being that also judges, it opens being up to the analogical, to the possibility of creative gestures of reconciliation within the world, to a power of discrimination strong enough to distinguish between death camps and hospices without loosening its embrace of creation's goodness. From the more secure vantage of a conventional metaphysics, eschatological faith is an insane act of speculative expenditure, one that casts aside all the hard-won profits of history's turmoils and tragedies at the prompting of an impossible hope: rather than the consummation of history's grand detour for the purpose of reappropriating truth and presence,[230] rather than telos, or synthesis, or reabsorption into the One,[231] the eschatological vindication of cre-

---

230. See Derrida, *Of Grammatology,* 10.

231. See Levinas, *Totality and Infinity,* 22: "[Eschatology] does not introduce a teleological system into the totality; it does not consist in teaching the orientation of history. Eschatology institutes a relation with being *beyond the totality* or beyond history, and not with being beyond the past and present."

ation is, once again, creation. The kingdom gives what is always given, in every moment; the gift remains simply the gift it always was.

But if the kingdom is not the consummation of history as such (the fruit of its totality), it is nonetheless involved with a particular history; the eschatological interruption of humanity's sinful narratives of power also occurs within time, in creation and covenant, in the election of Israel, the life of Christ, the constitution of the church. Over against false tales, God has declared the story of his peace, contradicting the claims of worldly power; the kingdom enters history from the future perhaps, but enters history nonetheless, in the form of a counterhistory, under the form of a subversive hope that forsakes the safe enclosure of the totality for the boundless beauty of the infinite. Eschatology opens the future as a horizon of hope, embraced within God's distance, precisely insofar as it takes leave of every purely speculative idealism, every attempt to discover a continuity between the stories that humanity tells of its metaphysical pedigrees and the ultimate order of things, so as to resituate humanity in a narrative that places both origins and ends in the hands of the transcendent God. The eschatological does not confirm any myth regarding the prerogatives of the creature, it casts no light upon his secret genealogies and forgotten appanages; it is for every soul a new thing, an event that may restore an unfolding history but does not simply recover a lost identity. In the light of Christian eschatology, nothing could seem falser to the church's tradition than, say, a sort of Eckehartian mysticism that would make of salvation simply the soul's return to its original self (which becomes the pattern of a certain style of idealism), rather than the advent within history of the possibility of a new, Christlike self, the form of one's true self beyond oneself, for which one was created and toward which one stretches out, the proper "essence" that one has never yet possessed. The eschatological light (which interrupts history at Easter) reveals — and inverts — the myth of ontological violence, but also the myth of an original self, prior to repetition, present to itself in the repose of a pristine immediacy. Again, our being is an ontic ecstasy, rising from nothingness, an arrival from nowhere, and so a judgment in each instant. The kingdom comes as a verdict laid against our claims to power, sufficiency for ourselves, and sovereignty over ourselves.

The history of Christ and the church — which is the presence of the last end in the here and now — may displace, change, or pass by other histories, or gather them into its own through acts that reconcile and renarrate, but it will not fulfill other histories; it is a word that reaches us from a divine future that does not involve itself in mythologies of the past, nor even in mythologies of a "destined" end. It might be argued that the eschatological shows even the biblical narrative of creation (which is *creation*, not mythic generation, and is therefore always oriented toward God's good ends, rather than rooted aetiologically in a cosmic or divine process) to be already an interruption of every self-aggrandizing saga concerning origins, every myth of aboriginal autochthony, every taxonomy that "places" persons within the hierarchy of totality. The kingdom is a judgment that falls across all things, as the future of all things in their particularity, and so disrupts decisively the tyranny of the universal; it reveals all things as unique moments within the glory of the infinite. This is why the eschatological is the true form of justice: as the language of judgment, it is also the affirmation of the "infinity" of the particular, of every other — the goodness of the "bad" infinite. It is when the absolute claim of the eschatological is resisted, in order to repair to the "realism" of the "middle," that the present good is often neglected, that the claim of the particular to justice is lost in the exigencies of prudence. To turn from the eschatological is to close off the present within economy, to move from the radical event of judgment to the rooted stability of institution, to become resigned to the limiting measures that ignore the call, and the threat, of the infinite; to forget that the eschatological verdict has been pronounced already, within history, and has raised up the crucified, is to resist the anarchy of charity.

As the vindication of a particular history, the kingdom is also an event of discrimination, a condemnation of all the falsehoods that enslave creation. The kingdom wears the aspect of damnation, as well as of redemption, and the language of hell enters Christian discourse alongside the evangel of peace; this is the shadow side of a gospel that promises the rescue of the world by way of a history in which God tells correctly the story that a sinful humanity tells awry, and so saves not by unifying the many strands of human history in a great synthesis but by electing one story as the truth of the world. Election, in this sense, always involves rejection. Hell is the name of that false history against which the true story, in Christ, is told, and it is exposed as the true destination of all our violence, by the light of the resurrection, even as Christ breaks open the gates of hell and death. Hell is with us at all times, a phantom kingdom perpetuating itself in the wastes of sinful hearts, but only becomes visible to us as hell because the true kingdom has shed its light upon history. In theological tradition, most particularly in the East, there is that school of thought that wisely makes no distinction, essentially, between the fire of hell and the light of God's glory, and that interprets damnation as the soul's resistance to the beauty of God's glory, its refusal to open itself before divine love, which causes divine love to seem an exterior chastisement.[232] Hell is the experience (a possibility in

232. See Maximus, *Quaestiones ad Thalassium* 59 (*PG*, 90:609A-B), on the eschatological encounter of all persons with the kingdom of God, either according to grace or according to dereliction; see also Origen, *Contra Celsum* 4.72; *Hom. in Ezech.* 3.7; *De principiis* 2.10.4; Gregory of Nyssa, *DAR, PG*, 46:97-105; and see Lossky, *Mystical Theology*, 178-79, 234-35.

each moment) of divine glory not as beauty, but as a formless sublimity; it is the rejection of all analogical vulnerability, the sealing off of the "self" (or the cosmos) in univocal singularity, the "misreading" of creation as an aboriginal violence. The "fire" of hell is that same infinite display of *semeia* by which God is always declaring his love, misconstrued (through rejection) as the chaotic sublime rather than the beautiful, not susceptible of analogical appropriation, of charity; it is the soul's refusal to become (as Gregory says) the expanding vessel into which the beauty of God endlessly flows. For exile is possible within the beauty of the infinite only by way of an exilic interiority, a fictive inwardness, where the creature can grasp itself as an isolated essence. Hell is, one might almost say, a perfectly "Kantian" place, where the twin sublimities of the star-strewn firmament above and the lofty moral "law" within remain separated by the thin tissue of subjective moral autonomy: where this tissue has become impervious to glory, the analogy of the heavens is not the transforming voice of God but only a mute simile, an inassimilable exteriority, and so a torment. Hell is the perfect concretization of ethical freedom, perfect justice without delight, the soul's work of legislation for itself, where ethics has achieved its final independence from aesthetics. Absolute subjective liberty is known only in hell, where the fire of divine beauty is held at bay, where the divine *apeiron* miraculously divests itself at the *peras* that, in Christ, it has already transgressed and broken open, and humbly permits the self to "create" itself. True, though hell is the purest interiority, it is also by contagion a shared interiority, a palpable fiction and common space superimposed upon creation, with a history of its own; but still, it is a turning in, a fabrication of an inward depth, a shadow, a privation, a loss of the whole outer world, a refusal of the surface. For Eastern Christian thought, in particular, it makes no difference here whether one speaks of death, sin, or hell: in each case one speaks of the same privation, the same estranging history, the same limit shattered at Easter; and hence there can be no aesthetic explanation of hell (something that a few of the Fathers occasionally foolishly attempted) that would make of it a positive moment in the exposition of divine beauty, a part of the universe's harmonious ordering of light and darkness. Hell cannot serve as an objective element of the beautiful — a source of delight — because it is an absolute privation of form and quantity; it has no surface, nor even a shadow's substance; its aesthetic "place" is the sealed outside of an inside. But destroyed by the infinite motion of Christ, it is now always to be consigned to the lake of fire (Rev. 20:14); hell is no place within creation, no event, though its history is everywhere told, its dominion everywhere suffered.

In a sense, then, the kingdom will be eternal superficiality, the beautiful "surfacing" of being, the endless liberation of difference into the light. Such is the promise in the doctrine of general resurrection: that creation, in which the

glory of God is given endlessly various and beautiful expression, is to be redeemed as such, as an aesthetic truth. In the general resurrection, says Augustine, God will be seen in the whole of created being, in all the bodies of the
saved (*De civitate Dei* 22.29); the kingdom's beauty will be this perfect loveliness
of the resurrected state (22.30), this lifting up of the world out of all hidden
depths.[233] As Balthasar says of Augustine's eschatology, "Only at the resurrection will the difference between *frui* and *uti* be abolished, will 'enjoyment' be
permitted to include not just the spiritual God but also his material creation, in
which he will henceforth be openly reflected. Only then will the analogical hierarchies of rhythmical systems be able to vibrate through the whole, as was
plainly the creator's intention."[234] The kingdom, as Romans 8 most clearly adumbrates, will be a restoration of the entire cosmos, in its integrity as God's
creation, as grace and glory. In its eschatology Christian thought most decisively breaks with every division between similitude and simulacrum, venturing forth and drawing nigh, the essential and the adiaphoral. Creatures exceed,
through their particularity, the similitude of every ideal reduction, and that excess is the open interval of analogy, of likeness in difference (rather than a likeness prior to difference); every true path of return leads not to the primordial
innocence of the ideal, but out into the free play of departing difference, which
God will raise up on the last day.

The kingdom, then, functions in Christian thought not as the moment of
metaphysical closure toward which history builds, but the truth that the good
of creation is creation itself, without need of any higher justification, any dialectical "remedy" for the ungovernable profusions of difference. Christian eschatology does not presage the termination or ideally purged coda of creation's
music, but assures that the motile theme given in creation will be given ever
anew, unfolded in the boundless generosity of its exposition; it is the promise
neither of the knowing silence toward which speculation makes its ceaseless
way nor of a concrescence of creation's harmonies in the roar of the absolute,
but of eternal music. The harmony of the kingdom is not the proper arrangement of essences, but a choral placing and yielding of voices; as Augustine says,
it is the combination of the universe's beauty in a great hymnody, with God as
the mighty composer (Epistle 138 *ad Marcellinus* 5). The motion of reconciliation in the Spirit, which is the motion that makes time beautiful, occurs within
time; this, at least, is the assurance given by Christian eschatology: that the particular is always included within the terms of reconciliation, that reconciliation
is not an *Aufhebung*, a tragic forsaking of the particular instance, but a
symphonia. The beauty of time is its openness to the novelty of peace, which

233. See Balthasar, *Glory of the Lord*, 1:439.
234. Balthasar, *Glory of the Lord*, 2:137-38.

can redeem every moment, "carry back" all discord into the complications of God's harmony. To quote John Meyendorff,

> One of the recurring themes in the Byzantine hymnography of Pentecost is a parallel drawn between the "confusion" of Babel and the "union" and "symphony" effected by the descent of the Spirit in tongues of fire. . . . The Spirit does not suppress the pluralism and variety of creation; nor, more particularly, does He exclude the truly personal experience of God, accessible to each man; He overcomes division, contradiction, and corruption. He himself is the "symphony" of creation, which will be fully realized in the eschatological fulfillment.[235]

To redeem each thing is to integrate it into the story of God's peace, and to rescue it from the stirring epics and sordid tales of violence (the way, remotely, a hammer that has been used as a weapon or in order to build a gallows is in a sense "redeemed" when employed instead to build a home for a poor man), and also to gather up time's moments of peace and charity in the beautiful cadences of the kingdom's music. The Holy Spirit always redeems memory, even in telling each story anew: he remembers feasts and those called to the feast, gestures of peace within time and those to whom peace is promised; the paradisal "repose" of the eschatological never forsakes history as such, but rather extricates all truths from the destructive fictions of sin. The new creation is justice, and so does not abandon the beauty of time to the holocaust of history. Christian eschatology could not stand more at odds with the idealization of history; it is an aestheticism without reserve, an eternal release of beauty, a perfect impartation of the gift whose departure is also already its return.

ii. The Last Adam

To conclude this minor dogmatics I shall turn once more to the theology of Gregory of Nyssa. Some might think Gregory an unlikely ally to invoke at this point, given that, on its face, his eschatology often looks indistinguishable from one or another species of metaphysical closure, an idealist recuperation of history's vagaries into rational "meaningfulness," at once a barely regenerate Platonism and a foreshadowing of German idealism. One might very well choose to view Gregory as the first metaphysician of history, the first thinker who allowed the Greek logos to be shaken by the radical historicality of Jewish and

---

235. John Meyendorff, *Byzantine Theology: Historical Trends and Doctrinal Themes* (New York: Fordham University Press, 1974), 174.

Christian Scripture, even perhaps a brilliant and innovative precursor of Hegel. For him, after all, the making and redemption of the world belong to the working out of a great "process," by which God brings to pass that perfect creation conceived and intended by him before all ages, and residing eternally in his will; all time is, says Gregory, an *akolouthia*, a gradual unfolding of God's eternal design in time and by way of change. Creation is twofold; or rather, one might speak of two creations: a prior (or eternal) creation that abides in God, as the end toward which all things are directed, for the sake of which all things are brought about; and a posterior creation, the temporal exposition of the divine model, its cosmic and historical effoliation, which from the creaturely vantage appears to precede the eternal form that, in fact, guides it. The idealist cast of such a scheme is scarcely difficult to see. It seems especially pronounced when Gregory speaks of the fashioning of humanity in the divine will: from eternity, he says, God has conceived of humanity in the form of an ideal "Man" *(anthropos)*, the archetype and perfection of the human, a creature shaped entirely after the divine likeness, neither male nor female, possessed of divine virtues: purity, love, impassibility, happiness, wisdom, freedom, and immortality.[236] By all appearances this is merely Christianized (and somewhat vulgar) Platonism. And yet, not so: this apparent idealization of humanity becomes at once unstable, and hastily divests itself of its ideality, where Gregory describes the first Man as comprising — as indeed being — the entire *pleroma* of all human beings, through all the ages, from first to last. In his reading of Genesis 1:26-27, Gregory understands the creation of humanity according to the divine image to refer not principally to Adam but to this fullness of humankind, comprehended by God's "foresight" as "in a single body" (*DHO* 16: 185C), fashioned after the divine beauty. Adam, however superlatively endowed with the gifts of grace at his origin, constitutes in Gregory's eyes only the first increment (so to speak) of that concrete community that, as a whole, reflects the beauty of its creator and that, in the fullness of its beauty, will come into being only at the end of its temporal *akolouthia*, when it will be recapitulated in Christ. While the parents of the race enjoyed a share in those attributes of the divine life that sin and death make inaccessible to a fallen humanity, in a wider sense it is only the entirety of the human race that reflects the divine, as now it exists in the purity of the divine wisdom, where it is comprehended "altogether" (ἀθρόως) in its own fullness (*DHO* 17: 189C). Here alone, in the solidarity of all humanity, has God fashioned a creature in the image and likeness of God: "Thus 'Man according to the image' came into being, the entire nature, the Godlike thing. And what thus came into being was, through omnipotent wisdom, not part of the

---

236. See C. N. Tsirpanlis, "The Concept of Universal Salvation in Saint Gregory of Nyssa," in *Studia Patristica* 17, vol. 3 (1982), 1132.

whole, but the entire plenitude of the nature altogether" (*DHO* 22: 204D).[237] Adam was fashioned, in some sense, in a state of perfection (*ICC* 15: 457-59), but the perfection of humanity, in a much more fundamental sense, will come about only in the fullness of time. It is this entirely novel coincidence in Gregory's thought of the concepts of *physis* and *pleroma* that marks an irreversible break from "Platonism's" myth of recollection, eidetic science as anamnesis, and the chasm dividing the intelligible and aesthetic worlds.

And yet, whatever its novelty, this still looks like an idealist metaphysics, anabstract or even proto-Hegelian "rescue" of the doctrine of creation from its ungovernable arbitrariness by way of an ultimate ideality. Gregory's reading of the creation narrative in Genesis bears more than a passing resemblance to Philo of Alexandria's, which also distinguishes the first account of humanity's creation from the second: the former, Philo (like Gregory) argues, concerns an ideal, divine Man, shaped in God's eternal counsels before the ages, while the latter concerns the actual race of mortal men and women.[238] For Philo, though, the primordial *anthropos* is most definitely a Platonic form: an interval remains fixed between the two creations, a *chorismos* between eternity and history, idea and image. In Gregory's exegesis, however, the primal Man is neither in any real sense "preexistent" nor finally transcendent of the plenitude of persons who come into being in the course of history; persons are neither shadows of, nor separated participants in, "Man," but are in fact the very substance of the creation God wills from before the ages.[239] Indeed, there is little in Gregory's thought at all that suggests too hard and fast a division between the ideal and phenomenal worlds; for him the intelligible realm (the spiritual order) is not the demesne of divine "ideas" as such, but of spiritual creatures, angels and souls. Gregory's exegesis of Genesis certainly resembles Philo's, but finally diverges from it radically: Gregory submerges the ideal in the historical rather than the reverse, while still allowing the "ideal" (which now should really be read as the "eschatological") to prevent the historical from assuming the aspect of a totality oriented toward an immanent end. The first creation stands over against — in judgment — any attempt to wrest a meaning or "destiny" from the limited arrangements and sinful ambitions of history by sacrificing the good of particular persons, because it is precisely the full community of persons throughout time that God elects as his image, truth, glory, and delight. At the same time, the very openness of history,

237. Γέγονεν οὖν κατ᾽ εἰκονα ὁ ἄνθρωπος, ἡ καθόλον φύσις, τὸ θεοείκελον χρῆμα. Γέγονε δὲ τῇ παντοδυνάμῳ σοφίᾳ οὐχὶ μέρος τοῦ ὅλου, ἀλλ᾽ ἅπαν ἀθρόως τὸ τῆς φύσεως πλήρωμα.

238. See Philo of Alexandria, *De mundi opificio*, in *Opera Quae Supersunt*, ed. Leopoldus Cohn and Paulus Wendland, 7 vols. (Berrlini: Reimeri, 1896-1930); reprint in 8 facs. (Berlin: W. de Gruyter, 1962-63), 1:38.

239. See G. B. Ladner, "The Philosophical Anthropology of Saint Gregory of Nyssa," *Dumbarton Oaks Papers* 12 (1958): 82.

404

thus liberated from its worldly end, also stands over against any idealism that would serve to reduce this perfect primordial creation to a bloodless abstraction. If the ideal and actual constitute not two realities but only two sides of one reality, then a kind of reciprocal critique must pass continually between them, so that neither can ever suffice to explain or "found" itself.

Which is to say that eschatology is where history's truth and history's disruption uniquely coincide. Still, within this very indistinction of ideal from actual, inasmuch as its unity occurs as an *akolouthia,* a certain distinction remains between the innocence of time and the violence of history, between the good creation God wills and the destructive fictions of a fallen world. This is the power of the eschatological, its prophetic irony, which can make every moment within time a moment of discrimination, a *critical* moment. Gregory's awareness of this takes, at one juncture, the somewhat whimsical form of a speculative mythology concerning how the multiplication of the species would have proceeded had we not sinned: but for the fall, he opines, humanity would have propagated itself in a more angelic fashion; God's foresight divided the race into two sexes so that, even when deprived of the properties necessary for celestial procreation (whatever those might be), humanity could bring the race to its foreordained plenitude (*DHO* 17: 189D). Gregory's "idealizing" prudery aside, the point to note here is that God brings the good creation he desires to pass in spite of sin, both in and against human history, and never ceases telling the story he intends for creation, despite our apostasy from that story. Prior to the fall humanity took its part in that retinue of spiritual creatures that eternally hymns God's glory (*IIP* 2.6: 86-87), but the departure of Adam and Eve from that company subjected all succeeding generations to an inhuman condition (*ICC* 8: 250-53; 12: 342-52) and diverted the history of the world from its true end. But for sin, God's design would have still unfolded, but peacefully, continuously, from potentialities established for the world in the beginning, according to an innate dynamism similar to those operating in the processes of the natural world (*De mortuis; GNO,* 9:49), and everything would have come without obstruction to partake of divine glory (*DAR* 105A). Sin, though, inaugurates its own sequence, an *akolouthia* of privation and violence, spreading throughout time from its own first seeds (*DV* 299), striving against God's love.[240] Humanity, as the *pleroma* of God's election, still possesses that deathless beauty that humanity, as a historical being, has lost; and God, seeing that beauty, draws all things on toward the glory he intends for them,[241] but according to a mystery

---

240. See A. J. Philippou, "The Doctrine of Evil in St. Gregory of Nyssa," in *Studia Patristica* 9 (1966), 252.

241. See *CE* 3.2: 74; *DP* 283B; *De infantibus praemature abreptis* (hereafter *DIPA*), *GNO,* 3.2: 82-85.

— a grace that does not predetermine the operations of a human freedom that cannot elude it.

Christ, the Father's express image, stands in relation to humanity from eternity; it is the beauty of the eternal Logos after whom the first Man is fashioned (*DHO* 16: 180D), to be the living body of Christ, its only head.[242] In entering into the plenitude of humanity, in assuming its creaturely finitude and its history, Christ orients humanity again toward its true end; and because this *pleroma* is a living unity, the incarnation of the Logos is of effect for the whole. Christ has, one might say, assumed the *pleroma*: his presence in human history is his presence within that coinherence, and so his glory enters into all that is human (*IITIF* 14). This is one of the points at which Gregory's theology opens out upon his notorious universalism: in the incarnation Christ implicates the entire plenitude in the pattern he establishes; such is the indivisible solidarity of humanity that the entire body must ultimately be in unity with its head, either the first or the last Adam.[243] This is the meaning Gregory takes from John 20:17: when Christ goes to his God and Father, to the God and Father of his disciples, he presents all of humanity to God in himself (*Refutatio confessione Eunomii*;[244] *GNO*, 2:346-47); and so Christ's obedience to the Father even unto death will be made complete only eschatologically, when humanity, gathered together in him, will be yielded up as one body to the Father in the Son's act of subjection, and God will be all in all (*IITIF* 16). The restoration of human nature, of course, is extended to creation only in the breaking of the bondage of death at Easter, from which the power of new life passes to all of humanity (*OC* 16: 48-49); Christ's resurrection inaugurates an *akolouthia* of resurrection, so to speak, in the one body of humanity (*RCE* 387): an unfolding that cannot now cease (given the solidarity of human nature) until the last residue of sin — the last shadow of death — has vanished (*IITIF* 15-16). But Easter will be complete only in the raising up of the entire body of humanity, in the eschatological restoration of creation.

For now, the mystical body of Christ, the church, is the only visible form of that redeemed nature, but the visible manifests the as yet invisible; Gregory divides his doctrine of the church (and so of salvation) into two dispensations, two gatherings: a gathering "in part" and another "of the whole" (*IITIF* 12-13; *In sanctum pascha*; *GNO*, 9:249-50), the former being that period during which the action of the Holy Spirit works out in the church the continuity of Christ's

---

242. J. Laplace, introduction to Gregory of Nyssa, *La Création de L'homme*, Sources chrétiennes 6 (Paris, 1943), 28.

243. See Jean Daniélou, "L'apocatastase chez Saint Grégoire de Nysse," *Revue des sciences philosophiques et théologiques* 30 (1940): 345.

244. Hereafter *RCE*.

resurrection and parousia, and the latter being the restoration of all things, when the single body of humanity will be recognizable as the body of the Logos. In the between times the church as a concrete and distinct history within history is the unity of the saved; but, as Balthasar observes, "the theological unity of the Mystical Body of Christ is entirely based on this philosophical unity. The total Christ is none other than total humanity."[245] The universalist implications of Gregory's thought are that much more obvious here: there can be no true human unity, nor even any perfect unity between God and humanity, except in terms of the concrete solidarity of all persons in the complete community that is, alone, the true image of God. Gregory's thought is never without a certain tension on this score, a stress between the forces of free historical contingency and God's eternal will. Humanity is one, as God first fashioned and eternally wills it, and cannot ultimately be divided; nor can any soul be properly redeemed — indeed, be human at all — outside of the human *pleroma*. On the other hand, even though each person is "objectively" implicated in the salvation Christ has wrought in human nature before any "subjective" appropriation of it (*OC* 32: 77-81), it is in each person, as he or she takes on the form of Christ, that the likeness of God also dwells in its fullness and is expressed (*CE* 1: 78-79). God shall be all in all, according to Gregory, not simply by comprising humanity in himself as the metaphysical "premise" of the human, but by way of each particular person, in each unique inflection of the *pleroma*'s beauty (*DIPA* 85-86); and yet his assumption of the human unfolds only within human freedom, within our capacity to venture away. Of course, for Gregory sin is always in some sense accidental to humanity, a privation, a disease corrupting the will, and so is the opposite of real human freedom, ultimately to be purged from human nature, even if needs be by hell (which is, according to Gregory — as is most clearly expressed in *De anima et resurrectione* — a period of purgation rather than final perdition). Evil is inherently finite, indeed is pure finitude, and so builds only toward an ending; it is a tale with an immanent conclusion; but in the light of God's infinity, its end is shown to be nothing but its own disappearance; when it is exhausted, when all shadow, chaos, hiddenness, and violence have been outstripped by the infinity of God's splendor, beauty, radiance, and delight, God's glory will shine in each creature like the sun in an immaculate mirror, and each soul — born into the freedom of God's image — will turn of itself toward the love of the Trinity. There is no other place, no other liberty; at the last, to the inevitable God humanity is bound by its freedom.

The eschatological kingdom will be, according to Gregory, a choral eter-

---

245. Balthasar, *Presence and Thought*, 87. See also A. H. Armstrong, "Platonic Elements in St. Gregory of Nyssa's Doctrine of Man," *Dominican Studies* 1 (1948): 115.

nity, a restoration of humanity to the universal hymnody that flows from and returns to God; when nothing is excluded from the good, when there can no longer be any exile, any sealed and unanswering interiority impervious to music and its complications, then the confession of Christ's lordship will rise up in one eternal harmony (*DAR* 72A-B) and humanity will be born as the creature God desires and conceives in the beauty of his Logos. Because he understands this coming into being of humanity "according to the image" in terms of a temporal unfolding, which makes the "ideal" and the actual each the "cause" of the other, Gregory is one of a very few theologians capable of viewing the history of the world in the light of salvation without resorting to some notion of sacral history set like an island in a sea of otherwise meaningless temporality (much as he does not think in terms of a particular saved humanity extracted from the mass of the reprobate): the story of Christ, even in its historical specificity, is also the story of all time in a quite literal sense, the story of the lordship of the Logos over the body of humanity.[246] Seen from the perspective of the kingdom, time is redeemed from our sinful histories, the story that every secular dispensation fails to tell is told at last, and the distinction between the ideal Man and the multiplicity of contingent persons throughout time disappears upon the horizon of God's good creation. The inevitability of Gregory's universalism is all the more obvious here: each person, as God elects him or her from before the ages (*DHO* 22: 207C-208B), is indispensable, insofar as the humanity God eternally wills could never come to fruition in the absence of any member of that body, any inflection of that beauty. Apart from the one who is lost, humanity as God wills it could never be complete, nor even exist as the creature who is fashioned after the divine image; the loss of even this one would leave the body of the Logos incomplete, God's purpose in creation unrealized. Obviously the shape of Gregory's anthropology looks Philonian, caught in the same penumbral interval between idealism and the biblical story; but this eschatological collapse of the distinction of ideal from actual sets his formulation apart from every predecessor. As Laplace justly remarks, "La pensée grecque n'était jamais parvenue à maintenir la liberté dans la nécessité, le temps dans l'éternité."[247]

The kingdom, as Gregory envisages it, will be a condition of accord, a unity achieved in the harmonious play of "the redeemed oneness of all, united

---

246. One might note here that Gregory in a sense offers a Christian answer to Hegel's understanding of universal history different from a more "Barthian" approach: he allows all history its place as the theater of God's ordination neither by making the violence of history a necessary negative probation nor by subordinating the merely particular to the synthetic; and he imagines the difference of God's true story from the stories of sinful humanity without making it seem as if the true story told in Christ is simply an intrusion upon worldly time, a radical rupture.

247. Laplace, 49.

one with another through their convergence upon the One Good" (*ICC* 15: 466).[248] The humanity that God wills from eternity and fashions after his likeness is a coinherence, a *perichoresis,* one might say, analogous to that of the Trinity. Gregory's "Man" of the first creation is not a Platonic ideal of which persons are shadows, much less an Aristotelian form that subsists solely in the individuals in which it is instantiated; it is a living community. The old idealism begins to dissolve in the narrative of creation and redemption; at the same time another idealism is forestalled, that of the dialectical recuperation of the universal from the provisionality of the particular. There really is not, in Gregory's thought, any sense in which the humanity of the first creation is an "ideal" reality at all; rather, it is an eschatological judgment that falls across every age of human history, the kingdom of peace in the light of which every other kingdom is revealed to be a tyranny; indeed, Gregory's eschatology could not be more profoundly anti-Hegelian, inasmuch as it recognizes no realm of historical indifference, no "bad" infinite, but in fact erases every distinction between the different (or indifferent) and the Same, between "transcendent" meaning and the beauty of being's surface, between speculation and display. Platonic beauty suffers defatigation in its transposition from the ideal to the phenomenal realm, Hegelian truth emerges from and rises above the interminable welter of the particular; but for Gregory the only site of the beautiful or true is in the entirety of creation's living body. Human history is thus embraced from beyond itself, receives its meaning from an end transcendent of it, and so is justified not by any sacrificial or prudential logic of its own, but by grace.

And if the "essence" of the human is nothing but the plenitude of all men and women, every "pure" essentialism is rendered empty: all persons express and unfold the human not as shadows of an undifferentiated idea, but in their concrete multiplicity and hence in all the intervals and transitions belonging to their differentiation (freed from sin); and so human "essence" can be only an "effect" of the whole. Repetition is the "ground" of presence. Every unlikeness, enfolded in the harmony of the Logos, manifests in an irreplaceable way the beauty of God's likeness. No stress remains between the ideal and the simulacral; just as every rose varies the "theme" of the rose, even so the human semblance is a sequence that differs and defers, toward its final truth; only eschatologically is it possible to speak of the presence of the human, and then as an "effect" of repetition, as a thematic and analogical verdict. The human "original," no longer an abstract paradigm, is the gift and fruit of every repetition, every peaceful difference and divergence; and it is only as this differentiating dynamism that the unity of the human "essence" is imaginable at all, as the

---

248. τότε εὑρίσκεται μονὰς τὸ σῳζόμενον, ἐν τῇ πρὸς τὸ μόνον ἀγαθὸν συμφυΐα, πάντων ἀλλήλοις ἑνωθέντων. . . .

unity of all persons in the Spirit, who is always bringing the great polyphony of creation to pass and ushering in the kingdom. And even in the kingdom that essence will not belong to us as a fixed *proprium;* our *epektasis* can know no surcease, no final capture of infinity's beauty. There will always be the eschatological within the eschaton, a continuous setting free of the creature from all recollection (*ICC* 6: 174), all anamnetic grounding in the absolute, a release into utter futurity. The eschaton brings nothing to a halt, returns nothing to its pure origin; it never secures beings within their own being; it is a perpetual venturing away from our world, our totality, into the real world of the infinite. The verdict of the resurrection will continue to occur, then, in every instant, always breaking the bonds of every apparent and representable essence, every pause within motion, every serenely static proportion; all our discourses of immanent truth — power, privilege, necessity — have been conquered in our one indivisible nature, and shown to be servile guardians of a boundary violently inscribed upon the infinite, which, in its glory, allows no boundary to persist. And if even the finality of death has been deprived of its authority, its power to consummate and complete, no refuge is left for our "essence": except there, in God, where we dwell "altogether." And so in Gregory's eschatology there is also no end of mediation or deferral (though not on account of the abysmal absence of the signified); there is no final synthesis or repose that leaves the incompletion of vestigia behind, or makes the mediation of creation's *semeia* obsolete. Signs and vestiges remain; creation's icons will not melt away when their meaning is grasped, sublated, ironic traces marking the place of their dissolution before a gnostic gaze. All expression is at the surface, and in the endless *epektasis* of the soul the surface will never be abandoned; the infinite openness of beauty and its evocation of a correspondingly infinite desire will never be raised into a realm beyond the free, aesthetic creativity of the God of infinite beauty.

My purpose, I should say, in discussing Gregory's eschatology is not to enter a brief in behalf of his universalism (Orthodox tradition does not authorize me to do so). My principal interest is in the power of Christian eschatology not only to assume the grammar of a certain metaphysical system, but to alter that system so radically from within as practically to reverse it, while yet "redeeming" its essence; this says much, certainly, about the real nature of theology, and about its "metaphysics." A conclusion to be drawn from Gregory's thought is that Christian eschatology (even when it borrows the shape of a kind of idealism) must inevitably subvert every presumptuous discourse that would strive to put an end to the deferrals of difference. The eschatological — which remains a word of hope, a paschal evangel that denies death its tragic splendor — functions as a promise that the verdict of God is on the side of the particular, the name and face of the one lost, that his justice is not a transcendental reconciliation between chaos and order, violence and rest, but a reconciliation of infinitely many sequences of difference. Which is to say that it is the promise that justice will never forget the other, that the other will always be blessed with an infinite regard and charged with an infinite worth: not because the other belongs to an abyss of the ethical, but because the other belongs to the infinite beauty of the surface; because, as this eschatology insists, the entire weight of the infinite in which all things share, this infinite and infinitely various music, rests upon each instance, requires every voice. This is a story, but one revealed at Easter to be the story that God elects, inasmuch as he is the God who never forsakes his beloved — who is the delight of God and the image of his glory. It must ultimately be, for Christian thought, that this paschal radiance, which breaks upon reflection not merely as promise but as the event that constitutes all Christian memory, exposes the falsehood of our purely worldly teleologies: for there is no good end immanent to a nature that we each simply privately possess, to which some may attain of themselves while others, also of themselves, fall short; nor is there some "higher" end achieved only when the lost, having discharged their limited roles in the drama, are abandoned to the past. Our only just and proper end is given to us all, as one, from beyond the worlds we fabricate to accommodate our violences. We own neither essence nor prerogative in ourselves, but belong from everlasting to Christ; and this is the highest freedom, for it is freedom from death, even the death we work in ourselves by our own wills. To know that liberty, we — our words — must be spoken anew in and by the Word; until that unending end that we await, though, our words may speak of him, invoke him on others, beckon others to him, peacefully — so long as they assume the style and cadence (revealed in Christ) of the infinite: which is eternally beauty and peace, and which may forever be traversed.

PART 3

Rhetoric without Reserve

Persuasion, the Tyranny of Twilight, and the Language of Peace

Vocasti et clamasti et rupisti surditatem meam, coruscasti, splendu-
isti et fugasti caecitatem meam, fragrasti, et duxi spiritum et anhelo
tibi, gustavi et esurio et sitio, tetigisti me, et exarsi in pacem tuam.

AUGUSTINE

I. THE WAR OF PERSUASIONS

In this book's "diegetic" interval, just past, I attempted to demonstrate (in a somewhat elliptical fashion, admittedly) that one may speak, within the Christian tradition, of a rhetoric of peace, of a practice of rhetoric that is peaceful, because rhetoric and beauty are both already narrated by Christian thought as peace, obedient to a particular understanding of the infinite: beauty is prior to sublimity and infinity surpasses totality. Moreover, the concrete form of Christian rhetoric — Christ, the Father's supreme rhetoric, his Word — appears within the terms of this Christian narrative of the infinite as the very form of peace, the infinite gesture of a love that simply exceeds the gesture of every violence brought against it, the real and visible beauty whose historical and aesthetic particularity invites response and variation and whose effect can inhabit time not simply as negation but as a practicable style of existence. Because he is no beautiful soul, no withdrawing and perishing beauty, Christ offers, in himself, a peace that enters history always as rhetoric, as a persuasion, as a gift that can be received only as a gift. But, this said, can persuasion ever be entirely peaceful? This story can be enunciated, but can it issue in the action it seems to promise? Can such a gift really be given?

413

This is a practical question, not simply a theoretical one. The claim that is made implicitly in and alongside every proclamation of the Christian evangel is that, although all secular discourses of meaning or truth belong to, or at least cannot escape, the circle of a closed economy of violence, of a war of persuasions whose guiding impulse is power, Christ freely crosses this circle to impart his peace without ceasing to be the true rhetoric and open proclamation of God, and yet without assuming the shape of violence. Can, though, Christians convert this claim into a genuinely efficacious practice? After all, Christ's crossing of this circle eventuated ineluctably in the cross itself, as the world's recoil against the advent of the beauty of the infinite; of course, theology's claim is that the resurrection shows that Christ overcomes the discourses of power that crucify not by a kindred violence but by way of the infinite motion of peace that is the shape of his whole life. Very well; but the question from which this book began concerned not only what Christians believe, but the power of the Christian story *to persuade.* Amid a war of persuasions, what form can be assumed by a persuasion that is peace, especially if it does not offer itself as a mere gnostic persuasion *away from,* offering escape from being's strife, but claims to reveal the very shape of creation as God intends and loves it? In the moment that this rhetoric is addressed to another, and encounters in consequence the intractability of another persuasion, it finds itself engaged in a kind of war, a struggle of voices each to suppress or displace the other; and in this moment, how does Christian rhetoric distinguish itself as a peaceful gesture that suffers this war, without merely abjuring from persuasion as such, and how does it comport and unfold itself in the midst of war as the practice of a peace more primordial than every war? The church has always known that the presence of Christ in history not only invites assent to the beauty of his form, but also provokes the violence of the powers of this world: "These shall make war with the Lamb, and the Lamb shall overcome them" (Rev. 17:14). But how does the Christian evangel make war upon war, so to speak, without becoming — insofar as it persuades *against* and *in favor of* — a form of coercion, deceit, or empire? (Christian history is obviously not entirely encouraging on this score.) Or to phrase the question differently, what name can be given to the rhetorical practice of the church that sets it apart from other styles of persuasion?

I should emphasize again that Christian thought is bound here, on account of its evangelical commission, to a perilous course; and all the prejudices of modern ethics are ranged against it. To quote Levinas, "Justice is the recognition of [the Other's] privilege qua Other and his mastery, is access to the Other outside of rhetoric, which is ruse, emprise, and exploitation. And in this sense justice coincides with the overcoming of rhetoric."[1] The ethical can be found, he

---

1. Emmanuel Levinas, *Totality and Infinity: An Essay on Exteriority,* trans. Alphonso Lingis (Pittsburgh: Duquesne University Press, 1969), 70-72.

says, only in a discourse that "is rupture and commencement, breaking of rhythm which enraptures and transports the interlocutors — prose."[2] For the slightly more sensible Derrida, as has been said, the final abolition of rhetoric is impossible and is imaginable only, in the end, as silence, the language of death; and so philosophy must enact its own violence against violence, and guard with tireless vigilance against its own impulses toward "totalization." The language of the ethical must of necessity be (if it is to be any language at all) a restless suspicion, a pious hesitancy, which is ceaselessly engaged in the work of subjecting discourse to the scrutiny of an "undeconstructible" justice. But Christian discourse is thoroughly "unethical," if these are indeed the terms of ethics: it is always in some sense the rhetoric of conversion, a campaign of persuasion; it addresses the other in the open intonations of a beckoning call, it speaks to the world with the most enticing eloquence it can command. It proclaims a form, a certain splendor, and so can never assume the polite and prosaic proportions of the Levinasian language of the ethical; but neither can it submit itself to a roving vigilance that, presuming to stand outside the circle of persuasion, attempts to hold the excesses of the rhetorical in check. So it has no recourse but to resist both the privative rigorism of an ethical language devoid of rhetoric (an impossibility in any event) and the prudent restraints of a "disinterested" surveillance of rhetoric; Christian thought denies the necessity of war, the violence of rhetoric as such, and so always constitutes a potential provocation to war.

Where two persuasions meet, one must remember, there is always the possibility of a violence somewhat different from the "violence of metaphysics," indeed prior to every metaphysics, every attempt to exert mastery over the real by reference to its "ground"; it is the violence that arises from the absence of every final ground, of final foundations, and from the consequent acceleration of attempts *to refer* in conditions of incorrigible provisionality — attempts to arrive at a final decisive pronouncement that might somehow circumvent language's ungovernable imprecision. Wittgenstein, who understood extremely well the shifting fluidity and instability of linguistic "foundations," and the limitations placed upon communicable meaning by the "rules" of usage belonging to particular linguistic practices, understood also the immense difficulties that arise in the encounter between two "language games" whose schemes of reference and meaning are not only incompatible with, but even incomprehensible to, one another. In *On Certainty* he reflects upon the possibility that one might find oneself confronted by beliefs and practices grounded in a view of reality so thoroughly alien to one's own that it would be impossible even to identify the "reasons" for the disagreement: if for instance we met a people who prefer to consult oracles rather than physicists, we might denominate their belief as

---

2. Levinas, 203.

"wrong," but in so doing we would merely be "using our language-game as a base from which to *combat* theirs."[3] "I said I would 'combat' the other man, — but wouldn't I give him *reasons*? Certainly; but how far do they go? At the end of reasons comes *persuasion*. (Think what happens when missionaries convert natives.)"[4] Wittgenstein perhaps fails adequately to address whether upon persuasion there might follow a cultivation of vision and reflection that, in its integrity and fullness, could supply reasons unavailable to the unconverted heart, but finally compelling in their "rightness"; but the dynamics of the encounter between two worldviews he describes with crystalline clarity: "Where two principles really do meet which cannot be reconciled with one another, then each man declares the other a fool and a heretic."[5] And it is just this cry of "heretic" (or better, "infidel") that is the threat of war, or of persecution or conquest, and that seems to invite the more detached and suspicious discourse of ethical restraint: to call, that is, for a kind of indefatigable and disinterested hermeneutical invigilation of rhetoric. After all, the "understanding" that is often sought between two worldviews is, in the end, a median struck between differing tropes, *figurae*, narratives, and metaphors; and so, often this understanding is really a misunderstanding that is forcibly suppressed by a rhetorical and aesthetic strategy that submerges the fissure of genuine difference in the interminable dissimulation of a seductive style, and thus simply allows each party to ignore the other — indefinitely. Even though there may be no ascertainable ground deeper than the linguistic surface where understanding or misunderstanding might come to rest — even if we are language all the way down — and the violence of persuasion does not consist in "alienation" from a "natural" condition, but merely in a semantic metabolism, a conversion of the text of the self, it remains nonetheless a motion of violence that some see the rhetoric of persuasion as always in danger of becoming. Perhaps, as a Christian might claim, it is not rhetoric as such that is violence, but only particular kinds of persuasion; but this in no way alters the truth that, in the absence of any sure metaphysical ground to which the difference of persuasions may be referred, and in light of the seemingly inevitable rhetorical invocation of grounds implicit in every practice of persuasion, it would seem an ethical necessity that every discourse of "truth" submit itself to the unquiet vigils of a consciously "ungrounded" hermeneutical suspicion. And after all, the great, multifarious "poem" of Christianity stands out in its particularity, a monument among many monuments, which means in some sense to displace and even consume

3. Ludwig Wittgenstein, *On Certainty*, ed. G. E. M. Anscombe and G. H. von Wright (New York: Harper and Row, 1972), ¶609.
4. Wittgenstein, ¶612.
5. Wittgenstein, ¶611.

other narratives, to overturn many other monuments as idols. A hermeneutical vigilance that stands on guard against the sheer sway of suasion, that resists the irresistible in any discourse of meaning, and that patiently seeks to deconstruct every hierarchy within totality appears, in a world of warring persuasions, as perhaps the only certain form of peace; not, of course, a final peace, but a prudent armistice, a pious practice of attentiveness that strives, as far as possible, against the silencing of any voice, however frail — which means, against the triumph of any voice, however powerful.

Before anything else, then, it would seem wise, and morally responsible, to consider the claims of this other order of peace, this restrained and restraining — chaste and chastening — metarhetorical vigilance, this "hermeneutics." Is it, perhaps — or could it be — peace?

II. THE VIOLENCE OF HERMENEUTICS

I should clarify, in advance of anything else, in what sense I employ the word "hermeneutics." I mean it in the sense given it by Heidegger and his heirs: the discipline of philosophy conceived as a patient consideration of the history of metaphysics and of its decline, an appropriation of the "history of being" under the aspect of dissolution, which seeks to emancipate thought from any commanding ontology, any temptation to seek out being's "ground." The hermeneutical project receives the testimony of the history of the West as the chronicle of the successive arising and passing away of metaphysical epochs, not in the hope of discovering a more original truth than metaphysics, but in order to grasp being's self-disclosure *as* dissolution, and so to bring thinking to a place beyond metaphysical violence. This is hermeneutics in the sense given the word by, for instance, Gianni Vattimo,[6] and in a sense compatible with what John Caputo calls "radical hermeneutics": a practice of interpretation that presumes to have had done with foundations altogether, and to be free in consequence to undertake its very principled deconstructions. "Hermeneutics" seeks to relinquish every "strong thought of being," to adopt a style of "weak

---

6. See Gianni Vattimo, "Toward an Ontology of Decline," in *Recoding Metaphysics: The New Italian Philosophy,* ed. Giovanni Borradori (Evanston, Ill.: Northwestern University Press, 1988); Vattimo, *The End of Modernity: Nihilism and Hermeneutics in Postmodern Culture,* trans. Jon R. Snyder (Baltimore: Johns Hopkins University Press, 1988); Vattimo, *The Adventure of Difference: Philosophy after Nietzsche and Heidegger,* trans. Cyprian Blamires with Thomas Harrison (Baltimore: Johns Hopkins University Press, 1993). See also Luca D'Isanto, "Gianni Vattimo's Hermeneutics and the Trace of Divinity," *Modern Theology* 10, no. 4 (October 1994): 361-64.

thought" (Vattimo's terms) that hears and responds to the textual tradition of the epochs of Western thought as a history of the decline of metaphysics; and inevitably it implicates theological tradition in its account of this epochal sending.

Though not always, one should add, from a presumed position of advantage. Vattimo, at least, in his recent turning (back) toward the "vicinity" of Christian faith,[7] has come to see the hermeneutical project, and its benign nihilism, not as a contradiction of Christian tradition but as its singular achievement, the effect of theology's own textual tradition. He has even come to see his account of the genealogy of nihilism, secularization, the decline of metaphysics, and the weakening of thought as a philosophical transcription of salvation history; Western thought, he asserts, has come to relinquish its every strong thought of being, and so comes to understand being not as absolute structure but as event, as the hermeneutical consequence of the *kenosis* of God in Christ — of the history, that is, of this announcement. The story of a God who creates out of love, not necessity, who becomes human to suffer violence rather than impose it, who is the one condemned rather than the one who condemns — this story, he says, has inverted our understanding of the divine, taught us to see being not as structure and hierarchy but as event, and shown us how to release our grip — charitably — on being conceived as substance, foundation, power, etc. Vattimo is all but unique among hermeneuticians in this way of viewing things, and his particular project at present may not be very germane to my argument, but one should take note of it and at least ask if this might be the model theology should adopt in its understanding of the relation of theology to the history of metaphysics. To some limited extent it should, most definitely; but one must be on guard, for followed to its end, it leads to a convergence of theology and nihilism (the absolute evacuation of God's transcendence) that is not very much better than the inanity of "death of God" theology, and that shares the latter's fundamental misunderstanding of the Christian concept of divine transcendence (though Vattimo, more intelligently, limits himself to a consideration of the history of an announcement within a tradition, and so avoids lapsing into apocalyptic parodies of Hegel). For Vattimo's talk of *kenosis*, quite contrary to theological tradition, is not balanced by any audible talk of exaltation; it seems to concern, therefore, only a kind of ontic "transcendence," the divine summit set atop the hierarchy of the totality, the speculative pinnacle of being, whose power a *kenosis* of the divine would indeed exhaust. However, as I have argued above, the truly ontological transcendence that Christian

7. See, for instance, Gianni Vattimo, *Belief,* trans. Luca D'Isanto and David Webb (Stanford: Stanford University Press, 1999); and Vattimo, "The Trace of the Trace," in *Religion,* ed. Jacques Derrida and Gianni Vattimo (Stanford: Stanford University Press, 1998).

thought introduced into Western thought is the infinite act of both *kenosis* and *plerosis,* as one, full in its self-outpouring, emptying itself in its imperishable *apatheia.* Vattimo is indeed right to read the history of nihilism as, in some sense, the effect of the Christian interruption of Western metaphysics, but he misinterprets that interruption as a mere inversion of the priority of transcendence and immanence, rather than the raising of the finite into the infinite. Is this latter not, though, the most important part of the story of metaphysics' decline: not merely a weakening of thought released by the announcement of God become a man, but the irresistible and "revolutionary" transcendence visited upon thought by the proclamation of the empty tomb? For Easter was indeed a revolution, an overthrow of powers and dominions; it brought about not the death of God but the death of many gods, the death of immanence. The gods have been emptied of their eminence entirely, but not the God who will be where he will be, who is the fullness of all being in its generosity and glory. Everything, according to the Christian announcement of redemption, has been lifted up now into an inescapable transcendence, uprooted from all "grounds," and we forget this *hermeneutical* truth if we continue to think of strength and weakness, or fullness and outpouring, or justice and mercy, or "transcendence" and immanence as merely opposed rather than reconciled in the infinity of God's supereminent actuality. This is a vital matter, even in terms of the largely ethical concerns that animate Vattimo's project. For does the weakening of thought always, even within the ambit of our peculiar Judeo-Christian textual and cultural tradition, necessarily weaken into charity? And is charity its own light, its own visibility? Are there not always more exuberant and violent nihilisms waiting to fill in the empty spaces where once stood what we thought were strong, enduring edifices of truth? It is perilous to imagine otherwise, and worse than perilous to forget that it was the announcement of God's true transcendence, of his power of judgment, and of the glorious exaltation of the crucified that teaches Christian culture to see in the weak and suffering and abject the power and glory of being, the special charges of a God of judgment, and the form of the one who has overcome the world. History delivers us to so many worldly projects of truth, within whose orders of visibility so many things can be reduced to a new invisibility: that which Christ has taught us to see as formerly we could not — the poor, the weak, the lame and halt, the oppressed — can so easily be hidden again behind such stable essences as, say, the commodity of cheap labor, the economic burden of the unemployed, the irrelevance of those who lack the power of purchase, the individual who is subordinate to the good of society. It is not metaphysical nostalgia, then, but fidelity to the true announcement of the death of the totality — Easter — to call upon Christ risen and reigning in glory to make the otherwise invisible irresistibly appear.

Setting aside Vattimo, though, and his extremely kindly intentions, I should frankly confess my own hermeneutical suspicion regarding hermeneutics; I might be forgiven, I trust, for wondering whether the desire to narrate the death of metaphysics (conceived, even under the aspect of an epochal sending, as a unitary history) is not often part of a strategy of power, serving a deeper, even perhaps unconscious desire to set sentinels at the boundary of every other narrative: not a rejoicing in the open and atelic play of difference, but a panoptic scrutiny that stands guard against every narrative that would narrate itself too fully. Indeed, is there any way to confine the narrative of the death of metaphysics to a kind of internal critique of the Western tradition, or will it not always inevitably become a kind of "colonial" discourse of its own, imperiously inscribing its negations across every other narrative? A critical soupçon of every metanarrative still constitutes a hermeneutical prejudice, an act of positioning and critique prior to the enunciation of any story, one that presumes it possesses an understanding of metanarrativity as such, and so is permitted to enforce a kind of silence — governed by a condescending irony that may even wear the demeanor of tolerance — that no claim to truth dare violate. But surely, then, it becomes a moral necessity to attempt to liberate the contingency and variety of different stories from the ever expanding ambitions of this monolithic history of metaphysics. A suspicion of every metanarrative is also a fatidic awareness of what sort of thing a metanarrative will always be, where it will always distinguish itself from more licit and finite stories. Surely the power to narrate the end of Western metaphysics is, by extension, a power to approach all narratives from a postmetaphysical vantage and to pronounce upon them — even in advance of their appearance — a final verdict. And one must ask whether such a verdict does not demand, as a "moral" necessity, a particular social regime: it is difficult to see how this style of restraint could fail to invite (if only indirectly) another, more pervasive, subtler, and more irresistible coercion. The only vigilance that can hold "totality" at bay, in the name of the plurality of difference, must be one that proleptically concludes every story that is told. As a private practice of hermeneutical hesitation, it cannot be simply a humble *Gelassenheit* of difference, but must also function as an advantage over the other, a knowledge in advance of how far the other's story may go before it becomes obviously myth, and so a knowledge of when other voices are to be ignored or merely humored, in their enchanting or annoying garrulousness. Such a piety of restraint can never be merely a private piety (any more than a language could be private), but must inevitably require a public space of discourse whose boundaries are assured by a very particular political arrangement, in the interest of a very particular form of ethics, and the result must be that within this space every narrative that would advance itself as truth must do so under the shadow of a dogmatic discourse of truthlessness. The truth of no truths requires of plurality that it be civil (according to a very specific conception of civility), that it restrain and subvert itself, that it come out of itself into a neutral space where cultural identity and tradition are negotiable property, even quaint artifacts. One can rightly ask whether the story of the twilight of metaphysics, which suspends thought indefinitely in a condition of crepuscular weakness, really constitutes a relinquishing of the supposed metaphysical presumption of the West to impose the finality of its narratives on every other narrative, or whether in fact it constitutes simply the most devious kind of metaphysical closure, a "total" regime in the guise of a debile and chastened hermeneutical history of secularization. After all, the West is the *Abendland*, most in ascendancy in the light of decline (or in a declining light); philosophy has always been a discourse, in some sense, of twilight, of endings; Minerva's owl, we are reliably told, flies at dusk. The danger that must attend the master narrative of endings is that all its good intentions will prove, in the end, only to conceal its ambitions behind its hermeneutical passivity, its narrative irredentism behind its "weakness," and its appetites behind an absolute surrender whose yielding indifference to narratives is (by virtue of its very plasticity) invincible.

This is in no way to deny the ethical impulse that may guide "radical hermeneutics," nor to deny that the history of metaphysics (conceived very narrowly as the history of Western philosophy) has indeed, for the most part, culminated in the dissolution of every strong concept of being (philosophically conceived). Nor should one overlook the quite palpable reality of the violence in which the metaphysical and the metanarrative have often been implicated: for the violence of metaphysics lies not simply in an abstract campaign to master the principles of the real, but in the actual violences of history, the imperial or colonial or prudential campaigns that have often sought to justify themselves by appeal to some more fundamental "truth." But even so, the pious practice of hermeneutical suspicion, though it appears to have disengaged itself from all foundations, is no less deserving of the scrutiny of Nietzschean suspicion: Might not the renunciation of power over the real also dissimulate a subtler kind of power, a final violence (or the violence of finality), the tyranny of twilight? After all, the deconstruction of Western metaphysics, and the attendant critical privilege of deconstructing every metanarrative, must be undertaken in such a state of structuralist abstraction that it is, by extension, a forcible interruption of every narrative precisely where it would take flight. A postmetaphysical hermeneutics of suspicion must stand — no less than the Hegelian gnosis — always farther along downstream, aware of the inevitable conclusion of all stories; and this is why it must be allied also to a very particular regime: insofar as it presumes to exercise no control over difference, it must have the form of a kind of critical *Gelassenheit* of all voices; but insofar as it resists the "totalizing" motion in every narrative, it also must mediate among all voices as the metanarrative condition of undecidability that is presumed before any discourse can articulate itself in the open. In order for there to be this letting be of different voices, a certain neutral space must first be secured: so much difference must be converted into indifference, so many voices must be suppressed; the consensus of the forum always excludes the overly garrulous fabulist, the storyteller who knows too much. It is not to be doubted, certainly, that this is the very form of ethical restraint; but it operates effectively only to the degree that it makes difference unthreatening — not by imposing total silence, but by setting the limits of intelligibility, the demarcation past which no narrative may pass without becoming an illicit discourse of impossible knowledge. Obviously a radical hermeneutics intends to suppress nothing by force; it seeks, probably in earnest, to be just a patient and humble craft of salutary suspicion, the most unambitious pursuit of liberation. But whom, or what, does it liberate?

The question must be asked, principally, precisely because a more or less "unfounded" discourse of suspicion always commences from a place prior to, and so also somewhat inattentive to, the difference of one story of truth from another. Christian rhetoric, by contrast, must start out from within this very difference, this interval between stories that cannot be resolved by reference to an incontrovertible ground of reference more basic than stories, nor resolved by a metanarrative of the unpresentable sublime that would demand of every story that it accept its status as a local and elective mythology. To give an example of this distinction: the Neoplatonic One spends its inexhaustible power and beauty in a descending scale of participatory radiance; the Christian Trinity does not merely descend or radiate its bounty, but imparts all things freely, creatively, and gathers all things into its infinite motion of gift and restoration, and knows no power that is not also the inexhaustible exhaustion of power, the giving of all and receiving of all; one narrative concerns the "loan" of being, but still with a certain collateral (funds, *fundamenta*, foundations), whereas the other concerns a gift of being that is radically groundless, that needs always to be surrendered to be received aright. To a critic predisposed by a structuralism of the metaphysical to see these as variants of a single "foundationalist" impulse, the distinction is perhaps interesting, but in no way constitutes a break within the history of metaphysics "as such" (which is, after all, a history of epochal breaks, but also of a doubling back in every case, and always of a forgetting of the ontological difference). But from the vantage of Christian thought, this distinction of stories is the very substance of freedom, the very shape of the peace the church offers, and an ontological hermeneutics of the history of metaphysics can serve only to obscure it; the practice of post-onto-theological critique is then perhaps best defined as a willful forgetfulness of the narrative difference. Yet it is precisely where one story diverges from another, or advenes upon another, that a path of liberation might possibly open up (and Christian thought, to state the obvious, understands its story as the story that alone truly unmakes the narratives of violence that hold sway over history). It is tempting to hope that a radical hermeneutics might act as a moderating force that could impose "peace" upon the space of difference, if not in the interests of justice, at least of prudence; but for Christians this pacification of difference's "site," prior to the advent of what genuinely differs, should be fled, as a violence that seeks to subdue the evangel, to reduce its audacious renarration of the world to just so much more exotic chatter at the world's margins, outside the boundaries of the forum.

What is at issue, of course, is power. According to John Caputo, the real aim of his postmetaphysical hermeneutics is an attack upon established power, its totalizing discourses, its supremacy over the narratives that might resist or seek to escape its embrace; it strives to make room for all voices, in order to make sure that debate is fair.[8] This, obviously, makes it sound as if he is advocating a strategy of simple liberalism, a social hygiene for preserving the openness of a marketplace of ideas from the imperial ambitions of unconstrained (and politically enfranchised) metanarratives. Nor does Caputo pretend that his project occupies a position beyond every mythos as such: his interest, he declares, is in advancing a certain very particular myth,[9] the myth of justice, and in inventing many small emancipatory myths that might disrupt the dominance of great stories of being, while exercising vigilance over these small myths as well.[10] But then again, there is surely something here of the familiar gesture of doubling back upon one's own discourse, to protect it preveniently from critique: having acknowledged that one's myths are myths, one is then free (with a clear conscience) to deploy them among the world's narratives, as limits imposed upon their "excesses." This is, in some sense, a gesture of occultation, concealing radical hermeneutics' capacity for rhetorical violence behind a veil of critical detachment. When, similarly, Derrida declares that "Justice . . . is not deconstructible" and that "Deconstruction is justice,"[11] it is supposedly because it is in the nature of justice that it make its claim on behalf of the other, prior to every narrative of the Same — this is its definition — and deconstruction (if it can be practiced) serves the ends of justice, in fact is the course of critical suspicion that justice must follow when great narratives threaten to overwhelm "alterity"; but it can also mean that a very particular practice of deconstruction has been placed beyond all deconstruction. And while a radical hermeneutics may seek only the

---

8. John Caputo, *Radical Hermeneutics: Repetition, Deconstruction, and the Hermeneutic Project* (Bloomington and Indianapolis: Indiana University Press, 1987), 260-61.

9. John Caputo, *Demythologizing Heidegger* (Bloomington and Indianapolis: Indiana University Press, 1993), 3.

10. Caputo, *Demythologizing Heidegger*, 38.

11. Jacques Derrida, "Force of Law: The 'Mystical Foundation of Authority,'" trans. Mary Quaintance, *Cardozo Law Review* 11 (1990): 957.

path of peaceful pluralism, where no voice is suppressed, it still perhaps hides within itself an impulse to subdue the very difference it attempts to emancipate; it invites, or at any rate foreshadows, a rule of law or (at the very least) a rule of legitimate discourse that would seek to contain all voices within a neutral paradigm of rational restraint. Yet this very paradigm may constitute a complete contradiction of the narratives for which it seems to make room; this particular species of toleration may, as likely as not, enact a subtle but quite devastating violence upon narratives that make claims in excess of the proportions of polite restraint. However admirable the ethical intentions of a radical hermeneutics, it should itself probably be disrupted by the particularity of all those narratives that should not consent to the constraints placed upon them by the "myth of justice," if it is a myth that merely governs the strife of persuasions according to a dogmatic metanarrative of truthlessness. At any rate, insofar as it tends to subsume so many narratives under a single history of metaphysics, and insofar as it attempts to preface every story with a story of undecidability, radical hermeneutics remains a metanarrative, a discourse of power, however much it dissembles itself as a kind of principled powerlessness.

This may seem a rather harsh judgment, but it is certainly not unwarranted. The violence of hermeneutics is the inevitable concomitance — a shadow — of a certain benign passivity; in faithfully receiving word of the end of metaphysics, in a condition of salubrious resignation, the hermeneutical consciousness also achieves an undeniable advantage. Like the neutral rationality of the Enlightenment's mythos, radical hermeneutics places itself beyond, in the place where every narrative would seek to transcend the condition of local myth, with a knowledge — before every advent — of what can or can never appear to view. It declares an end to the war of truths by resolving (or dissolving) every disagreement into its own truth; the hermeneutical space is an unassailable site, an Archimedean point that shifts every tradition that arrives away from the center. Whereas, for instance, Lyotard repeatedly asserts that all particular, local, and religious narratives should have their rights guarded against omnivorous metanarratives, he also directs some of his more excoriating observations against the "tribal narratives" that bring about war, and uses the Nazis as an example of what tribal narratives (like the mythology of the Aryan race) often bring to pass;[12] and he remarks that distinct communities banded about their names and narratives cannot be relied upon to resist the hegemony of capital, as the forms of resistance indigenous to such communities are as like as not to promote just this hegemony.[13] (Unasked, as scarcely needs be said, is

12. Jean-François Lyotard, *The Differend: Phrases in Dispute*, trans. George Van Den Abbeele (Minneapolis: University of Minnesota Press, 1988), 105.

13. Lyotard, 181.

whether the problem is "tribalism" as such or simply the particular traditions of quite specific tribes, and whether there might indeed be particular communities that possess languages and names that are *essentially* resistant of the political, cultural, and social evils that Lyotard deplores.) Caputo, with his "myth of justice," which supposedly protects the priority of the claims of the other over against every language of "essential" truth, observes at one point that "The whole idea behind the myth of justice is to avoid playing favorites, which is why the myth of justice is betrayed by locating a chosen people (the Jews), or the people of God (the Christians), as if some people were and some people were not God's, as if God prefers Jews to Egyptians, Christians to Jews, Europeans to non-Westerners, and so on. The whole idea behind justice is not to exclude anyone from the kingdom, which means the kingdom is nowhere in particular."[14] The import of such a remark is quite disturbingly clear: even if this myth of justice is intimately associated, in its origins, with the myth of a God of election, who chooses the other as his beloved rather than merely enfranchises the other with a univocal and inviolable otherness, it is ultimately a myth without topology or native dialect, it belongs to no people, it must forget the differences between peoples; Jews participate in justice, but only to the degree that they will consent to cease being Jews (after all, apart from the story of God's election of Israel, can Jews be Jews?). Is this liberating? Whom does it liberate, and for what? By Lyotard and Caputo both, one is reminded of how much unreflective conventional liberalism underlies the "radicality" of this hermeneutics, especially when it becomes a model for public discourse, and how much condescension: there is a point at which all distinct cultural narratives, subjected to the panoptic gaze of an unlocalizable "justice," can have only the character of nostalgia, ethnic recollection, local color, perhaps even the babble of savages, for whom we tolerantly make room; every faith is then a *devotio foci,* an accidental identity, to be practiced in a temenos set away from the realm of public concourse, guarded by lares and penates, a local paganism. But faiths and traditions all too often insist on being more than this: they make claims upon all of being, upon history, upon truth, and resist the place made for them at the margins of the forum, in the galleries where subdued exotic specimens are permitted to exhibit their colorful eccentricities. The danger that differing traditions present is real, it should be added, and the prudence of a postmetanarrative hermeneutics is perhaps the wise and restraining hand needed in a culture of tolerated (and so, by a reciprocal necessity, tolerable) plurality; but this should in no way obscure the truth that this hermeneutics is indeed a violence, enacted perhaps against violence (or the perceived threat thereof), but violence all the same. Moreover, it is a practice that necessarily ignores the sheer irreducible complex-

14. Caputo, *Demythologizing Heidegger,* 190.

ity of the relationship between community and identity, and between the particularity of the other and the particularity of a tradition; it overlooks the degree to which communities and distinct names are often the only form of resistance against "totality," and the degree to which metanarratives are the only way of liberation from metanarratives. There never really is, in the end, a neutral place or an unambiguously just perspective; there are, however, various stories of freedom, perhaps some far more liberating than others, over against which the "myth of justice" may itself often stand as an unjust limit imposed from without. This myth is indeed myth (Caputo is correct here), though its meta-metanarrative presumption is too easily converted into a forgetfulness of its own mythic origins and imperial ambitions, its own claim to narrate being with greater authority (even if it does so as a narrative of unsynthesizable dissolution), its own will to power. As it is, the hospitality afforded narratives by postmetaphysical pluralism (on this model) is rather like the glass of wine left for Elijah at Passover: a shock were the prophet to appear to claim his libation; and a shock whenever any narrative attempts to narrate itself to the end, as the truth to which others must pay heed.

Perhaps a certain distressingly facile elision already corrupts this discourse: Is it meaningful to talk of metanarratives as such, or even of local narratives as such, indifferent to the incompatible ambitions they harbor, the differing ends they pursue, the perhaps irreconcilable stories they tell? Is it really of any use to speak of a strategy of power, or the legitimation of power, in metanarrativity in the abstract? After all, power does not necessarily profit from an appeal to some metaphysical warrant for its exercise; it is often most at liberty when it narrates itself simply as power, as the romance of acquisition and of conquest. Metanarratives — or narratives of truth — are frequently fraught with restive moral ambiguities, intractable tendencies toward critical transcendence, and may just as well confuse, disrupt, ironize, or subvert the discourses of power that attempt to appropriate them (the church of the rich, for instance, again and again hears itself, not without a certain consternation, reciting the Magnificat). Power is often best served when it can demystify itself altogether, and effect a transvaluation of all values in the process: the market celebrates ruthless acquisition, without metaphysical premise; the empire exhorts legions to take up arms for the glory of dominion, not in the name of destiny; the socialist utopia wrings submission from the governed through confiscations, imprisonments, and tortures, not through its idealism — and acquisition or dominion or submission becomes the tautologous truth of a culture, the undeconstructible good that can never be deprived of its foundations because it makes no pretense of resting upon any. If the heavens are evacuated, the earth is thoroughly exploitable, endlessly fictile, a site where values are created by the exuberance of will. Here is where Caputo would want to set small mythologies at work breaking down the great stories of power, or where Lyotard would call for the unleashing of the differends; but such mythologies can avail very little against a power whose only mythos is power. Over against such a metanarrative only other metanarratives can stand, other narratives of being, other evangels of the good; a humble hermeneutics of suspicion fails here because it cannot really be (except through a metaphysical gesture it claims to deny itself) a different tradition of virtues, an openly different and unapologetic metaphysics.

Caputo's own attempts at a postethical ethics (so to speak) reveals the splendid futility of attempting to make intelligible any discourse of justice, over against discourses of mastery, in the absence of such a metaphysics. His recent work, especially *Against Ethics*,[15] is dominated by the idea of obligation, which (being a name for the infinite alterity of the other) confronts one from without in a moment of fragile suddenness, irreducible to any more foundationalist calculus of the ethical; "obligation happens" is Caputo's tireless refrain, which in the early pages of *Against Ethics* appears to be, at first, a mere stylistic device promising a fuller argument, but which at length acquires the unmistakable aspect of a frantic and insistent repetition of an unsupportable — but desperately desirable — dogma. Obligation happens, he says often and in a variety of ways, "in the twinkling of an eye," and no science of the ethical or metaphysics of the true can prepare one adequately for its advent. If, though, one steps back for a moment from all these obliging nictitations, one must realize that prior to every obligation glimpsed in the face of the other there must be a constant and complex optical preparation. Obligation never simply "happens," in point of fact, but always awaits one as something for which one has been made ready: again, obligation does not belong to a transcendent and unthematizable priority, some unlocalizable ubiquity of justice (like a saying prior to every said), but is a cultural artifact, prepared for one in advance by a particular language, practice, tradition, history, and cultural identity. Obligation, as well as the possibility of any response to obligation, is always fully narrated before one can be obliged; every obligation, therefore, is essentially fabulous, and so it matters which *tradition* one advances, which narrative of the other, which story of moral duty. Both the God of Israel and the thousand-year *Reich* claim obligation from their peoples, and there is no sense in which obligation (in any more neutral sense) precedes such narratives as these. Not that Caputo entirely fails to grasp this, but his moral earnestness proves here to be self-defeating. A scrupulous strategy of restraining the violence of persuasion is also a surrender to the inevitability of violence in the rhetorical; and so no recourse to — no hope in the possibility of — a rhetoric of peace is left open. Christian thought, how-

---

15. John Caputo, *Against Ethics: Contributions to a Poetics of Obligation with Constant Reference to Deconstruction* (Bloomington and Indianapolis: Indiana University Press, 1993).

ever, must pursue a more uncertain but surely less self-deluding course of action, staking its claims on nothing more universal (nothing any less particular,
that is) than its own story, its own revelation, its own beauty. Its narrative may
fail to convince, or be told poorly, but it will never imitate the practice of a
"pluralism" that asks one to suffer the reduction of one's cultural and narrative
particularity to something fundamentally indifferent, something superadded
to a mysteriously obliged and obliging subject who inhabits a "community"
where narrative differences are merely cultural residues; it will not insist that
otherness become a vagrant and aleatory identity when the other enters the
realm of ethical action, traversing an adiaphoral universe of cultural production, a world of opaque signifiers, eliciting and beholden to an "obligation"
whose claim is both absolute and indeterminate. The Christian evangel may desire the conversion of the other to the truth it proclaims, the other's passing
over from one city to another; but it does not demand that the other exist in
perpetual exile, outside of every city, except for occasional retreats to the refuge
of "private" or "local" practices. To guard against the violences of the polis, it
does not insist that all dwell in the desert.

This is not to say that from a Christian vantage the idea of a tolerant but
vigilant governance of the public space should simply be displaced by an idea of
public space as an ungoverned, uninvigilated strife of differing perspectives (a
space prepared for holy war); it is to say, rather, that Christian thought has no
views regarding the governance of a *neutral* public space at all, it has no belief
in or knowledge of an extranarrative site or a postmetanarrative peace, it is suspicious of every claim to neutrality. The only peace it knows, upon which it
stakes its hope, or according to which it can proceed is that which belongs to its
kerygma; it does indeed desire to convert all the world into the church, because
the church is (it believes) the true earnest of the world that God creates and
raises up. Christianity knows no peace but the peace of Christ, and has no word
to speak concerning the peace of "neutrality," the end of every metanarrative,
the hermeneutical cultivation of a humble, contrite, and crepuscular consciousness, disposed merely to witness the last traces of the departing light of
the Platonic sun as it descends beneath a far horizon. (And thus, for all its "absolutism," there is surely one kind of violence — modernity's or postmodernity's necessary suppression of absolute commitments — in which
Christian thought cannot participate.)

Almost every species of the postmodern seems prone, contrary to its
avowed intentions, to a return to the subject, to a lingering solicitude for the
last vestiges of a Cartesian or Kantian self, no matter what hygienes have been
employed to purge the subject of any particularly stable subjectivity, and no
matter how etiolated, in consequence, the idea of the self has become. Deleuze
still clings (with whatever irony) to a model of freedom that depends upon a

singularity whose special élan or force must expand to the limits of its power; the reverberation of difference in each instance still erupts from a somehow indivisible monadic point of departure, and even when the self — the body — is dismembered into an assemblage of "desiring machines," indifferently arranged, this does not mitigate the singularity of desire as an originary force, a kind of moral autonomy that ought not to be transgressed. Foucault resorts, ultimately, to a kind of Stoic interiority. Lyotard imagines some kind of positive liberty on the other side of tribalism and on "this side" of the sublime. Derrida's concern for the ethical priority of a subject, appearing now under the form of the other, indicates a border, a precinct, which must not be invaded. These are only traces, of course, largely denuded of any real texture; but the singularity of subjectivity — albeit in a condition of univocity — remains, ringed about by the unmediable sublime. There is really no other place for the practice of unreserved critique to come to rest, unless it chooses (in absolute consistency with itself) to forsake altogether the question of freedom or of the ethical. Of necessity, it depends upon and invokes a subjectivity from which every defining characteristic, every open and analogizable interval, has been excluded, a subject who is at most an ineradicable point of departure, or a terminus. If the self is the folded inside of an outside (to use the Deleuzean image), the person is then always a shifting and densely woven fabric, a texture incorporating incalculably many series, involving innumerable modes of expression: linguistic, cultural, "tribal," religious, and so forth. And yet, it would seem to follow, it is this entire fabric, this fortuitous convergence of series upon the surface, this "soul," that is displaced by a radical hermeneutics, that is always moved away from the center; the myth of justice, the hermeneutics of suspicion, in a sense lavishes its solicitude upon the claims of a "subject" (not so called, of course) that must be forcibly invented, through a progressive impoverishment of the surface, a constant dismantling of those very "grand narratives" in which persons actually arise.

And this is the greatest moral danger implicit in the pious and self-effacing practice of postmetaphysical hermeneutics: all the while that the claims of traditions are patiently unmade (and all traditions are in a sense implicitly unmade by the critique of onto-theology), the hermeneutician is engaged in dismantling cultures, identities, peoples, and persons — he is deconstructing souls. Persons are in some sense the creatures of their traditions, and it is for just this reason that one should call into question the ease with which a hermeneutics of suspicion sets limits to the claims that traditions may intelligibly make. The freedom, the name, even the face of the other appear with a terrible fragility, in a space opened up by stories, in fact by metanarratives: stories of being or of truth; this is the space that (potentially) liberates difference, allows it to become iconic, the face of the other, the name of another — of a difference that is not indifferent. But a critical vantage that claims to stand beyond all narratives, with the privilege of concluding all discourses where they threaten to overflow their assigned places, subjects the face of the other to its speculative iconoclasm. This raises a delicate and irresoluble ethical question concerning where, at what juncture, one may distinguish the individual from the narrative to which the individual belongs: when one tears away the veil of purdah, does one liberate another from bondage, or steal from her her face? In a sense every great metaphysical story is a narrative of the veil, of the fabric of metaphor and allegory that seems, in every culture or system, to conceal a certain invariable presence, a certain otherwise inaccessible truth; and the practice of a radical hermeneutics is the art of lifting the veil, or of, at any rate, stoutly resisting the authority of the veil, treating it instead as mystification rather than mystery. Which is to say that postmodern suspicion is a practice that suspends thought between face and veil: it cannot pretend to liberate a subjectivity it denies, but neither can it submit to the "truth" of purdah, the authority that veils, that at once depicts and contains the other. Confronted by the allegories and metaphors in which difference always arrives, by which otherness is always given shape, the peculiar privilege of a meta-metaphysical suspicion lies not simply in pointing out that the veil is not a face but only a veil, but in complaining that the very appearance of a veil is culpable insofar as it creates the illusion of a face — by fabricating the image of a veiled face.[16] This is the final condition of a dogmatic discourse of undecidability: precisely because this hermeneutical suspicion can come to rest on neither side of the veil, it can undertake its critique only by eliminating face and veil alike, by relocating the other in a nonplace, by drawing all otherness out into the space of the kinds of difference that can be governed as exchangeable instances of an abstract "alterity." Having passed through the disenchantments, the skepsis of the hermeneutical place, the other — decorticated, denuded, named now only "the other" — arrives where? It is, I repeat, a nonplace, a place of endlessly fluid boundaries, where persons are preserved solely as featureless instances of inviolable otherness, narrated in ab-

16. This suspense between face and veil, so to speak, between presence and metaphor, and the impossibility of liberating textuality or speculation from this suspended condition constitute in part the theme of Derrida's "White Mythology: Metaphor in the Text of Philosophy," in Jacques Derrida, *Margins of Philosophy*, trans. Alan Bass (Chicago: University of Chicago Press, 1982), 207-71. Metaphor figures in philosophy as an economy of the true, a loss of meaning for the sake of the recuperation of meaning; and so the apparent dissolution of the metaphor is always part of the metaphysical gesture; but Derrida's approach suggests the possibility of a second act of dissolution, a nonrecuperative destruction of metaphoricity by way of its own textual interminability, its own failure to refer, that might serve as a veil that can be lifted: a deconstruction that neither attempts to get "behind" metaphor nor to leave the metaphor intact as a metaphor *tout court* (an allegory of another, less "written" truth).

straction from those traditions to which they may, in the realm of private fixation, remain attached; it is, as it happens, the very place where Nietzsche's madman announced the death of God: the market.

III. THE OPTICS OF THE MARKET

I invoke the market here not as a preamble to any ideological critique of capitalism in the abstract (which would be no less vacuous than a critique of "power" in the abstract); nor, certainly, do I intend any denigration of property, production, or trade, which are all honorable enough if morally employed. I mean instead to describe a place that can accommodate within itself both capitalist and socialist "styles" of order (neither of which is, properly speaking, particularly hospitable of Christian commitments). The market transcends ideologies; it is the post-Christian culture of communication, commerce, and values characteristic of modernity, the myth by which the economies, politics, and mores of the modern are shaped, the ideal space where desire is fashioned; it is the place that is every place, the distance of all things, no longer even the market square, which is a place of meetings, a communal space, but simply the arid, empty distance that consumes every other distance. The market is that ubiquitous realm of endlessly proliferating images of the real that Vattimo calls the "transparent society,"[17] and much of the postmodern constitutes only the most uncontradictory ideological expression of its logic and its dominance of history's horizon. Radical hermeneutics, certainly, has all the marks of a necessary, "superstructural" hygiene of the market, a final speculative transition from the concrete figures — the particular optics — of certain premodern traditions, inexplicably lingering on in the public space, to the open, Heracleitean spectacle of the market's endless fluidity. When Caputo describes radical hermeneutics as a kind of humility, a frank expression of ignorance,[18] it is difficult not to conclude that, for him, this style of ignorance is the only acceptable form of humility, the only piety of social and ideological peace; which makes it a strangely imperious humility that he advocates (as his tirelessly sanctimonious tone makes unpleasantly obvious). And this is why it serves especially well (though at a removed and ideological level) to help clear the ground for the market: it obeys the logic of an age and a regime in which the agora has been disseminated throughout the polis, giving

17. See Gianni Vattimo, *The Transparent Society* (Baltimore: Johns Hopkins University Press, 1992).

18. Caputo, *Radical Hermeneutics*, 252-58.

shape to all real public identity. Caputo's talk of the "flux" and the "abyss" (his own names for the postmodern sublime)[19] is itself a metaphysics, surely: to name the flux is also to profess an understanding of the "logic" (the logos) of the aleatory, to name chaos as the metaphysical substance — the truth — that, once grasped by thought, excludes other and opposed truths, and exposes them as fictions. And one should (as Deleuze and others have) call this metaphysics by its proper name: Dionysian metaphysics, metaphysics in its primordial constitution — which is to say, *market* metaphysics.

The market, after all, which is the ground of the real in modernity, the ungrounded foundation where social reality occurs, makes room only for values that can be transvalued, that can be translated into the abstract valuations of univocal exchange. And in the market all desire must needs be conformed to commodifiable options. The freedom the market acknowledges and indeed imposes is a contentless freedom, a "spontaneous" energy of arbitrary choice; and insofar as this is the freedom that is necessary for the mechanisms of the market to function, every aspect of the person that would suppress or subvert this purely positive, purely "open" and voluntaristic freedom must be divided from the public identity of the individual, discriminated into a private sphere of closed interiority and peculiar devotion. To be prepared to enter the market, one must suffer this division between the "private" and the real, one must endure a metabolism from one to the other; for the indestructible power of the market — its ability to adapt almost anything to its abstract system of exchange — to accommodate "selves," so many aberrant desires must be suppressed or diverted into a discrete realm of extrapublic activity (quietly suppressed, that is: "subjectified," poeticized, finally dissolved into the ether of the private because they do not constitute matter for substantial transactions). However admirable its intentions, "radical hermeneutics" is merely one theoretical articulation of a transformation that is always already being effected by the market: persons (arising as they do from the often irreducible stresses of particular traditions, particular communities of speech and practice, even particular landscapes and vistas) must be reduced to economic selves, by way of a careful and even tender denudation and impoverishment; thereafter the "enrichment" of the person can occur only under the form of subjective choices made from a field of morally indifferent options, in a space bounded by a metaphysical or transcendental surveillance that views the person as utterly distinct from his or her aboriginal narratives, allowing these narratives the status perhaps of quaint fictions but preventing them from entering into the realm of the real on other terms (as, say, persuasions, forces of contention that cannot be reinscribed as part of the playful agon of the market). Radical hermeneutics, as a thin echo of the ideology of

19. See especially *Radical Hermeneutics*, 145-46.

the market, attenuated to the faint bat's squeak of "ethics," can preserve the "rights" of distinct communities and discourses only as a pressure constantly resisted, pushed to the margins of the real; and thus it can describe only an "emancipation" that occurs, without bidding, in every instant.

I am saying nothing very outlandish or even very original. After all, to stand at the end of modernity one must stand in the only place modernity has left us. Deleuze and Guattari, for instance, often openly embrace the "deterritorialization" and "decoding" of the market, its clastic and antianalogical exuberances, its dissolution of stable hierarchies and preserved sites;[20] as there can be no return to archaic models of domination, nor any resort to revolution (which is an impossible resolution), thought must seek to intensify the "schizophrenic" impulses of capitalism until capitalism itself — as a rigid system — shatters from its own energies. Truth be told, this faint residue of radicalism seems only absurd in the light of the market's power to assimilate and commodify almost any energy, to subdue any force, and doubly absurd insofar as it advances itself according to a logic already indigenous to the market (but so many French intellectuals are still embarrassingly obliged to believe Marxist diagnoses of capitalism's "contradictions"). Nonetheless, this all accords perfectly with the Deleuzo-Guattarian wish to define desire not as *manque,* but as a creative and productive ebullience:[21] this is the very logic of the market, at least as an engine of production (though the consumer's "need," of course, plays a secondary role, as part of advertising's bright pageantry). One might ask whether a great part of Deleuze's project is not, at most, a simple transfer of the myth of capitalism's "self-made man" to the realm of ontology. The market thrives on a desire that recognizes no commonality of needs, a desire that seeks to consume and to create an identity out of what it consumes, a desire that produces out of its own energy and in indifference to a shared proportion of the good that might limit invention or acquisition. A desire that expands to the limits of which it is capable: not an analogical desire for God or the other, but a desire for nothing as such, producing in order to desire more. Here one sees the necessary, if not always immediately apparent, synonymy of consumerism and nihilism: in our "society of the spectacle" (to use Guy Debord's phrase), the open field where arbitrary choices may be made among indifferently desirable objects must be cleared and then secured against the disruptions of the Good; this society must presume, and subtly advocate, the nonexistence of any higher "value" than choice, any truth that might order desire toward a higher end; de-

---

20. See, in particular, Gilles Deleuze and Félix Guattari, *A Thousand Plateaus,* trans. Brian Massumi (Minneapolis: University of Minnesota Press, 1987), 351-474.

21. See Ronald Bogue, *Deleuze and Guattari* (London and New York: Routledge, 1989), 88-89.

sire may posit, seize, want, not want — but it must not obey. Thus endless transvaluation is the law of the market, and its secret faith is in the impossibility of anything beyond this law; and as this law and this faith mark the triumph of the nothing, their "moral" logic is simply that of the absolute liberty of the will. Hence the freedoms that allow one, at one's discretion, to purchase puce draperies, to gape at pornographic magazines, to sell popular celebrations in song and film of brutal violence, or to destroy one's unborn child are all intrinsically "good" because all are expressions of an essential freedom of choice. The market expands in the constant invention of a nomadic desire that seeks merely the acquisition and then the disposal of interesting debris and agreeable conveniences, so that appropriation and dispossession become a perpetual economic oscillation; even substantial needs, like food, can be transformed into commodities, subordinated to the system of arbitrary exchangeability, bedizened with desirable emblems and runes. Thus it is tempting (and rather obvious) to see the Deleuzean insistence upon a discourse of univocity as merely expressing the logic of a system of univocal exchanges — the translatability of substantial (or illusory) goods into the abstract medium of currency (money or credit), which becomes the *true* possession — and of univocal selves — monadic quanta of financial power, originary instances of arbitrary will, whose expenditures are never teleological but always directed back toward the center, toward the market of innumerably many things. In the thought of Deleuze and Guattari, in fact, the lingering traces of Cartesian subjectivity are only intensified by the dismemberment of the "self" into various desiring machines, various expressions of the singularity of volition and desire, and made that much more conformable to the energies of the market (the mouth machine, for instance, that desires to eat — in abstraction from cultic or communal prescriptions, prohibitions, or pieties concerning foods — is a veritable font of such energies).

One wonders, really, whether this is not the narrative that the Nietzschean element in the postmodern most truly subserves. The market is not so much a vertical as a horizontal totality, a plane upon which everything can be arranged in a hierarchy of abstract equivalence, aleatory instances of desire or apathy; it is a totality that contains everything in a state of barren and indifferent plurality. It invites and preserves a vertical hierarchy of wealth and poverty, of course, but without reference to a stable ontological or "analogical" syntax: the realm of the real is at the level of horizontal transactions, from which social and economic positionings arise and into which they can just as easily sink again. It is the totality, in short, not of Apollo but of Dionysus (Apollo's other face). It may well be that in some sense what Nietzsche foresaw, what he prepared for (why God "died" for him), was modernity's postindustrial market. The myth of affirmation without negation, or of no negation except as part of a prior affirmation, the insistence upon evaluation and transvaluation (upon value) and upon the primordiality of the will, and so many other aspects of the Nietzschean narrative stand in curious compatibility with the mythos of the market. For all his solicitude for noble values, Nietzsche may prove, in retrospect, to have been the greatest of bourgeois philosophers: the active and creative force of will he praised may be really a mythic aggrandizement of entrepreneurial ingenuity and initiative; talk of the will to power, however abstracted and universalized, may reflect only a metaphysical inflation of that concept of voluntaristic punctiliarity that defines the "subject" to which the market is hospitable; the notion of a contentless and spontaneous activity that must create values describes, in a somewhat impressionistic vein, the monadic consumer of the free market and the venture capitalist; to speak of the innocence of all becoming, the absence of good and evil from being, and a general preference for the distinction between good and bad as a purely evaluative judgment is perhaps to speak of the guiltless desire of the consumer, the relativity of want, and that perpetual transvaluation that is so elegantly and poignantly expressed on every price tag, every declaration of a commodity's abstract value; a force that goes always to the limit of what it can do is perhaps at one with modern capitalism's myth of limitless growth and unbounded trade. Nietzsche, however much he detested bourgeois values, perhaps knew not which god he served[22] (as a Marxist might say, his ideology was the product of material forces he did not recognize). Seen in this light, it is clear why the figure of Christ presents such an intractable problem in *The Anti-Christ:* he is unmarketable, he produces nothing that can be brought into history's true arena (the strife of the market), his practices do not obey market functions; he is, simply enough, a bad consumer and entrepreneur, concerned with feeding the poor and comforting the sickly,

---

22. Nietzsche's avowed god, Dionysus, is of course an endlessly protean and deceptive deity and a wearer of many masks. When he makes his unannounced appearance at the end of *Beyond Good and Evil,* as its secret protagonist, whose divine irony has occultly enlivened its pages, he exercises his uniquely divine gift, the numinous privilege of veiling and unveiling, concealment and manifestation; he is the patron deity, appropriately, of the philosophical project of genealogy. But perhaps another veil remains to be lifted, and the god may be invited to step forth again, in his still more essential identity: Henry Ford. After all, Ford's most concise and oracular pronouncement — "History is bunk!" — might be read as an exquisite condensation of the theme of the second of the *Unzeitgemäße Betrachtungen* (see also *On the Genealogy of Morals,* trans. Walter Kaufmann [New York: Vintage Books, 1969], 1.10 and 2.1). And there could scarcely be a more vibrant image of univocity's perpetual beat of repetition — of eternal recurrence, the eternal return of the same — than the assembly line: difference here is certainly not analogical, but merely univocal, and the affirmation of one instance is an affirmation of the whole. It is, moreover, well documented that Ford was a devotee of square dancing, which is clearly akin to (perhaps descended from) the dithyrambic *choreia* of the bacchantes; Ford was a god who danced.

living like a mendicant, advocating the unconditional forgiveness of debts, treating money like Caesar's uncontested property (with an irresponsible air of indifference), and promiscuously producing and distributing good things like bread, fishes, and new wine outside the cycle of commodification and exchange. *The Anti-Christ* may well be the text that best marks the line of division between church and market as a line of enmity (another reason theology may be beholden to Nietzsche). None of the rhetorical ornaments of Christ's life — none of its shadow and light, pathos and joy — can be fitted to the pagan aesthetic of endlessly expansive power and Dionysus's heedless dance.

Opposed orders of desire are at issue here, and desire is the form of either freedom or servitude; persons are shaped by desire, as Gregory of Nyssa and Augustine understood, and so the nature of one's desire — what one sees as beautiful or desirable — is what the Christian evangel seeks to convert. The market, according to the order of desire it cultivates, apprehends being under the form not of the weightiness of glory but of immateriality; for, contrary to the frequent but unreflective characterization of the ethos of the market as simple "materialism," modern consumer culture subsists most essentially upon the etherealization of desire, a diversion from the concrete to the symbolic. A desire guided by material needs, after all, within the varying constraints of different cultures and traditions, would always be capable of a calculable degree of satisfaction; and so the modern market, as the field of the production of consumer goods, urges what is produced as, above all else, novelty and status, emblems and totems. The nothing is a veritable wellspring of sigils. One object of desire displaces another, each object becomes — according to function or fashion — obsolete, and yet the status of possession continues on; rather than concrete goods being themselves the primary objects of desire, actual palpable wealth, commended by their beauty or usefulness to the one who possesses them, they become simply the symbols of a wealth whose actuality is the abstract power of acquisition itself; it is the force that procures, rather than the splendor of what lies near at hand, that the market celebrates and feeds upon. The world of things becomes, in consequence, an endless array of indifferent instances — or rather, occasions — of the exercise of this acquisitive power. The market reverses the process of analogy, the making concrete of God's declaration of his glory in creation, and resists every vision of creation as glory, as the tangible display of God's *kabod*. Wealth becomes immeasurably light, the darkness between stars. The market appropriates the world in a gnostic fashion: everything as symbol or as waste, nothing as beauty; the process whereby the accumulation of possessions is also the disposal of possessions (a Carpocratian piety, perhaps), and whereby the material is transformed ceaselessly into a "spiritual" deposit of abstract wealth, culminates in a gnostic delirium, the constant acquisition of nothing by way of symbols and the constant reduction of symbols to nothingness again. The abstraction of the market, its lightness, is a fire that attempts to burn away the weight of glory as so much dross, as exchangeable tokens of wealth; unlike the fire of God, it does not transfigure but consumes. The market, then, is a particular optics, a particular order of vision. Its aesthetic of immateriality suspends all difference in the univocal formalism of the aleatory; all more refractory values — beauty, need, awe — are transformed into the universal value of price (the transvaluation of all values, endless evaluation). Within the world descried by such an optics, there is no theme to vary in the fabric of things, no distinct orders of beauty and grace, but only random series of simulacra whose unitive logic is uniform: exchange value. The particular pathology of the market, in consequence, is a kind of anaesthesia through inanition of the apparent, a painless and wonderless gaze, prey to moments of anxiety but immune to awe; the precise symbol of this anaesthesia, perhaps, would be not wine (which speaks of creation's goodness and tends to disorient the acquisitive rapacity of a keen mind) but aspirin (which speaks of the world's oppressive glare and thins the blood). The market makes of the world a spectacle of vanity: the nonspace of nonthings, a universal and proliferating immateriality, inhabited by a desire for nothingness under the aspect of an insatiable appetite for plenitude. But the fullness this desire seeks is an appropriation through disposal, a metabolism of matter into credit, pure sacrifice, the transformation of the world into symbol. It is the very antithesis, in short, of the infinite longing described by Gregory of Nyssa, which opens up creation as an endless parataxis of inappropriable but freely given beauty. In the sterile *es gibt* of the market, no distinction can be made between gift and disposal, mission and rejection, grace and dereliction; all being assumes the form of an exhausted or exhaustible commodity, a surpassed fetish, buoyantly thrown away because a phantasm (the future acquisition) continues to nourish the immateriality of desire. There is a special dynamism of nothingness here, a particular way of making everything and anything merely the outward aspect of nothing (ontological univocity indeed).

The question all honest Christian evangelism implicitly poses, then, is whether the sublimity of the market can possibly be disrupted by the indomitable event of beauty — of an infinite beauty that does not dissolve into the abstraction of value, or meaning, or formlessness, or fate, even in enduring death, but continues to be given as form and beauty, forever. The market's ideal order of vision is a vague and undetermined inattentiveness that is occasionally intensified into fixation upon some specific object by a sourceless and consequently insatiable desire; seeing is a process of serial distraction, straying from one point of ephemeral interest to another, a momentary agitation of vision that cannot and must not sustain the will's fascination. Theology must ask, though, whether the rhetoric of the form of Christ, this distinct beauty that inaugurates its own order of supplementation and extension, can enter into a world enclosed within this cycle of delirious fixation and distracted disenchantment. To be drawn, subversively, to the beauty of the divine is to adopt a style of vision whose intensity — whose hunger for the weight of glory — cannot be accommodated by the immateriality and lightness of the market's bloodless, dispirited desires. And to be drawn to the beauty of Christ is to encounter with joy the infinite intensity, resistance, and generosity of his form, its enduring and radiant particularity; but the market embraces only forms that can be dissolved, displaced, and replaced. Beauty, as such, is really not a marketable commodity, anyway, because it excites a love that is made perfect in dispossession, that requires distance, and that is awakened by the sheer gratuity of what is given; this is not to say that a kind of beauty does not often figure in the calculus of acquisitive desire, but the market thrives upon more conformable values. The commodification of art, for example, involves an emphasis upon such quantifiable but anaesthetic matters as authenticity, sheer novelty, and the potential for financial appreciation; modern "conceptual art" — that perfect coincidence of intellectual banality, technical incompetence, and gustative philistinism — answers the demands of the market (evanescence, intrinsic poverty of merit, insipience, vulgarity, imbecility, pomposity) as no other kind of "art" possibly can. Real art, though, in its true nature, by virtue of its intricacy, craft, and splendid inutility, repeats the gesture of creation, its gratuity, its generosity, its character as gift; art proclaims a delight more original than simple function. So the market quantifies art's "aesthetic" energy by way of a cult of authenticity, a passion for ideological propaganda, an obsessive concern for fashion and celebrity, and so forth, until our galleries become congeries of the trite, the tedious, and the depressingly vile. Insofar as beauty can resist revaluation as commodity, to whatever degree it can remain a grammar of weight, quantity, and glory, it is a revolutionary force; and the beauty of the form of Christ, insofar as it is a beauty without economy, that will not be exchanged for some more abstract set of values (that is resurrected, this is to say), and that enjoins such practices as bearing the burdens of others and forgiving their debts, is indefatigably resistant to the regime of "value." This would be no cause for alarm, obviously, if the church and the market did not both lay claim to the world.

It may seem that my argument has wandered far afield; radical hermeneutics, after all, neither desires nor is able to suppress anything by force; it is intended to function as suspicion only, and is certainly intended as a critique of every narrative of power, especially that of modern capitalism. But the market transcends the ideology of capitalism in any event; it is the province of neither classical capitalist "liberalism" (with its tendencies toward coarsening cynicism, demotic barbarism, and "social Darwinism") nor late modern state "socialism" (with its tendencies toward political authoritarianism, cultural infantilism, and ideological homogeneity), but determines the shape either generally may assume, as the economic and cultural reality with which either is always already now engaged and which, moreover, both serve. More to the point, while it can provide no critique that cannot be absorbed by the market (which is undeconstructible, in that it simply is the world it describes, it is the values it promotes, it creates the reality it proclaims), a radical hermeneutics can and does serve the ideological ends of the market, precisely because it aids in breaking down the inassimilable extravagances of precapitalist and presocialist traditions, and resists and ironizes the claims they make regarding truth or the good. To put the matter more simply, "radical" hermeneutics looks suspiciously like a species of liminal *semeiosis,* which aids in bearing persons over (in various states of privation) into the diversified identitylessness of the market; it wears the aspect of a passive soupçon perhaps, but even so plays its part in the violence of this necessary transformation, this invention of the abstract self, the unnarrated consumer. This hermeneutics, this great narrative of the death of metaphysics that is by extension an elegy pronounced over every story of truth, merely serves the market, as the latter forces back the pressures of other traditions to the margins of reality, causing identities to evaporate, to be burned off in a newly fashioned space of private meaning. Certainly there is no need to doubt the benign intentions that inspire such a hermeneutics; but Christian thought can be satisfied neither with the justice it pursues nor with the peace it would effect. The Christian evangel still stands apart, a word of contradiction that falls across philosophies of public accord, because the only justice and the only peace it knows is the infinite beauty of the form of Christ, which cannot be contained within the prudent economies of modernity. Radical hermeneutics remains simply another great story of the world, which the Christian evangel seeks, in some sense, to displace.

But, again, how can this displacement be a gesture of peace?

IV. THE GIFT OF MARTYRS

That the history of "metaphysics" has often been a history of various expressions, legitimations, and mystifications of power, and that speculative tradition has typically attempted to master reality by way of general principles, I would not care vigorously to deny (though I would add that they have also quite often been or done nothing of the sort). There can be no objection, in principle, to the practice of a patient genealogy of metaphysics that, within the very narrow ambit of a history of philosophy and of the dissolution of its thought of being, criticizes speculative metanarratives, great systems, and rationalist orthodoxies.

But the postmetaphysical discourse of suspicion has an end in view: it is truly "hermeneutics" insofar as it seeks the creation and endless expansion of a neutral space, a quasi-Gadamerian "merging of horizons," an expansion of understanding, albeit under the form of an understanding of the impossibility of understanding. The hermeneutical space is by definition extraterritorial, the pristine openness of the desert, the place of a peculiarly ascetic irony; but this should not obscure the fact of it accommodating a longing for a kind of empire, the wicked ascetic's etherealizing will to power, a desire to dissolve all territories into its twilight, until it has become the center. It remains an anaesthetic place, where beauty's illicit representation of things is dissolved, and where particularity is reduced to mere singularity. But Hermes is also a trickster god, a magus who ensorcels, a purveyor of *thaumata*. The merging of horizons — the prospect of a rationality that inhabits the place between horizons — is an optical trick, the deceiving trompe l'oeil that makes the distance a third place, untraversable except in the terms prescribed by the hermeneutical meta-narrative (in terms, that is, of the always partial negation and always incomplete restraint of rhetoric). But this hermeneutics does not lie outside every territory: it is itself a territory, a warlike state; thought never emerges from the discord of persuasions. A genuine "pluralism" would mean making no preparation against identities that trouble or even threaten us, faces that simply *are* the veil of purdah (and this no hermeneutics, however humble and deconstructive, is really able to do). Christian thought, though, when it is recalled to its nature as a kerygmatic suasion, has interest neither in the prudence of postmetanarrative hermeneutics nor in the passivity of an impossible pluralism, but must engage always in the telling of its own story, in the offer of the peace it knows over against many other models of peace (though discoveries of fortuitous — or providential — accord with other traditions, naturally, are also to be hoped for, as forms of *praeparatio evangelica*), and so engage in the practice of a persuasion that is also a practice of the peace it proclaims. Unlike the devotee of Hermes, the Christian (under the imperative of text and tradition) must frankly acknowledge the intentions of his or her discourse: the Christian evangel means to embrace all creation, and so must seek to evoke love from the other, the aesthetic rapture that captivates (or liberates) by its splendor. After all, the figure emblematic of understanding and conversion for Christian thought is not Hermes but the angel of the annunciation, the harbinger of an unimagined Other before whose advent the waiting soul must be laid open. Christian rhetoric must seek to induce this rapture, this reorientation of vision that lifts one into another order of seeing, that seizes one from oneself. That some of these metaphors come perilously close to the imagery of seduction or even of rape perhaps indicates the danger in any such open and unapologetic acknowledgment of the ends of persuasion (it will, at any rate, set off certain

440

predictable alarms), and Christian history proves that the Christian rhetoric of persuasion can easily be subordinated to some other discourse of power and violence. Nevertheless, theology has no choice but to cling to its own peculiar practice of persuasion, in order to resist the temptations of power (and in a history governed by sin, these temptations inhabit every moment); Christianity can only return to its understanding of peace, its unique style of rhetoric, as the sole source of accord; it must always obey the form of Christ, its persuasion must always assume the shape of the gift he is, it must practice its rhetoric under the only aspect it may wear if it is indeed Christian at all: martyrdom.

Christian thought learns that its rhetoric must never be a practice of coercion precisely because, in following the form of Christ (the Father's supreme rhetoric), it is always already placed on the side of the excluded, and must occupy this place as the place of triumph. By that trinitarian logic that is more extravagant than any magisterial hypotaxis of the high and low, Christian thought finds itself drawn over into the place of the crucified, addressing the nations from this place as the only place where peace is known, seeking to imitate Christ's renunciation of violence. Theology must, because of what its particular story is, have the form of martyrdom, witness, a peaceful offer that has already suffered rejection and must be prepared for rejection as a consequence. In resisting the myth of a hermeneutical neutrality that can govern persuasions from without, theology perhaps summons the specter of holy war, of the chaos of endless persuasion and repersuasion; but the only answer Christian thought can pose over against this apprehension is its own story of the inversion of violence, God's vindication of the crucified over against the orders that crucify, and its own urging to the world of the model of peace that Christ offers. Against the violence of rhetorics, it can do no more than offer a rhetoric of peace. The cross is not an ending, merely marking the closure of all metanarratives, awaiting translation into a speculative Good Friday more radical than even Hegel contemplated; rather, it inaugurates a world, the true world restored to itself, whose peculiar nature binds Christians to occupy, if they must, within this war of persuasions, the place of the warred against, the excluded. It would be comforting were Christian history always encouraging on this count — if, that is, "Christianity" had not often yielded to other, alien impulses, leaving the faith to be enacted most purely at the farmost margins of what history records — but this does not alter the truth that, for Christian thought, the only peace that puts an end to war is the form of Christ, and its power to persuade. Christ crucified thus must remain "metahermeneutical"; he stands outside modernity, outside the market, outside every human order of power, as a real and visible beauty. Nor can worldly power ever overcome him in his mystical body, because, again, the very gesture of the rhetoric of his form is one of donation, of martyrdom, and one that the powers of the world can suppress only through a violence that creates martyrs, and so confirms — contrary to all it intends — the witness of a peace that is infinite. In the time of sin, governed by an eschatological hope that has already been imparted in history but that is still also deferred, Christian rhetoric can be only a declaration of witness, and a gift. A gift of martyrs — which is the name that must, finally, be given to the Christian practice of persuasion — can never be returned violently, as the Same; because this gift is always peace and beauty, violence can "receive" the gift, but never return it.

This means, perhaps tragically, that Christian peace has no prudential or universal or systematic way of averting war (though neither has anything else), but can overcome violence only through conversion (which means also that Christians, posing persuasion against persuasion, are also always in danger of being won over by narratives of violence). Christian thought should be aware always of the risk of war, but should still nonetheless never consent to the illusory peace of "neutrality." Hermes, the messenger and exegete of the gods, always crosses an alien distance to bear tidings, always traverses a *chorismos;* but Christian thought announces a God who is himself the distance of all things, the impossibility of exile, the peace of the infinite. Truth is not, for theology, a place at which one arrives, leaving the space traversed as indifferent; all distance belongs to God and is claimed by Christian thought as the place where God's peace is to be shown; and so it is in the crossing of the distance (the style of traversal, the peaceful measure of love, the fashion of approach and arrival) that Christian truth is made known, in the degree to which it succeeds in renarrating that distance as love. This most emphatically does not mean that it is rhetoric as such that Christian thought must affirm (Christianity is not "liberalism" or "pluralism," but hospitality); it affirms only a particular rhetoric, a particular practice conformed to the peace of Christ; and it desires the freedom of other stories, in part, that they might be free to be defeated. Still, in this war of persuasions, Christians can struggle only by way of martyrdom, by surrendering their gift to others even in the moment of rejection. This is the peril and promise of Christian rhetoric: it endures, even in some sense invites and "wages" war, not because violence is inevitable but because the evangel, by claiming that violence is not necessary, transgresses the totality. Perhaps a liberal or hermeneutical suppression of the more extreme registers of innumerably many voices, proclaiming all their innumerably many persuasions, is the only wise rhetorical economy; but Christian thought is bound to a more dangerous course: war is not necessary, so there must be no economy. A letting be of strife, a striving in the militant pursuit of peace, is what Christian thought offers instead of a prudent hermeneutical piety: for the latter still belongs to the ancient story that says that all peace is the negation of war, while the former proclaims that all war is the privation of peace. In the face of the impasse described by Wittgenstein, the shouting of accusations over a distance of alienation between persuasions, Christian thought can still rely only on its own peculiar rhetorical stance, a peaceful encounter with the stranger and the offer of gifts across the distance (which refashions the distance as beauty and as peace). This is the rhetorical beauty of Christ the stranger, calling the apostles, speaking to Mary in the garden, joining the disciples on the way to Emmaus, meeting his apostles again on the sea strand, over a shared meal: always offering himself anew, always displaying his presence as an unanticipated gift and unhoped-for reconciliation. This is the style of a martyr's expenditure, which is made in the hope of a return that it is powerless of itself to effect, but which is also made by a soul committed to the grace of an infinite God who can always give souls to one another in the dispensation of his peace, in the shared scope of his infinite beauty. That such a gift can truly be given can be demonstrated only by ceaseless giving; the charter of Christian rhetoric remains Christ's exhortation: "freely ye have received, freely give" (Matt. 10:8). And of those who, in an earnest longing for peace, can urge only hermeneutical consensus, a silence that conceals its coercions, Christian thought can say only that "They have healed also the hurt . . . of my people slightly, saying, Peace, peace; when there is no peace" (Jer. 6:14; cf. 8:11). Christian rhetoric proclaims another — a more original and more inexhaustible — order of peace; but to do so it must follow after Christ, who has overcome the world (John 16:33), who came to cast fire upon the earth: would that it were already burning (Luke 12:49). Only by assuming the form of a ceaseless practice of peace, however — even in enduring the wounds always borne by the body of Christ — can Christian rhetoric demonstrate and persuade that this is, at the last, the fire of an infinite love.

Index